BRITISH THEATRE

*

VOLUME 3
Since 1895

This volume explores the rich and complex histories of English, Scottish and Welsh theatres in the 'long' twentieth century since 1895. Twenty-three original essays by leading historians and critics investigate the major aspects of theatrical performance, ranging from the great actor-managers to humble seaside entertainers, from between-wars West End women playwrights to the roots of professional theatre in Wales and Scotland, and from the challenges of alternative theatres to the economics of theatre under Thatcher. Detailed surveys of key theatre practices and traditions across this whole period are combined with case studies of influential productions, critical years placed in historical perspective and evaluations of theatre at the turn of the millennium. The collection presents an exciting evolution in the scholarly study of modern British theatre history, skilfully demonstrating how performance variously became a critical litmus test of the great aesthetic, cultural, social, political and economic upheavals in the age of extremes.

BAZ KERSHAW is Chair of Drama at the Department of Drama, University of Bristol. He is the author of *The Politics of Performance: Radical Theatre as Cultural Intervention* (1992) and *The Radical in Performance: Between Brecht and Baudrillard* (1999), and has published in many journals including *Theatre Journal*, *New Theatre Quarterly* and *The Drama Review.*

THE CAMBRIDGE HISTORY OF
BRITISH THEATRE
General Editor
PETER THOMSON, *University of Exeter*

The Cambridge History of British Theatre provides a uniquely author-itative account of the turbulent and often troublesome public life of performance in Britain. Whilst making full use of new research in a subject that is at the centre of current concern, the essays are designed for the general reader as well as for the specialist. Each volume is fully illustrated. Together, they offer a comprehensive and comprehensible history of theatre, of which plays are a part but by no means the whole.

The Cambridge History of British Theatre, Volume 1: Origins to 1660
EDITED BY JANE MILLING AND PETER THOMSON

The Cambridge History of British Theatre, Volume 2: 1660 to 1895
EDITED BY JOSEPH DONOHUE

The Cambridge History of British Theatre, Volume 3: Since 1895
EDITED BY BAZ KERSHAW

THE CAMBRIDGE
HISTORY OF
BRITISH THEATRE

*

VOLUME 3
Since 1895

*

Edited by
BAZ KERSHAW

CAMBRIDGE
UNIVERSITY PRESS

PUBLISHED BY THE PRESS SYNDICATE OF THE UNIVERSITY OF CAMBRIDGE
The Pitt Building, Trumpington Street, Cambridge, United Kingdom

CAMBRIDGE UNIVERSITY PRESS
The Edinburgh Building, Cambridge, CB2 2RU, UK
40 West 20th Street, New York, NY 10011–4211, USA
477 Williamstown Road, Port Melbourne, VIC 3207, Australia
Ruiz de Alarcón 13, 28014 Madrid, Spain
Dock House, The Waterfront, Cape Town 8001, South Africa

http://www.cambridge.org

First published 2004

Printed in the United Kingdom at the University Press, Cambridge

Typeface Dante 10.5/13 pt.   *System* LATEX2ε [TB]

A catalogue record for this book is available from the British Library

ISBN 0 521 65132 8 hardback

Volume 1: Origins to 1660
ISBN: 0 521 65040 2

Volume 2: 1660 to 1895
ISBN: 0 521 65068 2

Three volume set:
ISBN: 0 521 82790 6

Contents

Contents

Contents

Illustrations

Notes on contributors

JOHN BULL is Professor of Film and Drama at the University of Reading. His publications include *New British Political Playwrights* (1984) and *Stage Right* (1994), and he is general editor of *British and Irish Dramatists Since World War Two* (2000–).

COLIN CHAMBERS is Senior Research Fellow in Theatre at De Montfort University. His writings on British theatre include *The Story of Unity Theatre* (1989) and he has edited *The Continuum Companion to Twentieth-Century Theatre* (2002).

HAZEL WALFORD DAVIES is Professor of Theatre at the University of Glamorgan. Her publications on theatre include *Saunders Lewis a Theatr Garthewin* (1995), *State of Play: Four Playwrights of Wales* (1998) and *One Woman, One Voice* (2000).

CHRISTINE DYMKOWSKI is Reader in Drama and Theatre at Royal Holloway, University of London. Her extensive publications include articles on British women playwrights and directors and the book *The Tempest: Shakespeare in Production* (2000).

MAGGIE B. GALE is Reader in Theatre at the University of Birmingham. She has published many articles on women's theatre history and is author of *West End Women: Women and the London Stage 1918–1962* (1996).

VIV GARDNER is Professor of Theatre Studies at the University of Manchester. She has published extensively on women's theatre history and is co-editor, with Maggie Gale, of *Women, Theatre and Performance: New Histories, New Historiographies* (2000).

VERA GOTTLIEB is Emeritus Professor of Drama at Goldsmiths College, University of London. She has published extensively on twentieth-century British theatre and on Russian theatre.

NADINE HOLDSWORTH is Senior Lecturer in Theatre Studies at the University of Warwick. She has published articles on British theatre and edited collections of John McGrath's writings: *Naked Thoughts that Roam About* (2002) and, more recently, *Plays for England*.

SIMON JONES is Reader in Performance at the University of Bristol. He has published articles on contemporary theatre practice and is the director of the performance group Bodies in Flight.

DENNIS KENNEDY is Samuel Beckett Professor of Drama and Theatre Studies at Trinity College Dublin. His numerous publications include *Looking at Shakespeare* (2001) and he is editor of *The Oxford Encyclopedia of Theatre and Performance* (2003).

BAZ KERSHAW holds the Chair of Drama at the University of Bristol. His many publications on theatre include *The Politics of Performance* (1992), *The Radical in Performance* (1999) and a recent trilogy of essays on the ecologies of performance.

STEPHEN LACEY is Principal Lecturer in Performing Arts at Manchester Metropolitan University. His research interests include post-war British theatre and television drama and he is author of *British Realist Theatre* (1995).

JAN MCDONALD is Arnott Professor of Drama at the University of Glasgow. She has published extensively on Scottish and British theatre history, most recently on Scottish women dramatists and the nineteenth-century star performer Sarah Siddons.

STEVE NICHOLSON is Reader in Twentieth-Century Drama at the University of Sheffield. His extensive writings on political theatre include *British Theatre and the Red Peril* (1999) and a three-volume history of twentieth-century theatre censorship in Britain.

SOPHIE NIELD is Senior Lecturer in Drama, Theatre and Performance Studies at University of Surrey Roehampton. She gained a Ph.D. (on theatre and power) from the University of Manchester in 2002 and has published on space in performance.

ROGER OWEN is Lecturer in Theatre and Performance Studies at the University of Wales, Aberystwyth. He gained his doctorate (on Welsh theatre) in 1999 and has published articles on contemporary Welsh performance.

DEREK PAGET is Visiting Research Fellow at the University of Reading. He has written extensively on British theatre and television, particularly on documentary drama, and he is the author of *True Stories* (1990) and *No Other Way to Tell It* (1998).

THOMAS POSTLEWAIT is Professor of Theatre at Ohio State University. He is the author of *Prophet of the New Drama* (1986), editor of Bernard Shaw and William Archer's letters (2004), and co-editor of *Interpreting the Theatrical Past* (1986) and *Theatricality* (2003).

ADRIENNE SCULLION teaches in the Department of Theatre, Film and Television Studies at the University of Glasgow. Her research interests include Scottish cultural issues since the eighteenth century, dramaturgy and British women playwrights.

L I Z T O M L I N is Research Associate in the Performing Arts at Manchester Metropolitan University. She gained her doctorate at the University of Sheffield in 1997, has published articles on British theatre and co-founded the Open Performance Centre.

M I C K W A L L I S is Professor of Performance and Culture at the School of Performance and Cultural Industries, University of Leeds. He has published on British theatre history, on *Studying Plays* (1998), and more recently on 'Drama, Theatre, Performance'.

I O A N W I L L I A M S is Professor of Theatre, Film and Television Studies at the University of Wales, Aberystwyth. He has published widely on Welsh and other European theatre / literature, including editing the collected plays of J. Saunders Lewis (2000).

General preface

It is not the aim of the three-volume *Cambridge History of British Theatre* to construct theatrical history as a seamless narrative, not least because such seamlessness would be a distortion of the stop/start/try-again, often opportunistic, truth. Chronology has guided, but not bullied, us. The editorial privilege has been to assemble a team of international scholars able to speak with authority on their assigned (or sometimes chosen) topics. The binding subject is theatre, to which drama is a major, but not the only, contributor.

Each of the volumes includes some essays which are broad surveys, some which treat specific themes or episodes, some which are socio-theatrical 'snapshots' of single years and some which offer case studies of particular performance events. There is, of course, an underlying assertion: that a nation's theatre is necessarily and importantly expressive of, even when resistant to, the values that predominate at the time, but the choice of what to emphasise and what, however regretfully, to omit has rested with the volume's editor or editors. The aim has been to provide a comprehensive 'history' that makes no vain pretence to all-inclusiveness. The character of the volumes is the character of their contributors, and those contributors have been more often asked to use a searchlight than a floodlight in order to illuminate the past.

It is in the nature of 'histories' to be superseded. These volumes, though, may hope to stand as a millennial record of scholarship on a cultural enterprise – the British theatre – whose uniqueness is still valued. They are addressed to a readership that ranges from students to sheer enthusiasts. A 'history' is not the place for scholars to talk in secret to other scholars. If we have ever erred in that direction, it has been without the sanction of Victoria Cooper, who has shepherded these volumes through to publication with the generosity that is well known to all the authors who have worked with her.

Peter Thomson

xvi

Acknowledgements

Collaborative scholarly projects are often like flocks of migrating birds: they know where they want to get to – a 'new history', say – and they have a keen sense of the best route to get there, but many unpredictable factors will determine the nature and length of the journey. The flight of these particular essays to the bookshops has been especially perturbed by a key paradox in the writing of history, but especially recent history: when the history-bird cannot see the wood for the trees, a resort to the avian equivalent to 'slash and burn' will not improve its view, nor its progress. So first and foremost I must thank all the contributors to this volume, who have been unusually understanding of, and sensitive to, the difficulties of a complicated task; as well as being fabulously patient with our slow advance through the thickets and brambles, they have engaged wholeheartedly and often imaginatively with my, sometimes no doubt unreasonable, editorial demands. It would usually be invidious to single out any one of them, but the structure of the book allows me to thank Dennis Kennedy especially for his unerring guidance and sustaining good humour. Thanks too must go to the editors of the other volumes; we were never strictly a 'team', but thanks to Peter Thomson's trust, great good sense and impressively speedy editorial support it never felt like we were working alone. Closer to home, thanks are due to colleagues in the Department of Drama at Bristol, but especially to Janet Thumim for nimbly shifting resources to support the project, and to my remarkable postdoctoral research associates, Angela Piccini and Caroline Rye, who have been what every embattled academic editor must long for: brilliantly supple, strong, cool and supportive, especially as this project flew through the apex of its demand on my time. Special thanks must also go to my doctoral research student, Dafydd James, who assiduously helped to compile the chronology and bibliography right on schedule. The staff of the University of Bristol Theatre Collection were specially helpful in the search for illustrations, so thanks particularly to the keeper, Jo Elsworth, and to Louise Matter and Frances Carlyon, for their speedy and spot on support. Also, thank goodness, yet again I have been personally and professionally sustained beyond all reasonable measure to get my part of this whole thing done by Dr Gill Hadley, and by Eleanor and Logan. Without them it probably would not even have grown its feathers, let alone flapped its wings, and so attracted the interest and support of a significant number of the practising theatre artists who are named in these pages: many thanks to those for helping to source images and, much more importantly, for the high creativity that we have been privileged to write about. And, finally, we all have been incredibly fortunate that our commissioning editor at Cambridge University Press is Vicki Cooper: to have enough courage to trust us to complete the outward migration is one thing, as she must have known she could assemble a fit production team at the Press, but to have the vision to imagine how it might actually wing its way back into the public domain with much more than it started out with, thanks to everyone who contributed, is quite something else. To slightly paraphrase Samuel Butler, this was surely a case of the long-distance, high-flying flock being the egg's idea for getting more eggs.

Baz Kershaw
September 2003

Chronology

	Theatrical events	Political and social events
1895	Henry Irving is first actor to be knighted Elizabethan Stage Society founded by William Poel Oscar Wilde's trial; *An Ideal Husband* and *The Importance of Being Earnest* performed in London	
1896	Jarry's *Ubu Roi* performed in Paris Ibsen's *A Doll's House* performed in London Wilson Barrett's *The Sign of the Cross* performed in London	Lumière brothers bring Cinématographe to London
1897	Beerbohm Tree opens Her Majesty's Theatre J. M. Barrie, *The Little Minister*	
1898	New Century Theatre Company founded The Independent Theatre Company collapses Wyndham's Theatre opens Moscow Art Theatre founded Brecht born	
1899	The Stage Society founded Irish Literary Theatre founded by Yeats / Gregory	South African (Boer) War begins
1900	Craig directs *Dido and Aeneas*, Purcell Opera Society	Méliès makes *Jeanne d'Arc* (film)

	Theatrical events	Political and social events
	Max Beerbohm directs *Midsummer Night's Dream* Wilde dies in Paris	
1901	Apollo Theatre opens	Queen Victoria dies Accession of Edward VII
1902	Barrett, *The Christian King* Barrie, *The Admirable Crichton*	Education Act South African War ends
1903	New Theatre opens	Women's Social and Political Union founded by Emmeline Pankhurst First powered flight by Wright brothers
1904	Barker–Vedrenne seasons start at Royal Court Abbey Theatre founded by Miss Horniman RADA founded by Herbert Beerbohm Tree Barker–Archer publish National Theatre scheme Chekhov dies	
1905	Aldwych Theatre opens Tree establishes annual Shakespeare festival Barker, *The Voysey Inheritance* Irving dies on tour; Ibsen dies	
1906	Variety Artistes' Federation established Samuel Beckett born	
1907	Lena Ashwell takes over Kingsway Theatre Riots at the Abbey Theatre Barker's *Waste* refused licence Elizabeth Robins, *Votes for Women*	
1908	The Society of West End Theatre founded Actresses' Franchise League founded	Henry Ford produces first Model T car

	Theatrical events	Political and social events
	Craig's first publication of *The Mask* (to 1929)	
	Hamilton's *Diana of Dobson's* at the Kingsway	
	Horniman creates Manchester Repertory Company	
1909	Glasgow Repertory Theatre founded with British première of *The Seagull*	Parliamentary inquiry into censorship
		Kinematograph Act
	Elizabeth Barker, *Chains*	
1910	Diaghilev's Ballets Russes visits London	King Edward dies
		Accession of George V
	Reinhardt's productions of *Sumurun* (Coliseum) and *The Miracle* (Olympia exhibition hall)	
1911	Stage Society forms Repertory Theatre Association	Prison Reform Bill
	Liverpool Repertory Theatre started	
	Pioneer Players founded by Edith Craig	
1912	First Royal Command Performance of Variety	
	Githa Sowerby, *Rutherford and Sons*	
	Stanley Houghton, *Hindle Wakes*	
	Reinhardt's *Oedipus Rex* (Covent Garden)	
1913	Jackson founds Birmingham Repertory Theatre	
	Actresses' Franchise League founds first Women's Theatre Company	
	Shaw's *Androcles and the Lion* at St James'	
1914	Old Vic starts producing all Shakespeare's plays (to 1923)	World War One starts

	Theatrical events	Political and social events
	Glasgow Repertory Theatre closes	
	Shaw, *Pygmalion*	
1915	Barker's final Court Theatre season	
	Harold Brighouse, *Hobson's Choice*	
1916	Oscar Asche's *Chu Chin Chow* opens at His Majesty's Theatre (to 1921)	Easter Uprising in Dublin Introduction of Entertainment Tax
1917	Beerbohm Tree dies	Russian Revolution
1918	Nigel Playfair opens Lyric Theatre, Hammersmith	World War One ends General Election – Lloyd George forms coalition government Women granted vote
1919	William Bridges-Adams directs Shakespeare Memorial Theatre British Drama League founded	
1920	Scottish National Players Committee founded Shaw, *Heartbreak House*	Irish Civil War
1921	Shaw, *Back to Methuselah*	The dole (unemployment pay) started
1922	Scottish National Theatre Society founded	Irish Free State established Conservatives win General Election
1923	Oxford Repertory Theatre formed Terence Gray founds Cambridge Festival Theatre Sybil Thorndike in Shaw's *St Joan* Marie Stopes, *Our Ostriches* Death of Sarah Bernhardt	Conservatives hold power in General Election – Baldwin Prime Minister
1924	Edith Evans's Millament at Lyric, Hammersmith Barry Jackson's modern-dress *Hamlet*	First Labour government elected Ramsey MacDonald Prime Minister Conservatives regain power
1925	Peter Godfrey/Molly Veness open Gate Theatre	

Theatrical events	Political and social events
1926 Workers' Theatre Movement founded Theatre Managers' Association founded Shakespeare Memorial Theatre burns down Shaw receives Nobel prize for literature Shaw, *Mrs Warren's Profession*	General Strike BBC Royal Charter
1927 Arts Theatre Club opens	BBC formed
1928 Brecht sees Eliot's *Sweeney Agonistes* in London Moscow Art Theatre visits London Fortune and Piccadilly Theatres built League of Welsh Drama established R. C. Sherriff, *Journey's End*	Full emancipation for women
1929 Harcourt Williams directs Old Vic Company Jackson founds Malvern Festival Piscator publishes *The Political Theatre* Sean O'Casey, *The Silver Tassie* Noel Coward, *Bitter Sweet*	First talking films marketed Great Depression and Wall Street Crash General Election, Labour minority government, MacDonald Prime Minister
1930 British Actors' Equity formed League of Welsh Drama collapses	
1931 Lilian Baylis opens the new Sadler's Wells Compagnie des Quinze visits London First English performance of Wilde's *Salome* Coward, *Cavalcade*	Depression in Britain 2.5 million unemployed General Election, coalition national government under MacDonald
1932 Rupert Doone's Group Theatre founded Joan Littlewood's Theatre of	First National Workers' Movement conference Hunger marches in London

	Theatrical events	Political and social events
	Action founded	
	New Shakespeare Memorial Theatre opens	
	Lady Gregory dies	
1933	Guthrie's first season directing Old Vic Company	Hitler becomes German Chancellor
	Regent's Park Open Air Theatre opens	Reichstag burns
	Kurt Jooss's dance theatre visits London	
	Left Theatre founded	
	Curtain Theatre (Glasgow) founded	
1935	Theatre of Action becomes Theatre Union	Baldwin replaces MacDonald as Prime Minister
	First Ivor Novello musical at Drury Lane	Left Book Club founded
	Gielgud, Olivier, Ashcroft and Edith Evans in *Romeo and Juliet* at New Theatre	
1936	London Unity Theatre founded	Accession of George VI
	Guthrie reappointed to Old Vic Company	Spanish Civil War begins
	Novello, *Careless Rapture*	Television introduced on BBC services
		Saunders Lewis's arson at Penyberth
1937	Left Theatre collapses	Chamberlain replaces Baldwin as Prime Minister
	Olivier, Richardson join Old Vic	
1938	Auden and Isherwood, *On the Frontier*	Republic of Ireland
		Munich Crisis
1939	Group Theatre closes	Spanish Civil War ends
	ENSA established	Germany invades Poland
	MSU Players founded by Molly Urquhart	World War Two begins
	Yeats dies	
1940	CEMA established	Battle of Britain and the Blitz
	Scottish National Players collapses	Churchill replaces Chamberlain as Prime Minister

Theatrical events	Political and social events
1941 Old Vic Theatre bombed CEMA tour Old Vic Company (to 1944) John Stewart opens Park Theatre in Glasgow Glasgow Unity Theatre founded	BBC television service discontinued Germany invades Soviet Union
1943 Citizens' Theatre, Glasgow founded CEMA invests in Theatre Royal, Bristol	Churchill, Roosevelt and Stalin meet
1944 Urquhart's MSU collapses Conference of Repertory Theatres (CORT) founded	
1945 Theatre Workshop founded Old Vic Company at New Theatre Glasgow Citizens' move to Gorbals Peter Brook directs *King John* at Birmingham Rep J. B. Priestley, *An Inspector Calls*	World War Two ends Labour win general election – 146 majority, Clement Atlee is Prime Minister Welfare State legislation begins Arts Council of Great Britain founded
1946 Bristol Old Vic founded London Young Vic founded Jackson directs Shakespeare Memorial Theatre First university drama department, Bristol	BBC television service resumed
1947 London Old Vic Theatre reopens Joint Council of National Theatre / Old Vic formed Ena Lamont Stewart, *Men Should Weep* J. B. Priestley, *The Linden Tree* Granville Barker dies	First Edinburgh Festival
1948 British Theatre Conference Society for Theatre Research founded	National Health Service started

Theatrical events	Political and social events
Saunders Lewis's *Blodeuwedd* first performed	
Christopher Fry, *The Lady's Not for Burning*	

	Theatrical events	Political and social events
1949	Olivier and Richardson fired from Old Vic	National Theatre Act
	Berliner Ensemble founded by Brecht and Wiegel	
	Brecht's *A Short Organum for the Theatre*	
	T. S. Eliot, *The Cocktail Party*	
1950	Old Vic Theatre reopens	General Election, Labour majority 5
	RSAMD opens in Glasgow	
	Rose Bruford College opens in Edinburgh	
	Anouilh, *Ring Round the Moon* (trans. Fry)	
	Shaw dies	
1951	Pitlochry Festival starts (summer only)	General Election, Conservative majority 17 – Churchill Prime Minister
	Derby Playhouse opens	Festival of Britain
	Olivier and Leigh in *Anthony and Cleopatra*	
	Ivor Novello dies	
1952	Arts Council awards first playwright's bursary	Accession of Elizabeth II
	George Gershwin, *Porgy and Bess*	
	The Mousetrap opens	
1953	Theatre Workshop at Stratford East	Coronation Elizabeth II
	The Gateway established in Edinburgh	
	Terence Rattigan, *The Sleeping Prince*	
1954	Kenneth Tynan joins the *Observer*	Food rationing ends
	John Whiting, *Marching Song*	Commercial Television Act
	Dylan Thomas, *Under Milk Wood* (broadcast)	First hydrogen bomb exploded

	Theatrical events	**Political and social events**
1955	National Student Drama Festival established Theatre Workshop, Brecht's *Mother Courage* Arts Theatre, Beckett's *Waiting for Godot*	General Election, Conservative majority 60 – Anthony Eden Prime Minister Commercial television introduced
1956	Berliner Ensemble visits London (Palace Theatre); Brecht dies Jacques Lecoq school opens in Paris George Devine founds ESC at Royal Court National Youth Theatre founded John Osborne, *Look Back in Anger*	Russia invades Hungary
1957	Olivier in Osborne's *The Entertainer*	Suez Crisis, Anthony Eden resigns, Harold Macmillan becomes Prime Minister Wolfenden Report on homosexuality
1958	Belgrade Theatre, Coventry opens Moscow Art Theatre at Sadler's Wells Theatre Festival of Scottish Repertory Theatre Ann Jellicoe, *The Sport of My Mad Mother* Harold Pinter, *The Birthday Party*	Campaign for Nuclear Disarmament – first Aldermaston march European Common Market starts
1959	Nottingham Playhouse opens John Arden, *Sergeant Musgrave's Dance* Penguin launches New Dramatists series	Conservatives win General Election with 100 majority
1960	Peter Hall directs new Royal Shakespeare Company Pinter, *The Caretaker* First professorship of drama, Bristol	

	Theatrical events	**Political and social events**
1961	Arnold Wesker starts Centre 42 RSC leases Aldwych Theatre Beckett's *Happy Days* at Royal Court Martin Esslin's *The Theatre of the Absurd*	US invades Cuba Major nuclear disarmament demonstrations
1962	Chichester Festival Theatre opens, Olivier directs National Theatre formed at Old Vic, Olivier directs Victoria Theatre (in-the-round) opens at Stoke on Trent Welsh Theatre Company established Saunders Lewis's, *Tynged yr Iaith* lecture	Cuban Missile Crisis Commonwealth Immigration Act
1963	Jim Haynes opens Traverse Theatre, Edinburgh Nottingham Playhouse opens RSC, *The War of the Roses* (Hall/Barton) Theatre Workshop, *Oh What a Lovely War* First NT production, *Hamlet* at Old Vic	Macmillan resigns as Prime Minister – Douglas-Home takes over President Kennedy assassinated
1964	First world theatre season at Aldwych Edinburgh Civic Theatre Trust created Peter Brook, Theatre of Cruelty/*Marat Sade* Sean O'Casey dies	General Election, Labour majority 4 – Harold Wilson Prime Minister
1965	First TIE team, Belgrade Theatre, Coventry People Show and CAST founded Edward Bond's *Saved* prosecuted Trevor Nunn joins RSC	Abolition of Capital Punishment Jenny Lee first Minister of the Arts Vietnam War begins

	Theatrical events	**Political and social events**
	Close Theatre Club established in Glasgow	
1966	Nunn directs *Revenger's Tragedy* at RSC	General Election, Labour majority 97
	Gwenlyn Parry, *Saer Doliau*	Abortion legalised
	Joe Orton, *Loot*	Sexual Offences Bill legalises
	Edward Gordon Craig dies	homosexuality
1967	Octogan Theatre, Bolton opens	Entertainment Tax abolished
	Stoppard's *Rosencrantz and Guildenstern* at Old Vic	
	Peter Nichols, *A Day in the Death of Joe Egg*	
	Alan Ayckbourn, *Relatively Speaking*	
	Joe Orton murdered	
1968	*Hair* and *Oh! Calcutta* in West End	Lord Chamberlain's censorship abolished
	Jim Haynes founds Drury Lane Arts Lab	Russia invades Czechoslovakia
	John Fox founds Welfare State	Worldwide student protests
	Red Ladder Stage Company founded	
	Living Theatre's *Paradise Now!* in London	
1969	Conference of Drama Schools founded	British troops in Northern Ireland
	Traverse Theatre moves to Grassmarket, Glasgow	Bloody Sunday
	Royal Court *Come Together* festival	US moon landing
	Peter Nichols, *The National Health*	
1970	Young Vic Theatre opens	General Election, Conservative majority 31 – Edward Heath Prime Minister
	Peter Brook leaves to work in Paris	
	Trevor Griffiths, *Occupations*	Women's Liberation Group founded
	Olivier created Life Peer	Gay Liberation Front founded
1971	Trevor Nunn director of RSC	
	Birmingham Repertory Theatre rebuilt	

	Theatrical events	Political and social events
	Crucible Theatre, Sheffield opens	
	General Will Theatre Company founded	
	David Storey, *The Changing Room*	
1972	Arden and D'Arcy picket RSC	Direct rule of Northern Ireland begins
	Bush Theatre opens	
	Portable Theatre, *England's Ireland*	First miners' strike
		Over 1 million unemployed
	Jesus Christ Superstar in West End	
1973	Peter Hall director of NT	Britain joins EEC
	Women's Theatre Festival at Almost Free	Fuel shortages force three-day working week
	Richard Eyre director of Nottingham Playhouse	
	7:84 (Scotland) founded by John McGrath	
	Peter Shaffer, *Equus*	
1974	Other Place opens at RSC Stratford	General Election, Labour wins hung parliament – Harold Wilson Prime Minister
	Max Stafford-Clark founds Joint Stock	Miners' strike
	Women's Theatre Group founded	General Election, Labour majority 3
	Independent Theatre Council established	
	Tom Stoppard, *Travesties*	
1975	Riverside Studios opens	Margaret Thatcher leads Conservatives
	Gay Sweatshop founded	
	National Council of Drama training launched	Fall of Saigon
	Theatre Writers' Group forms	
	Alan Ayckbourn, *Bedroom Farce*	
1976	NT moves into South Bank complex	James Callaghan Prime Minister
	Monstrous Regiment founded	Association for Business Sponsorship of Arts founded
	Royal Exchange Theatre, Manchester, opens	Economic crisis

	Theatrical events	Political and social events
	Brenton, *Weapons of Happiness* at NT	
	Sybil Thorndike dies	
	Edith Evans dies	
1977	RSC open Warehouse in Covent Garden	Grunwick Print disputes, flying pickets
	Cottesloe Theatre opens at NT	
	Bara Caws established	
	Ayckbourn, *Bedroom Farce*	
	Terence Rattigan dies	
1978	Albany Empire arson attack	Saatchi and Saatchi campaign for Conservatives
	Hands joins Nunn directing RSC	
	Fringe unionisation begins	
	David Hare, *Plenty*	
1979	Comedy Store opened	Winter of Discontent – mass strikes
	Rebuilt Lyric, Hammersmith opens	General Election, Conservative majority 43 – Margaret Thatcher Prime Minister
	Belt and Braces / Dario Fo in West End	
	Martin Sher, *Bent*	Soviet Union invades Afghanistan
	Caryl Churchill, *Cloud Nine*	
1980	Howard Brenton's *Romans in Britain* at NT	Maze Prison, Northern Ireland – hunger strike
	David Edgar's *Nicholas Nickleby* at RSC	Reagan elected President in USA
	Steven Berkoff, *Greek*	
1981	First London International Festival of Theatre	Riots in Brixton, Toxteth, Moss Side
	Ewan Hooper forms Scottish Theatre Company	Maze Prison – second hunger strike, ten die
	Brith Gof (Aberystwyth) founded	Greenham Common Peace Camp
	Lloyd Webber / Trevor Nunn, *Cats*	
	David Edgar, *Maydays*	
1982	RSC moves into Barbican	Falklands War
	Tron Theatre opens in Glasgow	Channel 4 TV launched
	Caryl Churchill, *Top Girls*	Welsh television channel established

	Theatrical events	Political and social events
1983	Mayfest established in Glasgow Howard Barker, *Victory*	General Election, Conservative majority 144
1984	National Theatre Studio founded Cwmni Theatr Cymru collapses Lloyd Webber, *Starlight Express*	Miners' strike IRA bomb Downing Street Reagan re-elected
1985	John Godber, *Bouncers* RSC, *Les Misérables*	Miners' strike quashed
1986	RSC Swan Theatre opens Yvonne Brewster founds Talawa Jim Cartwright, *Road* Lloyd Webber, *Phantom of the Opera*	Greater London Council abolished
1987	British Theatre Museum opens Caryl Churchill, *Serious Money* Liz Lochhead, *Mary, Queen of Scots*	General Election, Conservative majority 80 'Black Monday' financial crash
1988	Richard Eyre director of NT 'British Theatre in Crisis' conference Deborah Warner directs *Titus Andronicus* Howard Barker, *The Bite of the Night* Timberlake Wertenbaker, *Our Country's Good*	Lockerbie air disaster George Bush elected US President
1989	Winsome Pinnock, *A Hero's Welcome* Beckett dies Olivier dies	Chancellor Nigel Lawson resigns Communism collapses in Eastern Europe Tiananmen Square protest
1990	Adrian Noble director RSC Stephen Daldry takes over Gate Theatre Howard Barker, *Scenes from an Execution* Bill Bryden, *The Ship* in Glasgow	Poll Tax riots – Thatcher resigns John Major Prime Minister Paris Summit ends Cold War Gulf War Glasgow is European City of Culture
1991	Theatre de Complicite, *The Visit* Alan Bennett, *The Madness of George III*	Yeltsin elected President of Russia Soviet Union becomes

	Theatrical events	**Political and social events**
		Commonwealth of Independent States
1992	Sam Mendes takes over Donmar Warehouse	General Election, Conservative majority 21
	New Traverse Theatre opens	War in Bosnia
	Stephen Daldry directs *An Inspector Calls*	Bill Clinton elected US President
	Brith Gof, *Haearn*	
1993	David Hare trilogy at NT	European Union Treaty ratified by Britain
	Sophie Treadwell, *Machinal*	
1994	Stephen Daldry takes over Royal Court	Genocide in Rwanda
	Max Stafford-Clark founds Out of Joint	National Lottery starts
	Edinburgh Festival Theatre replaces Empire Theatre	Channel Tunnel completed
	Jonathan Harvey, *Beautiful Thing*	Russia invades Chechnya
1995	Sarah Kane, *Blasted*	
	Jez Butterworth, *Mojo*	
1996	Royal Court Theatre moves to West End	Prince Charles and Diana divorce
	TOSG founded (devoted to Gaelic repertoire)	Clinton re-elected as US President
	Mark Ravenhill, *Shopping and Fucking*	
	Ayub Khan-Din, *East is East*	
1997	Trevor Nunn directs NT	General Election, Labour majority 179
	Shakespeare's Globe opens in London	Tony Blair Prime Minister
	Patrick Marber, *Closer*	Princess Diana killed
1998	Anthony Sher in *Winter's Tale* at RSC	House of Lords reformed
	Nicole Kidman in *Blue Room* at Donmar Warehouse	President Clinton impeached
1999	Sarah Kane dies	NATO bombs Kosovo
	TAG (Glasgow), Making the Nation project	Scottish Parliament established
		Welsh Assembly established

	Theatrical events	**Political and social events**
	Tricycle Theatre, *The Colour of Justice*	
2000	Watford, Salisbury and Coventry Theatres co-produce Brian Friel's *Translations*	London Millennium Dome fails Arts Council £100m grant increase
2001	*Shockheaded Peter* in West End	Sept. 11 terrorist attack on World Trade Centre

PART I

*

1895–1946

British theatre, 1895–1946: art, entertainment, audiences – an introduction

DENNIS KENNEDY

In 1895 three major figures in the history of British theatre came centre stage in revealing ways. Henry Irving, master of theatrical illusion and the most famous performer of the age, knelt before Queen Victoria and rose as the first actor in history to be knighted. Oscar Wilde, that Dubliner brilliant in his plays and impudent in society, had two productions running simultaneously in London: *An Ideal Husband* and *The Importance of Being Earnest*. G. B. Shaw, virtually unknown as a playwright, began a three-year mission of modernity and socialism as theatre critic for the *Saturday Review*. Shaw complained frequently that Irving, whom he greatly admired, wasted his talents on weak and insignificant work, and he was disturbed to find himself laughing mechanically at Wilde's masterpiece. Shortly after *The Importance of Being Earnest*'s brilliant opening, Wilde was in grave trouble with the law over his homosexuality. Just as his play marks the high point of Victorian comedy, so Wilde's trial signals a turn in the history of Victorian righteousness. Irving's knighthood and Wilde's disgrace: the poles of late Victorian attitudes to the theatre demonstrated within a single year, with Shaw as touchstone commentator.

Despite such anecdotal charm, 1895 does not distinguish the beginning of a new era for theatre in Britain. Yet in some ways it is fortunate that this volume on the twentieth century begins at a date not historiographically remarkable, for what most characterised the theatre in the 1890s was a determined insistence on security and continuity. There were few signs of change and fewer still that there soon would be. The early forays of theatrical modernism in Britain seemed to have had no lasting effect. Though the plays of the Scandinavian visionary of transition, Henrik Ibsen, had been seen in London and championed there by Shaw from 1889, no one could guess that Ibsen's social dramas would in a few years seem out of date. In the 1890s his more palatable propositions were already being naturalised by the principal writers of society 'problem' plays, Henry Arthur Jones and Arthur Wing Pinero. Just two years after American actress Elizabeth Robins brought *Hedda Gabler* to the London stage, Pinero's variation on its themes was a great success at the St James's Theatre in 1893. *The Second Mrs Tanqueray* moved Hedda's story into the upper reaches of British society, with George Alexander matching the darkly exotic Mrs Patrick Campbell in the roles of husband and the wife 'with a past' who has deceived him. The graceful worldliness that was Alexander's trademark, and the charged sensual implications of Mrs Pat's performance – Shaw called it 'wicked Pinerotic theatre' – showed a safe view of smouldering sexuality, since the female who was its creator and object would be destroyed.[1] Pinero's *The Notorious Mrs Ebbsmith* in 1895 repeated the casting but handled the 'woman question' differently by turning the plot of *Ghosts* on its head, giving Mrs Pat a marvellous transformation from bluestockinged New Woman to conventional female, burning her Bible and keeping her man through time-honoured sexual means. Similarly, Jones had turned Ibsen's *A Doll's House* upside-down in his 1894 adaptation *Breaking a Butterfly* (written with Henry Herman), which has the Nora figure learning her lesson and staying at home.

J. T. Grein had produced *Ghosts* for a small private audience as the opening salvo of the Independent Theatre in 1891, thus making him 'the best-abused man in London',[2] but it remained banned by the censor from public performance until World War One. *A Doll's House* was not staged in London until 1896. Few of Ibsen's later plays were seen in the commercial theatre in London. Why should they be, a manager might ask, when Pinero and Jones were raising the same social concerns without making the audience uncomfortable? The Ibsen movement of the 1890s, engineered chiefly by actresses committed to feminism and anxious for good roles not demeaning to their ideals, had little effect on dominant theatrical practice. Instead of the revolution that Shaw hoped the stage would foster, the major theatres resourcefully redirected Ibsen's interest in women to a conventional eroticism that maintained the status quo.

In 1895 the stylistic and thematic renovations of the first decades of the twentieth century were unimaginable in the London theatre. The audiences were highly varied, ranging from almost the bottom of the social scale to the very top: the Queen avoided the public theatre after Prince Albert died in 1861, but her heir, the hedonistic Albert Edward, Prince of Wales, was a frequent spectator. The spectrum of entertainment available was extremely

---

1 See Joel H. Kaplan, 'Pineroticism and the problem play: Mrs Tanqueray, Mrs Ebbsmith and Mrs Pat', in Richard Foulkes (ed.), *British Theatre in the 1890s: Essays on Drama and the Stage* (Cambridge University Press, 1992), pp. 38–58.
2 Michael Orme, *J. T. Grein: The Story of a Pioneer* (London: J. Murray, 1936), p. 88.

wide: sophisticated problem plays and comedies at the St James's, rough-and-tumble melodramas in the East End halls, the 'autumn melodrama' filled with technological marvels at Drury Lane, music hall songs and dances scattered throughout the capital and its suburbs, musical comedies at the Gaiety, Shakespeare at the Lyceum, blackface minstrels at St James's Hall, pierrots at the Palace and Royalty Theatres. No earlier period in the history of British theatrical performance provided such diversity of choice or appealed so widely across the social scale.

This introduction will look at some of the audiences for theatre after 1895, what they attended and why, and how they changed in the course of the first half of the twentieth century. The main outline of the picture is easy to draw: audiences diminished. From huge and varied assemblies in the many theatres at the turn of the century, they dwindled to smaller and relatively specialised groups by 1946. The chief reason, of course, was the competition provided after 1910 by the upstart cinema. But other factors were at play as well, including the modernist-driven division of the audience into aesthetically based segments, the effects of the two world wars and larger cultural and political changes in British society. For clarity, I will classify the highly varied theatrical diet into four types of entertainment, each notionally representing a different audience: the bourgeois theatre, the modernist theatre, the populist theatre, and the catch-all category of Shakespeare performance. In the first three sections I concentrate on the initial twenty-five years or so, when most of the patterns were established; the final section will look in more detail at the second half of the period, the years between the wars.

The bourgeois theatre

Theatre chiefly intended for middle-class audiences was dominant in both 1895 and 1946. 'Bourgeois' or 'middle class' must be understood in a broad way in this context, especially in the earlier years, extending from the *petit bourgeois* (say, shopkeepers) to the *haut bourgeois* (merchant bankers, self-made industrialists), and even into the reaches of the upper classes (aristocrats, the land-owning gentry). All the changes in this period did not affect the abiding importance of this group of theatre-goers as trendsetters, despite major alterations in what they were seeing. For example, the actor-managers who controlled the London theatre were overwhelmingly aware of the importance of middle-class gentility to their enterprise and usually worked to bolster it.

In 1895 the actor-manager system appeared unassailable, an industrial powerhouse of theatre, both logical and efficient. Up until the end of World

War One '[t]he actor in management was, indeed, the very symbol' of the period, wrote Allardyce Nicoll.[3] The system was perfectly in keeping with late Victorian notions of economic practice – and patriarchy. A single entrepreneur owned the acting and production company, owned the theatre or leased it for a long term, chose the plays or had them written to order, organised the productions and took the leading role. And actor-managers were overwhelmingly men. A few women became managers, often taking an entirely different approach: Emma Cons and Lilian Baylis at the Old Vic, Lena Ashwell at the Kingsway, Annie Horniman in Manchester, though of these only Ashwell was an actress.[4] The actor-manager would find and supervise the capital, take the risks and reap the rewards. The concept of the 'director' (or 'producer', as he would soon be called) as a functionary separate from the actors or playwright was unknown in Britain until after 1900. The actor-manager wielded the power of the director *avant la lettre*, and much more besides. He had to be an engaging or even charismatic performer, a businessman, a leader of personnel, a cultural touchstone and popular as a person with audiences all at once. The financial, artistic and social rewards could be great. With so much power in the hands of a single figure the practice was clearly open to trade abuse, though the abuse was probably not greater than in other areas of Victorian life regulated by private or family-run commerce.

Historical views of the actor-manager have been heavily influenced by the disdainful approach taken by modernist reformers, who believed that far too much of the life of a theatre was dedicated to the ego of the owner. There is no doubt that the actor-managers marked the enterprise of theatre-making – from playwriting to casting, from production economy to audience comfort – with their heavy individual stamps. The critic P. P. Howe in 1913 found the plays of Henry Arthur Jones badly affected by 'the trail of the actor-manager', which demanded as protagonist 'a bright, shrewd man of about fifty' who (in Act 3) decides 'the destinies of several persons' before (in Act 4) laying successful siege 'to a younger heart that has long held out against him'.[5] But while it is true that the hegemonic demands of actor-managers restricted stylistic and structural innovation, it is also true that they were in a tradition that had pleased audiences since the 1660s and had kept theatre attendance climbing throughout the nineteenth century.

3 Allardyce Nicoll, *English Drama 1900–1930: The Beginning of the Modern Period* (Cambridge University Press, 1973), p. 22.
4 See Tracy C. Davis, 'Edwardian management and the structures of industrial capitalism', in Michael R. Booth and Joel H. Kaplan (eds.), *The Edwardian Theatre: Essays on Performance and the Stage* (Cambridge University Press, 1996), pp. 111–29.
5 P. P. Howe, *Dramatic Portraits* (London: Martin Secker, 1913), pp. 74–5.

One of the greatest changes in this period was directly linked to the actor-manager system: the rise in the social position of performers. Henry Irving's knighthood is the most obvious sign that actors, at least at the top end, had moved from opprobrium at the beginning of the century to admired gentlemen at its close. Once Sir Henry had breached the wall of Victorian respectability there was no stopping; in the twentieth century performers of all types moved more and more firmly into the centre of social recognition and even political power. Between 1895 and 1922 actors were made knights at an average rate of about one every three years. But these men received the honour only partly for achievements as actors, as it was their contributions as managers that set them off from hundreds of other successful performers; they were not knighted as artists but as capitalists. And gender played its usual role: though a few non-managerial actresses received the equivalent honour of Dame of the British Empire, none of the female managers of the period were so rewarded.

Two examples will show what the general run of actor-managers were like. George Alexander (1858–1918) and Wilson Barrett (1846–1904) were opposites in thought and effect and entirely successful at what they did. Alexander started acting with Henry Irving at the Lyceum in 1881 and a decade later took over the St James's Theatre, which he ran with flair for over a quarter of a century, until his death. The St James's was admired by smart society in part because of its location in the fashionable section of Piccadilly but chiefly because its manager made his leading spectators feel as comfortable as in their own drawing-rooms. An astute cultural entrepreneur, Alexander capitalised on his location by selecting plays about society characters conducting lives parallel to those in the audience. His spectators were well aware of their positions in this social panopticon: 'The most expensive seats were occupied by Society with a capital "S", the less expensive ones by those who longed to be in Society, the least expensive by those who wished to see what Society looked like.'[6] Hesketh Pearson's view finely captures the symbiotic relationship of the British classes in the theatrical context.

Alexander and his company provided models of behaviour and dress for the audience. His actors and spectators operated as doubled figures in an exemplary world, with the plays of Pinero, Jones and Wilde the meeting ground of the real and the ideal, their characters righteously manipulating the status quo. As Joel Kaplan and Sheila Stowell have shown, the playhouse of this period became more and more illustrative of fashion, often using society couturiers to create the actresses' gowns that might be copied for wealthy patrons, and

---

6 Hesketh Pearson, *The Last Actor-Managers* (London: Methuen, 1950), p. 23.

something similar can be said about the stage settings and the gestural habits of the actors.[7] Everything surrounding a play at the St James's justified power and affluence: the manners of the theatre's attendants, the advertisements in the printed programmes (often from London's elegant clothiers and furriers), the drinks at the interval – even the box office manager, who always wore a top hat while on duty. Patrons in the stalls and dress circle were required to dress formally, just as they would for an elegant dinner; complimentary tickets at the St James's were printed on special cards with a sharp reminder that evening dress was essential for admission.

Alexander understood that his curious position as a society actor was dependent upon impeccable deportment and reputation. Though a kind man, he ensured that decorum went beyond the walls of the theatre, insisting that his actors who played society people on stage dress like them in their private lives, and when he discovered sartorial violators walking in public he threatened them with dismissal on the spot.[8] One is tempted to conclude that Alexander could not sufficiently distinguish between the fictions on his stage and the actors who portrayed them, who in reality obviously were not of the same social class as most of their prominent spectators. But no doubt he understood the difference well enough, for what concerned him were appearance and manners; he knew that the habit of the gaze was widespread in the life of the time, not restricted to the stage alone. He was careful to ensure that no scent of the street enter the refined aura of his theatre, which he treated not so much as a temple of culture – as Irving did the Lyceum – but as a church of social class, a space with precise performative functions, idealised as a regulator of distinctions and differences. In some ways his knighthood was the most unnecessary of the actorly honours, for Society already considered him one of 'us'.

The St James's was not unusual in requiring evening dress in the prime precincts of the house. All the theatres with social pretensions had done so since the middle of the nineteenth century at least and many would continue until World War Two, their interior architecture designed to display the formal fashions of patrons in the boxes, stalls and circle and to make nearly invisible the punters in ordinary clothes in the pit and galleries. Black tailcoat, white tie, stiff collar for the men – all evoking older styles – elegant and revealing long gowns for the women: in the Victorian and Edwardian ages attire was

---

7 Joel H. Kaplan and Sheila Stowell, *Theatre and Fashion: Oscar Wilde to the Suffragettes* (Cambridge University Press, 1994).
8 See Dennis Kennedy, 'The New Drama and the new audience', in Booth and Kaplan (eds.), *Edwardian Theatre*, p. 144.

the chief and most ready visual signifier of wealth and class. Before the time of mass-produced stylish clothes, only those with bags of money or significant lines of credit could afford to dress in a way acceptable for entrance to any area of high social life. (Accent and speech, of course, would signify just as well: Henry Higgins in *Pygmalion*, Shaw's parody of the English class system from 1914, finds Eliza's speech much harder to change than her dresses.) Spectators in cheaper seats had separate entrances in alleyways and separate bars for the interval, leaving the quality and gentlefolk undisturbed in their righteous otherness. Audience arrangements were quite different and much less formal in the East End theatres, in the suburbs and the provinces, but for managers like Alexander the distinctions of dress code, speech and behaviour – on both sides of the footlights – were central to the theatrical performance of class and wealth.

Wilson Barrett succeeded diametrically. He did not have a permanent theatre, he spent much time touring abroad, and his finances were often shaky. Successful in leading roles in melodramas in the 1880s, especially *The Silver King* and *The Lights o' London*, he is interesting chiefly because of *The Sign of the Cross*, which he wrote and opened in America in 1895 before bringing to London the next year. It is a Christians-and-lions melodrama of intense but fraudulent spirituality, with a heroic role for the manager in the form of Marcus Superbus, Prefect of Rome during Nero's persecution of 'the Galileans and Nazarenes'. A dissolute patrician, Marcus falls in love with Mercia, the virginal Christian always dressed in white, attempts to seduce her, shamelessly begs Nero for her life after she has been arrested, in desperation offering marriage and all worldly riches if she will renounce Christ. Of course she refuses. In the final scene, overwhelmed by her faith and piety, he recognises his sinful life, makes a last minute conversion as she declares the purity of her love for him, and they go together to face the lions in the arena. 'Come, my bride', he says at the curtain, 'come – to the light beyond'.[9]

The 'toga play' was a popular form at the end of the nineteenth century and became equally important for film, lasting there well into the 1950s. It is easy to disdain these works set in ancient Rome, as Victorian and Edwardian sophisticates indeed did, but they had enormous appeal on many levels of the social scale. They cleverly combined tropes about empire with titillating sexuality submerged in religious righteousness. As David Mayer reminds us, after a period of relative calm the last two decades of the century saw grave

---

9 Wilson Barrett, *The Sign of the Cross*, in David Mayer (ed.), *Playing out the Empire: Ben Hur and other Toga Plays and Films, 1883–1908; a Critical Anthology* (Oxford: Clarendon Press, 1994), p. 187.

unrest in the colonies, in Constantinople, Afghanistan and the Sudan; the press regularly reported these wars 'as conflict between Christian and pagan'. In a number of adventures that involved the Great Powers in the 1890s, the British were 'continually undecided whether to support Christian imperialism or to encourage pagan opposition to a potentially dangerous Christian rival'.[10] In this circumstance Rome elided Britain, the great ancient empire silently signifying the great modern one – but without any overt insistence that the fall of the first meant the likely decline of the second. Interestingly, the South African (or Boer) War ran more or less parallel to *The Sign of the Cross*, and Barrett took one of his numerous touring companies there during the conflict.

But the chief reason for the play's triumph was its religious theme, its fundamentalist or primitive Christianity strongly appealing to prevalent evangelical and chapel persuasions. Hence, Barrett received unrivalled worldwide attention; his biographer estimates that by the end of 1896 the play was seen by 70,000 people a week in Britain alone; it may even have been the most popular play of the nineteenth century. By the time of Barrett's death in 1904 it had been performed over 10,000 times around the globe and seen by over 15 million spectators who bought a further 2.5 million copies of the sixpenny novel version.[11] Even the sheet music of the Christians' hymn sold and sold, an early example of vertically integrated theatre merchandising. Many pious people who would not otherwise go near a theatre were drawn to watch the piece, and, once present, behaved with the kind of reverence reserved for church. Jerome K. Jerome reported a revealing incident involving proletarian admirers in Rochdale in 1896: 'I saw the rough cotton-factory workers slip off their clattering wooden shoes, and between acts steal softly about the pit and gallery in stockinged feet, as though, with *The Sign of the Cross* in the theatre, they trod upon sacred ground.' The Bishop of Truro wrote a preface to Barrett's novelised version, the Bishop of Norwich offered dispensation from Lenten observance for those of his flock who attended the play, and a vicar in Surrey published a sermon urging 'every man and woman in Croydon to go and see it'.[12]

If George Alexander was a kind of theatrical *flâneur*, ideally suited to the sophistication of the capital, Barrett was a rough and ready colonialist, a dramatic equivalent to Cecil Rhodes who, in our starting year of 1895, became one of the few persons in history to have a country named for him. A later Barrett

10 David Mayer, 'Toga plays', in Foulkes (ed.), *British Theatre in the 1890s*, p. 78.
11 James Thomas, *The Art of the Actor-Manager: Wilson Barrett and the Victorian Theatre* (Ann Arbor: UMI Research Press, 1984), pp. 134, 162.
12 Mayer, 'Toga plays', pp. 84–5.

play, *The Christian King*, about King Alfred but inspired by the South African War, played London briefly in 1902. In a curtain speech on the last night he came forward still costumed as Alfred to note that 'the colonies – especially South Africa – were knitting themselves ever closer bonds to the Mother Country'.[13] Jingoistic claptrap, of course, which rightly disgusted Max Beerbohm, but an indicator of the authority Barrett and his fellow actor-managers could assume, whether they appealed, like Alexander, to class consciousness or, like Barrett, to imperial ambitions.

Matters and manners were changing, however. By 1918 the force of the actor-manager system was spent, many of its remaining examples old-fashioned and unfit for the new theatrical world. London theatre rapidly came to be dominated by financial speculators who had no stake in a venue or company. Production costs and playhouse rents rose astronomically after the war. Like the cinema, theatre became more and more a monopoly enterprise, controlled by businessmen interested chiefly in short-term profit.

But that new world did not lose its hold on the bourgeois theatre. Musical comedy, a form that evolved in the 1890s from Victorian burlesque and the Gilbert and Sullivan operettas, grew apace in the Edwardian and war years, gaining in popularity and sophistication. George Edwardes at the Gaiety led its development, specialising in what Peter Bailey calls 'the rhetoric of the girl',[14] putting production on an industrial basis and attracting huge audiences with a combination of songs, frenetic stage activity, and tales about footloose yet ultimately decent single women. In another inflection of Empire, the orientalist musical fantasy *Chu Chin Chow* (1916) ran at His Majesty's Theatre for 2,238 performances over five years. Such distinctively English musical comedy remained a vital form, confirming a middle-class view of life for primarily middle-class spectators.

The drama of the interwar years remained essentially Edwardian in morality and theme because the dominance of bourgeois theatre was not seriously challenged by aesthetic renovation or political ideas. Stylish and smart, reflecting the surfaces of the modish 1920s, the plays and musicals of Noel Coward and Ivor Novello nonetheless appealed to attitudes parallel to those of George Alexander's audiences. It has often been pointed out that neither the subjects nor styles of mainstream British theatre were affected by the major European avant-garde movements of the period: German expressionism,

13 Quoted in Victor Emeljanow, 'Towards an ideal spectator: theatregoing and the Edwardian critic', in Booth and Kaplan (eds.), *Edwardian Theatre*, p. 162.
14 Peter Bailey, '"Naughty but nice": musical comedy and the rhetoric of the girl', in Booth and Kaplan (eds.), *Edwardian Theatre*, pp. 36–60.

Russian constructivism, Italian futurism, French symbolism and surrealism, international Dada, were all considered overheated foreign monstrosities.[15] Despite the fact that the horrors of the war were common knowledge, only R. C. Sherriff's *Journey's End* (1928) dealt directly with the trench experience, and the great English-language war play, *The Silver Tassie* (1929), was written by an Irishman, Sean O'Casey. Even J. B. Priestley's *An Inspector Calls* (1945), passionately committed to socialist reform, is centred on an upper-class dinner party and written in the accepted bourgeois style.

The modernist theatre

But if the bourgeois theatre continued unabated, the first ripples of theatrical modernism in Britain had washed in from Europe in the wake of the Ibsen movement even before 1895. When the Dutchman J. T. Grein founded the Independent Theatre Society (ITS) in London in 1891 he was imitating André Antoine's Théâtre Libre in Paris (1887), subtitling his enterprise 'an English Théâtre Libre'. Its purpose was to organise a small body of advanced play-goers as a private club, thereby avoiding both the dead hand of the censor and the economic perils of the box office. Actors were paid a token wage and performed on Sunday evenings in plays that were banned by the Lord Chamberlain or, more often, too small in their appeal to attract commercial managers. Choosing *Ghosts* as its first production was a calculated risk that quickly established the progressive nature of the enterprise. The audiences were always small: in the seven years of its life the ITS produced twenty-two plays but its membership never exceeded 175 and its income was barely £400 a year.[16] Though certainly not avant-garde in style, it was definitely forward-looking in its choice of repertoire.

Similar societies followed, all of them what Nicoll calls 'remedial' in nature in that they wished 'to correct defects in the current theatrical régime rather than to inaugurate something new'; each depended on the energies of a single person.[17] But in 1899 a group of theatre progressives organised the Stage Society; though this was not a trail-blazing endeavour either, it would nonetheless promote new plays on a regular basis and in circumstances less limited than those of the ITS. Two of the most important reformers of the period emerged from it, George Bernard Shaw and Harley Granville Barker,

---

15 See, for example, Simon Trussler, *The Cambridge Illustrated History of British Theatre* (Cambridge University Press, 1994), p. 288.
16 J. T. Grein in *Stage Society News* (25 Jan. 1907).
17 Nicoll, *English Drama 1900–1930*, p. 54.

whose careers were interlinked in the first decade and a half of the new century.

Though Barker was much more of a modernist in inclination, welcoming the innovations of European directors, without Shaw little reform of the English theatre would have occurred as it did. Like Wilde, Shaw was a Dubliner, but of very different birth: Wilde's parents lived a fashionable life in a fashionable part of the city, whereas Shaw was born, as he put it, in a street of downstarts. He eventually followed his mother to London, where he learned to live by his ample wits, describing his own reviews as 'a siege laid to the theatre of the XIXth Century by an author who had to cut his own way into it at the point of the pen'.[18] Theatrically Shaw was raised on the strong-blooded, full-bodied theatre of Barry Sullivan, a mid-Victorian touring tragedian, so even when Shaw's own plays were at their most talky he was looking for big acting and strong effects. Criticising Barker's directing of actors, Shaw wrote 'Keep your worms for your own plays; and leave me the drunken, stagey, brassbowelled barnstormers my plays are written for.'[19] But also he was probably one of the best-educated autodidacts of all time. Skilled in music and its analysis, a critic of sensitive and wide-ranging proportions, a master prose stylist, a political thinker and activist of prodigious and steady energies, the greatest playwright of the Edwardian period and the most famous of the twentieth century, he was a restless yet thorough personality – in his own phrase, 'an artist philosopher'.

Shaw's first play, *Widowers' Houses*, produced by ITS in 1892 for two matinées, dealt with the problem of slum landlordism; his second, *The Philanderer*, drew on his own love life but found no outlet; his third, *Mrs Warren's Profession*, about middle-class investment in organised prostitution, was banned by the censor. His prospects changed with the Stage Society; Shaw was a founder and with his plays and advice the association became an important force. Its opening production in 1899 was *You Never Can Tell*; the next year *Candida* established him further in the eyes of the small group of play-goers who thought themselves advanced. Like the ITS, the Stage Society performed on Sunday evenings, though it had more subscribers; in the second season it was pressured into doubling its membership to about 500, giving an added performance on Monday afternoons, and inviting the press to review its work. But clearly Shaw would not become the most important dramatist of the age based on two performances of each play, no matter how rapidly he turned them out.

18 G. B. Shaw, *Our Theatres in the Nineties* (London: Constable, 1931), vol. I, p. vii.
19 Bernard Shaw, *Letters to Granville Barker*, ed. C. B. Purdom (London: Phoenix House, 1956), p. 115.

Enter Granville Barker, more or less stage left. He acted the role of March-banks in *Candida*, one of a line of lover-poets he was especially good at; he also played Frank, another dreamer, in the society's production of *Mrs Warren's Profession* in 1902, the same month that he directed his own play *The Marrying of Ann Leete*, to the utter mystification of the critics. Actor, playwright and direc-tor at age 22, Barker also possessed a determined idea, to make the society – he later called it the Secessionist Movement – extend its work on a regular basis. He wrote to the critic William Archer in 1903 about a plan to hire the Court Theatre for 'a stock season of the uncommercial drama', meaning European writers such as Ibsen, Maeterlinck, Schnitzler – and Bernard Shaw.[20] The next year Barker went into management with J. E. Vedrenne, who took care of business matters, and opened the first of three seasons at the Court (1904 to 1907) that created a new model for London theatre.

Money was always short, rehearsals were at odd hours, and at first plays were given in matinées only, to provide opportunities for employed actors on their days off. Given these constraints, Barker's achievement is all the more remarkable. There were three main reasons, all flying in the face of the Victorian actor-manager system. First, the acting was 'ensemble' and paid much attention to the total effect of a piece, ensuring that minor roles were fully characterised and played with commitment. This was similar to Stanislavski's approach at the Moscow Art Theatre (though Barker was unaware of his work) and would become a dominant goal of many companies in the twentieth century. Critics frequently commented on the quality of the playing, noting that at the Court actors seemed much better than when they appeared elsewhere. No doubt this resulted in part from the pioneering spirit of the enterprise, but now it is easier to see that the role of director was the crucial new element; as the concept did not exist audiences could identify the good effects, but not their cause. Second, the scheduling ensured fresh performances: runs of each show were short, so that actors could not become tired of their parts or fall into the habit of repeating the same business and tricks night after night. Though forced by economic circumstances, the rapid turnover of repertory was a creative benefit. Third, and most important, the plays were innovative and of superior quality. The new scripts in particular were among the best and most interesting being written at the time, and none of the regular managers would have risked staging them. 'The plain fact is', said a general magazine during the first season, 'Mr Vedrenne has succeeded in drawing to the theatre

---

20 Letter, 21 April 1903, in Eric Salmon (ed.), *Granville Barker and his Correspondents* (Detroit: Wayne State University Press, 1986), pp. 41–2.

a class of playgoer for whom too scant consideration is shown by the theatrical managers; playgoers, I mean, with a purely artistic taste for the theatre'.[21] Some Ibsen, a little Maeterlinck, a few other European plays, new translations by Gilbert Murray of Euripides – practically speaking, the first professional productions of classic Greek drama in London. Included in the British work was the first play by the novelist John Galsworthy, a feminist play by the actress Elizabeth Robins and Barker's own *The Voysey Inheritance*, a great and bitter comedy about Edwardian morality.

But chief among playwrights at the Court, dangerously overshadowing the rest, was Bernard Shaw. Of the almost 1,000 performances in the three years of the enterprise, just over 700 were of eleven scripts by Shaw, all either new plays or new to London audiences. The first season was dominated by *Man and Superman*, with Barker as the wealthy revolutionary John Tanner, and *John Bull's Other Island*, Shaw's political paean to the land of his birth. *Major Barbara* came next, a masterwork of the Edwardian age about poverty and personal commitment, followed in the final season by *The Doctor's Dilemma*. The other Shavian plays consisted primarily of earlier, little seen works. Barker acted in most of the eleven productions; he also collaborated with Shaw in directing them.

The Court seasons established Shaw – who wrote his first play at age 36 and turned 50 in 1906 – as a major dramatist. That it had taken fourteen years reflects as much on the difficulty presented by Shaw's themes as on the conservatism of the actor-management system. Despite the common opinion at the time, Shaw's dramaturgy is fairly conventional, drawing on traditions of melodrama, dramas featuring the woman-with-a-past, Victorian comedy, even the toga plays. The difference was his persistent success in turning expected conclusions on their heads, in emphasising ideas, in using a dramaturgy derived from debate to establish conflict. These were not qualities admired by playgoers attracted to the work of Alexander or Barrett, not to mention George Edwardes. For many Edwardians ideas were dangerous, cleverness suspicious, artistic and social innovations repellent, especially in the theatre. They threatened to lead to an unknown and frightening modern world. So if Shaw was recognised by some as an important writer, he was also seen as an unholy fool, a circus clown firing a loose cannon. Further, throughout his career Shaw was committed to one issue above all others: an equitable redistribution of wealth. As a socialist he was far from radical – Fabianism advocated gradual change in the social structure, not violent revolution – but his political propositions

21 *Referee* (16 April 1905), 2.

were nonetheless horrifying to the well-to-do and the already rich. Yet despite such Edwardian suspicion he flourished as a dramatist, eventually reaching the wider audience he had always desired with *Pygmalion*, *Heartbreak House* and *St Joan*, just before and after the first World War.

Barker's subsequent career was not so fortunate. Between 1908 and 1915 he set up a series of managements with his actress wife, Lillah McCarthy, attempting to extend the Court principles. His ambition was to establish a permanent London company that would stage the best contemporary and older plays in repertory: a national theatre. But this could be accomplished only with substantial and regular subsidy, since it was eminently clear that an art theatre, a theatre including the 'New Drama', was not going to pay its way – just as in Dublin or Paris or Moscow. The art theatres there had secured private or public funding, but in England the theatre was viewed – by the state, by potential wealthy patrons, and most of all by the actor-managers – exclusively as a commercial enterprise. The war put an end to Barker's campaign; he gave up his stage work and concentrated on writing.

The audience for Barker's reforms, as for Shaw's early plays, was always problematic. The great paradox of the modernist avant-garde was that it wished to displace the comfortable bourgeois classes that the Victorian actors-managers had cultivated, through an aggressive aesthetic model that presented disturbing material. But a theatre must have an audience; the early modernists had somehow to attract the bourgeois spectators *and* make them uncomfortable. This kind of self-conscious élitism can work only when the élite, or an 'enlightened' state, will pay enough to maintain the cultural institution regardless of its politics or earned income. Modernism wished to replace a system of distinction based on class with one based on aesthetics; progressive, reformed or revolutionary spectators were to become part of the movement by opting into the avant-garde, their advanced status marked not by birth or wealth but by their choice of books, plays, music and art. A movement for democracy, yes, but one still based on educational privilege, as Bourdieu has shown,[22] and ultimately dependent upon an élite band of self-designated pioneers. 'I prefer addressing minorities', Barker said in 1909; 'one can make them hear better'. And in 1917, preparing to give up the stage, he admitted that 'I do believe my present loathing for the theatre is loathing for the audience. I have never loved them.'[23] This paradox of the audience lasted for most of the twentieth century.

22 Pierre Bourdieu, *Distinction: A Social Critique of the Judgement of Taste*, trans. Richard Nice (London: Routledge & Kegan Paul, 1984).
23 Granville Barker, 'Repertory theatres,' *New Quarterly* 2 (1909), 491; 1917 statement quoted in Michael Holroyd, *Bernard Shaw* (New York: Random House, 1989), vol. II, p. 175.

In the creative career of the third great British theatre reformer of this period, Edward Gordon Craig, the idea of an audience was even more paradoxical. Like Pablo Picasso or Ezra Pound, he was fascinated by tradition but worked against it, always on the fringes of the theatre system, a self-conscious oppositionalist. His influence in the twentieth century perhaps was as great as Stanislavski's, certainly greater than Barker's, though he directed very few productions. His ideas stemmed from Wagner's desire to create a *Gesamtkunstwerk*, a total work of art. He wished to move the fussy and over-decorated nineteenth-century theatre, the theatre of surface realism, into the realm of the abstract spirit – to put theatre on a par with serious music. Hence, Craig's starting point was eminently modernist: all the elements of theatrical production should work in harmony to create a unified aesthetic experience. Since this notion became doctrine for much of the century, it is hard now to recognise how fanatical it seemed in 1900.

An excellent draughtsman-designer, Craig proffered the idealism of the visual artist against the pragmatic reality of the Victorian stage. For him scenography came first, a vivid and untrammelled expression of the artist's vision, and the rest of a production would have to be hammered into compliance. Craig held it necessary that a single artist-director be in supreme control, selecting and adapting a text, designing, directing, governing the actors and all other elements of an activity that is notoriously collaborative. Never mind how positive the wayward creativity of actors, say, might be, Craig insisted they must adhere to the single vision that sought a non-naturalistic theatre purged of human flaws.[24]

Craig's first directing work was with the Purcell Opera Society (another 'remedial' group), and his productions of *Dido and Aeneas*, *The Masque of Love* and *Acis and Galatea* between 1900 and 1902 were remarkable for their visual effects. Significantly, he was working with amateurs who were willing to bend to his every command. But when his mother, the famous actress Ellen Terry, gave him an opportunity to restage her production of *Much Ado About Nothing* in 1903, she and the rest of the cast were unwilling to give up their professional actorly selves to his nascent directorly supremacy. The designs were wonderful for their fresh and evocative approach, but the result was a mish-mash of the old and the new, hurriedly mounted, and Craig was forced to realise that his avant-garde reforms would be heavily resisted from within the theatre industry.

24 See Denis Bablet, *The Theatre of Edward Gordon Craig*, trans. Daphne Woodward (London: William Heinemann, 1966); Christopher Innes, *Edward Gordon Craig* (Cambridge University Press, 1983).

Craig's ideal presented an especially serious challenge to the audience. Most performance in history has treated spectators as collaborators in the event, establishing a complicity with actors and action. Craig believed reciprocal engagement was a commercial sell-out, a form of prostitution, insisting with utmost conviction that the true artist must be a leader, dragging the audience, if need be, into a new world. When in 1905 Max Reinhardt engaged him to direct four productions at the Deutsches Theater in Berlin, Craig asked for complete artistic and financial autonomy. Reinhardt, a very savvy businessman, declined and the proposal came to nothing. But the incident was fateful, for it set the future course of Craig's career: moving abroad and losing opportunities. Soon he gave up all thought of working in England, in favour of writing and theorising, with very occasional productions in Europe. His influence would be conveyed through his books and the *Mask*, the journal he wrote and published from 1908 to 1929, which propounded the abstract and non-naturalistic theatre as a saving force.

Little of that influence affected British theatre. The Edwardians delighted in nostalgia, perhaps because the age was fraught with deep social uncertainty. Worries, worries everywhere: mounting fear of Germany and an invasion; trouble in the African and other colonies; home rule for Ireland; growing class and wealth divides at home; the New Woman, suffragism and gender reform – and all set against a social and political structure determined to appear constant. No wonder that Jones and Pinero and large-scale melodrama were attractive: they suggested the continuation of the nineteenth century. The wind of change was blowing steadily across the Channel nonetheless: modernist art, dance, music, theatre and literature were interpreting the world as constant movement. Notable modernist visitors to London in 1910 included a post-impressionist exhibition at Grafton Galleries, Diaghilev's Ballets Russes with Nijinsky and the exorbitant designs of Léon Bakst, Reinhardt's massive productions of *Sumurun* (at the Coliseum) and *The Miracle* (in the vast Olympia exhibition hall), followed in 1911 by his *Oedipus the King* (Covent Garden). A new world of colour and flux. As Virginia Woolf famously wrote, 'In or about December, 1910, human character changed'.[25]

The Edwardian feminist cause was similarly exercised about the idea of the audience. Strongly centred on the fight for female suffrage, the women's movement was interested in the theatre for its instructive virtues. Like the modernist reformers with whom they were often allied, feminists believed that

25 Virginia Woolf, *The Captain's Death Bed and other Essays* (London: Hogarth Press, 1950), p. 91.

THE FINEST STAGE CROWD OF RECENT YEARS: "VOTES FOR WOMEN."

Figure 1.1 Elizabeth Robins's *Votes for Women*, Court Theatre, London, 1907, directed by Harley Granville Barker. The Act 2 Trafalgar Square suffragist meeting scene.

the conservatism of bourgeois audiences was a fault that must be corrected by those with better knowledge and higher purpose. A number of suffrage plays dealt openly with gaining the vote or with the condition of women in employment, marriage or law, including *Votes for Women* by Elizabeth Robins (1907), *Diana of Dobson's* by Cicely Hamilton (1908), Elizabeth Baker's *Chains* (1909) and *Rutherford and Son* by Githa Sowerby (1912). Shakespeare was often viewed as more enlightened than contemporary dramatists. Cordelia in a 1909 *King Lear* 'seems more modern . . . than any heroine imagined by Pinero or Maugham', and in Barker's 1913 production of *The Winter's Tale* stylistic innovations were subsumed by a view of Hermione's unjust trial and Paulina's vehement retaliation as those of 'a militant Suffragette'.[26] Courageous protests by feminists in the playhouses were common, particularly over the harsh prison sentences for demonstrators and the horrible force feeding of hunger strikers,

26 Sheila Stowell, 'Suffrage critics and political action: a feminist agenda', in Booth and Kaplan (eds.), *Edwardian Theatre*, pp. 174–6; see also Sheila Stowell, *A Stage of their Own: Feminist Playwrights of the Suffrage Era* (Manchester University Press, 1992).

confirming how central the institution of the theatre was to progressives, whether modern aestheticists or political activists.

The battle lines were drawn over the issue of censorship as well. Reformers of all stripes found the power of the Lord Chamberlain to control which plays were seen in London intolerable, especially exercised as it was by a functionary called the Examiner of Plays whose decisions were arbitrary, absolute and often absurd. The aggravations of censorship came to a head in 1907 when Barker's play *Waste* was refused a licence because the plot centred on an illegal abortion. A campaign to abolish censorship followed, engineered by dramatists and led by Shaw, Barker and J. M. Barrie, which forced a parliamentary enquiry in 1909. But the actor-managers carried the most weight and they were firmly on the side of the status quo. For them a licence from the Lord Chamberlain established a play's suitability to their audiences; it also meant that managers were free from prosecution for obscenity. As so often in the years leading up to the war, the government decided that no action was the best course. The way to deal with recalcitrant problems – the woman question, the Irish question, the distant colonies – for both Liberal and Conservative régimes, was to leave them alone. Thus Shaw summed up the censorship inquiry: 'The art of contriving methods of reform that will leave matters exactly as they are.'[27]

These various strands of modernism came together in 1913 at the St James's Theatre in a way that seriously challenged the audience. Barker and Lillah McCarthy hired the theatre for a few months for another experiment in repertory, the main attraction being Shaw's Fabian toga play extravaganza, *Androcles and the Lion*. McCarthy had served her apprenticeship playing Mercia in *The Sign of the Cross* on tour; now she invested Shaw's Lavinia with a sense of parody that pervaded the production, satirising the older play. But the piece sat poorly in the St James's. Shaw's portrait inside the front cover of the programme faced an International Fur Store advertisement, Britain's leading vegetarian staring at an enticement for 'charming new designs made in Russian Sable, Chinchilla, Natural Musquash, and other fashionable furs'. Expecting Shaw's sympathy, suffragists seized the earliest opportunity for a demonstration. The *Manchester Guardian* reported that when the Roman captain claimed that Christians have only their 'own perverse folly to blame' if they suffer, the first night was interrupted by 'suffragette cheers from the gallery': they saw the plight of the Christians as a reference to their own cause, especially given government

---

27 Shaw, *Collected Plays*, ed. Dan H. Laurence (London: Bodley Head, 1971–4), vol. III, p. 677. See also Dennis Kennedy, *Granville Barker and the Dream of Theatre* (Cambridge University Press, 1985) pp. 91–8; Samuel Hynes, *The Edwardian Turn of Mind* (Princeton: Princeton University Press, 1968).

insistence that feminist hunger strikers in prison were themselves to blame for force feeding.[28] The *Guardian* reviewer was sure that the play had scandalised 'the most characteristic part' of the regular St James's audience, having heard words like 'vulgarity', 'blasphemy' and 'childish' around him in the house. From their perspective, the play should have been censored. In this volatile arena every gesture was loaded with a heavy freight of contention: Barker's most flagrant move was to place a sign near the box office window – whose manager still wore a top hat – that read, 'We should like our patrons to feel that in no part of the house is evening dress indispensable.'[29]

Populist theatre

The concept of a 'popular' theatre – one that appeals directly to the tastes of people in the social and economic classes below the bourgeoisie – is not easy to pin down. Throughout the nineteenth century most theatrical entertainment was 'popular' in the sense that it was the chief form of public diversion for most of the urban population. It was common, for example, to place animal acts or folk-dancing on the bill with *Hamlet*, and the same venue might be used for large-scale temperance meetings, fancy-dress balls and grand opera on different nights. Of course the public understood the cultural variation among events and between types of theatre, but aesthetic tastes were not as rigidly divided as they would become near the end of the century, when ever more specialised amusements enticed distinct audiences and modernism's insistent separation of high art from low further segmented the pool of spectators. Despite this tendency, it is a reasonable assumption that the classes were still mixed in many theatres before and after World War One. 'Bloods' and 'toffs' went slumming to the East End, the middle classes could delight in melodrama, some of the working classes attended bourgeois theatres in the West End, and almost everyone but the reformers liked musical comedy.

Traditionally discussions of popular theatre in the 1890s focus on the music hall, musical comedy, revues and melodramas in the smaller suburban houses. Until 1914 these were the chief attractions for working-class theatre audiences, though music hall in the Edwardian years was gradually gentrified to become the 'variety show' by managers intent on appealing to more comprehensive and respectable audiences, though not always successfully.[30] But there were other

28 *Manchester Guardian* (2 Sept. 1913), 6.
29 Reported in *The Standard* (3 Dec. 1913), 8.
30 See Dave Russell, 'Varieties of life: the making of the Edwardian music hall', in Booth and Kaplan (eds.), *Edwardian Theatre*, pp. 61–85.

paratheatrical entertainments directed towards the working classes, ranging from the circus and penny arcades through freak shows and mechanical peep-shows to boxing exhibitions and other sports. Since the 1880s spectating at sports, especially Association Football, had grown in appeal to men as part of the emerging 'proletarian leisure'.[31] Eventually, in the first decades of the new century, the rowdy, drunken male behaviour common in the Victorian music hall was forced out of theatres entirely and transferred to professional sport.

Then cinema changed everything. It abducted the popular theatre audience and never gave it back, though film was in turn overshadowed by television in the 1950s and 1960s. Cinema's arrival, though, was not a theatre-shattering blow; in the Edwardian years variety managers might have worried about the new form, but for a while it seemed that the two could co-exist. When the Lumière brothers brought their Cinématographe to London in 1896, it was logical that they demonstrate it at the Empire Music Hall. By 1908, however, there were a number of purposefully designed halls for film exhibition and their names have a certain naïve charm: the Bijou Picture Palace in Dulwich, the Electric Palace in Lewisham, the Electric Pavilion in Great Windmill Street and the Bioscopic Tea Rooms in Leicester Square.[32] After the Kinematograph Act of 1910, which increased safety by regulating film stock and exhibition procedures, cinemas sprang up everywhere. The music halls responded by including films as part of their bills; an act of self-defence equivalent to feeding the wolf in the dining-room. For the regular playhouse, the damage film did to variety at first seemed a blessing in disguise, since it was abolishing the drama's main competitor. Then the second big change occurred after 1927 with the introduction of talking films, and suddenly the theatrical establishment as a whole was undermined.

Why did cinema have such a devastating effect on variety and the theatre? Novelty played a part, of course, especially in the early years, and so did film's ability to create a convincing locale through photo-realism. It has often been claimed that the theatre of the end of the nineteenth century grew the seeds of its own destruction in that it had become more dependent on the type of technological marvels – the chariot race in *Ben Hur*, the train wreck in *The Whip* – that film could do much better. Through montage, film also added new notions of time and narrative that struck viewers as powerful. The magnification of the face and body of the actor, and particularly of the actress, increased

31 Alan Guttmann, *Sports Spectators* (New York: Columbia University Press, 1986), p. 105. See also Dennis Kennedy, 'Sports and shows: spectators in contemporary culture', *Theatre Research International* 26.3 (2001), 277–84.
32 Nicoll, *English Drama 1900–1930*, p. 41.

the voyeuristic pleasures of drama so greatly that they seemed to be an utterly new, erotically exciting and potentially dangerous spectator experience.

While these factors are important, the underlying reason for cinema's success with the popular audience was financial. An early full-length film could cost as much as a theatre production to make, and sometimes considerably more, but once the investment was made the subsequent costs were contained: reproduction was based on technical manufacturing models, distribution global (especially in the silent era) and exhibition cheap. The industrial basis of the actor-manager system, exemplified by the five touring companies for *The Sign of the Cross*, was nothing compared to the economic efficiency of film. At the spectator's end the difference in cost was great, and the ticket price affected manners and dress as well. Daphne Du Maurier caught the mood well in her memoir of her father, the 'gentleman actor' George Du Maurier, when she noted that around 1929 it became fashionable with all ranks of people to attend the cinema, 'where three and sixpence bought a comfortable chair, the right to smoke, and a programme packed with incident'. Hardly surprising that the advantages of the cinema 'weighed heavily in the balance with the twelve-and-sixpenny stall, the boiled shirt, and the long intervals that awaited the audience in the legitimate theatre'.[33] With a nine-shilling difference in the cost of a good seat, informal dress, no requirement to book in advance, and a novel and exciting form to boot, cinema was bound to win the argument with theatre. Thereafter theatre's particular claim would have to be staked on the value, intensity and spontaneity of live performance compared to the coolness of a mechanically reproduced and thoroughly commodified popular entertainment. More than anything else, film (then radio and TV) brought the dream of theatrical modernism to life: in the twentieth century a small, selective, dedicated audience replaced the huge numbers of spectators that had filled the Victorian theatres.

The justifications for theatre's retreat from a popular audience had already been provided by the modernist reformers, as we have seen. Shaw hoped for a large audience, participating fully in the making of some interesting films of his plays in the 1930s, but the general disposition of the progressives was closer to Barker and Craig. What matter if cinema drew off the popular audience for it left theatre free to do what they had always insisted it could do best: concentrate not on the material details of the *mise-en-scène* but on emotional and spiritual themes. In 1931 Barker wrote that theatre would survive in the

---

33 Daphne du Maurier, *Gerald: A Portrait* (London: Victor Gollancz, 1934), as quoted *ibid.*, 47.

face of its electrical competition because 'it satisfies some emotional hunger' not provided for by 'the new mechanical drama of the Movie and the Talkie'.[34] In the battle for the type of theatre that would dominate the twentieth century, modernism won by default.

The rise of the regional repertory companies provides a further major issue in relation to populist theatre. They were important, not as popular entertainment, but because they were part of a movement to extend and democratise the stage beyond the absolute control of the capital. The movement's initial inspiration and motivation came from Dublin, where the Irish Literary Theatre (1899) was founded as a nationalist initiative. W. B. Yeats and Lady Augusta Gregory created a rock-hard idea, that Irish culture and nationalism could be fostered by a drama and a style of performance that was specifically Irish, evoking both current political realities and an imagined past of ancient myths and heroes.

But it was only when a wealthy patron came aboard that the project could be put on a permanent basis through the creation of the Abbey Theatre in 1904, just a few months after Barker started the Court experiment in London. The benefactor was Miss A. E. F. Horniman, heiress to the Empire Tea fortune, who made possible the establishment of the first permanent repertory theatre (and first national theatre) in the British Isles. Nationalism proved to be a sticking point, however, for despite her immense admiration for Yeats, Annie Horniman thought that politics, especially Irish politics, should be separated from art. Unable to convince the founders, and aware of the resentment her support caused in some Irish quarters, she withdrew from the project.

Dublin's loss was Manchester's gain, for in 1907 she joined forces with the director Ben Iden Payne at the Gaiety Theatre in that city, and created the first repertory company in England. 'I want to teach these impossible people in Dublin', Miss Horniman said, 'that I have other fish to fry.'[35] A group of Glasgow citizens started a similar venture in 1909 and Liverpool followed in 1911. Two years later, the Birmingham Rep became the first company with a purpose-built theatre, led by a youthful Barry Jackson, heir to the Maypole Dairies. Significantly, the Stage Society set up a Repertory Theatre Association in 1911 to encourage and assist the movement.

The repertory initiative drew upon Barker's example in its attempt to find a way around the limitations of the commercial London managements and their

34 Granville Barker, preface to *Laurence Housman's Little Plays of St Francis*, 2nd series (London: Sidgwick & Jackson, 1931), p. viii.
35 Quoted in George Rowell and Anthony Jackson, *The Repertory Movement: A History of Regional Theatre in Britain* (Cambridge University Press, 1984), p. 36.

provincial touring patterns. High rents and extensive competition meant that a serious non-commercial theatre in the capital would need a large subsidy, but in the industrial cities of the north rents were much lower and the field open. Anxious to create a cultural environment to match their mercantile success, leading industrialists and merchants – or their children, in the cases of Horniman and Jackson – were willing to put up enough capital to support an alternative theatre.

The reps followed the model of the Vedrenne–Barker seasons of a stock system of production, in which each play had a limited run no matter how well or poorly the audience received it, and they drew on the Court's programming as well. Shaw was the mainstay, 'a rallying-point for them all', as George Rowell puts it, though Shaw's reluctance to grant rights to his latest work forced the reps to fall back on *Widowers' Houses* (frequently seen in Manchester), *You Never Can Tell* (Glasgow) and *Arms and the Man* (Liverpool).[36] Galsworthy, St John Hankin and John Masefield were also important for the regional theatres. The most significant development, however, was new plays from what became known as the Manchester School, especially *Hindle Wakes* (1912) by Stanley Houghton and *Hobson's Choice* (1915) by Harold Brighouse – 'Lancashire drama' written by Mancunians about characters who speak the local dialect. They were seen at the other reps as well and some, but especially *Hobson's Choice*, achieved national fame.

The Manchester School is the clearest sign from the repertory movement that the regions were providing something new and much more populist than the London theatre. But they were caught in an even more complicated audience dilemma and suffered even more at the hands of cinema. The reps were not bourgeois theatre by the standards of the capital, but neither were they wholly modernist or populist: they combined something of all three, and so struggled to find a dramatic repertoire and social role appropriate to the local circumstance. Some did not survive World War One, others were reinvented. Two of the most successful in the interwar years, the Birmingham Rep and the Cambridge Festival Theatre, were supported by wealthy private enthusiasts. And despite their populist urges, the issue of subsidy remained paramount.

The most significant populist work occurred in irregular entertainment projects customarily presented outside the regular playhouses and beyond the capital. These included some dramatic activity, especially in the small theatre troupes generically known as 'fit-ups', that toured to locations without

36 *Ibid.*, p. 35.

playhouses, erecting portable stages in the village hall or school and performing Shakespeare and melodrama in a markedly Victorian style. Though most troupes disappeared after World War One, some persisted longer. But drama was infrequently a part of most populist entertainments. Industrial workers and miners increasingly travelled by excursion train to flourishing seaside resorts such as Blackpool, Margate, Southend and elsewhere. There they would find relaxed and often unregulated performances concentrated on the seafronts and piers: blackface minstrels, pierrot shows, variety shows, musical ensembles, folk-dances, conjuring acts, Punch and Judy puppets.

The democratic social and political inclinations of many of these entertainments, evident in their direct appeal to audiences and supple resistance to modernity and commodification, laid some of the ground for the political theatre of the 1930s and after. This often sought to combine modernist aesthetics with Marxist analysis, as the Workers' Theatre Movement did through agitprop (agitational propaganda) and the Unity Theatre attempted with an international repertoire. Small-scale and perhaps timid in comparison with the vital political theatre of the Soviet Union and Germany, such companies nonetheless kept socialist reform and the class struggle on the agenda of British theatre. During World War Two theatrical and other amusements were regularly brought to factory canteens, community centres and even bomb shelters by Basil Dean's Entertainments National Service Association (ENSA, popularly known as 'Every Night Something Awful'), which was entirely funded by the state after 1942 as part of the war effort.

The national dramatist and the national theatre

The performance of Shakespeare reflects some of the main theatrical currents of the first half of the twentieth century and also highlights some of its more widespread ideological concerns. To begin with, Shakespeare was a focus of theatrical tension. The hyper-realist or 'upholstered' Shakespeare of Beerbohm Tree was dominant, localising every scene, cutting the text for the convenience of the sets and, famously, placing a forest, a grass carpet, and real rabbits on stage for *A Midsummer Night's Dream* (1900). But a counter-attack had been underway since the early nineties. William Poel, fanatically dedicated to the ideal of authentic performance, was attempting to rediscover the Elizabethan stage. Using Henslowe's sixteenth-century contract as his main source, in 1893 he built a replica of the Fortune Theatre that jutted out from the proscenium arch of London's Royalty Theatre for a production of *Measure for Measure*, with actors in Elizabethan costumes. In 1895 he founded the Elizabethan Stage

Figure 1.2 Shakespeare's *Twelfth Night*, Savoy Theatre, London, 1912, directed by Harley Granville Barker. Orsino's Court for 'Come away, death' Act 2, scene 3.

Society, yet another Sunday 'remedial' society, and moved the Fortune set to Burlington Hall for *Twelfth Night*, 'acted after the manner of the Sixteenth Century' claimed the programme. The opposition between Tree and Poel was complete: the first an utterly successful and conventional actor-manager, presenting a Shakespeare as cluttered and affected as a Victorian bourgeois drawing-room; the second working through his hatred of the commercial theatre by rigidly drilling the voices of amateur actors for one or two performances on a bare, open stage.[37]

'I don't go as far as Mr Poel; I think his method is somewhat archaeological; there is somewhat too much of the Elizabethan letter, as contrasted with the Elizabethan spirit.'[38] So said Granville Barker at the time of his own *Twelfth Night* (1912). Barker extended his progressive methods to Shakespeare by drawing on the innovations of Poel, for whom he had played Richard III in 1899.

37 See Robert Speaight, *William Poel and the Elizabethan Revival* (London: Society for Theatre Research, 1954); Cary M. Mazer, *Shakespeare Refashioned: Elizabethan Plays on Edwardian Stages* (Ann Arbor: UMI Research Press, 1981).
38 *Evening News* (3 Dec. 1912), 4.

He developed a simplified stage and abstract settings, eliminating long scene changes; he also avoided the over-inflated delivery of the Victorian classical actor to produce a swift style of speech that would speed the narrative. At the Savoy Theatre in 1912 he began with *The Winter's Tale*, a play unfamiliar to the critics, who were shocked as much by its loose narrative as by the production's modernism. 'Post-Impressionist Shakespeare', said A. B. Walkley of the *Times*, thinking of the eclectic visuals and the unlocalised but colourful sets. *Twelfth Night* followed the same year, a pared-down extravaganza spoken rapidly and gracefully, and *A Midsummer Night's Dream*, with the fairies all in gold from head to foot, completed the series in early 1914. In each case Barker and his designers had replaced Tree's literalism with a fanciful modernism indebted to Craig, Reinhardt and Bakst. The acting was clear and precise, the dialogue full of pace, the small roles emphasised – and a non-acting director very much in charge.[39]

Once staged, Barker's revisions could not be forgotten, even by those who found them abhorrent. But in an England at war, and in the peace that followed, Shakespeare was too valuable a commodity to leave to the modernists. His work, increasingly perceived as high culture's answer to the threats of the new disorder, became a secure foundation against European radicalism in the arts and an opportunity to recapture some pre-war certitude. This was apparent at the London Old Vic, the first theatre anywhere to mount every play in the canon. Directed mainly by Robert Atkins and Ben Greet – Shakespeareans of the old school – the project started in 1914 and concluded in 1923, the 300th anniversary of the first Folio edition of the plays. The simple settings had been influenced by Poel (and necessitated by economy), but Barker's colourful approach was nowhere in sight. Under the management of Lilian Baylis, the Old Vic between the wars proclaimed itself 'The Home of Shakespeare and Opera in English'. It was the most continuously successful of the alternative theatres in London, extending its operations to Sadler's Wells Theatre and insisting on Shakespeare as a high art replacement for lasciviousness and drink.

Stratford-on-Avon in the 1920s was not much different. The Shakespeare Memorial Theatre, opened in 1879 as the first theatre dedicated to the plays of a single dramatist, was more monument to the Bard than a working theatre. At the turn of the century Stratford celebrated Shakespeare's birthday each year with performances from the touring companies, often staged by Greet or Frank

---

39 For more detail see Dennis Kennedy, *Looking at Shakespeare: A Visual History of Twentieth-Century Performance*, 2nd edn (Cambridge University Press, 2001); Jonathan Bate and Russell Jackson (eds.), *Shakespeare: An Illustrated Stage History* (Oxford University Press, 1996).

Benson. Spectators attended out of a sense of duty, relishing participation in the rituals of bardolatry. The theatre acquired its first permanent director in 1919 in William Bridges-Adams, an improver in the Barker mould, who was hampered at every turn by the board of directors and so severely limited by budgets that he could institute no significant changes. Required to prepare six plays in four weeks, he was forced to use old prompt-books, thereby crystallising the blocking, characterisations and designs. A fire in 1926 put the operation into a converted cinema for six years, and when the new Shakespeare Memorial Theatre opened in 1932 the building was a great disappointment.

Bridges-Adams nonetheless managed to stage some interesting productions and, more importantly, gave free reign to Theodore Komisarjevsky. A Russian modernist who emigrated in 1919, his combination of showmanship and irreverence pleased audiences throughout the 1930s. *The Merchant of Venice* in 1932 had a painted Venice of leaning towers and Portia's room in Belmont rising on an elevator from beneath the stage floor. The *Comedy of Errors* in 1938 was acted in *commedia dell'arte* style in a toylike set and a clock tower that struck the wrong hour. Komisarjevsky was a great visual director, designing his own productions, but he was uninterested in social themes or political statements.

British Shakespeare generally in this period, but particularly in Stratford and London, backed away from connecting the national dramatist to the conditions of the contemporary world. Bridges-Adams's production of *Coriolanus* in 1933, three months after Hitler's accession to power, was indicative of this syndrome. Aware of the topicality of a play about a fascist Roman general with dictatorial inclinations, Bridges-Adams refused to allow politics to enter his interpretive field. He thought it 'shockingly improper' when an artist 'turns his stage into a platform and takes sides in the temporal issues that divide us'.[40] At a time when European Shakespeare productions were rife with political nuance, the director of the official theatre of Shakespeare in England was determined to remain aloof. He cut most of the political speeches, attempting to show it as 'a very simple play', aligning himself with the growing conservative opinion that strove to keep art out of politics and politics out of art.

A Shakespeare more consistently engaged with the world after the war could be found at two of the regional repertory companies. Barry Jackson's Birmingham Rep was especially important for developing new areas of programming and expanding into the capital; between 1919 and 1935 at least one Birmingham production played in London each year, some of them of remarkable quality. Jackson was more of an impresario than a director; he often left the directing

---

40 W. Bridges-Adams, *Looking at a Play* (London: Phoenix House, 1947), p. 32.

to A. J. Ailiff and concentrated on management. This was the case with his most notable production, the modern-dress *Hamlet* of 1925, which brought British theatre-goers face to face with a Shakespeare immediate and novel. In a world of speed and streamlining, of jazz and commercial flight, of art deco and consumerism, of novels such as *Ulysses* and *To the Lighthouse* and films such as *Potemkin* and *Metropolis*, suddenly Shakespeare seemed a function of the contemporary imagination. 'We have never succeeded in getting hold of the people for Shakespeare', Jackson said; 'our effort . . . is aimed at making the people of England believe today that the plays of Shakespeare are really good stuff – the right thing'.[41]

The first scene was played in near darkness to prevent laughter, so the second scene greeted spectators with bright light: evening dress for the court, monocles, war medals, cigarettes, butlers, the Queen in bobbed hair, and a lounging Hamlet in shabby dinner jacket and soft shirt. Jackson followed the fashion of the day: 'Hamlet Dons Plus Fours to Kill Laertes in Oxford Bags', said one photo caption in the *Observer*. Jackson's solution to museum Shakespeare was to speak and act the play in a thoroughly modern manner as well, as if it had been written by Noel Coward. His *The Taming of the Shrew* and *Macbeth* followed in 1928. Though neither was as successful as *Hamlet*, the three together marked the first time since Barker that Shakespeare in Britain had been treated in a manner that required spectators to reimagine their relationship with the Bard. Spectators responded well and so, surprisingly, did the critics. Jackson's loyal audience in Birmingham, as well as his private fortune, allowed him to continue to innovate through the next two decades. His other major achievements included Shaw's massive *Back to Methuselah* in 1923 and the founding of the Malvern Festival in 1929 to honour Shaw; for nine years Jackson managed this most successful British dramatic festival prior to the creation of the Edinburgh Festival in 1947.

The roll-call of famous actors who began at the Rep or worked there when young is mightily impressive: Peggy Ashcroft, Ralph Richardson, Laurence Olivier, Cedric Hardwicke, Paul Scofield. And it was Jackson who first grabbed the 20-year-old Peter Brook, fresh out of Oxford, to direct *King John* at the Rep in 1945, starting his professional and Shakespearean career. When Jackson took over the Shakespeare Memorial Theatre in 1946, he brought Brook and Scofield along and made the first moves to reverse the stultifying traditions of Stratford.

The Cambridge Festival Theatre was a very different enterprise to the Birmingham Rep but was even more engaged with Shakespeare. Founded

---

41 Quoted in Kennedy, *Looking at Shakespeare*, p. 110.

in 1926 by another wealthy enthusiast, Terence Gray, it had few of the robust qualities of the original regional companies and none of their interest in local work. It catered to the university audience in an aestheticist mode, running each production for the eight weeks of the academic term, providing the best restaurant in town, offering fine wines, and allowing its (mostly male) spectators to smoke during performances. Gray's project was to import the European avant-garde movement to Britain, and he went about it with the zeal of a recent convert. He remodelled the old Theatre Royal, Barnwell, making it the most up-to-date theatre in Britain by ripping out the proscenium and installing a permanent cyclorama, a revolving stage and the latest European lighting system. Gray stressed design, but in the abstract or presentational mode, often using simple shapes and unit sets. The Berlin expressionist director Leopold Jessner was his model. He engaged his cousin, Ninette de Valois, as movement director for his productions, and made clear his total opposition to the commercial theatre – 'the trade theatre', he called it – in his choice of repertory: Ibsen, the symbolist plays of Wilde and Yeats, even plays banned in London by the Lord Chamberlain.

But classic drama was Gray's strength, as it gave him all the freedom of invention an avant-garde director could desire. His productions of Shakespeare were unlike any others in Britain. His *Richard III* of 1928 followed in Jessner's footsteps, using a system of hollow cubes for an abstract set, arranged in different configurations on a revolving stage. He and his innovative lighting designer, Harold Ridge, did away with general illumination and relied instead on tightly focussed spotlights, picking out characters and throwing enormous shadows on the cyclorama in the expressionist mode. *Romeo and Juliet* the following year used flamenco costumes and seemed to be inspired by the films of Rudolph Valentino. But not all of his productions had the same intellectual rigour: unable to disguise his boredom with *The Merchant of Venice*, Gray had Portia deliver her mercy speech listlessly to a yawning courtroom and a Duke playing with a yo-yo. He hated criticism yet seemed to seek it by outlandish design decisions. In *As You Like It* (1928), for instance, Arden was black-and-white, Rosalind a Boy Scout and Celia a Girl Guide; the characters in *Henry VIII* (1931) were dressed as playing cards; and *Twelfth Night* was on roller skates.

In the 1930s Shakespeare in Britain returned to the control of actors. In some ways the great actors of that decade and of the war years revivified the traditions of the actor-manager. John Gielgud, Ralph Richardson, Laurence Olivier, Peggy Ashcroft, Sybil Thorndike, Flora Robson and Edith Evans led London productions that were created around their talents, and sometimes managed or organised projects themselves. Gielgud and Olivier were the most important Shakespeareans, with high-profile careers that spanned from the late 1920s until well into the 1980s. Gielgud's dulcet, romantic voice, which caressed and seduced words as if they were lovers, suggested that the text was somehow unmediated, conveyed directly from Shakespeare to the audience. Olivier's more modern approach gave a rougher, less musical sound to the verse that highlighted the actor's own intervention in the creation of meaning and left room for the intrusions of the contemporary world. The two created a deliberate rivalry in Gielgud's production of *Romeo and Juliet* in 1935 in London, with Ashcroft as Juliet and Evans as the Nurse. Olivier opened the run as Romeo with Gielgud as Mercutio – in keeping with their vocal strengths – then after six weeks they switched roles to fascinating effect. The set was by Motley, the group name for a team of women designers who became as important as the two star actors in British Shakespeare for the next generation.

British actors were becoming internationally famous again, not because of world tours but through Hollywood films, often of classic English novels or plays. Stage directors did not disappear, of course, even if their significance lessened under the bright glow of remarkable acting and powerful personalities. Tyrone Guthrie, who would revolutionise the approach to Shakespeare after World War Two by creating a series of open-stage theatres, directed a number of proscenium-bound productions at the Old Vic in the 1930s. One of these, *Henry V* in the coronation year of 1937, starred Olivier and used fanciful visuals that stuck with the actor: when he came to film the play in 1944 he expanded on the design and Guthrie's interest in the idea of national leadership during a time of severe threat. One of the most successful Shakespeare films ever made, Olivier adapted, acted in and directed *Henry V* as if the victory of the allies in World War Two depended on it. The film brought together a number of strands of British culture during the war: the relationship of art and entertainment to the national mission, the importance of cinema in conveying a chauvinistic message, the rising power of the star actor. Above all, it exhibited a humanist approach that united Shakespeare with what the allies took as the inherent virtue and moral supremacy of Britain during the war.

The most obvious effects of the conflict on London theatre were physical. Almost all theatres closed during the Blitz; the Shaftesbury, Queen's and the Little Theatre were destroyed by German bombs; the Duke of York's, the Royal Court and the Old Vic were badly damaged. Though some other venues had reopened by 1942, the repertoire was often drastically altered to accommodate the large numbers of soldiers on leave in the capital looking for light entertainment. More lasting were changes to the social habits of play-going. Curtain times were advanced from 8.30 to 6.00 p.m., so that spectators could go directly from work to the playhouse and still get home reasonably early; travelling the blacked-out streets did not encourage urban lingering. Formal evening dress was abandoned as a wartime measure, and never returned; the wonder was that it had lasted so long.

But the tension in Britain between modernism and the bourgeois theatre that had surfaced before the First World War was not resolved until after the Second. Modernist theatre, as Granville Barker had argued, could not exist on a permanent basis without major subsidy. Its audience might be zealous but the conditions of the marketplace remained inimical to reforms, especially after the rise of film. The growing socialist movement, culminating with the landslide election of a Labour government in 1945, should logically have continued the policy of benign neglect for a cultural institution that appealed to only a small segment of the population. Yet that government, busy with nationalising industries and creating a national health service, discovered also a commitment to the social value of high art. It established the Arts Council of Great Britain in 1946, an outgrowth of the Council for Encouragement of Music and the Arts, the national funding body established in 1942 that had subsidised ENSA. Soon the Arts Council was passing out public funds for artistic enterprises: for the first time the stage was treated like national museums, the railways and the water supply. No other development more clearly signals the end of an era of British theatre history. The new dispensation for theatre finance, which institutionalised modernism and culminated in the opening of a permanent and very expensive building for the National Theatre in 1976, finally gave form to Barker's dream of theatre at the start of the century.

2

The London stage, 1895–1918

THOMAS POSTLEWAIT

By the 1920s, after three decades of playwriting, Bernard Shaw (1856–1950) had finally attained the status of a major modernist writer. *Heartbreak House*, written during World War One, had opened in London in 1920. *St Joan* followed in 1923, and Shaw received a Nobel prize for literature in 1926. Since the 1890s Shaw had been creating a new kind of drama that blended the narrative genres of comedy, fable, history and romance with the rhetorical modes of disquisition, debate and declamation. London audiences, though at first slow to respond, had come to appreciate his unique wit and style, if not always his ideas. Shaw had become a celebrity, famous not only for the series of plays but also for his steady flow of wry pronouncements and grand pontifications. Peppering the English-speaking world with his thoughts on almost any conceivable topic of the day, from theatre reform to spelling reform, he challenged received opinions and traditions. And by means of his political activities in the Fabian Society, he helped to create the new Labour Party. Thus, through his plays and polemics, Shaw – the Irish outsider – had situated himself at the centre of London culture and society.

But Shaw and his plays had not always been celebrated, as he acknowledged in 1921. Asked to write a preface for the theatre criticism of J. T. Grein, Shaw used the occasion to reflect upon the austere beginning of his theatre career three decades earlier with the Independent Theatre Society. Founded by Grein, the ITS had helped to carry forward the 'alternative theatre movement' in London by staging Henrik Ibsen's *Ghosts* in February 1891 (a year and a half after Janet Achurch, Charles Charrington and William Archer had staged *A Doll's House*). The controversial production of *Ghosts* served as a catalyst for Shaw, who quickly wrote *The Quintessence of Ibsenism* (1891). Then a year later, having defined and defended Ibsenism, he premièred his first play, *Widowers' Houses*, which the ITS produced for two 'private' performances in order to circumvent the censor. From the vantage point of 1921, Shaw saw the 1890s as not only the beginning of his own career as a playwright, director and theatre

Figure 2.1 Bernard Shaw (1856–1950) in the 1890s.

critic, but also the turning point in the development of modern theatre in London. Grein's society had thus served as the avatar of the new:

Everything followed from that: the production of *Arms and the Man* [1894], Miss Horniman's establishment of Repertory Theatres in Dublin [1904] and Manchester [1907], the Stage Society [founded in 1899], Granville Barker's tentative matinées of *Candida* at the Court Theatre [1904], the full-blown management of Vedrenne and Barker [1904–7], Edie [*sic*] Craig's Pioneers [founded in 1911], and the final relegation of the nineteenth-century London theatre to the dust-bin by Barrie.[1]

1 Bernard Shaw, *The Drama Observed*, vol. IV, *1911–1950*, ed. Bernard F. Dukore (Pennsylvania State University Press, 1993), p. 1364; dates added.

In praising Grein, Shaw was putting in place a now familiar historical narrative that features a brave band of renegades – 'the Impossibilists' as he tagged them in 1895 – who battled for the new theatre.[2] These 'desperadoes' struggled to establish an alternative to the commercial stage, which was dominated by the powerful actor-managers of the West End theatres, especially Henry Irving.

Throughout the 1890s Shaw conducted a critical siege on the citadel of the Lyceum Theatre, which represented, in the presiding figure of Henry Irving (1838–1905), the theatrical establishment in all of its late Victorian respectability. Not even the charm and talent of Ellen Terry, Irving's co-star, could offset Shaw's animosity.[3] It mattered not that Irving – an outsider like Shaw – came from a working-class family, had spent years acting in the provinces and had only succeeded in joining the London theatre in the 1870s. By the 1890s he had established himself as the dominant actor-manager in the capital. Audiences packed the Lyceum to see spectacular productions of Shakespeare (*Richard III*, *The Merchant of Venice*, *Macbeth*, *Cymbeline*), sensational melodramas (Leopold Lewis's *The Bells*, Edward Bulwer Lytton's *The Lady of Lyons*) and grand historical pageants (J. Comyns Carr's *King Arthur* and Tennyson's *Becket*).

On 18 July 1895 Irving was knighted, and a day later theatre people packed the Lyceum Theatre in tribute to him. But Shaw would have none of this. He continued to see Irving as the enemy who was standing in the way of the new drama. Shaw's mission was to save British theatre from its worst temptation – the desire, both commercial and social, to please bourgeois and upper-class audiences. In his barbed theatre reviews he castigated the West End theatres because they were dedicated primarily to the commercial charms and calculations of the actor-managers, their productions making an aesthetic virtue and a social mandate of philistine values. Irving was frustrated by these attacks, but for the most part he avoided debate with Shaw, and he refused to stage any of Shaw's plays (though he toyed with Shaw over *The Man of Destiny*). Firm in his belief that his success and fame sanctioned his idea of the theatre, Irving scoffed at the Irishman's plays, ideas and behaviour. So, the new century began with each man convinced of his mission and disdainful of the other's accomplishments.

The age of Irving versus the age of Shaw: here we have the now familiar historical narrative that Shaw and the impossibilists put in place. Usually presented

2 *Ibid.*, vol. 1, p. 248.
3 On Shaw, Irving and Terry, see Michael Holroyd, *Bernard Shaw* (New York: Random House, 1988–92); W. Davies King, *Henry Irving's Waterloo* (Berkeley: University of California Press, 1992).

as a progressive battle, it records how the Edwardian theatre of modern drama and ensemble acting displaced the Victorian theatre of star actors and grand spectacles. In 1910, for example, P. P. Howe argued that there were two forces at work in the contemporary theatre: 'There is the force which treats the theatre as a trade to be exploited to the greatest possible profit, and there is the force which treats the theatre as an art.'[4] On one side of the divide, according to Howe, were most of the West End theatres; on the other side were the brave new theatre societies, occasionally supported by 'one or two among the managements' (p. 13). More recently, George Rowell has suggested that the turning point in this struggle came in 1905 when Irving died on tour, after having presented Tennyson's *Becket* at the Theatre Royal in Bradford. Back in London that day at the Vedrenne–Barker Court theatre, 'they had played a matinée of [St John Hankin's] *The Return of the Prodigal*, given [Shaw's] *John Bull's Other Island* in the evening, and rehearsed *The Wild Duck*. Irving's day – the age of the actor – was over. The age of the dramatist had begun.'[5]

Alternative histories?

This historical understanding, though in accord with certain modernist developments in the London theatres (and throughout Europe), is too formulaic, especially if it implies that the West End theatre of actor-managers became a diminished thing by the Edwardian era. Nothing could be further from the truth, as the series of knighthoods for actors confirms: Henry Irving (1895), Squire Bancroft (1897), Charles Wyndham (1902), John Hare (1907), Herbert Beerbohm Tree (1909), George Alexander (1911), Johnston Forbes-Robertson (1913) and Frank Benson (1916). During the same period only four dramatists were knighted: Francis C. Burnand (1902, a writer of burlesques; but better known and honoured as editor of *Punch*), W. S. Gilbert (1907), A. W. Pinero (1909) and J. M. Barrie (1913). At least from the perspective of the crown, actor-managers were the élite leaders of London theatre, with playwrights effectively cast in a supporting role.

Throughout the late Victorian and Edwardian eras, the West End establishment of actor-managers, lessees, impresarios and entrepreneurs controlled

---

4 P. P. Howe, *The Repertory Theatre: A Record and a Criticism* (London: Martin Secker, 1910), p. 12.
5 George Rowell, *Theatre in the Age of Irving* (Oxford: Blackwell, 1981), p. 7; for this historical perspective, see also W. Bridges Adams, 'Theatre', in *Edwardian England: 1901–1914*, ed. Simon Nowell-Smith (Oxford University Press, 1964) pp. 367–410.

London theatre.[6] The alternative theatre movement remained mostly a marginal development of limited influence. For example, during the parliamentary hearings on stage censorship in 1909, most of the new dramatists, including Shaw, Barrie, Harley Granville Barker and John Galsworthy, and some of the major theatre critics, including William Archer, testified against the Lord Chamberlain's powers, while almost all of the West End actor-managers and producers supported the system, for it allowed them to proclaim that their productions were sanctioned by the government.[7] So, while Ibsen's *Ghosts* and Shaw's *Mrs Warren's Profession* were denied public production because of their subject matter, sex farces and popular musicals, with their fetching girls, who sang and danced, played to full houses. The hypocritical standards of the system and its supporters maintained the economic health of the commercial establishment *and* the precariousness of the alternative theatre. How appropriate, then, that Charles Brookfield, who wrote naughty sex farces, was selected in 1911 to be the Examiner of Plays.[8]

West End theatres were organised to feature the performers, especially the actor-managers. Audiences came to the theatres expecting to see famous stars in well-crafted productions that delivered fine acting, elaborate set designs and sumptuous costumes.[9] Their expectations were usually satisfied by the West End managers, including George Alexander (1858–1918) at the St James's Theatre. He specialised in society dramas, social comedies, historical melodramas and an occasional Shakespearean comedy. Alexander acted in most of his productions, and he was supported admirably by some of the most celebrated actresses of his era, including Mrs Patrick Campbell, Evelyn Millard, Violet and Irene Vanbrugh, Eva Moore, Lilian Braithwaite and Julia Neilson.

Alexander always sought works that had the potential for a long run (and substantial profit). By contrast, Herbert Beerbohm Tree (1853–1917) tried to balance the commercial successes, such as *Trilby* (adapted in 1895 by Paul Potter

---

6 For celebratory histories, see W. Macqueen-Pope's books. For criticism, see John Pick, *The West End: Mismanagement and Snobbery* (Eastbourne: John Offord, 1983). For socio-economic analysis, see Tracy C. Davis, 'Edwardian management and the structures of industrial capitalism', in *Edwardian Theatre: Essays on Performance and the Stage*, ed. Michael R. Booth and Joel H. Kaplan (Cambridge University Press, 1996); Tracy C. Davis, *The Economics of the British Stage, 1800–1914* (Cambridge University Press, 2000).

7 'Report from the Joint Select Committee of the House of Lords and the House of Commons on the Stage Plays (Censorship)', in *Reports from Committees*, 1909, Parliamentary Papers, vol. 3.

8 For his views, see Charles H. E. Brookfield, 'On plays and play-writing', *National Review* 345 (Nov. 1911), and Samuel Hynes, *The Edwardian Turn of Mind* (Princeton University Press, 1968).

9 See Joel H. Kaplan and Sheila Stowell, *Theatre and Fashion: Oscar Wilde to the Suffragettes* (Cambridge University Press, 1994).

from George du Maurier's popular novel), with limited runs of Shakespearean productions and adaptations of famous novels (Dickens's *David Copperfield*, Tolstoy's *Resurrection*). Long runs bored him, so each year he alternated quick revivals of his repertoire with two or three new productions, including grand spectacles of truncated classics, such as Stephen Phillips's *Ulysses*. Tree's 1908 *Faust* production, written by Phillips and Comyns Carr, was one more attempt to signal that he had inherited the mantle of Henry Irving, whose earlier production of *Faust* had been written by W. G. Wills. Both Tree and Irving, preferring the demonic, played the role of Mephistopheles.

In 1897 Tree opened Her Majesty's Theatre, newly built from the revenues of *Trilby*. Besides his great skills at promoting his new theatre and himself, Tree was most accomplished as a character actor (Svengali in *Trilby*, Fagin in *Oliver Twist*). He was also successful as Falstaff, Malvolio, Shylock and Caliban, but inadequate as Hamlet, Macbeth and Othello. His Shakespeare productions, continuing the Irving tradition of cut texts and grand spectacle, defined the norm for Shakespeare in the Edwardian era, though he was challenged by Frank Benson, William Poel, Johnston Forbes-Robertson, Ben Greet and Harley Granville Barker, among others. But none of them could match his success with audiences. For example, the 1902 production of *The Merry Wives of Windsor*, starring Tree, Madge Kendal and Ellen Terry (whose partnership with Irving dissolved at this time), delighted audiences and was revived nine times between 1903 and 1912. Perhaps Tree's most significant achievement was an annual Shakespeare festival, initiated in 1905. Staged at the end of the season, it presented several plays in short runs. He also established an actor training programme that later developed into the Royal Academy of Dramatic Art. So, though profit and status were certainly the main forces driving the actor-managers of London theatre in this period, they were by no means all as philistine as Shaw pictured them.

The scale of London theatre

But the actor-managers did control West End theatres. Talented individuals like Alexander and Tree, who were also savvy businessmen, ensured that the approximately forty West End theatres remained a defining feature of London entertainment until after World War One. Charles Wyndham, for instance, was even more successful than Alexander and Tree in management; by the Edwardian era he was operating three theatres. And the careers of other actor-managers, including Arthur Bourchier, Gerald du Maurier, Cyril Maude and Fred Terry blossomed at this time. In 1908, accordingly, these leaders of the commercial theatres consolidated their control over production with the founding of the Society of West End Theatre. Confident and self-satisfied, the actor-managers, impresarios and entrepreneurs ratified their professional status and economic health.

They had much to celebrate. Between 1880 and 1920 twelve new theatres were built in and around the Strand, Charing Cross, Leicester Square, Shaftes-bury Avenue, Haymarket and Oxford Street. In addition, a handful of new theatres, such as the Comedy and the Court, went up beyond the central area.[10] Also, dozens of new restaurants, some owned by theatre entrepreneurs, opened in the West End, and a number of new hotels served the growing number of theatre-goers. The West End had become big business. By the Edwardian era the central theatre district, supported by the transportation networks of the metropolitan bus and tram service, the railways (with their ring of terminals) and the new underground system (Piccadilly and Leicester Square tube stations opened in 1906), brought together each evening, except Sunday, an audience of approximately 100,000 spectators, drawn from the 7 million Londoners and the many visitors to the city.[11] The money spent in the West End district contributed directly to the welfare of at least 10–15 per cent of the population of London. The modern entertainment industry had arrived with great commercial and social success. In response, though their struggles were more difficult and their successes piecemeal, the work-ers of the theatre industry – dancers, stage hands, actors, musicians, the-atre staff – began to organise for better wages and working conditions, but these battles did not deliver major benefits until unionisation in the following decades.

The successes of the commercial theatres are reflected in the number of opening nights. For instance, there were 281 West End productions in 1895, then 240 in 1900; 321 in 1905; 346 in 1910; 337 in 1915; and 240 in 1918, the last year of the war.[12] (In the early 1920s this pattern continued, but by the 1930s the numbers had begun to decrease noticeably, in part because of the major

---

10 See W. Macqueen-Pope, *Shirtfronts and Sables: A Story of the Days When Money could be Spent* (London: Robert Hale, 1953); A. E. Wilson, *Edwardian Theatre* (London: Arthur Barker, 1951); Diana Howard, *London Theatres and Music Halls, 1850–1950* (London: Library Asso-ciation, 1970); Raymond Mander and Joe Mitchenson, *The Theatres of London*, 3rd edn (London: New English Library, 1976); R. Mander and J. Mitchenson, *The Lost Theatres of London*, rev. edn (London: New English Library, 1976).

11 See Paul Thompson, *The Edwardians: The Remaking of British Society*, 2nd edn (London: Routledge, 1992); Jonathan Schneer, *London 1900: The Imperial Metropolis* (New Haven: Yale University Press, 1999). On the location of theatres in 1901, see A. E. Wilson, *Edwardian Theatre* (London: Arthur Barker, 1951), pp. 20–1.

12 See J. P. Wearing in the *London Stage* series (London: Scarecrow Press, 1985–95).

Table 2.1 *Extended performance runs, 1890–1929*

Production runs	Over 100	Over 200	Over 300 perfs.
1890 to 1899	169	58	25
1900 to 1909	192	73	39
1910 to 1919	308	138	70
1920 to 1929	406	191	93

growth of the film industry and professional sports.) The general rising scale of theatrical activity at the turn of the century is also indicated by the number of plays submitted to the Lord Chamberlain's Office: 297 in 1890; 466 in 1900; 604 in 1910.[13] But a better measure of West End success is revealed in the number of productions achieving extended performance runs during this era (table 2.1).[14]

There were also several dozen suburban theatres beyond the West End that provided performances nightly.[15] Throughout the year, catering to neighbourhood audiences, they staged a wide range of popular plays, especially melodramas and comedies. Moreover, in the 1890s approximately 35–40 music halls drew audiences nightly with their medley of singers, comedians, dancers, tumblers, magicians and animal acts. By 1914 close to sixty music halls were operating in London.

The spectators who filled the West End theatres could select from a steady flow of farces, drawing-room comedies, costume dramas, adventure melodramas, pantomimes, musicals and society dramas of high fashion. As the theatre critic William Archer (1856–1924) noted in early 1898, about 20 per cent of the productions in the West End that year were adaptations from the French theatre – mainly comedies, farces and musicals. Another 25 to 35 per cent were English comedies, farces and musicals. And society plays, melodramas and pantomimes provided yet another 25 to 35 per cent.[16] Each Christmas season the Drury Lane pantomime, which usually ran for several months, was a major holiday event. As well, two or three other West End theatres offered pantomimes during the holidays, and pantomime was also a popular feature at several of the suburban playhouses.

13 Hynes, *Edwardian Turn of Mind*, p. 215.
14 Pick, *West End*, p. 31.
15 For suburban theatres, see Howard, *London Theatres and Music Halls*; Mander and Mitchenson, *Theatres of London* and *The Lost Theatres of London*; Macqueen-Pope, *Shirtfronts and Sables*.
16 William Archer, 'Epilogue', in *The Theatrical World of 1897* (London: Walter Scott, 1898).

Figure 2.2 William Archer (1856–1924) in the 1890s.

A mixed economy

Much of this fare, though highly professional, was light and frivolous. But as the careers of Alexander, Tree and Wyndham illustrate, the West End was not merely the home of popular entertainments. Although modern drama in London primarily developed in the non-commercial theatre, the commercial theatre made significant contributions. Several West End playwrights, including Oscar Wilde, James Barrie, Arthur Wing Pinero, Henry Arthur Jones and Somerset Maugham participated in the dramatic renaissance, though they usually delivered their critiques of modern society in measured, if somewhat accommodating, voices.

Also, despite the significant differences in their theatrical agenda and aims, key people in the commercial and non-commercial theatres joined forces occasionally. How else, for example, can we make sense of the 1914 production of Shaw's *Pygmalion*, which premièred at Tree's His Majesty's Theatre? Directed by Shaw, it starred Tree and Mrs Patrick Campbell. The partnership was difficult for all involved, but they found a way to make the process work. An age of acting and an age of drama coalesced in the same production.

Many of the key figures customarily identified with the modern theatre movement, including Shaw, Wilde, Archer and Galsworthy, were quite capable of accommodating themselves to the commercial theatres. For example, Archer's melodrama, *The Green Goddess*, had long runs in London and New York, and later was made into a film. Likewise, dozens of actors combined successful careers in both the West End and the alternative theatres; and a number of the actor-managers – Tree, Alexander, Frohman and Dion Boucicault – contributed to the new theatre. Further, the Shakespearean repertoire during this era reveals a broad range of productions, with many actors performing in both the minor and the major venues.[17] In short, the historical narrative of philistines versus impossibilists offers an inadequate melodrama.

Many accomplished playwrights maintained their careers in the West End. For example, Oscar Wilde, though silenced in 1895, had written several successful plays of high style and delightful wit in the 1890s, and his comic masterpiece, *The Importance of Being Earnest*, was staged in 1895 by Alexander, who played the role of John Worthing. For a few years, following his disgrace, Wilde's plays disappeared from the stage; but in 1902, two years after his death, Alexander revived *The Importance of Being Earnest*, despite the possibility of public censure. He also revived the play in 1910 (316 performances).

Perhaps no playwright during this period gained greater success in the West End than J. M. Barrie, whose works satisfied almost everyone. Supported by Charles Frohman, the astute American producer who managed theatres in both New York and London, Barrie created his unique blends of fantasy, sentiment, and social commentary, beginning with *The Little Minister* in 1897 and continuing with a run of successes, from *Quality Street* (1902 – 457 performances) and *The Admirable Crichton* (1902 – 326 performances) to *Dear Brutus* (1917 – 363 performances). And nothing quite compares to the popularity of *Peter Pan* (1904 – 150 performances), which became a regular feature of the Christmas season each year. Many of the leading performers of the era starred in Barrie's

---

17 See Cary M. Mazer, *Shakespeare Refashioned: Elizabethan Plays on Edwardian Stages* (Ann Arbor: UMI Research Press, 1981).

plays, including Cyril Maude, Winifred Emery, Brandon Thomas, H. B. Irving, Violet and Irene Vanbrugh, Seymour Hicks, Ellaline Terriss, Gerald du Maurier, Lillah McCarthy, Mrs Patrick Campbell, Fay Compton and Nina Boucicault, the first Peter Pan.

The commercial stage was also the home of Arthur Wing Pinero and Henry Arthur Jones, who were usually produced by leading actor-managers (e.g., Alexander, Wyndham, Oscar Asche, Dion Boucicault). After beginning as a farce writer, Pinero took up social themes in *The Second Mrs Tanqueray* (1893) and *The Notorious Mrs Ebbsmith* (1895), both starring Mrs Patrick Campbell in career-making performances. He followed with a series of social dramas: *Iris* (1901), *His House in Order* (1906), *Midchannel* (1909). He also wrote the sentimental comedy on Victorian theatre, *Trelawny of the 'Wells'* (1898).

Henry Arthur Jones, who began his career writing melodramas, (e.g., *The Silver King* for Wilson Barrett in 1882), had some notable successes with not only comedies (*The Liars*, 1897; *Dolly Reforming Herself*, 1907), but also social dramas (*The Case of Rebellious Susan*, 1894; *Mrs Dane's Defence*, 1900). Jones continued to write social dramas throughout the Edwardian era, though he never matched the popular success of *Mrs Dane's Defence*.

Yet despite the accommodation that some of the West End actor-managers and producers made to the new social drama, they generally resisted the kinds of play that Shaw, Barker and others championed. The West End was quite modern, especially in its ability to package the social themes, fashions and values of the new consumer society, but it was not modernist. On and off the stage, these West End leaders represented the age and its sensibilities. In its political jingoism (dozens of imperialist melodramas), its reinforcement of the class system (the social dramas staged by Alexander and Wyndham), its representation of women (farces about suffragists) and its pervasive racism (hundreds of plays and musicals with racist and religious stereotypes of Asians, Jews, Muslims and Africans), London theatre generally reinforced the conservative – sometimes reactionary – rhetoric and values of the times. Not surprisingly, then, most of the actor-managers and their theatres, despite their measured support of some new endeavours, failed to meet the needs and values of a significant artistic and social minority.

Modernist alternatives

The division between modern consumerism and modernist sensibility generated a new alternative theatre during this era. This counter-movement and its leaders never attained dominance over London theatre, but they did succeed in changing certain aspects of the West End theatre industry. Working both inside and outside the theatre establishment, they created a new artistic movement, often international in its modernist dimensions and agendas.

This movement – partially constituted and consecrated by the genius of Shaw's plays and polemics – has generally been seen as 'the renaissance' of modern English theatre, as the theatre critic James Agate proclaimed in 1926: 'The years between the beginning of the century and the beginning of the war mark a period of the greatest dramatic energy in this country since the Elizabethans.'[18] William Archer concurred: 'In these twenty years [between 1895 and 1914] the English drama has become one of the most fertile and flourishing provinces of English Literature.'[19] For Agate, 'the great spur to the movement was the Vedrenne–Barker venture at the Court Theatre between 1904 and 1907' (p. 68). With Barker as producer, director, actor and playwright, and J. E. Vedrenne as business manager, the partnership staged a three-pronged attack on the conventional repertoire of the day: new plays by Shaw, Barker, Laurence Housman, John Galsworthy, St John Hankin, John Masefield, W. B. Yeats and Elizabeth Robins (the only woman playwright in the group); modernist works by foreign playwrights, including Ibsen, Maeterlinck, Hauptmann and Schnitzler; and three classical tragedies by Euripides, translated by Gilbert Murray: *The Trojan Women, Hippolytus* and *Electra*. The new drama and a new sensibility had arrived.

The Court seasons turned Shaw into the leading playwright of the alternative theatre in London: eleven of the thirty-two Court plays – and, more tellingly, 701 of 988 performances – were Shaw's.[20] Finally, after a long battle, Shaw had emerged victorious. As Arnold Bennett, the novelist and playwright, noted in 1909:

> It is remarkable that a man cannot write an essay . . . on the modern stage without bringing in the name of Bernard Shaw . . . He is a writer of genius, and before him, during the entire course of the nineteenth century, no British writer of genius ever devoted his creative power principally to the stage.[21]

This canonisation conveniently elides Shaw's Irishness, significantly contributing to subsequent histories which tend to downgrade or ignore the international contributors to the movement, or reduce them, at best, to the dominance

---

18 James Agate, *A Short View of the English Stage, 1900–1926* (London: Herbert Jenkins, 1926), p. 68.
19 William Archer, *The Old Drama and the New* (London: William Heinemann, 1923), p. 384.
20 See Dennis Kennedy, *Granville Barker and the Dream of Theatre* (Cambridge University Press, 1985); Desmond McCarthy, *The Court Theatre, 1904–07* (London: A. H. Bullen, 1907).
21 Arnold Bennett, *Cupid and Commonsense* (London: Frank Palmer, 1909), p. 29.

of the Irish: Shaw, Wilde, Yeats, Synge, Lady Gregory and so on. But William Archer and J. M. Barrie were Scottish, Grein was Dutch, actress Elizabeth Robins was American, translator Gilbert Murray was Australian, actress Lena Ashwell was Canadian and Barker himself was half-Italian. Several others, including Somerset Maugham, were raised and educated abroad; and, just as importantly, several came from working-class backgrounds, while playwrights Pinero, Alfred Sutro and Israel Zangwill were Jewish (though the last was the only one who asserted this publicly). As more or less conscious 'outsiders' most of these people also participated in the social and political events of the era: the suffrage movement, Fabianism and socialist causes, liberalism, anti-colonialism and Irish independence. The cultural 'renaissance' was also, in great measure, a political initiative.

Of course, it is debatable just how revolutionary and modernist the new British drama was, when compared to the drama of Ibsen, Strindberg, Chekhov, Gorky, Maeterlinck, Jarry, Hauptmann, Schnitzler and Wedekind. And the Court productions, while taking up young actors who had worked previously in other marginal companies, also hired a number of established actors from the West End, including Henry Ainley, Dion Boucicault, Dennis Eadie, Laurence Irving, Gertrude Kingston, C. Aubrey Smith, Kate Rorke and Irene Vanbrugh. And on occasion the Court featured celebrated stars: Ellen Terry in *Captain Brassbound's Conversion*, Mrs Patrick Campbell in *Hedda Gabler*. In time, some of the leading actor-managers, such as Tree and Alexander, benefited from the Court productions, which trained actors to work in ensemble.[22] Also, some of the actors in the Court productions, such as Louis Calvert, Lewis Casson, Harcourt Williams and Lillah McCarthy (the wife of Barker), became stars in their own right during this era.

The Court seasons provided the artistic turning point for not only Shaw but also Barker, who launched his substantial career as director, actor, playwright and producer. But the Court's achievements, substantial as they were, cannot be separated from the contributions of several other groups and individuals in the alternative movement. Their successes, like those of the Court, were usually critical rather than commercial. Funded primarily by idealism, most of these alternative theatre groups tended to unravel within a few years. For instance, the Independent Theatre Society (ITS), after its initial efforts in the 1890s with plays by Ibsen, Zola, Maeterlinck, Shaw, George Moore and a few others, collapsed financially and administratively in 1898. Likewise, the New

---

22 See H. Beerbohm Tree, *The Stage* (14 March 1907); reprinted in James Woodfield, *English Theatre in Transition, 1881–1914* (London: Croom Helm, 1984), p. 62.

Century Theatre Company (NCT) (1898–1904), founded by Archer, Elizabeth Robins, H. W. Massingham and Alfred Sutro, failed to make a substantial mark after producing Ibsen's *John Gabriel Borkman* in 1897. Only three inconsequential matinée productions of new plays followed during the next two years. Although Robins and Archer had distinguished themselves with their Ibsen productions in the 1890s, especially *Hedda Gabler* (1891) and *The Master Builder* (1893), the NCT staged only one production in the new century when it presented Gilbert Murray's translation of *Hippolytus* in 1904. Besides putting Euripides on stage (a task embraced subsequently by the Court Theatre), this production was notable for scenic effects that revealed the influence of Gordon Craig's modernist ideas, which were on display a year earlier in a London production of Ibsen's *The Vikings* (thanks to his mother's willingness to go into debt for him). The NCT folded, however, after this production.

Despite the NCT failure, Archer had made major contributions to the new theatre with his tireless campaigns for Ibsen (translations, reviews, essays and directing), his leadership in establishing high standards for theatre reviewing, his championing of a national theatre movement, his consistent fight against censorship, and his abiding friendship with Shaw. Likewise, Robins's major accomplishments included her Ibsen work as actress and producer, her playwriting (e.g., *Alan's Wife, Votes for Women*) and her substantial role in the suffrage movement. For both Archer and Robins, who complicated their partnership in the 1890s with a love affair, the job of being producers and fundraisers proved too demanding.

Far more successful was the Stage Society, which emerged in 1899 and became incorporated in 1904. Filling the vacuum left by the collapse of both the ITS and the NCT, it began as a subscription society with 300–500 members (including Shaw), and soon enlarged to over 1,000 subscribers, who were a cross-section of London artists, intelligentsia, socialists and feminists. Barker became involved early on, directing two one-act plays by Maeterlinck and acting in other plays.

Although the Stage Society lasted in name until the 1940s, its significant contributions occurred between 1899 and 1914, when it staged most of the European modernist playwrights and many of the emerging British and Irish playwrights. Among these, Shaw and Somerset Maugham made the shift to the West End theatres with several long-running productions. Indeed, in 1908 Maugham had four plays running there simultaneously. And in 1913 Arnold Bennett had two major hits: *Milestones* in 1912, co-written with Edward Knoblock (607 performances) and *The Great Adventure* in 1913 (673 performances; directed by Granville Barker and featuring Lillah

Musical comedy

So, the modernist movement, on several artistic fronts, began to emerge in London during the late Victorian and Edwardian eras, despite the commercial dominance of the West End actor-manager system. But during World War One the alternative theatre staled, as patriotism and chauvinism took over both country and stage. Even most of the suffragists became war supporters, and the theatre mainly reverted to its familiar West End patterns of musicals, farces, society plays, melodramas and pantomimes. A few theatre artists, encouraged no doubt by Shaw, were prepared to speak out against the carnage, yet Shaw himself had to wait for peace in order to stage *Heartbreak House*, written between 1914 and 1916.

Musicals and music halls, before and during the war, served as pleasing diversions from both modernism and the modern world. During this era the talented performers of these two forms of popular entertainment gained social acceptance. Dan Leno was invited to appear before King Edward VII and Queen Alexandra at Sandringham in 1901. Albert Chevalier was invited the next year. The royal recognition of music hall performers culminated with the Royal Command Performance of stars of the music hall at the Palace Theatre of Varieties in 1912 (though Marie Lloyd was excluded).

The increasing popularity and status of music halls and musicals, with many performers moving from the one to the other, signals another important feature of the London stage. Indeed, the full story of British theatre would be seriously incomplete without an account of the amazing success of musical comedy. The era was substantially defined by the creative energy and popularity of the musical, as William Archer noted in 1894, with prescient insight: 'This is the real New Drama . . . a form to be reckoned with, a form that has come to stay'.[24] Given its twentieth-century history, on stage and screen, this new genre of dance, song, sex and spectacle – which, unlike modernist theatre, was in great measure London born and bred – has proved to be one of the most significant forms of entertainment in the professional theatre.

Without question, the major London figure in musical comedy was George Edwardes (1855–1915). Called the 'Guv'nor' by his associates, Edwardes dominated the London theatre between 1895 and 1915. Overseeing his empire of writers, composers, designers, musicians and performers, the Guv'nor fashioned an almost unbroken string of long-running musicals, with three or four productions sometimes running simultaneously. With grand flair and

---

24 Archer, *Theatrical World of 1894*, p. 245.

indomitable success, he became, as Walter Macqueen-Pope proclaimed, 'a London institution'.[25]

Edwardes began his London theatre career in 1878 when Richard D'Oyly Carte hired him as a box office manager for the Gilbert and Sullivan productions. During the next few years, working at the Opera Comique and the Savoy, he learned how to produce and manage a show. In 1885 John Hollingshead, who ran the Gaiety Theatre, asked Edwardes to become co-manager with him. A year later Edwardes bought out Hollingshead and began his career of producing musical entertainment. In 1887 he formed another partnership, with Augustus Harris, and together (with financial support from Alfred de Rothschild) they purchased the Empire Theatre, a music hall in Leicester Square, turning it into an upscale venue that attracted a diverse social audience, predominantly male (attracted, in some cases, to the promenading prostitutes in the gallery). Edwardes soon bought out Harris, and became sole managing director.

The Gaiety was the home of the burlesque, which offered both gentle parodies and derisive imitations of famous plays, novels and contemporary figures. Like the pantomime, the burlesque featured a woman playing the lead male role. The beloved star in those years was Nellie Farren, supported by Fred Leslie, Katie Vaughan and Edward Royce. For several years Edwardes continued the Gaiety tradition of musical numbers, farcical routines and dancing girls. Then in 1892, after Leslie's sudden death and Farren's illness, Edwardes guided his team of writers and performers to create *In Town*, a new kind of musical comedy that condensed the burlesque and expanded the songs and social comedy. *In Town* also featured high-fashion costumes, a signature of the new musical comedy. A year later Edwardes dropped the burlesque (but not the farcical routines) in *A Gaiety Girl*, which delighted audiences with its blend of wit, appealing songs, popular performers and a parade of beautiful 'girls' in fashionable clothes. It played in London for 413 performances, then toured for six years. Out of disparate parts, the Guv'nor had created a new form of entertainment.

For the next two decades he produced a series of long-running, expensive musicals. Alongside the Gaiety Theatre, he began to use Daly's theatre in 1895, purchasing it in 1899 when Augustin Daly died. Right up to the war, there was always at least two of his musical productions running in London (as well as his variety shows at the Empire). And success led him to lease or purchase a third, fourth or fifth theatre to open new shows or to accommodate the transfer of long-running shows from the Gaiety and Daly's. His productions

25 W. Macqueen-Pope, *Gaiety: Theatre of Enchantment* (London: W. H. Allen, 1949), p. 12.

also toured, in Britain, the USA, Canada, Australia, South Africa and elsewhere in the British colonial and trade networks.

The Gaiety Theatre, which he rebuilt completely in 1903, was Edwardes's base for musicals with 'Girl' in the title; these frothy comedies always featured beautiful young women. And at Daly's he produced a series of up-market shows, also displaying women, including *An Artist's Model*, *The Geisha*, *San Toy*, *The Cingalee* and *The Merry Widow*. The musicals at Daly's, though often starring some of the same performers who first appeared at the Gaiety, gained a reputation for glamour and good taste. Both theatres, by the Edwardian era, attracted the social élite. Edwardes no longer sought the crowds that had filled the old Gaiety in the 1880s. Instead, when the new Gaiety opened in 1903, King Edward and Queen Alexandra were present; and in 1904 they graced the royal box at Daly's for the opening of *The Cingalee*. During the next few years the king seldom missed a new production, and he saw *The Merry Widow* four times.

The Gov'nor guided the development of the shows, but they were crafted by a production team of writers, lyricists and composers who regularly worked for him. The story or 'book' was usually written by James T. Tanner, Owen Hall (James Davis), Seymour Hicks and others; the lyrics by Percy and Harry Greenbank, Adrian Ross and a stable of other clever songsmiths; the music by Lionel Monckton, Ivan Caryll, Harry Greenbank and especially the tuneful Paul Rubens. Many of these people also developed musicals for other theatres, so London was dominated by their songs and scores. Later in his career, while still maintaining his English production teams, Edwardes also looked to Paris, Vienna and Berlin for works to purchase and transform. He achieved his biggest success in 1907 with his revised book for Franz Lehár's *The Merry Widow*. Featuring the beautiful Lily Elsie and the American comic Joe Coyne, who recited rather than sang his songs, the production ran for two years, followed by a very profitable tour in England and the United States.

Through a process of reinvention and refinement, Edwardes and his production teams had created the modern musical comedy. As Noel Coward later recalled:

> Musical comedy was, I believe, originally devised by the late George Edwardes as a happy compromise between the continental operettas of Lecocq and Offenbach, the early burlesques of the old Gaiety Theatre, and the healthy, clean-limbed but melodious high jinks of Gilbert and Sullivan. In my youth nearly all musical comedies had 'Girl' titles.[26]

26 Noël Coward, 'Foreword', in Raymond Mander and Joe Mitchenson, *Musical Comedy: A Story in Pictures* (London: Peter Davies, 1969), p. 7.

Coward correctly identified some of the historical sources, though his memory mislead him, for only sixteen of the sixty-three shows produced by Edwardes had the word 'girl' in the title.

Yet whatever the title, an Edwardes musical always displayed young women, trained to dance and sing with sexual allure. No matter what the venue, he delivered beautiful women in stylish clothes and seductive performances. Men and women alike flocked to the theatres to see the stately, fashionable girls. As Peter Bailey notes, Edwardes was 'the man most responsible for the exaltation of the woman as girl'.[27] The musicals were thus in the business of sexual exploitation.

Of course, Edwardes was not alone in this enterprise of making sex, song and spectacle both respectable and profitable: sexual enticement and innuendoes were an organising principle of much popular performance in various countries, especially since the mid nineteenth century. The twentieth century continued the process: a cabaret girl in Berlin or Paris, a Ziegfeld girl, a Busby Berkeley girl, a Las Vegas girl, an MTV girl. But Edwardes led the way in forging sexuality as the lure for an entertainment machine that appealed to all social classes. Perfecting the art of packaging sex as a commodity of entertainment, he unified the capitalist components of advertising, fashion and cosmetics. He groomed and instructed women on how to be displayed and desired, and he then placed them in a pleasing light comedy, set off by charming singers and clever comic performers.

The whole package was important, for besides highlighting the charming young 'girls' these new musicals attained much of their appeal from the singers, dancers and comic performers who became some of the most popular entertainers on the London stage: Seymour Hicks, Ellaline Terriss, Marie Tempest, Hayden Coffin, Letty Lind, Connie Ediss, Ada Reeve, Katie Seymour, Arthur Williams, George Grossmith, Jr., Edmund 'Teddy' Payne, Arthur Roberts, Evie Greene, Lily Elsie and the beloved Gertie Millar. The magnetism of their performances seeps through the memoirs like honey on toast. In 1951, reflecting on the 'far-off days' of a once cheerful London, the theatre historian A. E. Wilson equated the Edwardian era with 'the floating, willowy grace and good nature of Gertie Millar'. And Noel Coward, equally possessed by his fond memories, recalled his youth when he watched 'my adored Gertie Millar', a 'miraculous' performer and a 'beloved star, as magical as ever'.[28]

27 Peter Bailey, '"Naughty but nice": musical comedy and the rhetoric of the girl, 1892–1914', in *Edwardian Theatre: Essays on Performance and the Stage*, ed. Michael R. Booth and Joel H. Kaplan (Cambridge University Press, 1996), p. 38.
28 Wilson, *Edwardian Theatre*, pp. 11 and 17; Coward, 'Foreword', p. 7.

3

Provincial stages, 1900–1934: touring and early repertory theatre

VIV GARDNER

In the queer nondescript world of the theatre – neither art nor trade – today is a time of unrest . . . The old unhasting dynasties find themselves less secure . . . new managements are essayed . . . and there is a general disposition towards experiment . . . New theatres spring up, each more palatial than the last, as often as not in a world that has no use for them . . . There is even talk of a New Drama to put in them . . . and . . . the proud predominance of London itself . . . has been rudely shaken by a growing disposition on the part of the provincial capitals to provide a drama for themselves.[1]

P. P. Howe's description of the state of British theatre in the last years of the Edwardian era is, with hindsight, both true and misleading.[2] What is missing from his view is the later perception that this was both a luxuriant, golden era for theatre *and* a period of ideological and aesthetic 'revolution'. Critics and chroniclers, born in the late nineteenth century and growing up in the British provinces, often write with passion of their early experiences of the actor-managers who visited their towns and cities. But they also decry the commercial 'revolution' that mostly destroyed the actor-manager system after World War One, as well as championing the fragmented experiments that brought about another type of 'revolutionary change in the character of the theatre' in Britain.[3] Allardyce Nicoll describes this new theatre as 'possessed of an animating spirit the like of which the nineteenth century . . . had never known.'[4]

1 P. P. Howe, *The Repertory Theatre: A Record and a Criticism* (London: Martin Secker, 1910), pp. 11–12.
2 See Joseph Donohue, 'What is the Edwardian theatre?', in Michael R. Booth and Joel H. Kaplan (eds.), *The Edwardian Theatre: Essays on Performance and the Stage* (Cambridge University Press, 1996), pp. 10–34.
3 St John Ervine, 'Foreword' to Rex Pogson, *Miss Horniman and the Gaiety Theatre* (Manchester: Rockcliff Press, 1952), p. vi. See also: A. E. Wilson, *Edwardian Theatre* (London: Arthur Barker, 1951); William Archer, *The Old Drama and the New* (London: William Heinemann, 1923); J. B. Priestley, *Theatre Outlook* (London: Nicholson & Watson, 1947).
4 Allardyce Nicoll, *English Drama 1900–1930: The Beginning of the Modern Period* (Cambridge University Press, 1973), p. 3.

If that period was a golden one, it was because much of the radical experiment and lasting change originating then started in provincial cities such as
Dublin and Manchester, Liverpool and Birmingham – as well as in London. As
this chapter will show, Howe's picture was largely accurate. The expensive and
expansive theatrical palaces and new managements did indeed challenge the
'old unhasting dynasties', only to be challenged in turn by the 'insistent music
hall', the 'young Turks' dedicated to experiment, the increasing 'disposition'
of the provincial cities to assert their cultural independence of London and, in
due course, by the cinema.[5]

Most theatre histories of this period have concentrated on the London stage
and the more prominent repertory ventures in the large provincial cities,
mainly focussing on the period before World War One.[6] Whilst there are
many good local theatre histories, no overview of provincial theatre in Britain,
including the contribution of the touring companies that criss-crossed the
country during the first three decades of the twentieth century, has appeared.
Yet these companies provided the theatre experience of most people in Britain
in this period, whether it was Shakespeare, Shaw, musical comedy and society
drama, melodrama or farce.

The imprint of social and political change can always be found in the
theatre, such that the upheaval of World War One may be seen as a watershed,
bringing many practices to a premature close and accelerating the arrival of
others. But pre-war theatrical trends were interrupted rather than destroyed,
and continued after 1919, albeit in modified forms. Technological advances
were of considerable significance in this respect, as were the more significant
social trends. Peter Bailey has identified an increasingly robust and assured
leisure culture amongst the late nineteenth-century middle class liberated by
their success as entrepreneurs and professionals. He cites T. H. S. Escott's
observation that 'Only the commercial prosperity of England could have generated the new order from which the chief patrons of theatres and outdoor
amusements are drawn.'[7] This was a middle class at ease in the newly built
or refurbished theatres of Britain's urban centres, well catered for both in
the repertoire and architecture. The prosperity of commercial and industrial

---

5 See Donohue, 'What is Edwardian theatre?'; Nicoll, *English Drama 1900–1930*; J. C. Trewin
   Theatre since 1900 (London: Andrew Dakers, 1951).
6 Exceptions include: Nicoll, *English Drama 1900–1930*; George Rowell and Anthony Jackson, *The Repertory Movement: A History of Regional Theatre in Britain* (Cambridge University
   Press, 1984); L. J. Collins, *Theatre at War 1914–18* (London: Macmillan, 1998); Steve Nicholson, *British Theatre and the Red Peril: The Portrayal of Communism 1917–1945* (University of
   Exeter Press, 1999).
7 Peter Bailey, *Popular Culture and Performance in the Victorian City* (Cambridge University
   Press, 1998), p. 15.

cities such as Manchester and Birmingham produced an assertive regionalism, while similar developments in Dublin and Glasgow strengthened nationalism in Ireland and Scotland.

In the pre-World War One period the expansionist designs of the actor-managers, almost all of them London based, were matched by the colonisation of both the London and provincial stage by commercial managements with little or no interest in 'art'. Resistance to these trends can be detected in the provincial capitals by the mid 1900s, and the radicalism of the early Labour movement was echoed in the repertory theatres. There *were* clarion calls for a national theatre to be based, inevitably, in London; but also voices were raised for a truly national venture that served the whole country in the form of municipally funded theatres. World War One ended the dominance of the great actor-managers and of a number of the early repertory experiments. Challenged by an accelerated change in taste during the war – often pejoratively characterised as the 'Theatre of the Flappers'[8] – followed by the domination of American entrepreneurs and shows, then by the advent of new media (particularly the cinema), the actor-managers who persevered into the 1920s and 1930s increasingly complained about a lack of appreciation and anti-intellectualism among audiences. Serious theatre critics also echoed this complaint, as did the managers and advocates of the growing repertory theatre movement.

This chapter begins in 1900, the so-called heyday of the touring actor-manager, and ends in 1934. In that year Cecil Chisholm published his history of the repertory theatre movement,[9] Joan Littlewood and Ewan McColl set up the revolutionary Theatre for Action in Manchester, and that same city's second Repertory Theatre embarked on one of the most successful of post-war tours with Ronald Gow and Walter Greenwood's *Love on the Dole* (1934),[10] which ran until 1937.

The provincial experience 1900–1914: the actor-manager and the young Turks

With the decline of resident theatrical stock companies in the last decades of the nineteenth century,[11] the provincial theatre became dominated by touring

---

8 Frank Vernon, *The Twentieth-Century Theatre* (London: George Harrap, 1924), p. 118.
9 Cecil Chisholm, *Repertory: An Outline of the Modern Theatre Movement* (London: Peter Davies, 1934).
10 Date denotes first performance where known.
11 See Rowell and Jackson, *Repertory Movement*, pp. 6–15.

companies. Every city or town had a theatre or theatres, almost all now 'receiving' houses that were divided into number 1, 2 or 3 venues. The sophisticated rail network enabled companies to travel between these venues. Towns too small for a theatre building might be visited by a portable theatre for a couple of weeks or even a season, or a 'fit-up' company would play in 'a hall of some sort . . . Two-night stands, mostly; a melodrama one night, a farce the next, and then up and away'.[12] These touring stock companies, with their 'ready-made theatrical tailoring'[13] of both repertoire and characters, did not entirely disappear from the suburbs of larger towns and cities, and some portable theatre companies continued well into mid-century.

Also, most cities continued to support resident companies that featured invited 'star' performers in a wide range of plays, though a few specialised in the classics. A good example of the latter was Manchester's Queen's Theatre, where Richard Flanagan produced a Shakespeare season every year between 1896 and 1915. Elaborately staged and immensely popular, with London stars such as Margaret Halstan and Harcourt Williams in the cast, Flanagan did not eschew the less well-known plays, such as *Henry VIII* and *Cymbeline*, and in nineteen years the only ones he repeated were *Antony and Cleopatra* and *The Merchant of Venice*.[14] In 1908 the *Manchester Programme* defended Flanagan's home-grown product against the intruders: 'no touring company, however famous may be a particular "star" actor or actress . . . can come within miles of it'.[15]

However, there is ample evidence of the popularity of the productions touring to number 1 theatres. Actor-managers of both genders found eager audiences in the provinces. Most, like Oscar Asche, Mrs Patrick Campbell, Johnston Forbes-Robertson, Henry Irving, Herbert Beerbohm Tree and Lewis Waller, staged a mixed bill of Shakespeare and currently conventional drama. Each tended to have a favourite vehicle that ensured success: Irving in *The Bells* (1871); Tree as Svengali; and Forbes-Robertson as the Stranger in Jerome K. Jerome's *The Passing of the Third Floor Back* (1908). Others, like George Alexander, constantly replayed their successes of the 1890s, in society dramas such as *The Second Mrs Tanqueray* (1893) and romantic roles such as Rudolph Rassendyll in *The Prisoner of Zenda* (1896). Some successful London-based actor-managers

---

12 Harold Child, *A Poor Player: The Story of a Failure* (Cambridge University Press, 1939), pp. 24–5. For venues, see R. Douglas Cox, C. Douglas Stuart and William Martin, *Theatrical, Variety & Fit-Up Directory* (London: Whitton & Smith, 1904 etc.).

13 Rowell and Jackson, *Repertory Movement*, p. 8.

14 See Viv Gardner, 'No flirting with philistinism: Shakespeare production at Miss Horniman's Gaiety Theatre', *New Theatre Quarterly* 14, 55 (Aug. 1998), 220–33.

15 *Manchester Programme* (6 April 1908), 12.

failed in the provinces, while others rarely played London. Of the latter, the most successful were those such as John Martin-Harvey, who, with his wife Nina de Silva, cultivated a provincial following for romantic melodrama that lasted until the outbreak of World War Two. His last appearance, aged 76, was in his most popular role as Sydney Carton in *The Only Way* (1899), an adaptation of Dickens's *A Tale of Two Cities*.

Frank Benson was outstanding among the actor-managers in promoting and maintaining a consistently serious repertoire with his Shakespearean Company. By 1908 there were four Benson Shakespeare companies: the 'first' and 'three secondary and geographically eccentric companies, North, South and Midland'.[16] Although the high point of running four companies was short-lived, Benson continued to tour into the 1930s and gained a prodigious reputation, though his acting was not always rated very highly, and the management of his company, with its eccentric insistence on sport and recreation, was sometimes ridiculed. In A. E. Wilson's judgement

> [t]he value of Benson's services to the theatre can never be fully estimated. His passionate enthusiasm kept Shakespeare alive in the provinces. He took the drama to the remotest parts of the kingdom and no man ever did more to conquer the last lingering prejudices of the stage.[17]

Yet he rarely commanded higher than second-rank venues. Like similar companies, Benson's could not fully compete with the expensively staged London productions of the more successful actor-managements or 'the commercial managers for whom financial return was paramount and [who] were prepared to exploit both actor and audience in the process'.[18]

The formation in March 1900 of the Touring Managers' Association by a number of leading managers was symptomatic of growing industrial tension in the provincial theatre system. The need for managers to advance and protect their interests and establish a framework for arbitration had become greater as performers and other workers in both drama and variety companies began to form professional associations to articulate and negotiate their 'rights'. A Provincial Actors' Union was formed in 1907, soon becoming part of the Actors' Union, though it was not until the 1920s that provincial performers showed serious opposition to management.[19] The Touring Managers' Association included actor-managers such as Beerbohm Tree, Ben Greet and Louis

---

16 *Ibid.*, p. 161.
17 Wilson, *Edwardian Theatre*, p. 103.
18 Rowell and Jackson, *Repertory Movement*, p. 13.
19 See H. R. Barbor, *The Theatre: An Art and an Industry* (London: Labour Publishing, 1924).

Calvert, who were more interested in making good theatre than in making money, but increasingly it was dominated by commercial managers such as George Edwardes and Percy Hutchison.

A closer analysis of the nationwide repertoire is revealing both of audience demand and managerial response. In November 1901 the theatrical newspaper *Era* lists some 163 companies 'on the road', indicating, if not the quality, then the vigour and quantity of productions on offer throughout the country.[20] The range is enormous, and can be demonstrated by a brief comparison between George Alexander's company at the Opera House in Belfast and Muriel Wylford's company at the Grand Theatre, Southampton. Alexander's repertoire included a selection of his St James's Theatre productions of society drama, Shakespeare's 'most respectable comedies'[21] and, inevitably, *The Prisoner of Zenda*. Miss Wylford's company was apparently well established on the provincial circuit, as she claims to be booking 'London, Suburbs and No. 1 theatres only'. Her repertoire is clearly tailored to her histrionic strengths in emotionally vibrant drama: *The Second Mrs Tanqueray*, *Magda*, *Brother Officers* and the 'Only Authorised Version' of *Lorna Doone*.

In the *Era* listings a large number of productions are described as 'musical plays' or 'musical comedies'. There are two versions of *The Lady Slavey* (1893), and three each of *The Belle of New York* (1897), *Floradora* (1899) and *La Poupée*. Melodramas and the occasional 'powerful sensational drama of the present day' or 'romance of the divorce court' or 'woman's great play' are billed alongside an 'enormously successful farcical comedy' or the 'funnier than "Charley's Aunt"' comedy, *The Varsity Belle*. At least two productions deal with the recently ended South African Wars, including *A Woman of Pleasure*, which featured 'a scene outside the Government buildings at Pretoria with the balloon section encampment vividly introduced, and the villain and the injured wife ascend together into space in a monster balloon'.[22] Many of the advertisements boast similarly 'beautiful scenes', or 'new scenes', 'everything carried' or 'magnificent scenery carried for all acts', indicating that this production comes complete and will not rely on aged local 'stock' scenery.

A significant number of productions originate in London, and sometimes a management will tour two or three companies with the same production, like Hall Caine's *The Christian* (1907) from the Duke of York's Theatre playing in Dundee and Chester in the same week. Others claim a London star, like

20 *Era* (9 Nov. 1901); the total number of companies would have been greater, as the listings are advertisements paid for by the managers.
21 Hesketh Pearson, *The Last Actor-Managers* (London: Methuen, 1950), p. 31.
22 *Era* (9 Nov. 1901).

'Mr J. J. Dallas (from the Gaiety, Lyric, Avenue, Savoy, Lyceum) and the Best Farcical Comedy Company on Tour' or an unnamed but 'specially engaged West End cast'. But in this month (November 1901), the only front-ranking London actor-manager on the road is George Alexander. He is outnumbered by provincial stars with nationwide reputations, such as Millicent Bandmann-Palmer, in her thirteenth year of touring 'High-class Comedies, Tragedies and Standard Plays' and, on a more local level, Mrs Kimberley from the Queen's Theatre, Fleetwood, appearing with her husband's company in her own dramas, *A Sister's Sin* (1900) and *Bound to Win* (1901).[23]

A decade later, in November 1911, the picture is not dissimilar. Of 175 companies listed, most are touring popular, undemanding pieces. Musical comedies dominate, with three companies touring *The Arcadians* (1909) and three touring George Edwardes's *The Girl on the Train* (1910) and *The Chocolate Soldier* (1910). *Floradora* is now to be found at the Miners' Theatre in Ashington and the New Hippodrome in Accrington, both 'no. 3' venues. Benson is running three Shakespearean companies, though Shakespeare is not well represented generally. Only two other companies are listed as touring the Bard.[24]

A comparison of shows on offer in two similarly sized towns, in the north and south of the country, confirms the impression of a repertoire dominated by musical comedies and London tours. The Yorkshire spa town of Harrogate in 1911 had three touring venues, the foremost being the Grand Theatre and Opera House. The Grand had been designed by the prolific theatre architect Frank Matcham[25] and opened in January 1900, boasting a capacity of 1,300, electric lights and eight shops. The autumn season of 1911 included productions from the Gaiety, Wyndham's, Playhouse, Haymarket, New, Vaudeville and Prince of Wales's theatres in London. On offer were musical comedies from the Robert Courtneidge and George Edwardes companies, a new play by Hall Caine 'said to be drawing all London' to see it, two detective dramas, two new comedies (one 'farcical', the other 'charming') and an old favourite, Julia Neilson in *The Popinjay*, plus the 'sensational American Drama, *The Cowboy Thief* ' – 'a peg above melodrama', the review claims.[26] However, these populist offerings were offset by a week of Shakespeare from the Alexander Marsh Company, preceded by a series of lectures by Professor Moorman from the University of Leeds.[27]

23 *Ibid.*
24 *Era* (4 Nov. 1911).
25 See Brian Walker (ed.), *Frank Matcham: Theatre Architect* (Belfast: Blackstaff Press, 1980);
    Jack Read, *Empires, Hippodromes and Palaces* (London: Alderman Press, 1985).
26 *Harrogate Herald and Weekly List of Visitors* (Sept.–Dec. 1911).
27 *Harrogate Herald and Weekly List of Visitors* (16 Oct. 1911).

By 1911 Brighton was an established south coast resort, with seven theatrical and variety venues. Compared to Harrogate, it shows a more significant incursion by the 'insistent music hall' and the cinema, with at least one dedicated picture-house, the Théâtre de Luxe, and mixed bills at the Court Theatre of film and live drama. In November, while Sarah Bernhardt played the Hippodrome – 'the first time she has appeared on the boards of a local music hall . . . timed for the very height of the fashionable season' – Mr H. Hamilton Stewart's company was showing '*Alias Johnny Valentine* . . . a thoroughly healthy play about a reformed criminal' at the West Pier Theatre, and the Grand offered a melodrama starring 'Billy Butt's goat . . . a very intelligent animal . . . and a great favourite'. At the Theatre Royal, recently extended and refurbished and for decades Brighton's principal venue for dramatic theatre, George Edwardes's company was followed by George Dance's, both offering musical comedy.[28] In the previous week, though, the Theatre Royal had featured Diaghilev's Russian ballet company from the Imperial Opera House in St Petersburg and a 'flying matinée' of Shaw's *Man and Superman* (1903).[29] The latter was a relatively new phenomenon, fostered by the growth and speed of rail links. A successful production would, with a minimum of props and costumes, 'fly' to a provincial town and play a matinée before returning to give an evening performance, usually in London.[30]

This type of mixed repertoire, with the risky venture followed by the certain money-spinner, is indicative of the financial tightrope trodden by all, but more especially provincial, theatre managers. The situation was exacerbated in 1911 for the Theatre Royal by a dispute between the lessees and owners that resulted in a period of closure, plus a fire that had destroyed the dressing-rooms and costume stock.[31] This may account for the dearth of Shakespeare that year. None of the 'London greats' had been attracted to the theatre: only one production of *A Midsummer Night's Dream* and a visit of one week by Benson's company were seen there.[32]

Unsurprisingly, there were many who saw the commercial imperative and the dominance of the manager, actor or otherwise, as a *grande malaise*. In 1907 Harley Granville Barker wrote that '[i]t will need the establishment, not of one permanent repertory theatre, but of many and the operation of several years,

28 *Brighton Gazette* (Nov. 1911).
29 Antony Dale, *The Theatre Royal Brighton* (Stocksfield: Oriel Press, 1980), p. 85.
30 See A. E. Wilson, *Playgoer's Pilgrimage* (London: Stanley, Paul & Co., 1938), p. 55; Dale, *Theatre Royal Brighton*, pp. 45–6.
31 Dale, *Theatre Royal Brighton*, pp. 82–5.
32 *Ibid.*, p. 85.

to steady and correct this debauched market'.[33] This disaffection led to what Nicoll has described, somewhat hyperbolically, as 'a vast upsurge in which professionals and amateurs alike were swept forwards by a kind of unseen power . . . they exerted such a force as had never been experienced by a theatre in England'.[34]

The repertory 'revolution'

sir, – I am writing to inform you of a scheme which, it is possible, may form the nucleus of a city theatre, the idea of which, I am informed, has been mooted recently in Manchester. Miss A. E. F. Horniman, with myself as her general manager, hopes to form a repertory theatre in Manchester . . . we intend to produce no plays which are not sincere works of art . . . We have chosen Manchester because we feel that of all towns it is the one most ready for such an undertaking.[35]

Ironically, the first provincial repertory theatre was not a local initiative. As Ben Iden Payne indicates, Miss Horniman had chosen Manchester, but her initial preference had been for a London base. In 1909 she gave her assessment of the London repertory ventures to Constance Garnett:

The Mermaid Society scheme was not wide nor thorough enough . . . to take a hold on London & the Court Theatre made an audience is true, but too cultivated and restricted to fill that small theatre always & not large enough for the Savoy . . . I think that Miss Kingston [of the] 'Little Theatre' . . . will find that she is catering for a class who are often away from London & eats too much to have enough vitality left for good drama . . . My idea is to keep the Gaiety as *catholic* as possible (barring musical comedy) & to attract the wide circle of people who read intelligently and *earn* the money they spend on seats.[36]

London was too expensive and problematic for what she and others envisaged. However, Manchester had already been identified as a possible location for a new repertory theatre or even the new National Theatre as conceived by the theatre reformists of the period. The idea of a National Theatre (based in London) had been voiced in the 1870s; twenty years later George Bernard Shaw

---

33 W. Archer and H. Granville Barker, *A National Theatre: Schemes and Estimates* (London: Duckworth, 1907), p. viii.
34 Nicoll, *English Drama 1900–1930*, p. 54.
35 Ben Iden Payne to the Manchester papers (11 July 1907); cited in Pogson, *Miss Horniman*, p. 22.
36 A. E. F. Horniman to Constance Garnett, 13 April 1909, Harry Ransom Humanities Research Center, University of Texas at Austin.

had addressed the issue of municipal sponsorship of theatre in the London sub-urbs and the provinces.[37] When William Archer and Harley Granville Barker published *A National Theatre: Schemes and Estimates* in 1907 (first issued privately two years earlier), Archer averred that his views had not altered except in one or two areas.

> I would draw up a second set of figures, suitable to the foundation of an ade-quate repertory theatre in Manchester, Birmingham, or some such provincial centre. For it is to one of these cities, easier to stir to the expression of civic opinion, rather than to the monstrous and inarticulate London . . . that I look for the first practical step in theatrical organisation.

The whole enterprise would be more economical in the provinces, it would be easier to find a suitable theatre and '[p]laygoers there might be more ready to recognise the virtues of acting, vitalised under simpler methods of production, than would the pampered London public'.[38]

Manchester's readiness was in little doubt, but the foundations had been laid elsewhere: at the London Independent Theatre, in the Barker–Vedrenne seasons at the Court and Savoy Theatres, in the 'art theatres' of Europe and in Dublin at the Abbey Theatre. The latter had, as Jackson argues, 'a legitimate claim to be the first permanently established repertory theatre in the British Isles [*sic*], antedating Miss Horniman's venture by nearly four years'.[39] The emergence of the Irish National Theatre Society in 1903 offered a model for the future repertories. Its manifesto primarily committed it to 'create an Irish National Theatre, to act and produce plays in Irish or English, written by Irish writers, or on Irish subjects'.[40] The idea of an ensemble company with a clear identity was also important, as Frank Fay had written in 1901: 'What is the use . . . if we have to get English actors because we are too lazy to train Irish ones?'[41] However, the theatre 'had to stand outside the nationalist movement to make its mark on the theatre of the world'.[42] With a subvention from Miss Horniman, the society acquired and refurbished a small music hall in Dublin's Mechanics Institute to create the Abbey Theatre in 1904, formed a professional company in 1906 and 'made its mark' by touring extensively beyond Ireland.

---

37 George Bernard Shaw, *Saturday Review* (14 and 21 March 1896), reprinted in *Our Theatre in the Nineties*, vol. ii (London: Constable, 1931), pp. 67–79.

38 Archer and Barker, *National Theatre*, pp. xi–xiv.

39 Rowell and Jackson, *Repertory Movement*, p. 31.

40 *Ibid.*, p. 32.

41 *United Irishman* (20 July 1901), cited in Sam Hanna Bell, *The Theatre in Ulster* (Totowa, N.J.: Rowan & Littlefield, 1972), p. 9.

42 Maire Nic Shiubhalaigh, *The Splendid Years* (Dublin: James Duffy, 1955), p. 75.

In its turn, Manchester provided an ideal context as a provincial 'capital' for the new theatre. As Rex Pogson wrote:

> Not only was Manchester's theatrical history a long, and in many ways notable one; it was also the only provincial city in which a serious attempt had been made to introduce the 'new' drama . . . from 1893 to 1898 the Independent Theatre Society had periodically produced plays [there].[43]

It also had a newly formed Manchester's Playgoers' Club, an amateur repertory company in the Stockport Garrick and a nationally read newspaper in the *Manchester Guardian*, which employed serious critics of the stage such as C. E. Montague and later James Agate and Allan Monkhouse. Above all, it was a prosperous city with a strong confidence in its national and regional identity.

Payne and Horniman enlarged on their aims in a subsequent letter to the press. Their theatre was to be:

(a) A repertory theatre with a regular change of programme, not wedded to any one school of dramatists, but thoroughly catholic, embracing the finest writing of the best authors of all ages and with an especially widely open door to present-day British writers . . . provided that they have something to say worth listening to, and say it in an interesting and original manner.
(b) A permanent Manchester stock company of picked front-rank actors.
(c) Efficient productions.
(d) Popular prices.[44]

The opening five-week season took place in September 1907 in the Midland Hotel Theatre. This small stage in the recently built 'finest hotel in the world' seems an unlikely venue for such a radical venture. However, the season was chosen with great care to exemplify the new theatre's philosophy. It opened with Charles McEvoy's *David Ballard*, a modern realist drama of lower-middle-class life, which follows the battles between art and survival in the life of a would-be writer. Two European plays followed – Rostand's *The Fantasticks* and Maeterlinck's *Interior* – then two plays by women, Miss A. R. Williams's *The Street* (1907), described as a 'powerfully realistic play', and George Paston's contemporary comedy *Clothes and the Woman* (1907), and finally Shaw's *Widowers' Houses* (1892). The company were chosen for their commitment to the repertory project. Many had played in one of the earlier 'art theatre' ventures, either at the Court or, like Payne himself, in Benson's company and with William Poel's Elizabethan Stage Society. Some, such as Charles Bibby and Herbert

43 Pogson, *Miss Horniman*, pp. 24–5.
44 *Ibid.*, p. 26.

Lomas, were local actors; others, such as Sybil Thorndike, Lewis Casson and Basil Dean, were young and relatively inexperienced but went on to spread the repertory tradition. In this first season, only *Clothes and the Woman* provided a 'star' role – for Margaret Halstan, long a Manchester favourite – though later local 'stars' developed within the company. From the first the acting was singled-out for praise: 'The acting [in *Widowers' Houses*] was like Shaw's writing, which has no stupidities and no beauties. There was no virtuosoish working of any of the actors' special gift, but every intention of the play was understood and carried out.'[45] By 1909 and their first London season, the realism of the company's acting tradition was nationally known and recognised.

The opening season was deemed by most a success and Horniman proceeded to take her company on tour and to buy a building, the Gaiety Theatre. A six-week season was undertaken in the 'old' Gaiety before it was refurbished by Frank Matcham. The opening production by William Poel of *Measure for Measure* was, in Pogson's words, 'a daring stroke . . . in a provincial theatre in 1908, particularly by a company not yet sure of its public, and in a city wedded to a strong Shakespeare tradition of a very different kind'.[46] It signalled the Gaiety philosophy in an uncompromising way, in terms of choice of play, acting and aesthetics.

However, *Measure for Measure* was untypical in some respects. In its 22-year lifespan, the Gaiety, for all its reputation as the home of dour realism, played more comedy than drama, less Shakespeare than other classic texts and more new drama than old. Plays by Shaw, Galsworthy, Masefield and McEvoy were regularly staged and there were significantly more plays by women produced than at most other theatres. From the beginning, Horniman invited local authors to submit work to her:

> If Lancashire playwrights will send their plays to me I shall pledge myself to read them through [which she did]. Let them write not as one dramatist does, about countesses and duchesses and society existing in the imagination, but about their friends and enemies – about real life.[47]

By the outbreak of World War One the so-called 'Manchester School' was one of the distinguishing features of the Gaiety. Its most successful writers were Stanley Houghton, best known for such social comedies as *The Younger Generation* (1910) and *Hindle Wakes* (1912), and Harold Brighouse, who wrote

45 Cited *ibid.*, p. 34.
46 *Ibid.*, pp. 42–3; see also Gardner, 'No flirting with philistinism'.
47 Pogson, *Miss Horniman*, pp. 36–7.

realist dramas of Lancashire working- and middle-class life, such as *The Price of Coal* (1909) and *Garside's Career* (1914), as well as a prescient drama on the business of football, *The Game* (1913), and the generational comedy *Hobson's Choice* (1915).

The Manchester initiative was rapidly followed by the setting-up of repertory theatres in Glasgow (1909), Liverpool (1911), Birmingham (1913) and Bristol (1914). Though these were modelled on Manchester's example, each was developed from a different base and in a slightly different direction. The Glasgow Repertory Company, for example, was established by Alfred Wareing, who in 1909 set out to found a 'citizens' theatre in the fullest sense of the term'.[48] But unlike Manchester and Birmingham, it could never afford to buy a theatre. Its leasing arrangements with Howard and Wyndham at the Royalty Theatre were never satisfactory, and despite an adventurous repertoire that included the first production of Chekhov in Britain (*The Seagull*, 1909) it had difficulty mustering sufficient public support to compensate for parsimonious commercial agreements, with the result that it closed in the autumn of 1914.

Liverpool Repertory Theatre, too, came close to closure at the outbreak of the war. Having started well, with a significant profit of £1,600 on its first six-week season in 1911 at Kelly's Theatre, the repertory subsequently suffered from differences in the artistic ambitions of its director, company and 900 shareholders. Though able to buy a theatre, the Star Music Hall, renamed the Liverpool Repertory Theatre, its policies were always circumscribed by the caution of the shareholders. Basil Dean, fresh from the Gaiety, was its first director, but despite his desire to extend the 'repertory vision', the repertoire looked 'commercial' when compared to similar theatres. True, the 'standard' plays were presented – by Shaw, Masefield, Galsworthy and Barker – but the company's opening production, J. M. Barrie's *The Admirable Crichton* (1902), signalled some of the conservatism of its future programming. Pinero, Wilde, Henry Arthur Jones, even Robertson's *Caste* (1867), and classic comedies, for example by Sheridan and Goldsmith, were staged more often than in other repertories' bills.[49] Liverpool Rep did not develop local writing in the way that Manchester and Glasgow had succeeded in doing, but it did produce a number of plays that confronted local issues. The opening production at Kelly's Theatre of Galsworthy's *Strife* (1909), a play about relations between

48 Playbill for Scottish Repertory Theatre, in Bill Findlay (ed.), *A History of Scottish Theatre* (Edinburgh University Press, 1998), p. 211.
49 See Grace Wyndham Goldie, *The Liverpool Repertory Theatre 1911–1935* (London: Hodder & Stoughton, 1935).

Figure 3.1 A typical realistic repertory setting of the 1910s: *Street Scene*, 1913–14 at the Playhouse, Liverpool.

capital and labour, was played at a time of great unrest in the city's docks, and James Sexton's *The Riot Act* (1914), dealing with the strikes of 1911, aroused fierce debate. Grace Wyndham Goldie records how Sexton, himself Secretary of the National Union of Dock Labourers, had been part of the 1911 strike and '[h]ere were the events, negotiations and characters as he saw them'. She continues:

> Enormous interest was aroused in the town; men outnumbered women in the audience; dockers crowded the gallery. The author was much criticised, less for the quality of the play than for the sentiments he expressed. And he held a meeting in the town to defend his attitude.[50]

Ironically, in a city where labour relations were such that the actors playing the 'Labour sympathizers' in *Strife* were not invited to Lord Derby's opening night reception,[51] it was the suffragettes who caused Sexton the most trouble, for a negative portrayal of one of their number.

In the 1913–14 season Liverpool Repertory Theatre made a loss of £1,400, and at the outbreak of war the directors decided to abandon the project. However, the tenacity of the newly appointed director, Madge MacIntosh,

---

50 *Ibid.*, p. 92.
51 Whitford Kane, *Are We All Met?* (London: Elkin Mathews & Marrot, 1931), p. 103.

and a fellow actress, Estelle Winwood, prevented closure when a scheme was devised whereby the actors would form a 'Commonwealth' under which they were guaranteed a living wage as long as the theatre remained open, while 25 per cent of the receipts would be used to pay running costs for the theatre. Precarious as the arrangement was, it enabled the repertory to survive into the post-war period.

Birmingham, like Manchester, had the advantage of a single benefactor; but it differed from Manchester and the other pre-war repertory theatres in almost every other respect. Its roots were in an amateur group – as many post-war repertories were to be – the Pilgrim Players. This company formed in 1907 under Barry Jackson, the wealthy son of the founder of Maypole Dairies, in order to reclaim and present English poetic drama. Its repertoire was wide-ranging, from the Tudor *Interlude of Youth* to Yeats's *The King's Threshold* (1903). Such was the company's success and growing reputation that in 1911 they turned professional as the Birmingham Repertory Company, and in 1913 opened the first purpose-built repertory theatre in the country. The advantages of this were enormous, as the new venue seated 464 as against the 1,000-plus that the Gaiety, Royalty and Liverpool Repertory Theatres held. So despite a lack of municipal support and relatively small audiences, the company was always financially more stable than its peers. The key to Birmingham's success and survival, however, was that it 'possessed in Jackson a combination of patron and artistic director unique in British theatrical history'.[52] Jackson was an accomplished actor, director and designer; as patron as well as artistic/stage director, he could develop the company as he wished. His commitment to the new drama was as strong as that of other repertory directors, but he also championed Shakespeare,[53] Euripides and medieval drama.

The survival of Birmingham, unlike that of Manchester and Liverpool when the war began, was not in doubt. Manchester had already had to resort to a less adventurous repertoire by 1914, as steady support from the community was never forthcoming and audience figures fell, due in part to a successful touring policy which took favourite performers away from the city base. Liverpool survived through the war by the actions of its company. Glasgow and the short-lived Bristol repertory both closed in 1914, largely due to the war, but also because without adequate subsidy repertory theatre is a fragile project. John Palmer, writing in 1913 on 'The Future of the Theatre', argued that repertory was 'the only system whereby the theatre can be continuously kept

---

52 Rowell and Jackson, *Repertory Movement*, p. 50.
53 See Claire Cochrane, *Shakespeare at the Birmingham Repertory Theatre 1913–1929* (London: Society for Theatre Research, 1993).

in a healthy condition of experiment, discovery and honest work'.[54] The post-war period was to demonstrate he was right. The repertory ideal was to prove a more tenacious creature than the situation in the autumn of 1914 might have led even its strongest advocates to believe.

The theatre of the 'flappers'?

The impact of World War One on the provincial theatre was both immediate and long term, but its severity varied enormously. In North Shields '[t]he outbreak of war seems to have caused no inconvenience to the theatre beyond finding a company to replace the company booked for the week beginning August 10 and unable to reach the town'.[55] The reason was probably that the town's Theatre Royal had in 1910 reinstated a stock company which, together with occasional touring groups, played a repertoire largely of melodrama. The pre-war offering of *The Collier's Lass* (1914), a curious tale of 'the White Slave Trade and Pit Life', was easily replaced by *The Woman in Khaki* (1915) and *The Munition Girl's Love Story* (1915). By 1916 melodrama was supplemented by revue and even the imposition of an Entertainments Tax in that year, though resented, appears not to have affected audience attendances.[56]

There are many reasons for this increased populism of the repertoire. There was a common perception that the theatre had a contribution to make to the nation's morale, and so there was a shift towards a less demanding and, at times, propagandist repertoire. L. C. Collins argues that '[t]heatre was much more than a diversionary and escapist tactic . . . but, in order to justify its existence, [companies] had to produce a theatre that was seen to be purposeful and relevant'.[57] When the war itself was addressed it was, unsurprisingly, largely uncritically. Many plays – for example, *Shakespeare for Merrie England* (1915) at Worcester, and Manchester Tivoli's *Your Country Needs You* (1914) and *The Call* (1915) – supported the government's recruitment drive in the period before conscription was introduced in 1916. Others, with titles like *In the Hands of the Hun* (1915), demonised the enemy, and the spy drama became immensely popular. Anti-war tendencies at home were attacked in pieces like *Mrs Pusheen: The Hoarder* (1918) at Stoke's Alexandra Theatre and Glasgow Pavilion's anti-socialist drama, *John Feeney – Socialist* (1915).[58] Frank Benson

54 John Palmer, *The Future of the Theatre* (London: G. Bell, 1913), p. 75.
55 Robert King, *North Shields Theatres* (Gateshead: Northumberland Press, 1948), p. 126.
56 *Ibid.*, pp. 126–7.
57 Collins, *Theatre at War*, p. 3.
58 *Ibid.*, pp. 177–211.

on a scale unseen before. Though some military bases restricted access to places of entertainment, including Margate's Pavilion Theatre,[67] in the interests of discipline, many theatres offered forces personnel advantageous rates.[68] Entertainment meant the maintenance of morale, and most camps in Britain and Europe either provided their own or were visited by companies established for the purpose. Following successful initial projects at Oswestry and Kimnel Park, the producer Basil Dean was transferred to the Entertainment Branch of the Navy and Army Canteen Board, and by the end of the war the forces had purpose-built garrison theatres in many military camps. These theatres were serviced by companies covering everything from opera to farce, as well as providing venues for the troops' own amateur performances.[69]

The post-war legacy

> I think the public is growing tired of these restless, noisy, musical comedies from America. The hideous American voice is surely getting on the delicate nerves of the ear. Beauty and grace and melody may one day replace brutishness, angularity and nigger noise.[70]

That now offensive alliteration indicates the depth of Oscar Asche's irritation, in 1928, at the parlous state of the theatre. Perhaps, too, it was fuelled by the flimsy hopes of a breed in terminal decline, for though some actor-managers continued tours in the provinces well into the 1930s, hardly any had a London base; most were growing old, like Benson and Asche himself, and their business was becoming unprofitable.[71] Yet there was relatively little diminution of theatrical activity for most of the 1920s, though its nature *was* changing. In November 1926 the *Era* listed 269 companies on tour. Musical comedies constituted a significant number of these, with, for example, no less than three *No, No, Nanette*'s on offer. This was matched by other types of light entertainment, with three productions of Arnold Ridley's thriller, *The Ghost Train* (1925), and another three of Leon Gordon's 'vivid play of the primitive unvarnished life in the tropics', *White Cargo* (1923).[72] But a new category of show had emerged

---

67 Malcolm Morley, *Margate and its Theatres* (London: Museums Press, 1966), p. 135.
68 For example, see Ros McCoola, *Theatre in the Hills* (Chapel-en-le-Frith: Caron Publications, 1984), p. 69.
69 See Basil Dean, *The Theatre at War* (London: George Harrap, 1955), pp. 21–9.
70 Oscar Asche, *Oscar Asche: His Life, by Himself* (London: Hurst & Blackett, 1929), p. 210.
71 For example, see Nicholas Butler, *John Martin-Harvey: The Biography of an Actor Manager* (Wivenhoe: Nicholas Butler, 1997), p. 128.
72 J. C. Trewin, *The Theatre Since 1900* (London: Andrew Dakers, 1951), p. 169.

during the war; by 1926, 126 companies, almost half of the total, were listed as offering revue.[73]

Hence, the schism between commercial touring companies and those with a claim to 'art' had widened, even producing, in Asche's view, an erosion of the estate of 'proper' theatre itself: 'In provincial towns the theatre proper is hidden down side streets; there is no illumination to advertise their [sic] whereabouts [and] they have not had a paint brush near them in thirty years.'[74] He blames the blight on moneymen, on an influx of American managements and, compared to the burgeoning cinema, on high seat prices. He was by no means alone in his disaffection, as Daphne du Maurier's jaundiced comment on the 1920s makes clear: 'the sacred world of drama and comedy became a pit for profiteers and a juggling game for clumsy amateurs'.[75]

The actor-managers had lent a certain stability to theatre management, but as they were replaced by investors and speculators this largely disappeared. The resultant effects were less marked in the provinces, where there was greater continuity of theatre and company ownership, but even so, syndicalism and changes in management structures led to increased antagonism between performers and managers. In 1921 the Actors' Association became a trade union and many prominent members of the profession resigned. In 1924 an attempt was made to bring all sectors of the profession together in a single group through the formation of the Stage Guild. In the same year the Actors' Association tried to impose a 'closed shop' on the actor-managers and an antagonistic campaign was waged in many cities between the Association and the Guild, a clash that was not fully resolved until the end of the decade.[76]

Despite – or perhaps because of – the general shift towards commercialisation and populism, a number of touring companies emerged in the 1920s that extended the approach of the earlier repertory experiments by 'embracing the finest writing of the best authors of all ages and with an especially widely open door to present-day British writers'[77] and in taking that work to a broader audience. Though often struggling to find adequate financial support and large enough audiences, these companies had a significant influence on post-World War Two subsidised theatre. Perhaps the best known and

---

73 Era (10 Nov. 1926).

74 Ibid., 229.

75 Daphne du Maurier, Gerald, A Portrait (London: Victor Gollancz, 1934), p. 205.

76 Nicoll, English Drama 1900–1930, p. 39; see also Michael Sanderson, From Irving to Olivier: A Social History of the Acting Profession in England 1880–1983 (London: Athlone Press, 1985).

77 Pogson, Miss Horniman, p. 25.

most successful in this period was Charles Macdona's Bernard Shaw Repertory Company, which had been formed in the wake of the Shaw boom of the 1900s. Macdona held touring rights to almost all Shaw's plays and staged them with a semi-permanent company. The actress Margaret Webster joined it in 1924, by when Macdona had refined his version of 'real repertory' – a different play on every night – to an extraordinary degree: 'By the time the tour finished, nearly nine months later, we were doing eighteen [plays] . . . and I had played thirteen parts (some of them leads) and understudied twenty others.' Most frequently performed were *Man and Superman*, *The Doctor's Dilemma*, *You Never Can Tell* and *Pygmalion* – which, she deduces, 'represented fairly precisely the box office value of the plays; for Mr Macdona was not a man to let anything come between him and the box office'.[78]

Other touring 'repertory' companies played a mixed repertoire and had a more 'Utopian' imperative. The Lena Ashwell Players, for example, were formed in 1919 from a core of actors who had 'served in the War areas' in concert parties and repertories. To these were added recently demobilised men. Eventually based at the Century Theatre in Kensington, from there they toured regularly to the provinces with a range of repertory 'standards' and European classics. The plays were performed, in John Masefield's words, 'with a spirit and grace which I had not seen before in any English Company. They were doing something new, fitting to the new time, with a freshness and gaiety . . . linked in one of those comradeships of art which alter the thought of the world.'[79] The company was supported irregularly by local councils and 'The Friends of the Players', but it was Ashwell's view that, due to the Entertainments Tax and a lack of capital, 'years were mostly spent in losing money but we were quite convinced that the sacrifice was worth while'.[80] The Lena Ashwell Players were especially innovative in educational terms, as they 'rendered a great service to education in playing each year the Shakespearean plays that are set for public examination . . . [arranging] for school matinées of their forthcoming production[s]'.[81]

Another company with a similar agenda was the Arts League of Service (ALS) Travelling Theatre, also formed in 1919, which aimed to 'bring the Arts into Everyday Life'.[82] Under the leadership of Eleanor Elder the

---

78 Margaret Webster, *The Same Only Different: Five Generations of a Theatre Family* (London: Victor Gollancz, 1969), pp. 310–11.

79 Quoted in Lena Ashwell, *Myself a Player* (London: Michael Joseph, 1936), p. 246.

80 *Ibid.*, pp. 244, 248.

81 *Observer* (6 Nov. 1925).

82 Eleanor Elder, *Travelling Players: The Story of the Arts League of Service* (London: Frederick Muller, 1939), p. 7.

companies – there were two by 1925–6 – travelled by road throughout Britain visiting largely non-theatre venues (often the old 'fit-up' halls) with a wide repertoire of drama, dance and folk music. Their audiences were interestingly varied: 'an audience of colliers to-night, an audience of agricultural labourers to-morrow night, and . . . of retired Anglo-Indians on the third'.[83] In its ten-year lifespan the ALS produced a remarkable total of twenty-nine new plays, as well as six 'new to this country', including *Hagoromo* (translated from the Japanese by Ezra Pound in 1916) and plays by Martinez Sierra, Susan Glaspell and Thornton Wilder.[84] Again, like Ashwell, Elder was forced to disband the company in 1929, but argued that '[p]erhaps with more capital and less popularity the ALS might have done more for the propaganda [*sic*] of modern art – but it would have been at the expense of all it did achieve'.[85]

A number of new building-based 'arts' projects were created during the immediate post-war period. Some were amateur companies, such as the Maddermarket Theatre in Norwich, opened by Nugent Monck in 1921 as an Elizabethan stage playing classical and modern drama, or the Leeds Art Theatre, an ambitious venture founded in 1922 by Edith Craig and playing contemporary European drama as well as locally written plays, or Manchester's Unnamed Society, which had taken on the mantle of the Gaiety in 1916. Some, such as the Sheffield Repertory Company, were semi-professional. The two most influential, though not long-lasting, professional ventures were J. B. Fagan's Oxford Playhouse (1923–30) and Terence Gray's Festival Theatre in Cambridge (1926–33). The former, despite working in a 'dismal, gimcrack building', developed an exceptional reputation for acting amongst its young company. Fagan's emphasis was on producing less well-known plays from the classical and contemporary repertoires and on an intense, short rehearsal period that produced acting which, though 'rough and unpolished . . . strove to develop the style and mood of the play, and to reproduce the author's characterisation as exactly and vividly as possible'.[86] Gray, by contrast, placed the emphasis on the director. His theatre was 'unique amongst English theatres because its policy was based not on the choice of plays but on the manner of their production . . . The Festival was founded to wage war upon what [Gray] described as "the old game of illusion and glamour and all the rest of the nineteenth century hocus pocus and bamboozle"'.[87] Gray has been criticised for being at times

---

83 St John Ervine in *ibid.*, p. 249.
84 'Appendix', *ibid.*, pp. 251–62.
85 *Ibid.*, p. 248.
86 Norman Marshall, *The Other Theatre* (London: Theatre Book Club, 1947), p. 22; see also Rowell and Jackson, *Repertory Movement*, pp. 60–2.
87 Marshall, *Other Theatre*, p. 53.

Figure 3.2 Shakespeare's *Hamlet* in modern dress, from the Birmingham Repertory Theatre, 1925.

'merely wilfully eccentric – Sir Toby Belch and Sir Andrew Aguecheek on roller skates, Rosalind . . . as a Boy Scout and Celia as a Girl Guide', and for failing 'to encourage a single author to write a play for production',[88] but his emphasis on the director and on the visual provided the provincial – and British – theatre with an experimental project to match those of contemporary continental practitioners. In architectural terms, too, Gray was innovatory. He and his lighting designer, Harold Ridge, 'stripped [the acting area] of its surviving fittings and proscenium, and . . . the open stage was provided with a permanent, curved cyclorama, "built from two layers of hollow tiles curved with sirapite and surfaced with cement"'.[89] Few between wars theatres were to go as far as this, but Gray's influence stretched beyond World War Two to the civic theatre buildings of the 1960s and 1970s.

The development of the repertory theatres in the 1920s and 1930s was piecemeal but incremental. At the end of the war only two of the earlier companies were in existence, Birmingham and Liverpool, Manchester having ceased

88 *Ibid.*, pp. 66–8; see also Rowell and Jackson, *Repertory Movement*, pp. 62–6.
89 Rowell and Jackson, *Repertory Movement*, p. 62.

to function as such in 1917. These were joined in the 1920s by a significant number of other companies whose ethos was that of the traditional repertory – a commitment to a 'dramatists' theatre', a mixed repertoire of plays, a non-star company and accessible price structure. Variously called repertory or little theatres, they were to be found throughout the British Isles. And by the end of the decade many of the older local theatres, increasingly starved of touring fare and threatened by the cheaper cinema, had returned to the idea of a 'stock company', but one based on the newly established repertory principle.

In the 1928 *Stage Yearbook*, Alfred Wareing wrote: 'So gradually and so modestly has the Little Theatre Movement in the Provinces spread and developed that many are almost ignorant of its existence . . . and do not realise the significant change it portends.'[90] He discusses some sixteen examples. He congratulates Birmingham for 'stand[ing] forth as beacon and a guide', and praises Liverpool for '"stand[ing] on its own bottom" – what goes out on pay-days must come in at the windows of the pay-box'. Amongst the new enterprises, he cites Plymouth (founded in 1914) where now Shakespeare, 'Ibsen, Pinero and Barrie's plays rub shoulders with "Monty's Flapper" and "The Knave of Diamonds"' in weekly repertory;[91] Sheffield, whose largely amateur company had by 1926 been joined by four professional actors, Southend-on-Sea (1923), with a 'prodigious' record of plays produced (260 in five years); and Hull (1924) which despite having a stage 'no larger than the dining-room of a semi-detached house' had produced some remarkable work,[92] while Newcastle-upon-Tyne's People's Theatre, rarely deviated from a radical repertory playing Toller, Chekhov, Karel Čapek, O'Neill, Pirandello and Elmer Rice, as well as Shaw and Galsworthy.[93] Others, however, had to balance the more challenging plays with popular drama. The repertory companies continued to struggle into the 1930s, when the combined effects of the economic depression and the impact of cinema caused some to flounder.

In 1921 Miss Horniman had sold the Gaiety Theatre to a cinema company,[94] but Manchester's repertory venture did not collapse because of the silver screen; it had failed because audiences had been too small and the city had not

90 Alfred Wareing, 'The little theatre movement. its genesis and its goal', in L. Carson, (ed.), *The Stage Yearbook 1928* (London: The Stage, 1928), p. 13.
91 See also Trewin, *Theatre Since 1900*, pp. 163–6.
92 Wareing, 'Little theatre movement', pp. 13–34.
93 Norman Veitch, *The People's: Being a History of the People's Theatre Newcastle upon Tyne 1911–1939* (Gateshead on Tyne: Northumberland Press, 1950), pp. 193–209.
94 Pogson, *Miss Horniman*, pp. 173–6.

responded to her plea for £40,000 to offset the company's losses. The initial threat of the cinema was not to the drama, but to variety. In 1913 John Palmer and others could write confidently that

> Ten years hence it would not be necessary to talk at all about the kinemato-graph. But in the present boom, when actors are in a panic of starvation, and when critics are talking nonsense about the art of the film, it is strictly neces-sary to dissociate the future of the theatre from the future of the kinoplasticon. There is no competition.[95]

However, the advances in technology, in film narrative, in the superior and cheaper facilities that were offered by the purpose-built cinema, plus the advent of the 'talkies' in 1927 with *The Jazz Singer*, meant that by the end of the 1920s cinema had begun to make a notable impact on theatre audiences across the country.[96] Though radio drama was initiated in 1924 with a broadcast of Richard Hughes's *Danger*,[97] the effect of home entertainment on live performance was not significantly felt until the 1930s.

The Brighton Theatre Royal had maintained a healthy profit throughout the 1920s with a varied and popular touring repertoire, but in the early 1930s it had to close for extended periods. The Grand Opera House in Harrogate had similar difficulties maintaining a visiting programme, and like many other provincial theatres resorted to weekly repertory. In 1933 the Peacock family, who had owned the theatre since its opening in 1900, established the White Rose Players. After a difficult first six months, the theatre managed to create a strong enough following to sustain itself to the end of the decade. Elsewhere, whilst some theatres closed, 'unattached' repertory companies replaced the old touring companies and played for limited seasons on the provincial circuits. Cecil Chisholm lists fifteen non-resident repertory companies in 1934,[98] while the *Era* for May 1933 names twenty-three.[99]

The vicissitudes of both the provincial touring circuit and the building-based companies were to diminish by the mid-1930s. The repertory movement of the pre-war period had provided a model by which both the commercial and the art theatres were able to survive. Many of its principles – a dramatist's theatre, a revisioned and non-star stock company, a repertoire that included modern

95 John Palmer, *The Future of the Theatre* (London: G. Bell, 1913), pp. 16–17.

96 See Nicoll, *English Drama 1900–1930*, pp. 40–8.

97 BBC broadcast, 15 Jan. 1924; see Jean Chothia, *English Drama of the Early Modern Period 1890–1940* (Harlow: Longman, 1996), pp. 115–21, 248–60.

98 Chisholm, *Repertory*, p. 246.

99 Rowell and Jackson, *Repertory Movement*, pp. 73–4.

and classic plays, in some places a commitment to local drama (regional or nationalist), and accessible prices – were now a commonplace in the provinces. Touring survived, but much of this too had a local or repertory base. Whilst it would be untrue to say that London was no longer 'the centre of the theatrical universe', a significant shift had taken place in the theatrical axis, and the 'provincial stage' was no longer a mere satellite of the metropolis.

4

Popular theatre, 1895–1940

SOPHIE NIELD

The first ever Royal Command Performance of Variety took place in the presence of George V and Queen Mary at the Palace Theatre, London, on 1 July 1912. The acts included singers, ventriloquists, comedians and sketch artistes; jugglers, magicians and minstrels; classical ballet dancers and 'Tiller Girls'. The programme looked back to the robust and lively Victorian music hall, and forward to the new technologies of entertainment. It featured acts representing the rich seam of British popular performance in the first half of the twentieth century. Some started out in the music halls of the late nineteenth century – stars of pantomime and musical theatre – and some were to find fame in film, sound recording and radio.

Little Tich, a comedian, vocalist and actor, had begun his lengthy career in 1880 as a blackface minstrel performer, at the age of 12.[1] Four feet tall, and with his trademark 28-inch long boots, he became a star of the music hall. He performed for over seventeen years at the Tivoli Theatre in the Strand, where, in 1907, he was one of the 'Five Harrys' (his real name was Harry Relph; the other four were Harrys Lauder, Tate, Fragson and Randall). He was also a regular in pantomime at Drury Lane, appearing in 1891 on the same bill as Dan Leno and Marie Lloyd in *Humpty Dumpty*. For the Command Performance he appeared as 'The Gamekeeper and His Big Boots'.[2]

G. H. Chirgwin was also a blackface minstrel performer, having begun his career in 1861. He was billed as 'The White Eyed Kaffir' in reference to the distinctive diamond-shaped patch of bare white skin around one eye, a result – so tradition has it – of his accidentally rubbing off the black cork minstrel make-up from his face one night. He had been one of the most popular and loved of music hall performers, and in the 1880s he was regularly seen in pantomime

---

1 http://www.bigginhill.co.uk/littletich.htm (19 Oct. 2002); see also M. Tich and R. Findlater, *Little Tich: Giant of the Music Hall* (London: Elm Tree, 1979).
2 *Souvenir Programme, Royal Command Performance of Variety, Monday July 1, 1912*, Mander and Mitchenson Theatre Collection; ref.: Royal Variety sub-collection, 1912.

at the Britannia Theatre, London. He was 58 at the time of the Command Performance, and had been forty years on the stage.[3]

Vesta Tilley had begun her career even earlier than Chirgwin. She first cross-dressed at the age of 9 and became one of the best known and popular of late Victorian and Edwardian music hall and variety theatre acts. Her songs satirised both masculinity and class. During World War One she was to win the soubriquet 'England's Greatest Recruiting Sergeant', with songs such as 'Jolly Good Luck to the Girl who loves a Soldier' and 'Six Days' Leave'.[4]

George Robey gained his title of the 'Prime Minister of Mirth' in the years following World War One in revue with Violet Laraine, popularising such songs as 'If You Were the Only Girl in the World'. Robey enjoyed an uncommonly eclectic and wide-ranging career, including comic opera, Shakespeare and regular appearances as a pantomime dame. At the Command Performance he appeared as 'The Mayor of Mudcumdyke'.[5]

The singer Sir Harry Lauder, the first 'knight of the music hall', was also to become the first performer to entertain the troops in World War One.[6] He closed all his 1914–18 wartime shows with the famous song 'Keep Right On to the End of the Road', and also performed in 1939 for soldiers about to embark for World War Two.

Harry Tate began his career as an impressionist, including imitations of music hall performers such as George Robey and Dan Leno. He became most famous for his series of comic sketches, particularly 'The Motoring Sketch', in which, as a chauffeur, he and his 'idiotic son' fail to start a car. This sketch gave rise to the catchphrase 'Goodbye-e-e', which was later to inspire the World War One song of the same title. Roger Wilmut tells us that Tate also originated the catchphrase 'How's your father?', used as basis for improvisation during lulls in inspiration.[7]

Cecilia (Cissy) Loftus was, unusually, a star of both the variety and legitimate theatre. She had toured as a child with her mother Marie, 'the Sarah

3 http://www.the-music-hall.haisoft.net/smoh/index2.htm (19 Oct. 2002); see also H. Chance Newton, *Idols of the Halls* (London: Heath Cranton, 1928; facsimile reprint 1975).
4 http://pages.unisonfree.net/casselden.htm (19 Oct. 2002); see also S. Maitland, *Vesta Tilley* (London: Virago, 1986).
5 http://www.amaranthdesign.ca/musichall/past/robey.htm (19 Oct. 2002); see also P. Cotes, *George Robey* (London: Cassell, 1972); programme information, *Souvenir Programme, Royal Command Performance of Variety*.
6 http://www.usinternet.com/users/danixon/harry%20lauder.htm (19 Oct. 2002); see also G. Irving, *Great Scot!* (London: Leslie Frewin, 1968).
7 http://www.rfwilmut.clara.net/musichll/xtate.html (downloadable sound recording – 19 Oct. 2002); see also Roger Wilmut, *Kindly Leave the Stage: The Story of Variety 1919–1960* (London: Methuen, 1985).

Figure 4.1 The artistes of the Royal Variety Command Performance, 1912.

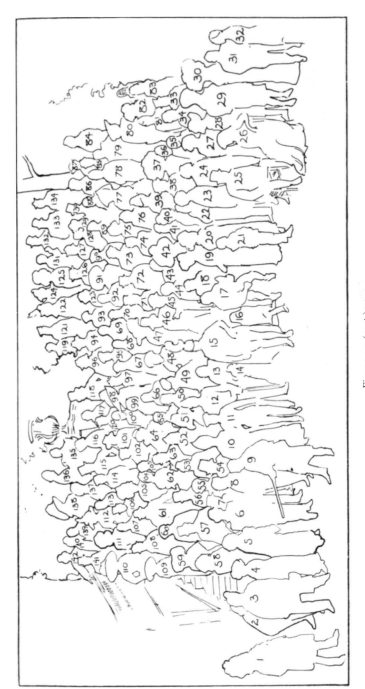

Figure 4.1 (cont.)

**The key to the large group above, with
the names of the artistes on the right**

1. Harry Blake.	49. Harry Lauder.	96. Harry Weldon.
2. Arthur Revell.	50. T. E. Dunville.	97. George French.
3. Harry Stelling.	51. Kate Carney.	98. Emilie D'Alton.
4. Alice Tremayne	52. Harry Tate.	99. Ella Retford.
5. M. Broadfoote.	53. Fred Emney.	100. Edmund Edmunds.
6. Cinquevalli.	54. George Bastow.	101. Albert Edmunds.
7. George D'Albert.	55. Joe Tennyson.	102. " Papa " Brown.
8. Charles Coborn.	56. Chas. Whittle.	103. Tom Stuart.
9. Harry Grattan.	57. J. W. Tate.	104. Harry Randall.
10. Wilkie Bard.	58. Clarice Mayne.	105. Marie Loftus.
11. Vesta Tilley.	59. Peggy Pryde.	106. W. J. Churchill.
12. Arthur Prince.	60. Tom Woottwell.	107. Harry Webber.
13. John Le Hay	61. Harry Champion.	108. R. H. Douglass.
14. Babs.	62. Minnie Duncan.	109. La Pia.
15. Harry Claff	63. Arthur Godfrey.	110. Florrie Forde.
16. Beatie.	64. Geo. Robey.	111. Florrie Gallimore.
17. G. H. Chirgwin.	65. Gus Elen.	112. Edith Evelyn.
18. Billy Williams.	66. Barclay Gammon.	113. Tom Clare.
19. Mary Law.	67. Albert Le Fre.	114. Ella Shields.
20. Pavlova.	68. Arthur Gallimore.	115. Harry Ford.
21. Jack Marks.	69. James Finney.	116. Flora Cromer.
22. George Gray.	70. Lupino Lane.	117. William Downes
23. George Leyton.	71. Chas. McConnell.	118. Charles Langford.
24. Edwin Barwick.	72. Joe McConnell.	119. J. W. Wilson.
25. Herbert Darnley.	73. Ed. E. Ford.	120. Deane Tribune.
26. Cecilia Loftus.	74. Cliff Ryland.	121. Bob Leonard.
27. Vasco.	75. Irene Rose.	122. Jennie Leonard.
28. Fanny Fields.	76. Fred Kitchen.	123. Cecilia Macarte.
29. Cruickshank.	77. Florence Smithers.	124. George Newham.
30. Diana Hope.	78. Arthur Lennard.	125. Fred Latimer.
31. Fred Farren.	79. Ryder Slone.	126. Joe Boganny.
32. Ida Crispi.	80. My Fancy.	127. Sydney James.
33. James Stewart.	81. Esta Stella.	128. Alf. Lotto.
34. Pipifax.	82. Gracie Whiteford.	129. Clara Lilo.
35. Panlo.	82a. Tom Edwards's Dummy.	130. Ernest Otto.
36. Charles Austin.	83. Fred Sinclair.	131. Gus McNaughton.
37. Marie Kendall.	84. Seth Egbert.	132. Fred McNaughton.
38. Fred Curran.	85. J. Alexandre.	133. Horace Wheatley.
39. Alfred Lester.	86. Harry Freeman	134. Arthur Rigby.
40. Novikoff.	87. Albert Egbert.	135. Albert Athas.
41. Percy Delevine.	88. W. F. Frame.	136. Carlton.
42. Harriet Vernon.	89. G. Hughes.	137. Marriott Edgar.
43. David Devant.	90. Dave Carter.	138. Lizzie Collins.
44. Harry Delevine.	91. Elsie Finney.	139. F. V. St Clair
45. J. W. Rowley.	92. Billie Bint.	140. Ada Cerito.
46. Martin Adeson.	93. Julia Macarte.	141. Fred Herbert.
47. Alexandra Dagmar.	94. Will Kellino.	142. W. Munro
48. Mrs. Adeson.	95. Jack Lorimer.	

Figure 4.1 *(cont.)*

Bernhardt of the Halls', and made her début at age 15 in 1891 with songs and impersonations of both male and female variety stars. Later, at the turn of the century, she appeared in both vaudeville and straight drama in New York before Sir Henry Irving contracted her to play Margaret in his 1902 revival of *Faust*. The *Era* reported that 'Miss Loftus was delightfully simple and sincere, and . . . displayed an amount of dramatic expression and power that astonished her most sanguine supporters'.[8]

The other Command Performance stars, while perhaps not all as well known, were the outstanding entertainers in their fields. The pianist Barclay Gammon; Alfred Lester, whose most famous song was 'Yes! We have no Bananas!'; 'Happy' Fanny Fields, singer and pantomime star; Fred Farren, the

8 *Era* (3 May 1902).

choreographer of the 1906 ballet *Cinderella* at the London Empire, dancing with Ida Crispi; Anna Pavlova, who appeared with members of the Imperial Russian Ballet; the juggler Paul Cinquevalli, who, according to the *Strand Magazine*, in 1897:

> played an orthodox, scientific game of billiards on his own sinewy person. The jacket is of real billiard cloth, with five beautifully made pockets of cord and brass wire. The sixth 'pocket' is the juggler's own right ear, and the game's 'spot' for the red ball is his forehead. His arms and knees serve as cushions, and wonderful cushions they are.[9]

There was comedy from Boganny's 'Lunatic Bakers' and sketch artiste Wilkie Bard, 'positively the first pierrot to earn £100 a week'.[10] Lastly, master magician and founding president of the Magic Circle, David Devant, performed illusions.

The Command Performance demonstrated the huge range of popular entertainment of the period, as well as the ways in which performers were able to move with relative ease between pantomime and musical comedy, West End and seaside entertainment, variety and legitimate drama. It also marks an important moment in the evolution of British popular performance towards 'respectability'.

This chapter explores the popular performance of the first four decades of the twentieth century from the perspectives highlighted by the Command Performance. Its various forms combined to create an increasingly 'respectable' industry. Simultaneously, it raised crucial contemporary cultural questions through a series of subtle and complex negotiations with its legislators and its audiences. It will be seen that changes in working practices were formalising in the industry, producing a professionalised and organised class of entertainers who would feed the new entertainment media later in the century. In this process, the question of 'licence' is important: in addition to legislative intervention, the interaction of performer and audience was a series of negotiations about the limits and possibilities presented by popular forms. I will suggest that Victor Turner's identification of liminality, the way that ritual creates a domain 'betwixt-and-between' quotidian norms, is a useful concept for interpretation of the often subtle and complex explorations of cultural questions staged by the popular acts and entertainments. I will focus in this analysis on the ways in which tensions regarding 'race' and gender were central to some of the most prominent entertainment forms of the time.

9 *Strand Magazine* 13 (Jan.–June 1897), see http://www.juggling.org/fame/cinquevalli/strand.html (Andrew Conway 1996; 12 July 2003).
10 http://www.the-music-hall.haisoft.net/smoh/smwbard.htm (19 Oct. 2002); see also Geoff J. Mellor, *They Made Us Laugh* (Littleborough, Lancs.: George Kelsall, 1982).

'Two shows a night and six matinées': regulating variety

The recognition of the variety theatre accorded by the Command Performance indicated, to an extent, its perceived distance from the Victorian music hall. 'Variety' was not an uncommon term in the nineteenth century, and as many music hall buildings were remodelled towards the turn of the century in response to increasing health and safety legislation, often they were reopened as Palaces of Variety. With dining and other facilities separated from the main auditorium, they were much closer to the design of conventional theatres. The chief characteristic of legislative intervention seems to have been pressure to make them more 'respectable'.

> In a period when local governing élites increasingly either shared or were influenced by the opinions of well-organised temperance and social purity lobbies, the music hall, with its close association with the drink trade, was increasingly vulnerable . . . Smaller halls were particularly susceptible to closure via the apparently neutral mechanism of increasingly stringent safety regulations, while newly erected halls were increasingly denied a drinks licence. The London County Council made this a formal policy in 1897 . . . the assumption of respectability marked the way ahead.[11]

The increasing syndication of halls under fewer managements (by 1914 around sixteen syndicates controlled 140-plus halls), and the widespread practice of having a 'second house' (an additional complete performance later in the evening) after about 1900 certainly altered the spontaneity and informality of nineteenth-century music hall. On stage, the programme became broader, with performers of sketches, magicians, cinematic presentations, strongmen and other novelty acts supplementing the music hall's more traditional fare of comic singers and solo acts. The adaptation and development of variety acts were not without regulatory incident. The long-running 'sketch question' is a case in point. Sketches were longer than their late twentieth-century counterpart, being akin to comic one-act plays. This led to legal difficulties under the terms of the 1843 Licensing Act, which did not permit the presentation of 'legitimate' drama in music halls. Eventually, in 1912, theatrical licences were granted to central London halls on condition that at least six variety turns accompanied any sketch presented.

---

11 D. Russell, 'Varieties of life: the making of the Edwardian music hall', in Michael R. Booth and Joel H. Kaplan (eds.), *The Edwardian Theatre: Essays on Performance and the Stage* (Cambridge University Press, 1996), p. 62.

These changes in working practices in the early part of the twentieth century were paralleled by moves towards unionisation made by many variety artistes. In 1907 the National Association of Theatre Employees and the Amalgamated Musicians Union formed a national alliance with the Variety Artistes' Federation (VAF) and went on strike.[12] The dispute centred on the status of artistes as self-employed professionals rather than 'employees', which was how the managements wished to regard them. The central point at issue was the exploitation of artistes in the two houses a night system, plus the expectation that they should perform in an additional matinée performance for no extra fee. Peter Honri gives a lively account of the dispute, including this 'protest' song:

> Some people visit halls where the artists are on strike,
> But I ain't one of them, not me;
> If a fellow starts to fight for his freedom and his right,
> I'm going to back him up, you see . . .
> Rule Britannia, Britannia rules the waves,
> Two shows every night and six matinées![13]

Managers with a number of halls under their control were in the habit of transferring artistes without prior notice, and altering times of acts without consent. Further, as artistes were encouraged to sign contracts with a management (rather than continue the informal practice of dealing personally with an individual manager) they faced contractual agreements that prevented them from giving performances in other theatres nearby. The VAF sought to limit the ban to venues within a one-mile radius of the employing theatre, and for a duration of three months. The strike ran for three weeks and was avidly reported in the VAF publication the *Performer*: 'Paragon. Everybody out at 7.45. Orchestra played, but no artists appeared. Money returned. Canterbury. No show. The sponge was thrown up at 7.45 and the Canterbury is hushed and still'.[14] Arbitration lasted twenty-three days in April and early May before an agreement was reached on 14 June. The artistes won most of their demands.

By the time of the Command Performance, therefore, the popular entertainment industry was organising itself along quite significantly different commercial lines than had existed in the previous century. 'Respectability', however, was not only something pursued by the professionalisation of the industry,

12 See L. Rutherford, '"Managers in a small way": the professionalisation of Variety Artistes, 1860–1914', in Peter Bailey (ed.), *Music Hall: The Business of Pleasure* (Oxford University Press, 1986).
13 Peter Honri, *Working the Halls* (London: Futura, 1976), p. 115.
14 *Ibid.*, p. 120.

licensing agencies and commercial interests. It was also of concern to the popular audience, and a consideration of this raises questions about the nature of 'popular performance'.

'Popular' performance and liminality

It is not easy to specify exactly what was classed as 'popular' in any particular period. Generally, though, 'popular' has been a term used to identify practices that fall outside the canon of 'high' culture. As Raymond Williams argued in 1958, historically 'high' culture was attached to levels of literacy and education that were inaccessible (and generally still are) to the majority of people. 'High' culture was something to be brought to 'ordinary people' to raise the quality of their sensibilities and behaviour. This positioned 'popular' cultural forms by default as degraded: 'lesser', 'lower', 'inferior', 'vulgar'. However, as Morag Shiach points out, neither side of this widely used binary is adequate to providing a definitive account of the popular arts in any given historical period.[15] At the turn of the twentieth century it was not uncommon for *Hamlet* to feature on the same programme as performing animals or other speciality acts.

Williams also points out that '[it] is still much too early to conclude that a majority (i.e. "popular") culture is necessarily low in taste. The danger of such a judgement is that it offers a substitute righteousness – the duty of defending a standard against the mob.'[16] Indeed, it would seem that what is deemed 'acceptable' in any given historical moment hinges on more subtle negotiations than those available to the law. The tension between acceptability and unacceptability, between what can and cannot be spoken, is both complex and one of the key determining factors of 'popular' forms.

In the eighteenth and nineteenth centuries the development of industrial capitalism displaced the 'natural' rhythms of medieval feudalism, and repositioned 'leisure time' as gaps in the working rhythms of labour and capital: evenings, weekends, Bank Holidays, the 'Wakes weeks' or summer closure of the factory or workplace. Such moments were not so much a break from the disciplines of labour and the identities it creates, but rather were still circumscribed by those disciplines and the relationships produced by them.

Working-class people would holiday with family, neighbours, co-workers, even whole communities. During Wakes weeks in the northern English

---

15 Morag Shiach, *Discourse on Popular Culture: Class, Gender and History in Cultural Analysis, 1730 to the Present* (Cambridge: Polity Press, 1989), p. 15.
16 Raymond Williams, *Culture and Society 1780–1950* (Harmondsworth: Penguin, 1958), p. 298.

industrial towns, for example, whole streets or factories would decamp to the seaside. While some holiday licence was no doubt expected, social identities were not left behind, and this had implications for how far popular performance could push the boundaries of the acceptable.

Seaside pastimes and performances, for example, certainly disrupted late Victorian modes of organising behaviour. People no doubt enjoyed the sights of 'bathing beauties', smirked at sexually suggestive songs and jokes in the pavilions and theatres, displayed themselves on the beach or promenade. Yet whilst the comic forms of the period were certainly committed to corporeality as a source of transgressive humour, it would be wrong to assume an unquestioning acceptance of libidinal pleasure, either by the licensing agencies or by audiences. The working class and working middle classes of this period were deeply concerned with respectability.

As D. G. Wright notes, 'traditional orthodoxy holds that, as the élite of skilled workers achieved relatively higher incomes and living standards, so it assumed aspirations and values that were characteristically middle-class'.[17] He continues: 'the concept of respectability was closely bound up with independence . . . [and] something more than a crude weapon of social control in the hands of the employing class, for it functioned as an instrument of working class liberation'. Rather than being an imposed value, the desire to be 'respectable' was driving the formation and evolution of working-class cultural practice. As G. Best observes of late Victorian working-class communities, respectability provides 'a sharper line by far than that between rich and poor, employer or employee, or capitalist and proletarian'.[18]

So whilst the body, say, was presented and represented in popular performance in ways that exceeded everyday norms, the degrees of excess were still circumscribed by sets of shared knowledge about what was 'appropriate' in public culture. Hence, popular performance may be seen as a continual negotiation of reputable or disreputable status for its audiences, producers and artists. As such, it is revealed as a series of forms within which contemporary cultural anxieties affecting sexuality, gender, 'race' and work are explored.

Victor Turner's identification of the 'liminal' as the transient, shifting point where meaning is open to alteration – 'the betwixt-and-between',[19] neither-this-nor-that domain of culture – may enable us to see more clearly the kinds

17 D. G. Wright, *Popular Radicalism: The Working-Class Experience 1780–1880* (London: Longman, 1988), p. 166.
18 G. Best, 'Mid-Victorian Britain 1851–1875', in *ibid.*, p. 166.
19 Victor Turner, *Dramas, Fields and Metaphors* (Ithaca: Cornell University Press, 1974), p. 13.

of cultural and social tensions explored by popular performance. A detailed examination of some of the most prominent of these forms – blackface minstrels, pierrot shows, musical comedy – will suggest the ideological slipperiness of British popular performance in the early twentieth century as it engaged the cultures of its times. And of all the places where popular forms flourished, the seaside was perhaps the most liminal of all.

The rise of the seaside resort

The development of the railways in the latter half of the nineteenth century brought an influx of holidaymakers to the seaside, and a large industry developed to provide a range of entertainment for them. Sixty-seven joint stock companies were set up between 1863 and 1919 to build or run seaside theatres, opera houses or music halls.[20] The companies identifiable as resort-based entertainment enterprises established between 1870 and 1914 numbered 263. But, as John Walton argues, the holiday industry in Blackpool and other resorts was shaped by municipal corporations at least as much as it was by the entrepreneurs of popular theatre.

> Except where natural attractions were sufficient in themselves, entertainments had to be provided to suit the tastes of the best-paying or most-desired class of holidaymaker; and the regulation of streets and beach had similarly to be tailored to match the preferences of the chosen visiting public.[21]

Although on occasion municipal entertainment was provided for 'lower-class visitors whose contribution to the local economy was important but unattractive', most civic intervention aimed to protect the interests of a defined (or self-defined) 'respectable' clientèle. The large number of working-class visitors to the resort towns undoubtedly led to the provision of more leisure space – promenades, piers and so on. However, there is substantial evidence of attempts on the part of resorts to organise popular pastimes spatially along class lines. In 1899 the Local Board of the East Yorkshire resort of Bridlington was involved in a parliamentary hearing to support their introduction of a threepenny charge to an enclosed area of the promenade on the grounds that '[it] is of the greatest importance to the town that the better class of

20 http://www.gosforth3.demon.co.uk (19 Oct. 2002); see also Lynn Pearson, *The People's Palaces: Britain's Seaside Pleasure Buildings 1876–1914* (Buckingham: Barracuda, 1991).
21 John Walton, 'Municipal government and the holiday industry in Blackpool, 1876–1914', in *Leisure in Britain*, ed. John Walton and James Walvin (Manchester University Press, 1983), p. 162.

visitors should have a secluded place where they can go away from the rough excursionists who come there in swarms during the season'.[22]

Pier pavilions were added to what initially had been rather ornate landing stages from the 1880s. Later, piers became whole worlds of entertainment in their own right, with shops, tearooms, aquaria and theatres. Lynn Pearson notes that the boom years for theatre construction in seaside resorts around Britain were 1896–9 and 1908–14.

> Seaside theatres were required to be adaptable and were often reconstructed as entertainment fashions changed. Some combined circus rings and stages, while those with flat floors and side stages were used for ballroom dancing and music hall and, when the cinema became popular, many small halls mixed bills featuring variety acts and films.[23]

In eclectic styles, designed to catch the attention of the passer-by who might otherwise be distracted by the many other entertainments available, one of the most significant considerations for a seaside theatre building was durability. A popular medium was therefore terracotta. Pearson reports that the Southport Opera House (1890–1, designed by Frank Matcham), the New Palace Theatre, Plymouth (1898, Wimperis and Archer) and the Marine Palace of Varieties at Hastings (1897–99, Ernest Runz) were all faced in buff terracotta.

Purpose-built cinemas, too, began to proliferate after about 1908, a trend encouraged by the Kinematograph Act of 1909. This legislation insisted on strict and particular fire and safety regulations; particular because of the high inflammability of film stock. As well as joint stock companies investing in cinema building, new cinema chains, such as Provincial Cinematograph Theatres Ltd (1909) and National Electric Theatres (1908), invested heavily in seaside picture-houses. The young Charles Cochran managed the Gem Cinema in Great Yarmouth, built by Arthur S. Hewitt in 1908, and ran continual film shows daily from 11 o'clock in the morning to 11 o'clock at night.[24]

So, by the early decades of the twentieth century resorts were as popular for the range of diversions they offered as for the beach itself. Rhyl in 1913 advertised itself as offering 'Bathing, boating and fishing, croquet, bowls, tennis, golf, concert bands and theatrical performances, hippodrome entertainments, cinematograph films, skating rink, water chute, miniature, scenic and figure-of-eight railways, coach and motor tours, steamboat excursions.'[25]

22 *Ibid.*, p. 163.
23 http://www.gosforth3.demon.co.uk (19 Oct. 2002); see also Pearson, *People's Palaces*.
24 http://www2.arts.gla.ac.uk (19 Oct. 2002).
25 Eric J. Evans and Jeffrey Richards, *A Social History of Britain in Postcards 1870–1930* (London: Longman, 1980), pp. 123–4.

Clearly there was a very high premium on novelty in this plethora of distractions, but, paradoxically, familiarity was an essential ingredient too. For in the seaside liminal zone the push-and-pull of danger and safety, excess and security, as much in the forms as in the buildings, was a vital attraction. And in this context the blackface minstrels and the whiteface pierrots seemed to provide an abundance of both.

From blackface to whiteface: minstrels and pierrots

'Blackface' or burnt cork minstrelsy (so-called because burnt cork was used to create the black face) was introduced from America to the British stage in the mid-nineteenth century, initially through solo performances in music hall programmes, but it rapidly evolved as a company form. By the final quarter of the century the minstrel show had developed its own set of theatrical conventions. It was completely respectable, 'family' entertainment, with a particularly sentimental tone. In his familiar history of the genre, Harry Reynolds reports that the famous nineteenth-century troupes – Christy's Minstrels, the Moore and Burgess Minstrels, the Mohawk Minstrels – were complemented by at least three all-female troupes and, notably, the Metropolitan Police Minstrels, in their fifty-fifth year at the time of writing in 1927.[26]

The minstrel show was usually in three or four sections. The first part featured comic exchanges between the on-stage co-ordinator, 'Mr Interlocutor' (often, adding an extra racial resonance to the form, in whiteface[27]), and the 'corner' men, Tambo and Bones, who sat at the ends of a loose semi-circle of six or eight performers. The first section concluded with a musical presentation of operatic numbers or plantation songs. This was followed by the 'olio', a variety show within a show, when skills of tumbling, singing, dancing, skits, ballads, magic tricks and recitation were demonstrated. The 'afterpiece' was often a burlesque or a cod lecture – called a 'Stump Speech' – on current affairs. The final section, the 'walkaround', generally consisted of singing, both solo and choral.[28] The instruments – fiddle, bones, tambourine, banjo and strill

---

26 Harry Reynolds, *Minstrel Memories: The Story of Burnt Cork Minstrelsy in Great Britain from 1836 to 1927* (London: Alston Rivers, 1928), pp. 198, 214.

27 http://www.britannica.com/blackhistory/micro/396/3.html (19 Oct. 2002).

28 Michel Pickering, 'White skin, black masks', in J. S. Bratton (ed.), *Music Hall: Performance and Style* (Milton Keynes: Open University Press, 1986), pp. 70–91; see also, Michael Pickering, 'Mock blacks and racial mockery: the "nigger" minstrel and British imperialism', in J. S. Bratton, Richard Allen Cave, Breandan Gregory, Heidi J. Holder and Michael Pickering, *Acts of Supremacy: The British Empire and the Stage, 1790–1930* (Manchester University Press, 1991), pp. 179–236.

(a portable harmonium) – were imported from the American tradition of minstrel shows, and the banjo in particular was to become extremely fashionable in British popular culture in the 1920s and 1930s. The performances were successful in a wide range of venues. By the turn of the century minstrel shows had become a staple at both St James Hall, Piccadilly and the Elephant and Castle Theatre in London, but they were also especially famous as seaside entertainment. However, as the century turned the minstrels were gradually supplanted on the promenades and beaches by 'whiteface' pierrot troupes, and this reveals something of the ambivalences and contradictions present in popular performance as it responds to changes in its environment.

The convention for early minstrel shows on the sands was usually the setting up of a circle of low boards similar to a circus ring. The audience simply gathered outside the ring, but at appropriate points a member of the troupe would go round to collect money in a bottle – hence the term 'bottling'. This had more functional than novelty value: money is hard to remove from a bottle. It would be broken after the performance in the presence of the whole troupe.

Clearly, burnt cork minstrelsy is extremely problematic in its representation of race, consisting as it does of white actors in exaggerated make-up, playing 'black' men and women, performing a particularly sentimental and inauthentic version of a culture born of slavery. However, some American scholars have argued for a more complex interpretation, which sees the minstrel show as sometimes undermining the inherent racism in the stereotyping of blackness by white actors.[29] The role of minstrelsy in British culture similarly has been analysed by Michael Pickering, who points out that the stereotypical images of black people carried a rather different set of cultural connotations in Britain than in the United States. Whilst not downplaying the damaging effect of such stereotyping to Victorian and Edwardian views on race (and the perpetuation of those images and stereotypes into the twentieth century), he interprets the presentation of, for example, the lazy black plantation hand as an antithesis of constructions of 'whiteness'. In other words, rather than black and white identities *per se* being placed in tension in minstrelsy, the figure of the black plantation hand in British blackface is about work and not-work, calling into question the disciplines of labour experienced by the white working-class audiences.

---

29 See Eric Lott, *Love and Theft: Blackface Minstrelsy and the American Working Class* (Oxford University Press, 1993); Dale Cockrell, *Demons of Disorder: Early Blackface Minstrels and their World* (Cambridge University Press, 1997).

> White men put on black masks and became another self, one which was loose of limb, innocent of any obligation to anything outside itself, indifferent to success . . . and thus a creature devoid of tension and deep anxiety. The verisimilitude of this persona to actual Negroes . . . was at best incidental. For the white man who put on the black mask modelled himself after a subjective black man – a black man of lust and passion and natural freedom (licence) which white men carried within themselves and harboured with both fascination and dread.[30]

Whilst this would support the case that popular performance is always a form in which tensions of various kinds are explored and pressurised, minstrelsy was not only performed by white men in black masks.

Examples of such varied ambivalence can be found in the early years of British minstrelsy. In 1861 an advertisement for Messrs Wolfenden and Melbourne's 'Annual Gratuitous Tea Party and Ball to 500 Old Women and their last Gala' in the Zoological Gardens, Hull, listed the Alabama Minstrels as a 'Troupe of Real Blacks' with Negro melodies, dances and conundrums.[31] Harry Reynolds mentions hiring a black performer in his own troupe of minstrels in the early twentieth century, and a troupe of real black minstrels appeared in Morecambe in the same period.[32] In the United States the great blues vocalists Ma Rainey and Bessie Smith were both minstrel performers early in their careers. Clearly the fact that access to entertainment careers was only available for performers of colour in the theatrical medium of the minstrel show is deeply problematic. Yet the presence on the popular stage of a black performer in blackface cannot help but highlight, as it were, the 'betwixt-and-between' status of the mask: neither black nor white, but rather raising questions about the relationships between colour, identity and representation.

The case that blackface minstrelsy represented something more than a stereotyped 'blackness' is also indicated by the self-defined 'coon' performers who did not adopt blackface. J. S. Bratton describes the hugely successful, albeit more sexually explicit, 'coon' act of the male impersonator Bessie Wentworth, who 'did not black up, but relied on costume and lyrics to evoke the stereotype of the African-American male plantation slave'.[33] It is significant to an

---

30 N. I. Huggins, *Voices from the Harlem Renaissance* (Oxford, 1980), pp. 253–4, cited in Bratton (ed.), *Music Hall*, p. 88.

31 Facsimile poster (Hull: Humberside Libraries, 1984).

32 Reynolds, *Minstrel Memories*, p. 231; Baz Kershaw, *The Radical in Performance: Between Brecht and Baudrillard* (London: Routledge, 1999), pp. 140–53; Michael Pickering, '"A jet ornament to society": black music in nineteenth-century Britain', in *Black Music in Britain*, ed. Paul Oliver (Milton Keynes: Open University Press, 1990).

33 J. S. Bratton, 'Beating the bounds: gender play and role reversal in the Edwardian music hall', in Booth and Kaplan (eds.), *Edwardian Theatre*, p. 89.

understanding of popular theatre, then, that both the ambivalences of colour and gender implied by this act are apparent in the performances of the white-faced pierrot troupes.

In the seaside resorts the minstrels were almost completely ousted by the pierrot shows around the turn of the century, with some notable exceptions, such as 'Uncle Mack' (J. H. Summerson), who worked the sands at Broadstairs in Kent until 1938. Many blackface minstrel troupes actually transmuted into whiteface pierrots. In Saltburn in the 1890s the Whitby troupe Mulvana's Minstrels were hugely popular with visitors to the resort. Three of the original troupe – Bert Grapho, Billy Jackson and Phil Rees – later returned as pierrots. The Waterloo Minstrels, working in Bridlington at the same time, became the Waterloo Pierrots.[34]

The very first troupe of pierrots had been started in 1891 by Clifford Essex, a singer and banjo player. Based on a *commedia dell'arte* character introduced by Guiseppe Giratoni to Paris in the 1660s, the distinctive costume had been seen in London in the popular 1891 mime *L'Enfant prodigue* at the Prince of Wales's Theatre. Bill Pertwee reports that 'Pierrot became the order of the day. The tasteful white costume of loose blouse, ornamented with pom-poms, the equally loose pantaloons, the natty shoes and the black silk handkerchief . . . around the head . . . surmounted by the conically-shaped hat fairly "caught on".'[35] The distinctive 'white face' was achieved by the application of a mixture of zinc and lard.

The relationship of 'whiteface' pierrots to 'blackface' minstrelsy is reflected in the specific reference to whiteface in company names, most explicitly, Will C. Pepper's White Coons (started in 1899 in Hove). Pepper was not the only one to make an overt connection to the minstrel shows. Fred White ran a troupe of White Coons at Bognor Regis for several seasons. It is probable that some of these troupes had been minstrel companies and so retained reference to the genre in their names. This also seems to indicate that, by the turn of the century, the use of terms such as 'coon' had become disconnected from their earlier connotation of colour, becoming shorthand for a particular style of popular programme.

The pierrot shows comprised various 'turns' which varied from company to company, depending on the talents of the troupe's members. Usually, audiences could expect to enjoy songs, instrumental turns, comic backchat and sketches,

---

34 Mave Chapman and Ben Chapman, *The Pierrots of the Yorkshire Coast* (Beverley, East York: Hutton Press, 1988), pp. 25, 65.
35 Bill Pertwee, *Pertwee's Promenades and Pierrots: One Hundred Years of Seaside Entertainment* (Newton Abbot, Devon: Westbridge, 1979), p. 12.

dancing and displays of particular skills, such as juggling. Companies for the most part were based in particular resorts, returning summer after summer to perform on the sands or promenade. In the early decades of the century, touring from resort to resort became more usual. Touring inland, especially in the winter, began about 1910. On the beach, the weather and the water sometimes got the better of the show. The Waterloo Pierrots in Bridlington were pictured in the *Police Gazette* in sopping wet costumes, having had to pull their waterlogged stage from the sea. They left for drier venues in 1909. In 1912 huge freak waves lashed down on the sands at Redcar, soaking the audience and performers of the Redcar Follies.[36]

The most famous of the pierrot men, sometimes called 'The King of the Pierrots', was Will Catlin (William Fox), who started up in Scarborough in 1894 with Catlin's Favourite Pierrots, later the Royal Pierrots. Catlin was one of several pierrot entrepreneurs who eventually ran a string of troupes under different managers around the country, and many ex-Catlin men went on to start their own companies. Catlin's all-male pierrots were always meticulously turned out, and he also encouraged them to present themselves as bachelors, although many were married: they were on strict instructions never to be seen walking arm-in-arm with a lady. Catlin seems to have had great skills in this kind of promotion and entrepreneurship, sometimes applied somewhat ruthlessly. For example, the first troupe of pierrots in Scarborough was Sidney James's Strolling Players, one of whose members, Tom Carrick, started the White Musketeers in the 1890s. In 1906 Catlin bought up all the rights to perform on the sands for 'a bob a nob' – a shilling a day for each performer – and Carrick was forced to take his show to the outdoor skating rink. Catlin was also the first to have postcards of his troupe printed and available for sale.

Although Catlin was strict in insisting that his troupes were all-male, many companies had women performers, dressed, at least in the early years, in identical outfits to the men, producing a notably liminal blurring of gender through the androgynous costumes. George Royle's Imps (later the Fol-de-Rols), playing Whitby from 1907, featured Sybil Glynne and Lora Lyndon; even earlier, in 1899, Bert Grapho's Jovial Jollies at Saltburn contained at least four female performers. As the distinctive make-up and costume was abandoned in later years, leaving behind 'whiteness' as a performative metaphor in favour of the more formal – and conventionally gendered – dress of the concert party, women continued to play an important role.

36 Chapman and Chapman, *Pierrots of the Yorkshire Coast*, pp. 68, 16.

Figure 4.2 A publicity postcard for Tom Carrick's Pierrots, Scarborough, 1905.

Typically, given the entrepreneurial nature of seaside entertainment, councils were quick to respond to the popularity and money-making possibilities of
pierrots. In 1901 the Jovial Jollies were paying a fee of £10 to Saltburn Council
for their pitch for a season, but by 1906 this had risen to £50. In 1903 Scarborough Corporation was already charging £650 in fees for pitches on the sands,

Piccadilly, was not free of trouble. The 'respectable' woman ran the risk of being taken for a 'working girl' – a telling euphemism in the context of the 'Girl' shows. It is clear that the productions dealt in such ambiguities. Peter Bailey argues for a sexual 'knowingness' implicit in the lyrics of many of the musical comedies, which undercut the 'innocence' of the women in the story.[39] This emphasises a key quality in the liminalities of popular forms: tensions can be displayed that would not be acceptable elsewhere. It also activates a spatial knowledge, as the theatres were located in areas where prostitution and the sex industry were rife. Women would have more awareness (whether welcome or not) of sexual activity than they would 'properly' be expected to acknowledge. Thus popular performance explores the tension between what is 'supposed to be' and what 'is': like Turner's 'betwixt-and-between' domain, it represents one account while simultaneously incorporating another, more 'true to life', but un-speakable.

Within the supposed propriety conferred by the status of being a 'performance', many of the narratives of the 'Girl' shows facilitated ambiguously 'legitimate' display of the female body in a state of partial undress. The action, for example, might be transferred from the workplace to the seaside, permitting the Chorus to appear in scanty bathing dresses, and neatly activating the liminal place-image of the seaside in the story. Whilst the actresses themselves were presented in the press and elsewhere as disciplined and respectable working women, the profession of the actress is mobilised in the fiction in a much more morally dubious light: *The Shop Girl* (1894) included a sequence with scantily clad show girls from the 'Frivolity Theatre', whose role as actresses explains and excuses their attire and behaviour.

This tension between representation and the 'real' speaks to continuing anxiety about women's presence in the public sphere. The heroines of these shows, as Bailey observes, are not 'women': they are 'girls', and further, 'girls' who aspire to be 'ladies'. It is perhaps significant that in yet another instance of the ambiguities generated between the actress and her role, Forbes-Winslow, in his history of Daly's, sees fit to record all the former Daly's or Gaiety Girls who married into the nobility: the Countess of Orkney, Lady Churston, Countess Polett and several others are all cited as at one time or another having been managed by Edwardes.[40]

A more explicitly hostile response to women's emancipation can be found in the work of the Melville brothers, who assumed control of Irving's Lyceum

---

39 Peter Bailey, '"Naughty but nice": musical comedy and the rhetoric of the girl, 1892–1914', in Booth and Kaplan (eds.), *Edwardian Theatre*, p. 48.
40 D. Forbes-Winslow, *Daly's: The Biography of a Theatre* (London: W. H. Allen, 1944), p. 133.

in 1909. By then they had already written and produced a string of lurid melodramas, highly popular with London and regional patrons alike, with titles such as *The Worst Woman in London* (1899), *The Ugliest Woman on Earth* (1903) and *The Girl who Wrecked his Home* (1907). Of course, 'girls' in the Melville brothers productions are allowed to be 'women', but only if they are ugly or dangerous. Being a 'woman' is clearly not something to which a respectable female aspires. Nevertheless, there are clearly liminalities at play in the relationship between the performer as 'working woman' and the representation of women produced in and through her performance. This idea can be usefully expanded by an analysis of a key convention of musical comedy, the chorus line.

Musical comedies were justly famous for their chorus lines of high-kicking 'girls', and the name most closely associated with them was John Tiller. Tiller began his career presenting a quartet of child dancers, the Four Sunbeams, at the Prince of Wales Theatre in Liverpool in 1890: they executed a 'rigorous and regimented routine to the tune of Mamma's Babee'.[41] With his wife, Jennie, he opened the Tiller School in Manchester shortly afterwards, the first of a series of schools dedicated to drilling chorus dancers like a *corps de ballet*. Derek and Julia Parker note that it took three months of very hard work to turn a competent dancer into a Tiller Girl.[42] They learned 'tap-and-kick' routines, originally termed 'fancy dancing' and later known as 'precision'. The routines consisted of a series of rigorously choreographed movements, in straight lines and geometric figures, executed by a line of identically dressed dancers.[43]

By the turn of the century, Tiller was supplying most musical comedies with choruses, and by the 1920s his alumni were performing regularly in Europe and America. Troupes of Tillers included the Plaza Girls, Lawrence Tillers, Carlton Tillers and the Palace Girls, who appeared at the Royal Command Performance in 1912. Tiller's troupes appeared in the Ziegfeld Follies of 1922 and inspired the famous Rockettes. Pantomime, too, 'continued to require annual infusions of Tiller Girls, recruited locally to join established Tillers throughout the country. There would be six weeks of "Panto Classes" during which new girls would be put through their paces, learning to tap and "getting

41 http://www.fortunecity.co.uk (chapter 7, 'Burlington Bertie' – 19 Oct. 2002); see also Derek Parker and Julia Parker, *The Story and the Song: A Survey of English Musical Plays, 1916–78* (London: Chappell, 1979).

42 http://www.btinternet.com/~nigel.ellacott.htm (19 Oct. 2002); see also Derek Parker and Julia Parker, *The Natural History of the Chorus Girl* (London: Trinity Press, 1975).

43 http://www.streetswing.com (19 Oct. 2002).

their kicks up".'[44] S. Kracauer discusses the particular disciplines of the chorus line through his notion of the girls as 'mass ornament'. He argues that the obliteration of individuality that the chorus routine attempts parallels exactly the experience of the worker in modern industrial capitalism.

> These products of . . . distraction factories are no longer individual girls but indissoluble girl clusters whose movements are demonstrations of mathematics . . . The structure of the mass ornament reflects that of the entire contemporary situation . . . it is conceived according to rational principles which the Taylor system merely pushes to their ultimate conclusion. The hands in the factory correspond to the legs of the Tiller Girls.[45]

Interestingly, Bailey mentions the reminiscences of some of Tiller's chorus girls, who spoke 'a little wryly, of being "Tillerised" by (his) system' – a direct play on 'Taylorising', F. W. Taylor's method of organising factory production line systems.[46]

There is a limitation in this analogy, however. An important point about the alienation of the worker in systems of mass production is that 'the relation the workers can establish between their actions and the whole production process is highly abstract: they can see the final objects they are producing but do not have a holistic perception of them'.[47] Kracauer, in comparing the legs of the Tiller Girls to the 'hands' in the factory, is proposing that 'the unified body is dismembered by a repetitive "geometrical activity" . . . repeating like a machine the movements someone else (the big boss, the big brother, the big male) has designed'.[48] Whilst there is certainly an appropriate point here about the gendering of the Tiller process, and it is true to say that the chorus line is intended to work as a 'collective' or 'unit', the parallel really only exists in the way the performance is perceived. The Tiller Girls all perform all the actions: they are not necessarily alienated from their own experience of the dance.

Bunty Gordon, a Tiller Girl in the 1940s, recalled:

> the precision dancing and the rehearsals were very very hard. At the Tiller School, the rehearsal room had mirrors all round. You would start with two Tillers dancing together, then three, four, five and gradually build the line up

---

44 http://www.btinternet.com/~nigel.ellacott.htm (19 Oct. 2002); see also Parker, *Natural History of the Chorus Girl*.
45 S. Kracauer, *The Mass Ornament*, trans. Thomas Y. Levin (Cambridge, Mass.: Harvard University Press, 1995), pp. 75–8.
46 Bailey, '"Naughty but nice"', p. 40.
47 http://www.sas.upenn.edu (19 Oct. 2002).
48 *Ibid.*

and when you have been used to dancing in your own style for years, it is very difficult to discipline yourself to be as one in a troupe. In a line-up of twenty-four girls, it takes a great deal of control to keep absolutely together.[49]

The sense of ownership felt by the dancers for the precision of their performance would seem to undercut any interpretation of them as cogs in a machine. The performance itself can certainly be critiqued in terms of its representational practices: 'identical' and 'indistinguishable' units of femaleness overwriting the women who are at work there. Nevertheless, the inevitable provisionalities and potentialities of live performance would always seem to offer the opportunity to disrupt uniformity. The very discipline of unity itself draws attention to the way individuality is being controlled by the performer – so the audience may well look for it all the more.

It would seem that in the forms of early twentieth-century British popular theatre one of the major negotiations enjoyed by workers-as-audience 'at play' was about the status of players 'at work', with both contributing to the refiguring of the entertainment industry as both respectable diversion and profession. Yet within this general trajectory, the liminal status of popular performance continued to enable exploration of cultural questions and anxieties, and to put pressure on what could and could not be 'spoken' within the wider culture. After all, respectability can never finally be 'arrived at': it is always itself held in tension as the culture of which it is part evolves. Rather than being evidence of a pale interregnum between two richer periods, the types of popular performance that flourished in these turbulent years illuminate the social, political and cultural functions of popular performance generally. In raising debates and posing questions about social and cultural boundaries, in exercising the liminal dynamics of the popular, the forms of blackface minstrelsy, pierrot shows, musical comedy, variety and the rest are major components of a much longer history. The forms of popular theatre between the 1890s and 1940s were indebted to their Victorian predecessors but also provided a seedbed for popular uses of the new electronic media in the second half of the twentieth century. One might even suggest that live entertainment as a whole in this period was a liminal phenomenon, providing new kinds of 'betwixt-and-between' for the evolution of popular performance itself.

49 http://www2.arts.gla.ac.uk (19 Oct. 2002).

5

Case study: Cicely Hamilton's
Diana of Dobson's, 1908

CHRISTINE DYMKOWSKI

Diana of Dobson's, by Cicely Hamilton, was one of the undoubted hits of British theatre in 1908, proving both a popular and a critical success. Mischievously subtitled 'A Romantic Comedy in Four Acts',[1] the play made its audiences laugh at the same time as it made them think about theatrical convention, voyeurism, the 'living-in' system for shop employees, sweated labour and capitalism, homelessness and unemployment, double standards and the nature of marriage. The number of issues with which it engages may seem formidable but, as one reviewer wrote, Hamilton

> has driven her lesson home with almost brutal frankness . . . [yet] has not fallen into the error of making everything subservient to the lesson she seeks to inculcate as so often obtains in 'plays with a purpose' . . . [S]he has so adroitly 'gilded the pill' that the work in itself is simply delightful and of absorbing interest.[2]

Almost unanimously, critics hailed it as fresh and original, blending realism and romance, and doing so with considerable wit.

Before exploring the play, its issues and contemporary reception, it is worth examining the circumstances of its production. After three weeks in rehearsal,[3] *Diana* opened at the Kingsway Theatre, London, on Wednesday 12 February 1908, the second offering of Lena Ashwell's management there. Ashwell, who was a leading actor, had taken over the small theatre on a long lease, renamed and redecorated it. Her announced policy was

---

1 Cicely Hamilton, *Diana of Dobson's: A Romantic Comedy in Four Acts* (New York: Samuel French, 1925); reprinted in *New Woman Plays*, ed. Linda Fitzsimmons and Viv Gardner (London: Methuen, 1991), pp. 27–77. All further references are to the latter edition.
2 *Newcastle Weekly Journal* (12 Sept. 1908), II, 116. Unless otherwise indicated, all reviews quoted are from press clippings in two of Lena Ashwell's scrapbooks ('1907–April 1908' and '1908', identified respectively as I and II), Theatre Museum, London.
3 *Daily Telegraph* (20 Jan. 1908), I, 173, announced the start of rehearsals on 20 January.

to alternate Plays of serious interest with Comedies, and to produce at Matinées pieces which, while worthy of production by reason of their artistic merit, would not perhaps interest a sufficient number of the public to warrant their being placed in a regular evening Bill. Thus . . . I hope to form a Repertory of Plays likely to appeal to the varied tastes of my Patrons.[4]

In addition, Ashwell was committed to establishing an ensemble company under the direction of fellow-actor Norman McKinnel and to discovering new, younger dramatists. For the latter purpose she employed a play-reader to deal with unsolicited manuscripts, ensuring a departure 'from the orthodox manner of relying upon the efforts of a recognised clique of dramatists'.[5] She was further concerned to raise the standard of entr'acte music, substituting serious classical and modern music 'for the usual light melodies' and including the 'works of younger composers who [were] struggling to obtain a hearing'.[6]

As manager, Ashwell showed as much concern for the audience's needs as for her own artistic ideals. She rearranged the seating so that all places, including those in the pit and the gallery, were 'numbered and reserved';[7] the innovation meant that audiences for those cheaper areas no longer had to queue outside the theatre and then, once inside, scramble for the best spot available. She also abolished cloak-room fees and, although charging for programmes, ensured their value by including portraits of the players and information about the music played, the theatre, cab fares, tube stations, trams and horse and motor bus routes; for one reviewer, it was the only theatrical programme worth paying for.[8] She made the 573-seat theatre one of the most comfortable in London; with prices starting at one shilling, it was also one of the most reasonably priced.[9] Similarly, by making afternoon teas a special feature at 'a fair price' of 'sixpence inclusive', Ashwell brought this usually 'expensive luxury' within the reach of more play-goers.[10] She also seems to have solved the vexed issue of matinée hats; whereas Robert Courtneidge at the Queen's resorted to an 'ultimatum' printed on matinée tickets that they were sold 'on condition' women remove their hats, Ashwell relied on 'humour', displaying the following notice on the proscenium fire curtain: 'The management beg to

4 Ashwell's policy pamphlet (9 October 1907), Theatre Museum, London.
5 *Daily News* (22 Jan. 1908), I, 174.
6 *New Album of Modes* (Jan. 1908), I, 178; and policy pamphlet (9 Oct. 1907).
7 Policy pamphlet (9 Oct. 1907).
8 *Public Opinion* (25 Jan. 1908), I, 17.
9 *Bystander* (29 April 1908), II, 6. One shilling (1909) = c. £2.45 (1999).
10 Policy pamphlet (9 Oct. 1907); quotations are from the *Bristol Times & Mirror* (9 May 1907), II, 14.

thank those ladies who have so kindly removed their hats and allowed others behind them a clear view of the stage'. It 'worked like a charm'.[11]

Ashwell's memoirs makes clear the idealism that inspired her venture: rebelling against commercialism, she wanted to 'sweep the profession clean of all artificial standards of value, all inhibiting control by the aristocracy of the profession. Room must be made for the unknown author, for experiments with new lighting, for new ideas of scenery.'[12] However, she also makes clear her self-interest, asserting that male actor-managers had kept 'the attention of the public on [themselves] as the centre of attraction' (p. 131). In reviewing *Diana of Dobson's*, the *Observer* agreed that its author was 'fortunate in the fact that London has one of its theatres just now under an actress-manageress's control. By reason of the relative insignificance of the male characters of her new play no actor-manager would have cared to produce it' (16 Feb. 1908, I, p. 199).[13] Ashwell reversed the situation: her play-reader, Edward Knoblock, reports that among the 'Definite rules' given to her hopeful authors was the stipulation that the play contain 'a good part for a woman'.[14] Even before the play opened – with Ashwell of course in the title role – the press was announcing 'a most unusual thing [about it] – the proportion of women to men is altogether excessive, the former numbering seven and the latter only three'.[15]

The play's focus on women – and working women, at that – might be expected, given Cicely Hamilton's own politics. Born into the impoverished middle class in 1872, she had earned her own living from an early age as teacher, translator, writer of hack romances and detective stories, journalist and actor. Although an active supporter of women's struggle to obtain the vote, she was not, as were many better-off women of her class, merely a suffragist; she held to a more broadly based feminism, which recognised that the vote alone would not change the central fact of women's social and economic oppression.

Hamilton began writing plays in 1906, having spent ten years on the provincial stage, usually playing the 'heavy' in melodramas. In that year her one-act play, *The Sixth Commandment*, was used as a curtain-raiser by Otho Stuart, who advised Hamilton to conceal her sex in order to avoid getting a bad press. The following year the Play Actors society staged two others, *The Sergeant of*

---

11 *Weekly Dispatch* (17 May 1908), II, 39, and (29 May 1908), I, 264; the final quotation is from the *North Mail* (20 March 1908), I, 249. Ashwell's successful solution was noted even in Paris: see *Gaulois* (2 May 1908) and *Le Gil Blas* (6 May 1908), II, 17.

12 Lena Ashwell, *Myself a Player* (London: Michael Joseph, 1936), p. 141.

13 See also *Morning Advertiser* (12 Sept. 1908), I, 115.

14 Edward Knoblock, *Round the Room: An Autobiography* (London: Chapman & Hall, 1939), p. 87.

15 *Daily Telegraph* (20 Jan. 1908), I, 173, and many others.

Hussars and *Mrs Vance*.[16] *Diana of Dobson's* was her first full-length play, written 'in the interval between pot-boilers'.[17]

Hamilton's distaste for 'the sugary treatment' and 'utter sloppiness of the admired type' of female character ensured that Diana Massingberd is no traditional romantic heroine. And although the play in which she features uses many of the conventions and settings of romantic comedy and melodrama, it is not conventional. The deployment of familiar motifs in unfamiliar ways perhaps accounts for discrepant reactions to the play, with one critic calling 'theatrical' what another calls 'realistic'; the act endings provoked similar disagreement.[18] In any case, its first audience, who had been led by Ashwell's stated policy to expect a straightforward comedy, found itself delightedly ambushed by a

> strong [play], compelling . . . attention and sympathy . . . from first to last. The story is not a hackneyed theme, and its developments are by no means easy to anticipate, while the dialogue throughout is brisk, incisive, and lucid . . . with force and character . . . quite out of the common.[19]

This unconventionality is the main focus of the rest of the chapter. A brief act-by-act synopsis of the play's salient features indicates the surprising turns of direction it took for its original audiences. Close analysis of reviews aims to reconstruct significant aspects of the production and its contribution to the play's thematic power and social relevance; it also offers a fuller understanding of its significantly varied contemporary reception, highlighting how theatrical convention and genre were subverted and what consequences that had for the creation of meaning.

Bedtime at Dobson's

The play opens in a dreary dormitory of Dobson's 'large suburban drapery establishment', where weary workers are beginning to turn in for the night:

> As the curtain rises the stage is almost in darkness except for the glimmer of a single gas jet turned very low. A door opens . . . *Miss Smithers* enters and gropes her way to the gas jet, which she turns full on. The light reveals a

---

16 *Stage* (23 Jan. 1908), I, 175.

17 Cicely Hamilton, *Life Errant* (London: J. M. Dent, 1935), p. 61; following quotations pp. 57–8.

18 See *Wallasey News* (12 Feb. 1908), I, 195; *Weekly Times & Echo* (16 Feb. 1908), I, 201; *Western Morning News* [Plymouth]; *Bradford Argus*, both (13 Feb. 1908), I, 194, 196.

19 *Financial Times* (12 Feb. 1908), I, 194. The date suggests this was written after the final dress rehearsal, to which an audience of 'all that was most representative in the artistic world of London – artists, politicians, playwrights, journalists, leaders at the bar' – had been invited. *Throne* (15 Feb. 1908), I, 197.

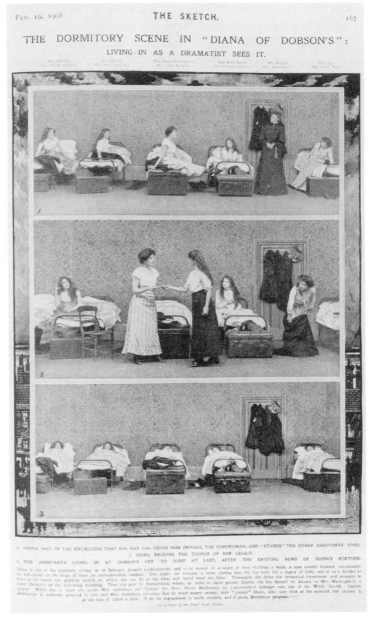

Figure 5.1 *Diana of Dobson's*, Kingsway Theatre, London, 1908. Three moments from the dormitory scene. Diana – Lena Ashwell – confronts Miss Pringle; Diana takes the unexpected letter from Miss Morton; the curtain is raised momentarily (and extratextually) to show the women asleep.

bare room of the dormitory type. Very little furniture except five small beds ranged against the walls – everything plain and comfortless to the last degree.

(p. 35)

Reviews fill in the grim picture: 'a more depressing apartment, with its cheap iron bedsteads [and] broken chairs . . . could hardly be imagined'. Damp came through the walls of the 'dingy' room, where there were tin trunks at the foot of each bed and 'exactly one towel and one washstand for the five "young ladies"'. Whilst one reviewer complained that the scene lacked 'verisimilitude' because of the 'scanty' furniture, another felt it 'too painfully realistic to be exaggerated'.[20] In fact, if the set were a distortion, it erred on the generous side: one audience member from Bath explained that 'living-in' was 'fifty times worse than it is portrayed', with the room shown on stage six times as large as most dormitories that contained five beds, and with single rather than the more usual double occupancy of the beds themselves.[21]

The widespread 'living-in' system was not, of course, a voluntary arrangement. As a contemporary, William Anderson, put it,

> No aspect of shop-life tells more against individuality and freedom than the living-in system – that curious arrangement which permits the management to assume that grown people are little boys and girls who cannot take care of themselves . . . Employers pretend that [it] endures because they are deeply concerned about the moral welfare of the employés [sic] . . . I am all the more sceptical about moral considerations when . . . the employers make about £1,000 in cash profits on the board and lodging of every 100 assistants.[22]

The issue was pertinent in 1908: the same night the play opened, the Amalgamated Union of Shop Assistants had organised a meeting at Queen's Hall to protest against the system.[23] It was even more timely when the play was revived early the following year: after sitting for more than two and a half years, the parliamentary committee set up to look into the truck system of wages had recently presented its report, which included a 'mass of evidence' about the living-in system.[24]

20 *Manchester Courier* (13 Feb. 1908), I, 189; *Daily Chronicle* (13 Feb. 1908), I, 189; *Throne* (14 March 1908), I, 245; *Yorkshire Daily Post* (13 Feb. 1908), I, 196; *Sportsman* (13 Feb. 1908), I, 190.
21 *Shop Assistant* (16 May 1908), II, 34.
22 William C. Anderson, '"Diana of Dobson's": the shopgirl's characteristics and conditions', *Woman Worker* 2, n.s. (12 June 1908), 10. See also Wilfrid B. Whitaker, *Victorian and Edwardian Shopworkers: The Struggle to Obtain Better Conditions and a Half-Holiday* (Newton Abbot: David & Charles, 1973), pp. 8–30.
23 *Manchester Guardian* (13 Feb. 1908), I, 190.
24 Whitaker, *Shopworkers*, p. 26. See also *Reynold's Newspaper* (17 Jan. 1909), II, 232; *Westminster Gazette* and *Morning Post*, both (12 Jan. 1909), II, 220 and 228.

As Dobson's workers prepare for bed, they reveal the harshness of their working conditions. Kitty Brant 'sighs wearily, and flings herself down on her bed' (p. 35). Diana, sharp-tongued and bitter, comes in 'feeling murderous' at having been fined again for the 'Usual thing – unbusinesslike conduct' (p. 37). She rails against her 'totally inadequate salary' of 'thirteen pounds a year' – 'five bob [shillings] a week – with deductions . . . for fourteen hours' work a day' (p. 39). This miserable picture was not exaggerated: according to Anderson, women workers faced excessive working hours (seven-day weeks of ninety-five hours in tobacco and sweet shops), scant wages (average eight shillings a week) and an 'elaborate system of fines and deductions (some business[es] have lists of from 100 to 200 separate offences punishable by fines ranging from 2d to 2s 6d)'.[25] Hamilton had '"attended meetings of the Shop Assistants' Union and listened to burning tales of their grievances"', but she still had to correct one of her facts after the first night: the forewoman levied a fine of 3d on each of the women for having the 'Gas burning after eleven o'clock at night' (p. 43) instead of the 6d it would have actually cost.[26] Many of the fashionable audience looked 'very pained and shocked' when Ashwell delivered Diana's ironic 'Hurrah for life!' as she contemplates her unchanging future (p. 40); others clung to the belief, despite the play's evidence to the contrary, that capital is the friend rather than the enemy of labour.[27]

Diana, however, soon discovers that her future holds more than she has anticipated, at least temporarily. Unexpectedly inheriting £300 from a distant and intestate cousin, she resolves to spend it on 'a crowded hour of glorious life' (p. 42). *The Stage* (13 Feb. 1908, p. 23) thought it unintelligible that a 'sensible, matter-of-fact girl' like Diana would decide to buy a month of luxury with her inheritance, but another critic found there was 'more in the amount . . . than meets the eye . . . [By its] largeness in comparison with her shop-girl's wages . . . this £300 serves the Fabian purpose of pointing the moral of wealth and poverty, while doing good service as the hinge of the plot besides'.[28] Crucially, the amount Diana inherits is not substantial enough to change her standard of living: invested 'in something really safe', it would return only 'nine or ten pounds a year at the outside' (p. 41). However, as a sum of money to spend, its buying power transcends the merely material. Diana's decision

---

25 Anderson, "Diana of Dobson's", p. 10. 2s 6d is two shillings and six pence; there are twelve pence in a shilling and twenty shillings in a pound.
26 Interview with Cicely Hamilton, *Weekly Dispatch* (23 Feb. 1908), I, 219.
27 *Clarion* (24 Feb. 1908), I, 249; see also *Lady's Pictorial* (22 Feb. 1908), I, 216, and *Horse and Hound* (21 March 1908), I, 249.
28 L. Haden Guest, *New Age* (26 Feb. 1908), 356.

'to have everything' she wants while the money lasts shows that she 'grasp[s] what money really is':

> It's power! Power to do what you like, to go where you like, to say what you like. Because I have three hundred pounds in my pocket, I shall be able tomorrow to enjoy the priceless luxury of telling Dobson to his fat white face, what we all whisper behind his mean old back – [.]   (p. 42)

The first act's focus on women shop workers, and the elevation of one to heroine, was unusual. However, such characters were not totally unrepresented in theatre and literature: several reviewers allude to W. B. Maxwell's 1905 novel *Vivien*, which painted a clear picture of a shop-girl's life and 'its moral perils', and to 'T. Baron Russell's powerful [1898] "shop girl" novel, "A Guardian of the Poor"'.[29] The shop-girl had also 'glided and pranced through the musical comedy', but now here was 'a serious attempt to present [her] on the stage, not as a lay figure or a farceuse, but as a creature of flesh and blood'.[30] Since the theatre of the time overwhelmingly focussed on upper-class life – for example, in 1908 Somerset Maugham had four society plays enjoying long West End runs – Hamilton's play had 'the great advantage of striking what [was] practically new ground for dramatic cultivation'.[31]

The first act also stood convention on its head by paradoxically using the women's preparations for bed as a way of de-eroticising the act of undressing.[32] The idea was a daring one, especially as striptease itself originated in an 1894 sketch, called 'Le Coucher d'Yvette', which was subsequently 'much imitated'.[33] Reviews, however, often show surprise that what might have been shocking, indelicate or risqué was in fact none of these things. Most found the undressing inoffensive, emphasising its realism and naturalness, elements that worked against voyeurism or sexual titillation: 'There is a naïve, simple frankness about this scene that puts to shame any thought of an appeal to

---

29 *Illustrated London News* and *MAP*, both (22 Feb. 1908), I, 215 and 211; see also *Lady's Pictorial* (22 Feb. 1908), I, 216.

30 *Dundee Telegraph* (4 March 1908), I, 232.

31 *Era* (15 Feb. 1908), I, 198; see also *MAP* (22 Feb. 1908).

32 The way the undressing contributes a double dynamic to the scene became very clear when I directed the play in the Department of Drama and Theatre, Royal Holloway, University of London (March 1987): first, it allows the characters to demonstrate physically the effects of their soul-destroying labour rather than merely to talk about it; second, the need to make themselves ready before the gas is turned out dramatises one of the ways in which the living-in system infantilised adult workers. Rehearsals also showed that the emphasis on tiredness and the careful handling of the undressing itself removed any danger of sexual titillation. See also Sheila Stowell's *A Stage of their Own: Feminist Playwrights of the Suffrage Era* (Manchester University Press, 1992), pp. 80–1.

33 Laurence Senelick, 'Nudity', in *The Cambridge Guide to Theatre*, ed. Martin Banham, updated edn (Cambridge University Press, 1995), p. 802.

naughtiness.'[34] Since the text calls for one character, Kitty Brant, to undress completely, a description of how the actor managed to do so discreetly is instructive:

> She removed her stockings with a delicate modesty, so that not even an ankle was visible in the process; and then, having taken off the first layer or so of her other garments, she threw over her head a pink flannel 'nightie'. Then her hands were seen busily at work under cover, and presently she produced from under the 'nightie' a neat and comprehensive bunch of feminine underduds, which she deposited carefully at the foot of the bed before scrambling in between the sheets. The operation was performed with the most charming simplicity and delicacy in the world.[35]

The much remarked hideousness of Kitty's modest nightgown also attests that costuming itself subverted audience expectation about intimate female apparel. Furthermore, reviews recognised 'real dramatic interest in the situation', with the different ways in which the women undid their hair and handled the various false puffs and switches that went into it helping to flesh out their characters: 'All that which goes to make up the modern coiffure is ruthlessly cast aside or brushed, as the temperament of the girl suggests.'[36] It is worth noting that the actors, besides buying their own clothes in order to characterise and give variety to the women, did much to develop the scene themselves;[37] Christine Silver, for example, made Kitty Irish.[38]

Besides divorcing the act of undressing from one of sexual display, this first scene had varied effects on its audience, and a few reviewers suggested that gender issues helped to determine the disparate responses. For example, the *Irish Independent*, who saw Ashwell on tour, thought that Hamilton had 'rather miscalculated the comic effect of that dormitory scene. Instead of the scene bringing home the squalid environment of Diana it merely amused the audience. It caused parterre girls to blush and the Johnnies to leer' (22 Sept. 1908, II, p. 122). In contrast, the *Observer* felt such 'feminine intimacies . . . [were] deliberately calculated to embarrass the masculine spectator' rather than the female (16 Feb. 1908, I, p. 206). Other critics simply found the scene moving: the business was 'so well treated that only the grimness and fierce humour of the

---

34 *Daily Chronicle* (13 Feb. 1908), I, 189; see also *Morning Post, Standard, Daily Graphic*(?), *Morning Leader*, all (13 Feb. 1908), I, 186–7 and 195; *Star* (n.d.), I, 185; *News of the World* (16 Feb. 1908), I, 205.
35 *Pick-Me-Up* (7 March 1908), I, 202.
36 *Manchester Courier* (13 Feb. 1908), I, 189; *Winning Post* (15 Feb. 1908), I, 198.
37 Interview with McKinnel, *Weekly Dispatch* (23 Feb. 1908), I, 219.
38 *Daily Chronicle* (13 Feb. 1908), I, 189.

affair impressed the audience, and the pathetic tragedy, also, of the toilet of the stately young ladies'.[39]

Conventional views of undressing inform some reports, although these were in the minority. One reviewer imagined that most people would 'question the motive and taste of the authoress', but still realised that 'a simple frankness about it . . . puts to shame any thought of an appeal to the baser feelings'.[40] Another critic used the scene's sexlessness to assert a masculine voyeuristic prerogative:

> None of the girls at Dobson's, with one solitary exception, are particularly good-looking, so the fact that five of them undress and creep into their respective beds with a becoming sense of the proprieties which would not bring a blush to the cheek of even a highly susceptible censor is not likely to fill this theatre with a crowd of mere curiosity seekers. Nor is the lingerie and underclothing generally of the young ladies of a sort to establish Dobson's in the eyes of feminine beauty as a remarkably chic and up-to-date establishment.[41]

His desire to subvert the scene's point testifies to its having achieved the desired effect.

The romance begins

Whilst the first act aroused expectations of a realistic problem play focussing on the living-in issue and showing the influences of Ibsen and Zola,[42] the second and third acts take place at the fashionable Hotel Engadine in the Swiss mountains, where Diana is enjoying her glorious month of luxury. Diana's ease in such a setting made reviewers both wonder and justify how a shop worker could manage so well amongst smart society.[43] Certainly, Hamilton took care here to overturn the theatrical stereotype of the 'adventuress', the original (and ironical) title of the play: instead of appearing 'as the familiar type of charlatan, making mistakes and being vulgar', her 'conversation differs from those about her only in its expressions of sympathy with Cook's tourists'; she was 'impetuous, revolutionary, and careless in the best sense of the word'.[44]

39 *Sketch* (19 Feb. 1908), I, 206.
40 *New Zealand Graphic* (4 April 1908), II, 33; see also *Leeds Mercury* (13 Feb. 1908), I, 194.
41 *Yorkshire Daily Post* (13 Feb. 1908), I, 196.
42 See *Reynold's Newspaper* (16 Feb. 1908), I, 200; *Lady's Pictorial* (22 Feb. 1908), I, 216; *London Chat* (29 Feb. 1908), I, 224.
43 See *New Age* (26 Feb. 1908), I, 228; *The Statesman* [Calcutta] (n.d.), I, 245; *Standard* (13 Feb. 1908), I, 186.
44 *Birmingham Post* (13 Feb. 1908), I, 192.

However, few reviewers thought Diana so likeable, and her character attracted even more comment than her social skills, with many critics finding her hard and unpleasant – another far cry from the usual heroine of romantic comedy. She appeared 'admirably decisive if needlessly harsh', 'downright, wilful, and it must be owned rather self-absorbed' – in all, simply 'very unlovable'.[45] Whilst complaints that Diana could have been drawn more softly emphasise critical sensitivity about the theatrical representation of 'woman', some critics nevertheless recognised her as 'Fundamentally . . . real', with 'a character as [interesting] as it is [difficult]'.[46]

In telling contrast to the privileged setting of the hotel, the play remains firmly fixed on the relationship between labour and capital, between working and leisured classes. Seemingly a fashionable and wealthy widow – Diana recognises that 'You're ever so much freer when you're married' (p. 43) – her company is sought by two other holiday-makers: the newly ennobled Sir Jabez Grinley, who owns a chain of shops in which she once worked, and the Hon. Victor Bretherton, who recently resigned his Guards commission, since (in his aunt's words) his private income of 'a miserable six hundred pounds a year' is insufficient 'to keep up the position' (p. 45). The 'miserableness' of his income is, however, imaginary: in 1910, G. D'Aeth 'established seven social groupings by reference to income, occupation, housing, social customs, and education'. The Oxford-educated Victor would have been near the top, in category F, which 'included the heads of firms, professional men and administrators, earning at least £600 per annum, who had usually received a university education'.[47] Victor's unearned income is anything but paltry.

Diana's meetings with the moneyed guests allow Hamilton to make a number of telling points about the exploitation of labour: the way to wealth, argues Diana, is 'to get other people to work for you for as little as they can be got to take, and put the proceeds of their work into your pockets' (p. 53). Some commentators deduced Hamilton's 'socialistic leanings', as well as her feminist perspective, but praised her subtlety: 'The characters express some strong opinions on debateable points but – and I can recall no parallel to the achievement – Miss Hamilton makes them do this without appearing to preach at the audience and without showing which of her creatures voices her own

---

45 *Observer* (16 Feb. 1908), I, 199; *Illustrated London News* (22 Feb. 1908), I, 215; *Westminster Gazette* (13 Feb. 1908), I, 188.
46 *Westminster Gazette* (13 Feb. 1908), I, 188; *Illustrated London News* (22 Feb. 1908), I, 215.
47 Donald Read, *England 1868–1914* (London: Longman, 1979), p. 399, citing G. D'Aeth, 'Present tendencies of class differentiation', *Sociological Review* (Oct. 1910).

views.'[48] Furthermore, her writing had 'sufficient virility to give the lie to Mr Bernard Shaw's dictum that a London audience will not listen to long speeches on the stage'.[49] Others also characterise Hamilton's writing as virile, perhaps unconsciously linking masculinity and politics. Some reviewers even covertly transform Hamilton into a man.[50]

A proposal fails

Act 3 opens with Diana, her money nearly gone, making plans for a hurried return to London. Her imminent departure precipitates two proposals, one from Sir Jabez, whom she turns down despite his 'Forty thousand a year, to say nothing of the title' (p. 60), and the other from Victor. Diana realises that Victor's aunt has assumed her legacy is her monthly income and mistakenly deduced that 'Three hundred pounds a month . . . is three thousand six hundred a year' (p. 56), thus misinforming her nephew about Diana's financial circumstances. Diana therefore honourably 'consider[s] [his] proposal of marriage unspoken' until she has undeceived him (p. 65). Victor complains about being 'put in a deuced awkward position' and accuses Diana of being an 'adventuress' (p. 67), a charge that the *Standard* indignantly refuted: 'she is not – she has spent her own money and owes no one' (13 Feb. 1908, I, p. 186). Diana rounds on Victor with some home truths, pointing out that in hoping to marry a rich woman *he* is the adventurer, that working to support oneself is more admirable than marrying for money, and that without his private income he would be unable to survive (pp. 67–9).

This scene was one of the production's highlights, with the actors taking seven (or even nine) curtain calls after it on opening night.[51] It helped at least one reviewer to accept Diana as a very different kind of heroine from the norm:

> The character . . . is very neatly drawn; we have a girl naturally clever, fairly educated, ambitious with no means of gratifying her ambition, and with the mark of her years of drudgery upon her. The lack of refinement, the vulgarity

48 Respectively, *Bradford Argus* (13 Feb. 1908), I, 196, and *Civil & Military Gazette* [Lahore] (13 March 1908), I, 282. On the play's feminist sensibility, see *Era* (15 Feb. 1908), I, 198; *Gentlewoman* (22 Feb. 1908), I, 217; *Birmingham Post* (29 Sept. 1908), II, 130; *Christian Commonwealth* (29 Jan. 1909), II, 237.
49 *Bradford Argus*; see also *Western Morning News* [Plymouth] (13 Feb. 1908), I, 194.
50 See, for example, *Wallasey News* (12 Feb. 1908), I, 195.
51 *World* (19 Feb. 1908), I, 206; *Pall Mall Gazette* (13 Feb. 1908), I, 190.

if you will . . . [when] Diana stands and shouts, and insults . . . seems at first to
strike a jarring and unnatural note, but one ultimately admits that her manner
has truth in it and is based on probability.[52]

This contrast between theatrical stereotypes and real women reminded
another reviewer of Ibsen, while a third called it a 'magnificent tirade . . .
worth any number of Socialistic pamphlets'.[53]

However, Diana and Victor's exchange made some reviewers feel cheated
in their expectations of romantic comedy. B. W. Findon complained that
Hamilton had allowed

womanly prejudice to run away with her . . . [so] that we are face to face with
a serious problem, instead of being confronted with an amusing episode . . .
[T]he girl makes no allowance for the awkward predicament of the man . . .
[T]he poor fellow is not allowed to get a word in edgeways [sic] . . . In dealing
with a piece which purports to be a 'romantic comedy' I ought not to be
discussing a problem of sex; I ought to be congratulating Miss Hamilton on
her finesse and wit as a writer of comedy.[54]

Some reviewers complained that Hamilton did not 'sufficiently [clarify] that
[Victor] loved Diana for herself alone', or vice versa.[55] Others were surprised
that the first hint of how the two characters regard each other came only
in Diana's exit line: when Victor wonders why she had anything to do with
him, she 'bitterly' responds that 'It would have been very much better for
me if I hadn't' (p. 69). There was 'a world of emphasis in the sad way in
which [Ashwell made] the remark, for she show[ed] clearly that, in spite of
her apparent contempt for the gallant captain, he has found at least a corner
of her heart'; other critics mention a 'touching little break in her voice' and
a 'hidden tear'.[56] Given the disparate perceptions of the pair's feelings toward
each other, Ashwell's handling of this business must have been subtle and helps
to account for the very different final views of the comedy's 'romance'.

The 'romantic' trick is turned

When Act 4 opened on the Thames Embankment, a 'favourite *mise-en-scène* [*sic*]
among old-fashioned authors of London melodrama', the surprised audience

52 *Musical Standard* (22 Feb. 1908), I, 23.
53 *Lady's Pictorial* (22 Feb. 1908), I, 216; *Daily Chronicle* (13 Feb. 1908), I, 189.
54 *Morning Advertiser* (13 Feb. 1908), I, 188. The *Daily News* (13 Feb. 1908), I, 191 also defended
Victor.
55 *Planet* (22 Feb. 1908), I, 211; see also *Stage* (13 Feb. 1908), 23, and others.
56 *Pick-Me-Up* (7 March 1908), I, 202; *Morning Leader* (13 Feb. 1908), I, 195; *People* (16 Feb.
1908), I, 200.

Figure 5.2 *Diana of Dobson's*, Kingsway Theatre, London, 1908. On the Embankment, the chance meeting of Diana and Victor (C. M. Hallard) is followed by their engagement breakfast.

expected 'a tragic termination to the story'.[57] Three figures huddle asleep on a bench 'in the small hours of a November morning' (p. 70). One of them is Victor who, stung by Diana's parting words and setting out to disprove her, is discovering that she was right: he explains to an ex-army comrade, the police constable who had tried to move him on, that 'For the last three months I've been trying to earn my living by the sweat of my brow – net result, a few odd jobs at the docks and a shilling for sweeping out an old gentleman's back garden. My present profession is that of a cab chaser' (p. 71). Allowed by the policeman to stay, he is eventually joined by a shabbily dressed woman who turns out to be Diana, now 'homeless and penniless' and 'half starved' after losing a job through illness. After various misunderstandings and explanations, Victor, acknowledging that £600 a year is 'not only enough for *one* to live upon – it's ample for *two*' (p. 76), again proposes to Diana, who eventually (but tacitly) accepts. With a shilling borrowed from the policeman, they celebrate their

57 *Daily News* (22 Jan. 1908), I, 174, and *Bradford Argus* (13 Feb. 1908), I, 196.

reconciliation with a breakfast of 'two cups of coffee and thick slices of bread and butter' from a nearby coffee-stall (p. 77). The final image of the play parodies Robertsonian cup-and-saucer comedy: Ashwell and C. M. Hallard, who played Victor, spent 'two minutes in an ecstacy [sic] of munch and gulp'.[58]

Hamilton's 'romantic comedy' thereby seems to end as it should, with a projected marriage between lovers, but many reviewers expressed misgivings about this conventionally happy conclusion. Some objected because they doubted the two would be happy together, while others considered the ending too formulaic for such a thoughtful play.[59] In fact, this debunking of romance was precisely what one might expect from the future author of the feminist analysis *Marriage as a Trade*.[60] Hamilton had prepared for it carefully throughout the play by subverting the characteristic story motifs of nineteenth-century romantic comedy: as outlined by Martin Meisel, the 'opposition between youth and age', 'a Cinderella-Galatea motif of transformation and testing' and 'misalliance between classes'.[61] In *Diana of Dobson's* the busy snooping of the older generation (Victor's aunt) presents no real obstacle to the match; the hero's own unwillingness to marry a woman without money constitutes the threat. Nor does Cinderella-Diana have to prove herself worthy of Prince Charming-Victor – rather the opposite. Although he fails Diana's challenge to earn his own living, upper-class Victor rises to the greater one of learning respect for working people.

Besides undermining romantic comedy conventions, Hamilton also ensures that the play's dialogue underlines the point that marriage is all too often the only trade women can ply. In this she was especially in tune with the more radical thinking of her times. Carol Dyhouse comments that 'Marital relationships were the subject of intense discussion amongst feminists' in the period, with Edward Carpenter's 1896 work, *Love's Coming of Age*, proving 'a highly important stimulus to feminist discussions of marriage'.[62] In the theatre, 1908 also saw the first productions of J. M. Barrie's comedy *What Every Woman Knows*, in which the capable Maggie Wylie is so desperate to marry that her father and brothers 'buy' her a husband, and of Bernard Shaw's

58 *Times of India* [April 1908?], I, 274.
59 See *Daily Telegraph* (13 Feb. 1908), I, 191; *Stage* (13 Feb. 1908), 23; *Sporting Times* (15 Feb. 1908), I, 197; *Irish Independent* (22 Sept. 1908), II, 122; *Manchester Courier* (13 Feb. 1908), I, 9; *Western Morning News* [Plymouth] (13 Feb. 1908), I, 194.
60 Cicely Hamilton, *Marriage as a Trade* (London: Chapman & Hall, 1909; rpt. London: Women's Press, 1981).
61 Martin Meisel, *Shaw and the Nineteenth-Century Theater* (Princeton University Press, 1963), p. 161.
62 Carol Dyhouse, *Feminism and the Family in England 1880–1939* (Oxford: Blackwell, 1989), pp. 145–6.

farcical discussion play *Getting Married*, which Max Beerbohm described as 'a conspectus of the typical tragedies and comedies caused by the marriage laws in twentieth-century England'.[63] Because Hamilton focusses on the economic realities behind supposed romance, the prospective marriage that ends *Diana of Dobson's* has a double edge: it delivers the expected 'happy' ending, but the unease generated about the very nature of matrimony discourages the audience from simply accepting it in accord with convention – as so much contemporary comment testifies.

Although Hamilton subverts the tragic expectations raised by the Embankment setting, its miserable atmosphere pervades the play's final scene. Some reviewers recognised that, paradoxically, the melodramatic location gave the romantic comedy a hard and realistic edge, the *Financial Times* arguing that 'the Registrar-General's returns, with their grim insistence that one in every four of the population dies in the workhouse, bear out the truth of the author's picture, and refute any charge of exaggeration' (12 Feb. 1908, I, p. 194). The transformation of melodramatic conventions to produce subtle but hard-hitting social and political comment is especially achieved through the Old Woman who is Victor's and Diana's bench-mate for much of the final act. Beryl Mercer's performance in this small part, besides being universally praised, received attention out of all proportion to her time on stage. Hamilton had made the 'beggar woman . . . almost Zolaesque in its truthfulness', and in Mercer's 'make-up and acting she was so realistic that it made one shudder to watch her'; she was a 'draggled old waif whose gin-voiced "Dearie!" sound[ed] so veritable an echo from the slums'.[64] The issue of unemployment was prominent in 1908, with Winston Churchill (then president of the Board of Trade in Asquith's cabinet) believing it 'was especially "the problem of the hour"'.[65] The opening night audience would certainly have been conscious of it, as newspapers concurrently reported various marches of the unemployed and parliamentary debates on the subject.[66]

Despite its serious concerns, *Diana of Dobson's* was a great theatrical success: it ran for 143 performances at the Kingsway, with Ashwell only bringing the production to an end in order to rest before touring with it.[67] During 1908 and

---

63 *Saturday Review* (23 May 1908), reprinted in Max Beerbohm, *Around Theatres*, 1924 (London: Rupert Hart-Davis, 1953; rpt. New York: Simon & Schuster, 1954), p. 510.

64 *Throne* (14 March 1908), I, 245; *Throne* and *Observer* (16 Feb. 1908), I, 199.

65 Quoted in Read, *England 1868–1914*, p. 465.

66 See, for example, *Times* (31 Jan. 1908), *Morning Post* (11 Feb. 1908), and *Times* (12 Feb. 1908).

67 J. P. Wearing, *The London Stage 1900–1909* (London: Scarecrow Press, 1981), vol. 11, p. 634; *Morning Post* (12 Jan. 1909), II, 228. Ashwell revived the play at the Kingsway in 1909 for a further thirty-two performances.

1909 four other companies toured Britain with the play, and productions were scheduled in the United States, Australia and South Africa.[68] Its success in a market that favoured light comedy, musical plays, and stirring melodrama is testimony to Hamilton's skill in embedding a wide-ranging social critique in an ostensible romantic comedy. As innumerable reviews confirm, she made the fashionable part of her audience face unpalatable truths about social and economic injustice without compromising her own feminism or patronising those she championed. She breathed fresh life into tired conventions, creating 'a delightful play, fresh, light, and sparkling, yet absolutely earnest and challenging at the heart of it'.[69] No seriously engaged playwright could hope to do more.

68 Besides Ashwell's London company, which travelled to major cities, there were also the Principal, North, South, and Midland companies; see *Stage* (6 Aug. 1908) and *Health* (8 Aug. 1908), both in II, 99; *Brighton Herald* (6 Feb. 1909), II, 241. For foreign productions, see *Sheffield Independent* (7 Aug. 1908), II, 98. Hamilton, *Life Errant*, p. 62, remarks that the play 'ran for years in the provinces'.
69 *Daily Chronicle* (13 Feb. 1908), I, 189.

6

A critical year in perspective: 1926

STEVE NICHOLSON

This, then, is the situation in 1926. A large part of the London theatre is given up to plays about dope fiends and jazz-maniacs; other large tracts are abandoned to the inanities of musical comedy. Roughly speaking, three-fourths of the London stage is closed to persons possessed of the slightest particle of intellect or the least feeling for the drama . . . Yet – and this is the thing I want most to say – there never was a time when the general interest in, and preoccupation with, the drama was bigger both in London and throughout the country.[1]

Britain came closer to outright class war in 1926 than at any other time in the twentieth century, and theatre, as one of the principal media through which ideas were disseminated, was a crucial battleground in the struggle. A few years earlier, a play called *The Right to Strike* had led to arguments and fighting in the auditorium, articles in the *Times*, polls by the *Daily Mirror*, extracts being performed in church, and the intervention of Buckingham Palace. 'One feels', wrote the *Saturday Review*, that the author, if he had liked to do so, might quite easily have provoked a riot'.[2] It is only necessary to see how concerned the Censors were about licensing plays for public performance to realise how significant theatre was seen to be in preventing or encouraging class conflict. In 1925 a licence had been refused to Strindberg's *Miss Julie* partly because of its 'very questionable theme in these days of the relations between masters and servants',[3] and in 1926 Noel Coward's *This Was a Man* suffered the same fate at the hands of the Lord Chamberlain and his Advisory Board:

---

1 James Agate, *A Short View of the English Stage, 1900–1926* (London: Herbert Jenkins, 1926), pp. 113–14.
2 *Saturday Review* (9 Oct. 1920), 292–3. Ernest Hutchinson's *The Right to Strike* ran in the West End in the autumn of 1921. See Steve Nicholson, *British Theatre and the Red Peril: The Portrayal of Communism 1917–1945* (Exeter University Press, 1999), pp. 33–9.
3 Lord Chamberlain's Correspondence Files – *Miss Julie*. See Steve Nicholson, '"Unnecessary plays": European drama and the British censor', *Theatre Research International* 20, 1 (spring 1995), 30–6.

Every character in this play, presumably ladies and gentlemen, leads an adulterous life and glories in doing so. The only exceptions are two servants who are kept busy mixing cocktails. I find no serious purpose in the play, unless it be misrepresentation. At a time like this what better propaganda could the Soviet instigate and finance?[4]

In January 1926 the theatrical newspaper the *Era* described theatre as 'a necessity' in helping to preserve a peaceful society: 'Its soothing influence during the darkest days of the war was admitted on every hand, even by responsible Ministers, who broadcast the opinion that amusements were indispensable to the people.'[5] A report by the government's education committee published a couple of months later claimed that theatre could function as more than a mere distraction and play an active role in creating peace; it was, they said, 'an unrivalled instrument for breaking down social barriers and establishing friendly relations', with the potential to 'bring some element of healing and of reconciliation into the warring elements in our national life'.[6]

Yet 1926 was also the year in which the Workers' Theatre Movement emerged with a commitment to use performance as a weapon in the class war: 'In other countries we use the theatre; it is a splendid servant. But we British . . . leave the theatre in the boss's hands, allow him to spread dope far and wide . . . graft boss ideas on the working class bodies.'[7] Whether as means of escape, as moral educator, as weapon of revolutionary propaganda, or as healer of social discord, rarely can performance have been so widely attributed with the power to influence decisively both individuals and society, and it is this which makes 1926 a particularly significant year in British theatre history.

The threat of revolution

The General Strike of May 1926 lasted for little more than a week before the Trades Union Congress capitulated to Baldwin's government and abandoned the miners to fight alone; it had, of course, been the culmination of the protest and discontent that had emerged in the aftermath of World War One to challenge the fundamental economic basis and class divisions within society.[8] Whilst the strike was specifically about the wages and working conditions of

---

4 Lord Chamberlain's Correspondence Files – *This Was A Man*.
5 *Era* (6 Jan. 1926), 10.
6 Great Britain Board of Education, Adult Education Committee, *The Drama in Adult Education* (London: HMSO, 1926), pp. 120, 198.
7 Jack Loveman, *Young Worker* (9 Oct. 1926), 4.
8 The strike lasted from the 4th to the 12th of May; the miners capitulated in November.

miners, general strikes had famously been used as a deliberate and partially successful strategy against governments in a number of European countries, including Sweden, Belgium and Germany. For many within the political establishment and the ruling classes, the very concept embodied the ultimate threat of a Soviet-style revolution and the loss of power to a proletarian dictatorship. As the strike threatened, a *Daily Mail* editorial requested 'all law-abiding men and women' to put themselves 'at the service of King and country',[9] and after its victory, the government was quick to introduce legislation to outlaw future general strikes.

It is an indication of their perceived importance in maintaining morale and normality that, as soon as the strike started, London theatres were immediately targeted with hoax phone calls purporting to come from the government and instructing them to suspend performances. The lack of public transport and fuel did force some theatres to close, but most continued to function through the strike, and many managers provided private cars to ferry their casts to work. Neither side in the political struggle doubted the importance of the theatre; Johnston Forbes-Robertson, the president of the Stage Guild, later boasted that, but for the combined work of the Stage Guild and the Theatrical Managers' Association, 'not only would thousands of actors and actresses have been thrown out of work, but the country would have been deprived of that mental diversion which is such a safeguard in times of unrest'.[10] The Left, meanwhile, argued that the government had made systematic and 'sinister' use of the media: 'Recognising their importance as strike-breakers they encouraged the capitalistic theatres to carry on (as at wartime when they were used to gas the public into sympathy with government war aims).'[11] Forbes-Robertson even suggested that the industry offered a unique model of harmony that others might imitate; in the theatre, he claimed, 'managers, artists (i.e., employers and employees)' were united in their pursuit of the same ends.[12]

Perhaps surprisingly, economic debates and plays warning of the dangers or impracticalities of revolution penetrated even some of the mainstream theatres in 1926. In March *Mrs Warren's Profession* received its first fully public performance, after being refused a licence for nearly thirty years, with Shaw adamant that 'the economic situation so forcibly demonstrated by Mrs Warren

---

9 Quoted in C. L. Mowat, *Britain Between the Wars, 1918–1940* (London: Methuen, 1955), p. 308.
10 Johnston Forbes-Robertson, letter in the *Times* (19 May 1926), 17.
11 *Sunday Worker* (6 June 1926), 8.
12 Forbes-Robertson, letter in the *Times*.

remains as true as ever in essentials today'.[13] An interesting comparison with Shaw's analysis of a hypocritical society driving women into prostitution and then condemning them was *The Gold-Diggers*, an American comedy about mercenary young chorus women revelling in the lucrative and pleasurable pastime of obtaining money and jewellery from men without giving anything in return. Meanwhile, *First Blood* by Allan Monkhouse, *A Place in the Shade* by Ian Rankine, *The Forcing House* by Israel Zangwill, *What Might Happen* by J. F. Maltby and *Yellow Sands* by Eden and Adelaide Philpotts all focussed on political struggle and revolution.[14] The Monkhouse and Zangwill plays were almost tragic in tone, but it was the comedies of Maltby and the Philpotts that were presented by West End managements. *Yellow Sands* ran for sixteen months, showing how a Devonshire fisherman who wants 'to see the guillotine set up on this beach' is converted from his naïve communist ideals into a recognition that capitalism works for the benefit of all.[15] Similarly, audiences at the Savoy Theatre laughed at Mrs Patrick Campbell in Maltby's dystopian satire set in a post-revolutionary society in which rich and ignorant workers abuse their power over newly impoverished aristocrats, who pathetically attempt to maintain the forms of their previous existence:

> LADY STRONG-I'-TH'-ARM: I hope this tea will be strong enough for you, we only used it for breakfast this morning.
> LADY TOTTENHAM: Oh – quite, quite! Strong tea is so bad for the nerves . . .
> LADY STRONG-I'-TH'-ARM: I am afraid I cannot offer you anything to eat.
> LADY TOTTENHAM: Oh, we never eat anything in the daytime.[16]

The narrative and the tone, especially, of these two plays suggest an almost breathtaking complacency on the part of West End audiences – that the threat of revolution need not be taken seriously. Perhaps this was a desperate escapism from an alternative too awful to contemplate, as the *Sunday Times* review of *Yellow Sands* surely signals: 'The time is not yet, in the theatre, when we shall cease to believe that a legacy of four thousand pounds can turn the most frenzied Communist into a rapturous Individualist.'[17]

---

13 Author's note, 2 March 1926, programme for Strand Theatre production of *Mrs Warren's Profession*.
14 See Nicholson, 'Appendix,' *British Theatre and the Red Peril*.
15 Eden Phillpotts and Adelaide Phillpotts, *Yellow Sands* (London: Duckworth, 1926), p. 12. Opened Haymarket Theatre, 3 November 1926; over 600 performances.
16 H. F. Maltby, *What Might Happen: A Piece of Extravagance in Three Acts* (London: Stage Play Publishing Bureau, 1927), p. 5.
17 *Sunday Times* (7 Nov. 1926), 6.

A contested repertoire

The West End was increasingly berated by critics for its obsession with 'infantile and trivial' material performed by 'over-grown boys and girls' to 'the wrong sorts of audience'.[18] Just as the political conflict in the country derived from an economic system primarily designed to increase profits for owners and managers, so it was theatre managers and their obsession with profit who were blamed for the perceived lack of intelligence in the commercial sector. In pursuit of financial success, managements increasingly concentrated on musical comedies and revues, many imported from America, which relied for their appeal largely on the attractiveness of the chorus lines: 'Where formerly the performance was carried out by trained artists, the stage is now invaded by young ladies who can sing a little and dance a little.'[19] The critic James Agate drew an absolute distinction between theatre, 'an economic proposition', and drama, 'an aesthetic proposition', and summed up the prevailing philosophy as 'No money for serious drama: bags of it for tosh.'[20] Such criticism came not only from 'highbrow' critics; the *Era* insisted that theatre 'should not be regarded as a mere business speculation', and under the headline 'WHAT IS WRONG WITH THEATRE?: Commercialism Ousting Art' complained that the energy and creativity that had flourished under the old actor-manager system had been 'superseded by a newer spirit introduced by men of money and leisure whose interests in the theatre are the box office receipts and the relegation of the real art of the profession to the background'.[21]

However, although Agate complained that those who took an intelligent interest in the theatre 'never have any money' while those who 'have money never take an intelligent interest in the theatre', there did exist an alternative to the mainstream in the so-called 'highbrow' theatre. Even discounting the work of Noel Coward and Ben Travers, an assiduous London theatre-goer in 1926 could have seen plays by Strindberg, Pirandello, Toller, O'Casey, Kaiser, Čapek, Turgenev, Gorki, Gogol, Sophocles, Molière, Wycherley, Goldsmith, Granville Barker, Galsworthy, Lawrence, Barrie, Malleson, Joyce, O'Neill, Shaw and Shakespeare, and just about everything Chekhov ever wrote. Many regional theatres also offered alternatives and those in Liverpool, Birmingham, Bristol, Bath, Norwich, Sheffield, Leeds and York were frequently ambitious in their approach. The spring season at Leeds Civic Theatre, for example, included

---

18 S. P. B. Mais, 'A short view of the modern English stage', *Theatre World* (Dec. 1926), 30–1.
19 *Era* (24 Feb. 1926).
20 Agate, *Short View*, p. 45.
21 *Era* (6 Jan. 1926), 10.

Everyman, *Oedipus Rex*, a Japanese Noh play and Elmer Rice's *The Adding Machine*, with admission throughout the season by voluntary donation and audiences based around group bookings from factories, workshops and educational organisations. The continuing and often passionate debate over 'the national theatre problem'[22] and state subsidy was far from producing any practical results, yet even in the face of moral, political and economic censorship some theatres and managers took responsibility for educating and broadening public tastes. Thus whilst the West End had become a 'sickly plant', its decline frequently traced to the escapism demanded by audiences during World War One, by 1926 there was also much confident talk of a new 'dramatic renaissance' and a 'great revival' in serious theatre.[23] Sean O'Casey's *The Plough and the Stars*, having provoked riots in Dublin, opened in London on the day the General Strike collapsed and ran for well over 100 performances to great acclaim. In presenting O'Casey with an award for 'the most moving and impressive drama' produced in the last twenty years, Lord Oxford declared that theatre audiences – 'one of the most intelligent classes in the community' – had at last become 'heartily sick' of the 'thinly disguised indecencies' that had come to dominate the stage.[24]

One producer who consistently challenged mainstream repertoires and theatrical conventions was Terence Gray, who in 1926 published his personal manifesto *Dance-Drama: Experiments in the Art of the Theatre* and opened the Festival Theatre in Cambridge to put his theories into practice. The theatre's approach was determinedly anti-naturalistic, as Gray sought to abolish the barrier between stage and auditorium by removing the proscenium and introducing a revolving stage, a 14-metre high cyclorama, advanced lighting technology and steps as wide as the auditorium to allow acting on multiple levels.[25] Gray also set out to undermine what he called 'the tyranny of words' dominating British theatre, employing a permanent director of choreography since 'the use of the human body rather than the intellectualised spoken word is the medium that is most essential for dramatic art'.[26] His first production was Aeschylus's *Oresteia*, staged, he announced, 'almost expressionistically' to avoid the still prevalent conventions of the nineteenth-century commercial theatre: 'The performance will be stylised rather than realistic, abstract rather

---

22 *Times* (17 April 1926), 13.
23 Both phrases from a British Drama League lecture by critic and playwright St John Ervine, *Times* (1 Jan. 1926), 6.
24 *Times* (24 March 1926), 11.
25 *Festival Theatre Review* 1, p. 1.
26 Terence Gray, *Dance-Drama: Experiments in the Art of the Theatre* (Cambridge: Heffer, 1926), p. 27.

than representational, ritualistic rather than inspirational. It will partake a little of the character of a dance, and the people . . . will seem puppets, majestic mannequins'.[27] Gray took inspiration from Craig and Appia, but though the revolution he sought was in aesthetics rather than politics, his unequivocal insistence that theatre was an art which had unfortunately given birth to 'the bastard species of entertainment' embodied an implicit criticism of market capitalism; it was, he said, the direct result of commercial imperatives that 'inferior machine-made plays by hack writers and money-seeking adventurers' had gradually 'choked out of existence the genuine art of the theatre'.[28]

The dramatic revival

'Who now doubts the genuineness of the dramatic revival?' asked the *Times* rhetorically, in a leader column of April 1926.[29] The newspaper was in fact echoing the conclusions of a 240-page report on the place of drama in national life, compiled by the Adult Education Committee of the Board of Education and published by the government, which despite its assumptions and omissions is a remarkable documentation of dramatic activity across the country. Among the report's recommendations were the subsidy of 'Little Theatres' and amateur societies, and the introduction of drama classes by local authorities and of theatre lectureships by universities. 'Our claims on its behalf are high', said the report: 'Drama can be under right conditions a most potent instrument of moral, artistic and intellectual progress, and under wrong conditions an equally potent instrument of moral, artistic and intellectual degradation.'[30] Whilst acknowledging the merits to be derived from watching good, professional productions, the report's tone became positively evangelical when discussing the benefits of active participation, and the church, the Labour Party, educational institutions and even prisons were said to be amongst those already using drama to turn people into 'better citizens'.[31] The supposedly non-political goal assumed by the report was national unity, and it therefore warned against 'the production of plays designed either to expose the fallacies of capitalism or to emphasise the unquestionable character of its benefits'.[32] By contrast, it particularly celebrated the opportunities provided by amateur theatre for people of different classes and backgrounds to work alongside each

27 Gray, 'The *Oresteia* of Aeschylus', *Festival Theatre Review* 1, pp. 3–5.
28 Gray, *Dance-Drama*, p. 9.
29 *Times* (17 April 1926), 13.
30 Great Britain Board of Education, *Drama in Adult Education*, p. 9.
31 *Ibid.*, pp. 113–14.
32 *Ibid.*, p. 160.

other, citing companies such as the Bournville Dramatic Society for Cadbury employees, which used drama to promote harmony between management and workers: 'All classes of employees take part in the work of the Society on an equal footing. As an example, an apprentice in the laboratory had a leading part in a play produced by the head of his own department; in the subsequent production the roles were reversed. The producer of a recent production was a piece-rate setter.'[33] So at a time of social division, the committee defined participation in theatre as a binding force, offering a brief carnival of escape that would not disrupt the underlying social order. It also conveniently assumed that class conflict was rooted in individual misunderstandings, and that through 'the reconciling power of the theatre' participants would come to understand that 'the same troubles and trials come alike to all sections of the community'.[34]

The committee was chaired by the Reverend R. St J. Parry and contained several other clergymen, at a time when the church itself was becoming increasingly convinced of the power of theatre to influence audiences. The London Public Morality Council, whose president was the Bishop of London, had set itself the task of preventing what it called 'The Poisoning of Youth', by restricting 'the presentation of undesirable plays'.[35] The Archbishop of Canterbury, meanwhile, preached a sermon on theatre's 'ennobling power' and insisted that it could do 'untold good for the common life' provided only that it 'was kept high toned, pure and strong'.[36] Both the Bishop and especially the Archbishop were in frequent consultation with the Lord Chamberlain regarding theatre censorship. A book published in 1926, *Drama in Education: Theory and Technique*, focussed on how theatre could best be used to promote a Christian understanding of the world. 'Drama has once again been called to the service of the Church as a means of teaching spiritual truths',[37] wrote Grace Overton, insisting that plays performed 'must be ethically sound' and should 'agree with present-day standards of moral and religious conduct'; it was just about acceptable to include 'immoral conduct and wrong attitude', provided these are clearly seen to 'meet with inevitable punishment'.[38]

---

33 *Ibid.*, p. 117.
34 *Ibid.*, p. 170.
35 See correspondence between the London Public Morality Council and the Home Secretary, *Times* (4 and 13 March 1926).
36 Speech at 27th anniversary meeting of the Actors' Church Union, 18 May 1926, *Times* (19 May 1926).
37 Grace Overton, *Drama in Education: Theory and Technique* (London: Century Company, 1926), pp. 45–6.
38 *Ibid.*, p. 133.

If religion was discovering the potential of theatre to propagate ideas, then so too were political organisations. The previous year had seen the formation of both the London Drama Federation by Labour MPs and professional theatre workers, and the Independent Labour Party's Arts Guild, which declared its intention to involve the working class in theatre. In 1926 the ILP published an essay by Arthur Bourchier, famous actor-manager and owner of the Strand Theatre, where he had staged Sunday evening political events. In *Art and Culture in Relation to Socialism*, Bourchier posited a future society organised along socialist principles, in which municipal and state-supported theatre would ensure that the production of good plays would not depend on the occasional whims of philanthropists. He contrasted this with the current 'sordid, money-grubbing state of society' in which art and culture could only be 'judged and accounted for by the self-same standards that rule in the most commercialised part of our commercialised society'. Under capitalism, says Bourchier, theatre has become 'an after-dinner resort' and an escape from the 'dispiritingly monotonous toil' in which so many are engaged; given that 'we cannot conduct our economic life according to one system, and possess a theatre that belongs to another', it is inevitable that most performances are 'to be enjoyed only by leaving one's brains in the cloakroom'.[39]

Much of the work performed by groups linked to the Labour Party dealt with social issues from a broadly left-wing perspective; Miles Malleson, who was influential in developing the ILP programme, had insisted that 'we shan't do only propaganda plays; but neither shall we be scared by the word', which he defined as 'the dispelling of . . . ignorance'.[40] Plays by Shaw, Galsworthy, Čapek and Malleson himself featured strongly in the repertoire. But according to a recent analysis, the people involved saw this primarily as 'cultural enrichment for those participating' and 'worthwhile for its own sake no matter what the content'. There was little or nothing revolutionary in the form, the content or, perhaps, the implications of such work.[41]

By contrast, the Workers' Theatre Movement (WTM), which was allied to the British Communist Party, committed itself to a much more didactic and explicitly propagandist approach. Huntly Carter, one of its early instigators and theorists, noted in January 1926 that the previous twelve months had seen 'the beginning of a keen struggle between the bosses and the Workers for

---

39 Arthur Bourchier, *Art and Culture in Relation to Socialism* (London: ILP, 1926), pp. 4–12.
40 Miles Malleson, *The ILP and its Dramatic Societies. What They Are and Might Become* (London: ILP, 1925), pp. 4–5.
41 Ian Saville, 'Ideas, Forms and Developments in the British Workers' Theatre, 1929–1935', Ph.D. thesis, City University (1990), p. 7.

possession of the theatre'.[42] The WTM was generally dismissive of the work of Labour groups, describing the plays they produced as 'compounds of diluted liberal politics, mawkish sentimentality, and middle-class snobbery' which 'no self-respecting group of Worker players would want to produce'.[43] Even writers such as O'Casey, Toller and Kaiser were dismissed as 'intellectual playwrights' who were of little direct use to workers since whatever their sympathies, they were 'unable to put an embargo on their own mental kinks'.[44] Carter, who in 1925 had written *The New Spirit in the European Theatre*, had some awareness of revolutionary theatrical techniques and forms developed in the Soviet Union and elsewhere in Europe; he recommended that the WTM should experiment with the collective creation of scripts, and suggested adapting existing scenes and plays and drawing on historical and current events to construct living newspaper sketches, to be performed outside factory gates or on street corners. In February a 'Red Concert' was staged involving music and sketches, and in April the branch that became a spearhead for the movement over the next few years, the Hackney Labour Group under Tom Thomas, gave its first performance. The General Strike and its aftermath gave further impetus to the WTM, for Carter insisted that the government had recognised the importance of commercial theatre as a strike-breaker and believed that a better prepared and more effective workers' theatre would have been able to 'counteract the forces of reaction' controlling the media.[45]

Shakespeare on strike

Not for the first or last time, Shakespeare became the focus of a political struggle. The authors of *Drama in Adult Education* had placed particular emphasis on his plays, which 'however little they may attract the West End of London never fail in their attractiveness to a popular audience'.[46] Unsurprisingly, Shakespeare was appropriated to the cause of peace and reconciliation, since his plays were rooted in 'the elements of beauty, order and harmony'[47] and contained 'a basis of common experience and common humanity which destroys any barrier

---

42 *Sunday Worker* (10 Jan. 1926), 8.
43 *Sunday Worker* (11 July 1926), 8.
44 *Sunday Worker* (18 July 1926), 8.
45 See Saville, *Ideas, Forms and Developments*; Richard Stourac and Kathleen McCreery, *Theatre as a Weapon: Workers' Theatre in the Soviet Union, Germany and Britain, 1917–1934* (London: Routledge & Kegan Paul, 1986); Raphael Samuel, Ewan MacColl and Stuart Cosgrove, *Theatres of the Left 1880–1935* (London: Routledge & Kegan Paul, 1985).
46 Great Britain Board of Education, *Drama in Adult Education*, p. 42.
47 *Ibid.*, p. 162.

erected by social conventions'.[48] Predictably, the *Sunday Worker* was more hostile, seeing in the Old Vic production of *As You Like It*, 'a queer, rambling, inconsequential sort of play, full of ludicrous love episodes',[49] and responding to the technically innovative radio transmission of scenes from *Henry VIII* by declaring that 'seldom, if ever, was there so much class propaganda packed into a play'.[50] Its astute argument continued: 'those who denounce propaganda in the theatre and who praise Shakespeare should study his plays over again', pointing out that his working-class characters were primarily used for comedy and clowning, and that as a 'defender of the propertied interests' his plays inevitably 'come down heavily on the side of the rising merchant class and the monarchy'.

For many in the cultural establishment, the most important theatrical event of the year occurred in March, when the Shakespeare Memorial Theatre in Stratford was destroyed in a fire. The cause of the fire was never properly identified, and in his essay on 'Shakespeare and the General Strike', Terence Hawkes provocatively remarks that it occurred just one week after an announcement that *Coriolanus* would be staged there for the annual celebration of Shakespeare's birthday.[51] Whilst, as Hawkes makes clear, only a reductivist approach to this text could yield a politically unambiguous production, in the spring of 1926 the on-stage confrontations would certainly have signalled real-life contemporary conflicts. Hawkes points out that on the very day that *Coriolanus* opened in the substitute venue of Stratford's cinema, Stanley Baldwin was holding urgent meetings with the coal owners and the miners: the Prime Minister went to dinner 'having almost colluded in a decision to precipitate the strike' just as actors representing the rebellious and armed citizens of Rome took to the stage in Stratford.

The fire resulted in new attempts to construct Shakespeare as the voice of England and social unity, as national and international appeals were made for donations to restore the Memorial Theatre. In November, as the miners' strike was inexorably crushed, a major fundraising event was staged at the Drury Lane Theatre, consisting of extracts from Shakespeare's plays performed by 'star' actors for an audience that included the King and Queen. The souvenir programme contained a poem in the form of an address from 'William Shakespeare to John Citizen', which claimed the bard as an ally not of 'soldiers, emperors and statesmen' but of the 'breathing multitudes'. It ended with the

48 *Ibid.*, p. 115.
49 *Sunday Worker* (7 March 1926), 6.
50 *Sunday Worker* (14 Feb. 1926), 8.
51 Terence Hawkes, *Meaning by Shakespeare* (London: Routledge, 1992), pp. 42–60.

AN APPEAL TO THE NATION.

SHAKESPEARE (*to Polonius Punch*). "GOOD MY LORD, WILL YOU SEE MY PLAYERS WELL BESTOWED?"

[Cheques made payable to the "Punch" Stratford Memorial Theatre Fund and addressed to the Secretary, 10, Bouverie Street, E.C. 4, will be gratefully received and handed over to the National Fund inaugurated by *The Daily Telegraph*.]

Figure 6.1 One response – from *Punch* – to the fire that destroyed the Shakespeare Memorial Theatre in 1926.

call 'Master Citizen, your arm in mine!' However, the front cover carried two lines from Hamlet which it is unlikely the organisers could have selected without realising the political overtones:

Masters, you are all welcome . . .
Come, give us a taste of your quality.[52]

As I have shown, the Workers' Theatre Movement generally saw Shakespeare as irrevocably on the side of the ruling class. However, two days before this matinée, the *Sunday Worker* printed an enthusiastic review of a script which it described as 'the most striking political satire since Gulliver's Travels'. This was nothing less than 'the famous scene between Brutus and Mark Anthony [*sic*] in Shakespeare's Julius Caesar, modernised in terms of the mining crisis'.[53] 'An Oration over the Dead Body of a Miner' is set 'at the funeral of a miner done to death being given burial under the auspices of the Trades Union Congress'. The Labour MP and former union leader J. H. Thomas is cast as the treacherous Brutus, and the miners' leader A. J. Cook as Anthony, rousing the trade unionists to take up the cause of the dead miner.

The coalowners
Have told you the miner was avaricious;
If it were so, it was a grievous fault
And grievously the miner answer'd it . . .
He was my friend, faithful and just to me:
But the owners say he was avaricious;
And the owners are all honourable men.
He hath hewed many tons of coal from the mire,
The profits did the coalowners' coffers fill:
Did this in the miner seem avaricious?[54]

Despite occasional linguistic lapses, the oration was a well-written and potentially effective piece of propaganda, which successfully harnessed Shakespeare's poetic and theatrical rhetoric to speak about the most contemporary and emotional of political issues. The *Sunday Worker* described the script as 'extremely suitable for presentation by Workers' Theatre groups' and

---

52 Souvenir Programme, 'Special Matinée' at Theatre Royal, Drury Lane, 9 November 1926. The poem is published in full in Ashley Dukes, *The World to Play With* (Oxford University Press, 1928).
53 *Sunday Worker* (7 Nov. 1926), 8.
54 'Socrates' [pseud.], *An Oration Over the Dead Body of a Miner: With Apologies to the Shade of Shakespeare* (London: Workers' Publications, 1926).

The 1926 production of *Bethlehem* is striking above all for its integration of political passion with religious morality, and of classical text with agitational propaganda. But it also imitated some of the techniques of the European political and cultural avant-garde:

> The stage had no curtain. There was no change of scenery as the lighting was arranged to pick out the action of the play when it passed from the miner's cottage to Herod's palace or to the stable. The stage had steps leading into the auditorium from where many dramatic entrances and exits were made . . . the producers had carefully studied many of the methods now being used so successfully by Meyerhold in his theatre in Moscow.[58]

'The doom of the drama and the British theatre has seemed to hang in the balance during the past year', wrote the *Stage Year Book* at the start of 1927.[59] Ashley Dukes similarly concluded that 'drama, for the hundredth time in its history, stands at a crossroads', in terms of its content, its form and its purpose: 'The everyday theatre, although only dimly aware of dramatic movements and their origin, nevertheless feels the uncertainty of changing times. The old subjects have lost their allurement, the old impulses are enfeebled.'[60] Meanwhile, in December 1926 Prime Minister Stanley Baldwin was roundly cheered for a speech in which he warned the directors and chairman of the newly formed BBC that 'the whole progress of civilisation' depended on ensuring that images broadcast across the Empire would not propagate what he called 'false ideas'.[61] Baldwin was obviously correct to anticipate that in the future it would be recorded and electronically transmitted, rather than live, performances that would have the greater potential to influence audiences internationally. Yet the most remarkable thing about live performance in Britain in 1926 is how many people of such different persuasions were committed to it, or in some cases even frightened by it.

58 *Ibid.*
59 *Stage Year Book*, 1927, p. 1.
60 Ashley Dukes, *Drama* (London: Williams & Northgate, 1926), pp. 237, 243.
61 Reported in full in the *Times* (17 Dec. 1926), 7.

7

The London stage, 1918–1945

MAGGIE B. GALE

The London stage of 1918–45 has often been characterised as pandering to an undiscerning audience, waiting with baited breath to be entertained by the latest frivolous or escapist offerings of the day – but this is an overly simplistic reading. To begin with, it condones an assumption that our contemporary interpretations of theatre in the period are that much more sophisticated and somehow nearer the 'truth' than those of people who were actually a part of it. Moreover, underlying such readings is a failure to understand the complexities of an interwar society that was transformed by enormous social and cultural upheavals over a very short period of time. This chapter reflects upon key issues raised in an analysis of the London stage between the two world wars, in three sections. Firstly, it investigates historiographical approaches to the history of theatre during the era, looking at the nature and social significance of drama for its audiences. Secondly, it examines the growth of theatre as an industry, owned and managed by a new class of entrepreneur, in the light of arguments about a new commercialism versus a belief in theatre for arts' sake. Thirdly, it proceeds to give an outline of popular themes and genres in playwriting and performance, including an examination of audiences, and closes by looking at government and state intervention in the making of theatre during the period.

British people experienced endemic social paradoxes during the interwar years, with the country plunged into hardship at the same time as benefiting from technological and social development. The nation was in a state of shock after the massacres of World War One, victory soured by the fact that a whole generation of young men had been killed. As the 1920s progressed, more and more people felt that the huge number of deaths had all been for nothing and, as fascism began to take hold of Europe by the early 1930s, many anticipated the hardships of another war. In the same period Britain experienced years of industrial strife – including the General Strike in 1926 – elected its first Labour government in 1924, and felt the economic reverberations of the Wall Street Crash in the late 1920s. Alongside these difficulties, however, came tremendous

Other theatres

The commercial theatres constituted the financial backbone of the British theatre industry during the first half of the twentieth century. However, in an astute analytical move, Norman Marshall, a leading theatre producer and historian of the interwar period, coined the term 'other theatres' for projects that thrived beyond the economics of the London commercial theatre. Some of the other theatres produced revues and musical shows, but many experimented with drama by new writers from Britain and abroad. West End programming policies were seen by many in this sector as representing the tastes of an élite constituting a 'timid and reactionary commercial theatre'.[15] Yet the other theatres often fed the commercial theatre market, constituting a 'trying-out' ground for new plays and playwrights.

The other theatres comprised subscription clubs, that produced Sunday night and sometimes Monday afternoon performances, and small independent theatres; such organisations had been formed, argued Marshall, in 'self-defence against the standards of commercialism'.[16] The subscription club theatres usually operated on a non-profit basis. This enabled them to avoid the censorship dealt out by the Lord Chamberlain's Office and to take risks in producing plays by unknown or commercially unviable writers. In London such independent producing companies, which blossomed during the 1920s and 1930s, included the Stage Society, the Pioneer Players, the Three Hundred Club and the Venturers. The small independent theatre buildings included the Embassy, the Everyman and the Gate. Together the other theatres provided a platform for experiment and a partial alternative to the West End monopoly.

The Sunday play-producing societies also provided the opportunity for professional and amateur to work together. In addition, many of the playwrights and professional performers worked in both the commercial and the other theatres, sometimes alleviating the tedium of West End engagements by Sunday performance projects. Some of the societies were formed by professionals; some, such as the Three Hundred Club, were set up by play-goers whose taste significantly differed from that of the Lord Chamberlain's Office and West End theatre management. But by the beginning of World War Two, the majority of these societies were no longer functioning, the difficulties produced by professional performers' touring and rehearsal schedules, plus inadequate budgets, having proved insurmountable.

---

15 Norman Marshall, *The Other Theatre* (London: John Lehmann, 1947), pp. 14–16.
16 *Ibid.*

The independent theatres, such as the Everyman, the Embassy, the Arts Theatre and the Gate, mostly produced new and experimental plays. They were usually funded by subscription – in part to avoid censorship, in part to avoid the constraints of commercialism – so wages were low and sometimes non-existent, while facilities were minimal. The theatres were very small, with limited audience capacity. The Gate, founded by Peter Godfrey and his wife Molly Veness in 1925, had a stage only half a metre high in order to allow height for sets. It was 'little more than a large garret holding an audience of eighty crammed together on cruelly narrow and uncomfortable seats'.[17] Productions had short runs and actors often left for better paid assignments in larger theatres. There was some inverted snobbery amongst theatre critics about the work of the Gate and other independent theatres: their productions were not populist enough and were far too 'highbrow' for the majority of theatre-goers. But these 'private' productions quite often transformed plays into popular 'classics', which were later adapted into films. The general consensus among devotees was that their job was to keep theatre alive by refusing to pander to commercial dictates – even though many productions went on to successful West End transfers. Philip Godfrey's opinion was shared by many: 'the studio or art theatre exists to prevent dramatic art from being wiped out by the commercially minded. Unlike ordinary theatre goers, the supporters of art theatres have dramatic convictions'.[18]

Women playwrights and changing audiences

The class make-up of theatre audiences changed significantly during the inter-war years, and the numbers of women attending live performances increased. In the years immediately after World War One a number of commentators, led by St John Ervine, critic and sometime playwright, claimed that the London stage was being overrun by 'Flapper' audiences: young women with a new-found independence. This characteristic of audiences was at first considered a leftover from wartime theatre, but even as late as the mid-1930s critics and commentators noted that plays were being produced in order to please 'the feminine first-nighters' or that women went to the theatre for their 'regular dream-hour off'.[19] Critics like Ervine felt that the new women audiences

---

17 Ibid., p. 42.
18 Philip Godfrey, *Back Stage* (London: George Harrap, 1933), pp. 160–70.
19 See *Era* (11 Dec. 1935); John Carey, *The Intellectuals and the Masses* (London: Faber & Faber, 1992), p. 87.

were adversely affecting the drama especially, which was somehow becoming 'feminised'.

Of course, women playwrights did not dominate the London stages of 1918–45, though they did hold a steady grip on the numbers of plays in production. When there was an explosion of new writing by new playwrights, many of them were women. It was fairly common for plays to be co-written by a man and woman, often a husband and wife team, such as Fryn Tennyson Jesse and Harold Harwood in the 1920s, or Aimée and Phillip Stuart, whose work dominated the West End in the early 1930s. Even allowing for team writing, the statistics that evidence a gender shift in the population of playwrights in these two decades are especially telling: the percentage of productions of plays by women and mixed sex teams on the London stage rarely fell below 12 per cent, and at times – such as in 1927, 1936 and 1945 – rose higher than 20 per cent. Also, on average, plays in the West End by women were as likely to run as long as those by men, or even longer. During World War Two, for example, there were fewer London productions of plays by women, but they ran for longer.[20]

Interwar women playwrights, customarily considered both conservative and commercial, have been largely neglected by later critics and historians. This is partly explained by the fact that commentators in the period tended to sideline their plays as being of 'specialist', that is, female or domestic, interest and thus of little literary worth. A few women playwrights, such as Dodie Smith and Clemence Dane, may have become familiar to theatre enthusiasts by the turn of the millennium, but there are many more whose work has been largely ignored. Gertrude Jennings, Aimée Stuart, Gordon Daviot, Esther McCracken, Joan Temple, Margaret Kennedy, Fryn Tennyson Jesse, Harriet Jay and Naomi Royde Smith, for example, were all familiar names to West End audiences, many of them writing hit after hit, which were often made into films. And this list does not include American women playwrights, such as Rachel Crothers, Sophie Treadwell, Rose Franken and Edna Ferber, whose work made a significant impact on the London stage.[21]

So who were the audiences that welcomed this widening range of playwrights? Changes in the class structure of London audiences can be gauged through organisations such as the Gallery First Nighters. This was not a new

20 See Maggie B. Gale, *West End Women: Women on the London Stage 1918–1962* (London: Routledge, 1996), pp. 10–13.

21 See *ibid.*, and Maggie B. Gale, 'From fame to obscurity: in search of Clemence Dane', in Maggie B. Gale and Viv Gardner (eds.), *Women, Theatre and Performance: New Histories, New Historiographies* (Manchester University Press, 2000), pp. 121–41.

phenomenon, but between the wars it organised itself into a loosely formed 'club'.

> The wise dramatist takes the gallery very seriously. He expects to find full enthusiasm there . . . I do not suppose anyone goes to the gallery except for one purpose, and that is to see the play and its players . . . the audience in the gallery . . . start by giving more comfort, time and hard-earned shillings and they are eager to be rewarded . . . the author looks with satisfaction upon a crowded gallery. There he can count on a response.[22]

These were enthusiasts who regularly attended the opening nights of productions, occupying the cheapest seats in the gallery or the 'Gods'. One such enthusiast, Fred Bason, a 'confirmed and incorrigible galleryite', edited a collection of 'experiences and opinions' of galleryites and claimed that 'the Gods' denoted the power they had in deciding the fate of a play, rather than the height of the gallery in the theatre. Galleryites caused much consternation amongst critics, who regularly complained that they were noisy and disrespectful, or simply in disagreement with their own 'high-brow tastes'. Whilst many of the interwar critics came from either an Oxbridge or an otherwise privileged background, the galleryites did not.[23] Galleryites – largely from the upper working classes or from the itinerant population, for example, foreign students – were not shy in voicing their opinions, seeing themselves as a kind of theatrical family, debating the pros and cons of various plays and often, more importantly, individual performances. For Fred Bason, galleryites were interested in the intricacies of theatre production, going to the theatre not just to pass the evening before late dinner in a fashionable restaurant, as he assumed many of the well-to-do audiences in the stalls did. He even argued that the 1920s and 1930s had produced a new breed of critical gallery audience who wanted to 'seek knowledge – not sentiment' and that through their presence new kinds of plays and dramatists had emerged. He identified Noel Coward, Miles Malleson, Frank Vosper, Patrick Hamilton, John Van Druten and H. M. Harwood amongst others, as playwrights who fitted the bill: they had all written successful, sometimes controversial, 'really good plays with backbone in them'.[24]

'Fandom' was not new to the theatre, but it thrived in London between the wars as more theatres produced more plays as part of a 'star-driven' production

22 Somerset Maugham, 'Foreword' to Fred Bason, *Gallery Unreserved* (London: John Heritage, 1931), pp. xv–xvi.
23 See W. J. Macqueen-Pope, *The Footlights Flickered* (London: Herbert Jenkins, 1959), pp. 33–6.
24 Bason, *Gallery Unreserved*, pp. 16–17.

system. This star system, based on a specialist development of the earlier actor-manager role, was enhanced by the new film industry, which relied on the commodity of star performers to sell cinema seats. The interwar years produced an increasing number of actors who moved freely between theatre and film, and they became a key factor in live performance – vehicles for selling a play regardless of its author. Actors such as Laurence Olivier, Ralph Richardson, Peggy Ashcroft, Jessica Tandy, Leslie Howard, Charles Laughton, Vivien Leigh, and so on, in some ways drew the theatre and cinema industries closer together, but also pushed them further apart in others.

Many felt that the star system and the cinema together were killing the theatre, which seemed in danger of becoming an imitation of film, with its sensationalist and escapist leanings. Theatrical publications, such as the *Era*, by the mid-1930s had moved away from theatre and variety towards cinema and film; though judged by the production rate of the London stage, there was still a sustained public interest in the glamour, liveness and intellectual stimulation of theatre. Nevertheless, the cinema, and more particularly the American film industry, had begun to dominate the cultural consumption of British audiences.

Cinema

The cinema, more than any other cultural phenomenon, was seen as the greatest threat to theatre. In the mid-1920s there had been reaction from the theatre profession to the new radio industry, with attempts to ban the broadcast of some live performances. But cinema's visual qualities, in a culture which was becoming increasingly visually oriented, made it a far more tangible opponent. The new form cut across class barriers. Almost everyone went to the cinema, largely seeing the same films, so that 'as a leisure activity the cinema superseded the music hall and competed, not unsuccessfully, with pub, church and political meeting'.[25] By 1929 there were some 3,300 cinemas in Britain, under the ownership of such companies as Gaumont and British International, the two controlling chains until the establishment of Odeon in 1933. By the late 1930s some 20 million British people attended the cinema weekly, with an estimated 25 per cent going twice or more each week.[26] The programmes would often change twice weekly and might include cartoons and newsreels.

25 Noreen Branson, *Britain in the Nineteen Twenties* (London: Weidenfeld & Nicolson, 1975), p. 229.
26 Noreen Branson and Margot Heinemann, *Britain in the Nineteen Thirties* (London: Weidenfeld & Nicolson, 1971), p. 253.

Inevitably, the popularity of cinema worried theatre managements, but it also provided a new avenue of expression for playwrights and more lucrative work for actors and actresses. The cinema industry borrowed, absorbed and exploited the star system, feeding on popular stage successes by making them into films for mass distribution. The rise of cinema, though, hardly depleted London theatre audiences in this period, and it reached a far wider class of audience than either the commercial or the other theatre venues. It is also worth noting that critics, practitioners and theorists were already talking of the theatre as being in a state of crisis well before the cinema achieved mass popularity; a crisis supposedly caused by the lack of government support for a system that was aesthetically, as opposed to economically, driven. Theatre as a live art, however, could not be replaced by the cinematograph, and although by the mid-1940s the two were clearly inherently connected, most commentators had realised that the similarities of film to theatre, and therefore its potential threat, were crucially offset by its differences.

Musicals and revues

A singular characteristic of the London stage between the wars was the growth in musical comedies, variety shows and revues. Often these were linked to, or played upon trends in, popular film and vice versa; but also, especially in the case of revue, they drew on the Victorian and Edwardian world of music hall: short sketches and turns by skilled performers adding up to an evening's entertainment. Some historians have suggested that the British musical lacked the satirical and political bite of its American counterpart in the 1930s; it was typified by escapism and the parading of scantily clad females.[27] *Chu Chin Chow* (1916) was the most successful of the period: Oscar Asche's loose adaptation of the Ali Baba story from *The Arabian Nights* (often staged as a pantomime in the nineteenth century) was just the first in a series of long-running orientalist musical entertainments. But James Ross Moore has argued that revue became the era's 'most vital, influential and innovative form of musical theatre [which] honed the skills of librettists and playwrights and stretched the versatility of its stars, people like Gertrude Lawrence, Jack Buchanan, Jack Hulbert, Cicely Courtneidge and Beatrice Lillie, subsequently leading performers in all the Era's media'.[28] Revues consisted of songs, playlets and sketches and often promoted the latest dancing or music crazes, in the 1930s even playing host

27 James Ross Moore, 'Girl crazy: revue and variety in interwar theatre', in Barker and Gale, *British Theatre Between the Wars*, pp. 88–112.
28 *Ibid.*, p. 89.

Figure 7.1 That's entertainment in the early 1930s: Noel Coward's *Cavalcade*, Drury Lane Theatre, London, 1931.

to the new ballet. The late 1910s and early 1920s proved lucrative for key producers of these shows, such as André Charlot and C. B. Cochran. Certain theatres – for example, the Comedy, the Playhouse and the Vaudeville – became revue venues. The producers often rebuilt the theatre interiors, adding new stage machinery to create the spectacular shows. Revue veterans such as Noel Coward and Ivor Novello went on to create and star in a new wealth of British plays with music in the late 1920s and early 1930s, the best known being Coward's *This Year of Grace* (1928), *Bitter Sweet* (1929) and *Cavalcade* (1931), and Novello's *Careless Rapture* (1936) and *The Dancing Years* (1939).

From the mid-1930s a more politically astute form of revue developed. Intimate rather than spectacular, *This Year, Next Year* at the Gate Theatre was the first of the 'topical, witty and satirical' revues which became especially popular.[29] The Gate revues used the talents of writers and performers such as Herbert Farjeon, Robert MacDermot, Diana Morgan, Hermione Gingold, Ronnie Hill and Geoffrey Wright. Norman Marshall – who took over the tiny,

29 Marshall, *Other Theatre*, p. 109.

Figure 7.2 That's entertainment in the late 1930s: *The Gate Revue*, Gate Theatre, London, 1939.

makeshift Gate Theatre from Peter Godfrey in 1934 – saw their success as dependent upon a coherent mixture of forms: 'if a revue is to have any style of its own it must be the expression of a single person's taste, not an indigestible hotchpotch resulting from a dozen people's suggestions and prejudices'.[30] In the late 1930s Marshall transferred one of the Gate revues to the Ambassadors, where it ran for two years. Ernest Short, theatre critic and historian of the time, identified a key value of the Gate's revue performances in their actors' abilities as ensemble players exploiting the 'ways of intimate and inexpensive revue'.[31] Whereas West End musicals during the 1920s to some extent borrowed in style and appeal from cinema, revue offered an overt social commentary through an intimacy that perhaps is at the heart of all good theatre.

Plays: themes and genres

It was not only the structure of the theatre system that defined what was produced, but also the style and content of the plays. A maxim coined by James Agate in 1926 – 'the drama is an aesthetic phenomenon, the theatre is an economic proposition' – acutely exemplifies the gap that apparently had opened up between theatre as glamorous entertainment for profit and theatre

---

30 *Ibid.*, p. 120.
31 Short, *Sixty Years of Theatre*, p. 277.

as the realisation of dramatic texts with stylish narrative and serious meanings.[32] Similarly, Lynton Hudson observed that at the 'end of the Twenties there were no great kinds of play and no grand manner of acting' and that the 'kind of play most popular during the Thirties was the domestic, adramatic play . . . it belongs to the lap-dog class'.[33] His comments indicate nostalgia for a style of presentation and content which belonged to the late nineteenth century and an unwillingness to evaluate positively the work of non-commercial theatres, as well as a refusal to come to terms with the fact that theatre had begun to develop the economic structures of a twentieth-century capitalist industry. That the 'adramatic, domestic play' – usually authored by a woman or male-female team – was popular somehow guaranteed a lack of aesthetic value and a state of disintegration in the drama generally.

The conventions of the well-made 'realist' play changed very little during the interwar period, but the writers and the issues on which narratives were focussed changed a lot. In the 1920s and 1930s historical or chronicle dramas were sporadically in vogue – plays that loosely reworked factual narratives to recreate national and international figures of the past. John Drinkwater's *Abraham Lincoln* (1919) was an early example, followed by others like Gordon Daviot's (pseudonym of Elizabeth Mackintosh) *Richard of Bordeaux* (1931) and, in the early 1930s, numerous plays about the Brontes. Usually the idioms of language and character type were modern, suggesting a search for national heroes in a post-empire world, a craving for a clear national identity following the social fragmentation of World War One.

There were also numerous farces and thrillers, detective plays, 'sex plays' which tuned into public debates about gender and morality, and professional dramas about working people in their occupational environments. Although the upper and middle classes still provided the main narrative focus of the drama, there was an increasing shift of interest – pioneered by pre-war writers such as Stanley Houghton and Elizabeth Baker – towards the lower middle classes who inhabited the growing suburbs, the new white-collar workers and their families. The style was realism, the setting often the drawing room, the front parlour, or in the case of historical dramas the Great Hall or Chamberlain's office.

In 1935 the literary critic Camillo Pellizzi bemoaned the loss of the so-called play of ideas, claiming that audiences for the 'well-made plays' of the commercial theatres were there out of curiosity, vicarious desire for the lives

---

32 Agate, *Short View of the English Stage*, p. 20.
33 Lynton Hudson, *The Twentieth-Century Drama* (London: George Harrap, 1946), p. 64.

of people who were, in reality, remote.[34] But changes in the constitution of the audience suggest that plays such as *The Fanatics* (1927), *London Wall* (1931), *Nine Till Six* (1930) and *The Dominant Sex* (1935) were so successful because they represented the new audiences, who were predominantly lower middle class. Pellizzi proposed that audiences endured the dramas rather than learnt from them, implying that theatre history should be about 'worthy' texts. Jon Clarke gives a good summary of how drama from the period traditionally has been viewed:

> British 'naturalistic' theatre in the first half of the twentieth century has often been criticised as sentimental, thematically dated and lacking in creativity . . . such assessments are based on highly restricted concepts of literature and theatre, and also a narrow textual analysis approach to literary and cultural criticism.[35]

In the interwar period there were numerous critics, such as Hannen Swaffer or St John Ervine, who drew a distinction between the playwright who worked with the needs of the audience in mind – the populist craftsman – and the dramatist who was a poet – the refined artist. This approach to analysis is one that persists even today. Jean Chothia, for example, proposes that innovation and experiment happened only beyond the West End theatres. For her, the 'inconsequent entertainment' provided by the West End is worth analysis only because there was cross-fertilisation between commercial and non-commercial practices.[36] From the perspective of the twenty-first century, it may be more productive to look at what people actually went to see, the contexts in which they went to see it, and why.

Thrillers and 'sex plays'

Thrillers and detective plays enjoyed a particular popularity during the interwar years. Camillo Pellizzi saw the thriller genre as a mixture of Grand Guignol and the American 'drama of action' and suggested in 1935 that the English somehow had a propensity for enjoyment of such plays: 'in the damp and capricious climate of England, the thrill is a need which is universally felt, and is hence an institution', a reaction 'with the nerves against the heaviness and boredom of

---

34 Camillo Pellizzi, *The English Drama: The Last Great Phase* (London: Macmillan, 1935), p. 284.
35 Jon Clarke and Margot Heinemann, *Culture and Crisis in Britain in the 1930s* (London: Lawrence & Wishart, 1970), p. 219.
36 Chothia, *English Drama of the Early Modern Period*, pp. 88–125.

the environment'.[37] Whilst this assessment implies that English audiences are passive and easily pleased, John Stokes proposes that audiences sought pleasure in the virility and cunning of such upper-class heroes as could be found in Sapper's *Bulldog Drummond* (Wyndhams Theatre, 1921). For Stokes, characters like Drummond provided a 'dramatic interest [which] was unashamedly spurred by violence'. Such heroes showed the officer class forcefully relocating themselves in a post-war society that had clearly betrayed them.[38] Indeed, other thrillers and detective plays fed an audience apparently eager for a challenge, both to their nerves and to their intellects. Plays such as Edgar Wallace's *The Ringer* (1926), Frank Vosper's *Murder on the Second Floor* (1929), A. A. Milne's *The Fourth Wall* (1929), Emlyn Williams's *A Murder Has Been Arranged* (1930) and *Night Must Fall* (1935), and Patrick Hamilton's *Rope* (1929) and *Gaslight* (1939) portrayed perversely attractive criminals and murderers through narratives woven with intricate puzzles in powerful – sometimes sexual and often violent – atmospheres, and these proved very popular with inter-war audiences. Pellizzi's notion of thrillers providing 'a slight shiver in the bones . . . a little internal electrical discharge – something like a sneeze' ignores the powerful attraction of such plays for an audience struggling to come to terms with the aftermath of World War One, the seeming lack of value in life and the power of fear.[39] The main roles in these plays often were taken by performers well known for their 'thriller' acting – Gerald du Maurier, Charles Laughton and Emlyn Williams. Williams played the lead, Dan, in his own play *Night Must Fall* (1935), which ran for over 400 performances. Ernest Short argues that Dan, who walks around with the severed head of his first victim in a hatbox, sees *himself* as a victim of life's circumstances and uses his perfected criminal skills to get back at fate and at a society which he feels has failed him. Short recognised the philosophical and psychological complexity underpinning much of the thriller genre, where crime was often framed as an aesthetic activity with its own seductive forms.[40]

Such interpretations suggest a far more sophisticated audience than Pellizzi imagined. Similarly, many plays that have been seen conventionally as 'mere' domestic comedies – supposedly a 'degeneration' of the 'comedy of manners' – show that London audiences were concerned with contemporary issues,

---

37 Pellizzi, *English Drama*, pp. 278–9.
38 John Stokes, 'Body parts: the success of the thriller in the inter-war theatre', in Barker and Gale, *British Theatre Between the Wars*, p. 42.
39 Pellizzi, *English Drama*, p. 279.
40 Short, *Sixty Years of Theatre*, pp. 320–1.

albeit indirectly through the notional 'realist' framework of the well-made play. Freud's ideas feature in populist form, through dramatisations of sexual impulse, behaviour and morality. Far too many plays focussed on marriage and gender relations to list here, but any account would include Noel Coward's *The Vortex* (1924), *Fallen Angels* (1925) and, of course, *Private Lives* (1930), plus Frederick Lonsdale's *Spring Cleaning* (1925) and *On Approval* (1926). Many of the women playwrights of the period, often summarily dismissed as 'domestic comedy' writers, also dealt with gender – especially between generations of women and quintessentially between pre- and post-World War One women. I am thinking here particularly of G. B. Stern's long running *The Matriarch* (1929) and Margot Neville's *Heroes Don't Care* (1936). The plot of the latter centred on the exploits of a strident woman explorer – originally played by a young Coral Browne – who outwits all her male and female adversaries. Certainly the psychology of sex, and the new-found freedom to talk about it, was very much part of the cultural currency of the 1920s and 1930s, finding a rightful place on the stages of London.

In 1927 John Van Druten questioned the almost automatic appellation of 'sex play' as applied to so many new productions dealing with gender negotiations. For Van Druten, the theatre was 'reaping the harvest of a long period of separation' between physical and romantic love.[41] He suggested that audiences might be more enthusiastic about theatre if playwrights portrayed life as a whole, rather than being enticed by some vain hope of witnessing a seduction on stage. Interestingly, however, a number of Van Druten's plays may be seen as sex plays. *Young Woodley* (1928) – originally banned in England for its portrayal of public-school life – portrays a schoolboy infatuated with his teacher's wife; he is eventually expelled for attacking another boy who is teasing him about his infatuation. The play deals with a male adolescent's growing awareness of his own sexuality and the sexuality of those around him and it is frank in its detail.

Miles Malleson's *The Fanatics* (1927) – which somehow managed to escape the censor's blue pencil, to the astonishment of a number of critics of the day – centres on sexual behaviour and life choices. John Freeman, wanting to be 'free' of any traditional familial obligations, has ambitions to break away from the family business and become a writer. He has befriended an older woman who talks openly about her various sexual partners; meanwhile, his sister Gwen wants to live with a man before she marries him. This was a

41 John Van Druten, 'The sex play', *Theatre Arts Monthly* (11 Jan. 1927), 23–7.

jerkily – all the time . . . he hurls the ledger with such force that the door is smashed clean open, so that he can walk through.)[45]

Refusing to be just a 'bee in a glass cage', Cornelius exits on a positive note, with the kind of fighting spirit that was to become more common in later plays of the period.

Official and government intervention

State intervention in the theatre industry operated throughout the period, both overtly and covertly, in the form of censorship, but it was only towards its end that state funding began to influence the stage. The Lord Chamberlain's Office had power of veto over what could be performed in public theatres. This directly affected a good deal of what was staged, and because the censorship policies were not always clear they may have indirectly influenced everything else. Some plays, often by foreign authors, such as Pirandello's *Six Characters in Search of an Author* (banned initially in 1922) and Strindberg's *Miss Julie* (not given permission for public performance until 1939), now considered classics, were often prohibited for very ambiguous reasons.[46] Whilst plays such as Malleson's *The Fanatics* (1927) and Shairp's *The Green Bay Tree* (1933), although dealing overtly with risky issues about sexual freedom and choice, were licensed for public performance. Hence, exactly how censorship shaped what was on the London stage is difficult to ascertain, and it is very difficult to know how it determined what was not seen. Some people in the industry held on to the belief that theatre needed policing by people with the 'appropriate moral tastes' and opinions. Others thought that managements and audiences should be left to decide for themselves, especially as the Sunday Societies and independent club theatres avoided censorship by operating membership-only audience schemes. It is also likely that some of the socially better-connected production companies would have had, at times, privileged access to the Lord Chamberlain's Office and its decision-making processes. The significance of the censorship of twentieth-century British theatre has not, until relatively recently, received much scholarly attention. Cultural materialists such as Alan

---

45 J. B. Priestley, *The Plays of J. B. Priestley*, vol. III (London: William Heinemann, 1950), pp. 67–8.

46 See Steve Nicholson, 'Unecessary plays: European drama and the British censor in the 1920s', *Theatre Research International* 20, 1 (1995), 30–6. This chapter was completed before the publication of Steve Nicholson's two-volume account of twentieth-century stage censorship.

Sinfield have begun to address this through exploring the censorship of 'gay drama' from the perspective of post-liberationist sexual dissidence, but the extent to which they can account for the specific repercussions in patterns of production, say, is limited by a focus on common themes and ideological issues.[47] Much still needs to be done to map the other types of impact the censor had on theatre and performance.

The government did not intervene with financial aid for theatre until the 1940s, but its earlier taxation policies had a problematic effect on theatre production. The key tax on professional theatre was the 1916 Entertainment Tax, primarily a wartime emergency measure based on gross box office receipts rather than profit, which ensured that the state would benefit from the run of a play, even if it lost money for the management. In 1924 the tax was abolished on all seats under the price of one shilling and threepence, but this was more beneficial to the cinema than to the theatre, which proportionally had fewer seats at or below this level. By 1942 the Entertainment Tax was charged at 33.3 per cent, but exemption was given to companies with 'educational policies'. This change only really helped already established, large companies which could produce financially risky plays with star performers already on their books: profits could be transferred to another satellite company, owned by or closely connected to the original partly educational company. Hence, state fiscal intervention had advantages, but in the main only for production companies that were already in a profitable position.

When the London theatres closed down as part of the total blackout in 1939, many actors who were not conscripted into the army worked for the state-sponsored association ENSA (Entertainments National Service Association). Some well-known producers, most notably Basil Dean, directed the development of ENSA, providing entertainments for the troops.[48] CEMA (Council for the Encouragement of Music and the Arts) was established as a permanent organisation with grants from the wartime coalition government and the Pilgrim Trust in 1940. CEMA initially mostly supported touring productions for the regions, but as the war wore on it began to put funds into buildings, particularly the London and Bristol Old Vic theatres. This shift in policy had a significant impact on the development of CEMA's 1946 successor, the Arts Council of Great Britain.

Inevitably, during World War Two patterns of production on the London stage were transformed. Theatres were shut down just for a short while at

---

47 See Alan Sinfield, *Out on Stage: Lesbian and Gay Theatre in the Twentieth Century* (New Haven: Yale University Press, 1999).
48 See Basil Dean, *The Theatre at War* (London: George Harrap, 1956).

the beginning of the war and the West End was severely affected by the blitz thereafter; the arts and subscription companies gradually petered out. The star system was still the main motor of production managements such as H. M. Tennent, but many actors and playwrights were engaged in war-related work, either providing entertainment for the forces or making propaganda in the film industry. As a result, variety acts and revue shows became much less common on the London stage. A few interwar playwrights – for example, Terence Rattigan and Rodney Ackland – continued to be produced during and after the war, but very quickly the plays of 1918–45 began to appear outdated.

Yet the London stage between 1918 and 1945 had been very lively indeed. It underwent a swift transformation in who held economic and managerial control, from the old-style actor-manager akin to factory owner to the new-style consortia of entrepreneurs typical of later capitalism. Paradoxically, such different monopolies were in part responsible for the proliferation of so many independent and private play-producing organisations, often run by amateurs or semi-professionals, interested in aesthetic experiment and ideological issues and linked into the traditions of European drama and theatre. Although there was relatively little experiment with the form of playwriting, plays of ideas, revues offering politically or socially astute commentary, plays which grappled with crucial social issues – such as women's changing social roles, gender nego-tiations, sexual choices and the psychology of violence in a post-war society – all found favour amongst audiences who were perhaps less conservative than has been conventionally assumed by critics and historians. For those audiences the London stage, while clearly in some senses escapist, was a potent location of intellectual and social challenge.

8

Social commitment and aesthetic experiment, 1895–1946

MICK WALLIS

There have been theatres in which social commitment and aesthetic experiment work in tight tandem. The most familiar and sharpest example is probably that of Brecht. But whilst this chapter touches on practices that align quite well with the Brechtian model, it has a more complex and fragmentary story to tell. There are a number of reasons for this. In general terms, in this period of British theatre there were also instances of aesthetic experiment for its own sake, of progressive belief wedded to 'conservative' forms, and of conservative ideology wedded to 'progressive' forms. The analysis of theatre practices that follows mirrors that range of possibility. And whilst most of them, in different ways, were part of the great 'modernist' project of the first half of the twentieth century, each had a particular and often complex relationship to its own historical moment. Their experiments negotiated quite specific rhetorical engagements with audiences, typically by exploiting theatre's quintessential capacity as a reflexive and ironic apparatus.

More specifically, this chapter deals with theatrical phenomena that are marginal in a double sense. First, whilst the impact of modernity in this period – at once exhilarating and alienating – was potent in Britain, the burgeoning of *European* modern theatre movements was only faintly reflected there. This was despite fairly frequent visits, mostly to London, by such influential foreign companies as Diaghilev's Ballets Russes (1910–14), the Moscow Art Theatre (1928), the ensemble Compagnie des Quinze (1931) and Kurt Jooss's dance theatre (1933). This faintness of European influence was due, I suggest, to three main factors – the absence of state subsidy for the arts, the strength of the commercial theatre and the relative lack of an earlier leftist theatrical tradition. These factors partly explain the second marginality, as all the practices discussed here were *institutionally* marginal in British theatre.

Since that double marginality made for fragmentation – there is little evidence of extended concrete connections, let alone anything we might call a unifying 'movement', between many of these theatres – there is no one clear narrative to tell. Hence this chapter offers a number of independent accounts, which are placed roughly in chronological order and which move along a political spectrum from liberal to leftist practices. This strategy aims to enable the reader to identify differences and similarities that produce some thematic threads. Thus, we will be concerned with institutional status; with aesthetic questions that address textual and rhetorical effects such as repetition, doubling and quotation; with scenography and *mise-en-scène*; and with the work of the actor and his/her co-workers in the theatrical ensemble. Also, the idea of 'their theatre and ours' echoes as a sub-theme throughout, drawing out contrasts between, say, literary and scenic aesthetics, British and European influences, working-class and middle-class appeal, men's and women's issues, popular and official approaches in the making of theatre.

Liberal innovations

At the opening of Ibsen's *Ghosts*, Mrs Alving alarms Pastor Manders with her reading habits. London audiences in 1891 might reasonably have surmised that the books on Mrs Alving's table are works of feminism, radical philosophy, liberal politics and possibly also naturalist fiction. These are socially committed cultural products, ones associated with the broad pressure for reform of public and private institutions articulated by a critical fraction of the north European middle class in the last quarter of the nineteenth century. Stage naturalism was one formal articulation of that pressure. So in Britain in the 1890s audiences seeking a drama overtly engaged with serious contemporary issues would rarely look to the commercial stage. The actor-manager system still dominated, and favoured the long run rather than innovation, relying heavily on spectacle and promoting the star player over the ensemble. Moreover, the censorship of the Lord Chamberlain stood firmly in the way of radical content.

Progressive actors, playwrights, critics and intellectuals sought two broad solutions to these problems. One was the institution of an endowed theatre that would be free of commercial concerns: some called for private subscription, others state subsidy – the movement towards a National Theatre had begun. The other was to create a club that would mount unlicensed performances on a non-commercial basis in whatever theatre might be available. A progressive bourgeois cultural formation was working towards theatrical institutions through which a new committed drama might be sustained, either in outright opposition or as a declared adjunct to conservative commercial fare on the British stage. So what happened in Britain to the radical potentials of both naturalism and Ibsenism?

It was with a production of *Ghosts* in 1891 that the Dutch playwright-manager J. T. Grein and the Irish poet-playwright George Moore inaugurated the first British institution of the 'new' drama, the Independent Theatre. Its declared aim was 'to stimulate the production of new, original English plays independent both of the censor and of commercial, profit-oriented management'.[1] Moore and Grein themselves differed in perspective on the new aesthetic. Moore believed that a genuine new theatre would best emerge from the music hall. Here was a truly popular theatre, 'incarnate with the . . . living world', whose existing comic sketches and business were the basis for a new drama dealing directly with life. Grein, in contrast, stressed that he wanted to 'nurture realism' but only 'of a healthy kind'.[2] But for both, dramatic form would eschew the artificial manipulations of the well-made play and the scenic aesthetic would refuse superficial sumptuousness in costume and set.[3] In the event, *Ghosts* was chosen as the company's opening play as a deliberate challenge to the censor – an act both of direct defiance and of cunning promotion. Even so, the Independent Theatre quickly proved to be politically moderate, a loose association of people 'united . . . only in their unconscious alienation from the popular mainstream'.[4]

The Independent and its successors, such as the Stage Society, were self-consciously 'literary' theatres. Principally, this was an alignment with the seriousness and progressive nature of naturalism.[5] But Simon Shepherd rightly argues that at the heart of the 'new' drama movement was in fact an anti-theatrical animus – anything on stage other than the direct replication of life was deemed to be excessive and false.[6] The job of the stage was to deliver the dramatic text; in tandem they were to approximate everyday life. Thus, the drama of bland plausibilities, as Raymond Williams characterises the decayed naturalism of the British stage,[7] was a formula for ostensible relevance and easy recognisability, rather than challenge and engagement. It merely continues the domestication of the stage begun by the Bancrofts and Robertson in the 1860s. However, John Stokes stresses that while the Independent Theatre

---

1 J. T. Grein and George Moore, quoted in James Woodfield, *English Theatre in Transition 1881–1914* (London: Croom Helm, 1984), p. 43.
2 *Ibid.*, p. 40.
3 John Stokes, *Resistible Theatres: Enterprise and Experiment in the Late Nineteenth Century* (London: Paul Elek, 1972), p. 127.
4 *Ibid.*, p. 115.
5 *Ibid.*, p. 116.
6 Simon Shepherd, 'The unacceptable face of theatre', in Simon Shepherd and Peter Womack, *English Drama: A Cultural History* (Oxford: Blackwell, 1996), pp. 219–48.
7 Raymond Williams, 'Social environment and theatrical environment: the case of English naturalism', in *Problems in Materialism and Culture* (London: Verso, 1980), pp. 125–47.

was a coterie institution, it was by no means insular. Its mission was to disturb in order to reform. It stimulated debate, promoted and then published new writing. It aimed to force the British public sphere to recognise its own parochialism. Yet, whilst it directly facilitated Shaw's break into theatre with *Widowers' Houses* (1892), it is worth noting that Shaw only stepped in because the steady flow of new writing the theatre had hoped for did not emerge.[8]

The Independent Theatre was wound up in 1898, never having established a permanent home. But its founding was, as Stokes says, an annunciatory event – its example was followed. In 1893 Charles Hughes, a close friend of tea heiress theatre patron Annie Horniman, formed an Independent Theatre Society in Manchester. In London there followed the New Century Theatre and the Stage Society, founded in 1897 and 1899 respectively. These theatres began to broaden the base of aesthetic possibility in Britain, and the Stage Society, particularly, is notable for staging symbolist and other post-naturalist European plays.

Many women were active in bringing the new European drama to Britain. For example, Kate Santley risked the censor's retribution by letting London's Royalty Theatre for private performance; Janet Achurch mortgaged future wages to mount *A Doll's House* at the Novelty.[9] Gay Gibson Cima argues that, especially in performing Ibsen, a new generation of women actors – products typically of liberal education rather than theatrical families – negotiated a sphere of relative creative independence. She demonstrates how Robins's playing of Ibsen in the 1890s 'enabled contemporary audiences to see the performance of gender as a series of repeated melodramatic acts'. The institution of what we now call 'psychological acting' by these women actually entailed a 'consciousness of performance': the actress demonstrated, on behalf of women in the audience, how they were required to play out allotted and damaging roles.[10] Robins was one of the first in a new wave of actress-managers, followed for instance by Edy Craig, whose Pioneer Players (1911–25) specialised in woman-centred drama.[11]

Meanwhile, the Actresses' Franchise League (AFL), founded in 1908 to campaign for women's suffrage by theatrical means, fashioned a workable realism, music hall monologue and burlesque, pageantry and a kind of skeletal symbolism into effective campaigning forms. Politically non-aligned, the League

---

8 Stokes, *Resistible Theatres*, pp. 141ff.
9 Woodfield, *Theatre in Transition*, pp. 39, 44, 59.
10 Gay Gibson Cima, *Performing Women: Female Characters, Male Playwrights and the Modern Stage* (Ithaca: Cornell University Press, 1993), pp. 20–59; quoted pp. 53 and 49.
11 Julie Holledge, *Innocent Flowers: Women in the Edwardian Theatre* (London: Virago, 1981), pp. 105–63.

provided affirmative propaganda to both constitutional and militant suffrage societies. The early staple of the AFL was plays based on the social drama, depicting sexual inequality in general terms. Inez Bensusan's *The Apple* (1910) eloquently depicts the preferential treatment of middle-class sons over daughters, not only through the dialogue but most crucially through physical action – as the man smokes, the women do domestic work. After 1911, the year in which Prime Minister Asquith killed off the modestly progressive Conciliation Bill, AFL plays became more politically focussed, typically very portable two-handers designed to deliver debate on specific issues of sexuality and gender.

The founding of the AFL followed two decades of campaigning against inferior conditions for women within the profession. The lecture at an AFL members' meeting on the proposition that the present 'stage conception of women' was 'conventional and inadequate' is just one instance of another repeated complaint.[12] The eventual founding of the Women's Theatre Company by the AFL in 1913 marks an attempt to right both these wrongs. Yet in order to find sufficiently demanding roles, the company had to resort to male playwrights. And the advent of World War One cut short the possibility of developing a women's dramaturgy in this new context.[13]

Continued aesthetic ferment – other theatres

Once the dramatic conventions and institutional logic of the commercial stage had been breached, other models of dramatic writing and stage practice quickly followed. The Stage Society, for example, presented Ibsen's later plays – plus Strindberg, Hauptmann, Maeterlinck and others. One important complement to the independent theatre initiatives was the early repertory movement, and the free theatre was strengthened by a number of clubs and societies formed between the wars. By 1925 the Stage Society was one of a dozen 'Sunday societies' operating in London, extending its repertoire to expressionism and constructivism. A number of marginal commercially run theatres were also committed to experiment.

The Gate Theatre broke ground in being the first private theatre club to mount runs of plays for two to three weeks, in contrast to the Sunday societies. It eventually displaced the Stage Society. Under Peter Godfrey's management (1925–34), it pioneered the international theatrical avant-garde in

12 Vivien Gardner (ed.), *Sketches from the Actresses' Franchise League* (Nottingham: Nottingham Drama Texts, 1985), pp. 1–5; quoted p. 3.
13 Holledge, *Innocent Flowers*, pp. 92–7.

London. A graduate of circus clowning and Ben Greet's Shakespeare experiments, Godfrey determined with his wife Molly Veness to open a theatre for expressionist drama. They secured the top floor of a ramshackle warehouse in Covent Garden, forcing the Gate into club status primarily because the premises were unlicensable. Godfrey developed his own expressionist style: a permanent black background, minimum props and furniture and non-illusionist lighting. For new premises in Villiers Street (1927) he built a stage occupying one-third of the floor space. A steeply raked auditorium brought the audience into very close contact with a low platform stage. For actors, this 'combined most of the advantages of the theatre with those of the radio and the cinema' – they developed a fleet style capable of nuance and close-up intimacy.[14] But by 1934 'advanced' taste had overtaken Godfrey – the vogue returned to 'realism'.

A small-part actor with an enthusiasm, Nigel Playfair converted a derelict music venue into a fringe commercial theatre, the Lyric theatre, Hammersmith (1918–33), where he 'amuse[d] himself by producing the plays he liked in the way he liked'.[15] Playfair pursued his taste for deliberate artifice through a string of productions of eighteenth-century plays, which made the Lyric famous. The 'Lyric style' was characterised by clean design lines, semi-permanent sets and costumes in primary colours. It also broke the barrier of the fourth wall, patently accepting the presence of the audience. Meanwhile, at the Everyman, Hampstead (1920–6), Norman Macdermott made use of Edward Gordon Craig's 'screens' against black velvet curtains in a programme of new plays and revivals reminiscent of Barker and Vedrenne's at the Royal Court (see pp. 174–6 below). He specialised in Shaw, mounted Coward's *The Vortex* (1924), introduced Eugene O'Neill to the London stage and even achieved some influence over West End programming.

J. B. Fagan's Oxford Playhouse (1923–9) furnished a mostly undergraduate audience with modern classics on an apron stage, in a deeply uncomfortable shack. The presentational acting was fumbling but fresh, Fagan being 'too scrupulous . . . to be capable of smearing a veneer of polish over unfinished work', as was the case in the majority of repertory theatres.[16] It was here in 1925 that Chekhov's *The Cherry Orchard* (1904) first won favour on a British stage, the 'sociologically minded' Stage Society audience having been unimpressed by its London première in 1911. Also in 1925–6, Theodore Komisarjevsky made influential productions of Ibsen, Chekhov and Gogol at

14 Norman Marshall, *The Other Theatre* (London: John Lehmann, 1947), p. 46.
15 *Ibid.*, p. 32.
16 *Ibid.*, p. 22.

Figure 8.1 Terence Gray and Doria Paston's design for the Cambridge Festival Theatre production of Sophocles' *Antigone*, 1931.

Philip Ridgeway's Barnes Theatre, a converted cinema. The subtle variations of tone and tempo, the primacy of mood over detail, the romantic over realism, contrasted sharply with the meticulous exactitude and 'glittering efficiency' of West End naturalism.[17]

Marshall notes that while most European capitals established a 'producer's theatre' in the 1930s, only Terence Gray's Cambridge Festival Theatre (1926–33) came near to that ideal in Britain.[18] The wealthy Gray converted a Regency playhouse into a venue where he could wage war on both illusion and glamour. He developed an open minimalist stage consisting of levels backed by a bare cyclorama. In place of scenery he built abstract structures reminiscent of functionalist architecture, approaching Soviet constructivism. Their purpose was to articulate the grouping of actors. Gray declared that his business was not to interpret but to create, and that he would evolve a fresh technique of acting. But his highly stylised productions lacked substance for most, and Gray quickly was seen as a single-minded eccentric.

Allardyce Nicoll pairs the 'horizontal' international influences on British dramaturgy and stage practice early in the century with the 'vertical' force brought to bear by academics and others trawling through historical forms

17 *Ibid.*, p. 219.
18 *Ibid.*, p. 53.

for new stimulus or reform.[19] Thus, the Stage Society founded the offshoot Phoenix Society (1919) specifically for historical revivals. Significant impetus towards the open stage came not only from Craig and via Yeats's fascination with the Japanese Noh drama, but also from William Poel. Starting in 1881 with a production of the first quarto *Hamlet* on a bare platform at St George's Hall, London, and later founding the Elizabethan Stage Society (1895–1905), Poel made repeated attempts to recreate the physical conditions of the Elizabethan (as opposed to picture frame) stage, further challenging the spectacular realism then in dominance.

Granville Barker

By 1904 the independent theatre movement had achieved no significant impact on the commercial repertoires, so the playwright-actor Harley Granville Barker determined – at the Royal Court Theatre (1904–7) – to make what was to become the last significant attempt in this period to square the circle of making uncommercial theatre work commercially. J. E. Vedrenne, who already was a manager at the Court, joined Barker as business manager. Whilst he hoped for an enlightened national theatre, Barker perceived a need for something mid-way between the free theatres and the run-for-profit theatres. He proposed an extended stock season of uncommercial plays, mainly as a subscription exercise, but open to the general public and with modest seat prices. Each run would be long enough to get press notice, but short enough to maintain freshness and interest.

By the end of the third season the Court, as Dennis Kennedy demonstrates,[20] was established as a home for intellectual and socially committed drama. A new, ensemble style met new writing in a new commercial apparatus involving a new programming rhythm. But there were limitations and compromises. Shaw – the chief backer – dominated the repertoire. Matinées limited the audience to those without day jobs. Successful plays transferring to evening performance had to be recast. Actors' fees were low and rehearsals unpaid. The subscription scheme collapsed and prices rose. Delighted by the success of Shaw's *John Bull's Other Island*, Barker was dismayed to see its targets – politicians from both sides and King Edward himself – chortling smugly in the stalls.

---

19 Allardyce Nicoll, *English Drama 1900–1930: The Beginnings of the Modern Period* (Cambridge University Press, 1973), p. 118.
20 Dennis Kennedy, *Granville Barker and the Dream of Theatre* (Cambridge University Press, 1985).

But by 1907 Barker's attempt to create new work as a benign parasite on the profit-based theatre business was thriving. With Vedrenne, he decided to raise the stakes on his knife-edge enterprise at the Court by moving to the bigger Savoy Theatre in the West End. There he produced two famous seasons, 1907–8 and 1912–14, which proved economically disastrous. Costs were higher, the audience missed the intimacy of the Court, the shows looked shabby in the light of traditional West End standards. But the seasons were aesthetically highly innovative and Barker's production methods introduced significant new creative approaches to the British stage.

His treatment of cross-casting gender in *Twelfth Night* (1912) provides a good example: 'To tell a woman to begin her study of how to play a woman's part by imagining herself a boy may seem absurd; but it is the right approach nevertheless.'[21] In its original casting, of course, the play plays with gender: a young man plays Viola, who disguises as a young man. We might argue that Shakespeare thus 'defamiliarises' convention and destabilises gender categories – or instead that he fetishises sexual difference. But for 250 years after the Restoration, until Barker's production at the Savoy in 1912, 'Viola' mostly had been a titillating breeches part.

Barker eschewed such established routines. His wife Lillah McCarthy, cast as Viola, reopened the dynamic mobility of gender signals invested in the part. Similarly, Barker refitted the Savoy to approximate the spatial logic of Shakespeare's stage, but he avoided a 'return' to Elizabethanism in the manner of Poel *and* any temptation to domesticate Shakespeare to modern realism. Rather, he sought an active and playful relationship with the terms of the text's original playfulness. The one full-stage set of the production – for Olivia's garden – was militantly both emblematic and modern, with lurid colours and futuristic shapes, which audiences likened to confectionery. Groupings and gestures, while 'natural' to the action, declared themselves as compositions. For long passages, actors remained motionless. This production's success with both the public and critics was a breakthrough for Barker, and for the British (not only Shakespearean) stage. The term 'stylisation' is insufficient to capture its mode of active apprehension of a cultural object at once familiar yet also strange, both close yet also distant.

The comprehensive vision shaping all elements of production is a directorial one, and effectively Barker installed the role of director on the British stage. Where the independent theatre had subdued the theatricality both of the stage and of the actor, Barker helped reinstate theatricality, by himself

---

21 Harley Granville Barker, 'Shakespeare's dramatic art', cited *ibid.*, p. 138.

becoming the co-author as director of what is recognisably now a *theatrical* (not simply a literary) text. Hence, Barker worked, aesthetically and socio-politically, at highly significant margins. The Vedrenne–Barker seasons helped create a new but limited commercial audience, one identified by an artistic taste for theatre. Women predominated in the audience, their seriousness lampooned as cultism. Barker was heckled on stage: 'That precarious amalgam of Shavians, Fabians, feminists, lovers of the Court idea, theatrical pioneers – was repudiating its leader for invading the West End'.[22] Barker had hoped that his own play *Waste* (1906–7) would prove a mainstay at the Savoy. Peter Womack distinguishes it as a radical departure within the terms of the new realist writing, a play that escapes sententiousness and unsettles the audience, since 'the extreme individuation of the dramatic languages' puts 'all the available moral categories at risk'.[23] But the play was censored and the books, in the end, did not balance. Barker's work at the margins of both form and formation has left him curiously marginalised: both famous and relatively neglected.

Agit-prop

A large working-class crowd has gathered at the factory gates. A flatbed truck provides a platform. The troupe of six performers 'marches on well-disciplined, singing enthusiastically and in well-marked rhythm'.[24] The song which opens the ten-minute sketch identifies their company name and reminds the crowd how Workers Theatre Movement (WTM) groups 'show you how you're robbed and bled', how 'speed-up / And unemployment, / Have brought starvation to our door'. But the target in this sketch is more than direct exploitation: it also attacks the ideological means by which the capitalist class maintains its hegemony:

> With stage and film-show,
> They're always striving,
> To hide from you the real class-war.
> (p. 139)

Tom Thomas's *Their Theatre and Ours* (1932) stages a confrontation between workers' theatre and capitalist theatre and film. The latter are derided by

---

22 Kennedy, *Granville Barker*, p. 30.
23 Peter Womack, 'Naturalism', in Shepherd and Womack, *English Drama*, p. 263.
24 Tom Thomas, *Their Theatre and Ours* (1932) in Raphael Samuel, Ewan MacColl and Stuart Cosgrove, *Theatres of the Left 1880–1935: Workers' Theatre Movements in Britain and America* (London: Routledge & Kegan Paul, 1985), p. 138.

means of 'burlesque inset scenes', which are to be strongly contrasted with 'the serious passages' (p. 142). The movement between passages is swift; players change role in an instant. Whilst the sketch criticises mass entertainment films ('Miss Greater Garbage'), it has learnt the power of montage from the cinema. And whilst it attacks the jingoism of the later music halls, the burlesque that delivers the attack has its roots deep in Victorian music hall culture. As in the Soviet Union, Germany and the USA, British agit-prop (agitation-propaganda) synthesises modernist experiment and the traditions of popular performance.

Another Thomas sketch, *Something for Nothing* (1932), demonstrates how workers are denied the fruits of their intelligence. A factory worker hits on an idea to improve productivity. It gets passed up through five levels of management, each of which calls it daft but each of which then claims it as their own. It finally reaches the Board of Directors. Each successive 'scene' repeats the same exchange: enthusiastic suggestion met by flat put-down. If repetition is one part of the aesthetic, crescendo is another: as we rise up the hierarchy, the fawnings become more exaggerated and the accents more bizarre. The music hall characterisations are held within an abstract, consciously 'modern' aesthetic whose formal characteristics both draw attention to the sketch's own artifice and *work* aesthetically to provide pleasure in performance itself. In what at first might seem a paradox, this 'linear' aesthetic itself connotes efficiency. Thomas and others insisted that WTM troupes be precisely drilled. A typically arresting sight would be a group of uniformed players – wearing neat workplace overalls – acrobatting into a perfectly sculpted chevron of bodies poised for action. This swift but tight control embodies the optimism, aptitude and power of young women and men with future vision.

Agit-prop has a double aim: to call for action (agitation) and to spread revolutionary political understanding (propaganda). Stourac and McCreery (from whom the following is drawn[25]) judge these two Tom Thomas sketches unusual in their successful attempt to deliver an argument, rather than simply sloganising. Oversimplified sectarianism was a double problem for the WTM. First, because sketches needed to be short, to grab attention at a factory gate from the back of a lorry, at a break in a meeting – and to avoid the police. They captured the essence of things by dealing in types or stereotypes. But brevity and cartoon typifications militate against refinements of analysis, and always push propaganda towards crude slogans. Second, because the fierce official

25 Richard Stourac and Kathleen McCreery, *Theatre as a Weapon: Workers' Theatre in the Soviet Union, Germany and Britain, 1917–1934* (London: Routledge & Kegan Paul, 1986), pp. 238–9.

political line of the WTM made an appeal to the unconverted very difficult. A sketch might attack the very union a worker had long fought for, for collusion with the bosses – all in a matter of minutes. So most sketches were predicated on preaching, usually very well, to the converted. British agit-prop in the 1930s was strong on agitation, weak on propaganda.

The energy of the form reflects the urgency and volatility of the political circumstance, however. Disgusted by the betrayal of workers by the Labour Party and trade union leaders in the 1926 General Strike, Tom Thomas left Labour and joined the Communist Party. The Hackney Labour Dramatic Group, which he had recently founded to promote socialist ideas, was transformed into the People's Players, a cornerstone of the nascent WTM.

After three formative years, from 1929 the WTM expanded significantly, with several groups established in London, northern England and Scotland. The sharpest growth, paralleled by organisational consolidation, came in 1930–2 with a period of increased working-class militancy. The first National WTM Conference was held in 1932. Members were typically young people aligned with, if not always members of, the Communist Party. White-collar workers predominated in the south, proletarians in the north, though many were unemployed. Stourac and McCreery list some sixty groups in the UK, but caution that many were short-lived and that collaborations were customary.[26]

In the summer of 1932 the WTM Central Committee reported on the condition of the movement. Its propositions include:

- The workers' theatre is a conscious weapon of the workers' revolution expressing their struggle in dramatic form.
- Agit-prop needs minimal apparatus, is portable and flexible. Its performers deploy class understanding rather than specialised skills of impersonation.
- Direct address and close proximity to the crowd embody the fact that players and audience share oppression and so might share a way of overcoming it.[27]

The leadership insisted that whilst naturalism might be explored, agit-prop was yet to be fully developed. But events overtook them.

The WTM's militant revue form derived in part from contacts abroad, especially Germany. *Their Theatre and Ours* was a fundraiser in support of delegates to the 1933 Moscow Olympiad, where agit-prop troupes from several countries met to exchange ideas and to be judged. Moscow held two major disappointments. First, the British contingent came last, being considered amateurish.

26 Ibid., pp. 203–44 passim, p. 305.
27 Samuel et al., Theatres of the Left, pp. 99–105.

Second, the Moscow leadership was now calling for a return to a more naturalistic form. And some British troupes, notably the Rebel Players, were coming to feel that naturalism could get closer to everyday reality. Middle-class theatre professionals were associating with some troupes, their 'theatrical' expertise diluting political imperatives. But most crucially, in 1933 the Communist Third International made a *volte-face* and called for class collaboration rather than struggle. The rapid growth to power of fascism, which would destroy all hope of socialism unless it was defeated, now necessitated a popular front against that threat. The Communist Party would lead it. Class struggle was suspended and classical agit-prop had had its day.

The WTM had been the theatre of 'class against class'. But the most benign attitude it ever gained from the Communist Party was a sort of avuncular indulgence: the party was disinclined to regard cultural work as politically significant. Whilst politically Communist, the WTM was never an official organ of the party, and neither was a parallel project – Left Theatre – nor their successor, the Unity Theatre movement.

Left Theatre and Montagu Slater

Left Theatre was a declared attempt to synthesise aesthetic experiment with socialist politics. It was founded in 1933 around a core group – André van Gyseghem, Barbara Nixon and Montagu Slater – and later associated with the radical journal *Left Review* (established 1934). The aim was to provide professional productions of socialist plays to working-class audiences. Its shows typically opened in the West End and then toured to town halls in working-class districts of London. Left Theatre's means of survival are familiar: it was founded as a club and the actors were professionals working for nothing except occasional expenses. In 1936 it formulated plans for a cultural and political centre housing a permanent repertory company in a working-class district. Clearly, this would require continuing subsidy. But cultural work – even that closely engaged with contemporary struggles – must compete with other priorities: in the same year the Spanish Civil War began, and subscriptions were lost as radicals put their money directly into the Republican cause. Left Theatre wound up in 1937.[28]

Left Theatre aimed to draw on a wide range of influences old and new, in the expectation that new social content would stimulate new aesthetic

---

28 Bernadette Kirwan, 'Aspects of Left Theatre in England in the 1930s', unpublished Ph.D. thesis, Loughborough University (1989), p. 224.

forms. But there were difficulties. Inadequate rehearsal time and small budgets limited the choice of plays, kept production standards low and experimentation modest. There was not a consensus about its broad political policy. Bernadette Kirwan contrasts the views of two executive committee members: whereas Tom Thomas thought that the militant WTM political line was here finding useful support in the middle class, Barbara Nixon saw Left Theatre as part of a wider left, liberal and amateur movement set to resist commercialism and refurbish theatre's cultural function.[29]

The first five productions were of imported plays, including Okhlopkov's *Mother* (after Gorki), which focussed on working-class women's experience, but audiences wanted plays dealing with immediate English issues. A play-writing competition in 1935 was won by Slater's *Easter 1916*. Slater's substantial achievement is the development of forms for a committed Communist content. Steve Nicholson identifies three principal stylistic elements: the juxtaposition of broad realism with a poetic register typically managed by chorus and aural effects; the scripting of visual imagery integrated with the spoken text; and 'the blurring of the gap between the fictional world on-stage and the reality of the audience'.[30] In Slater's next play, *Stay Down Miner* (1936), about contemporary stay-down strikes in South Wales, the audience are once cast as strike-breaking blacklegs, and in the last scene as a sympathetic courtroom crowd urged from the witness stand to 'join Wales!' (p. 264). The audience is drawn to confront its own complicity with class and imperial repression, and challenged to create solidarity with the miners. Yet complicity is not used just to blame. In Slater's realist register, social typification renders the blacklegs as unsympathetic but comprehensible: he figures them as products of a total system that is the ultimate foe. And Slater characteristically folds in a powerfully heroic poetic register, verbally and visually, as in the magnificent passage when mine workings come to figure the struggle of all oppressed people to carve their liberation from a recalcitrant history.[31]

Slater's is a unique theatre of its time, resisting both the tenuous appeal to transcendence of some poetic stages and the too easy totalisations of some Communist theatre. It embraces the autonomy of the audience in potential comradeship, carefully modulating theatrical registers to share analysis, vision

---

29 *Ibid.*, p. 196.
30 Steve Nicholson, 'Montagu Slater and the theatre of the thirties', in Patrick J. Quinn (ed.), *Recharting the Thirties* (London: Associated Universities Press, 1996), p. 209.
31 Montagu Slater, *Stay Down Miner* (1936), in John Lucas (ed.), *The 1930s: A Challenge to Orthodoxy* (Brighton: Harvester Press, 1978), pp. 251–3.

and the difficulty of struggle. It is great aesthetic innovation because it is deeply informed by a searching, reflexive ethics.

Unity and the Army Bureau of Current Affairs

London Unity Theatre, the Communist Party-aligned amateur dramatic club that opened in 1936, displaced the WTM and soon replaced Left Theatre. Its ascendance was part of the general shift from class politics to the cross-class Popular Front. London's was just one of over a dozen Unity Theatres in Britain, of which Bristol, Glasgow, Sheffield and Merseyside are perhaps the most notable – a geographical spread that reflected a widening left-ideological alliance. In a related change, the aesthetic drive from the Communist International at this time was towards socialist realism. But as Raphael Samuel begins to admit,[32] commentators who claim that the displacement of the WTM by Unity constituted a total retreat from *aesthetic experiment* to curtain-stage naturalism are mistaken. London Unity's foundation principally as a club for progressively minded amateurs fostered an experimental attitude. It also allowed for political uncertainty and a degree of concern for theatrical, and eventually West End theatrical, success.

Montagu Slater himself contributed to Unity's *Busmen* (1938). Its 'Living Newspaper' form, developed in tandem with the Federal Theatre Project in the USA, was a means of making campaign documentaries on urgent topical issues – in this case, a transport strike. *Busmen* utilises cinematic cutting and interpolates verse and comic sequences in a series of gestic episodes. Jack Lindsay's *On Guard for Spain* (1937) is perhaps Unity's most famous 'mass declamation', a lyrical outgrowth of agit-prop's hortatory choric address. It adds extended poetic metaphor to documentary fact and direct audience address, and, through sheer length, the reach of epic. Revised to keep up with the progress of the Spanish Civil War, *On Guard* was performed in theatres and often outdoors, raising popular consciousness and funds, and sustaining morale.

Eager to encourage worker-writers, London Unity produced taxi-drivers Robert Buckland and Herbert Hodge's first play, *Where's That Bomb?* (1936). This is a political burlesque that satirises reactionaries *and* ridicules agit-prop rhetoric as personal pomposity. Similarly, Hodge's *Cannibal Carnival* (1937) is a wild cartoon that both attacks class society and offers a comic pastiche of the Marxist grand narrative. This strategy of ironic evacuation (treating the serious

---

32 Samuel *et al.*, *Theatres of the Left*, pp. 61–4.

unseriously while withholding commitment to any 'true' ideological position) results from Hodge's insistence that progressives should resist self-importance. He described *Cannibal Carnival* as a 'vulgar spectacle'.[33]

Colin Chambers provides an extended picture of London Unity's bold and various formal innovations. For example, *Babes in the Wood* (1938) attacked the government's policy of appeasement with fascism by turning pantomime into a vehicle for political satire through pastiche.[34] It dared direct scatological satire at living individuals: Prime Minister Chamberlain appears as 'Chamberstrain'. Its huge success marks it as a clever ruse to repair the embattled Popular Front; but also as delicious scandal – well-heeled West Enders attended in eager hordes.

Unity was the first theatre in London to reopen after war was declared in 1939, and initially maintained its criticism of government policy through revues (*Sandbag Follies* and *Turn Up the Lights*, 1939) and a second political pantomime, *Jack the Giant Killer* (1940), while O'Casey's *The Star Turns Red* (1940) was a striking testament to class-militant Communism, lurching from realism through verse to expressionism. A mobile group later toured solidarity shows to shelters in goods yards, tube stations and railway arches, spawning a women's company, the Amazons, in 1943–4. Thanks to its expertise in Living Newspaper, some of Unity's leading practitioners, including Bridget Boland, André van Gyseghem and Mulk Raj Anand, were invited by the Army Bureau of Current Affairs (founded in 1941 to provide educational programmes for the forces) to set up the Play Unit in 1943. In the first six months it performed fifty-eight shows to 20,000 troops. Jack Lindsay and Ted Willis's *It Started As Lend Lease* (1945) begins as if it is simply a lecture justifying the method whereby the US funded UK armaments. But the lecturer/Narrator is quickly interrupted by the Clerk who, through a series of illustrative scenes, continually questions the 'truths' that the Narrator is trying to demonstrate. The dialectical commentary both admits and negotiates any suspicions the audience may have that they are indeed being fed army propaganda. It also opens up the debate sufficiently for a surreptitious leftist spin on the topic. The war ended before an army investigation into political bias in the Play Unit could report.[35] Meanwhile, by 1945 Unity was reduced to an unoriginal repertoire and soon

---

33 Mick Wallis, 'A draught through the Front: Herbert Hodge, the Popular Front and the BBC', in Ros Merkin (ed.), *Popular Theatres?* (Liverpool John Moores University Press, 1996), p. 259.
34 Colin Chambers, *The Story of Unity Theatre* (London: Lawrence & Wishart, 1989), pp. 165–79.
35 *Ibid.*, p. 203; see also Dan Rebellato, *1956 and All That: The Making of Modern British Drama* (London: Routledge, 1999), p. 62.

after both the London and Glasgow branches began to harbour ambitions to turn professional.

The Group Theatre

Emerging in 1932, the Group Theatre was originally the brainchild of the young director Tyrone Guthrie and the dancer Rupert Doone, who imagined an ensemble committed to actor-centred art in emulation of the Compagnie des Quinze. Founded on a co-operative and free-flowing basis, the Group never achieved financial stability. Doone can safely be considered the key member. He provided physical training through a synthesis of classical ballet technique and the new central European dance of Jooss and Wigman, but geared to actors. Its aim was a physical precision and fluidity that was wholly committed to expressivity, through which performers trained to a 'sensual awareness' in the totality of body and mind might respond to material drawn from morality plays to new experimental drama.

The Group offered its members the prospect of one day earning a living making art, an art moreover with social commitment, and a British theatre that at last might match those of mainland Europe. But also it wittily saw that the variety halls of London, even though now thoroughly commercialised, still embodied qualities that such a radical theatre might use: intimate to the point of identity with the audience, so side-stepping the superficial mimicries of naturalism by dealing directly and vigorously with its world.[36] The Group wanted to emulate the playful immediacy of the halls.

As its chief historian Michael J. Sidnell recounts, the widely experienced Doone had worked briefly with Cocteau, whose theatre already approximated to forms that would later emerge from new dance. Cocteau's performer is actor, dancer and singer; designers, writers, director and performers work co-operatively to create a 'poetic' theatrical event, immanent in its commitment to presentation rather than representation. As Doone said, there is 'no such thing as an interpretative art: the actor does not interpret the poet's words, he recreates them'.[37] Accordingly, the Group staged poetic dramas specially written for them by T. S. Eliot, W. H. Auden and Christopher Isherwood, and had Nugent Monck and Michel St Denis as guest directors, plus Benjamin Britten as composer of incidental music. This was the aesthetic avant-garde of

---

36 John Allen, 'Foreword', in Michael J. Sidnell, *Dances of Death: The Group Theatre of London in the Thirties* (London: Faber & Faber, 1984), pp. 17–21.
37 Quoted in *ibid.*, p. 46.

interwar London, dedicated to serious experiment in the European manner, but with a British twist.

Perhaps the general level of innovation of the Group fell short of its European cousins, but Auden and Isherwood's contributions can be seen as constituting an exceptional case of something approaching the continental idea of 'total theatre' in Britain. In *The Dog Beneath the Skin* (staged by Doone at the Westminster Theatre in 1936), Alan Norman is a middle-class Everyman from Pressan Ambo, a quaint English village presented through a brittle pastiche of 1920s musical comedy, a genre that was itself a pastiche of middle-class life. The local stray dog accompanies his quest across Europe in search of the missing local heir, Sir Francis. The journey is a ruse for a satirical montage depicting Europe's descent into barbarism. Sir Francis eventually reveals himself to Alan by climbing out of the dogskin. When they return to Pressan, it is in the throes of fascist enthusiasm. Sir Francis had known it was like that all along; that was why he hid in the panto costume.

Here is another kind of critical inversion akin to those of radical naturalist and polemical Communist theatre, as bourgeois culture's endemic up-ending of the truth is righted and the ideological veil is, as it were, pierced. Alan and the audience must look more clearly to see everyday English fascism, present or in potential. Simultaneously, the picaresque form delivers a mixture of stereotypical cartoon and poetic play that maps out capitalism's alienation of human value and its drive towards war. Alan falls in love with a mannequin, chorus girls are eaten, a liturgy is sung to a famous surgeon, and so on. The two elements of critical inversion and satirical excess fuse together to expose England's collusion in European fascism.

If *The Dog Beneath the Skin* trades in the lure of aesthetics, Auden and Isherwood's next collaboration, *The Ascent of F6* (1937), investigates the powerful and dangerous magnet of the male hero. Both plays are about collusion in the romance of domination, so critical deconstruction is unstageable without a self-reflexive irony that contests the possibility of speaking concrete truth on the English stage. Urgent political necessity – reaction to rising fascism – encounters the frailty of the human desiring machine, both subject and agent of politics. Fascism might easily be dug out of the village greensward, but desire, animated through a theatrical excess that itself threatens domination, makes the position from which to address and eliminate it crucially uncertain.

T. S. Eliot was doubtful that the Group Theatre had achieved truly vibrant poetic substance, as he held that the only basis on which serious dramatist and audience might meet was shared belief, and the only viable options were the Church and Communism. Yet Eliot found at the Group a poetic theatre corresponding to Yeats's synaesthetic experiments in *Plays for Dancers*, and one drawing on popular theatre forms – the vitality of music hall, for example – for experiments in serious analysis that approximated the self-reflexive strategies of modernist poetry. This offered Eliot two things at once: the overwhelming 'presence' of total theatre, an aesthetic doubling of his central religious themes of transcendence; and a rhetorical means whereby to negotiate those themes in an age of disbelief. Like Auden, Eliot was suspicious of aesthetic lures. His solution in *Murder in the Cathedral* (Canterbury Festival, 1935) was to excise movement, gesture and scenography to arrive, paradoxically, at a severely ascetic, liturgical form. If Auden and Isherwood's practice of the poetic stage is centrifugal, deconstructive, Eliot's practice here is centripetal, totalising. Aided by Doone, he arrived, not back at Yeats's mythic swoon in synaesthesia, but at the word echoing back on itself on a stage now purified of theatrical noise. Initiating the ritual is the Chorus: women of Canterbury, half blessed with a bovine prescience, dimly aware of the magnificence about them. The mass is not quite worthy of the Mass.

As Sidnell suggests, it is both apt and somewhat paradoxical that Eliot and Auden were the main literary poets gravitating towards the Group.[38] And, symptomatic of the cross-fertilisations at work in the Group Theatre in the 1930s, both Yeats and Brecht were in the audience for Eliot's *Sweeney Agonistes* (Group Theatre, 1934). We might also note two divergences. Whilst Auden and Eliot learned from each other in the making of poetic theatre, their paths diverge from the moment of Auden's *Dance of Death* (1934), which celebrates the death-throes of the British bourgeoisie. And Auden and Isherwood, in their love of aesthetic excess, diverged from Brecht as he left *épater les bourgeois* gestures behind to develop the pared down Epic of a patently Marxist theatre.

From the Red Megaphones to Theatre Workshop

In May 1946 Theatre Workshop toured to Butlins holiday camp at Filey, Yorkshire. *Uranium 235* reviewed the history of science up to Hiroshima through a complex mixture of styles in a flexible staging developed over fifteen years of experiment. It went down a storm with the working-class audience. The company's founders, Ewan MacColl and Joan Littlewood, had achieved a poetic theatre committed to working-class politics. The audience took it on their own terms: they cheered as if it were a variety show. *Uranium 235* and other

---

38 *Ibid.*, pp. 257–60.

early Theatre Workshop plays still retained the energy and directness of the Red Megaphones, the Salford WTM troupe that MacColl had formed in 1931.

The development from agit-prop to Theatre Workshop is instructive. After 1933 the Red Megaphones, like other WTM troupes, felt pressured to move indoors: the rise of fascism demanded that broader political issues be addressed, and this required a more sophisticated theatre. Indoor theatre needed lighting, and their research led them to Appia, whose 'musical' approach to light influenced all their subsequent shows. It is ironic that the key aesthetic tactic of Wagner's mystificatory *Gesamtkunstwerk* led these revolutionaries to a leftist theatrical poetry. But the street played an equally significant part, as the shapes of outdoor spaces (such as the steps in front of the public baths) were translated indoors to create an abstract stage of levels and areas where lighting could cinematically cut between scenes.

The Red Megaphones re-formed as Theatre of Action, now including director Joan Littlewood, for their first indoor production in 1934. Tiring of agit-prop's 'denunciatory broadsides',[39] the collective had found in the American play *Newsboy* an epic dramaturgy geared to depicting the plight of the unemployed in the context of world events. The criticism of British WTM amateurism at the 1933 Moscow Workers Olympiad had made the need for training clear. This was reinforced by the fact that Newsboy is a dancer's part, and answered in good measure by Littlewood's knowledge of Laban technique.

At a WTM conference they attended in 1934, a naturalistic anti-war play *Hammer*, staged by two of the London groups, was promoted as an example of a 'new' aesthetic line capable of articulating complex political material in new political conditions. Theatre of Action rejected this seeming retreat to the curtain stage and threw themselves into increased experimentation. Crucially, their autodidactic imperative led them to Leon Moussinac's *The New Movement in the Theatre* (1931), a rich compendium of modern European stage designs. In its 'Introduction', R. H. Packman writes that just as Le Corbusier conceives of the house as a machine to live in, so 'we must learn to think of the theatre as a machine to act in'.[40] Hence, they came to emulate Meyerhold in their 'Ballet with Words' *John Bullion* (1934), a total reworking of *Hammer* utilising a mixture of styles 'borrowed from agit-prop, constructivism and expressionism' and including both choreographed action and slide projections.[41]

---

39 Ewan MacColl, 'The evolution of a revolutionary theatre style', in Howard Goorney and Ewan MacColl (eds.), *Agit-Prop to Theatre Workshop: Political Playscripts 1930–50* (Manchester University Press, 1986), p. xxix.
40 R. H. Packman, 'Introduction', in Leon Moussinac, *The New Movement in the Theatre: A Survey of Recent Trends in Europe and America* (London: Batsford, 1931), p. 12.
41 MacColl, 'Evolution', p. xxxv.

The collective re-formed once more as Theatre Union in 1936, after a Theatre of Action split. Significant for this account is the creation of back-projection for their restaging of Piscator's version of *The Good Soldier Schweik* in 1938. Their 'Living Newspaper' *Last Edition* (1940) broke completely from the formalities of conventional staging, embracing the audience on three sides. Its sweeping address of matters as disparate yet connected as pit disaster, unemployment, the Spanish Civil War and Munich was achieved through a rich amalgam of styles including dance-drama, agit-prop satire, folk, burlesque, pageantry and mass declamation in an 'overall effect . . . not unlike a fast-moving variety show'.[42]

Theatre Union was one of the many casualties of World War Two. Re-formed yet again in 1945 as Theatre Workshop, the collective – an 'organisation of artists, technicians and actors'[43] – determined to 'create a form which was infinitely flexible', able to 'move backwards and forwards in time and space as . . . with . . . film'.[44] Thus *Uranium 235* hurtles between styles, partly because it was hastily written but principally to keep the contract with the audience dialogical, open. The stage 'negotiates' with its audience, as when a pastiche ballet is used half-jokingly to deliver a lesson in atomic physics. Indeed, pastiche continually threatens to undermine the ground of any statement or role. In a manoeuvre frequently deployed in the 1930s, actors in *Uranium 235* declare the levels of roles they play, as part of their commitment to truth-telling; but in joining this scheme, the Scientist makes a pompous fetish of it: 'In the course of putting on this chiton I have ceased to be a twentieth-century physicist, gone through a transition phase of being myself playing an actor . . . '.[45] The critical faculties of the audience are kept active; everything is to be questioned and evaluated.

Derek Paget describes Theatre Workshop as 'the Trojan horse through which European radical theatre practices from the 1918–1939 period entered post-war Britain'.[46] Whilst he stresses the European dimension, their eclecticism was wide. They gathered dramaturgical forms from the long tradition of popular theatres, which for MacColl included the Greek and Renaissance theatre as well as contemporary working-class entertainment.

---

42 *Ibid.*, p. xlv.
43 Theatre Workshop, 'Manifesto', in Howard Goorney, *The Theatre Workshop Story* (London: Eyre Methuen, 1981), p. 42.
44 MacColl, 'Evolution', p. 1.
45 Goorney and MacColl, *Agit Prop to Theatre Workshop*, p. 82.
46 Derek Paget, 'Theatre Workshop, Moussinac, and the European connection', *New Theatre Quarterly* 11, 43 (Aug. 1995), 212.

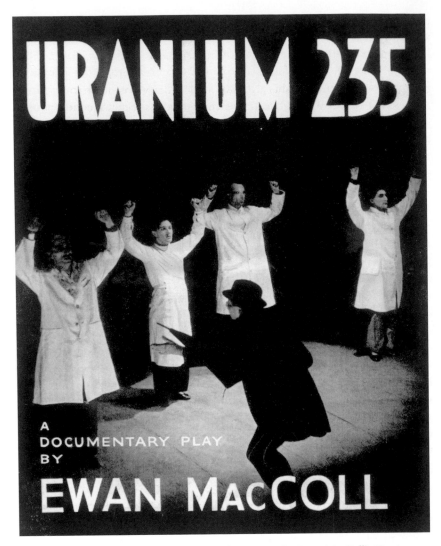

Figure 8.2 Theatre Workshop – programme front cover for Ewan MacColl's *Uranium 235*, 1946.

MacColl attributes their pursuit of cinematic techniques to the recognition that working-class folk *like* Hollywood – and for some good reasons.[47]

As a working-class company, the collective regarded theatre as a complex tool to be mastered. They attended to the technicalities of the stage and to

47 MacColl. 'Evolution', p. xlviii.

their own bodies as parts of its mechanism. Whilst Theatre Union attracted a broader class mix of collaborators, somewhat in the spirit of the Popular Front, the principal commitment in 1946 remained to working-class audiences. Theatre Workshop's achievement of their very characteristic form of social expressionism[48] contrasts sharply with London Unity's recourse to Shaw and Ibsen for the 1945–6 season. The difference is between a focussed collective with clear political aims and a club for progressives with a nervous eye on official Communist Party policy over the war, which was contradictory.[49] Theatre Workshop's continuing post-war difficulty was that, while it emerged as state subsidy began, it was repeatedly denied support by the middle classes holding the purse-strings.

Edward Gordon Craig in context

In his 1931 'Introduction' to Moussinac's book, R. H. Packman makes an evaluative distinction between two main trends in modern scenography. He castigates the *pictorial* trend, characterised by the collaboration between theatre directors and fine artists and typified by Bakst's designs for Diaghilev, where actors and the rhythmic action of the stage are encumbered and upstaged by painterly objects. But he celebrates the *architectonic* stage, in which architecture and theatre are brought into productive synthesis through their shared concern with volume, light, rhythm and the human body.[50] Within the architectonic trend, we can again distinguish two tendencies. One is typified by Craig and Appia, a *monumental* approach that tries to access transcendent value and in which the messiness and contingency of the actor's body must be overcome. The other is the *functional* approach of Copeau and Meyerhold, in which the stage setting is declared a 'machine for acting'.

A mid-1930s book on *The Changing Theatre in Europe* refers to over thirty scenographers in Russia and Germany-Austria and half as many in Italy and Spain.[51] Just Craig is listed for England. Granville Barker would credit only Craig (besides Poel) as influence; Norman Macdermott at the Everyman Theatre, Hampstead, and some other independent arts theatres directly emulated him; Yeats used a model of the 'screens' when composing his *Plays for Dancers*; and Craig's influence is apparent in Gray's work at Cambridge. But

---

48 Raymond Williams, *Culture* (London; Fontana, 1981), p. 177.
49 Stourac and McCreery, *Weapon*, p. 261.
50 Packman, 'Introduction', pp. 7–13.
51 Thomas H. Dickinson, *The Changing Theatre in Europe* (London: Putnam, n.d. [c. 1937]).

Craig's major direct influence was on the European mainland, and enthusiasm for his vision in British theatre was tellingly marginal.

Craig's aim for the theatre was that it should eschew literary ambitions and resume its identity as a fine art. Following on from an apprenticeship on Irving's Lyceum stage (until 1897), his early designs for two productions by Martin Shaw's marginal Purcell Operatic Society (1900–2) first introduced his radical ideas for a poetic theatre. He hoped, in vain, that commercial backers might back art for its own sake. Thus, another key determinant on Craig's developing aesthetic is his own 'abstraction': away from practical stage work in order to exhibit, publish and experiment; away from Britain to settle in Florence. Such isolation from the intractabilities of everyday theatre-making was especially conducive to his conception of the 'Artist of the Theatre'; the ideal form, as it were, of the Stage-Director.

On the Art of the Theatre (1911) derides the compartmentalised practice of the contemporary stage, in which writer, musician and painter exercise their separate skills. Craig looks forward instead to a true synthesis of action, scene and voice – three new unities – from which would 'spring so great an art, and one so universally beloved, that I prophesy that a new religion will be found contained in it'.[52] In the same volume the famous essay 'The Actor and the Über-Marionette' elevates acting to an almost holy status: 'Its ideal will not be the flesh and blood but rather the body in a trance – it will aim to clothe itself with a death-like beauty while exhaling a living spirit' (pp. 84–5). In sum, Craig's was a theatre of unities that reached for totality and transcendence. The shifting architectonic masses in his stage designs gesture towards a loosely specified ultimate principle, shimmering between poetry and religion. And linked with the vision of transcendence in Craig's self-assigned role as stage-modernity's prophet is the idea of progress itself.

Craig's totalising and abstract commitment to transcendent principles is clearly cognate with Wagnerian ideals. It also chimes somewhat with Poel's purifying retreat from modern vulgarity, in favour of an idealised 'popular' Renaissance synthesis. In more abstract terms, it arguably also resonates with agit-prop's strident clarification of social structure, both in its dramaturgy and its simplification of staging, with its transcendent principle rooted in the Marxist grand narrative. And a linked grounding can be found in Naturalism's gesture to scientific objectivity. So the question of ultimate guarantees – either transcendent or grounding – often haunted these theatres and their

---

52 Edward Gordon Craig, *On the Art of the Theatre* (London: William Heinemann, 1911), p. 123.

performances. The key dynamic with respect to Craig is between a theatre actively engaged with social transformation and a dream of a theatre that might somehow transcend the social, an autonomous art and pseudo-religion.

Conclusion

If these diverse practices have not been conducive to the telling of a single narrative, perhaps they are amenable to the drawing of an ideological-stylistic map. It shows contingencies everywhere: the swift way in which modernist forms followed on the heels of naturalism, and the often rather blunted way in which either found expression in Britain; the anti-theatrical impetus of the 'new' drama; the consolidation of commercial theatre around entertainment value and surface realism, with various private clubs and marginal enterprises attempting the new. But also perhaps it reveals linked perspectives: a range of practices from dilettante experiment on one hand to thoroughgoing innovation or direct political engagement on the other; within the politically engaged, a spectrum of aesthetics shaped according to political and class affiliation; and dotted here and there a few high points in the integration of aesthetic experiment with clear political purposes, even then plagued by contradiction, as in the continued domination of men over theatrical enterprises that in their different ways reached towards unity and/or equality. Viewed any which way, in this period the English theatres of social commitment and aesthetic experiment produced a wonderfully diverse domain.

PART II

*

SCOTTISH AND WELSH THEATRES, 1895–2002

9

Towards national identities: theatre in Scotland

JAN McDONALD

Country: Scotland. Whit like is it?
It's a peatbog, it's a daurk forest.
It's a cauldron o'lye, a saltpan or a coal mine.
It you're gey lucky it's a bricht bere meadow or a park o'kye
Or mibbe . . . it's a field o'stanes.
It's a tenement or a merchant's ha'.
It's a hure hoose or a humble cot. Princes Street or Paddy's Merkit.
It's a fistfu' o' fish or a pickle o' oatmeal.
It's a queen's banquet o' roast meats and junketts.
It depends. It depends . . . Ah dinna ken whit like your Scotland is. Here's mine.
National flower: the thistle.
National pastime: nostalgia.
National weather: smirr, haar, drizzle, snow.
National bird: the crow, the corbie, le corbeau, moi![1]

Liz Lochhead's celebrated prologue to *Mary, Queen of Scots got her Head Chopped Off* (1989) provides an apposite epigraph to a history of twentieth-century Scottish theatre. The choric commentator, La Corbie, the crow, with whip in hand is a personification of the topic: 'an interesting, ragged, ambiguous creature in her cold spotlight'. Her speech contains a series of oppositions, topographical ('peatbog' or 'coal mine'), socio-economic ('tenement' or 'merchant's ha'') and moral ('hure hoose' or 'humble cot'). This may be seen as reflecting a pattern of binaries that has existed in Scottish theatre itself, and an analysis of its achievements and failures in representing a fluid set of national identities.

This chapter will trace the development of indigenous theatre in Scotland in the twentieth century, without ignoring the foreign influences that shaped it. The history may be divided into two main parts, the watershed being

---

1 Liz Lochhead, *Mary Queen of Scots got her Head Chopped Off* (Harmondsworth: Penguin, 1989), p. 12.

around 1950. Indigenous playwriting and production in the first part is largely amateur. In the second part an embryonic profession burgeoned into a major cultural industry, as a result of the introduction of state funding after World War Two, the creation of a professional training school for actors in 1950, and the promotion of Scottish dramatists, initially through radio, in the 1960s and 1970s.

In the first half of the century there is a marked binary schism between national identity as represented through narratives of the Highlands – historical and mystical in theme and tone – in contrast to those of the Central Belt, which tend to be contemporary, realistic and working class. But both focus on local heroes, whether defeated Jacobites or socialist agitators; both frequently depict a 'lost cause', whether Bonnie Prince Charlie's defeat at Culloden or the workers' capitulation in the miners' strike; both express regret for the passing of some unspecific golden age. For the second half of the century, a binary analysis is less productive although not wholly irrelevant. The rapid development of professional theatre, particularly since 1960, and exposure to international influences fostered a multiplicity of styles and subjects. The productions and plays that I analyse are selected to demonstrate major contrasting trends and to dramatise the philosophy and structure of the companies that created them.

Given these developments, the critical methodology of the 1980s that used 'Scotch Myths' tropes – viz. Tartanry, Kailyardism and Clydeside-ism[2] – is generally inappropriate. Scottish theatre and media have expanded far beyond these concepts. The terms, though, are not wholly redundant. Their interest now lies in how theatre practitioners have engaged with the 'myths' as myths, not as history or as signifiers of cultural inferiority, but as raw material for drama. Dramatists in the 1980s and 1990s were particularly adept in revisioning the past, in the process shedding new light on old critical categories.

It is tempting to map the peaks and troughs of Scottish theatre on to those of the Scottish Nationalist Movement. Surges of indigenous theatrical activity often predated periods of political activism, perhaps indicating new growth in national self-esteem that was first articulated on the stage. The 1920s, when

2 'Tartanry' generally locates Scotland's 'tragic past' in the Highlands, a wild and romantic land of brave men and mystic women, as in Sir Walter Scott's novels. 'Kailyardism' depicts small town life in a sentimental manner, with pithy and endearingly eccentric characters enjoying an idealised parochialism, as in J. M. Barrie's novels. 'Clydeside-ism' focusses on the Central Belt region of heavy industry (ship-building, coal mining, engineering) and the 'Hard Man', characterised by militant left-wing politics, heavy drinking, religious bigotry, violence and the marginalisation of women. See Colin McArthur (ed.), *Scotch Reels: Scotland in Cinema and Television* (London: British Film Institute, 1982); John Caughie, 'Representing Scotland: new questions for Scottish cinema', in *From Limelight to Satellite*, ed. Eddie Dick (London: British Film Institute and Scottish Film Council, 1990).

the Scottish National Party was founded, saw the most vibrant activity from the Scottish National Players. In the 1970s, when the promise of revenue from 'Scotland's' oil led to growing demands for independence, the Citizens', Royal Lyceum and Traverse Theatres flourished, and 7:84 (Scotland) was launched. Thatcherism in the 1980s was anathema to the Scots, not only because of its monetarist economic policy but also because of its apparent determination to convert a Scottish nation into a province of little Englanders. The resultant discontent informed the campaign for devolution throughout the 1990s, when both established theatre companies and a plethora of new young talents fuelled the emergence of a range of national identities that strengthened political assertiveness.

The relationship between 'political autonomy' and 'national identity' is complicated, in that Scotland's relationship with Britain's Westminster Parliament was a series of negotiations for increasing independence achieved over 300 years. The 1707 Act of Union retained Scotland's religious, educational and legal systems, and since 1939 and the creation of the Scottish Office in Edinburgh many agencies were devolved, not least the Scottish Arts Council in 1994. The restitution of the Scottish Parliament in 1999 was just another step in the devolution of political power, albeit a very important one.

The poet C. M. Grieve (*aka* Hugh MacDiarmid), a prime mover in the so-called Scottish Renaissance in literature of the 1920s, wrote, 'it must be recognised that the absence of Scottish nationalism is, paradoxically enough, a form of Scottish self-determination'.[3] Extending this paradox, one might observe that the nature of Scottish theatre, and of theatre in Scotland, certainly has been 'self-determined', but it may not be 'nationalistic'. My coda on 'A Scottish National Theatre' touches on this problematic.

Independent of London?

At the beginning of the twentieth century theatre in Scotland, as in England, was dominated by London touring companies, depicting a world-view alien to Scottish audiences. A *Glasgow Herald* editorial of 1909 declared: 'The visit of the first London touring companies to Glasgow in 1845 must be regarded as the first instalment of the sacrifice of a national birthright.'[4]

So it is ironical that the first serious attempt to make Glasgow theatrically independent was much indebted to a London model, namely, Harley

3 C. M. Grieve (1927), cited in Christopher Harvie, *Scotland and Nationalism*, 3rd edn (London: Routledge, 1998), p. 34.
4 *Glasgow Herald* (27 Feb. 1909).

Granville Barker's Royal Court seasons from 1904 to 1907. The Glasgow Repertory Theatre, founded in 1909, was ideologically and administratively shaped by Barker's success. The Court repertoire was adopted almost wholesale, particularly plays by Shaw, Galsworthy and Masefield. Twenty-six out of eighty actors who worked at the Rep in its first six years were veterans of the Court, and its two principal directors, Madge McIntosh and Lewis Casson, were former Court actors. The 'best' of the London theatrical scene was undoubtedly preferable to the hackneyed commercial imports, but the sheer excellence of the Court repertoire militated against one of the declared aims of the new Glasgow Company:'To encourage the initiation and development of a purely Scottish Drama by providing a stage and acting company which will be peculiarly adapted for the production of plays, national in character, written by Scottish men and women of letters.'[5]

The clamour for an indigenous drama was encouraged by the successful production of Irish plays by the Abbey Theatre in Dublin. But if the influence of the Court was problematic, the model of the Abbey was dangerous. The Irish company had visited Glasgow in 1907 and its enthusiastic reception motivated production manager Alfred Wareing to launch the Glasgow Rep by soliciting contributions from Glasgow citizens to finance the venture. But the Rep had neither the benefit of Abbey benefactor Annie Horniman's fortune nor the talent of established indigenous writers on which to draw. There were also, as ever, very great political differences between the two countries: Ireland was on the brink of a political and cultural revolution; Scotland, or the industrialised Central Belt at least, was very much part of a thriving British Empire.

Enthusiasm for the emergence of a 'Scottish Synge' led to a constant demand for Scottish plays that could not be met overnight. Many critics did not want 'tartan plays' at all, but pressure continued on the Glasgow Repertory Theatre to deliver 'a Scottish theatre equal to the Irish one in national spirit and possibly superior to it in breadth of artistic horizon'.[6]

The Repertory Theatre tried hard to encourage indigenous drama: on average three new Scottish plays were produced every season. These were published in a series entitled 'Repertory Plays', whose foreword claimed: 'The productions by the Scottish Repertory Theatre, produced to satisfy a highly critical and fastidious audience, contain a high percentage of plays that have literary merit, style and construction. They are not ephemeral.'[7] That last judgement sadly has proved wide of the mark: the only text to survive with

5 *Ibid.*
6 *Glasgow Herald* (26 March 1909).
7 The 'Repertory Plays' were published by Gowans & Gray, London.

any reputation is J. A. Ferguson's one-act historical drama, *Campbell of Kilmohr*. Directed by Lewis Casson in the 1914 season, it had many of the qualities that permeated Scottish drama in the first half of the twentieth century: the representation of Scottish history (it is set in the aftermath of the 1745 Jacobite Rebellion), the tension between the romantic Highlanders' self-sacrifice and idealism and the Lowlanders' opportunistic materialism and sly treachery, and the use of poetic and highly figurative language.

Some cultural commentators have argued that the Lowlanders lost their Scottish identity by 'selling out' to the English for financial gain, thus marginalising the west and north of the country while looking to the Highlander to provide a 'true' and 'noble' icon of Scotland.[8] Ferguson dramatises this schism, but there is no irony or overt authorial critique of romantic heroism in the play. The valorisation of the son's 'heroic' death, with which it ends, seems yet another celebration of a Scottish defeat, an indulgence that perhaps has gripped the nation too often. Yet *Campbell of Kilmohr* is a neatly constructed drama with an opening sequence that arouses suspense and a grim twist to its bitter conclusion. Whether or not, as the preface claims, it 'does for Scottish History what Lady Gregory's work has done for Irish History' remains in doubt.[9]

Glasgow Rep's most innovative production was the British première of Chekhov's *The Seagull* in 1909. The principal architect of the success was the guest director, George Calderon, a former diplomat who knew Russia well and who had witnessed Stanislavski's productions at the Moscow Art Theatre. The Rep Company's acting was universally praised largely because 'the ensemble was so perfect' and actors 'subdued themselves to the prevailing tone'.[10]

Despite occasionally styling itself as a 'Scottish Repertory Theatre', the Rep focussed its activities in Glasgow, the 'Second City of the Empire', and the impetus for its founding arose from civic, rather than national, pride. Much was made of the fact that it was the first theatre in Europe to be funded by subscriptions from 'citizens', albeit Glaswegians were not notably supportive through attendance at productions. The Repertory Theatre closed with the outbreak of World War One, ironically after its 1913–14 season had been the first one to make a profit. Its assets were handed over to the St Andrew's Society – an organisation of patriots who were by no means political

---

8 See David McCrone, *Understanding Scotland* (London: Routledge, 1992); Ian Donnachie and Christopher Whatley, *The Manufacture of Scottish History* (Edinburgh: Polygon, 1992); Cairns Craig, *Out of History* (Edinburgh: Polygon, 1996).
9 J. A. Ferguson, *Campbell of Kilmohr* (London: Gowans & Gray, 1915), p. 7.
10 *Glasgow Herald* (4 Nov. 1909).

Figure 9.1 A classic amateur set piece of the 1930s: Gordon Bottomley's *Ardvorlich's Wife*, Scottish National Players, 1930.

nationalists – clearly in the hope that, when peace returned, a new theatrical venture might be launched.

The age of the amateur

Between 1914 and 1943 the amateur movement was responsible for virtually all theatrical activity in Scotland. The first significant company was the Scottish National Players (SNP), established under the aegis of the St Andrew's Society, which had criticised the Glasgow Rep's perceived failure to encourage native Scottish drama. In 1920, using part of the Rep's final season's profits of some £700, it established the Scottish National Players Committee, with aims later stated in the company's newsletter: 'to develop Scottish National Drama through the production by the SNP of plays of Scottish life and character; to encourage in Scotland a public taste for good drama of any type; to found a Scottish National Theatre'.[11] In January 1921 an amateur group performed

11 Constitution of the Scottish National Theatre Society, 16 January 1922. Copy in the Scottish Theatre Archive (hereafter STA), Special Collections, University of Glasgow. See also Karen Marshalsay, 'The quest for a truly representative native Scottish Drama', *Theatre Research International* 17, 2 (summer 1992), 109.

three short plays, including John Brandane's *Glenforsa*, at the Royal Institute in Glasgow, and in November two full-length plays followed at the Athenaeum Theatre. After this successful launch, the Scottish National Theatre Society was formed in 1922.

The Players performed three or four productions per year in hired theatres in Glasgow, but their most significant innovation was country-wide touring, largely under the directorship of Tyrone Guthrie from 1927. The repertoire on the weekly tours included items of mime, songs and sketches as well as full-length dramas. This touring policy was particularly important in a country in which the distribution of population is so uneven, and it was extremely influential in encouraging amateur dramatic activity throughout Scotland, leading to the establishment of the Scottish Community Drama Association.

The SNP produced some 130 plays in the thirteen years of its existence, just over half of which were new works. Popular authors were John Brandane (*Glenforsa* and *The Glen is Mine*, 1923), Reston Malloch (*Soutarness Water*, 1926), Gordon Bottomley (*Gruach*, 1922) and Robert Bain (*James the First*, 1925). It also premièred James Bridie's first play *Sunlight Sonata* (1928), but he took his subsequent work to Barry Jackson at Malvern and later to London. A company stalwart, Reah Murray Denholm, stressed that inspiration came 'from the Dublin Abbey Theatre . . . not from the much beloved but dead and gone Glasgow Repertory Theatre'.[12] Once again worship of the Abbey set Scottish theatre on an aberrant tack: rural Scotland became the locus of the great new Scottish drama, the industrial centre was largely ignored and nostalgic obsession with the 'lost causes' of Scotland's history gained dominance over a more democratic and engaged dramaturgy.

An assessment of the SNP's repertoire and style can be gained through a comparison of one of its greatest successes, John Brandane's *The Glen is Mine*, which had 175 performances, with one of its Reading Committee's rejections, *In Time o' Strife* by Joe Corrie. The refusal of Corrie's play was symptomatic of the SNP's belief that Scottish identity was grounded in the hills and the heather rather than in the pit and the coalfield villages. It may be, too, that the professional middle-class members of the committee were antagonistic to the representation of a working-class community written in a direct style. Yet, despite their fundamental differences in social and political outlook, *The Glen is Mine* and *In Time o' Strife* display singular similarities of form.

Both plays depict small communities under threat. In *The Glen is Mine*, this comes from the young Laird's plan to flood the glen so that his mining project

---

12 R. M. Denholm, *Scottish Player* 4, 32 (1926), 1.

can be powered by hydroelectricity. The only obstacle is Angus's croft, and the play enacts the battle of wits between the crofter and the evictors. *In Time o' Strife* is set towards the end of the miners' strike in 1926, when months without wages have driven the community to near starvation so that some believe that there is no option but to return to work. In both plays, the ideological clash – progress versus preservation, survival versus solidarity – is centred in the romantic liaison of a young couple. In *The Glen is Mine*, Mungo is on the side of progress, science and discovery. Morag upholds 'the old ways of the Highlands':

> MORAG: It's the clean life and the healthy – not the scum and the dirt of the cities.
> MURDO: Learning, Morag! Civilisation. That's the town, not the country.[13]

The old nineteenth-century moral polarisation of rural innocence and urban vice is replayed with a Scottish accent. In *In Time o' Strife*, Wull Baxter too supports progress: he realises that the old way of life is doomed. He wants to emigrate to Canada with his fiancée, Jenny. She, however, under pressure from her family and friends, cannot become the wife of a 'blackleg'.

Both plays open with a song. The sounds of Angus's bagpipes playing the pibroch known as 'The Glen is Mine' introduce the action and give the play its title; strains of 'We'll hang every blackleg to the sour apple tree' to the tune of 'John Brown's Body' permeate the Smiths' home in Corrie's play. Each piece of music introduces the theme. Angus's Glen *is* his at the outset and remains so at the end. With his Highland cunning he is able to outwit the lairds and their agents. The reprise of the tune at the end of the play confirms his ownership.

The marching song in *In Time o' Strife* also has significant connotations for the play as a whole. The fragile solidarity of the workers is not motivated by any commitment to international socialism. What ultimately keeps most of them on strike is what might be described, at best, as a sense of community and, at worst, as a fear of what the neighbours will say about a blackleg. Wull's pragmatic arguments fall on deaf ears: the people of Carhill have courage to fight alongside their neighbours, but cannot stand against them. Few of the strikers have any understanding at all of socialist principles. Bob's repeated cry, 'It's a revolution that's needed here', becomes a running gag, picked up by young Lizzie for comic effect. No one knows what the 'dictatorship of the proletariat' really means. The closing speech, to the strains of 'The Red Flag', may indicate the growth of an international political consciousness, but

---

13 John Brandane, *The Glen is Mine* (London: Constable, 1939), p. 2.

it seems simplistic, even perfunctory, a standard utterance of one of those indomitable working-class mothers that people much of Scottish theatre:

> JEAN: Keep up your he'rts, my laddies, you'll win through yet, for there's nae power on earth can crush the men that can sing on a day like this.[14]

Joe Corrie was himself a miner from Bowhill in Fife and formed the Bowhill Players together with members of his family and other miners and their wives in order to raise money for the soup kitchens in the General Strike of 1926. *In Time o' Strife* was written in the following year, and after its rejection by the SNP he toured the play extensively within Scotland with his amateur group, renamed the Fife Miner Players. The power of these performances and the impact of the directness and sincerity of the acting gave the production almost legendary status in Scottish theatre. Paradoxically, in breaking away from the type of drama favoured by the SNP, Corrie provided a new prototype that was to have considerable influence on Scottish playwriting, namely, the drama of working men in an industrial society.

The SNP flourished under a series of distinguished directors: A. P. Wilson, from the Abbey; Frank D. Clewlow, from the Birmingham Rep; and Tyrone Guthrie, whose brief period with the company brought it much respect. It was a very good training ground for actors, some of whom later participated in the professional theatre, and it had a considerable impact on the development of radio drama in Scotland that helped create the climate in which professional initiatives could flourish. In 1933 a proposal that the Players should become professional was rejected and its backers, Brandane, Bridie and T. J. Honeyman, left the board. The company went into liquidation in 1934 and although some of the players decided to carry on, it had foundered by 1940. A further effort to revive it after World War Two failed after one production.

The SNP, like the Glasgow Rep, was one of Scottish theatre's 'fruitful failures', or, as some might say, 'lost causes'. Tyrone Guthrie's assessment is apposite, 'an enterprise that never really fulfilled its purpose', but which certainly was 'one of the links in the chain which will ultimately result in some form of indigenous drama in Scotland'.[15]

Three other amateur groups, however shortlived, had a significant impact, notably in acting but also in playwriting. The Curtain Theatre was founded in Glasgow in 1933 by performers including Grace Ballantine and Molly Urquhart. Their tiny playing space, seating about 65–70 people, was an L-shaped drawing-room in a large Victorian terraced house. The members believed that little

---

14 Joe Corrie, *In Time o' Strife* (Edinburgh: 7:84 Theatre Company, 1982), p. 67.
15 Tyrone Guthrie, *A Life in the Theatre* (London: Hamish Hamilton, 1960), p. 48.

could be done to promote a Scottish drama until its makers had a theatre of their own. The Curtain 'discovered' the playwright Robert McLellan, presenting his first full-length play, *Toom Byres*, in 1936. His masterpiece, *Jamie the Saxt*, was premièred by the group at the Lyric Theatre in 1937. McLellan – whose later works *Torwatletie* (1946) and *The Flouers o'Edinburgh* (1948) were produced by Glasgow Unity at the Edinburgh Festival Fringe – was a talented comic dramatist, but his commitment to 'Lallans' (a fictitious language) has mitigated against recognition of his plays outside Scotland.

Molly Urquhart founded the semi-professional MSU players (named after her initials) in a renovated church in Rutherglen, near Glasgow, in 1939. Her aim was to create 'another Little Theatre in Scotland where talented players can be given an opportunity to play in their native country . . . The new theatre also hopes to foster Scottish playwrights'.[16] Both objectives were met in part during the five years of the company's existence, although many actors who began their careers in Rutherglen, such as Eileen Herlie, Gordon Jackson and Nicholas Parsons, did not choose to stay 'in their native country'. Nonetheless, Urquhart's gift, according to Parsons, of 'making actors out of people – railway workers, students, teachers, housewives and children', certainly strengthened the indigenous pool of performers.[17] She attempted to reinstate Joe Corrie by producing his play *Dawn*, a domestic drama set against the background of World War Two, but it was banned by the wartime censor for being insufficiently anti-German. The MSU Players were reasonably successful but were always in rather a precarious financial position. James Bridie offered tempting opportunities of regular professional work at the Citizens' Theatre to Molly Urquhart and other regular company performers, such as Duncan Macrae, and the venture was wound up in 1944.

The Curtain's house manager, John Stewart, a Glasgow businessman, opened up the house next door in 1941 and named it the Park Theatre. The Park was an amateur club and presented a standard repertoire of plays by Shaw, Maugham and Priestley, but it also staged the work of a new playwright, James Shaw Grant, whose dramas, such as *Tarravore* (1948), were very much in the Brandane mould. The Park turned professional in 1948 and undertook an extensive tour, which included Pitlochry in Perthshire. There Stewart founded the 'Theatre in the Hills' in a large tent in 1950. By the end of the century, housed in a splendid theatre, the Company had become a valuable tourist attraction.

---

16 Helen Murdoch, *Travelling Hopefully. The Story of Molly Urquhart* (Edinburgh: Paul Harris, 1981), p. 63.
17 *Ibid.*, p. 122.

Other ventures in the late 1930s and early 1940s demonstrate the gradual swing from amateurism to professionalism that was consolidated after World War Two. The tiny Byre Theatre in St Andrews began as the St Andrews Play Club in 1933 under the leadership of A. B. Paterson. It became the St Andrews Repertory company in 1940, employing a professional director, and later benefited from state support to produce a season of plays in repertory from April till December each year. Almost at the end of the 'age of the amateur' two further professional theatres were founded, one in Perth by Marjorie Dence and David Steuart in 1935, and one in Dundee by Robert Thornley in 1939. These were run initially on the lines of provincial English repertory companies, but grew to develop a distinct role in theatre in Scotland.

A people's theatre and a citizens' theatre

The 1940s was a highly significant decade for Scottish theatre. State support facilitated the creation of professional indigenous theatre, and the foundation of the Edinburgh International Festival in 1947 brought world-class companies to the Scottish capital, providing a cosmopolitan audience for Scottish practitioners. Two new theatre companies were founded, Glasgow Unity Theatre in 1941 and the Citizens' Theatre, set up by dramatist James Bridie, in 1943. These ventures had very different theatrical and social philosophies and have often been represented as being in conflict, as indeed they sometimes were, but their coexistence prefigured the later diversity of Scottish theatre. They shared a common audience and a common pool of actors.

Unity was an amalgamation of several amateur groups in Glasgow, most of which had a clear left-wing or anti-fascist political agenda. The outbreak of World War Two brought them together as many of their members were conscripted and numbers declined. Throughout the various manifestos of Unity in the press, in its programmes and in its publicity material the same key phrases are repeated: 'ordinary working people' (as actors, writers and audience); 'the group ideal'; 'social criticism'; 'entertainment and education'; 'a native theatre'; 'a People's Theatre'. Their motto came from Gorky, whose *The Lower Depths* was one of Unity's major successes: 'Theatre is the school of the people, it makes them think and it makes them feel.' At the outset there was no particular commitment to a Scottish repertoire. The aims on the application form for membership were

> To present plays which, by truthfully interpreting life as experienced by the majority of the people, can move the people to work for the betterment of society.

To train and encourage producers, actors, and playwrights in accordance with the above principles.
To devise, import and experiment with new forms of drama.[18]

Initially, the company's work fell into two strands: one group took revue-style shows to hospitals, works, canteens and barracks, while a second produced full-length plays which were broadly socialist, although not specifically propagandist. The repertoire included work by Clifford Odets, Sean O'Casey, Shaw and Ibsen. Increasingly, Unity began to stage new Scottish drama, such as Robert McLeish's *The Gorbals Story* (1946), Ena Lamont Stewart's *Men Should Weep* (1947) and George Munro's *Gold in his Boots* (1947). The social and political concerns of the Scottish *urban* working-class were dramatised for the first time.

After the success of *The Gorbals Story*, a professional or 'full-time' company was created for touring, with two 'part-time' groups left in Glasgow. This schism heralded the demise of the company in 1951. Unity never had a permanent home, performances generally taking place in the Athenaeum Theatre, rented for each show. Its finances were always uncertain and not all of its productions were of a high standard, but it did give some of the citizens of Glasgow a theatre that reflected their everyday existence. The form was social realism in dramaturgy, production and acting, for Unity had close links with the New York Group Theatre and shared its debt to Stanislavski and the Moscow Art Theatre. Unity actors such as Russell Hunter, Roddy McMillan and Ida Shuster, who all began as amateurs, were to contribute greatly to the developing Scottish professional theatre.[19]

James Bridie's Citizens' Theatre took its name from a programme note of the Glasgow Repertory Theatre, which claimed that it was 'a citizens' theatre in the fullest sense of the term'. Nonetheless, in conceiving the new company, Bridie observed: 'The Citizens' Theatre is not taking any old or new repertory movements as its model. It is out to establish something which has not yet been attempted and it will take time.'[20]

The prime movers in its creation and the members of its first board of management were drawn from the Glasgow artistic and intellectual establishment and from the local business community. Several public meetings were held to

---

18 A collection of ephemera, including press cuttings, programmes, etc., relating to the Glasgow Unity Theatre is held at the STA.
19 See John Hill, 'Glasgow Unity Theatre: the search for a Scottish people's theatre', *New Edinburgh Review* 40 (Feb. 1978), 27–31.
20 Cited by T. J. Honeyman in 'Backward glance', in *A Conspectus to Mark the Citizens' 21st Anniversary as a Living Theatre* (Glasgow: Citizens' Theatre Ltd, 1964), p. 7.

launch the project, whose aims were: first, to present plays of didactic and artistic merit; second, to establish a stage for Scottish dramatists and actors; and third, to found a Scottish drama school. A private subscription raised £1,500 and CEMA (Council for the Encouragement of Music and the Arts) gave a guarantee against loss. A Citizens' Theatre Society was formed and within a fortnight it had a thousand members. There was still no available theatre, and Bridie had to fall back on the Athenaeum. There were problems too over the appointment of a director. Bridie approached over nineteen people before settling for Jennifer Sounes, a comparatively inexperienced producer. She was English, as were all the directors of the Citizens' during Bridie's lifetime.

The company was launched in 1943 with a production of Bridie's *Holy Isle*, before a distinguished audience including the Lord Provost of Glasgow and Sir Lewis Casson, the last director of the old Glasgow Repertory. He congratulated Bridie and his board on their magnificent courage in starting this enterprise in wartime. The first-night euphoria was subsequently dispelled by a disastrous production of Goldsmith's *The Good Natured Man*, but fortunately Paul Vincent Carroll's *Shadow and Substance* saved the day, and the first season ended without the company having to draw on the CEMA guarantee. In 1945 Harry McKelvie offered Bridie a ten-year lease of the Princess's Theatre in the Gorbals at a very low rent, and the Citizens' was established in the building it occupied into the twenty-first century.

During Bridie's time there were some brilliant successes. Theatrical legends were created with *The Tintock Cup* (1950 – by Bridie, George Munro and others), Sir David Lindsay's *The Three Estates* (1948 – for the second Edinburgh Festival, directed by Tyrone Guthrie), plus Bridie's *The Forrigan Reel* (1944) and *The Queen's Comedy* (1950). There were also some very respectable plays by Scottish dramatists Robert Kemp and George Munro. Yet Bridie's biographer, Winifred Bannister, called the theatre 'an Anglo-Scottish bairn dressed in the kilt for special occasions'.[21] Bridie himself had said that 'the Scottish theatre must grow from the seed to the root and from the root to the tree. Transplanting will not serve.' But he was forced to transplant by the shortage of Scottish plays of quality and the lack of qualified Scottish directors. This policy left an uncomfortable legacy for his successors.

Two plays that encapsulate the style and philosophy of Unity and the Citizens' are Robert McLeish's *The Gorbals Story* and James Bridie's *The Anatomist*. Both texts might be classed as 'problem' plays: *The Gorbals Story* addresses a social issue of direct relevance to the underprivileged; *The Anatomist* deals

---

21 Winifred Bannister, *James Bridie and his Theatre* (London: Rockcliff, 1955), p. 251.

Figure 9.2 An image of the professional classes: James Bridie's *The Anatomist* at the Gateway Theatre, Edinburgh, 1956–7.

with an ethical dilemma for the professional middle classes. The first play mirrors the importance to Unity of community solidarity in artistic as well as political endeavours, whereas a powerful individual dominates the second (as the Citizens' certainly was during Bridie's lifetime).

The Gorbals Story was written to raise awareness about the problems of homelessness and overcrowding in Glasgow following World War Two. Its first performance was preceded by a speech from squatters' leader P. A. McIntyre, making the case for more and better houses before an audience that included the Lord Provost and other civic dignitaries. The drama aimed to demonstrate how living in appalling social conditions led to poor health, frustration, violence, sectarianism and heavy drinking. The production was a paradigm of Unity's concerns: the absorption with social issues; the focus on the community rather than on the individual; the use of popular variety show techniques in the mixing of comedy, pathos and music in short scenes rather than a continuous narrative. The first performance in Glasgow was at the Queen's Theatre, a variety house at Glasgow Cross, a working-class area. The socialist paper, *Forward*, described it as 'a period piece from the rollicking days when music-hall was an art form of the common folk. It is a suitable setting for the people's drama.'[22] *The Gorbals Story* in both form and the social context of its venue was popular political theatre.

Bridie's *The Anatomist* is based on the murders committed in Edinburgh in 1828–9 by the Irish resurrectionists Burke and Hare, who supplied the flamboyant Dr Robert Knox (via his janitor) with corpses for his lectures on anatomy. Bridie uses history to explore an ethical issue that is still topical: should medical science be allowed to break legal and moral proscriptions in its endeavour to save human life. This is a problem for the professional middle classes who have the leisure and the educational capital to debate it. It was a problem that Bridie, as the medical doctor O. H. Mavor, might well have encountered personally.

Both *The Gorbals Story* and *The Anatomist* present a meaningful image of Scotland. The land of 'the heather and the kilt' is replaced by working-class protest and middle-class ethical debate. For the Glasgow audiences for both the Unity and the Citizens' – and these were by no means discrete – the Tartanry of earlier dramas was irrelevant. A comment by Peggie in *The Gorbals Story* is particularly apposite: 'Ach, Scotland doesna mean much tae Glesca folk, Hector – yon pictures they print on boxes o'shortbread – big blue hills and coos that need a haircut.'[23]

Eastward Look; the land is bright!

After the creative flourish of the 1940s the following decade was rather a bleak time, as theatres closed, audiences declined and no new dramatists emerged to match Bridie or the Unity playwrights. Writers such as Alexander Reid and T. M. Watson became tangled up in an unproductive debate about the use of Scots that far from liberating creativity, inhibited it. Whilst the English theatre had found a 'new wave' in drama at London's Royal Court Theatre, there was no equivalent impetus in the Scottish theatre to reinvigorate the repertoire of Perth, Dundee and the Glasgow Citizens'. Scotland had to some extent already experienced the shift from the drawing-room to the kitchen in the work of Corrie, McLeish and Stewart, and so the 1956 'revolution' heralded by Osborne's *Look Back in Anger* was hardly significant.

The only positive development was the consolidation and growth of a pool of excellent professional actors, trained in the amateur companies and at the new College of Drama in Glasgow, which had been founded, following James Bridie's campaigns, in 1950. Also, the Wilson Barrett Company, which played

22 *Forward* (7 Sept. 1946).
23 Robert McLeish, *The Gorbals Story* (Edinburgh: 7:84 Publications, 1985), pp. 21–2.

seasons in Glasgow and Edinburgh from 1941 to 1955, although never focussing on indigenous drama, provided many Scottish amateurs with a first-class training. Such 'graduates' included Eileen Herlie, Edith McArthur, Robert Urquhart and John Young.

Two initiatives in the 1950s, ostensibly designed to encourage indigenous playwriting, sought to do so by harnessing the talents of popular actors, Duncan Macrae and Stanley Baxter. Macrae established his own company, Scottishows, in 1952 in collaboration with the playwright T. M. Watson, with the twin objectives of 'championing' Scottish playwrights and touring to areas with no access to mainstream theatre, ending the season at the Edinburgh Festival Fringe. The venture, financed personally by Macrae and Watson, was a reasonable success, largely thanks to Macrae's superb comic gifts, but Watson's plays *Bachelors are Bold* (1952) and *Johnny Jouk the Jibbet* (1953) were extremely lightweight, while Bridie's *Gog and Magog* (1954) and Alexander Reid's *The World's Wonder* (1955) were both revivals. A comment in the *Scotsman* is perceptive: '[t]he annual quest for Scottishows is not so much for the ideal Scots comedy as the ideal Scots vehicle for Duncan Macrae'.[24] In 1956 the impresario Henry Sherek, building on the Wilson Barrett model of alternating between Glasgow and Edinburgh and exploiting the talents of Macrae and Stanley Baxter, ran a twelve-week season of ten Scottish plays, all revivals, between April and June. This was designed as a pilot to see if Scottish drama could be a commercially viable proposition. Sherek did not lose money, thanks largely to Macrae's success in a much cut *Jamie the Saxt*, but he did not see fit to repeat the experiment.

An excellent company of Scottish actors, including Tom Fleming, Lennox Milne, Roddy McMillan and occasionally Macrae, assembled at the Gateway Theatre in Edinburgh under the chairmanship of the dramatist Robert Kemp in 1953. The repertoire included plays by Robert McLellan, Alexander Reid, T. M. Watson and Kemp. The Gateway, though, apart from providing opportunities to Scots actors in a barren period, had little lasting influence on Scottish theatre. Moultrie Kelsall, seeing the company as the linear successor of the Scottish National Players, blamed this on the unwillingness of other companies to give the plays premièred at the Gateway subsequent productions.[25]

The Scottish Committee of the Arts Council, concerned with the health of Scottish theatre generally and with the lack of touring product in particular, planned a subsidised Festival of Scottish Repertory Theatre in 1958 in which

24 *Scotsman* (23 Aug. 1953).
25 Moultrie Kelsall, *The Twelve Seasons of the Edinburgh Gateway Company, 1953–1965* (Edinburgh: St Giles Press, 1965).

the companies exchanged productions. Dundee contributed Sartre's *Crime Passionel*; Perth, Shaw's *Caesar and Cleopatra*; Citizens', Chekhov's *The Cherry Orchard*; and the Gateway, Robert Kemp's *The Penny Wedding*, the last being the only financial success, as well as the only Scottish play. The 'Festival' was never repeated. The imposition from above of a national strategy for Scottish theatre did not work then, nor has it since.

The bright hope of the following decade came from Edinburgh, specifically from the old Lyceum and the new Traverse. In 1960 Howard and Wyndham sold the Lyceum to a developer, Meyer Oppenheim, who had plans to create an arts complex on the site, which included the Usher Hall. Horrified at the potential loss of two major venues for the Festival, the Edinburgh Corporation bought the Lyceum after prolonged negotiations and in 1964 the Edinburgh Civic Theatre Trust was created. Members of the trust, largely dominated by city councillors, included the playwrights Robert Kemp and Alexander Reid from the Gateway, which was incorporated into the new venture. The appointment of Tom Fleming as artistic director in 1965 suggested that this was to be 'Gateway Mark 2', but Fleming saw the need for an international repertoire in the capital's theatre, and the first season included Brecht's *Galileo* and two plays, *Police* and *Out at Sea*, by the Polish dramatist Sławomir Mrożek, directed by Jan Kott. The Scottish flavour came in Victor Carin's adaptation of Goldoni's *Servant o' twa Maisters*. For its first Festival, the Lyceum Company presented a highly controversial version of Aristophanes' *The Birds*, *The Burdies* by Douglas Young. Transposing a classical Greek comedy into Scots vernacular and substituting contemporary Edinburgh for ancient Athens seemed an excellent idea for an international festival, but though the exotic settings and costumes received enthusiastic plaudits, the critics were deeply divided and audiences were small. Following this, the board insisted that a reading committee vet the choice of plays. Fleming resigned.

The board was luckier than it deserved to be in Fleming's successor, Clive Perry. An astute financial manager, he also had the vision to appoint three talented associates while at the Royal Lyceum between 1967 and 1976: Richard Eyre, Bill Bryden and Peter Farrago. Eyre mounted a series of excellent productions, frequently of new dramas, including John McGrath's early play, *Events While Guarding the Bofors Gun* (1965). In the early years, neither Eyre nor Perry evinced much interest in promoting a specifically Scottish drama. (This was to emerge strongly when Bryden became associate director.) Nonetheless, the Scottish Arts Council approached the Lyceum in 1970 with a view to establishing a major drama company on a par with Scottish Opera and Scottish Ballet. Perry presented a plan to SAC, but it was never implemented.

The opening of the Traverse in 1963 was a significant event not just for Edinburgh and Scotland but also for British theatre as a whole, for this was among the first new-style professional club theatres (members only) and became the model for many more. Described as an opportunity for audiences to see avant-garde or fringe shows all the year round, it was the brainchild of Jim Haynes, an American whose paperback bookshop had become the hub of alternative arts in the city. Together with Richard Demarco, whose plethora of artistic initiatives had delighted and scandalised the Edinburgh establishment for many years, Haynes founded a theatre that would be free from the Lord Chamberlain's censorship. The Traverse began in a former brothel in James Court. It had a small playing space with seats set on either side, hence the name. Initially its programme was not designed to promote Scottish work, but to bring to Edinburgh audiences adventurous international theatre. Max Stafford-Clark, for example, brought the American La Mama Troupe, inspiring a series of performances devised by the Traverse Company, one of the most successful being *Dracula* in 1969. But it was not so much what the Traverse did that was important, it was what it stood for – a vibrant, slightly risqué, exclusive group of young people with a passion to change the theatre in Scotland and the world. The company moved to a larger venue in the Grassmarket in 1969.

Meanwhile, at the Citizens' there was talent and dissension in equal measure. Throughout the 1960s, certain productions rose meteor-like above the rest of the standard repertory. There was Iain Cuthbertson's production of Pirandello's *Henry IV* with Albert Finney in 1963 and Cuthbertson's own brilliant performance as Armstrong in the première of Arden's *Armstrong's Last Goodnight* (1964). This was directed by Michael Blakemore; he was also responsible for the première of Peter Nichol's *A Day in the Death of Joe Egg* and Brecht's *The Resistible Rise of Arturo Ui* with Leonard Rossiter, both in 1967.

Two years earlier the Close Theatre Club had been established in a property adjacent to the Citizens'. Inspired by the Traverse, it held 150 seats usually arranged on three sides of the stage. The programme included plays by Jean Genet, Marguerite Duras, Olwen Wymark, Harold Pinter, Sam Shepard and Peter Weiss. Very few plays by Scots authors were presented: Tom Wright's *There was a Man* (1966) and Joan Ure's *I See Myself as This Young Girl* (1968) had some success.

These initiatives of the 1960s – two new experimental theatres and a new company at the Lyceum – were important institutional changes that were soon to bear fruit. There was an increase in indigenous writing but, most significantly, an increasing awareness of international theatre influenced both the repertoire and the *mise-en-scène* of Scottish theatre companies. After the doldrum fifties, the sixties set the scene for a flourishing theatrical culture in Scotland during the next thirty years.

'Blood and glitter' – 'tears and sweat' – 'socialists and saints'

The North Sea oilfield developments instilled in many Scots the idea that their nation was potentially wealthy and turned the hitherto marginal Scottish Nationalists into the viable political party that gained eleven seats in the 1974 General Election. The failure of the Devolution Referendum in 1979 temporarily dashed hopes of political independence, but for many theatre practitioners the momentum towards cultural autonomy was accelerated. Despite insidious changes in arts funding under Thatcherism, Scottish theatre blossomed in unprecedented ways. The imaginative and creative intelligence of theatre practitioners (still mostly men) determined to make the prevailing conditions work for their enterprises, rather than wait for ideal circumstances.

Giles Havergal in 1969 inherited the Citizens' Theatre at the lowest point in its history, with diminishing audiences and debilitating strife between artistic directors and the board. Appointed because he had resuscitated the theatre at Watford, he repeated the hitherto successful formula of modern classics with celebrated actors in his first season in Glasgow. It failed, not artistically, but financially. Paradoxically, this was liberating for Havergal and his designer Philip Prowse, who determined that 'If nobody likes what we do, we can do what we like.'[26] The repertoire consisted of European and British classical plays, deconstructed, translated, adapted and reconstructed by dramaturg and dramatist Robert David MacDonald, the third member of the directorial triumvirate.

Prowse's spectacular sets incorporated Meyerholdian mirrors, all-encompassing draperies, monochromatic elegance and vertiginous architecture. Sumptuous costumes in black and white with occasional flashes of scarlet and gold enabled actors to 'present' rather than 'become' their characters. This was a young company, described by Michael Coveney as 'beautiful and noticeably short of talent in the traditional sense'.[27] Cross-gender casting was common, producing some remarkable performances such as Jonathan Hyde as Lady Bracknell, David Hayman as Lady Macbeth and Rupert Frazer as Madame in Genet's The Maids. Predictably, the Citizens' suffered attacks from

---

26 Michael Coveney, The Citz: 21 Years of the Glasgow Citizens' Theatre (London: Nick Hern Books, 1990), p. 37.
27 Financial Times (2 Feb. 1973).

an outraged Glasgow bourgeoisie. A more significant reaction came from Scottish playwrights, none of whose work was presented during the first twenty years of the triumvirate's reign. Robert David MacDonald was Scottish by birth, but his theatrical influences were European rather than 'Scottish'. The Citizens' of the 1970s and 1980s was called a 'theatre of obsession', 'a coterie theatre of high esoteric camp', 'a discotheque of a theatre', 'a theatre of blood and glitter' and, more aptly, 'a house of illusion'.[28] Its aesthetic eschewed naturalism, overt social comment and solemn moralising, yet the elegance and style barely concealed a purposeful puritanism that eventually struck a chord with Scottish audiences.

Meanwhile, the Royal Lyceum in Edinburgh, under the influence of Bill Bryden, was promoting a new vein in ethnic drama. The first breakthrough came with Stewart Conn's *The Burning* (1971), which uses Scottish history to illuminate contemporary consciousness. Bryden went on to direct his own play, *Willie Rough* (1972), based on his grandfather's experiences in the Clydeside shipyards in World War One, which, like Roddy McMillan's *The Bevellers* (1973), owed much to the working-class dramas of Joe Corrie and Unity Theatre. Hector MacMillan's *The Sash* (1973) explored religious bigotry in Glasgow and became a popular commercial success. As a director, Bryden encouraged a rugged style of ensemble playing from the company of Scottish actors, including Rikki Fulton, James Grant, Roy Hanlon, Fulton Mackay, Roddy McMillan and Paul Young. Regrettably for the women performers, such as the talented Eileen McCallum and Jan Wilson, the militant masculinity of the new Scottish drama did not fully engage their potential. The patriarchal, hierarchical management of the Lyceum contrasted sharply with the Citizens' androgynous egalitarianism, which the Edinburgh company despised, as Michael Coveney reported:

> At the Citizens' everyone is on an equal wage of thirty pounds. But one of the Lyceum actors does not consider the work they do as being proper professional theatre anyway; 'dressing up in make-up and funny clothes, that's just amateur stuff . . . there is an undisguised animosity towards the Citizens' felt by those senior actors who played in Glasgow in their younger days.[29]

Havergal's gentle riposte was to describe the Lyceum Company as a band of 'ethnic lovelies'.[30]

28 Jan McDonald, 'The Citizens' Theatre Glasgow, 1969–1979 – a house of illusion', *Maske und Kothurn* 29 (1983), 204.
29 Michael Coveney, 'Pushing on to a national theatre', *Plays and Players* 21, 7 (April 1974), 30.
30 Quoted in Alasdair Cameron, *Twentieth-Century Scottish Theatre: A Study Guide* (University of Glasgow Press, 1988), p. 122.

Figure 9.3 Concerned with their craft: Robert David MacDonald's *Chinchilla*, Citizens' Theatre, Glasgow, 1977.

A comparison of the Lyceum's *The Bevellers* (1973) with the Citizens' *Chinchilla* (1977) demonstrates how the strengths of each company constituted fundamental differences in their artistic and organisational philosophies. *The Bevellers* is a 'work' play securely pitched in the naturalistic mode in its careful reconstruction of a basement workshop in a Glasgow glass company. The action is confined to one day, the pattern of the work schedule dictating dramatic structure. Elegiac in tone, the play portrays men who are, in varying degrees, bonded through their craftsmanship as demand for their skills is diminishing. The community is strictly hierarchical: the unseen 'boss' occupies a room above the workshop to which only the foreman, Bob, has access, and then only when summoned.

In contrast, Robert David MacDonald's *Chinchilla* is set in times 'Past', 'Present' and 'Future', on a Venice beach where the characters are surrounded by the 'paraphernalia of leisure'. The visually arresting setting connotes the beach, as well as a ballet studio, a desert, a playground and a mindscape. As in *The Bevellers*, the characters are concerned with their craft, in this case, dance and movement, but despite their fitful quarrels, conducted largely in Wildean aphorisms, it is made clear that for them success is grounded in their collaborative effort: 'This company is founded on the talents of every man and woman working in it, coming together to create something none of them could have conceived, let alone achieved, on his own. That is a miracle we pull off more times than we have a right to.'[31] In *The Bevellers* a hierarchical 'community' is disintegrating while in *Chinchilla* a supportive collective flourishes, yet in both plays women are marginalised or represented as dangerous, perfidious creatures without an understanding of, or holding aspirations at odds with, the professional satisfaction and sexual fulfilment of a male domain. Like McMillan's bevellers, MacDonald's artists are vulnerable, their craft or art a fragile endeavour: perhaps the 'ethnic lovelies' and the 'watchable beach boys' could be brothers under the skin.

The Lyceum's commitment to indigenous drama was reinforced by Stephen MacDonald, who succeeded Perry in 1976 and continued to promote Scottish writers as he had at the Dundee Repertory Theatre. In 1977 the chair of the Royal Lyceum's board, Ludovic Kennedy, announced that it was the Scottish National Theatre 'in waiting'. This somewhat hubristic claim was received rather coolly by the rest of the theatre in Scotland; no Scottish National Theatre could ever have the sobriquet 'Royal'. Meanwhile, Chris Parr at the Traverse – known as 'St Chris' to the Scottish Society of Playwrights, founded in 1973 – was championing a group of distinguished Scottish writers. Outstanding achievements include John Byrne's *The Slab Boys* (1978) and Tom McGrath's *Animal* (1979), both frequently revived. Many new plays of the seventies were broadcast, thanks to Stewart Conn, then drama director of BBC Scotland, and subsequently published in a collection entitled *A Decade's Drama*.[32] For the first time in the twentieth century a canon of Scottish plays was deemed worthy of preservation and dissemination.

In 1973 John McGrath launched 7:84 (Scotland) with *The Cheviot, the Stag and the Black, Black Oil*. McGrath was a Marxist and the company ostensibly ran on socialist principles, with equal wages and an equal voice for all, although McGrath's political and aesthetic philosophy dominated and it seems that he had the final decision regarding writing and acting. The company included his wife Elizabeth McLellan, and actors Alex Norton, John Bett and Bill Paterson, all three of whom appeared in Billy Connolly's *The Great Northern Welly Boot Show*, which in theatrical form prefigured *The Cheviot* in 1972. *The Cheviot* had an amazing impact on its first audience at a conference in Edinburgh entitled 'What Kind of Scotland?' Presented as work-in-progress, it may have been

---

31 Robert David MacDonald, *Chinchilla*, in *A Decade's Drama* (Todmorden, Lancs: Woodhouse Books, 1980), p. 86.
32 *A Decade's Drama* includes Stanley Eveling's *Mister* (Lyceum, 1970), John Byrne's *Threads* (Traverse, 1976), C. P. Taylor's *Walter* (Traverse, 1977) and others.

the excitement generated when actors take risks with new material that in part produced the standing ovation. The conference topic could also explain why many at the predominantly academic gathering may have interpreted the show as being about Scottish national identity rather than international socialism. There was a similarly rapturous reception at the Scottish National Party's annual conference. The play incites the audience to join with the performers in attacking exploitative authority, but many Scots saw that authority as being vested in the hegemony of London and south-east England rather than in international capitalism. Nevertheless, the strong reception of the show in village halls and community centres throughout the Highlands and Islands was undiminished by critical debate as to the nature of the 'enemy'. Audiences enjoyed participating in a brilliantly presented theatrical experience that affirmed beyond doubt that an 'enemy' existed and still needed to be resisted.

The triumph of *The Cheviot* was followed by other plays by McGrath, such as *The Game's a Bogey* (1974), about the legacy of the Scottish Labour leader James Maxton, and *The Little Red Hen* (1976), which explored the role of women in socialist politics. In 1977 the company was allowed a fallow year by the Scottish Arts Council (SAC) when McGrath took a sabbatical at the University of Cambridge, giving lectures which were published as *A Good Night Out*.[33] In 1978 the musically orientated members of the company, Dave Anderson and David McLellan, formed a splinter group, Wildcat, which had a less overt political agenda. 7:84 continued with two more successful plays by McGrath: *Joe's Drum* (1979), about the failure of the Scots to achieve a devolved government and the election of a Tory government at Westminster, and *Blood Red Roses* (1980), a history of working-class militancy, traced through the political growth of a woman activist. In the early 1980s, however, as Catherine Itzin had argued, 'it was questionable . . . how long it was possible to persist in doing this kind of theatre when the external political circumstances showed no indication of responding or changing in a socialist direction'.[34]

Meanwhile, two new venues for middle-scale touring had been built, in Stirling (1971) and in Inverness (1974), and the repertory theatres had been prospering. Perth, for example, under the redoubtable Joan Knight, played to capacity audiences with a general repertoire; Pitlochry, under Kenneth Ireland's stewardship, presented six (safe) plays in six days to the tourists. The close of the 1970s was a period of optimism for theatre in Scotland: attendances

---

33 John McGrath, *A Good Night Out – Popular Theatre: Audience, Class and Form* (London: Methuen, 1981).

34 Catherine Itzin, *Stages in the Revolution: Political Theatre in Britain since 1968* (London: Eyre Methuen, 1980), p. 128.

were rising and local authorities were emerging as staunch supporters both in terms of capital grants for renovation and new buildings and in revenue grants to companies.

However, the election of the Thatcher government in 1979 was to have a significant effect on theatre in Scotland. SAC policy developed in three ways: first, theatre companies were expected to find alternative sources of funding through box office income and business and commercial sponsorship; second, the monitoring of companies, particularly focussing on boards of management financial control, was intensified; and third, the SAC's Drama Committee was invited on several occasions to devise a blueprint or strategy for theatre in Scotland. The Committee (and many members of the Council) unsuccessfully tried to resist the first; it was forced into complying with the second; and, in the main it failed dismally in the third, for Scottish theatre practitioners showed that they could not (and should not) be so instructed with regard to their location or policy.

This new climate led to the rise and fall of the Scottish Theatre Company. In the early 1980s there was a shortage of large-scale touring product in Scotland, although companies such as Wildcat, Borderline and Communicado and, of course, 7:84 (Scotland) were active in smaller venues. In 1981 the actor Ewan Hooper, following two years of research funded by the SAC, was given £50,000 by the Council to mount a season of Scottish plays, and the Scottish Theatre Company was duly formed specifically to present the work of Scottish writers, to establish a repertoire of existing Scottish plays, to commission new work and to tour widely throughout Scotland.[35] The company was based in Glasgow, with a plan to play in repertoire with Scottish Ballet and Scottish Opera at the Glasgow Theatre Royal. But it was primarily the touring remit that proved problematic: there were too few large-scale receiving houses in Scotland to yield sufficient revenue, and they customarily hosted commercial productions featuring television personalities. The managements were in the main out of sympathy with the STC's artistic vision.

The first season opened in Stirling with Scottish adaptations of Molière's *L'Ecole des Femmes* and Ibsen's *Ghosts* alongside Tom McGrath's *Animal* and Bill Bryden's *Civilians*. It was a qualified artistic success but an unmitigated financial disaster. By the end of the second season the deficit had risen to about £120,000. Hooper resigned and Tom Fleming, veteran of the Lyceum, took over in 1983. The company's major success was a revival of *The Three Estates* at the

---

35 Ewan Hooper, 'A New Scottish Theatre', unpublished manuscript (1981), STA.

Edinburgh Festival, which toured to Poland in 1986. On the surge of euphoria that followed, some saw the company as the elusive Scottish National Theatre. But critical acclaim and nationalist fervour could not outweigh on-going financial problems. In 1987 the Scottish Theatre Trust, which administered the company, announced that it had ceased trading. Other theatre companies in Scotland mourned its demise, but only briefly. The enterprise had been imposed from above, never had much grass-roots support, and attitudes to a quasi-national company were ambivalent.

Another near catastrophe of the 1980s was 7:84 (Scotland). The group's Clydebuilt season in 1982 revived such classics of working-class theatre as George Munro's *Gold in his Boots*, Corrie's *In Time o' Strife* and most successfully Ena Lamont Stewart's *Men Should Weep*. (Giles Havergal's brilliant production established the play firmly in the Scottish canon.) But the season had produced a large deficit, and a total failure in an adaptation of Aristophanes' *Women in Power* mounted by an offshoot company, General Gathering. In subsequent years, as 7:84 (Scotland)'s touring schedules from 1981 to 1987 show, fewer productions were toured to non-theatre spaces and audience numbers fell, at a time when theatre attendances in Scotland as a whole had increased by almost 50 per cent.[36] By 1988 the company was subsidised at a higher rate per seat than any other touring group in Scotland.

The SAC intimated that revenue funding would be withdrawn from the company in the following year, charging it with poor financial management, unsatisfactory administration and composition of the board, and a perceived decline in the standard of artistic output. 7:84 (Scotland) was allowed to appeal against this decision. Jo Beddoe, appointed general manager in April 1988, underlined this point: 'The Arts Council were looking for a reason to keep it going, but it had to be a good reason.'[37] John McGrath resigned, claiming that the SAC's decision was based on political considerations.

David Hayman, a regular Citizens' actor, Gerard Kelly and Jo Beddoe took over. With management structures and financial control redefined, the company focussed on encouraging new writing. Rona Munro's *Bold Girls* (1990) was one result, but financial stability was restored largely by a revival of Hector MacMillan's *The Sash* (1973) and *No Mean City*, an adaptation of H. Kingsley Long's novel (of 1935) about the Glasgow slums. The philosophy of the new

---

36 Greg Giesekam, 'Review of *The Politics of Alternative Theatre in Britain, 1968–1990*, by Maria DiCenzo', *Comparative Drama* 33, 3 (fall 1999), 414.

37 Quoted in Tom Maguire, 'Under new management: the changing Direction of 7:84 (Scotland)', *Theatre Research International* 17, 2 (summer 1992), 132.

régime was described as 'based on the socialist traditions of the working class . . . modern, non-sectarian and aligned to no single political party'.[38]

In 1983, with the support of Glasgow District Council, a group of enthusiasts – including Feri Lean, formerly of 7:84, and Alex Clark, former general secretary of Equity in Scotland – founded Mayfest, designed as a community arts festival. This venture became the second largest arts festival in Britain but foundered on financial problems in the 1990s. Another group of enthusiasts determined to revive the old Close Theatre, destroyed by fire in 1973, literally built with their own hands a new venue in the Tron Church. From tentative beginnings in 1982, Glasgow's answer to the Traverse blossomed into a writers' theatre, particularly under the directorship of Michael Boyd. Many Scottish playwrights, such as Marcella Evaristi, Sue Glover and Rona Munro, received great encouragement and the Tron staged several plays by the Québecois dramatist Michel Tremblay. Bill Findlay and Martin Bowman's translations of Tremblay's *joual* dialect into Scots demonstrated that the 'language problem' that bedevilled indigenous drama in the 1950s had become an asset. Moreover, a new generation of dramatists flourished at the Traverse under Jenny Killick. Peter Arnott's *White Rose*, Chris Hannan's *Elizabeth Gordon Quinn* and John Clifford's *Losing Venice* were produced in 1985. All these have been performed outside Scotland, proof that Scottish theatre was now gaining an international status. Facilitated by the foundation in 1982 of the Scottish Theatre Archive at Glasgow University Library, the increasing national and international strength of Scottish theatre was also reflected in the growth of scholarly publications on drama, theatre history and production analysis.[39]

Cultural capitals

The health and vitality of theatre in Scotland in the 1990s makes it impossible to summarise adequately the various strands of its diversity. The eight building-based companies – the Citizens' and the Tron in Glasgow, the Royal Lyceum and the Traverse in Edinburgh, the Repertory companies in Perth, Dundee and Pitlochry and the Byre in St Andrews – continued to operate. Four companies

---

38 *Ibid.*, 133.
39 See Bill Findlay (ed.), *A History of Scottish Theatre* (Edinburgh: Polygon, 1998); Joyce McMillan, *The Traverse Theatre Story 1963–1988* (London: Methuen, 1988); Christopher Whyte (ed.), *Gendering the Nation* (Edinburgh University Press, 1995); Randall Stevenson and Gavin Wallace (eds.), *Scottish Theatre Since the Seventies* (Edinburgh University Press, 1996); Douglas Gifford and Dorothy McMillan (eds.), *A History of Scottish Women's Writing* (Edinburgh University Press, 1997); Valentina Poggi and Margaret Rose (eds.), *A Theatre that Matters: Twentieth-Century Scottish Drama and Theatre* (Milan: Unicopli, 2001).

toured to a range of venues throughout the country: 7:84, Borderline, Communicado and TAG (Theatre About Glasgow). All these companies received revenue funding from the SAC. But also there was a plethora of emergent companies; for example, Theatre Babel, Theatre Cryptic, Suspect Culture, Boilerhouse, LookOut and Vanishing Point. Tosg (a Scots Gaelic word meaning 'ambassador') founded in 1996, is devoted to a Gaelic repertoire. Some of the younger groups focussed on physical theatre, others on site-specific productions, others on devised work, others on the dramas of one young playwright. Clyde Unity, for example, under its director John Binnie, also a playwright, presented several plays on gay and lesbian themes that successfully toured to community venues as part of a consciousness-raising exercise. LookOut's resident dramatist was Nicola McCartney, who also wrote for the Traverse Theatre and for 7:84. David Greig, a prime mover in Suspect Culture, gained an international reputation for his plays. There was growing interest in providing theatre for, and with, people with special needs: examples included Fablevision and Birds of Paradise in Glasgow, and in Edinburgh, Theatre Workshop and Lung Ha's.

New links between diversity and international status were indicated at the Edinburgh International Festival in 1998 when the Citizens' presented *The Robbers* by Schiller (translated/adapted by Robert David MacDonald), while the Lyceum showed Calderon's *Life is a Dream* (translated by John Clifford) and new plays by Scottish dramatists Liz Lochhead and David Harrower were part of the Traverse's programme. When the Festival began in 1947 no Scottish company was considered good enough to be invited, which is why Glasgow Unity had to gatecrash the capital's party and found the 'Fringe'.

Developments in the 1990s might best be summed up under three headings: space, funding and playwriting, each having a bearing on the other. In Glasgow, the decade saw the creation of four new theatre spaces, and substantial refurbishment of two existing ones. In 1988 Peter Brook selected a 100-year-old factory where Glasgow trams had been built – appropriately renamed the Tramway – as the best venue for his epic production of *The Mahabharata*. The aesthetics and ethics of this cultural appropriation remain questionable, but it had two major repercussions for theatre in Glasgow. Both the Glasgow District Council and Strathclyde Regional Council realised, firstly, that the impact of the arts on the economy and image of the city could be very significant indeed, and secondly, that the Tramway could be a unique resource, particularly for Glasgow's year as European City of Culture in 1990. It became a permanent theatre, hosting performances by world-renowned directors and companies, including Robert Lepage and Theatre Répère from Quebec, the

Wooster Group from New York, the Maly Theatre from St Petersburg, and several return visits by Brook with both theatre and opera. Scottish companies used it successfully too, notably John McGrath's quasi-historical epic, *Border Warfare* (1989), staged by Wildcat, and Communicado with Liz Lochhead's *Jock Tamson's Bairns* (1990), an irreverent look at that perennial Scottish institution, the Burns' Supper. The City of Culture celebrations also inspired the opening of another unlikely 'found space' for theatre in the warren of tunnels that formed the undercroft of Central Station. The Arches, a venue shared by theatre-goers and 'clubbers', provided an unusual ambience. It hosted many innovative young companies and was the venue for the annual National Review of Live Art.

The popularity of the Tramway and the Arches with young audiences led the directors of the Citizens' to respond by converting its foyer into the Stalls Studio, seating 60, and the Circle Studio, which seated 120. In 1995 Irvine Welsh's *Trainspotting*, adapted by Citizens' actor Harry Gibson, began its successful career in the Circle Studio, bringing a new audience to this 'multiplex' theatre. In Edinburgh the new Traverse opened in 1992 with two auditoria, while the old Empire was reborn as the Edinburgh Festival Theatre in 1994, with international-standard production facilities and a glittering glass façade.

Scotland benefited greatly from National Lottery funding, introduced in 1994, with the Byre Theatre, the Tramway, the Tron and the Citizens' receiving major refurbishments. It also helped the creation of new playing spaces for higher education and professional training at the University of Glasgow, the Royal Scottish Academy of Music and Drama and Queen Margaret University College in Edinburgh. Ironically, there was a simultaneous decrease in revenue funding to put shows on the stage. In 1996 the SAC reacted to this anomaly with a 'New Directions' fund, designed to encourage new work, improve accessibility and participation, and enhance training and professional development. One beneficiary was Dundee Repertory Theatre, which gained substantial sums to promote its community programme and later to establish a permanent ensemble company.

The Local Government (Scotland) Act 1994, implemented in 1996, provided a major blow to Scottish theatres through massive cuts in arts funding. In 1994–5 Scotland's local authorities gave £47.6 million to the arts but by 1996–7 this had been reduced to £35.7 million, a cut of 25 per cent. The consequences for theatre were very serious, particularly in Strathclyde and Lothian, where regional council support had been strong. The Citizens' and the Tron in Glasgow and the Lyceum in Edinburgh suffered most. It was doubtful that their losses could be redeemed by an increase in sponsorship.

In the final two decades of the twentieth century commentators noted two significant developments in Scottish playwriting.[40] Firstly, a substantial and growing body of dramatic writing was building up, diverse in subject matter and style, and a recognisable community of Scottish playwrights had been established. Also, the pattern of one major writer working exclusively with one company – Bridie at the Citizens', McGrath with 7:84 (Scotland), for example – was being replaced by several companies drawing from the community of playwrights. Secondly, the issues addressed on stage were no longer exclusively Scottish, but embraced international concerns while retaining a national perspective. Adrienne Scullion has described the shifts in the cultural dynamic that increasing independence brought, asserting that contemporary dramatists met these demands 'by telling stories . . . that are *both* international and outward-looking *and* essentially and immediately committed to work within and about Scottish society'.[41] The prophetic words of director Sandy Neilson, in a television interview in 1981, were being fulfilled:

> In any form of development in drama, you're going to go through . . . playwrights writing about, first of all, their own identity . . . [a] fairly introspective sort of drama – who are we?, who are the Scots? . . . Surely we have an identity and a voice of our own. Then, eventually, that gets written out and . . . we can then go on and expand the subjects to become truly international, yet with a distinctive Scottish voice.[42]

This 'globalisation' of Scottish drama is evidenced in three ways. First, in the number of new plays from Scotland which have been translated or received productions abroad: for example, the works of David Greig, David Harrower and Liz Lochhead. Secondly, in the widening interest by Scottish writers in translating European classics specifically for production in Scottish theatre, of which Lochhead's versions of Molière's *Tartuffe* (1980) and *The Misanthrope* (2000), and Edwin Morgan's translation of *Cyrano de Bergerac* (1992) are prime examples (prefigured by Robert David MacDonald's translations and adaptations of Schiller, Goethe, Lermontov and Goldoni at the Citizens'). Thirdly, in an increase in Scots playwrights' engagement with European culture: for example, in John Clifford's *Losing Venice* (1985), David Greig's *Europe* (1993) and

---

40 See Peter Zenzinger, 'The new wave', in Stevenson and Wallace, *Scottish Theatre Since the Seventies*, pp. 125–37; Randall Stevenson, 'Perfect days: Scottish theatre at the millennium', in Poggi and Rose, *Theatre that Matters*, pp. 111–119; Adrienne Scullion, 'Self and nation: issues of identity in modern Scottish drama by women', *New Theatre Quarterly* 17, 4 (Nov. 2001), 373–90.
41 Scullion, 'Self and nation', 388.
42 Quoted in Stevenson, 'Perfect days', 117.

Chris Dolan's *Sabina!* (1996); in Marcella Evaristi's *Commedia* (1982) and Ann Marie di Mambro's *Tally's Blood* (1990), which drew on their Scottish-Italian backgrounds for subject and form; and in Rona Munro's *Bold Girls* (1990) and Nicola McCartney's *Laundry* (1994), both set in Northern Ireland, while the latter's *Heritage* (1998) re-examined conflicting national identities in the context of immigrants to Canada.

Whilst sterile preconceptions of the true nature of a 'Scottish play' were happily dispersed in cultural diversity, the rapid growth in the number and quality of Scottish playwrights was evolutionary rather than revolutionary. As the writers embraced the wider world in their plays, they simultaneously drew on the slow emergence of an indigenous dramatic tradition in the twentieth century. By revisioning and reconstructing the dominant themes of earlier works, they fostered more flexible and more inclusive Scottish cultural identities.

Women dramatists in particular, concerned with gender as well as with political identity, took a lead in refashioning the predominantly male canon. The strong tradition of romantic historical drama that nostalgically privileged Mary, Queen of Scots and Bonnie Prince Charlie plus the Jacobite rebellions was recast by Liz Lochhead in *Mary, Queen of Scots got her Head Chopped Off* (1989) and by Sue Glover in *The Straw Chair* (1988). Each play exploits historical icons – the beautiful, wronged Mary and the brave patriotic Jacobites – to explore contemporary themes of power, personal and political, and the marginalisation and silencing of women. Male writers such as John McGrath in *Border Warfare* (1989) and Bill Bryden in the *Big Picnic* (1994) readdressed the genre of the history play through innovative staging and spectacular theatrical effects.

The myths and legends of the Highlands and islands that inspired the Scottish National Players, epitomised in Neil Gunn's *The Ancient Fire* (1929), were likewise appropriated by, for example, Sue Glover in *The Seal Wife* (1980) and Rona Munro in *Piper's Cave* (1985) and *The Maiden Stone* (1995). The first two plays examine the myth of the selky – the seal who turns into a woman – by reframing it as a paradigm for female mutability, women's capacity for change and rebirth being contrasted with male inflexibility. *The Maiden Stone*, re-evaluating the legend of the kitchen wench turned into stone to save her from the devil, explores issues of maternity and female sexuality.

The celebration of male communities in, for example, Roddy McMillan's *The Bevellers*, Bill Bryden's *Willie Rough* and John Byrne's *The Slab Boys*, was countered by female 'equivalents'. Women writers, notably Rona Munro in *Bold Girls* (1990) and Sue Glover in *Bondagers* (1991), focussed on communities of women, inclusive and mutually supportive communities that lack masculine rites of initiation.[43] Other new writers recasting the stereotypical characters of earlier drama included Marcella Evaristi in *Commedia*. In contrast to earlier idealisations of the mother as an all-cherishing, all-sacrificing stalwart pillar of family solidarity – such as Peggy in *The Gorbals Story*, Jean in *In Time o' Strife* and Maggie in *Men Should Weep* – Evaristi's Elena breaks free from the received role of an Italian widow, engages with a younger lover, and transforms the 'kitchen' into a site of carnival and anarchy. The 'tenement' play was critiqued in Munro's *Your Turn to Clean the Stair* (1992), where the working-class solidarity celebrated by McLeish, Stewart and others is replaced by mutual suspicion and fear as a psychological murder mystery unfolds and undermines preconceptions of a supportive community. Chris Hannan, in *Elizabeth Gordon Quinn* (1985), also challenged the myths of the indomitable mother and of working-class camaraderie in urban tenement culture. Randall Stevenson suggests that Hannan might be 'the man finally to lay the ghost [of Sean O'Casey] to rest'.[44]

Finally, earlier celebrations of the Glasgow 'Hard Man', a self-destructive violent folk hero, were attacked in a short but moving piece, *The Letter Box* (1989) by Ann Marie di Mambro, in which male physical abuse is exposed in a monologue by a battered wife speaking to her child. The exploration of gender identity was also extended by several writers who took the gay community as their subject, most notably John Binnie in *Killing Me Softly* (1987), *A Little Older* (1992) and *Backgreen Belter* (1994), and in Rona Munro's *Saturday Night at the Commodore* (1989) and Ann Marie di Mambro's *Brothers of Thunder* (1994). Liz Lochhead's *Perfect Days* (1998) employs Binnie's favoured device of exploring homosexuality in the context of a male–female friendship.

Many playwrights in Scotland at the end of the twentieth century could legitimately claim international status. Some, indeed, were more celebrated abroad than at home.

Coda: a Scottish National Theatre?

The cry for a Scottish National Theatre has risen sporadically in Scotland's past and, like a lament on the bagpipes, vanished into relatively thin air. Many of the ventures touched on in this brief history laid claim to the title, but none has permanently made it their own.

43 See Adrienne Scullion, 'Female pleasures and masculine indignities', in Whyte, *Gendering the Nation*, pp. 169–204.
44 Randall Stevenson, 'In the jungle of the cities', in Stevenson and Wallace, *Scottish Theatre Since the Seventies*, p. 108.

In the wake of the Referendum in Scotland in 1997 that empowered the Westminster government to implement the creation of a separate legislative assembly, there was in many areas of Scottish public life a new impetus towards collaboration and inclusion. The Federation of Scottish Theatre, founded in 1955, had been little more than a talking shop for well-established building-based theatres, but in the new political climate, and with the advent of so many innovative groups, it became an agent that potentially could unite all companies in a federal national theatre. In contrast, the increased measure of national independence also brought with it, in the manifesto of the Scottish National Party, a renewed demand for a Scottish National Theatre, a flagship company that would 'make a set' with Scottish Opera and Scottish Ballet.

Those in favour of a Scottish National Theatre believed it would strengthen reassertions of national identity by providing an 'emblem of nationhood'; it would also bring Scotland culturally into line with other nations. Others argued that Scotland must set its own theatrical agenda, and not become a victim of residual cultural imperialism by aping institutional structures that were appropriate to other nations at other times. In addition, there was the problem of what image of nationhood a Scottish National Theatre would present. Were it to follow the pattern of its English counterpart in London, it would universalise the taste of the cultural hegemony rather than foster the cultures of subordinate groups. The radical tradition in Scottish politics, and in Scottish theatre, militated against the establishment of such an institution.

The majority of members of the Federation believed that there already was a national theatre, existing in the rich diversity of companies that were active in the country, and promoted this by including in their programmes a note which read: 'The ____ theatre or company is a member of the Scottish National Theatre Community.' The majority of practitioners wished the Scottish National Theatre to be the sum of its constituent parts, celebrating Scotland's 'mongrel culture' and its mongrel theatre.

Developing this idea, the Federation submitted a formal proposal to the Scottish Arts Council in August 2000. The essence of the suggested model was

> a National Theatre for Scotland as an independent commissioning body which works in a similar way to the Edinburgh International Festival. It would have a remit to commission work from theatre artists and companies of all scales and disciplines . . . This work would make up seasons or programmes of a National Theatre for Scotland which would be toured to audiences throughout Scotland.[45]

45 Federation of Scottish Theatre, *Proposal for a National Theatre for Scotland* (Edinburgh: Federation of Scottish Theatre, June 2000), p. 5.

Subsequently, an independent working group was set up by the Scottish Executive to conduct a feasibility study into the establishment of a national theatre organisation for Scotland. The group reported in 2001, endorsing the Federation's vision of the National Theatre as 'a creative producer', but pointing out that such a scheme could not 'by itself solve the problems of under-investment in Scotland's theatre infrastructure'.[46]

By this point the Federation's members were becoming increasingly concerned that, unless substantial further funds became available, the scheme would inevitably founder. The Executive, following a general review of theatre in Scotland, in 2002 allocated an additional £3.5 million over the following three years in order to build up an infrastructure. Hence 2004 was set as the year in which the Executive wished a National Theatre, building on existing companies, to begin operations. The Scottish National Theatre Community may be, like all communities, an 'imagined' one in Benedict Anderson's sense, but then what else is theatre but someone's imaginings?[47]

46 *Scottish National Theatre: Report of the Independent Working Group*, May 2001, introduction by David Smith, p. 5.
47 Benedict Anderson, *Imagined Communities* (London: Verso, 1983).

10

Case study: Ena Lamont Stewart's
Men Should Weep, 1947

NADINE HOLDSWORTH

Glasgow Unity first performed Ena Lamont Stewart's *Men Should Weep* at the Athenaeum Theatre, Glasgow on 30 January 1947. After the company closed in 1951, the play fell into obscurity until John McGrath staged a rewritten version for 7:84 (Scotland)'s 1982 Clydebuilt Season. The long absence of this play from the public arena is remarkable considering that it provided a major theatrical landmark for the representation of Scottish, class and gender identities. This chapter takes the opportunity offered by these two texts, productions and their critical reception to make a transhistorical comparison of the relationship between theatre and its wider context. Taking the play's central thematic framework of gender politics, poverty and notions of community, my argument explores how these two productions intersected with and revealed a great deal about their immediate social, political and economic landscapes. By highlighting Glasgow Unity's and 7:84's distinct use of staging, theatrical apparatus and acting techniques, I also aim to illuminate the responsiveness of performance to historical change.

Prior to writing her first play, *Starched Aprons* (1945), which deals with the trials and tribulations of everyday hospital life, Lamont Stewart was frustrated with the trivial and irrelevant representations she witnessed in post-war Scottish theatre: 'I came home in a mood of red-hot revolt against cocktail time, glamorous gowns, and under-worked, about-to-be deceived husbands. I asked myself what I wanted to see on the stage, and the answer was "life". Real life. Real People. Ordinary people.'[1] One of the few companies addressing Lamont Stewart's concerns was Glasgow Unity, which under its artistic director, Robert Mitchell, rejected the London-led, middle-class theatrical diet dominant in Scotland at the time. Discarding the retreat into nostalgic images of historical settings and rural idylls prevalent in the portrayal of

---

1 Ena Lamont Stewart, programme note, 1947 production of *Men Should Weep* (Glasgow Unity), Scottish Theatre Archive (hereafter STA), Special Collections, University of Glasgow.

'Scottishness' – Tartanry and Kailyard – Glasgow Unity promoted a 'people's theatre' that addressed topical socio-political issues and the experiences of the urban working class of Scotland and, in particular, Glasgow. Mitchell nurtured authentic self-representation by working with indigenous talent to produce a social realist 'native drama' that engaged with the specificities of its locale and audience. For example, Glasgow Unity's great triumph was Robert McLeish's *The Gorbals Story* (1946), which drew on his experience of living in the slums of the Gorbals in a forceful polemic on the contemporary housing crisis. In the same year that McLeish's play was produced, Mitchell commissioned Lamont Stewart to write about a working-class woman trying to bring up her family during the Great Depression of the 1930s. *Men Should Weep* was the result.

Set in a tenement flat in the Gorbals district of Glasgow, the protagonist is Maggie Morrison, a working mother of seven children whose teetotal husband John is unemployed. Their children suffer the diseases of poverty: Christopher has rickets and Bertie has tuberculosis. They share responsibility for the care of John's mother with his acerbic sister Lizzie, and their already cramped conditions are made worse when their son, Alec, has to move in with his wife Isa after their tenement collapses. The action focusses on Maggie's struggle to cope with the pressures of extreme deprivation aided by support from her independent sister, Lily, and help from a community of working-class women. The situation reaches crisis point as the family unit begins to disintegrate when their daughter Jenny leaves home and Bertie is hospitalised. At the beginning of Act 3 the tone temporarily brightens as John finds a job, but by the end of the play Bertie dies, John steals from Lily and returns to drink, Alec kills Isa, Granny is forced into the poorhouse, Jenny returns destitute and Maggie dies in childbirth. This catalogue of doom was, of course, a risky dramatic tactic: teetering close to melodrama, the play demands a strong production to rescue it from overstatement.

A new realism

In 1947 stage representations of a Scottish socio-economic underclass were rare and to secure the support of a working-class Glasgow audience it was vital that the overall design and performances were credible. Glasgow Unity's production stressed the accuracy and poignancy of its depiction by employing a social realist form, and the effectiveness of its documentary imperative was achieved by several key factors. Firstly, Lamont Stewart drew extensively on observations and overheard conversations to generate authentic dialogue, later recalling that being a receptionist at Glasgow's Royal Hospital for Sick Children

Figure 10.1 In the crowded tenements of the Gorbals: Ena Lamont Stewart's *Men Should Weep* at the Glasgow Unity Theatre, 1947.

'afforded me a splendid, if often harrowing, opportunity to indulge in blatant eavesdropping'.[2] This quality connects *Men Should Weep* to the pre-war 'mass observation' documentary movement, which was concerned to acknowledge and record the life of everyday working people, while Glasgow Unity's staging made the production a precursor to the 'kitchen sink' realism of the post-1956 theatrical 'revolution'.

Employing a conventional box set, the usual setting of a middle-class drawing-room was replaced by a slum tenement dwelling replete with real furniture, a kitchen sink, cheap trinkets and props, all serving to authenticate the scene. The production created an environment of deprivation and cramped conditions by fulfilling the text's demand for furniture 'piled high with a miscellaneous collection of household and personal effects' and 'a row of well-worn nappies'.[3] The claustrophobic overcrowding of people metaphorically and literally living on top of each other was also theatricalised by the 'dunt' – knocking – on the ceiling from the tenement above or holler through the window that summoned the neighbours. The constant cries of children,

2 Ena Lamont Stewart, programme note, 1982 production, *Men Should Weep*, 7:84 (Scotland), STA.
3 Ena Lamont Stewart, 'Men Should Weep', original unpublished manuscript, p. 1, STA.

Granny's wailing, fighting neighbours, Bertie's hacking tuberculosis cough and calls of hunger punctuated the action. The function of these effects in highlighting extreme socio-economic hardship was strengthened at the start of Act 3, when an uncluttered kitchen and newly purchased items – including a wireless sounding out jazz rhythms that replaced the cries of the needy – signalled John's success in securing employment.

The acting similarly articulated a Scottish, working-class presence. A review in the *Scotsman* commended the energy, commitment and localism of the performers: 'Here is Glasgow humour, quick, raw, homely, at its best, and it is "put over" with punch and vigour by a company of outstanding ability'.[4] The use of broad Glaswegian dialect, idioms and local humour aimed to encourage identification in the audience. Countering the conventional middle-class association of regional dialect with restricted vocabulary, the articulate speech of the characters sought to empower the audience by implying pride in its linguistic heritage. This effect was enhanced by the performers' familiarity with the rhythms and tones of the demotic dialogue, which captured the verbal richness and witty, quick-fire banter of the Glasgow streets. The liberating vitality of Glaswegian vernacular and the peoples' self-deprecating humour in the face of adversity is celebrated in the opening scene:

GRANNY: I'll be awa soon . . . Aye. It'll no be lang afore I'm awa. Aye. Ma lif's ebbin. Ebbin awa.

MAGGIE: Och, it's been ebbin ever since I met ye; but the tide aye seems tae come in again.[5]

The critic for the *Glasgow Herald* applauded the impact of Lamont Stewart's 'excellent dialogue, salty and full of the local idiom' and her 'sense of humour',[6] although this was not a unanimous response. The *Daily Record*'s critic dismissed this comic element as a weakness: 'Mrs Stewart has achieved the sordidness and squalor which exists in Glasgow's East End, but unfortunately an error is apparent in an excess of comic relief which incites the audience to humour when tragedy holds the boards.'[7]

The tragic aspect was most at risk in the final act, as the melodramatic and sentimental resolutions of the narrative placed a strain on the social realist production. One review suggested that events were 'well-told . . . (with the obvious exception of a highly dramatic murder scene)'[8] – this involved Isa

4 Anon., 'Men should weep', *Scotsman* (31 Jan. 1947), 6.
5 Ena Lamont Stewart, *Men Should Weep* (London: Samuel French, 1983), pp. 1–2.
6 Anon., 'Tenement life on the stage', *Glasgow Herald* (31 Jan. 1947), 6.
7 Anon., 'First performance of "Men Should Weep"', *Daily Record* (31 Jan. 1947), 6.
8 Anon., 'Men should weep', *Scotsman* (31 Jan. 1947), 6.

and Alec's violent battle staged against an emotive soundtrack of Salvation Army Christmas carols. Similarly, the relentless presence of infant mortality, death in childbirth and human despair throughout Act 3 was bleakly counterpointed by the unremitting sound of the neighbours fighting upstairs. As the *Scotsman* argued, the sheer volume of tragic events paradoxically undermined authenticity as 'the sequence of tragedy and distress is hardly likely to occur in any single household'.[9] The denouement, especially, placed the production perilously close to domestic melodrama. But this quality is surely indicative of the play's place in the immediate post-war history of Scotland, as a sense of stasis and pessimism seems to have dominated the period.

Nevertheless, many reviews referred to the success of the production as a 'powerful sociological document'[10] and even accused Glasgow Unity of concentrating too much on social authenticity at the expense of theatricality. Typical in this respect is a review from the *Bulletin*: 'the piece lacks drama. It reports, and very accurately, a series of incidents in the life of the Morrisons. But mere reporting never made a play.'[11] It is also historically interesting that the predominantly male critics steadfastly ignored Lamont Stewart's challenging treatment of gender, an aspect that was central to the success of the play thirty-five years later. However, even a brief survey of the social conditions that produced the real tragedy of the Gorbals indicates why Lamont Stewart should have taken such dramaturgical risks.

Historical context

Men Should Weep clearly engages with the climate of hardship faced by many working-class communities in the 1930s, which was principally caused by the unprecedented increase in unemployment as traditional coal, steel and shipbuilding industries collapsed. This economic decline hit the north and the lowlands of Scotland in particular, as John Stevenson and Chris Cook highlight: 'whereas Glasgow [had] a total of 89,600 unemployed in 1936, Birmingham, a city of comparable size, had only 21,000'.[12] Another pressing issue in Scotland was the disproportionately high level of dilapidated housing and overcrowding. In *No Gods and Precious Few Heroes* Christopher Harvie quotes a 1935–6

---

9   *Ibid.*
10 *Ibid.*
11 Anon., 'Unity play lacks drama', *Bulletin* (31 Jan. 1947), 3.
12 John Stevenson and Chris Cook, *Britain in the Depression: Society and Politics 1929–39*, 2nd edn (London: Longman, 1994), p. 69.

survey which disclosed that 22.5 per cent of Scottish homes were overcrowded compared to 3.8 per cent in England.[13] In turn, poor living conditions, coupled with malnutrition, ensured the spread of diseases such as tuberculosis, rickets and anaemia that contributed to many premature deaths.

In the post-World War Two context, memories of the Depression and the 'war effort' produced widespread support for the social welfare reform recommendations made by the Beveridge Report of 1942. The election of a Labour government in 1945, with a majority of 146, ensured legislation for the foundation of the Welfare State, but its implementation proved complex and slow, and in some areas working-class living conditions actually deteriorated. In the same year that *Men Should Weep* opened, Glasgow Councillor Harry McShane produced a report highlighting the 98,000 Glasgow families awaiting relocation to council housing and forced to suffer insanitary accommodation, infestation and chronic overcrowding.[14] He also linked these conditions to the high rates of maternal and infant mortality still evident in the deprived Gorbals area, which 'of the thirty-eight wards in the city . . . is either at the top, or second from the top, when, each year, the figures relating to infant mortality are made known'.[15]

Lamont Stewart tackles all these macro-political concerns through the micro-environment of the Morrison family unit, echoing *The Gorbals Story* by establishing a voice and representation for people usually restricted to nameless and faceless statistics. Through its relentless portrayal of the blatant and the insidious consequences on family life of chronic poverty, *Men Should Weep* served as an urgent rallying cry for the implementation of the Welfare State. In terms of material conditions and patterns of consumption, the absences are palpable – not enough food, no hot water and no space to live comfortably. An enforced culture of make do and mend characterises the existence of the Morrison family and their neighbours.

The hardships faced by women raising families in poor socio-economic conditions is predominant in contemporary social surveys, such as Margery Spring Rice's *Working-Class Wives* (1939), which concludes that 'there are three inter-connected factors which cause the life of the working-class housewife to be too difficult and strenuous. The first is poverty, the second ill-health and the

---

13 Christopher Harvie, *No Gods and Precious Few Heroes: Scotland 1914–1980* (London: Edward Arnold, 1981), p. 70.

14 Harry McShane, 'Glasgow's housing disgrace (1947)', in *Labour and Class Conflict on the Clyde 1900–1950*, ed. Robert Duncan and Arthur McIvor (Edinburgh: John Donald, 1992), p. 28.

15 *Ibid.*, p. 42.

third lack of trained knowledge.'[16] In many ways Lamont Stewart theatricalises Spring Rice's findings; for instance, Maggie's aversion to the hospital reflects the survey's results concerning women avoiding the professional public sector services from a fierce sense of pride and a fear of being judged and found wanting. Maggie's unplanned pregnancy and death in childbirth also supported calls for the dissemination of contraceptive advice made by the Women's Co-operative Guild. Conversely, the play departs from the story of subordination revealed by Spring Rice's account and chimes strongly with more recent feminist research, such as Elspeth King's *The Hidden History of Glasgow's Women*.[17] Eschewing the conventional characterisation of working-class women as helpless victims of circumstance, this study documents how the city's communities engaged in collective resilience, resistance and resourcefulness. Lamont Stewart's images of women sharing meagre resources and a common search for dignity in *Men Should Weep* are true to life.

A notable omission in Spring Rice's account is discussion of the role of men in determining the living conditions of working-class women. In contrast, *Men Should Weep* presents a penetrating critique of patriarchy, while simultaneously addressing a crisis in traditional constructs of working-class masculinity. Lamont Stewart attacks the sexual division of labour, as John's failure to help in the domestic arena clearly implicates him in Maggie's downtrodden existence of childbearing, child care, parent care, incessant domestic toil and her cleaning job. However, she does not offer a simplistic attack on men per se. Clearly, many men were humiliated by the failures of industrial capitalism, and *Men Should Weep* captures the destabilising, demoralising and disempowering impact of unemployment on the traditional male role. The male characters display aggressive posturing in their attempts to reassert their masculine identity, whether through excessive drinking and/or domestic violence. Whilst ignoring his domestic responsibilities, John steadfastly clings to a mythic head of the household role, even as he is constantly undermined by Lily's presence. These brave scenes must have made uneasy viewing for the working-class men in the audience, forced to confront a head-on expression of their culpability and, according to performer Eddie Boyd, a 'feminist element in a great big macho city'.[18] Robert Mitchell subsequently claimed that this unease influenced the limited commercial success of the production:

16 Margery Spring Rice, *Working Class Wives: Their Health and Conditions*, 2nd edn (London: Virago, 1981), p. 188.
17 Elspeth King, *The Hidden History of Glasgow Women: The New Factor* (Edinburgh: Mainstream, 1993).
18 Eddie Boyd, interview with Birmingham Film Workshop (1983), STA, tapes 37–8.

it was such an indictment of men's responsibilities in the home that . . . Well, they liked it at the start, they laughed at the funny bits . . . But it was so near home in Glasgow . . . It was hitting the man in Glasgow . . . Well, somehow they didn't go 'you must see that'.[19]

In response, Glasgow Unity's publicity targeted a female audience by hailing the piece as 'The play every woman must see'.[20] Thirty-five years later the accuracy of the depiction was confirmed during a discussion at the Clydebuilt Season, when a female member of the original audience recalled her shock at seeing her life on stage and the giggles of recognition which rippled across the women in the audience.[21]

7:84 (Scotland)'s revival of *Men Should Weep*

Lamont Stewart rewrote *Men Should Weep* in 1974, but it did not receive another production until 7:84's 1982 Clydebuilt Season. Research by the company uncovered several other plays expunged from Scottish theatre history, a selection of which formed the celebratory season, which was designed, according to John McGrath, to display the diversity, 'cultural breadth and maturity of the Scottish Labour Movement'.[22] Staged at Glasgow's Mayfest and the Edinburgh Festival, *Men Should Weep* was joined by Joe Corrie's *In Time o' Strife* (1927), George Munro's *Gold in his Boots* (1947) and Ewan MacColl's *Johnny Noble* (1945). With the exception of *Men Should Weep*, the emphasis was on revival; for example, David Scase was invited to reconstruct the folk-ballad style of Theatre Workshop's première production of *Johnny Noble*, in which he had played the title role. In contrast, *Men Should Weep* was transformed to highlight the disturbing correlation of the play's subject to the contemporary socio-economic results of Thatcherism as, once again, traditional industries collapsed, unemployment figures soared and the dismantling of the Welfare State was a frightening possibility.

Directed by Giles Havergal of the Glasgow Citizens' Theatre, *Men Should Weep* was distanced from the other period pieces in the season, not only by Lamont Stewart's rewrite, but also by the director's treatment of it in performance. A largely forgotten play was quickly hailed as an important 'state of the nation' piece as it toured major venues in Scotland before embarking on a five-week run in London at the Theatre Royal, Stratford East.

19 Robert Mitchell, interview (1967), STA, tape 60.
20 Publicity flyer, *Men Should Weep*, STA.
21 'Women in Scottish People's Theatre', Clydebuilt discussion, 17 May 1982, STA, tape 71.
22 John McGrath, programme note, 1982 production.

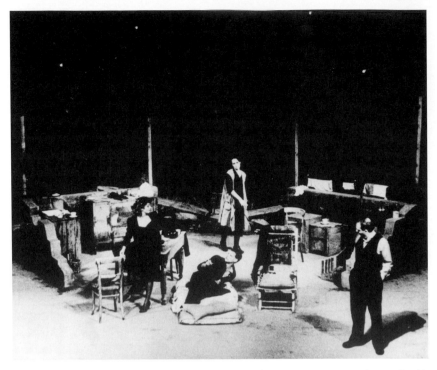

Figure 10.2 The Gorbals slums as collective wasteland: Ena Lamont Stewart's *Men Should Weep* staged by 7:84 Theatre Company (Scotland), 1982.

Unlike the other productions in the Clydebuilt Season, *Men Should Weep* also signalled something of a departure from 7:84's overt Marxist agenda, as it did not directly attack the social organisation of society or provide a call for collective political action. Nevertheless, the play's current political ramifications were emphasised as it toured against a backdrop of dissent and industrial action. Programme information included extracts from Muriel Brown and Nicola Madge's book *Despite the Welfare State* (1982), which documents research into deprivation and disadvantage in late twentieth-century Britain:

> roughly ten million people are suffering from poverty, over four million of them in families with children . . . three million are currently unemployed. One million eight hundred thousand households are living in physically unsatisfactory housing conditions in terms of over-crowding, shortage of amenities or general unfitness.[23]

23 Muriel Brown and Nicola Madge, *Despite the Welfare State* (London: Heinemann, 1982), cited in programme note, 1982 production.

On 22 September 1983, a National Day of Action, the company gave a benefit performance for the National Health Service Strike Fund. At the end of this performance Elizabeth MacLennan, who played Maggie, appealed to the audience to learn from history and to unite behind the Labour Movement:

> it is well to remember that the advances in Health and Welfare – albeit inadequate – that have been achieved since the Thirties were due to the unremitting and successful struggle of the Labour Movement . . . Today's vicious Tory government is intent on dismantling all that . . . We will not accept this . . . We will not go back to the 1930s.[24]

It is instructive to compare this call for resistance at the close of the 1982 production with the exhibition of working-class fatalism that concluded the original one, when Jenny comforted her father with 'It's no your fault – it's jist the way things are.'[25] Resignation to limited opportunity is replaced by a positive vision of the indestructibility of communities faced with dire socioeconomic conditions; the play is newly inflected by the post-1979 context, as oppositional campaigns and resistance were manifest in the social, industrial and personal arenas.

Gender matters

Whereas in 1947 the only reference to gender politics in reviews of *Men Should Weep* was in Winifred Bannister's comment that 'this bitter vitriolic tirade against the male of the species is its greatest weakness',[26] the success of 7:84's production in large part seems to have derived from the strengthened feminist commitment of Lamont Stewart's new version. In the early 1980s the play was resonant with the continued shift in Britain from collective class-based politics to the bid for individual autonomy of identity politics. More particularly, the focus on Scottish, working-class women engaged with new revisions of feminism, as theorists such as Michele Barrett and bell hooks heralded a pluralist women's movement that recognised other forces than sexuality in the construction of gender, such as class, race and geographical location. Despite the obvious improvements for women in health, education and opportunities since the 1930s, the production also offered a damning indictment of continuing oppression. As Arthur McIvor argued, 'Female subordination and economic

---

24 Elizabeth MacLennan, *The Moon Belongs to Everyone: Making Theatre with 7:84* (London: Methuen, 1990), p. 115.
25 Ena Lamont Stewart, unpublished manuscript, p. 61.
26 Cited in Linda MacKenney, 'Introduction', *Men Should Weep* (Edinburgh: 7:84 Publications, 1983), p. xiv.

dependency within the home . . . the maldistribution of resources within the family and the survival of chauvinist attitudes and patriarchal values continue to characterise the Scottish family.'[27]

Informed by current feminist thinking, Lamont Stewart's revised version enhances the strength, resilience, experience and voices of the female characters. The conclusions of the original principally reduced women to the status of absent victims: Maggie and Isa are dead, Mrs Bone suffers continuing domestic violence behind closed doors and Jenny returns destitute from a life of prostitution to take up the matriarchal role left vacant by her mother's death. In the modified final act, the women characters survive as participants in the decision-making processes of their own lives. Rather than being punished for their threat to the family unit and patriarchal order, Isa succeeds in leaving Alec, while Jenny returns happy and unrepentant of her attempts to achieve self-determination. Jenny thus represents the self-assured, proactive presence of a modern woman who, unlike her mother, has the confidence to question the hospital's refusal to permit Bertie's release back to a slum dwelling. It is Jenny who, ironically replete with the economic rewards of 'living in sin', has the means to reunite the family by extricating them from their squalid home. However, the ultimate triumph of the feminist reworking occurs when John rejects Jenny's 'whore's winnins': Maggie rounds on him to secure an emancipation denied to her in the original. Beginning with gentle persuasions and placating gestures, she challenges his sexual politics, unflinchingly humiliating him with evidence of his double standards and her defiantly independent spirit: 'Whit wis I, when we was coortin, but your tart? Let me, Maggie, g'on, let me! I'll mairry ye if onythin happens . . . Aye. I wis your whore . . . But mebbe it's a right bein a whore if ye've nae winnins.'[28]

Elizabeth MacLennan, who played the part in the 7:84 revival, was active in the growing women's movement in Scotland, and she has explained that the decision to stage *Men Should Weep* was informed by an increasingly assertive feminism and by the previous treatment of Lamont Stewart. In Britain feminist theatre critics have highlighted how patriarchal theatre history has discarded women's experience and contributions, a factor Lamont Stewart was painfully aware of: 'Of cours [sic] it hurt, let's not mince our words. Men select the plays that are put on. They are more likely to put on a play by a man than a woman.'[29]

---

27 Arthur McIvor, 'Gender apartheid? Women in Scottish society', in *Scotland in the 20th Century*, ed. T. M. Devine and R. J. Finlay (Edinburgh University Press, 1996), p. 195.
28 Stewart, *Men Should Weep*, p. 73.
29 Cited in MacLennan, *Moon Belongs to Everyone*, p. 112.

Hence the revival of *Men Should Weep* was part of a larger feminist project of recovering a 'lost' tradition of women's theatre practice.

Shifting histories

In rewriting the final act, Lamont Stewart removed the potential for melodrama that proved problematic in the original production, paving the way for a consistent social realist treatment. However, the ways in which director Giles Havergal combined the committed political vision of 7:84 with the 'stylised finesse', as Michael Billington called it,[30] that was his trademark at the Citizens' Theatre, are worth considering for the light it may throw on the malleability of performance to shifting historical factors. Whereas Mitchell's naturalistic production firmly rooted *Men Should Weep* in a specific socio-economic context, Havergal adopted a stark neo-epic/expressionist style to dehistoricise and decontextualise his production. The design rejected 'authentic' historical scenery in favour of a sparse domestic area enclosed by a high, rickety structure of broken furniture and raised stage levels, denoting a bleak industrial landscape. This staging resulted in a dominant image of the Morrisons and their neighbours as engulfed by a poor urban environment unlocated in a specific time or place. As Billington noted: 'Havergal's production . . . avoids archaeological realism. Geoff Rose's set is a grey pile of dilapidated junk from which the characters emerge like so many ghosts . . . neighbours circle round like swooping birds.'[31] Releasing the characters from the confines of a realistic slum dwelling produced an industrial wasteland evocative of both the 1930s and the early 1980s.

Rather than aim for historical accuracy, Havergal used costume, props and colour for symbolic effect. For example, when Maggie reveals Bertie has been hospitalised, MacLennan stood in the doorway, his tiny clothes clutched in her hands – sad signs of her failure to hold the family unit together. MacLennan has commented on the significance of this physical gestus for the impact of the moment: 'I used to carry his clothes in a bundle, folded, with his wee boots on top. In reality they would have fitted a four year old, while, according to the text, Maggie's son is about eight . . . But the shoes were very small and defenceless, and that was what mattered.'[32] Havergal utilised other alienating conventions of anti-illusionist performance, such as actors observing scenes when not performing and an epic, gestural acting style.

30 Michael Billington, 'Madonna of the Gorbals', *Guardian* (3 Sep. 1982), 10.
31 *Ibid.*
32 MacLennan, *Moon Belongs to Everyone*, p. 130.

During rehearsals Havergal encouraged performances determined by social circumstance rather than psychological motivation and, in a marked departure from the original, stressed the need for emotional economy against overindulgent sentimentality. MacLennan remembers: 'I had to pare everything away . . . I told Giles after one particularly exhausting rehearsal that I felt like a big bag of icing sugar being forced to write my name out of a tiny nozzle. At one opening night in my good luck card he sent me one in an envelope.'[33] Drawing more specifically on 7:84's style, Havergal reanimated the strong Scottish traditions of variety, pantomime and music hall. Performers experienced in the popular comedy skills of timing and direct delivery to the audience, enhanced the near vaudevillian interludes crucial to the humour of Lamont Stewart's text, no better illustrated than when Edie's knickerless state is exposed:

LILY: Pull up yer stockings. Have ye nae suspenders?
EDIE: *Suspenders?* No.
LILY: Well, have ye nae garters?
EDIE: No, Auntie Lily.
LILY: Well, have ye nae eleastic in yer breeks?
EDIE: I've nae breeks.[34]

Direct address was introduced to disrupt naturalistic exchanges, allowing an inclusive relationship to develop with the audience as the barrier of performer–spectator was transgressed. This device also meant that key speeches could provide an ironic commentary on the characters' situation. According to Linda Mackenney,[35] during Maggie and Lily's exchange of insults about the limits of their respective roles in life, the performers invited the audience to consider their own conduct, as the following was delivered directly to them:

MAGGIE: Servin' dirty hulkin' brute o' men in a coocaddens pub.
LILY: Livin' in a slum and slavin' efter a useless man an' his greetin' weans.
MAGGIE: They're my weans! I'm workin for ma aun.
LILY: I'm *paid* for ma work.[36]

One aspect of Havergal's direction firmly locates his treatment of the play in its new context. During this period, Margaret Thatcher's Conservative government was determined to undermine the collective principles and responsibilities central to *Men Should Weep*, favouring instead a kind of radical individualism. In defiance of this cultural shift, Havergal continually emphasised the

---

33 *Ibid.*, p. 116.
34 Stewart, *Men Should Weep*, p. 5.
35 MacKenney, 'Introduction', p. xi.
36 Stewart, *Men Should Weep*, p. 8.

significance of community through the near continuous presence of the neighbours, who, like a Greek chorus, observed and commented on events. This effect was further enhanced through the exaggerated orchestration of voice and choreographed ensemble formations, for example as the women neighbours eavesdropped and drank tea in unison. The production highlighted the collective experience of deprivation, rather than the dissection of one family's subjugation to poverty that had been central to Glasgow Unity's production.

In sharp contrast to the reviews of Unity's version, critics were almost unanimously united in admiration of the production's combination of socio-political relevance, emotional impact, skilled theatricality and popular entertainment. Billington declared it to be 'living proof that popularity and high definition skill can go hand in hand',[37] while Michael Coveney found 'a grim dramatic proposition . . . transfigured by imaginative design, brilliant playing and real interpretive flair'.[38] However, Eddie Boyd found the 'softened up' ending 'a betrayal' of the political intent in Glasgow Unity's interpretation of the first version of the play. He argued that, to be true to the characters' historical situation, the claustrophobia of poverty could only end in the way it had in the original – with fatalistic bleakness.[39] Nonetheless, 7:84's revival did put *Men Should Weep* back on the theatrical map, so that it is now generally acknowledged as a classic. In a poll organised by the Royal National Theatre in 1999 it was voted one of the most significant 100 plays of the twentieth century. This was an ironic achievement for Lamont Stewart, Glasgow Unity, 7:84 (Scotland) and the play, which all rejected the London-led, middle-class theatrical diet usually served up by the major British theatres. Yet still, this was a long overdue recognition of an innovative and thought-provoking play that continues to offer a coruscating and relevant socio-political critique.

37 Billington, 'Madonna', p. 10.
38 Michael Coveney, 'Edinburgh Festival', *Financial Times* (6 Sept. 1982), 10.
39 Boyd, interview (1983).

Towards national identities:
Welsh theatres*

IOAN WILLIAMS

For a good part of the last hundred years theatre in Wales has been prejudiced by the dominance of one imported model – 'good quality mainstream theatre in the literary tradition from Shakespeare through Ibsen and Shaw to our contemporary writers' – and by the widespread assumption that no indigenous theatre existed until the Arts Council assumed the responsibility for creating it.[1] This is the more ironic because Wales had produced in the relatively recent past an indigenous theatre which demonstrates that it can flourish without the advantages of wealth and cultural continuity, on the basis of a distinctive and particularly vibrant compact between audience and performer. This was the theatre of the *Anterliwt*, which flourished in rural Wales during the later eighteenth and the earlier nineteenth centuries. Satirical and celebratory, moralistic and indecent, the texts produced in this theatre projected the immediate realities of contemporary rural life against the background of traditional moral teaching. Written or adapted for particular occasions, they were presented in improvised spaces by two or three performers, amongst whose performative skills the ability to turn an appropriate song to a popular tune, Welsh or English, clearly ranked highly. Because the society it served lacked the wealth needed to create permanent structures and practices, this indigenous folk theatre disappeared completely when its social base was undermined. The example of the Anterliwt reminds us that the fundamental condition of theatre is the existence of a social group or groups within a cultural community who see it as in their interests to function as an audience.

In spite of the widely held view that Welsh theatre is comparatively new, the last century has actually seen the emergence of three further indigenous theatrical models. The earliest of these, the Drama Movement (1911–39), also involved a close collaboration between audience and performers. Even the

---

* A glossary of selected Welsh terms is included at the end of this chapter.
1 *The Arts in Wales: Priorities into Practice* 7, 2 (July 1984); see also David Adams, *Welsh Nation, Nationalism and Theatre: The Search for Cultural Identity* (Llandysul: Gomer, 1996), p. 42.

most charismatic performers who rose to public attention in the movement were never more than exceptional proponents of common performative techniques, developed and perfected in memorial halls and chapel vestries throughout rural Wales. They sustained a representative performance mode under especially disadvantageous conditions, willingly accepted by all parties concerned on the understanding that what was to be represented was not the conditions of their common life but the mythology that underlay their view of the world.

The Theatre of National Consensus (1949–76) depended on a different kind of compact, though one to which many of the same social groups involved in the Drama Movement also contributed. Roger Owen has observed how different groups in Wales have urged the importance of theatre as an indicator of national status and achievement, and of mainstream professionalism on the English or European models, sometimes in collaboration, sometimes in competition with one another.

> In discussing and describing the professional theatre, people tended to link professionalism and nationalism, until the belief was established – almost unconsciously – that the Welsh professional theatre was also a national theatre.[2]

Between the late 1940s and the mid-1970s several cultural groupings came together in different combinations, in various attempts to set up a professional, text-based national theatre, culminating in the establishment of Cwmni Theatr Cymru, which for a short time was accepted by many as representative of a genuinely 'national' theatre, if not its perfected embodiment. Significantly, both the performance style and the repertoire of that company were acceptable with minimal modification in the performance spaces available on radio and television and in the National Eisteddfod, the annual Welsh-language competitive cultural gathering.

In the work of the theatre groups making up the Third Theatre (1976–90) there were clearly distinguishable tendencies towards community theatre on the one hand and towards highly innovative, devised work on the other. However combined, these elements could be traced to a common preoccupation with the task of creating a new sense of the relevance of theatrical practice among the increasingly fragmented Welsh-speaking communities.

---

2 Roger Owen, 'Y ddefod golledig?: theatr, cymdeithas a chymreictod yn y Gymru Gymraeg 1945–1990', Ph.D. Thesis, University of Wales, Aberystwyth (1999), p. 134 (translation mine).

The different strands of activity in these three models of theatre are part of a complex pattern in which ethnic or linguistic factors are far less important than whether audiences and writers who share a given body of theatrical practice also share an awareness of how that practice relates to the wider context of national culture. Given that, the relative importance of dramatic authors is established neither by the subject matter of their plays, nor even their literary value, but by the assumptions they share with their audiences. So for this study, J. O. Francis is more important than Emlyn Williams, with whom he shared a common first language and similar dramatic material, because for a time in the second and third decade of the twentieth century his writing was part of a body of theatrical practice integral to a distinctively Welsh culture.

Defined in that way, 'Welsh theatre' excludes both imported forms of English theatre and the dramatic literature sometimes identified as Anglo-Welsh.[3] That is not to deny their importance as manifestations of the cultural identity of Wales considered comprehensively as a geographical or social unit. Certainly, it would be possible to put together a respectable body of 'Anglo-Welsh' dramatists, who have contributed substantially to the overall pattern of theatrical activity in Wales. This would include J. O. Francis (1882–1956), Emlyn Williams (1905–87), Richard Hughes (1900–76) and Gwyn Thomas (1913–81); and amongst later writers Dannie Abse (b. 1923), Alun Richards (b. 1929), Frank Vickery (b. 1951), Dic Edwards (b. 1952) and Ed Thomas (b. 1961). No such grouping, however, can be said to have written with reference to a distinctive theatre, in the sense I have begun to develop here.

The same criterion determines the relative importance of dramatists and practitioners like Lord Howard de Walden and Mike Pearson, *vis-à-vis* English-medium dramatists like Gwyn Thomas. De Walden, born in England of Welsh descent, played an important role over a number of years in stimulating writing and discussion about what Welsh theatre in either language might become. Mike Pearson, an Englishman whose knowledge of Welsh language and culture has sharpened his awareness of his rural Lincolnshire origins, has developed a body of innovative performance that has impacted strongly on theatrical practice across the linguistic divide in Wales.

---

3 For histories of English theatre in Wales, see Cecil Price, *The English Theatre in Wales in the Eighteenth and Early Nineteenth Centuries* (Cardiff: University of Wales Press, 1948); *The Professional Theatre in Wales* (University College of Swansea Press, 1984); 'Some Welsh theatres 1844–1870', *National Library of Wales Journal* 12 (winter 1961), 156–76; 'Portable theatres in Wales', *National Library of Wales Journal* 9 (summer 1955), 66–92; also, Simon Baker, 'The wounds of possibility: Welsh drama in English in the 1960s and 1970s', in *Staging Wales: Welsh Theatre 1979–1997* ed. Anne-Marie Taylor (Cardiff: University of Wales Press, 1997), pp. 8–18.

By the end of the last millennium the continuing fragmentation of Welsh communities had reduced the importance of linguistic divisions. Well into the twentieth century, Welsh-speaking communities could think of themselves as sharing an unbroken cultural tradition closely identifiable with the Welsh language itself. Welsh readers saw no difficulty in relating writers like D. J. Williams (1885–1970; from Carmarthenshire) and Kate Roberts (1891–1985; from Carnarvonshire), even though their characters spoke dialects they might scarcely have been able to understand. Since at least the 1970s, however, the impact of continuing fragmentation of the Welsh communities on Welsh speakers has led to the adoption of new defensive strategies.[4] At the same time, large-scale economic and social change has produced a degree of cultural convergence between the two linguistic communities, eroding many of the factors that sustained terms such as 'Anglo-Welsh'. In the last two decades of the twentieth century it became increasingly pointless to distinguish between writers such as Ed Thomas, Dic Edwards, Gareth Miles and Sion Eirian on the basis of language alone.

The Drama Movement, 1911–1939

If the Welsh-speaking communities were quite bereft of traditional forms of theatre in the decades following the Anterliwt's decline, a succession of phenomenally successful preachers ensured that they were well provided with dramatic excitement. It may well be that jealousy of their status as performers fuelled the rabid opposition of these religious leaders to indigenous forms of popular entertainment. The career of one of the greatest Methodist preachers, John Elias (1774–1841), popularly known as the 'Pope of Anglesey', is paradigmatic: his preaching festivals, attended by thousands, shared many of the characteristics of the secular festivals that they replaced.[5] Certainly the growing power of Nonconformist religion in Wales throughout the nineteenth century was part of the same social development that led to the eventual victory of liberalism. The phenomenal development of the Drama Movement in

---

4 See J. W. Aitcheson and H. Carter in *The Welsh Language 1961–1981: An Interpretive Atlas* (Cardiff: University of Wales Press, 1985), and *A Geography of the Welsh Language 1961–1991* (Cardiff: University of Wales Press, 1994). See also Meic Stephens (ed.), *The Welsh Language Today* (Cardiff: University of Wales Press, 1973), and Janet Davies, *The Welsh Language* (Llandysul: Gomer Press, 1993).

5 See Edward Morgan, *John Elias: Life, Letters and Essays* (Edinburgh: Banner of Truth Trust, 1973), and R. Tudur Jones, *John Elias: Prince Amongst Preachers* (Bridgend: Welsh Evangelical Society, 1975).

the early twentieth century was a later stage in the continuing realignment of the groups who gained advantage from the on-going social change.

The great Liberal victory in the elections of 1868 was founded on an interpretation of cultural, social and political history that identified Welshness with the characteristics of a monolingual – and fictional – Nonconformist peasantry: 'y werin bobl'.[6] An integral part of that process was the adoption of a sentimental, modernistic theology by the Nonconformist churches. Once that had been done, Nonconformist leaders, depicting themselves as the heirs and representatives of the romanticised *gwerin*, were free to develop a political programme that advanced their own class interests on the basis of the highest moral and religious standards.

Some of the religious leaders who promoted this change were also novelists, fleshing out the new mythology with characters and situations purporting to be drawn from life.[7] Most important among them was Daniel Owen (1836–95), whose novels embodied the tension resulting from attempts to mediate between the new liberalism and attitudes and values derived from the Calvinist past. The earliest creative response to the demand for theatre towards the end of the nineteenth century was the adaptation of scenes from Owen's novels for the stage.[8] The best original texts produced at this time draw on the same material. Richard Williams's *Helynt Hen Aelwyd: neu Helbul Taid a Nain* (c. 1890), for example, is virtually a dramatic footnote to Gwilym Hiraethog's novel, *Helyntion Hen Deiliwr* (1877). It presents the comic tension between an older peasant community and a younger, revisionary generation that is resolved by the marriage of the lovers and celebrated to the mutual satisfaction of both the characters and the audience by a song from the successful suitor.

The Drama Movement was part of a wider national movement which produced a widespread feeling that Wales required a dramatic literature and a prestigious theatrical institution in order to sustain its national self-respect. The two idols of the nation, O. M. Edwards and Lloyd George, both took advantage of the stage of the National Eisteddfod to pronounce to that effect, the one in Caernarfon in 1894, the other six years later in Bangor. The first creative outcome was a series of idealised presentations of Welsh history, in

6 'Y werin bobl' is roughly equivalent to 'the ordinary folk', but with quite different resonance. The key word is *Gwerin*, which loses its initial consonant after the definite article, some of whose force is implied by words like *Gweriniaeth*, which translates 'Republic'.

7 See Ioan Williams, *Capel a Chomin* (Caerdydd: Gwasg Prifysgol Pantycelyn, 1991); H. T. Edwards (ed.), *A Guide to Welsh Literature c. 1800–1900* (Cardiff: University of Wales Press, 2000).

8 D. Tecwyn Lloyd, 'Daniel Owen ar y llwyfan', *Llên Cymru* 10 (1968–9), 59–70; 'Gwir gychwyn y busnes drama 'ma . . .', *Llwyfan* 8 (spring/summer 1973), 5–8.

the 'Drama Cantatas' of Beriah Gwynfe Evans (1848–1927). His *Owain Glyndwr* (1897) won a prize of £10 offered at the Llanberis Eisteddfod in 1879 for a drama 'written in Shakespearean mode' and was presented the following year by an *ad hoc* company formed by the Eisteddfod committee. This group later established itself as the Llanberis Company, the first of its kind to perform substantial dramatic texts. A revised version of the play was later performed as part of the celebrations of the investiture of the Prince of Wales (Carnarvon, 1911), which is a good indication of the kind of compromise that underlay Beriah Evans's romantic nationalism.

There was a steady increase in dramatic activity throughout the Welsh community between 1890 and 1911, often organised within and around the chapels of the various Nonconformist churches. I have taken 1911 as the beginning of the Drama Movement, because in that year Lord Howard de Walden offered a prize of £100 designed 'to stimulate . . . attempts at expression in dramatic form', and the poet and critic W. J. Gruffydd (1881–1954) published an article, 'Drama for Wales', which could stand as a declaration of intent on the part of the generation of new playwrights whose work was to feed the growing movement.[9] Two years later Gruffydd produced his first play, *Beddau'r Prof-fwydi*, which he staged himself in Cardiff, with students from the University College of South Wales. The university connection is important. By 1911 university education had increased the cultural gap between the newly conscious Nonconformist élite and the monolingual peasantry from whom they claimed their inheritance. At the same time the demoralising failure of liberalism to satisfy the nationalist programme it had promulgated sharpened critical attitudes among young graduates aware of the achievements of the Drama Movement in Ireland, contemporary developments in English drama and the socially critical functions of European naturalism, especially as practised by Ibsen.

De Walden's competition stimulated the production of a coherent group of new plays. In 1912 J. O. Francis won with the political play *Change*, written in English, though often performed in Welsh. In 1913 the prize was shared between R. G. Berry (1869–1945) for *Ar y Groesffordd* and D. T. Davies (1876–1962) for the one-act *Ble Mà Fa?* and the full-length *Ephraim Harris*. These plays present more or less violent collisions between the old and the new value systems, but while the victory of the latter may be delayed or even doubtful, it is always quite unambiguous. The most common confrontation is that between the formalistic Calvinism of the narrow-minded and often

9 De Walden quoted in O. Llew Owain, *Hanes y Ddrama yng Nghymru 1850–1943* (Lerpwl: cyhoeddwyd ar ran Cyngor yr Eisteddfod Genedlaethol, 1948), p. 107; W. J. Gruffydd, 'Drama i Cymru', *Y Beirniad* i (1911), 49–54.

Figure 11.1 The full cast of the first production of W. J. Gruffydd's *Beddau'r Proffwydi*,
University College of South Wales, 1913.

hypocritical Nonconformist deacon and the broader, humanitarian theology
of the younger generation. This clash is sometimes complicated by references
to the traditional enemies shared by the rural *gwerin* and their educated successors – the Anglican, anglicised landlord, sometimes provided with a distracting
daughter!

The confrontation is engineered in different ways by the different writers.
In *Ble Mà Fa?* it arises from the question the bereaved (and naïve) widow of a
young miner puts to the visitors who come to comfort her – where will he
spend eternity, given his rejection of Calvinism? In *Beddau'r Proffwydi*, Gruffydd
resorts to an anachronistic poaching episode to motivate a collision sufficiently
violent to justify his hero's expressionist rage. Berry derives dramatic tension in *Ar y Groesffordd* from the situation of a minister who risks losing his

position and souring his view of life by choosing a wife of whom the deacons disapprove.

Of these dramatists, J. O. Francis came closest to a genuinely Ibsenite analysis of the reality of social and cultural conflict, but even in *Change* he is unable to answer the questions he makes his characters ask. The weak and ineffective Gwilym Price, who represents the playwright's view, is saved from a lingering death from tuberculosis only by a strike-breaking soldier's bullet, as he tries to drag his demagogic brother to safety. After that the remaining brothers self-righteously and self-indulgently go their separate ways, leaving their parents bitter and lonely. No one in the play develops the ability to criticise himself, nor does the author himself show any awareness that his own vague humanism provides no point of resistance to destructive pressures within the individual or in social life.

Taken together, these types of play were the raw material which fed an explosion of dramatic and theatrical activity in Wales in the period immediately before and after World War One. Strikingly, the war itself had virtually no effect on the subject matter of the plays produced, which showed little awareness of the forces that were tearing Wales apart, and continued to direct their criticism at enemies who no longer existed. The Nonconformist deacon, for example, who plays such a dominant part in the plays of the Drama Movement, was actually a peripheral figure in Welsh life years before the turn of the century. J. O. Francis recorded the embarrassment of his generation of would-be subversives when, far from bringing the remains of their once formidable power to bear against the new critical drama, the deacons were eager to take part in it. 'What is the poor playwright to do', he asked, 'when, having written a part that is a furious attack on deacons, the deacons come forward and earnestly beg the privilege of acting it?' Even *Beddau'r Proffwydi*, the movement's heaviest gun, was produced, financed and loudly applauded, noted Francis, 'by a body in which nine men out of ten might one day be giving out the announcements'. In other words, they would be deacons themselves one day, even if they were not already! What could the dramatist do in those circumstances, 'but go home and think again'.[10]

The criticism brought to bear throughout the new drama actually sustained the establishment of liberal ministers and socialist teachers, who welcomed it enthusiastically as the raw material for a concerted cultural project. Almost within moments of the appearance of works like *Change*, *Beddau'r Proffwydi* and *Ble Mà Fa?* drama groups and companies sprang up to perform them in

10 J. O. Francis, 'The deacon and the dramatist', *Welsh Outlook* (June 1919), 158–60.

villages and towns from one end of Wales to the other, often competing in the increasing numbers of festivals and *eisteddfodau* and sometimes even undertaking semi-professional touring programmes. Through the 1920s and the 1930s, according to one otherwise indefatigable commentator, the performances of these groups were too numerous to record, spreading beyond Wales to every English city with a substantial Welsh community, where every chapel had its company and took part not only in competitions, but also in lectures and training programmes designed to effect improvement in every aspect of dramatic art.[11]

At the time few contemporary observers were aware of any tension between the different aims and attitudes involved in all this activity, partly because the amateur theatre was widely regarded as a lower stratum, there to provide raw material in the form of outstanding performers and increasingly discriminating audiences for the new professionalism developing in the Welsh-speaking theatre. However, whilst a degree of progression certainly existed for the talented performer, amateur theatre actually supported a series of practices that were incapable of development and inaccessible to 'improvement'.

A good part of the immediate popularity of the new drama was its adaptability to performance in village halls and vestries with only the shallowest of playing areas and the most rudimentary technical facilities. Innumerable photographs of the period suggest a performance style well adapted to these circumstances, which quickly came to be seen as an intrinsic part of the whole theatrical project.[12] Tellingly, challenges to this prevailing style of presentation could attract a sharper response than any attempt to revise the fundamental attitudes on which the new drama was based, as Saunders Lewis discovered through his experience as stage-manager for the 'National Theatre' which the Cardiff Cymrodorion Society tried to establish in 1922. The reviews of the opening programme, which included Lewis's own new play, *Gwaed yr Uchelwyr*, and D. T. Davies's *Y Dieithryn*, fell into two clearly marked categories. *The Welsh Outlook* and the radical paper *Y Darian* welcomed Saunders Lewis's new play as a conscious attempt to revise the Liberal version of history and to introduce non-representative design practice borrowed from French directors such as Dullin, Jouvet and Baty. Critics in the *Western Mail* and the *Cardiff Times*, clearly resenting the play's political bearing, were angered by his abandonment of representational *mise en scène*:

11 Owain, *Hanes y Ddrama*, 143.
12 See Hywel Teifi Edwards, *Codi'r Llen* (Llandysul: Gomer, 1998).

The stage itself was somewhat novel, no attempt having been made to represent the ordinary walls, fireplaces, pictures &c., a few curtains, with the necessary openings in place of doorways, sufficing for these. This I am informed, was done of set purpose, but what the purpose was, I have failed to discover. There is no doubt some esoteric meaning in all this and it is hoped that in time we may be initiated into the secret. Meanwhile we share the feelings of the prominent Welshman who, when he saw the curtained walls, exclaimed, 'Great heaven, what is this?'[13]

After *Gwaed yr Uchelwyr* Saunders Lewis withdrew from active involvement with the theatre until 1936, at least partly because of his frustration with this combination of political conservatism and incorrigible amateurishness.

Throughout the twenties and thirties there were attempts to develop the Drama Movement into a platform for launching a National Theatre. The League of Welsh Drama, for example, established in 1928, aimed to develop a common resource base for Welsh drama and new training programmes, in preparation for the long-wished-for National Theatre. The League expired in 1930, but within three years the indefatigable Howard de Walden was chairing another committee charged with the duty of setting up a 'National Playhouse', with the aim of providing a professional touring company. Sharply criticised for the weakness of its Welsh-language work, this company also came to an end by December 1934.

Whilst the activity of the groups – some 350 of them, at least, according to J. Ellis Williams[14] – continued unabated until the outbreak of World War Two, the creative impulse behind the Drama Movement had come to an end a decade earlier. Some good plays in the earlier mode were produced through the twenties and early thirties – David Matthew Williams's (Ieuan Griffiths, 1900–70) *Dirgel Ffyrdd* (1933) redirects the standard satirical treatment from the deacon to the councillor. Idwal Jones's (1895–1937) *Pobl yr Ymylon* (1927), based on the exchange of roles between a disillusioned preacher and a spiritually ambitious tramp, is a particularly interesting variation on old themes. But the underlying health of the movement can be measured in the deterioration of dramatists like D. T. Davies, whose *Pelenni Pitar* (1925) is a disastrous attempt to write a comedy of modern life, and the fact that praise was lavished on writers like J. Eddie Parry. A partial exception is J. Ellis Williams (1901–75), but

---

13 *Western Mail* (15 May 1922), 6; cf. *Cardiff Times and South Wales Weekly News* (20 May 1922), 12.
14 J. Ellis Williams, *Inc yn fy Ngwaed* (Llanybie: Llyfrau'r Dryw, 1963), p. 113.

even his most serious play, *Ceidwad y Porth* (1927) failed to achieve a convincing analysis of human behaviour in contemporary Wales.

Theatre of National Consensus, 1949–1976

As early as 1960, George Davies, looking back over the devastating decline of the Drama Movement in his native Rhondda, insisted on the essential connection between language and theatre in Wales. The Drama Movement, he argued, which offered to actors and audiences a picture of the life of the individual projected against the life of the nation, had been destroyed by the same economic and social factors that were destroying the language. The only future for theatre in Wales was within a new linguistic community, put together out of the ruins of the past. Davies advocated, consequently, the establishment of a new 'Marginal Theatre', which could be created by student performers taking old and new work out to new audiences, in markets, pubs, in the street and on the Eisteddfod field.[15] This idea contained a seed that was to grow strongly only after another fifteen years had passed.

The Drama Movement was finally finished off by the arrival of television in the mid-1950s, but its obituary was effectively written by J. Saunders Lewis in the League's own magazine, *Y Llwyfan*, in 1928.[16] He endorsed the general suspicion that including English- and Welsh-language drama within the same institution would undermine the latter, but argued that its survival was of little significance, given its lack of artistic ambition. What he looked for was a professional theatre, committed to achieving the highest artistic standards across the whole range of theatrical crafts.

In a sense there had always been an underlying consensus in respect of the innate insufficiency of the national amateur movement. For de Walden and Saunders Lewis alike, the pattern to be imitated was the English professional stage, though Lewis preferred on the whole to refer to continental models. However, it was only when the amateur theatre was in evident decline that the movement for a national, professional theatre began to concentrate the attention of the majority of people actively involved in Welsh-speaking theatre. In the late 1940s and early 1950s theatrical festivals were established at Garthewin and Llangefni, for which Saunders Lewis himself created a series of plays that could be measured against the highest standards. Though still amateur, these festivals aspired to professional standards of performance and production and were partly funded by the Arts Council on that basis.

15 George Davies, 'Drama yr Ymylon', *Drama* (Gwanwyn 1960), 23–6.
16 Saunders Lewis, *Y Llwyfan* 4 (June/July 1928), 49–50.

It has often been regretted that, as Wilbert Lloyd Roberts put it, Wales was the only country in the world 'where television came before theatre',[17] particularly because of the part the broadcasting media have played in undermining Welsh language and culture. From the first, however, efforts were made by the Welsh theatre communities to take positive advantage of the media and to incline the often intransigent British Broadcasting Corporation towards a recognition of Welshness. From the 1950s onwards networks of patronage and production grew, reflecting the fact that the BBC, the National Eisteddfod and the pressure groups working in the interests of Welsh theatre had arrived at a general consensus concerning the nature and function of drama. The result was a text-based theatre, adapted equally well to the larger school halls in towns across Wales, to commercial theatres and to television and radio studios, on most occasions without any perceptible adjustment of style. This Theatre of National Consensus provided the stage for the drama of J. Saunders Lewis, John Gwilym Jones and Gwenlyn Parry and led to the establishment of Cwmni Theatr Cymru.

Though a National Theatre had been the dream of many closely involved with the Drama Movement in the early decades of the century, the project acquired a new impetus towards the end of the 1950s, when the BBC developed an interest in training actors proficient in Welsh. The Arts Council had supported the establishment of a permanent company at Swansea from 1948, initially under the direction of Lionel Harries, and subsequently a number of *ad hoc* companies had been set up to perform at Garthewin and Llangefni and to tour, including, from 1949, Chwaraeyddion y Genhinen. The shortage of actors and actresses who could perform naturally in Welsh, which revealed itself increasingly towards the late 1950s as a result of this activity, stimulated Arts Council interest in the project to create some sort of national repertory theatre.[18] At the same time the National Eisteddfod had become increasingly conscious of its function as a showcase for Welsh drama.

In 1959 Saunders Lewis joined an action group – soon to be named the St David's Trust – formed by the actor and scriptwriter Clifford Evans, with the aim of raising funds to establish a National Theatre in Cardiff. The architect Elidr Davies was commissioned to produce a design, which by the early 1960s seemed about to be realised, though opposition grew among those who suspected that a theatre established in Cardiff would be predominantly English

17 Cited in Elan Clos Stephens, 'Drama', in Meic Stephens (ed.), *The Arts in Wales* (Cardiff: Welsh Arts Council, 1979), pp. 239–96.
18 Arts Council of Great Britain, *Ends and Means: 18th Annual Report* (London: Arts Council of Great Britain, 1963), p. 70.

in medium and ethos. In 1962 the Welsh Committee of the Arts Council set up the Welsh Theatre Company, under the directorship of Warren Jenkins, which soon undertook Welsh-language projects. In 1963 the Arts Council and the BBC co-commissioned a new Welsh play 'suitable for both television and stage'.[19] Subsequently *Y Tad Afradlon*, by Tom Richards, was toured by Herbert Davies of the BBC with a cast of actors who with one exception were on BBC contracts. In 1966 the Arts Council recorded that 'one of the most helpful developments' of previous years had been the growing cooperation between the Welsh Theatre Company and the BBC, which had led to the establishment of a group of six young actors who worked with the BBC director, Wilbert Lloyd Roberts, as Honorary Assistant Director of the Theatre Company.[20] This *ad hoc* partnership culminated in the setting up of Cwmni Theatr Cymru, independently incorporated as the Welsh National Theatre Company (Cwmni Theatr Cenedlaethol Cymru), though soon obliged to drop the term 'National' as a result of legal action brought by the St David's trustees.[21] From then on Lloyd Roberts established Cwmni Theatr Cymru as a showcase for Welsh drama and as a training company. Saunders Lewis's disgust with the Arts Council's part in this process did not prevent him from allowing the company to present *Problemau Prifysgol* at the Barry National Eisteddfod in 1968, an implicit acknowledgement that its work satisfied the requirements of professional theatre.

It is ironic that well before that campaign had begun there had been developments in amateur theatre which suggested a potential for a quite different future for Welsh theatre. The social and political analysis offered in James Kitchener Davies's *Cwm Glo* (1935) swept away the mythology that the amateur theatre had served. Shocked by its portrayal of the reality of social life in the coalfield during the years of industrial decline, the judges at the National Eisteddfod at Neath in 1934 withheld the prize, though they identified it as the best play in the competition. No doubt that added to its popular success when Kitchener Davies staged it with his own Cwmni'r Pandy, but in the longer term *Cwm Glo* has not been successful on the stage, because the quasi-naturalist mode inherited from the Drama Movement was too crude a theatrical instrument to accommodate sophisticated social criticism.

---

19 Arts Council of Great Britain, *State of Play: 19th Annual Report* (London: Arts Council of Great Britain, 1963–4), p. 70.
20 Arts Council of Great Britain, *Key Year: 21st Annual Report* (London: Arts Council of Great Britain, 1965–6), p. 45.
21 See Stephens, 'Drama', pp. 239–96.

In his next important play Kitchener Davies challenged both the fundamental cultural assumptions and the production practices of the Drama Movement. Set in the ruins of Glangors-fach on Michaelmas Eve, 'in any year of the century', *Meini Gwagedd* (1944) presents two groups of long-dead characters condemned to revisit the world which destroyed them. In the contrast between these two groups Kitchener Davies develops a powerful critique of the cultural and social assumptions central to contemporary Welsh culture, though the drama is impaired by the fact that because the two groups occupy the same place at different times their on-stage relationship is incapable of dynamic development.

Awarded the prize in the competition for a short play in the Eisteddfod at Llandybie in 1944, *Meini Gwagedd* was staged for a specially selected audience at Lampeter by Cardiganshire Drama Committee in May of the following year. For some of those involved, this was an event of great potential significance. Acting in the play made D. Jacob Davies feel that he was in contact with something sinister and devilish he could not quite explain to himself: 'All I can say is that . . . the more I familiarized myself with the words and the more I saw the words taking flesh in the characters, the more I was aware of the evil spirit that is an inextricable part of the play'.[22] Reviewing the production, Dewi Llwyd Jones claimed it was indisputably 'the most significant play yet written in Welsh', though its dramatic effect was limited by its inherent structural weakness and by the circumstances in which it was presented. Ironically, the very incompleteness of the experiment left him full of confidence for the future of Welsh drama, if it could be widely adopted as the model for a series of experiments, rather than the preferred Arts Council option of touring Shakespeare productions.[23] In the event, however, the Arts Council's loyalty to the models of mainstream British theatre remained firm for many years, while radio commissions became an increasingly important element in stimulating innovative theatrical activity.

Kitchener Davies's best play, *Swn y Gwynt sy'n Chwythu* (1952), is a complex dramatic monologue, commissioned and broadcast by BBC radio. It had been radio commissions from the BBC's Alan Oldfield Davies that had brought Saunders Lewis back to playwriting following the famous 'Fire in the Llyn'. In 1936, in company with the writer D. J. Williams and the Revd Lewis Valentine, Lewis set fire to building materials gathered at Penyberth bombing range, in

22 D. Jacob Davies, 'Llwyfannu meini gwagedd', *Y Gehinen* 4, 3 (Haf 1954), 218.
23 D. Llwyd Jones, 'Drama arwyddocaol', *Y Faner* (23 May, 1945), 5.

reaction to the government's lack of response to widespread Welsh protests about what was regarded as the desecration of an important historical site. Afterwards the three men gave themselves up to the police. A jury at Carnarvon failed to reach a verdict in the subsequent trial, but a second attempt at the Old Bailey resulted in terms of nine months imprisonment for all three. This event was a turning point in the development of the Welsh national movement and had crucial repercussions in the Welsh-language community at large.[24] After the fire at Penyberth everyone in the Welsh-speaking community consciously faced the problem of living in a society in which their language and culture were being more or less systematically eroded. Like any other existential crisis, this deeply affected not only those not satisfied, as Saunders Lewis put it, to live on daily bread alone; it became the central preoccupation of contemporary literature in the Welsh language.

The BBC commission Lewis worked on while awaiting his second trial, resulted in the *vers libre* play *Buchedd Garmon* (1937). After his release from Wormwood Scrubs another radio commission occasioned *Amlyn ac Amig* (1940), which was later staged in the theatre his Catholic friend Robert Wynne had set up in a converted coach house at his estate in Garthewin.[25] His satisfaction with this production (February 1946) led him to complete an earlier unfinished verse play, *Blodeuwedd* (October 1948), which not only won unprecedented literary status for Welsh drama, but also marked the emergence of a new theatre.

Blodeuwedd provided Welsh theatre with a range of subject matter closely related to mainstream European culture and determined the dominant theatrical mode of what elsewhere I have referred to as Saunders Lewis's 'straitened stage', on the model of French neoclassic drama, rather than the expansive theatrical mode of the directors of the French Cartel whose work he had earlier admired.[26] After *Blodeuwedd*, he wrote a series of plays for Garthewin, culminating with *Siwan* (1954), a treatment of the traditional material of Welsh historical drama. His next play, *Gymerwch Chi Sigarét?* (1955), which abandoned verse and took up a contemporary subject drawn from the press, was first performed by the company of actors established by the Welsh Committee of the South Wales branch of the Arts Council and was staged at the 'national' drama festival at Llangefni (September 1955). His subsequent plays – *Brad* (1958), *Esther*

24 See Alun R. Jones and Gwyn Thomas (eds.), *Presenting Saunders Lewis* (Cardiff: University of Wales Press, 1973).
25 See Walford Davies, *Saunders Lewis a Theatr Garthewin* (Landysul: Gomer, 1995).
26 Ioan Williams, *A Straitened Stage: A Study of the Theatre of J. Saunders Lewis* (Bridgend: Seren Books, 1991).

(1959), *Excelsior* (1962) and *Problemau Prifysgol* (1968) – were commissioned for performance at the National Eisteddfod or for presentation on BBC television.

In the 1960s Saunders Lewis produced two contrasting but equally radical commentaries on the cultural situation underlying the productive collaboration between the Arts Council, the BBC, the Eisteddfod and the audiences of the theatre festivals. These were the broadcast lecture *Tynged yr Iaith* (1962) and a play, *Cymru Fydd*, commissioned by Bala National Eisteddfod in 1965 and performed there by Cwmni Theatr Cymru in 1967. *Tynged yr Iaith*, which proposed that unless drastic, radical and widespread action was taken, the battle for Welsh language and culture might as well be lost, stung many of the young supporters of Cymdeithas yr Iaith Gymraeg into direct and positive action. *Cymru Fydd* embodied Saunders Lewis's belief that the structures underpinning Welsh culture, including the drama as he had attempted to practise it, had already been destroyed. It followed that the grounds for the consensus which had provided the audience for the dramatic literature he had produced no longer existed.

Saunders Lewis's subsequent career seemed to confirm this: although productions of his major plays were a staple part of the artistic programme of Cwmni Theatr Cymru between 1965 and 1984, all six of his plays after *Cymru Fydd* were written for radio or television. Always something of an outsider in Wales, from the mid-1960s he seemed increasingly marginalised and in the 1970s his plays were widely criticised for their mannerism and conservatism of dramatic method. During those years critics and audiences looked to the work of two other major writers, John Gwilym Jones (1904–88) and Gwenlyn Parry (1932–91), who seemed to provide comforting evidence of the continuing strength and flexibility of the social and cultural groupings contributing to Welsh theatre.

Self-confessedly and cheerfully an amateur, John Gwilym Jones wrote as an unpretentious man of the people, closely in touch with the prejudices, the mannerisms and above all the speech of the village in Arfon where he spent most of his life. In contrast to Saunders Lewis's professedly élitist commitment to the literary language, he seemed to guarantee Welsh theatre's ability to adapt and to democratise, maintaining its vital capacity to reflect the experience of the national audience that had come together during the 1950s and 1960s. From another point of view, however, John Gwilym's career as a dramatist reflected the same fundamental trend towards isolation and fragmentation presaged in *Cymru Fydd*. His earlier plays presented a psychological critique of family relations, gradually developing into a more abstract analysis of the human condition. This was most successfully achieved in his penultimate play,

Ac Eto Nid Myfi (1976). Here a complex process of self-examination in the central character is the vehicle of a critique of the social and psychological problems produced by traditional Nonconformist culture in rural Wales. However, this is achieved only at the cost of idealising certain characters and is expressed in language permeated by the very cultural values under attack.

His last play, *Yr Adduned* (1979), commissioned for the National Eisteddfod at Carnarvon in 1979, depicts a more extreme condition of self-alienation and takes the process of theatrical alienation a substantial step further. The action arises from a dialogue between Ifan 1 and his alter-ego Ifan 2, who represents his creative imagination. The occasion is Ifan's attempt to come to terms with his inability to fulfil the promise made to a friend now dead, that he will write a commissioned play.

A powerful and effective piece, *Yr Adduned* stretches theatre to breaking point. It works because of the complex web of cultural reference and cross-reference which John Gwilym Jones weaves into the dialogue between Ifan 1 and Ifan 2, and through the flashbacks that open up his memories. This web enmeshes and implicates the audience, winning their willing acceptance of the reconciliation of existential *angst* and traditional certainty which Ifan 1 achieves while Ifan 2 is by his side. But when Ifan 1, alone on the stage, addresses directly to the audience the play's final words – 'Gone . . . gone . . . gone . . .' – relegating closure to the world of memory and imagination, it is revealed as nothing more than a temporary displacement of that immediate social reality in which the audience's language and culture is still being inexorably eaten away.

The plays of Gwenlyn Parry (1932–91) relocate Welsh drama to the hedge-less, fenceless world Kitchener Davies had made of the Rhondda Valley in *Sŵn y Gwynt sy'n Chwythu* – the same meaningless world Saunders Lewis's hero, Dewi Rhys, had protested against in *Cymru Fydd*. Parry's characters belong to lower social groups than those of his predecessors and speak a more demotic language. They also inhabit a world from which religion and traditional moral-ity have departed, except in the form of unavoidable and unpalatable truths.

His first full-length play, the comedy *Saer Doliau* (1966), forced the Eisteddfod audience into its first direct confrontation with the techniques of absurdism, though it still turned on the traditional confrontation between conservatism and revisionism. Together with subsequent plays, it was accepted into the repertory of Cwmni Theatr Cymru, though not without some protest.[27] *Tŷ ar y Tywod* (1968) was commissioned for the Barry Eisteddfod in 1968, where it

27 Owen, 'Y ddefod golledig?', pp. 242–57. On *Tŷ ar y Tywod*, see *Llwyfan* 2 (Gwanwyn 1969), 10.

was performed by Cwmni Theatr Cymru under Wilbert Roberts's direction, in preparation for a BBC television production directed by George Owen. *Y Ffin* was commissioned for performance by Cwmni Theatr Cymru at Dyffryn Clwyd National Eisteddfod in 1973, recorded for broadcasting on BBC television some months later and then taken on tour.

No doubt much of this success was due to the dramatist's mastery of the same Arfon dialect John Gwilym Jones had employed, which naturalised the inconsequential dialogue and irrational behaviour of his characters. But audiences must have sensed that his drama was central to the cultural project at the heart of the Theatre of Consensus. This is clear in the case of *Y Tŵr* (1978), which inculpates the audience in exactly that existential crisis which John Gwilym Jones's Ifan had tried to work out in his own head. Nothing in this play mitigates the pain and distress the characters bring on themselves and each other, nor the audience's awareness of it. Gwenlyn Parry's achievement was that he was able to dramatise the mutual need that conditions the selfish individuality of his characters – as John Gwilym Jones's Ifan 2 had put it, the fact that without other people, individuality has no shape or substance.

By the time Gwenlyn Parry's last play, *Panto*, was staged at the Fishguard National Eisteddfod in 1986, the social and institutional foundations of the Theatre of Consensus had been almost entirely destroyed. By 1968, with the establishment of the commercial Harlech Television Company, the pattern of broadcasting in Wales, as in the rest of Britain, was changing. The Eisteddfod remained much the same, but public assessment of its role as a showcase for Welsh drama had been fundamentally changed by the programme which led to the building of new theatres associated with educational institutions in Aberystwyth (1972), Harlech and Cardiff (1973) and Bangor (1975) and others funded by local authorities in Felinfach (1972), Mold (1976) and Milford Haven (1977).[28] The new burden imposed by those buildings was partly responsible for a change in the attitude of the Welsh Arts Council, but more importantly criticisms of Cwmni Theatr Cymru's artistic policy were becoming frequent, while audiences were beginning to decline.

When, in 1981, the Welsh Arts Council arbitrarily reduced Cwmni Theatr Cymru's annual grant from £253,000 to £175,000, its action found support both from the wider theatre audience and those actively involved in performance and production. This was by no means the end of the company, however. When Wilbert Lloyd Roberts resigned in 1982 after eighteen years as its

---

28 See Arts Council of Great Britain, *Housing the Arts in Great Britain: Parts 1 and 2* (London: Arts Council of Great Britain, 1959/61); also Stephens, 'Drama', pp. 262–3.

Figure 11.2 A key example of Welsh Third Theatre: Brith Gof's *Haearn*, Tredegar, 1992.

director, his successor, Emily Davies, tried to recreate on the larger stage the intimate working environment that had enabled her to work so successfully with students in the Department of Drama at the University of Wales, Aberystwyth. For the two years that remained she maintained two separate groups of actors, creating mainstream productions and innovative work side by side. But without effective financial management this proved impossible, in spite of the high quality of the work. By 1984 the company's financial difficulties were serious and no clear conviction existed within the funding council that support should be continued.

Third Theatre, 1976–1990

By the mid-1970s there was a strong feeling among younger practitioners that what the mainstream Welsh theatre Cwmni Theatr Cymru represented was no longer relevant. The primary reason for this was the continuing crisis of the language, under pressure from economic changes that were eroding its social base. The new theatre buildings themselves aggravated underlying problems by isolating theatrical activity from the remaining Welsh-speaking groups. Another factor was the alienation of audiences, who were developing increasing appetites for Anglo-American commercial media culture, from drama which identified existential problems they refused themselves to recognise. Finally, traditional concepts of Welshness were no longer relevant to new, urban, Welsh-speaking social groups and particularly to younger people, who enjoyed opportunities and challenges demanding new words and new skills.

It might seem ironic that this background of decline was the setting for a confident new theatre movement which seemed to grow stronger as the political and social situation deteriorated. That irony, however, tends to conceal certain continuing changes. At least as far as theatre was concerned, in the 1960s and 1970s Welsh culture became outward-looking and assimilative in ways without precedent. This trend had contributed to the difficulties of Cwmni Theatr Cymru almost from the first, generating a demand for progressive and radical projects. As Roger Owen puts it, battling through the 1960s to establish a professional, mainstream theatre, successive directors of the company found themselves in the 1970s 'trying to answer demands for a marginal, relevant theatre.'[29] Pressure from younger actors obliged both Wilbert Lloyd Roberts and Emily Davies to maintain an expensive experimental programme, which the Arts Council saw as an interference with the primary business of the company.

29 Owen, 'Y ddefod golledig?', p. 234.

When a meeting was held on the Eisteddfod field in August 1986 to consider whether some elements of a National Theatre might be saved from the ruins of Cwmni Theatr Cymru, few voices were raised in favour. Dafydd Ellis Thomas, Member of Parliament for Merionethshire, argued that it was precisely the 'marginal' groups which survived the collapse of the company that represented the true 'national' theatre of Wales.[30] The predominant view at the 1986 meeting was that the new groups represented a radically new kind of theatre, independent of theatrical buildings and free from the demands of dramatic literature. The point was also made, by the director and educationalist Emyr Edwards, that if Cwmni Theatr Cymru incorporated a view of theatre which was not intrinsically Welsh, the same was true of groups that drew their inspiration from a European tradition no longer new and, by the middle and late 1970s, arguably no longer relevant.[31] To argue, however, that the influence on young Welsh practitioners of Grotowski, Tadeusz Kantor or Eugenio Barba was equivalent to that of mainstream English theatre in earlier decades, was to miss a very substantial point. New Welsh theatre practice in the seventies related more directly to social and cultural circumstances in a rapidly changing world than either the 'First', established theatre, or the 'Second' theatre of the avant-garde.

Barba first formulated his notion of the Third Theatre in a lecture at an international workshop on theatre research in Belgrade in 1976, attended by members of the recently established Cardiff Laboratory Theatre set up by Mike Pearson in Cardiff in 1973.[32] For practitioners in the emergent worldwide alternative theatre, who eschewed traditional professionalism, Barba claimed: 'theatre is a means to find their own way of being present . . . to seek more humane relationships among men, with the purpose of creating a social cell inside which intentions, aspirations and personal needs begin to be transferred into actions'.[33] Barba's programme applied to the situation in Wales in the 1970s primarily because it asserted a link between existential and ethical needs and economic and cultural deprivation. Whilst the lack of continuing support for Cwmni Theatr Cymru betrayed a widespread feeling that the theatrical establishment was unable or unwilling to address the real cultural and social crises of modern Wales, the marginality of young practitioners,

---

30 See David Hughes, 'The Welsh National Theatre: the avant-garde in the diaspora', in Theodore Shank (ed.), *Contemporary British Theatre* (London: Macmillan, 1996), pp. 138–51.
31 Emyr Edwards, 'Tristwch ein Theatr', *Y Faner* (5 Sept. 1986), 4.
32 These were Inga Bjarnason, Richard Gough, John Hardy, Mike Pearson, Gerry Pyves, Sian Thomas and Nigel Watson.
33 Cited in *Maskarade. The Journal for the Cardiff Laboratory Theatre* (summer 1977).

lacking administrative power and access to funding, seemed a guarantee of commitment. The fragmentation of the Welsh-speaking community, under pressure of social and economic changes for which the cultural establishment had no answer, seemed a phenomenon favourable to the development of new theatres, closer to regional and social groupings than Cwmni Theatr Cymru, or any other 'national' institution, could ever be. Suddenly Welsh Wales acquired metaphoric and paradigmatic potential, not only for indigenous practitioners trained in youth theatres and new university courses, or in Cwmni Theatr Cymru's experimental Adran Antur, but for increasing numbers of outsiders, for whom learning the language was a passport to a world in which technical experimentation could be imbued with social and cultural meaning.

The new theatre that emerged in Welsh-speaking Wales during the 1970s was flexible and mobile, focussing attention on the here and now of the performer, rather than on the fictionalised other space of dramatic literature. It offered, consequently, a mechanism for the generation of new audiences and new cultural experience. Its ethos was close to that of the theatre in education (TIE) movement in England, whose methods and procedures were easily and profitably adapted in Wales from 1971, with the formation of the Breconshire TIE group, later to become Theatr Powys. From 1976, when the Welsh Arts Council took the decision to encourage the establishment of TIE groups in every one of the Welsh counties, the movement grew. Throughout the 1970s TIE was one of several distinguishable strands within the youth programme of Cwmni Theatr Cymru, which included projects like *Y Pibydd Brith* (1968–9) and *Twm o'r Nant – Ei Bobl a'i bethau* (1972) and in the work of the Adran Antur (from 1975), both clearly distinguishable from its mainstream programme. Their interconnectedness was also a general feature of Welsh performance work from the mid-1970s. For example, Theatr Gorllewin Morgannwg, recognised throughout Wales for its distinctive combination of agit-prop and cabaret techniques, was originally established as a TIE company in 1981, but subsequently developed a unique combination of community, educational and satirical theatre. In the same period, Cwmni Cyfri Tri – set up by a group of Aberystwyth graduates following a project they completed with Cardiff Laboratory Theatre to adapt traditional material to a new, physically based theatrical language – merged seven years later with the TIE company Theatr Crwban to form Arad Goch, which pursued a new, wider educational programme.[34]

The mainspring of the theatre produced in Wales outside Cwmni Theatr Cymru in the period after 1976 was either devised performance relevant to

34 Taylor, *Staging Wales*, pp. 189–90.

the immediate demands of the audience, or writing commissioned by a group of performers. Overall, it was motivated by two fundamental ambitions; to create a new audience and a new mythology. Of the two dominant companies, Bara Caws was reminiscent of the bread and cheese of the *gwerin*, Brith Gof of faint memories of traditional practices and values. Despite these differences of emphasis, however, they were both involved in an attempt to establish a new theatrical compact with Welsh-speaking communities.

Bara Caws was set up in 1977 by a group of talented performers who had worked within Cwmni Theatr Cymru under Wilbert Lloyd Roberts's direction, on shows such as *Byw yn y Wlad* (1975). From 1977, with the satirical review *Croeso i'r Roial*, initially presented to a late–night audience in the football club at Wrexham National Eisteddfod, they established a strong rapport with their audience. This continued through a number of popular shows for adults and children during 1978 and 1979 and reached its highest point with two devised pieces, *Bargen* and *Hwyliau'n Codi*. Roger Owen argues that in spite of the relationship they created with specific audiences in Gwynedd, Bara Caws never practised community theatre in the sense that the creative impulse behind their work was generated within a specific locality.[35] Their most successful shows exploited material which had already achieved the status of national myths, even though it related to the experience of specific communities. *Bargen*, for example, was in effect a reworking of the treatment given to the great quarrymen's strike at Bethesda in T. Rowland Hughes's novel, *Chwalfa* (1946).

Throughout the 1980s and 1990s Bara Caws sustained the popularity they had earned with audiences in Gwynedd and further afield with a series of often experimental shows, presented in the same informal, interactive style as *Croeso i'r Roial*. *Zwmba!* (1986) and *Salem ar Sêl* (1988) took sardonic views, respectively, of the world of rugby and the residue of Nonconformism in consumer society. *Siarad Hefo'r Wal* (1990) analysed contemporary views of marriage within a parody of television game shows. Reviews often referred to the slickness of performance and the sheer entertainment value of the product, though as time wore on comments about lack of development and over-emphasis in the scripts became more frequent. Marylyn Samuel's comment on *Os Na Ddaw Blodau* (1990) is typical: 'Instead of hammering out the message, it would be better to let it become apparent gradually as the situation develops.'[36] But at the end of the twentieth century Bara Caws remained a force to be reckoned with in the overall theatrical scene in Wales.

---

35 Owen, 'Y ddefod golledig?', pp. 264–70.
36 Marylyn Samuel, *Golwg* 2 (7 Sept. 1990), 110.

When Mike Pearson and Lis Hughes-Jones left the Cardiff Laboratory The-atre to create Brith Gof in Aberystwyth, in 1981, they set out to explore some of the central myths that had informed Welsh identity, using the techniques of physical theatre. Adapting methods learned from Japanese theatres, in 1981–3 they tested the relevance of exotic performance modes to material drawn from the *Mabinogi*, including the legends about Blodeuwedd and Rhiannon. By 1985 they described their aim as being 'to develop a new, vibrant and distinctive theatre tradition in Wales . . . relevant and responsive to the percep-tions, experience, aspirations and concerns of a minority culture.'[37] Then in 1983, collaborating with Cwmni Theatr Cymru on the *Gernika!* project at the Anglesey National Eisteddfod, they discovered the material which provided an overall frame for their activities during the next few years, under the loose generic heading borrowed from Goya's *Los Desastres de la Guerra*. *Rhydcymerau* (1984) and *Patagonia* (1992), represented a return to the central preoccupation of Welsh culture with its own survival, but the link with Welsh communities was weakening, even before the company moved back to Cardiff in 1988.

Their 1989 project, *Gododdin*, proved that Brith Gof could win an inter-national reputation, but from that time onwards commentators increasingly questioned their commitment to Welsh culture and their respect for audi-ences within Wales. The period from 1981 to 1988 had in fact seen a significant shift of emphasis in their work. By the late 1980s they still aimed to create a relevant and responsive theatre challenging to Welsh audiences, at the same time announcing an increase in site-specific work and a greater emphasis on music.[38] Though *Gododdin* was a success in Wales, criticisms of self-centredness and self-indulgence in *EXX-1* (1989), another of the *Trychinebau Rhyfel* projects, brought their relations with Welsh audiences to their lowest point and probably began the process that culminated in the Arts Council's decision to withdraw support.

Brith Gof's co-director, Cliff McLucas, later explained that *EXX-1* was designed to raise questions for the group, rather than the audience, describing it as one of the 'major lurches, ruptures and fractures' by which they effected their passage to 'new landscapes'.[39] The subsequent reorientation, manifested in shows like *Pax* (Edinburgh, 1989; Aberystwyth, 1991) and *Haearn* (Tredegar, 1992), developed new aspects of site-specific performance, emphasising fracture at the expense of the closures associated with *traditional* theatrical events. Staged in the disused Tredegar iron foundry, where audiences could

---

37 Brith Gof, *Brith Gof: A Welsh Theatre Company: 1981–85* (Aberystwyth: Brith Gof, 1985).
38 Brith Gof, *Brith Gof: A Welsh Theatre Company: 1985–88* (Aberystwyth: Brith Gof, 1988).
39 *Brith Gof Y Llyfr Glas* (Cardiff: Brith Gof, 1995), 35–6.

relate the deliberately disjunctive performance to the reshaping of human identity within the cauldron of heavy industry, *Haearn* showed the group could still forge a strong rapport with its audience. Meanwhile, however, they were becoming increasingly frustrated with the concept of performance as 'product', rather than a process reflecting their own 'fractured, complicated and sophisticated' mode of living.[40]

By 1995 the wheel which Mike Pearson and Liz Hughes Jones had started to turn in 1981 had been deliberately brought full circle.[41] At the beginning of Brith Gof's progress, Welshness offered a territory in which the dissociated identities individuals brought to performance could be integrated in new ways. Within fifteen years, as the audiences defining that territory broke up into smaller, less coherent groupings, the hybridisation of the site-specific project was presented as a paradigm of Welshness itself. By then a Brith Gof project could mean anything, 'negotiating its identity' in other places, irrespective of any cultural or social considerations proper to its place of origin. Only simpler, mechanistic groups, Cliff McLucas explained, believed that it was still possible 'to talk about things, and tell the truth, and communicate, and all these kinds of things.'[42]

Conclusion: endings – and beginnings?

No doubt Bara Caws and Brith Gof initially looked to create audiences similar to those Barba envisaged for the Third Theatre, 'whose powers of reception are particularly rich . . . more open to the displays of the imaginary than many intellectuals'.[43] However, as traditional audiences declined and young people drifted increasingly to the largely Anglicised and urbanised south, and as television culture took firmer hold of the popular imagination, it became increasingly obvious that the cultural revolution necessary to produce this 'third' audience would never take place. By the 1990s, in a new political environment in which funding policies seemed about to descend into permanent chaos and confusion, the Third Theatre's confident, creative activity had definitely come to an end.

The problem of consolidating an audience from among the Welsh-speaking communities dogged not only the new performance groups, but also more

---

40 *Ibid.*, 58.
41 Lis Hughes Jones left Brith Gof in 1992, at around the same time as the composer John E. R. Hardy, who had joined in 1987, four years after Clifford McLucas joined the company as scenographer.
42 *Brith Gof: Y Llyfr Glas*, 70.
43 Cited in *Maskarade*.

Figure 11.3 Act 3 of Gwenlyn Parry's *Y Tŵr*, from Ceri Sherlock's Theatrig touring production, 1987.

mainstream theatrical ventures. Under Graham Laker's direction from 1990 to 1997, Cwmni Theatr Gwynedd, set up in Bangor in the aftermath of Cwmni Theatre Cymru's closure, offered a varied, text-based programme with three elements – the 'classical' Welsh text, an adaptation of a modern European classic and new Welsh drama – only to see audiences consistently declining. Significantly, as the century drew to a close the greatest successes from the point of view of attendance were adaptations of the novels of T. Rowland Hughes (*O Law i Law*, 1986) and Daniel Owen (*Enoc Huws*, 1989) and a version of the phenomenally popular television comedy, *Awe Bryncoch* (1993).

Cwmni Theatr Gwynedd survived through the end of the twentieth century and seemed likely to continue, in spite of the Welsh Arts Council's proposal that it merge with Bara Caws to form a company committed to the production and performance of new texts. Another innovative company, working with the director Ceri Sherlock, met a worse fate. The title, Theatrig, suggested the general thrust of its programme; to create interpretations of traditional Welsh and European texts that would challenge the audience to explore new ways of looking at them. But though it succeeded, with technically striking and provocative productions of *Blodeuwedd* (1985), *Peer Gynt* (1987), *Y Tŵr* (1987) and *Hamlet* (1988), the company failed to convince the Welsh Arts Council that they merited continuing support. Its end may well have been hastened by director-performer Rhys Powys's decision to follow his innovative adaptation of Beckett's *Waiting for Godot* with the experimental productions *Adwaith* (1989) and *Anfadwaith* (1990).

Though it might seem unlikely that the period dominated by Bara Caws and Brith Gof would produce a large number of new plays, the writing of new drama continued unabated, partly because of the efforts of companies such as Hwyl a Fflag a Dalier Sylw and partly because of the relative financial security offered by the numerous independent production companies founded to serve the Welsh television channel S4C. Writers like Gareth Miles, Sion Eirian and Michael Povey continued to produce new work, while writer-directors like Ed Thomas and Sera Moore Williams set up and sustained their own production companies (respectively, Y Cwmni, 1987, and Y Gymraes, 1993).

Looked at in the overall context of Welsh and English theatre work in Wales, this new drama revealed a convergence within the two communities. As for the now not-so-new Third Theatre companies, it could be said that the transition from Cwmni Theatr Cymru's *Byw yn y Wlad* (1975) through Brith Gof's *Rhydcymerau* (1984) and their later site-specific projects like *Once Upon a Time in the West* (1996) and *Lla'th (Gwynfyd)* (1997) marked a hasty and disorganised development from modernism to post-modernism.[44] Welsh-medium drama and performance work at the end of the twentieth century reflected an on-going reassessment of the relationship between individual identity and social practice. Whilst earlier writers ultimately sought forms of closure that celebrated the inter-dependence of identity and social practice, cemented by language, dramatists writing as the millennium turned tended to interpret cultural practice and tradition as restrictive and oppressive mythology. For example, both Ed Thomas and Gareth Miles, the former primarily through English, the latter through Welsh, developed iconoclastic analyses of current mythologies valid across traditional cultural and linguistic boundaries. Simultaneously, gender issues brought together the English-language group Man Act and the feminist Magdalena project (both formed from within Cardiff Laboratory Theatre) with the Welsh-language company Y Gymraes, set up by Sera Moore Williams after initial experience with Cwmni Cyfri Tri and several years as an actress with Brith Gof.

In Wales at the beginning of the twenty-first century post-modernist discourse about the life-enhancing potential of a freer choice of identities drew strength from the powerful commercial forces that favoured the exploitation of digital technology. Digital art found enthusiastic supporters among practitioners and administrators eager for a panacea for the ills experienced by performing arts in a society subject to ever-increasing fragmentation. Whatever English and American practitioners might find in digital art as an alternative to audience-based theatre, however, it was hardly likely to offer much to a beleaguered, minority culture that had survived so far because of the integrative force generated by its various mythologies. Welsh-language culture more than ever needed collaborative art forms in which to create and maintain its own imaginative spaces. But it would take something stronger than optimism to feed a conviction that an audience which could dictate the form of *another* Welsh theatre was already beginning to emerge.

Glossary

Ac Eto Nid Myfi	*And Yet Not Me*
Adar Heb Adenydd	*Birds Without Wings*
Adran Antur	Venture Section
Adwaith	*Reaction*
Amlyn ac Amig	*Amlyn and Amig*
Anfadwaith	Evildoing

44 See Meic Pearson, 'Welsh heterotopias', *New Welsh Review* 21 (1993), 19.

Anterliwt	Interlude
Ar y Groesffordd	*At the Crossroad*
Arad Goch	Red Plough
Awe Bryncoch	*Come on Bryncoch!*
Bara Caws	Bread and Cheese
Bargen	*Contract*: a quarryman's 'bargain' was the patch of slate which he was allowed to work.
Beddau'r Proffwydi	*The Graves of the Prophets*
Ble Mà Fa?	*Where is he?*
Blodeuwedd	*Flowerface*
Brad	*Treachery*
Brith Gof	Faint Recollection
Buchedd Garmon	*The Life of Garmon*
Byw yn y Wlad	*Living in the Country*
Ceidwad yr Porth	*The Doorkeeper*
Ceredigion	Cardiganshire
Chwalfa	*Dispersal*
Chwaraeyddion y Genhinen	*The Leek Players*
Croeso i'r Royal	*Welcome to the Royal*
Cwm Glo	*Coal Valley*
Cwmni Cyfri Tri	'Counting Three' Company
Cwmni Theatr Cenedlaethol Cymru	Welsh National Theatre Company
Cwmni Theatre Cymru	Welsh Theatre Company
Cwmni'r Pandy	The Pandy Company. Originally a fulling mill; Pandy is now a common place name
Cymdeithas yr Iaith Gymraeg	Welsh Language Society
Cymru Fydd	*Future Wales*
Dalier Sylw	*Take Note*
Dirgel Ffyrdd	*Secret Ways*
Gwaed yr Uchelwyr	*Noble Blood*
Gwerin	Folk / People
Gymerwch Chi Sigaret?	*Cigarette?*
Haearn	*Iron*
Helynt Hen Aelwyd	*Trouble on an Old Hearth*
Helyntion Hen Deilwr	*Vicissitudes of an Old Tailor* [novel]
Hunangofiant Rhys Lewis	*Autobiography of Rhys Lewis*
Hwyl a Fflag	Sail and Flag
Hwyliau'n Codi	*Raising Sails / Moods*

Lla'th (Gwynfyd)	*Milk (Bliss)*
Llwyfan	*Stage* [magazine]
Mabinogi/Mabinogion	Various titles for the collection of medieval legends including the stories of Blodeuwedd, Rhiannon and Branwen
Meini Gwagedd	*Empty Stones*
'Nid Ffyr Minks a Bocsys Chocolate ddylai'r Theatr fod'	'Theatre ought not to be all Mink Stoles and Chocolate Boxes' [interview article]
O law i law	*From Hand to Hand*
Os Na Ddaw Blodau	*If No Flowers Come*
Panto	*Pantomime*
Pelenni Pitar	*Peter's Pills*
'Pethau sy'n Aros yn y Cof	'Things that Remain in the Memory'
Plaid Cymru	*The Party of Wales*
Pobl yr Ymylon	*Marginal People*
Problemau Prifysgol	*University Problems*
Saer Doliau	*Doll Doctor*
Salem ar Sêl	*Salem for Sale*
Sgwar Un	*Square One*
Siarad Hefo'r Wal	*Talk to the Wall*
Siwan	*Joan*
Swn y Gwynt sy'n Chwythu	*Sound of the Blowing Wind*
Theatr Crwban	Tortoise Theatre
Theatr Gorllewin Morgannwg	West Glamorgan Theatre
Theatr Powys	Powis Theatre Company
Theatrig	Theatrical
Trychinebau Rhyfel	*Disasters of War*
Twm o'r Nant, Ei Bobl a'i Bethau	*Thomas 'y Nant', his People and his Concerns*
Tŷ ar y Tywod	*House on the Sand*
Tynged yr Iaith	*Fate of the Language* [lecture]
Whare Teg	Fair Play
Y Cwmni	The Company
Y Cymro	*The Welshman* [weekly newspaper]
Y Darian	*The Shield* [radical newspaper]
'Y ddefod golledig?'	This title turns on a play of words, literally 'The Lost Ritual' (defod), rather than ' . . . sheep' (dafad)
Y Dieithryn	*The Stranger*
Y Ffin	*The Boundary*

Y Gododdin	A series of odes attributed to the poet Aneirin, which tells the story of a disastrous Brythonic campaign dated in the sixth century
Y Gymraes	The Welshwoman
Y Pibydd Brith	*The Pied Piper*
Y Pwerdy	The Powerhouse
Y Tad Afradlon	*The Prodigal Father*
Y Tŵr	*The Tower*
Y werin bobl	The common people
Yr Adduned	The pledge

12

Case study: refashioning a myth, performances of the tale of Blodeuwedd

HAZEL WALFORD DAVIES

No text has stimulated a wider spectrum of theatrical presentations and adaptations in Wales than the story of Blodeuwedd, the woman made of flowers, from the fourth of the medieval tales known as the Four Branches of the Mabinogi. Indeed, from 1948 onwards the changing face of theatre in Wales is mirrored in the different stagings of the Blodeuwedd story. This chapter explores the varying cultural moment of each major production based on the myth.

The full range of tales, the Mabinogion, has long been regarded as the crown of Wales's classic imaginative literature. First translated in three volumes by Lady Charlotte Guest in 1846, then issued as a popular single volume in 1877, the tales became much more widely available in 1948 through Gwyn Jones and Thomas Jones's now standard translation. In the early 1950s Dylan Thomas, aware that his own first name came from the Mabinogion, in *Under Milk Wood* has the Revd Eli Jenkins speak of an ancient Llareggub, 'before the Celts left the Land of Summer and where the old wizards made themselves a wife out of flowers'.[1] The Mabinogion have been a major source for Welshlanguage and non-Welsh writing alike, the most popular tale remaining that of Blodeuwedd.

The tale has immediate dramatic force. Arianrhod, the mother of Lleu Llaw Gyffes (the fair one with the deft hand) condemns her son to three fates, the third being that he should never have a wife 'of the race that is now on this earth'.[2] Math, the ruler of Gwynedd, and the magician Gwydion, decide to provide Lleu (later adapted to 'Llew') with a wife: 'they took the flowers of the oak, and the flowers of the broom, and the flowers of the meadowsweet, and

---

1 Dylan Thomas, *Under Milk Wood*, ed. Walford Davies and Ralph Maud (London: J. M. Dent, 1995), p. 60.
2 Anon., *The Mabinogion*, trans. Gwyn Jones and Thomas Jones (London: Everyman, 1992), p. 68.

from those they called forth the very fairest and the best endowed maiden that mortal ever saw . . . and named her Blodeuedd'.[3] During her husband's absence from his court in Ardudwy, Blodeuwedd falls in love with Gronw Pebr, the lord of Penllyn. The two plot Lleu's death and Gronw Pebr stabs him with a spear. Lleu, however, escapes death by turning into an eagle. He is discovered by Gwydion and restored to human shape. Within a year he returns to his court to wreak revenge on Gronw Pebr. Blodeuwedd attempts to escape but is captured by Gwydion, who turns her into an owl, a bird of darkness who must never dare show her face 'in the light of day, and that through fear of all birds'.[4]

The myth gained a renewed major currency in Welsh in 1948 with the performance of Saunders Lewis's play *Blodeuwedd* by the Garthewin Players in a theatre converted from a barn on the Clwyd estate of the landowner R. O. F. Wynne. A major Welsh text was interpreted – even repossessed – by Wales's greatest Welsh-language literary-cultural figure of the twentieth century, and in an aristocratic setting that threw long class and political shadows across Welsh culture. The valency of all subsequent dramatic presentations based on the Blodeuwedd myth is both energised and challenged by this fact.

Saunders Lewis's play had itself been a long time in the making. The first two acts were published in the Welsh-language literary periodical *Y Llenor* in 1923 and 1925. But it was only in 1947 that Lewis revised those acts and completed *Blodeuwedd*, following an invitation from John Morris Jones, the director of the Garthewin Players – a group of amateur actors drawn from all over Clwyd – to write a play for the company. It had its first performance at Garthewin on 15 October 1948. Of course, the years separating the writing of the two halves had been cataclysmic ones in world history, as in Lewis's own life. He had become politically active as one of the prime founders in 1925 of the Welsh Nationalist Party (now Plaid Cymru). He had been imprisoned in Wormwood Scrubs for a powerfully symbolic act of arson in 1936 at an RAF bombing school at Penyberth in Lleyn, as a result losing his post as lecturer in the Welsh Department at University College, Swansea.

It seems, too, that the shadow even of World War One lay on Lewis's first impetus for writing the play. He was excited at seeing Sybil Thorndike as Euripides's Medea at the Liverpool Repertory Theatre in 1921. In February 1922 he wrote to his future wife that he had found 'a kindred character'[5]:

3 *Ibid.*, p. 68.
4 *Ibid.*, p. 74.
5 Saunders Lewis, 'By way of apology', *Dock Leaves* 6 (1955), 10.

There's a glorious theme, taken from the Mabinogion, the faithlessness of
Flowerform, the girl the magicians made of flowers. I take advantage of her
nature origin to make her a fey heroine, one who follows her instincts like all
creatures of earth, careless what disaster she may bring on others.[6]

'Careless what disaster': the between-wars context deepens the dark shades of
the tale. But also Racine's *Andromaque* (1668) was relevant. Not long after the
play's first publication Lewis wrote to a friend, 'Did you ever read Act IV of
Racine's *Andromaque*? There's quite a bit of Hermione in Blodeuwedd also.'[7]
And almost a year after the first performance of the play at Garthewin he wrote
to R. O. F. Wynne that he was convinced that a Welsh audience would 'listen
to a Racinian kind of tragedy, and that is what I attempted in *Blodeuwedd*'.[8]

Wynne's theatre at Garthewin provided Lewis with an approximation of
the ideal performance space he had outlined in 1919 in an article on Welsh
drama.[9] The small intimate theatre had been adapted from a remarkable
eighteenth-century barn in 1937. The barn's roof rested on two handsome
brick arches, one of which formed a discrete proscenium arch. The stage was
low and connected to the auditorium by two shallow steps running the whole
width of the arch, with no footlights and no fixed seats. In the Garthewin
Players, Lewis believed he had also discovered a company of actors who
could speak his verse without the mannered presentation that characterised
Eisteddfod recitations, increasingly influential at the time. He also found in
Morris Jones an amateur director who recognised the prime importance of
the verse and who, in his staging, would leave a great deal to the imagination
of the audience.

Jones's set for *Blodeuwedd* liberated the actors from the naturalistic clutter
that characterised amateur productions in Wales in the first half of the twentieth century. Llew's fort in Ardudwy was represented by simple stone-effect
flats and plain drapes, and the furniture consisted of a wooden stool, bench
and table. Stage left and right, raised steps provided additional playing levels.
Colour was provided by an oversized heraldic shield representing a burning sun and the Welsh dragon rampant, and by plain but bright costumes.
Blodeuwedd's gown and cloak with their blue and green shot-silk effect, over-
laid with gold braid, combined her 'flower' origin with her status as Llew's
wife, and Gronw Pebr's parti-coloured tunic suggested his divisiveness. The

---

6 Mair Saunders Lewis *et al.* (eds.), *Letters to Margaret Gilcriest* (Cardiff: University of Wales
   Press, 1933), p. 483.
7 Nerys Ann Jones, 'Golwg Newydd ar Flodeuwedd', *Taliesin* 65 (1988), 82–3.
8 Hazel Walford Davies, *Saunders Lewis a Theatr Garthewin* (Llandysul: Gomer, 1995), p. 325.
9 Saunders Lewis, 'The present state of Welsh drama', *Welsh Outlook* 6 (1919), 302–4.

restriction of post-war clothes rationing guaranteed that the costumes, made from dyed Bolton sheeting, echoed the simplicity of the set.

Lewis had written the play in the hope 'that some day and some where there might be a Welsh-speaking Sybil Thorndike', who ideally should be dark-haired and able to speak the lines without theatricality.[10] The actress Ellen Wyn Jones was cast as Blodeuwedd. She gave the audience repeated glimpses of the character's changeability and frustration, and her loneliness was reinforced by her standing apart from other characters and hesitating near windows and doors as if anxious to make her escape. What she failed to embody was the character's dangerous sensuality and the fierce physicality of her relationship with Gronw Pebr. When the production later toured, the failure to show the various facets of Blodeuwedd was criticised by a reviewer at the University of Wales, Bangor. But at Rhos another review argued that the play was offensive enough as it was, since there were 'already too many tales of marital infidelity in the newspapers without dragging them onto the stage from the mythology of ancient times'.[11]

Other reviews were positive and particular praise was given to Morris Jones's directorial skills. He, however, had been disappointed that his plan to mix theatrical styles had been scotched even before rehearsals. In *The Mabinogi* Llew can be killed only when standing by a riverbank under a thatched roof with one foot on a goat's back and the other on the edge of a water trough. Morris Jones wanted to dispense with these details and present the killing as a mime in slow motion on a dimly lit stage. He wrote to Lewis to ask for his approval. Lewis's reply pictures a painfully realistic set:

> The setting of Act 3 is very simple. A riverbank; in the centre back, – a tree (or not) and a trough similar to a pig-trough, about 2 or 3 feet high; length about 4 feet (depends on the stage); the edge sufficiently thick for Llew to stand on it . . . It's possible to get hold of an ordinary bathtub and to colour it roughly and it will do wonderfully, or an old cistern or something of the kind to represent the trough.[12]

All this contradicted his statement in a letter to Jones, a month previously, that a director should be free 'to do as he sees fit'.[13]

Towards the end of the rehearsal period, however, Morris Jones and R. O. F. Wynne put their own stamp on *Blodeuwedd*. Lewis's text had ended with

---

10 Lewis, 'By way of apology', 10.
11 Anon., *Rhos Herald* (12 Feb. 1949).
12 Davies, *Saunders Lewis*, p. 316.
13 *Ibid.*, p. 315.

the off-stage mocking laughter of Blodeuwedd. But they persuaded Lewis to replace this with the eerie, drawn-out screech of an owl. This screech in the total darkness of the eighteenth-century barn in the middle of the Clwyd countryside must have been a chilling experience. It was, though, a dramatic device that Lewis was later to condemn as melodramatic.

Lewis, who was present on the opening night, wrote to congratulate the company on 'a brilliant performance'.[14] His first criticism came eight months later and it clearly intimates that he and the director did not share the same vision.

> Morris Jones made two separate acts of my Act 1. I didn't like to intervene, for he was producer. But my own conception was that when Blodeuwedd asks Rhagnell [the maid] for her arm to go to welcome Gronw the lights should go out, then in a $1/2$ minute lights on again showing Gronw facing her and the audience, from the top step on the right, and, if possible, a spot light on him. That would at once allow the intensity of the meeting, and follow the Mabinogi story – a point of importance to the play in the Welsh original and to a Welsh audience.[15]

Eight years later, in 1956, after writing further plays specifically for the company, he came to the conclusion that his dramas were 'not appropriate for ordinary Welsh companies', adding cryptically, 'the companies themselves are of the same opinion'.[16]

Restagings of *Blodeuwedd*

Blodeuwedd's success was significant in Welsh theatre history, since it led to the highly regarded annual Garthewin Welsh Drama Festival, supported by Sybil Thorndike amongst others, and attracting Welsh dramatists such as John Gwilym Jones and Huw Lloyd Edwards. It also attracted several of the best amateur companies from Wales.[17] In R. O. F. Wynne, the Welsh Nationalist and Catholic squire, Lewis had found a congenial patron. For several years after the production of *Blodeuwedd* at Garthewin, Lewis enjoyed 'a settled home, a Welsh Stratford where the pilgrims of drama shall gather'.[18] Indeed, in March 1952 the editor of the *Western Mail* could declare confidently, 'what Malvern was to Shaw, Garthewin is now to Saunders Lewis'.[19]

---

14 *Ibid.*, p. 322.
15 *Ibid.*, p. 325.
16 Saunders Lewis, '*Gymerwch Chi Sigaret?* (Llandybie: Llyfrau'r Dryw, 1956), p. 9.
17 See Davies, *Saunders Lewis*, pp. 203–8, 343–5.
18 Lewis, 'Present State', 304.
19 Anon., *Western Mail* (3 March 1952).

Five years after the Garthewin première, F. G. Fisher, a playwright, amateur director and schoolmaster at Llangefni, Anglesey, chose *Blodeuwedd* as the spring 1953 offering of the Llangefni Drama Society at the local grammar school. This was a production that relied heavily on realistic detail in the creation of a museological medieval hall. The fussy 'period' specificity of the set, of the costumes, of the eating, drinking, taking off of boots and cleaning of swords by the wood-magician Gwydion, robbed the play of its base in legend and turned it into a domestic drama. As Fisher admitted in a programme note to his next production of *Blodeuwedd* in 1964 at Theatr Fach Llangefni, his earlier attempt had taken no account of the mythical dimensions of the play. This time he opted for a bare minimalist stage and relied on shifting light effects and Lewis's poetry. In one sense, this might be seen as Wales's new cultural confidence in the unadulterated adequacy and currency of its own myths in that optimistic decade. Even so, the production was a conventional re-enactment of the text and there was no attempt to create new theatrical perspectives. Instead, this 'safe' production emphasised the primacy of the verse.

Perhaps the most misconceived production of Lewis's *Blodeuwedd* was that of the bilingual touring company Theatr yr Ymylon (Fringe Theatre) in 1975. The guest director was D. J. Thomas, a former drama producer at the BBC in Cardiff. He instructed Christine Pritchard as Blodeuwedd to see the character as a combination of Cleopatra and Lady Macbeth. She was to be a grand tragedienne with all the other characters in subservient supporting roles. There was no hint in this magnificent diva of Lewis's rootless, wild creature. The production aimed at a grand, operatic version, an impression reinforced by the costumes, created by a designer with the Welsh National Opera Company. In the 1970s the newly burgeoning Arts Council was encouraging a 'professionalism' designed to fill the large public stages in the newly built arts centres of university campuses. Theatr yr Ymylon's production reflected this new institutional copiousness. Hence, Blodeuwedd entered on stiletto heels wearing a long blonde wig and a sumptuous dress, with heavy, ornate rings on her fingers: every inch the statuesque beauty. But the formality and stiff folds of the dress did not allow Pritchard the freedom of movement to interpret the primal sensuality of the role. The redeeming feature of the production was the excellent interplay between Pritchard and Olwen Rees as mistress and maid. During a pre-tour rehearsal, immediately after the scene where Blodeuwedd attempts to strangle the maid, Saunders Lewis himself leapt to his feet, clapping and shouting 'Bravo!'

The first effective reinterpretation of *Blodeuwedd* was by Emily Davies in 1977 at the Department of Drama, University of Wales, Aberystwyth. Davies cast Siwan Jones, Lewis's granddaughter, in the title role of a production that was then commissioned for presentation at the Bute Theatre, Cardiff, during the 1978 National Eisteddfod of Wales. Davies was the first director to highlight the difference between the two halves of *Blodeuwedd*. Her production's first half underlined the Racinian, metrical mode of the play while the second half, with its greater flexibility, allowed the young actors greater opportunities for action and movement. Davies argued that

> a naturalistic interpretation of the play would be absurd. *Blodeuwedd* with its roots in legend is mystical. It's a play that insists on its audience's awareness that it must be interpreted through the senses as well as the intellect. The sensuous, dangerous world of nature is ever present in the play.[20]

Accordingly, she ran open-air workshops in the countryside, in Penllyn (Gronw Pebr's domain) and Ardudwy, the actual locale of the play. She also did a great deal of mask work 'in order to release the students from their everyday selves. Indeed, it was as a result of these mask workshops that the actors discovered who was controlling the action in Lewis's play.'[21] She was also the first to dispense with the proscenium arch in a presentation of *Blodeuwedd*. John Meirion Morris designed a set that allowed the audience to sit in a semi-circle skirting a circular space, suggesting simultaneously a ring, a womb, a crown and a prison. At other times, it gave the impression of a magic circle, containing and entrapping Gronw Pebr in Blodeuwedd's spell. During these scenes Blodeuwedd was a wild, wily creature, encircling her prey. Her dark and dangerous nature was echoed in the dissonance of the accompanying music: the harsh and jarring sounds of an untuned keyboard. Throughout the production the lights were dim, menacing and unrealistic. Davies set the characters in the misty world of myth and magic rather than in the daylight world of men.

Davies had consulted Lewis about the final scene and he had said that she should make it clear that it is Blodeuwedd, not her husband, who wins the last argument of the play. In her production, therefore, it was Nature, misused and manipulated by man, that had the final authoritative say. There was no melodramatic owl screech, but the final image pointed to the danger and power of the natural world. Blodeuwedd's costume was the fine silk dress that Dorothy Tutin had worn as Katharine in *Henry V* at the Old Vic in 1951: the long, jagged sleeves of the hand-me-down costume, when extended, suggested enormous wings. At Gwydion's command 'Enter the darkness and join the

---

20 Emily Davies, unpublished interview with Hazel Walford Davies (1988).
21 *Ibid.*

owls', Blodeuwedd opened her arms and the dimly lit circular set seemed to be entirely taken over by a dangerous and menacing bird of the night.

New adaptations

In 1979 Mike Pearson directed an open-air presentation of the Blodeuwedd myth at the National Eisteddfod at Caernarfon. Pearson was founder of the Cardiff Laboratory Theatre, whose work was heavily influenced by Artaud and Grotowski in seeking to create an archetypal theatre language. In this *Blodeuwedd* the tale was divided into several independent scenes introduced by a narrator, a combination of Everyman and Showman. The use of this intermediary freed the company from being slavishly bound to the original. Each scene was stylistically very different, as Pearson explained:

> Thus, a scene using two-dimensional cardboard puppets was followed by one with actors playing the same characters. It was as if each scene began the story afresh using a different technique. Even the most difficult images then became possible as there was no limit on the means to be used. The hunt scene was a number of cardboard dogs running above a screen.[22]

The screen was central to the performance, since it provided a focus for the audience and a backdrop for the actors. The cardboard puppets appeared over the top of it, extraordinarily shaped heads could push through it and, dismantled and shaken, it became the water in which Blodeuwedd's companions drowned as they attempted to escape from Llew's castle. Also, the performance utilised several aspects of Welsh culture. A brass band played Welsh folk-tunes, there was harmony singing and the tradition of animal disguise was woven into many of the episodes. These were mixed with traditions from other cultures: one episode featured the Japanese *bunraku* manipulation technique, with the actors themselves as the puppets. The goat in the scene of the killing of Llew was a piece of sacking and a skull on a pole. Pearson wanted to create a theatrically naïve performance where complexity could come from the audience's interpretation. It was a production that attracted fascinated audiences of adults and children, offering new images of an old tale. Pearson summed it up as 'an elaborate counterpoint of elements drawn from Celtic mythology and Welsh ethnological sources, using a range of techniques uncommon in Welsh theatre. It was a fragmented, imagistic and idiosyncratic visual interpretation made accessible by a vernacular narration.'[23]

22 Mike Pearson, 'Blodeuwedd', unpublished document.
23 *Ibid.*

There were two further innovative adaptations of the myth in the early 1980s, by the Cardiff-based company Moving Being and by Brith Gof. Moving Being's bi-lingual open-air production, *The Mabinogi*, was presented at Cardiff Castle in 1981 and at Caernarfon Castle in 1983. It was devised, directed and choreographed by Geoff Moore, the company's founder and artistic director, who explained: 'the composition of the Company reflected [a] desire for a new language with actors, dancers and musicians in combination with visual artists, not contributing stage design, but working with the art forms of the twentieth century, projection, film, video, electronics.'[24] This production enhanced the multi-media style of the company and involved the participation of several local groups, both amateur and professional. It was a dynamic mix of pageant, dance, music, drama, tale-telling and spectacle. Before and during the show the audience joined in a medieval fair, mixing with troubadours, mummers, falconers, craftsmen, cooks, fortune-tellers and an apothecary. At both Cardiff and Caernarfon full use was made of the battlements, the castle green, the moat and the gates. Original music was commissioned from two musicians representing different aspects of the Celtic bardic tradition. The Scotsman Robin Williams, co-founder of the Incredible String Band, contributed recorded pieces based on Celtic motifs, and the Welshman Geraint Jarman, positioned high on the castle walls with his reggae-influenced rock band, provided live music.

The highly successful 1981 show was reworked for Caernarfon in 1983. Opening within the castle walls at dusk, by the time the action reached the Blodeuwedd myth, darkness had fallen, and the playing area was lit thereafter by blazing fires and flaming torches. The smell of brazier wood-smoke filled the air and curled around the stage, itself a simple timber structure. Blodeuwedd was in tableau on a medieval theatre cart, levelled up to the stage. Her costume was in the Noh theatre tradition, with enormous sleeves supported by sticks held by the actress. At the key moment, when the curse was pronounced on her, these 'arms' which crossed her body and were painted with flowers, suddenly opened out as large wings, covered on the inside with feathers. Simultaneously a hood, designed as the face of an owl, was lifted over the actress's head. As she stood from her seated position, the entire image seemed to rise into the air, as the cart was pulled away into the surrounding darkness.

In presenting *The Mabinogi* as a bi-lingual production, Moving Being sought to reveal the sharp aspects of the language divide and elements in the medieval

---

24 Geoff Moore, *Moving Being: Two Decades of Theatre Ideas* (Cardiff: Moving Being Ltd, n.d.), p. 25.

myths that still operated within Welsh culture. In the cultural tensions of early 1980s Britain, the show was a unique Welsh cultural event: in the politically charged venue of Caernarfon Castle, a solid symbol of suppression, it celebrated Wales's inviolable identity as represented by its ancient myths.[25] The Arts Council of Wales had suggested that the Welsh Tourist Board's Festivals of Castles would provide the ideal opportunity for a revival. But as Moore noted:

> Unfortunately no one at the Tourist Board twigged that the castles all around Wales that they were proposing to celebrate for the tourists, were built by the English to keep the Welsh down . . . Caernarfon Castle . . . [was] . . . not only one of Europe's finest medieval fortresses built to confirm Edward 1st's victory over Llywelyn, the last Welsh Prince, but also the site of the Investiture of the English usurper from the House of Windsor.[26]

Before each performance, to draw attention to these contradictions, Moving Being dissociated itself from the festival by offering the stage to Cofiwn (Let us Remember), the protest group that had objected to the festival. The invitation was not taken up.

Brith Gof's 1982 *Blodeuwedd* was a touring production designed for school and village halls in Ceredigion. The set was a 2.5-metre square polished wooden floor with a colourful canopy suggestive of Balinese village settings. As the same portable stage was used for each performance, the choreography could be exact and detailed. The audience was close to the action on three sides of the stage, so that the players' relationships with them were constantly varied. Set in the middle of each hall, the small stage created an intimate enclosed world. The only prop was a small table at the back, set out with masks, mostly from Ceylon. The pig and bird masks highlighted different movements in the tale, and at the same time created an exotic display from another culture.

The rationale for the production sprang from a number of sources. During 1980 Brith Gof's co-founder and director, Mike Pearson, had spent time in Tokyo with a master of Noh theatre. Pearson used the figure of the Japanese warrior as a resource for the character of Gronw Pebr, who became a *kendo* fighter, dressed in black with a fencing mask, with red *kumadori* make-up in the corner of the eyes and carrying a *bokken*, a wooden Japanese sword. Brith Gof co-founder Lis Hughes Jones played Blodeuwedd. She had studied the Balinese *Legong* dance and adapted it for the final transformation of Blodeuwedd into an owl, attaching a pair of wings to her wrists. Her courtship dance with Gronw

---

25 Moving Being, *The Mabinogi*, programme note (1983).
26 Moore, *Moving Being*, p. 47.

Figure 12.1 Oriental influences on *Blodeuwedd*: Brith Gof, 1982.

Pebr was particularly powerful, as the winding and unwinding of the long sash of her elaborately patterned dress and the positioning of her fan became part of the seduction process. Nia Samuel, dressed in a dinner suit, was the narrator. She guided the audience through the main episodes, and in response to her words the characters enacted the tale. At times she sang the words as a folk-song, at others she announced events in town-crier style. David Baird created the music in full view of the audience, using three synthesisers simultaneously. The score had a wide range, varying from oriental instrumental to Welsh folk-song traditions.

Brith Gof's amalgamation of styles attempted to discover what form an alternative Welsh theatre could take. In a small country, lacking a wealth of dramatic material, Pearson believed the Welsh had to look for other sources of theatrical sustenance. His *Blodeuwedd*, by introducing the exotic alongside the familiar, attempted to animate Eugenio Barba's idea of the 'Third Theatre', seeking through a physical and imagistic *mise en scène* to transform the intimate venues that were familiar to their audiences into 'magical' spaces.

Jeremy Turner, artistic director of Cwmni Cyfri Tri (Count Three Company), in 1987 devised a version of Lewis's *Blodeuwedd* text for a teenage audience. Turner had toured Wales with Barba's Odin Teatret in 1980 and the experience convinced him that Welsh audiences should be given the opportunity to react instinctively rather than intellectually to a performance. By the late 1980s he was creating theatre that produced potent images of Wales and which invited audiences, of young people in particular, to respond imaginatively to the action. His adaptation of *Blodeuwedd* aimed to merge deconstructed sections of Lewis's text seamlessly into a contemporary theatrical presentation entitled *Tyfu* (*Growing*).

The production included residences in secondary schools aimed to enable young people to come to terms with their sexuality, emotions, loneliness and sense of identity. With the actress Catherine Aran he dismantled Lewis's text, using only the lines that illuminated or illustrated the seven sections of *Tyfu*: identity, instinct, belonging, love, sexuality, fear and loneliness. In the single-character presentation everything was seen through the eyes of Blodeuwedd, a woman with no past, no childhood, no relations, no roots, no morality. Her role was to question the audience, asking them to explain to her the experience of loving and being loved, the nature of childhood, the advantages of belonging to a family and a community. Aran's delivery of the short passages from the text had no hint of the rhetorical or declamatory: Lewis's lines and the more colloquial elements of the production sat easily together. Turner's interpretation made a classic 'syllabus' text accessible and relevant, and it showed 'that it was possible to play with plays constructively'[27] within a classroom as well as a theatre.

Back to the text

Ceri Sherlock directed two different productions of Lewis's *Blodeuwedd* in 1985 and 1992 respectively. Theatrig presented the first, and the second was with the Actors' Touring Company, in partnership with the Sherman Theatre, Cardiff. Theatrig's existence was brief (1984–1990), and during its lifetime its repertoire consisted of challenging interpretations of European and Welsh classical texts. *Blodeuwedd* was the company's first adaptation of a Welsh play, chosen because Sherlock felt it afforded ample opportunity to provide a social critique. He believed the play could successfully adopt Brechtian techniques to highlight the political ideas that he had detected in its structure.

The production aimed to illustrate the fact that the play had been written in two very different periods. Sherlock considered that Lewis's personal experiences between 1923 and 1947 had produced a major stylistic shift in *Blodeuwedd* from a drama of ideas to a drama of action. In the second half of the play Blodeuwedd is out of control and propelled along a route that has destruction as its inevitable end: Nature's revenge on man. The point is underlined in Sherlock's programme note for the ATC/Sherman production: 'At the ending of . . . *Blodeuwedd*, that which man has created out of nature cannot be destroyed, it may only like some piece of waste matter be hidden in the night, a constant reminder of what civilization has done to the universe.'[28] In this 1985 *Blodeuwedd* there was a radical difference in presentation between the two halves. The first two acts took place on a minimalist bare stage opening out towards two pools of real water. They aimed to present the essence of the characters in movements partly derived from *kabuki* theatre. On his first appearance, Gronw Pebr adopted the formal, heroic *kabuki* 'mie' stance; subsequently a gold-clad dancer represented the passion between him and Blodeuwedd emblematically. The second half was naturalistic: real plants, trees and moving water reminding spectators of the living force of the natural world. Blodeuwedd's transformation was prepared for by the actress's high-energy physical performance, as if she was in the grip of an implosion, a powerful metamorphosis. Sherlock dispensed with the melodramatic owl-call at the end. He had noted that owls often make menacing hissing

27 Jeremy Turner, unpublished interview with Hazel Walford Davies (1999).
28 Ceri Sherlock, *Blodeuwedd*, programme note (1992).

noises: a hiss, suggesting revenge and danger, filled the final moments of this production.

The 1992 *Blodeuwedd* used an English translation of Lewis's play by the poet and dramatist Siôn Eirian. This time Sherlock's attempt to register the stylistic change between the two halves led, in the opinion of one critic, to an uneven production, 'treading as it does an uneasy path between epic stylisation and intimate naturalism'.[29] Several critics also noted that the young actors from the Actors Touring Company failed to encompass the darker undertones of the play: 'while their young voices catch the daredevilry, they are short on the range and the sound of murky experience'.[30] Less austere than his earlier version, for several scenes Sherlock drew on the medieval romance tradition and Burne Jones and turn-of-the-century symbolist painters influenced the design. Blodeuwedd wore several costumes, their range of colours representing her journey. The men's costumes, like the set, were a blend of medieval and modern. Sherlock's images of the violence unleashed by man's meddling with nature were amongst the most impressive moments of his two productions. At the end a powerful Blodeuwedd was the focus of the audience's attention, precisely because, in Sherlock's opinion, Lewis 'in the second half of the play . . . [had given] all the power to Nature and Desire, the core of his central character'.[31]

By the turn of the millennium, no significant production of Lewis's text, or any other version of the tale, had been performed since Sherlock's 1992 staging. Theatre in Wales during the last decade of the twentieth century had little of the excitement and energy of the early amateur companies, and the innovation and eagerness of the new companies formed during the late 1970s and 1980s seemed to be evaporating. Sherlock, however, planned to return to Blodeuwedd and his work as a director in film and television suggested a new approach appropriate to the fragmented times: 'you can see in the explosive fissures in Saunders Lewis's verse . . . manipulation, communication breakdown, exploitation, time contraction / elongation / replay, and the present imprint of mythic time'.[32] Here is striking confirmation of the hold the story has on the imagination, so that it remains as challenging in the era of technological representation as it had in the medieval world of oral transmission out of which it first sprang.

29 Marie Lewis, *Cambrian News* (20 Nov. 1992).
30 Jeremy Kingston, *Times* (7 Oct. 1992).
31 Ceri Sherlock, unpublished interview by Hazel Walford Davies (1993).
32 Ceri Sherlock, personal correspondence to Hazel Walford Davies (May 2001).

Figure 12.2 The killing of Llew in *Blodeuwedd*: Actor's Touring Company / Sherman
Theatre, Cardiff, 1992.

PART III

*

1940–2002

13

British theatre, 1940–2002: an introduction

BAZ KERSHAW

British theatre in the second half of the twentieth century was probably more consistently volatile than at any other time in its long history. This is not surprising. After an initial collapse, the number and diversity of types of theatres and companies grew substantially, especially from the 1960s to the 1990s. Moreover, as theatre was still the art form most directly engaged in the public sphere through its face-to-face encounters in the live event, that growth gained energies from the huge cultural, social, political, economic and technological transformations that coursed around the globe as the millennium drew closer. Yet simultaneously the significance of theatre was subject to growing uncertainty and doubt, not least among the ranks of its practitioners. As other cultural forms – including performance – became ubiquitous, British theatre, despite its growth, seemed to lose much of its traditional authority in society. Then in the digital age that emerged in the final three decades of the century perhaps it faced its nemesis. The seductions of the new media not only vastly outstripped the theatre numerically, they also became insinuated into the production-consumption circuits of the live event itself, maybe inflecting its perceptual-cognitive processes with subtle confusions. When Nicole Kidman slipped out of her dress in *The Blue Room*, David Hare's version of Arthur Schnitzler's *La Ronde* at London's Donmar Warehouse Theatre in 1998, did the audience simply enjoy a mega-film-star in the raw, so to speak, or did the powerful qualities of her filmic persona make a kind of cross-media palimpsest of her flesh, especially as she was set on a 'stage [that] shimmers in blue light and neon signs, with film captions and crackling electronic sounds to signal the time taken before orgasm'?[1]

Such complexities push theatre historiographies into especially contested territory, in which every bid for accurate generalisation has to be qualified,

---

1 Nicholas de Jongh, *London Evening Standard*, cited http://www.albemarle-london.com/blueroom.html (10 Aug. 2003).

possibly to the point of disappearance. Hence the general narrative of British theatre's volatility, decline and possible rejuvenation that shapes this chapter is only one of many potential stories. This results from the more or less likely 'fact' that in the late twentieth century the so-called developed countries of the world entered a post-modern period in which 'history' was 'without a subject',[2] so that 'histories' became provisional assemblages of the detritus of the past, forever open to reassembly and reinterpretation. For every account of theatre *circa* 1940–2002, there is, almost certainly, a counter-account.

As a consequence, the way we envisage the theatre in context may have to be rethought. So if, for example, theatre is not a 'mirror' of the social, if it is not a 'slice of reality' abstracted for inspection, if it is not a 'laboratory' for investigating the human – how should we think of it? In 1972 Raymond Williams analysed the evolution of 'drama in a dramatised society' brought about by the spread of film, television and radio; he saw it as instilling the flux of 'drama', previously provided by the separate domain of theatre, into the textures of everyday life.[3] Just twenty years later the American performance theorist Richard Schechner argued that performance was replacing theatre so that 'the staging of written dramas . . . will be the string quartet of the twenty-first century: a beloved but extremely limited genre'.[4] It is not yet known if this will prove to be the case, but there can be little doubt that towards the end of the twentieth century the mediatisation of society had fabulously extended the dramatising process identified by Williams.

In Britain and elsewhere, that process was also massively reinforced by a widespread transition between the 1940s and the 1990s from economies based on industry to ones based on service and information. That transition encouraged the aestheticisation and then the theatricalisation of cultural exchange, so that performance, as it were, slipped out of the theatre to become wholly integral to all aspects of social endeavour. Moreover, the global spread of liberal democracy did not bring about the end of history, as some claimed,[5] but its reliance on mass persuasion in regular contests between political parties reinforced the theatricalisation of the social. These forces, bearing through the fantastic proliferation of media brought about by the emergence of global market

---

2 David Ashley, *History Without a Subject: The Postmodern Condition* (Oxford: Westview Press, 1997).
3 Raymond Williams, *Writing in Society* (London: Verso, 1991), pp. 11–21.
4 Richard Schechner, 'A new paradigm for theatre in the academy', *Drama Review* 36, 4 (1992), 8.
5 Francis Fukuyama, *The End of History and the Last Man* (Harmondsworth: Penguin, 1992).

economies, engendered the performative society.[6] In such a society the theatre is positioned paradoxically: it tends to lose whatever made it previously so special, but it also can become the cultural equivalent to what ecologists call 'edge phenomena', places fostering especially diverse life forms, such as riverbanks or deep-sea volcanic vents. So if we think of theatre systemically as integral to wider ecologies we might fashion a general narrative of its history (or histories) that acknowledges something of the 'nature' of the performative society.

However, it may seem perverse, especially given that 'history' probably now 'has no object', to attempt a general narrative of British theatre *circa* 1940–2002. Surely it would be 'safer', even 'more accurate' to provide a series of discrete impressions selected from 'significant moments' of theatre in the period: the première of *Look Back in Anger* in 1956, the emergence of alternative theatre in 1968, the opening of the National Theatre in 1976? Yet such a method could well miss the continuous flux of interdependencies between, say, theatres and companies, economics and aesthetics, state institutions and artists and so on, that characterises culture when it is viewed, literally, as an ecology. So what follows is an attempt at identifying the main interacting energies of theatrical change in this sixty-year period. I concentrate on four main factors to give shape to the narrative. Firstly, state subsidy and its influence in the structure of the theatre estate, leading eventually to proliferation and diversity. Secondly, new opportunities for creativity in the theatre, especially through the formation of new sectors and innovations in production. Thirdly, the growing impact of technology and mediatisation on the practices and status of theatre. And fourthly, theatre audiences and their changing roles. The first three of these are woven into the general narrative; the fourth is presented in three separate short sections, each dealing with distinct periods in which audiences were encouraged to assume different roles: as patrons, then clients, then customers. Through this contrast – continuous flow as against periodisation – I hope to exemplify the historiographic presumptions that inevitably come strongly into play in histories of the relatively recent past, especially histories of a phenomenon so excitable and volatile as British theatre between 1940 and 2002.

In the wake of war

World War Two had an immediate and long-lasting impact on the distribution of theatre in Britain. All theatres were closed by government order and after

---

6 Baz Kershaw, 'Dramas of the performative society: theatre at the end of its tether', *New Theatre Quarterly* 17, 3 (August 2001).

they reopened the Blitz ensured that West End playhouses were just 'touring dates' until 1941: in 1940 the actors' union Equity reported that only 26 of its 1,500 members usually employed in the metropolis were at work there.[7] The vast bulk of wartime performances took place outside London: by 1942 factories, military bases and other venues nationwide were receiving around 4,300 entertainments a year, *plus* productions of plays, a level generally sustained through to 1945.[8] This potential foundation for a truly popular national theatre was laid by three organisations: ENSA (Entertainments National Service Association); the civilian Drama Section of CEMA (Council for the Encouragement of Music and the Arts); and the Play Unit of ABCA (Army Bureau of Current Affairs).

ENSA (founded in 1938) organised tours of light entertainment to military and then civilian venues, at its height in 1944 regularly employing 4,000 artists.[9] The CEMA Drama Section from 1940 organised concerts and more traditional theatrical fare for touring. The Old Vic Company, for example, transferred to Burnley in 1940, then Liverpool, from where it toured standard repertory fare to villages and small towns: in Wigan *Othello* was the town's 'first straight play in twenty years'.[10] The Pilgrim Players, directed by Martin Browne, were a little more adventurous, with plays by James Bridie, D. H. Lawrence and Henri Ghéon: venues included a barn attached to Ellen Terry's cottage in Kent.[11] The ABCA Play Unit was founded in 1943 and its companies, staffed entirely by armed forces personnel, toured short and serious shows to thousands of military units for the rest of the war.[12] Also, from 1942 CEMA had begun buying into theatrical real estate, most significantly at the Theatre Royal in Bristol, then the Lyric Theatre, Hammersmith.[13] This policy was the basis of Laurence Olivier's post-war success with the Old Vic companies and, eventually, the building of the National Theatre in 1976. It also introduced a structural tension into the theatre system that shaped its ecology through to the

7 Andrew Davies, *Other Theatres: The Development of Alternative and Experimental Theatre in Britain* (London: Macmillan, 1987), pp. 125–7.
8 Robert Hewison, *Under Siege: Literary Life in London 1939–45*, rev. edn (London: Methuen, 1988), p. 180.
9 Richard Fawkes, *Fighting for a Laugh: Entertaining the British and American Armed Forces 1939–1946* (London: Macdonald & Jane's, 1978), p. 13.
10 Davies, *Other Theatres*, p. 127.
11 Peter Billingham, *Theatres of Conscience 1939–53: A Study of Four Touring British Community Theatres* (London: Routledge, 2002), p. 46; Henzie and E. Martin Browne, *Pilgrim Story: The Pilgrim Players, 1939–1943* (London: Frederick Muller, 1945).
12 Peter Noble, *British Theatre* (London: British Yearbooks, 1946), p. 96; Fawkes, *Fighting for a Laugh*, pp. 103–10.
13 Charles Landstone, *Off-Stage: A Personal Record of the First Twelve Years of State-Sponsored Drama in Great Britain* (London: Paul Elek, 1953), pp. 43–9, 86–8.

Figures 13.1a & b Two versions of theatre touring in wartime Britain: (a) the Pilgrim Players prepare to leave Dartington, Devon (1940) and (b) leaving Ashford, Kent after a school performance (1941).

millennium, between expensive building-based production mostly oriented towards London and low- to medium-cost touring that could be available anywhere.

Following the war a moderately complicated pattern of approaches to making theatre emerged, ranging from seaside summer variety to avant-garde experiments in arts theatres. A few pierrot companies survived into the 1950s, such as Ernest Binn's Arcadian Follies at Skegness and Alan Gale's Wavelets at

Redcar,[14] while blackface minstrelsy, remarkably, was revived in the 1960s with the BBC's *Black and White Minstrel Show*. But post-war holiday taste preferred the more 'sophisticated' fare of musical variety, which gained strength from the growth of light entertainment on radio and early television, as artistes such as Stanley Holloway, Tony Hancock, Joyce Grenfell and many more traded across the media. The 'little theatre' tradition continued, mostly in London, where venues for experiment included the Arts Theatre Club, the Mercury Theatre and the left-wing Unity Theatre, which also had branches in Bristol, Liverpool, Glasgow and elsewhere. However, the fact that in 1948 both the Arts Theatre – with Christopher Fry's *The Lady's Not for Burning* – and Glasgow Unity – with Robert McLeish's *The Gorbals Story* – transferred shows to central London theatres is significant.

London's West End was dominated by a capitalist consortium known as the Group: it owned the majority of theatres and managed a small number of producing companies. H. M. Tennent Ltd was foremost among the latter, staging lavish, star-studded versions of modern classics (*Lady Windermere's Fan*, 1945), the occasional new play (Williams's *A Streetcar Named Desire*, 1949), translations (Anouilh's *Ring Round the Moon*, 1950) and a string of American musicals, starting with *Oklahoma* in 1947. It is telling, then, that in 1950 the Shakespeare Memorial Theatre invited Tennent's chief producer, 'Binkie' Beaumont, onto its Board of Management, and he followed this with six years (1962–8) on the board of Olivier's National Theatre.[15] This very minor event, when juxtaposed with the Arts and Unity Theatres' transfers, suggests a powerful systemic shift that served to draw virtually every professional company into the hegemony of West End production values: 'the best star actors, exquisite sumptuous costumes, highly elaborate, superbly designed sets, tightly controlled, sure-footed productions'.[16]

The post-war strengthening of London theatre was gained at the expense of the regions. Estimates of the number of commercial companies touring beyond London immediately after the war range as high as 250.[17] By the early 1950s those solely touring had dropped to around forty-three, though there were about a further hundred for-profit repertory companies resident in

---

14 Geoff J. Mellor, *Pom-Poms and Ruffles: The Story of Northern Seaside Entertainment* (Clapham, Yorks: Dalesman, 1966), pp. 22–3, 10.
15 Martin Banham, 'Hugh (Binkie) Beaumont', *The Cambridge Guide to Theatre*, updated edn (Cambridge University Press, 1995), p. 80.
16 Sally Beauman, *The Royal Shakespeare Company* (Oxford University Press, 1982), p. 189.
17 *The Stage Year Book 1949*, p. 30, cited in George Rowell and Anthony Jackson, *The Repertory Movement: A History of Regional Theatre in Britain* (Cambridge University Press, 1984), p. 84.

regional theatres for periods varying from a few weeks to a year.[18] Yet by 1956 the total for all types of commercial company had fallen to around fifty-five.[19] This was in line with a steady fall in the number of cinema attendances per annum, from around 1.6 million in 1946 to just under 0.45 million in 1961.[20] Television is usually cited as a major factor in this decline in public pleasures, as TV ownership was boosted greatly by the 1953 coronation of Elizabeth II and by 1961 75 per cent of families had 'the box'.[21] But the influence of the Arts Council on the reps, though small scale and highly focussed, was possibly of equal significance to that sector's general instability. N. V. Linklater relates how the Council in the 1950s offered small subsidies to a selection of the commercial repertory companies in order to increase rehearsal time and 'improve standards',[22] a strategy wholly in line with the 'Few but Roses' policy that it operated from the 1940s to the 1960s. The unsubsidised companies could not compete against such an advantage and the majority rapidly closed, producing a collapse of regional touring that was almost total, soon followed by a major depletion of the country's stock of theatre buildings: by 1970 around a hundred theatres had closed down and only thirty main touring venues were left.[23] Two important effects resulted: London's place in the theatre system was hugely strengthened; and the way was opened for the growth of subsidised, civic theatres in the regions.

In the 1940s the between-wars repertory ideals of Miss Horniman and Barry Jackson had survived in the few regional theatres – Birmingham, Bristol, Cambridge, Sheffield and Glasgow among them – which generated a reputation for 'high-minded seriousness and lofty anti-commercialism'.[24] Aesthetic snobbery, cultural prestige, economic instability and outmoded management practices combined to produce a steep ranking in the 1950s among the richest West End theatres, the leading not-for-profit building-based repertory companies, the main London-based managements mounting commercial tours, and the generality of down-market short-term resident or touring box-office-driven reps. It was the base of this hierarchy that collapsed, thus creating a cultural perturbation in which a new, more professionalised system of subsidised and

---

18 John Pick (ed.), *The State and the Arts* (Eastbourne: John Offord, 1980), p. 80.
19 Rowell and Jackson, *Repertory Movement*, p. 87.
20 British Film Institute website: http://www.bfi.org.uk/facts/stats/alltime/uk_admissions.html (12 Feb. 2003).
21 Arthur Marwick, *British Society Since 1945* (Harmondsworth: Penguin, 1982), p. 121.
22 Pick, *State and the Arts*, pp. 82–3.
23 *Ibid.*, pp. 95–6.
24 John Elsom, *Post-War British Theatre*, rev. edn (London: Routledge & Kegan Paul, 1979), p. 11.

commercial theatre based on buildings could flourish. Such a system was unlikely to provide theatre as a people's art, even if the majority of the population was, theoretically, in reach of appropriate venues. The promise enshrined in the Arts Council's founding charter – 'to increase the accessibility of the arts to the public throughout Great Britain',[25] which ENSA, CEMA and ABCA had shown could be a reality – was utterly compromised. Theatre as a democratic benefit was undermined both by high-power commercial managements and by the very guardians in the Council who had been appointed to protect it.

Buildings and London: the twin poles of power that dominated British theatre throughout the 1960s and until well into the 1970s. Hence, the collapse of touring in the 1940s and 1950s is invisibly embedded in Olivier's vision of a theatre system that needs 'headquarters' in major cities; that is to say, theatre buildings.[26] A national theatre conference, chaired by J. B. Priestley, in 1948 confirmed this faith in 'bricks and mortar', plus a system of imagined strategic links between them, as being at the heart of theatrical life, in turn reinforcing Arts Council support for Olivier's ambitions for the Old Vic companies as the next stage leading to a concrete edifice: the National Theatre.[27] The mass closure of regional theatres paradoxically helped to germinate notions of a future featuring new replacements: if architect-designed council estates were possible, why not theatres? The theatrical establishment – as represented by West End managers, star actors, up-and-coming directors (such as Peter Brook), and even the tail-end of the actor-manager tradition still continued by the likes of Donald Wolfit – obviously had vested interests in this evolution, which powerfully resonated with the post-war theme of a national effort to rebuild 'Great Britain' itself into a stable and prosperous entity. But in the late 1940s the Old Vic project ran into difficulties and so George Devine and the English Stage Company at London's Royal Court Theatre, founded in 1956, came to provide a model for theatrical consolidation in Britain. Devine, however, was faced with a twofold challenge: he not only had to create a new type of theatre, but also a new kind of audience.

Audiences in the 1940s and 1950s

In the interwar years mainstream audiences were usually treated by theatres, and probably thought of themselves, as patrons. Generally, two traditions of

25 Pick, *State and the Arts*, p. 3.
26 Noble, *British Theatre*, pp. 3–4.
27 J. B. Priestley, *Theatre Outlook* (London: Nicholson & Watson, 1947), pp. 77–81; Davies, *Other Theatres*, pp. 147–8.

patronage ran in parallel. Firstly, there was a popular tradition that stretched back to the melodramas and music halls of Victorian England, in which audiences were particularly demonstrative. Secondly, there was a more genteel tradition, initiated by the Bancrofts at London's Prince of Wales's Theatre in the late nineteenth century, and then growing in importance as repertory theatre managers aimed to attract the burgeoning middle classes.[28] In both traditions audience patronage implied audience power – the patron assumes a right will be met – and this no doubt contributed to the tendency in pre-World War Two audiences – especially in the form of the 'gallery first-nighters' – sometimes to take matters into their own hands.[29]

Dan Rebellato has shown how all this began to change in the period immediately following World War Two.[30] The popularity of theatre during wartime meant that it continued to attract a good cross-section of the population, and audiences had a moderately wide repertoire of activities to indulge in, including drinking tea and eating biscuits in the auditorium. These audiences then seem to have felt pretty free in expressing their views of the show: shouted comments, booing and yells of approval were common practice, and a wide range of laughter was in play. In the 1950s the propriety of this freedom was increasingly debated, with writers such as Noel Coward, J. B. Priestley and Terence Rattigan defending the right of the audience to express judgement however they wished. In contrast, some journalists and, not surprisingly, many actors argued for more decorum: in 1952, for example, Sybil Thorndyke stormed 'Sometimes I feel like spitting at the audience because of the noise made by unwrapping chocolates'.[31]

So the conventional picture of audiences dominated by middle-class etiquette in the 1940s and 1950s is a far cry from their actual practices. The messy edge between stage and auditorium in much of post-war mainstream theatre was an arena of vitality and potential growth. The patrons of theatre were exercising an assumed right because that role made them the arbiters of taste; as Rebellato puts it, 'this self-consciousness in the audience is a recognition of collective identity and collective power'.[32] How ironic, then, that as the theatre estate shrank its attendant audiences were threatened with a reduction in their participation and power, and in the self-same period that a new kind of

28 John Pick, *The West End: Mismanagement and Snobbery* (Eastbourne: John Offord, 1983), pp. 117, 119.
29 See chapter 7, above, pp. 152–4.
30 Dan Rebellato, *1956 And All That: The Making of Modern British Drama* (London: Routledge, 1999), pp. 104–9.
31 *Ibid.*, p. 108.
32 *Ibid.*, p. 105.

democracy, one that went beyond enfranchisement to reach for a redistribution of resources through the Welfare State, was struggling for legitimacy in Britain.

After the Royal Court

Conventional histories routinely cite John Osborne's *Look Back in Anger*, staged by the English Stage Company at the Royal Court Theatre in its first season in 1956, as the play that unleashed a new age of great British drama. But the first *literal* foundations of the success of the 'new wave' playwrights were laid two years later and 100 miles further north by Coventry City Council, which opened the brand-new Belgrade Theatre in 1958. The Belgrade's chief significance, though, is *not* that it was the first new playhouse built since the new Shakespeare Memorial Theatre had been opened in 1932; that accolade must go to Middlesborough Little Theatre, constructed for local non-professional groups in 1957 and paid for by industrial and private donations.[33] Rather, the Belgrade is important because it was primarily funded through the Local Authority by ratepayers: it was the first purpose-built Welfare State theatre. There followed a flurry of publicly financed new theatre buildings, conversions and renovations – including, for example, the Bolton Octagon, Chester Gateway, Ipswich Wolsey, Leicester Haymarket, Worcester Swan Theatres; and in London the Shaw, Young Vic and National Theatres – until, by the late 1970s, there were about sixty such mainstream-style theatres in towns and cities throughout England, plus several more in Scotland and Wales. If other newly created, dedicated venues for performance are added, such as studios in arts centres, pub theatres and small alternative theatre venues, then the total for the period rises to well over a hundred.[34] In just twenty years the loss of the old commercial touring theatres was, roughly speaking, 50 per cent replaced by civic repertory playhouses and 50 per cent by a new miscellaneous mix of venue types – virtually all of them dependent on state subsidy. The council housing estates had been matched by a theatrical equivalent.

Virtually all of the new repertory theatres enshrined both civic pride and a democratic ethic: the frontages and foyers invariably (but usually unostentatiously) aimed to impress, while fan-shaped auditoria, thrust or flexible stages, low differentials in seat pricing and other attempts at 'accessibility' were commonplace. Moreover, many had resident companies, played in repertory and,

33 Pick, *State and the Arts*, p. 86.
34 *Ibid.*, p. 87.

from 1965, founded theatre-in-education companies, all aimed to consolidate identification with the local community. Through the 1960s and 1970s the levels of funding from the Local Authorities, the Arts Council and the new Regional Arts Associations showed some inevitable fluctuations, but the build-up in the system of public grant-giving ensured mostly that subventions were, to all intents and purposes, guaranteed. This was indeed the theatrical *sector* of the Welfare State, in principle broadly egalitarian, in general orientation pitched as a 'service' for the workers needed in the fast-growing industries forged in 'the white heat of technological revolution' imagined by newly elected prime minister Harold Wilson in 1964 as the 'age of affluence' got well and truly under way.[35]

By 1969 there were at least fifty-two subsidised repertory companies operating in Britain,[36] and of course they varied in the detail of their repertoire, management, economics and audiences. Yet the policies of the majority were pretty uniform, as they modelled themselves, more than less, on the Royal Court Theatre. From the outset they were run by artistic directors with the power to hire and fire, to choose the plays, to dictate the stage style and so on. This elevation of theatre artists to the ranks of state or local authority employed professionals on regular salaries went hand-in-hand with adulation of the playwright – living and dead – as a sage for the times. Powerful new partnerships, virtually always male, were struck between writers and directors, consolidating the reputations of theatres and exploiting new opportunities in film and television. London led the way with Tony Richardson and John Osborne, Peter Hall and Harold Pinter, William Gaskill and Edward Bond, John Dexter and Arnold Wesker. Exceptional actors, less tied to buildings than their off-stage colleagues, became highly skilled itinerant entrepreneurs of the public persona, slipping with apparent ease (but often consummate creative *élan*) across the borders between the boards, the screens and the glossy magazines. So subsidy increasingly became a springboard to personal riches, even fortunes. And gradually, as the not-for-profit egalitarian theatre estate of the new reps progressed into the 1970s, it became a cultural zone of acute institutional inequalities.

These in-growing contradictions between the founding principles and actual practices of the publicly funded theatre system eventually, in the 1970s, generated strong reactions among the emergent ranks of alternative theatre practitioners. Yet the repertory theatres' audiences of the 1960s, judged against the

35 Marwick, *British Society Since 1945*, p. 115.
36 Rowell and Jackson, *Repertory Movement*, p. 90.

probability that their numbers held steady because 'more . . . were attending though less frequently',[37] were apparently acquiescent in the whittling away of their powers. At best, this may be interpreted as gratitude for the new largesse in state and local authority provision; at worst, it may indicate pleasure in becoming willing suppliants at the new civic shrines to an increasingly haughty and self-interested art. Either way, in retrospect the artists' confident habitation of the new buildings *as a system* expressed a professionalisation that undermined the democratic purposes which had informed that system's creation. And increasingly, from the late 1950s into the 1970s, the regional building-based companies, besides appealing to their local communities, aimed for transfers to the West End.[38] Hence, the 'new wave' of post-1956 playwriting and the production methods it stimulated, for all its revitalising and quasi-democratic fervour, became integral to a deeply reactionary, systemic undertow. Where there were clear exceptions to these developments, such as at Peter Cheeseman's Victoria Theatre at Stoke-on-Trent and at the Liverpool Everyman under Alan Dosser, they served to highlight the rule of the emergent hierarchy. This tension in British theatre was one cultural response to the Labour government's fulsome embrace of a mixed economy in which socialist and capitalist principles supposedly were in rapprochement.

Meanwhile, the West End thrived, in part because some of its impresarios in the late 1950s and early 1960s – Donald Albery, Michael Conron and Oscar Lewenstein among them – premièred plays by the likes of Brecht, Dürrenmatt, Robert Bolt and John Mortimer, which were subsequently staged in subsidised theatres.[39] This belies the conventional view that West End theatre in this period was a moribund playground for the privileged, who continued to dress up in order to peer into a world of butlers, French windows, tea and tennis that somehow mirrored their own, or at least what they would like their own to be like – but only partly. The dress suits, long gowns and associated couture continued as influential motifs on both sides of the (actual) footlights well into the 1960s, though frequently they were pretty transparent cover for the open secret of queer sexual dissent on theatrical display, the stage as the original 'glass closet'.[40] Also, despite the mundane taste of much of the homegrown commercial drama, there was no small number of fabulous actors eager to shape plays to *their* purposes. Laurence Olivier, John Gielgud, Ralph

---

37 *Ibid.*, p. 128.
38 *Ibid.*, pp. 126–7; Pick, *West End*, p. 168.
39 Pick, *West End*, p. 163.
40 Rebellato, *1956 and All That*, pp. 155–91.

Richardson, Fay Compton, Peggy Ashcroft, Coral Browne and the rest apparently saw no necessary demarcation lines between the established commercial and new subsidised theatres, any more than did the new generation of 'star' directors such as Peter Brook and Peter Hall. In line with the affluence delivered by the mixed economy, the 'top' theatres in the late 1950s and 1960s became hothouses in which the newly professionalised cultural entrepreneurs flourished. Hence, Hall engineered the transformation of the Shakespeare Memorial Theatre into the Royal Shakespeare Company in 1960, astutely seeing that the repertory ideal of an ensemble company plus a London base at the Aldwych Theatre were necessities if the 'national playwright' was to have a stage on a par with the nascent National Theatre.

When the latter finally materialised as the National Theatre at the Old Vic in 1963 under Olivier's direction, the critical functions of the theatre in society were already in the process of institutionalisation in the civic repertory theatres. The appointment of Jenny Lee as the first ever Minister for the Arts in 1964, when Labour returned to power after thirteen years of Tory rule, was emblematic of the new dispensation. Hence, if a theatrical 'revolution' *had* been effected by the 'angry young men' of the 1950s, it was quickly domesticated by a speed-up in the quasi-nationalisation of the arts in the following decade. Once that had been mostly achieved it was time – because relatively safe – to get rid of the Lord Chamberlain and a censorship régime that had been in place for 231 years. The blue-pencil role was abolished in 1968. The new freedom allowed the American musical *Hair* a moment of quasi-revolution as its singing and dancing cast shed all their clothes on stage; but perhaps the more telling production historically was the 'opportunistic trash'[41] imported from America by the literary advisor of the National Theatre, Kenneth Tynan, which eventually found its way into the West End: the 'nude revue', *Oh! Calcutta!*[42]

Such a view of the late 1960s 'overthrow' of stage censorship in Britain may seem unduly jaundiced. Tynan was right, of course, to attack 'the Royal smut hound' as responsible for some of the 'rot that . . . plagues the British theatre',[43] and it took bravery and determined efforts from major theatre artists, such as Edward Bond and William Gaskill, to bring the agent of state censorship down. Yet there was a resounding 'absence of jubilation when the Theatres

---

41 Richard Eyre and Nicholas Wright, *Changing Stages: A View of British Theatre in the Twentieth Century* (London: Bloomsbury, 2000), p. 313.
42 Dominic Shellard, *British Theatre Since the War* (New Haven: Yale University Press, 1999), pp. 147–8.
43 Kenneth Tynan, 'The royal smut hound', in Micheline Wandor, *Look Back in Gender: Sexuality and the Family in Post-War British Drama* (London: Methuen, 1987), p. 78.

Act became law'.[44] *Hair* opened at the West End's Shaftesbury Theatre on the day after the law came into force, prompting Charles Marowitz to argue that the show 'is about everything that is going on at the moment'.[45] But that 'everything' must of course include the operations of the state in exercising its powers. 'Liberalisation of censorship', notes Arthur Marwick, 'had been one of the most striking products of the combination of radical protest and measured judgement'.[46] If the theatre had offered radical protest through the content of plays such as Arden's *Live Like Pigs* (1958) and Bond's *Early Morning* (1968), then the state simply continued in the process of applying the measured judgement that had brought about the legalisation of abortion, homosexual acts (at least in private) and divorce. Besides, the government had nothing much to fear from the dominant forms of British theatre, because by the late 1950s and through the 1960s its audiences had been well and truly tamed.

Audiences in the 1950s and 1960s

The audience's role as patron, Dan Rebellato argues, began to change with the creation by George Devine of the English Stage Company at the Royal Court Theatre in 1955. Symptomatic of this shift was the appointment of an 'audience organiser' to arrange group visits, a function with a subtly disciplinary agenda. Devine set about making a theatre that would be superior to the audience, in which poor box office would demonstrate not something wrong with the theatre, but with the public. This meant stripping the audience of any assumed authority, but particularly the right of the patron to arbitrate taste: Lindsay Anderson, Associate Director (on and off) from 1959 to well into the 1970s, had proposed that the phrase *'Judge not* should be inscribed on (every Royal Court) programme'.[47] It became almost a matter of faith to deny the audience a dignified identity as a basis of judgement: John Osborne recalls Devine peering through the curtain at the auditorium on the first night of *The Entertainer* (1957), and urging 'There you are, dear boy, take a look out there . . . What do you think, eh? Same old pack of cunts, fashionable arseholes. Just more of them than usual, that's all.'[48]

---

44 Nicholas de Jongh, *Politics, Prudery and Perversions: The Censoring of the English Stage 1901–1968* (London: Methuen, 2001), p. 240.
45 Charles Marowitz, quoted in Arthur Marwick, *The Sixties: Cultural Revolution in Britain, France, Italy and the United States, c.1958–c.1974* (Oxford University Press, 1998), p. 358.
46 *Ibid.*, p. 734.
47 Lindsay Anderson, 'Vital Theatre', *Encore* 4, 2 (Nov.–Dec. 1957), pp. 10–14, quoted in Rebellato, *1956 and All That*, p. 110.
48 *Ibid.*, p. 112; but cf. Philip Roberts, *The Royal Court Theatre and the Modern Stage* (Cambridge University Press, 1999), pp. 48–50.

The other side of the coin to this disgraceful disdain was the elevation of the professional artist to become an aesthetic expert who knows what is good for the public. Rebellato points out that this casts the audience as *client*, a role defined by an assumption of automatic deference to the expert. Such an attitude was necessary to its on-stage concomitant, often promoted by Devine, in the artist's 'right to fail'. This elimination of any ethical recourse to accountability in retrospect can be seen as an extraordinary move in the context of an emergent publicly subsidised, state-approved theatre system. Yet this redefinition of the artist's 'integrity' was reinforced significantly by the growth of Arts Council bureaucracies in the 1960s and 1970s, which had a vested interest in the valorisation of the professional.[49] From this perspective, the famous 'arm's-length principle' in the funding system, which was supposed to protect the Council and 'its' artists against political interference, may seem more like a way of avoiding responsibility to the public. This new kind of professionalism, and the attitudes that went with it, swiftly spread through British theatre – the new civic repertory companies, the national theatres and even parts of the West End – from the late 1950s even through to the early 1980s.

So the earlier authority of the patron was gradually hollowed out, audiences became 'better behaved' in auditoria that had been shorn of everything that might distract from the paying of proper attention, and applause began to increase in importance as the main mode of expression. This narrowing range of response in the audience was produced by a kind of surreptitious redefinition of its membership as a function of an increasingly hierarchical and meritocratic cultural system. This is part and parcel of changes in the wider sphere of the social in the 1960s and 1970s in, for example and paradoxically, the expansion of the universities. So another angle of interpretation for Wilson's celebrated 'technological revolution' would be that he was making the hallmark of the expert – including such technicians of the cultural as George Devine – into a guarantee of the highest and most desirable standards in every social domain.[50] Viewed from this perspective, Devine's famous claim that 'You should choose your theatre like you choose a religion' has a sinisterly despotic ring about it.[51]

---

49 Robert Hutchison, *The Politics of the Arts Council* (London: Sinclair Browne, 1982), pp. 44–50; Roy Shaw, *The Arts and the People* (London: Jonathan Cape, 1987), pp. 75–88.

50 The first ever Government Ministers for Technology and for the Arts were appointed in 1964: see Kenneth O. Morgan, *The People's Peace: British History 1945–1990* (Oxford University Press, 1992), pp. 239–40.

51 Irving Wardle, *The Theatres of George Devine* (London: Eyre Methuen, 1978), p. 279.

Into the 1970s

Like 1956, 1968 has often been portrayed as a watershed year for British theatre. In this interpretation the new 'alternative' venues and groups founded in 1968 and immediately after become tinged with the warm red glow of counter-cultural 'revolution', fired-up by worldwide student riots against 'the military-industrial complex', particularly those of the Parisian 'événements de Mai'. It was this radical fervour that led in the 1970s to the fabulous spread of hundreds of small theatre groups in Britain and elsewhere in the developed world. There were also, of course, some especially handy new inventions: lightweight sound and lighting equipment, the Transit van and extending motorway networks, all of which became available in the 1960s, just as the wartime baby boom generation was growing into maturity. So the British alternative theatre movement, as it was commonly called by the mid-1970s, was produced by a curious conjunction of capitalist technology and revolutionary politics. And like the proverbial cuckoo, it grew to have a profound and long-lasting effect on British theatre as a whole.

For example, for most of the 1970s alternative theatres increasingly siphoned a good deal of creative talent away from the repertory theatres and gradually increased their share of the total available grant aid.[52] This exacerbated the 'financial stresses and strains' of the reps,[53] whose size and buildings made them more vulnerable to instabilities in the national economy, and that led to a reduction in the scale and permanence of their companies and a narrowing of their repertoires, though this did not affect audience numbers overall.[54] The sparse audience surveys for the 1960s and 1970s suggest that the tradition of middle-class attendance for repertory theatre still held good, though in some areas, such as the central industrial belt of Scotland and parts of the north of England, and for some shows, particularly those with 'local' content, the proportion of working-class attendees reached as high as 10 per cent.[55] For alternative theatre practitioners, though, such statistics just served to prove the rule that the typical repertory theatre audience was yet another example of the already privileged benefiting at the expense of everyone else!

The reps' financial problems, however, gave an advantage to the two national companies. With a disproportionate share of the total subsidy for drama (e.g.,

52 Baz Kershaw, *The Politics of Performance: Radical Theatre as Cultural Intervention* (London: Routledge, 1992), p. 50.
53 Rowell and Jackson, *Repertory Movement*, pp. 96–7, 108–9, 114–15.
54 Kenneth Cork, *Theatre IS for All: Report of the Inquiry into Professional Theatre in England, 1986* (London: Arts Council of Great Britain, 1986), pp. 8–9.
55 Rowell and Jackson, *Repertory Movement*, pp. 120, 128–9.

55 per cent in 1974–5),[56] the nationals could employ larger casts on longer contracts and thus stage a wider repertoire. By the mid-1970s they were virtually the only companies in England – the Nottingham Playhouse, then under the directorship of Richard Eyre, was one of the few exceptions – that could produce large-scale 'state-of-the-nation' plays, a fact that drew a number of leading playwrights who had started out in alternative theatre, such as Howard Brenton, David Edgar and David Hare, firmly into their ambit. Hence Brenton's *Weapons of Happiness*, directed by Hare, became the first new play to be staged in the National Theatre's South Bank complex after it opened in 1976. The ambivalence of such success echoed in the curiously phrased claim by Brenton that his cast and production team were like 'an armoured charabanc full of people parked within the National walls'.[57] But this was more than the one-day excursion suggested by his choice of vehicle: Hare, Brenton, David Edgar, the director Buzz Goodbody and others were simply the advance guard of a growing group of alternative practitioners, including in the 1980s directors such as Declan Donellan, Simon McBurney and Deborah Warner, who engaged the hegemony of the great institutions from the inside.[58]

A powerful driver in this process – a quasi-nationalisation of dissent, perhaps – was the emergence and consolidation in the 1970s of a clear hierarchy of companies in the state-subsidised theatre system. Of course, this had existed to some extent from the inception of public funding, but the rapid development of alternative theatre in the early 1970s, and its success in making inroads into Arts Council and, especially, Regional Arts Association budgets, ironically added strong bottom-up pressure for differentiations of status among producing companies. This effect was exacerbated by developments in the largest companies, as the nationals especially required large subsidy increases to stay in play on the increasingly competitive global theatre circuit. A crude but highly accurate indicator of the nature of the hierarchy were the lists of core revenue and project grants disbursed by the Arts Council to various types of theatres. From these it is evident that by the mid-1970s the pecking order was pretty well fixed, and it would remain so for the next couple of decades. A straightforward comparison between 1977–8 and 1987–8 for seven selected companies – the two nationals, two regional reps, three alternative

---

56 Pick, *West End*, p. 169.
57 Howard Brenton, quoted in 'The man behind the Lyttleton's first new play,' *Times* (10 July 1976).
58 Colin Chambers, *Other Spaces: New Theatre and the RSC* (London: Eyre Methuen, 1980), pp. 26–33; Theodore Shank, *Contemporary British Theatre*, updated edn (London: Macmillan, 1996), pp. 205–22.

Figures 13.2a & b Fortress theatre: architect Dennis Lasdun's monumental National Theatre on London's South Bank, opened 1976.

Table 13.1 *Arts Council grants distributions, 1970s and 1980s*

	1977–8	1987–8
National Theatre	£2,770,593	£7,811,400
RSC	£1,365,000	£5,197,000
Bristol Old Vic	£227,000	£423,500
Northcott, Exeter	£92,000	£227,250
Welfare State	£46,000	£103,000
The People Show	£19,000	£55,000
Forkbeard Fantasy	£1,200	£36,170

groups (two with touring grants, one with a project grant) – demonstrates the point.[59]

These monies, of course, would be augmented from other sources, such as local authority budgets and sponsorship, but the 'stamp of approval' provided by Arts Council subsidy mostly ensured that the differentials were reinforced by those other funding streams. Such a strong consolidation of rankings through-out the system produced increasing competition to climb the individual career ladder at the top end, and increasing fragmentation of the alternative theatre as a movement, as companies struggled not to fall off it at the bottom.[60] It also contributed to the classification of companies and venues as members of fairly distinct sectors in British theatre; for example, by the early 1980s 'alternative theatre' included 'middle-scale' and 'small-scale' touring theatre groups, as well as 'community theatre' and 'puppet theatre'.

The remarkable growth of total subsidy in the 1970s also impacted on com-mercial theatre, especially in the West End. The oil crisis of 1973 and consequent world recession undermined tourism and increased production costs, gradu-ally, during the second half of the decade, making theatres 60 per cent more costly to run.[61] Predictably, the commercial managements responded by play-ing safe, in two main ways: by falling back on tried and tested formulae, such as 'proven playwrights' (Peter Nichols's *Chez Nous*, 1974) or 'plays from the past' (Terence Rattigan's *Cause Célèbre*, 1977), and by taking an increasing number

59 Arts Council of Great Britain, *A Year of Achievement: 33rd Annual Report and Accounts 1977/78* (London: Arts Council of Great Britain, 1978), pp. 56, 59–63; Arts Council of Great Britain, *43rd Annual Report and Accounts* (London: Arts Council of Great Britain, 1988), pp. 65–7.
60 Baz Kershaw, 'Building an unstable pyramid: the fragmentation of British alternative theatre', *New Theatre Quarterly* 9, 36 (Nov. 1993), pp. 341–5.
61 Cork, *Theatre IS for All*, p. 82.

of transfers from the subsidised theatres. Alan Ayckbourn's career provides a singular marker in this respect: from *How the Other Half Loves* (staged in his Scarborough theatre in 1969, transferring to London's Lyric Theatre in 1970), through *Absent Friends* (Scarborough, 1974; Garrick Theatre, 1975), to *Just Between Ourselves* (Scarborough, 1976; Queen's Theatre, 1977) and beyond, the master of genteel middle-class angst was an important prop for an ailing West End, as well as for the regional reps.

The full extent of the symbiotic interests increasingly shared by subsidy and capital in the 1970s may be inferred from two contrasting cases. In 1977 *Bedroom Farce* was the first Ayckbourn play to be staged by the National Theatre, directed by Peter Hall no less, and the first National production to transfer to the West End (Prince of Wales' Theatre). Three years later another transfer suggested a complete erosion of the demarcation lines between theatre sectors: the left-wing alternative theatre Belt and Braces Roadshow staged their touring production of Dario Fo's *Accidental Death of an Anarchist* at Wyndham's Theatre, by invitation of West End impresario Ian Albery. But the combination of reduced costs and tried and tested productions, home-grown in the West End or imported from elsewhere, did not solve the commercial managements' problems. Throughout the 1970s there were always up to eight (out of the forty-five or so) West End theatres closed at any one time, and by the end of that divided decade the generally parlous state of commercial theatre was ripe for rescue by a new kind of politics.

Enter the Iron Lady, stage right

Led by Britain's first woman prime minister, Margaret Thatcher, the neo-Conservative government elected in 1979 set about a reform of the economy and state institutions that was more radical than any proposed by previous administrations in the post-World War Two period. The conventional view in most theatrical quarters, and one that persisted into the twenty-first century, has been that Thatcherism was the worst news ever for the arts. Reactionary and intolerant of both criticism and cultural difference, especially those of sexuality and race, it was the closest Britain had ever got to fascism in government. Yet if the new Right's policies were abhorrent to most theatre enthusiasts, their actual effects in the 1980s were by no means entirely bad news.

This was the first decade in which systematically collated statistics for British theatre became available and they appear to demonstrate that its proverbial adaptability had not diminished. Between 1983 and 1988–9 there were significant gains in the system.[62] For example, whilst grants to the two national theatres fell in real terms, for the rest of English subsidised theatre overall they grew by around 40 per cent, eventually reaching a combined total subsidy of about £40 million; business sponsorship through the Arts Council Incentive Scheme grew from £0.35 million to just over £1 million; overall box office income for all theatres, subsidised and commercial, almost doubled from £79 million to £149 million. In regional subsidised building-based theatre, despite an almost 50 per cent rise in average ticket prices, the number of seats sold held steady at around 2 million per year; while in London, for both commercial and subsidised theatre, a similar price rise did not deter attendances, which rose from around 8 million in 1981 to almost 11 million per year in 1989. In other words, whatever it *felt* like to be making theatre under Thatcher – and there were rising cries of 'crisis' throughout the 1980s and into the 1990s – the theatrical system generally, and especially in London, responded well to the tough new fiscal challenges of monetarism and 'value for money'.

This was the decade in which the digital revolution really began to take hold. For example, in the four years between 1985 and 1989 sales of pre-recorded *analogue* video cassettes rose from £15 million to about £300 million, but in just three years ownership of digital CD players rose from 1 per cent (1986) to 9 per cent (1988) of British households, while trade deliveries of digital audio CDs rose from none in 1982 to almost 42 million units in 1989.[63] The flood of new media was bound to destabilise the psychic economy of theatre, even as increasing numbers of its artists worked across the growing diversity of recorded and live arenas. A major revision of Arts Council policy in 1984 exacerbated anxieties, as it led to a decimation of small-scale touring by political theatre companies as a result of grant cuts in 1984–5.[64] But it was on the building-based companies that the Tories' economic policies had the most sustained impact. Despite the strong growth in subsidy, improved box office income and rising levels of sponsorship achieved by the fifty or so regional reps, their costs continued to outstrip the hard-won rise in earnings, and coherent programming became an administrative nightmare. So whilst some

62 The numbers/statistics are from: Andrew Feist and Robert Hutchison, *Cultural Trends in the Eighties* (London: Policy Studies Institute, 1990), tables 1.8, 1.13, 1.2; Andrew Feist and Robert Hutchison, *Cultural Trends 1990* (London: Policy Studies Institute, 1990), tables 1.9, 1.12.
63 Feist and Hutchison, *Cultural Trends in the Eighties*, table 4.1, fig. 13.
64 The initial list for cuts is to be found in Arts Council of Great Britain, *The Glory of the Garden: The Development of the Arts in England* (London: Arts Council of Great Britain, 1984), p. 26.

of these theatres, such as those in Bristol, Birmingham, Manchester, Glasgow, Cardiff and a few other cities, were historically of 'major' status, by the mid-1980s their production budgets were not sufficient to achieve the standards or product range of the nationals.[65] In 1986 the first major report on the state of English professional theatre since the early 1970s provided dismal reading, particularly for the regions: an impoverished repertoire, dilapidated buildings, disgracefully low wages, proportionately more money to the nationals, a rising threat to diversity, and so on – 'The Theatre in England has reached a critical point which must not be allowed to become a crisis.'[66] Its recommendations to government for significant increases in subsidy fell on deaf ears. But the system, and therefore the generality of companies, was to grow stronger as it adapted to an environment that was so inhospitable.

To some extent the national companies seemed to share in the misery. The Royal Shakespeare Company moved into its new London base at the Barbican in 1982, only to be greeted by near universal dismay about the unfriendliness of the building. Continuing under Peter Hall, the National Theatre suffered a series of setbacks, from a £150,000 bill for damage caused by the on-stage water-tank for Alan Ayckbourn's *Way Upstream* (1982) bursting and flooding the auditorium to the enforced closure due to financial shortfall of the experimental Cottesloe Studio (1985). But these misfortunes, in retrospect, seem like mere irritations when set against the successes of some great acting and amazing musicals. At the RSC, Michael Gambon, Judi Dench, Anthony Sher, Kenneth Branagh and others created a string of remarkable performances in classics and new plays alike, some of which gained lucrative access – Sher's 1984 *Richard III*, for example – to the cultural marketplace that was forming among 'global' cities around the world.

It was the modern musical, though, which best proved that monetarism was oblivious to traditional cultural categories. Primarily a product of the West End in the early years of the decade, specifically Andrew Lloyd Webber's *Cats* (1981) and *Starlight Express* (1984), the formula was quickly picked up and exploited by Trevor Nunn in the RSC's *Les Misérables* (1985), its international success helping to ease some of the RSC's financial difficulties. But it was the commercial impresario Cameron Mackintosh who became the presiding genius of the genre, with shows like *The Phantom of the Opera* (1986), *Miss Saigon* (1989) and *Martin Guerre* (1995) running in identical productions in cities on three continents and more. This was the new live global art form for the early digital

---

65 Cork, *Theatre IS for All*, pp. 17–19.
66 *Ibid.*, p. 4.

era, massively popular and profitable because – like a good film – utterly reliable in delivering its effect no matter where it was seen. The success of the British musical was a global phenomenon that revivified the West End and rescued the national theatres from potential financial ruin as a result of continuing government hostility. And the export of cultural product was matched by an influx of cultural consumers. Towards the end of the decade tourists made up over 40 per cent of West End audiences.[67] But this widening of its constituency was not the only force that, yet again, was transforming the audience.

Audiences in the 1980s and 1990s

The treatment of audiences during these two decades was paradoxical.[68] Most mainstream theatres were transformed by a wholesale redesign of their 'interface' with the public. Especially through advertising, point of sale and front-of-house services, audiences were flattered, wooed, even pampered. Many theatres adopted quasi-corporate identities, complete with obligatory logos, implying that audience loyalty was important to them. Ticket buying was made easier by box office computerisation and credit card payment, and pricing policies reflected a greater awareness of untapped markets through subscription and discounting schemes. Niche marketing aimed to bring in different audiences for different shows, but also the notion of theatre as a cultural drop-in centre spread, as foyer areas were redesigned to make them more 'welcoming' and bar and restaurant services were developed. Supplementary entertainment such as foyer cabaret, art exhibitions, film screenings and music events became commonplace. All this indicates the theatre's environmental responsiveness, and it would appear to have produced a democratisation of cultural resources, an increase of accessibility. The audience was regaining some of its authority through its spending power as a customer.

As a collection of customers, the audience had a growing number of performance-related commodities to attend to, for there was a remarkable proliferation of theatre sales lines: T-shirts, badges, hats, posters, pennants, playscripts, cassettes and videos of the show. The performance would become a fading memory, but its traces were registered in countless objects, the consumption of which might magically recapture the moment of gazing at the stars on stage. The theatre became a new kind of emporium where products could

67 Feist and Hutchison, *Cultural Trends in the Eighties*, fig. 7.
68 See Baz Kershaw, 'Framing the audience for theatre', in *The Authority of the Consumer*, ed. Russell Keat, Nigel Whiteley and Nicholas Abercrombie (London: Routledge, 1994), pp. 166–86.

substitute for performance, becoming props in a cultured lifestyle. Through all these processes the pleasures of *theatre-going* gained as much emphasis in the consumption of theatre as any enjoyment of the performance itself. The power of performance was being challenged by the peripherals of theatre as it transformed into a service industry with subsidiary retail outlets, and the commodification of theatre was achieved by reshaping the theatre client in the image of the consuming shopper.

In this paradoxical system the audience appears to regain the power it once had as a patron: in a *service* relationship it is the customer who always calls the tune. But the price of such consumer power is the turning of the audience into an object of consumerism. The contract created by the modified conventions of the theatre experience transforms the audience itself into a commodity for someone else, as its bodies embody the ideology of theatre as a commodity form. This is the case even if, as is often argued for post-modernist cultural practice, the audience entertain the theatre ironically, with a self-reflexive awareness of themselves as the consuming commodity.[69]

In the consumerist theatre the quality of applause is an index of a widening chasm between performance and the theatre's critical potential in society, because applause becomes fatally tinged with a narcissistic self-regard. The standing ovation becomes an orgasm of self-congratulation for money so brilliantly spent, the desultory clap becomes an increasingly rare event as it is an admission of income wasted. Hence, what Lyn Gardner claimed of West End first-night audiences at the start of the twenty-first century probably applied almost everywhere: 'The applause . . . usually bears no more relation to the merits of the show than the response of proud parents to the infant school nativity play.'[70] Ironically, as the theatre experience appeared to grow richer through greater variety in theatres and styles, so the truer measure of its quality – range and flexibility in audience interaction – was impoverished. To risk overstatement by putting the case especially bluntly: towards the end of the twentieth century the ecology of theatrical performance was polluted by audience egotism, and socio-political critique all but evaporated from theatres in the heat of an orgy of compulsive narcissism.

Proliferating practices

It was not just the commercial and bigger subsidised companies able to mount high-investment, large-scale populist product that benefited from the

69 Nick Kaye, *Postmodernism and Performance* (London: Macmillan, 1994), p. 56.
70 Lyn Gardner, 'Just sit down and shut up', *Guardian Saturday Review* (14 Oct. 2000), 4.

entrepreneurial ethos of the 1980s: many new small-scale independent companies were formed, such as Made in Wales Stage Company (1982), Theatre de
Complicite (1983) and Forced Entertainment (1984). A good number of these
flourished, sometimes combining co-productions with building-based companies and tours abroad, both through British Council programmes that included
a broadening range of styles and through the growing network of international
festivals, such as the well-established annual ones in Avignon and Madrid, and
from 1981 the biennial London International Festival of Theatre. One type of
theatre that benefited greatly from festivals, growing substantially in the 1990s,
was street performance, which by the turn of the century was a must-have for
seasonal and/or themed celebrations in towns and cities throughout Britain.[71]
Another was heritage theatre, ranging from summer Shakespeare in the park
to interactive drama with interpreters in period costume: at Wigan Pier heritage centre you could get a chillingly forceful telling-off from the teacher in
the Victoria schoolroom.

Throughout the 1980s and into the 1990s there was a growing proliferation of
approaches to making performance both inside theatre buildings and beyond.
Some of its causes could no doubt be found in the vastly burgeoning competition from the digital media – CDs, DVDs, minidisks, PCs, laptops, hand-helds,
cellphones and the rest. Hence, theatres frequently reaffirmed the pleasures of
live performance in their advertising and 'branded' themselves as distinctive,
especially in London: the English Stage Company makes Shakespeare 'the
hottest ticket in world theatre'. There was also a significant growth in the
numbers of graduates from theatre and performance courses in colleges and
universities – by the millennium there were at least sixty institutions offering
full-time programmes – and these often included practices that drew on avant-
garde, alternative and independent theatre traditions for inspiration. Also the
distinctions between different sectors of the theatre industry – metropolitan,
regional, mainstream, alternative, medium- and small-scale touring and so on –
were breaking down as artists increasingly worked across them.

There was a blurring between live performance and digitally recorded
media, both in terms of aesthetics and institutional structuring. Live events
from theatre through popular music to sport increasingly involved technologies of representation as part of their appeal, from the huge live TV playback
screens at football matches to the surtitles skittering across the pixel panels
at foreign-language operas. The miniaturisation of digital technologies – such

---

71 Anthony Dean (ed.), *Street Arts: A User's Guide* (Winchester: King Alfred's College
Press/Independent Street Arts Network, 2003), pp. 25–8.

as high-quality video cameras, some no bigger than a bean – developed alongside the myriad small production companies that flourished as the monopoly of the national radio and television networks gave way to 'narrow-casting' and a more flexible system of franchising and subcontracting that made it easier for actors, directors, designers and other theatre artists to cross the newly permeable boundaries between media régimes. The fabulous spread of the World Wide Web and 'dot com' industries gave global distribution to desktop movie-making and live event broadcasting. More amorphously, the traditional demarcation lines between theatre and social life were increasingly blurred through a growing emphasis on image, style, design and service in almost all public and private domains. This aestheticisation of everyday life usually had a performative component so that, in a sense, theatre – or, more accurately, theatricalisation – was everywhere. These were the key techno-institutional components of the emergent 'performative society', rendering the theatre system of the 1990s especially complex as part of wider social and political processes, and causing it to be shot through with contrary forces. Even a consideration of its most concrete attribute – the physical estate of buildings – reveals considerable cultural contradictions and paradoxes.

Following the Arts Council's abandonment of its 'Housing the Arts' schemes in the late 1980s, theatres across the land entered a period of neglect and often speedy dilapidation. This coincided with a growing recognition in the Council and local civic authorities, subsequent to the publication of the first large-scale assessment of the economic benefits of the arts in Britain in 1988,[72] that theatres could be a high-profile focus for urban regeneration schemes, especially in city centres. When Margaret Thatcher was replaced by John Major as Prime Minister in 1990, this kind of instrumentalist justification of 'culture' led to a small upturn in overall subsidy levels for the arts, and a string of short-term Arts/Heritage Ministers (four in four years)[73] began to notice the huge infrastructural problems that monetarism had produced in cultural institutions. Accordingly they set about planning for a National Lottery, via which 'new money' would be provided for the arts and other 'good causes', such as sport and heritage, and it was finally introduced to an eager populace in November 1994. Estimates of the Lottery's total turnover were placed at around £1.5 billion per year, which would generate £150 million for disbursement to the

---

72 John Myerscough, *The Economic Importance of the Arts in Britain* (London: Policy Studies Institute, 1988).

73 Richard Luce (1989–90), David Mellor (1990–1), Tim Renton (1991–2), Peter Brooke (1992–4).

arts;[74] but the gambling public proved even more active than anticipated, and by 1996–7 the Arts Council Lottery schemes were awarding over £363 million to 732 organisations for capital projects.[75]

In the second half of the 1990s many theatres were renovated or rebuilt – including, amid great controversy, the Royal Opera House, Sadler's Wells Theatre and the Royal Court Theatre, which together received 61 per cent of the total £228.3 million of Lottery money distributed to 338 organisations in 1994–5[76] – and even a few new ones were constructed, such as London's Globe Theatre (1996), the Theatre by the Lake in Keswick, Cumbria (1999) and the New Byre Theatre in St Andrew's, Scotland (2001). But the restrictions on Lottery funding to capital projects, plus a continuing decline in the real terms value of total revenue grant aid, meant that many companies lacked the money needed to create productions that would fill the improved buildings with performances. A number of theatres were forced to 'go dark' for variable periods, including the recently renovated experimental Green Room in Manchester and the Cambridge Arts Theatre in 1997,[77] the year in which Tony Blair and New Labour were elected with a landslide victory. Chris Smith, the new government's first Minister for Culture, quickly instituted the Lottery A4E (Arts for Everyone) scheme, which allowed contributions to theatre revenue costs, but at a relatively low level. It took until 2000, and yet another Arts Council national review of theatre provision,[78] before significant increases to the total Arts Council grant and some semblance of a coherent balance between subsidy for buildings and productions was introduced.[79] Ironically, the influx of large Lottery grants had created instability and uncertainty for the whole theatre system in the 1990s. From this perspective, Simon Trussler's overarching evaluation seems accurate: 'a decade of distorted values and misplaced priorities'.[80]

The most spectacular example of cultural disequilibrium in the 1990s was the Royal Opera House, which in 1995 was awarded the largest arts grant in the

74 Robert Hewison, *Culture and Consensus: England, Art and Politics Since 1940* (London: Methuen, 1997), p. 298.
75 Arts Council of England, *51st Annual Report and Accounts 1996–97* (London: Arts Council for England, 1997).
76 Paul McCann, 'The trouble starts with a million pound windfall', *Independent on Sunday: Focus* (24 Aug. 1997), 14.
77 *Ibid.*
78 Arts Council of England, *The Boyden Report* (London: Arts Council of England, 1999).
79 Arts Council of England, '£100 million more for the arts', *Arts Council News* (Aug. 2000), 1.
80 Simon Trussler, *The Cambridge Illustrated History of British Theatre* (Cambridge University Press, 1994), p. 377.

Lottery's first year – £55 million – for a complete refurbishment, but two years later the company ran into major financial difficulties, which revealed astonishing levels of management incompetence and accumulating deficit. Amidst rising accusations of unbridled élitism, the ROH tried hard to rebrand itself as accessible and accountable, introducing extended low-price ticket schemes, a large video screen in Covent Garden showing selected operas 'live', and even allowing national television network screening of *The House*, a behind-the-scenes documentary series made during the mismanagement muddle that had triggered the bad press in the first place! Such cultural 'leakiness' – a deliberate blurring of existing media and socio-cultural boundaries – was encouraged by government policy for the arts at every level of subsidy. Hence from its inception many of the small A4E grants were 'targeted' at local community and grass-roots organisations, and for the first time since World War Two amateur theatre became eligible for state support. A4E projects ranged from turning Manchester metro trams into mobile art galleries to drama workshops in hospitals and prisons, and from the creation of community circuses to theatre work with the growing numbers of homeless people on the streets of every city. As the Secretary for Culture said in 1997: 'Art . . . and cultural enrichment should be part and parcel of everything we do and everywhere we go. I want to encourage cultural activity to come to the people'.[81]

The drive for the democratisation of creativity was official policy and inscribed in the Lottery schemes – the public must get back some of what they squander in a programme of 'cultural enrichment' – but this was a public conceived very differently to earlier notions of 'the people' which implied a unified populace. The segmentation of the audience for theatre achieved in the 1980s through niche-marketing continued into the 1990s and filtered into participatory drama programmes and other local community-oriented projects. The results, especially in the regions, were frequently impressive. For example, at the West Yorkshire Playhouse in Leeds its first director, Jude Kelly, with a background in alternative theatre, successfully set about making it both a 'national theatre' of the region and a centre for local community drama. As well as attracting rising and established stars to act in challenging plays, by the turn of the millennium the theatre was successfully undertaking a two-year project to involve different groups from a nearby housing estate in a long-term creative partnership.[82] This reflects a strong trend in building-based repertory companies throughout Britain in the 1990s, many of which, like

---

81 Chris Smith, *Creative Britain* (London: Faber, 1998), pp. 44–5.
82 Dick Downing, *In our Neighbourhood: A Regional Theatre and its Local Community* (York: Joseph Rowntree Foundation, 2001).

Dundee Repertory Theatre and the Torch Theatre in Milford Haven (Wales), created energetic education or 'outreach' departments that mounted carefully designed activities for an impressive variety of community groups.

There was also a resurgence of regional touring, especially towards the end of the decade. For example, the north of England offered a challenge to the RSC from 1992, by proving that 'regional Shakespeare' could be popular through the tours of Barry Rutter's Northern Broadsides company, often to non-theatre venues but also to leading proscenium-arch theatres from Newcastle-upon-Tyne to Bath. From Cornwall the peripatetic Kneehigh Theatre, founded in 1980, offered a fabulous mix of visual spectacle and intelligent storytelling in a combination of winter touring to conventional theatres, including a co-production with the NT of Nick Darke's *The Riot* in 2000, and large-scale outdoor summer shows. A significant number of companies founded in the 1970s developed distinctive styles, such as Horse and Bamboo (1978, masks and myths), Tara Arts (1976, Asian reinterpretations of European and Indian classics), Paines Plough (1975, new writing), IOU (1976, visual performance) and The Sphinx (1973 – formerly Women's Theatre Group – new writing by women). Such groups transcended traditional institutional and aesthetic differences between 'mainstream' and 'alternative' approaches to making theatre, showing that systemic uncertainty could be countered effectively by artistic vision and levels of production skill that matched those of the national theatres. In their various ways they, and many others like them, prefigured in the cultural sphere the shift towards diversity and decentralisation that culminated institutionally in the creation of the Welsh Assembly and the Scottish Parliament in 1999.

Yet though these regional initiatives drew a growing proportion of the total theatre subsidy away from the metropolis, the National Theatre and the Royal Shakespeare Company continued to absorb the lion's share of the state's largesse under both Tory and New Labour administrations. There were for both organisations, in contrast to the ROH, gains in stability as the 1990s progressed. Richard Eyre took over the NT from Peter Hall in 1988, when it became the Royal National Theatre. He forged a successful programme which included his own productions of David Hare's 'state of the national institutions' trilogy of *Racing Demons* (1990), *Murmuring Judges* (1991) and *The Absence of War* (1993), and a revival of *Guys and Dolls* (1996); impressive revivals of classics by visiting directors, such as Stephen Daldry's *An Inspector Calls* (1992), Phillida Lloyd's *Pericles* (1994), Deborah Warner's *Richard II* (1995 – with Fiona Shaw as the King); strong new plays, from Alan Bennett's *The Madness of King George* (1991) to Patrick Marber's *Closer* (1997); and experimental pieces by visiting companies such as Theatre de Complicite and Tara Arts. This well-balanced programming was shifted towards greater populism by his successor, that master of modern musical staging, Terry Hands. Meanwhile at the RSC Adrian Noble followed on as director from Hands in 1991, further fostering some very impressive acting talents, including Anthony Sher, who extended his already remarkable range in *Tamburlaine* (1992), *Cyrano de Bergerac* (1997) and *The Winter's Tale* (1998). The success of Noble's policy to create a strong cross-generational ensemble company – in the early 1990s he recruited highly accomplished actors Robert Stephens, Alec McCowen and Derek Jacobi, who began their careers in the 1960s – was regularly troubled by financial difficulties that were usually resolved by the high levels of sponsorship that the Shakespearean flagship theatre could command. As the millennium passed, both national theatres looked set to sail safely on into sustainable futures, partly secured by their place in the globalised marketplace for high-profile 'international' cultural product.

As in the 1980s and earlier, the rest of London's subsidised theatre supported the nationals through the work of a new generation of talented directors and playwrights. Mostly originating in the smaller arts theatres such as the Orange Tree, the Gate and the Almeida, directors such as Stephen Daldry, Sam Mendes, Simon McBurney, Neil Bartlett and Katie Mitchell imported experimental performance techniques into the Royal Court, the Lyric, Hammersmith, the RSC, the RNT and elsewhere. Other directors such as Dominic Dromgoole at the Bush Theatre, Max Stafford-Clark with his Out of Joint touring company and Ian Brown at the Edinburgh Traverse were primarily responsible in the early to mid-1990s for bringing the fresh 'new wave' of 'in yer face' playwrights to the English stage: Jonathan Harvey, Sarah Kane, Jez Butterworth, Mark Ravenhill and the rest.[83] By such means were the established subsidised theatres of London and beyond, from the smallest to the greatest, partly revitalised. They also contributed to an increase in diversity of styles and topics in West End theatres, through transfers of emollient musicals, 'shocking' new plays, innovative stagings of classics and imaginative imports from the regions, such as the amazing *Shockheaded Peter*, a co-production between independent company Cultural Industry, West Yorkshire Playhouse and the Lyric, Hammersmith, which transferred to the Piccadilly Theatre in 2001, then the Albery in 2002.

The commercial theatre of the 1990s was as well sustained by a more fundamental systemic shift, in which the top directing and acting 'stars' of

---

83 Aleks Sierz, 'Cool Britannia? "In yer face" writing in British theatre today', *New Theatre Quarterly* 14, 4 (Nov. 1998).

state-funded theatre created for-profit production companies of their own. Ex-NT directors Michael Bogdanov and Michael Pennington in 1986 had established the English Shakespeare Company, followed two years later by Kenneth Branagh's Renaissance Theatre Company and the eponymous Peter Hall Company. Of these, Hall demonstrated the greatest consistency and staying power: by 1997 he was mounting a repertory season at the London Old Vic that would have pleased even Granville Barker, as it included Barker's *Waste*, Chekhov's *The Seagull* and a sell-out *Waiting for Godot* that transferred with great success to Broadway – an approach that ensured the Hall company survived into the new millennium. Hence innovative devised shows and strong productions of repertory standards leavened the usual West End diet of modern musicals, safe new plays (Tom Stoppard, Michael Frayn, Alan Bennett and of course Alan Ayckbourn) and occasional revivals of classics, but were as well joined by exotic imports and unusual one-offs. The imports included a string of American mega-film-stars – from Dustin Hoffman as Shylock (1989) to Nicole Kidman in *The Blue Room* (1998) – who were prepared to take enormous pay reductions for the allure of playing 'live' on the London stage. In the early years of the new millennium some of the imported one-offs showed that commercial diversity might even open up new areas of, say, sexual and gender debate in the global public marketplace of culture. On the one hand (so to speak), in 2000 Australians Simon Morley and David Friend at the Whitehall Theatre used full-frontal nudity in practising the gentle art of 'genital origami' in *Puppetry of the Penis*; on the other hand, in 2001 at the New Ambassadors Theatre each week a new three-woman cast, often including major celebrities, significantly extended feminist entertainment in American Eve Ensler's *Vagina Monologues*.

Hence, as British theatre progressed into the twenty-first century it seemed to be enjoying unprecedented levels of success. Artistically and economically there were more opportunities for its artists, both in Britain and abroad, than ever before. Even the government appeared to continue to be taking it seriously as an important element in the burgeoning variety of 'cultural industries' that were now said to be close to the centre of the nation's health and prosperity. So had audiences moved beyond the narcissism of consumerism and had British theatre discovered a new confidence about its place in the performative society?

Conclusion

Two highly contrasting events marked the start of the new millennium. In 2000 the British cultural industries produced a hugely expensive and farcical failure: the Millennium Dome in London, constructed at a cost of some £800 million supposedly to show off the country's cultural riches, was a total and resounding flop, with only 4.5 million of the projected 12 million paying visitors passing through its turnstiles by the end of the year. Nine months later, two passenger aircraft were crashed into the twin towers of the World Trade Center in New York, creating a tragic global disaster almost beyond category. The terrorist attacks on September 11 caused unspeakable suffering, followed by a destabilisation of the global political and economic system of a kind and scale never experienced before. Every aspect of culture, first in the developed economies and then in the rest of the world, was affected. For example, international tourism was severely undermined and by the end of the month London theatres were reporting a 15 per cent drop in audience attendance.[84] Of course, compared to other aspects of the aftermath of September 11, their predicament was relatively insignificant. Yet, in an assessment of how British theatres were activated as part of the ecologies of wider cultural systems it is telling that it took less than two months for London's Soho Theatre to stage a series of specially commissioned ten-minute plays reacting to the news.[85] Was there something new in the general environment of British theatre that facilitated such a speedy response?

To assess this we need to look back briefly to the 1990s, for in exactly the same period as the theatre in Britain was enjoying an efflorescence of aesthetic and institutional creativity there were mounting cries of 'crisis' from both practitioners and commentators. Some of this anxiety was no doubt founded on the almost always parlous economics of theatre, which as it flourished artistically produced – as did the wider economy fostered by New Labour – increasing disparities between its very rich and relatively poor artists. But also those disparities were perhaps part of more fundamental instabilities in the theatre system. By 1999 even the Arts Council of England was warning that

> At the start of a new century, a number of theatres are slipping towards financial, managerial and artistic crisis . . . The 1986 Cork Report concluded that 'theatre in England has reached a critical point which must not be allowed to become a crisis'. . . ACE's 1996 'Policy for Drama of the English Arts Funding System' raised broadly similar issues. In many cases the crisis is either here or just over the horizon.[86]

84 http://www.london.gov.uk/mayor/londonline/docs/londonline2.rtf (10 Aug. 2003).
85 Michael Billington, *Guardian Saturday Review* (24 Nov. 2001).
86 Arts Council, *Boyden Report*, p. 10.

Such was the perceived seriousness of the situation that in August 2000 the Council announced an increased government subvention of an extra £100 million for the arts spread over the following three years.[87]

But there were qualities in the earlier complaints of the jeremiahs that suggest much more than a temporary panic about making ends meet. As the millennium approached there was a steady series of publications which suggested that something much more fundamental than the infrastructure of the theatre industry was at risk. In 1997 Peter Ansorge, with many years experience producing television scripts by Alan Bleasdale, Dennis Potter and others, expressed acute concern about British playwriting. He ends a long list of reasons to be *cheerful* about the theatre of the 1990s with 'much of this bravura is based on false perception. Our drama is in fact less confident and adventurous than twenty years ago'; hence there is a 'struggle for survival in our theatres'.[88] In 1999 Peter Hall wrote: 'the theatre of the Nineties reveals a failure to respond to society's actual needs . . . [but] . . . I think the creative madness of the British will ensure that theatre will continue in some shape or form. But this will only be after huge convulsions'.[89] In 2000 Michael Kustow, first arts commissioning editor for Channel 4 television as well as a producer for Hall, argued in a book entitled *Theatre@Risk* that 'Theatre . . . may be undergoing life-threatening mutations . . . I am therefore warning against endangered theatre, theatre subsumed by webs and networks'.[90] In the same year Sir Richard Eyre ended his history of twentieth-century British theatre with 'what is at stake today is the survival of theatre itself . . . [but] [t]he case for the survival of theatre can only be made by the art itself'.[91] False perception, creative madness, convulsions, webs and networks, a dying theatre having to save itself: these heated phrases suggest a threat that is somehow viciously awesome.

What defences had theatre against such a threat, whatever its nature? The consensus among these high-profile prophets was that the essential quality of theatre is its liveness. This is its strength and its glory, the source of its unique persistence and its guarantee of survival in the future. But always in these writings at the moment that power is celebrated there looms a shadow, or

87 Arts Council, *Arts Council News* (Aug. 2000), 1.
88 Peter Ansorge, *From Liverpool to Los Angeles: On Writing for Theatre, Film and Television* (London: Faber, 1997), p. 134.
89 Vera Gottlieb and Colin Chambers (eds.), *Theatre in a Cool Climate* (Oxford: Amber Lane, 1999), p. 109.
90 Michael Kustow, *Theatre@Risk* (London: Methuen, 2000), p. xiii.
91 Eyre and Wright, *Changing Stages*, p. 378.

more precisely a chimera. It is just barely submerged in the title of Ansorge's book – *From Liverpool to Los Angeles* – which transparently translates into 'from gritty reality to tinsel town'. It is in Peter Hall's 'The theatre in America is virtually dead . . . Film is the art of this century'.[92] It is in Michael Kustow's view that 'In a prefigured response to impending digital culture, arresting visual pieces . . . have begun to appear in the theatre . . . Theatre cannot ignore the perceptual changes of the new technology'.[93]

It may be that these eminent addicts of the live event, finely tuned to movements that transform the pulse of a culture's life, sensed that an impending generic revolution was underway, and one that might indeed deliver the end of theatre as it has been known since the Greeks. Was this because the new mutation of representation promised by the end of the analogue age was already changing the nature of the live itself? Was there a paradigm shift happening in the exchange between technology and live theatre during the last three decades of the twentieth century?

At the advent of the reproductive visual media – of photography, film, television – technology was largely geared to the scale of the human form. But in the twentieth century a difference emerged, most sharply identified by Walter Benjamin in the 1930s,[94] in which reproduction by mechanical media signalled an end of the special qualities of art. Human 'aura', most powerfully found in the live event, was lost in the inhuman gaze of technical devices. But also the image of the human figure in an instant could be massively magnified by close-ups or shrunk to a speck in cosmic infinity. The qualities and scale of the human, and by implication any values we might attach to it, increasingly was less of a determining factor in representation. Then in the 1970s and 1980s a new phase in this long history began. It was characterised by a single factor – the shift from analogue to digital systems of reproduction – but its ramifications for culture (and for global politics) were innumerable.

Here was a medium in which the progressive degradation of the original copy, either through material decay or through serial copying, is an almost totally negligible factor. Moreover, the contents of the digital media are open to infinite manipulability, they can be 'reorganised, remade, enhanced, distorted and presented again on demand'.[95] Even more fabulously, as those contents are at root just strings of numbers they 'require no inspiring or originating

---

92 Gottlieb and Chambers, *Theatre in a Cool Climate*, pp. 109–10.
93 Kustow, *Theatre@Risk*, p. 206.
94 Walter Benjamin, 'The work of art in an age of mechanical reproduction', in *Illuminations*, trans. Harry Zohn (London: Fontana, 1992).
95 Anthony Smith, *Software for the Self: Culture and Technology* (London: Faber, 1996), p. 96.

reality'[96] *and* they can create forms of reproduction that are highly immersive and interactive – computer games, training simulators, virtual reality systems. In this new and fast-developing environment, in the final decades of the twentieth century, perhaps it is not surprising that the foremost British theatre-makers were seized with such desperation. In the emergent digital age live performance in theatres and elsewhere could seem like the last bastion of the truly human, to be protected from the digitised world and its threats to fading notions of the human, at all costs.

Perhaps this account of the theatre system in the digital age is a touch too melodramatic. Perhaps the sense of crisis in the British theatre industry as the millennium turned was produced by its apparent inexorable incorporation into market consumerism. Perhaps it was simply that live audiences had mostly given up on critical awareness in their narcissistic enjoyment of a flourishing art form, severing it from social responsibility. Speculation is inevitable as we search for explanations about such recent pasts. Yet in the longer history discussed in this and the following chapters, there may well be grounds for hope about the theatre's future, and by extension the future of the human. So the probability that for most people in the world the *actual* disaster of September 11 was unimaginable, even given the plethora of disaster films that appeared in the 1980s and 1990s, is not necessarily cause for gloom. The same was certainly true of the full extent of the evil of Hitler's Nazi régime in the death camps, yet even there and in similar places earlier, we now know that theatre was made and enjoyed.[97] In London at the outbreak of World War Two the theatres were closed down – as they were in New York after September 11 – but they soon reopened and played an important part in the defeat of Nazism. So the volatility of the British theatre system in the second half of the long twentieth century, from an ecological point of view, may be taken as a sign of its acute responsiveness to the wider environment of the performative society. And its continuing vitality in the first years of the twenty-first century, as well as the cries of crisis arising from a willingness to look disaster in the face, may suggest a new potential for critical engagement in the dilemmas of the digital age.

96 *Ibid.*
97 Michael Balfour (ed.), *Theatre and War 1933–1945: Performance in Extremis* (Oxford: Berghahn, 2001), part 3.

14

The establishment of mainstream theatre, 1946–1979

JOHN BULL

Mainstream theatre is such a major feature of the cultural landscape in Britain that it scarcely ever merits discussion as an idea, and yet it is significantly absent as an entry in the four most substantial contemporary dictionaries of the theatre.[1] It is as if its constitution, its shape and its location were so obvious as to need no placement. Its apparent transparency as a concept is, however, highly problematic and contentious. For many contemporary analysts whose central concern is with performance rather than theatre, the simple fact that a piece takes place in a conventional theatrical space would seem to justify the descriptive tag 'mainstream'.[2] For others there is a perceived need to make distinctions between a 'serious' mainstream tradition and other occupants of the theatrical space, popular theatre and the avant-garde.[3] The use of the qualifying 'serious' does not in itself greatly aid in an attempt at definition, but it does point to the way in which mainstream theatre seeks to assert itself as centrally offering a drama that is capable of sustaining debate. It is this sense of centrality that is most important in considering the development of mainstream theatre in post-World War Two Britain, for as this centre changes, so perforce must the rest of the theatrical apparatus.

To define mainstream theatre it is necessary to do so largely in terms of what it is not, since – at any time in post-war history – it appears to account for a substantially high proportion of the theatrical fare on offer, and it thus occupies a complicatedly wide spectrum. It sets itself in conscious opposition to any contemporary notion of an avant-garde and, in particular, it seeks to

1 Martin Banham (ed.), *The Cambridge Guide to Theatre*, updated edn (Cambridge University Press, 1995); Phyllis Hartnoll (ed.), *The Oxford Companion to the Theatre*, 4th edn (Oxford University Press, 1983); Terry Hodgson (ed.), *The Batsford Dictionary of Drama* (London: Batsford, 1988); Dennis Kennedy (ed.), *The Oxford Encyclopedia of Theatre and Performance* (Oxford University Press, 2003).
2 See, for example, Baz Kershaw, *The Politics of Performance: Radical Theatre as Cultural Intervention* (London: Routledge, 1992).
3 See, for example, John Bull, *Stage Right: Crisis and Recovery in Contemporary British Mainstream Theatre* (London: Macmillan, 1994).

avoid the ideological commitment of an overtly politically constructed theatre. In Peter Nichols's 1987 play, *A Piece of My Mind* – the chief concern of which is the playwright's extreme distaste for the state of contemporary theatre – the central character, a word-blocked playwright, is interviewed by the parodied figure of a Swedish academic, seeking to establish firm distinctions:

> Do you see your plays as advocating revolution like those of David Mercer, Edward Bond, Trevor Griffiths, David Edgar, John McGrath, John Arden, Margaretta D'Arcy . . . Willy Russell, Caryl Churchill, Howard Barker . . . David Hare, Howard Brenton . . . or do you see them as supporting the status quo like those of Alan Bennett, John Osborne, Robert Bolt, Michael Frayn, Julian Mitchell, Tom Stoppard, Christopher Hampton . . . Charles Wood, Peter Nichols and Bob Tail?[4]

The two sardonically presented lists are offered in the belief that the audience will recognise not only the individual playwrights (with the exception of Bob Tail, who simply follows Rag and Tag), but also the terms on which the formal separation has been made. It would be easily possible to construct other, equivalent divisions. What Nichols's bitter accumulation of theatrical 'schools' serves to emphasise is precisely the way in which post-war British mainstream theatre has contained a series of oppositional strategies. For, whilst the 'serious' mainstream has defined itself against the avant-garde, it has also aimed to be thought popular *and* eschewed the notion of 'populism'. However, this in itself does not distinguish it from commercial populist theatre – the pantomime, the accessible musical, the farce – any more than it does from the products of the subsidised theatre.

Even so, British mainstream theatre does not offer a model that will allow it to be located as either the product of a particular historical period or as offering a consistent stylistic content. Mainstream theatre is a constant, but it is a constant that is always changing in response to its changing context. It is, then, similar to the tradition of popular music in that it is continually altering its shape by assimilating elements originally conceived as alien, or even in opposition, to it. The issue has been complicated by the fact that 'serious' mainstream theatre has an uneasy relationship with popular theatre.[5] For instance, it is not difficult to identify the musical *Starlight Express* as an example of popular rather than 'serious' mainstream theatre, but the situation is more problematic when we consider the career of Alan Ayckbourn, after Shakespeare the most

---

4 Peter Nichols, *A Piece of My Mind* (London: Methuen, 1987), pp. 34–5.
5 See John Bull, 'Popular/mainstream theatre', in *Popular Theatres?*, ed. Ros Merkin (Liverpool: John Moores University Press, 1996), pp. 19–31.

During the last twenty years few Irish dramatists have been in any way exciting technically. More often, however, our dramatists today are guilty of a worse defect than mere lack of technical proficiency. They are inclined to shirk the painful, sometimes tragic problems of a modern Ireland which is undergoing considerable social and ideological stress.[12]

Thus, in what follows I will be looking primarily at the centrally positioned forest, and perhaps insufficiently at the span of differentiated trees. Historiographically, this is a reflection of British mainstream theatre in the decades following World War Two, during which it aimed to construct itself through hegemonic consensus.

In the wake of World War Two

In a brief foreword to a book on the state of theatre in 1946, Laurence Olivier was in an up-beat mood, seeing it as so full of 'notable talents . . . vitality and enthusiasm' that it was comparable to 'the glorious Restoration period'.[13] At the turn of the millennium this reads as a somewhat strange remark, given the fairly general acceptance in British theatre histories that the post-war theatrical scene was pretty vacuous. This view had been enshrined, in particular, in the critical writings of Kenneth Tynan, who wrote in 1954, 'The bare fact is that, apart from the revivals and imports, there is nothing in the London theatre that one dares discuss with an intelligent man for more than ten minutes', and that there was no sign 'of a native playwright who might set the boards smouldering'.[14] He was not alone in this view: in an account of the first five years of theatrical activity after the war, J. C. Trewin concluded, 'As I write now, in the spring of 1950, the need for new playwrights with something to say and the means to say it, is still the first anxiety of the theatre'.[15]

So, how are we to reconcile these diametrically opposed opinions? Firstly, by realising that in one sense Olivier was correct. At the outbreak of war in 1939 the government's first instinct had been to close the London theatres. With the active help of the Council for the Encouragement of Music and Arts (CEMA), formed in 1940, many London productions toured the provinces (as they tended then to be called). Almost immediately, however, the London theatres began

---

12 Thomas Kilroy, 'Groundwork for an Irish theatre', *Studies: An Irish Quarterly Review of Letters, Philosophy and Science* 48 (summer 1958), 195.

13 Laurence Olivier, 'Foreword', in Peter Noble, *British Theatre* (London: British Yearbooks, 1946), p. 4.

14 Kenneth Tynan, *Curtains* (London: Longmans, Green, 1961), p. 85.

15 J. C. Trewin, *Drama 1946–50* (London: Longmans, Green, 1951), p. 8.

to reopen. In January 1940 Noel Coward's *Design for Living* reopened at the Savoy Theatre, following a provincial tour, and by the summer of 1941, after the Battle of Britain had been effectively won, London theatre began to revive in earnest. In that year Coward's *Blithe Spirit*, directed by the author, opened and went on to enjoy the longest wartime run. Audience attendances fell in 1944 with the arrival of the V-bombs, but on the day that the war finally ended thirty-six theatres were open in London's West End.

Hence, at least in London, the ending of the war saw a continuation of a long, virtually unbroken tradition of theatrical activity that stretched back to the early part of the century. Although about one-third of London's theatres were destroyed or badly damaged by bombing,[16] this did not fundamentally alter the situation. The opportunity was not taken to rebuild for a modern age, and the predominant model for West End theatres remained Victorian or Edwardian, in itself symbolic of a desire to hold on to the past. For instance, the Queen's Theatre suffered such severe bomb damage in 1940 that it had to be reconstructed; but, although the backstage areas were built to a contemporary design, the proscenium arch was replaced, and the auditorium rebuilt in a quasi-Edwardian style. Furthermore, there was little in the way of new theatre construction in the post-war years, with only the Mermaid (1959), the Royalty (1960), the Prince Charles (1962), the Mayfair (inside the hotel – 1963) and the New London (1973) being built. However, Camden Council was responsible for three small new theatres: the Young Vic (1970), Hampstead Theatre Club (1970) and the Shaw (1971).[17] These venues, along with other 'alternative' playing spaces, would do much to alter what was on offer in mainstream theatre in the 1970s.

When Olivier talks of a new golden age, he is referring to the revival of classical plays, not the staging of new ones, and he is thinking of the theatre almost exclusively in terms of the panoply of actors that he knew. In this sense Tynan is accurate in his recall that in the 1940s and early 1950s 'theatres . . . belonged to the actors'.[18] It also belonged to the impresarios, the most important of whom, 'Binkie' Beaumont of the H. M. Tennent Company, had twelve plays running in eight theatres as the war ended. Within a year that number had doubled.[19] The control of the London theatre by Beaumont and his rivals, who were generally interested above all in the theatre as a vehicle for star actors,

---

16 John Pick, *The West End: Mismanagement and Snobbery* (Eastbourne: John Offord, 1983), p. 141.

17 Ronald Hayman, *The Set-Up* (London: Eyre Methuen, 1973), p. 57.

18 Kenneth Tynan, *A View of the English Stage* (London: Davis-Poynter, 1975), pp. 9–10.

19 Richard Huggett, *Binkie Beaumont: Eminence Grise of the West End Theatre 1933–73* (London: Hodder & Stoughton, 1989), p. 323.

significance of these venues lay in their relationship with the commercial theatre, and particularly in the ways in which they gradually encouraged it to stage 'serious' new dramas.

New influences

It is easy to see that this symbiosis between the commercial theatres of London and the smaller theatres and regional reps as providers and receivers did little to promote the work of new or controversial playwrights. However, new writers did begin to emerge, although not in great numbers at first. One such was William Douglas Home, whose career effectively started in 1947 with *The Chiltern Hundreds*, a country-house comedy with an aristocratic Labour candidate being opposed in an election by his horrified and Conservative-supporting butler. This was a somewhat obvious plot device in a West End theatre not in sympathy with the kind of change promised by the post-war Labour administration of Clement Atlee. Douglas Home's play serves well as an indication of the way in which post-war theatre in England was intent on preserving the links with a pre-war society, with only the most token of gestures towards the present. Hugh Hunt puts the point well: 'Between 1946 and 1956 British theatre was largely living on its past both in subject matter and in staging.'[28]

There was some avant-garde work staged at venues like the Mercury Theatre in Notting Hill, which premièred the verse dramas of Ronald Duncan and T. S. Eliot, so that Philip Barnes is right to stress the importance of 'the less sensational, and certainly less known or popular, experimental theatre which emerged in the years immediately following the war'.[29] However, more generally, the emphasis was on the perpetuation of a theatrical world that, by the early 1950s, began to look increasingly out of step with the political and cultural changes of the post-war period. The dominant fare was provided by writers who had already been established before the war, by revivals, by American musicals – there were fourteen American plays and musicals running in London in 1955[30] – and by European imports. Indeed, one of the more heartening features of this period was the tours of companies to Europe under British Council sponsorship, a part of the movement towards a restitution of a sense of a united Europe. From 1951 the theatre impresario Peter Daubeny started

---

28 Hunt, *et al.*, *Revels History*, p. 49.
29 Philip Barnes, *A Companion to Post-War British Theatre* (London: Croom Helm, 1986), p. 3.
30 Hunt, *et al.*, *Revels History*, p. 50.

to bring European companies to London, culminating in the first of several highly successful World Theatre Seasons at the Aldwych Theatre in 1964.

This takes us nearer to the heart of the worries raised by Tynan. In complaining that there was no sign 'of a native playwright who might set the boards smouldering', he implied that there were plenty of *'non-native'* playwrights who could and were. Tynan was writing three years after the 1951 Festival of Britain and only one year after the coronation of Elizabeth II – perhaps even the young firebrand felt a touch of the nationalistic fervour that accompanied these events. When, in his reappraisal of the period, Dan Rebellato comments on the extent to which the work of foreign writers such as Jean Giraudoux, Ugo Betti and, in particular, Jean Anouilh accounted for so much of the new theatre staged in the 1950s, he is easily able to find critics from that period in agreement with Tynan, noting (correctly) that they saw this as a fact to mourn rather than celebrate.[31]

Apart from revivals, musicals and foreign importations, mainstream British theatre in the immediate post-war years came to rely on a diet of thrillers, farces and, for slightly more upbeat matter, drawing-room dramas and comedies that did nothing to threaten a theatrical status quo clearly out of tune with the changing cultural climate. As John Russell Taylor suggested, 'The drawing-room comedy was above all a theatrical pattern based on a social pattern; essential to its effect was the imaginative presence of a rigid convention of behaviour against which everything (in certain classes at least) would always be measured and judged.'[32] So, another problem for the critics was that post-war British theatre looked increasingly nostalgic, celebrating – or in some cases mourning – a world of social privilege that no longer reflected that of the 'centrist' classes beginning to build the new political consensus. It was inward-looking, self-obsessed, reflecting an insularity that was both class and geographically based. The failure of the theatre to respond to the challenge of rebuilding Britain according to a new social design pushed it into an increasingly entrenched position. Attempts by writers such as Terence Rattigan to discuss larger social and moral issues were generally doomed by the limitations of social locale – of both their characters and audiences – imposed by the established theatre. The traditional audience was well satisfied with both the level and the narrowness of the debate, but the institution of mainstream theatre was looking ever more unrepresentative in the changing order of society.

---

31 Dan Rebellato, *1956 and All That: The Making of Modern British Drama* (London: Routledge, 1999), see especially pp. 127–54.
32 John Russell Taylor, *The Rise and Fall of the Well-Made Play* (London: Methuen, 1967), p. 139.

which disagreement could take place. Hence, Ionesco's world is a nightmare vision of the life and culture of the French *bourgeoisie*, and it allowed a displacement of social critique – it is the *French* under attack – that made it attractive to a British theatre audience dedicated to a non-progressive political perspective. Absurdist theatre certainly influenced British drama, but by striking a responsive chord in a theatre already moving in its direction.

Harold Pinter's early plays were frequently claimed to owe much to the absurdists, as in this review of his 1959 double-bill of *The Dumb Waiter* and *The Room* at the Royal Court: 'What can already be applauded are his successes in finding minutely observed English personages to fill a structural framework borrowed from the continental avant-garde.'[37] Pinter had seen *Waiting for Godot* in 1955 and at least one of Ionesco's plays by the time *The Birthday Party* was premièred in 1958.[38] But the extent of the influence is insignificant; more importantly, critics and audiences could 'place' Pinter's 'comedies of menace' as a part of an absurdist school. By 1960 he had a commercial success with *The Caretaker*, which transferred from the Arts Theatre to the Duchess Theatre in the West End, to universal critical acclaim. His *The Homecoming* (1965) transposed the two-man struggle of the earlier play to a domestic context, effectively linking the new mainstream with its predecessor. Hence, that stalwart of the old mainstream, Terence Rattigan, reflected ruefully in 1967, 'It's a bit of a joke to think of the writers whose names were used to belabour me. John Osborne and Harold Pinter, for example. Two superb craftsmen, both writers of exceptionally well-made plays. They'd be annoyed if anyone suggested otherwise.'[39] Rattigan's plays were successfully produced through the 1960s. Even Noel Coward, more obviously a part of the earlier mainstream, enjoyed something of a revival with a rapturously received West End production of *Private Lives* in 1965, being followed a year later by his trilogy, *Suite in Three Keys*. Yet if the transition is seen in terms of an adaptation of the 'well-made play', it is equally clear that a break with the past was also created by the new playwrights' locus of social concern. Set alongside the kitchen sink, in the 1960s Rattigan's and, especially, Coward's plays were looking increasingly like nostalgic costume dramas.

In the second half of the 1960s Tom Stoppard garnered success similar to Pinter's when, in 1967, *Rosencrantz and Guildenstern are Dead* had its first

---

37 *Times* (3 July 1962).
38 See 'Harold Pinter's Recollections of his Career', in *British Theatre in the 1950s*, ed. Dominic Shellard (Sheffield: Sheffield Academic Press, 2000), p. 71; *Times* (3 July 1962).
39 *Sunday Times* (January 1967).

professional production, by the National Theatre Company at the Old Vic. Stoppard's play links *Hamlet* with *Waiting for Godot*, literally foregrounding the role of the two eponymous courtier friends / spies – quasi-Elizabethan stand-ins for Vladimir and Estragon – and allowing most of the major action of Shakespeare's play to be dimly heard off stage. That Stoppard should draw from an historically classic text and ally it with a play already established as a classic of the contemporary avant-garde is a perfect example of the way in which the mainstream reconfigures itself in order to survive, guaranteeing intellectual credibility to what had started life almost as an undergraduate revue piece. Another playwright, James Saunders suggested to Stoppard how he might develop the earlier version. Significantly, Saunders had had a major West End hit with his absurdist exercise *Next Time I'll Sing to You* in 1963, which opens with two characters, Dust and Muff, complaining that every evening they have to repeat the same lines. So Stoppard's use of *Waiting for Godot* was symptomatic, rather than unique, and it is not surprising that in 1967 Charles Marowitz could describe *Rosencrantz and Guildenstern are Dead* as an 'existential comedy whose ur-text like *The Caretaker* is *En Attendant Godot*'.[40] The overnight success of Stoppard's play was in no small part due to the pioneering work of Pinter, for it was staged in a mainstream theatre whose audiences were fully primed to expect and savour permutations of absurdism.

These absurdist borrowings had helped to facilitate – in parallel with the naturalist experiments of the 'new wave' – a movement down the social scale. But, whilst exponents of the naturalist school, such as Arnold Wesker and Shelagh Delaney, sought to depict and analyse proletarian culture, the British absurdist playwrights placed their action squarely in the world of the expanding *bourgeoisie* that would provide the mainstream theatre's new audiences. And the city suburbs were the setting most favoured in their satirising of the upwardly-mobile aspirations of the new middle classes.

One of the most successful productions of this kind was Giles Cooper's *Everything in the Garden*. Staged by the Royal Shakespeare Company at the 350-seat Arts Theatre Club in 1962 as part of an experimental year in an alternative space, it transferred almost immediately to the Duke of York's Theatre in the West End. Even as early as this, a major subsidised company saw the advantages of creating a kind of mini-Royal Court partly aimed at lucrative transfers that would subsidise its future and potentially less popular work. The Arts' status

40 Quoted in Thomas Whittaker, *Tom Stoppard* (London: Macmillan, 1983), p. 43.

as an established theatre club also allowed the production of plays that might have been banned by the Lord Chamberlain.

Cooper's play questions the moral foundations of middle-class marriage through a young couple, Bernard and Jenny Acton, who are obsessed with the acquisition of material goods. It deals with issues of sexuality – Jenny takes a job in a brothel, alongside her female neighbours, to help pay for the goodies; of racism – the brothel madam is a Polish Jew, producing a recurrent tone of anti-Semitism in the neighbourhood conversation; and of gender – the husbands set up a committee to put the prostitution on a proper business footing. The action even concludes with the 'necessary' killing of an outsider figure, an artist, who has stumbled on the community's secret. Earlier plays in the genre include T. M. P. Frisby's *The Subtopians* (1961), David Turner's *Semi-Detached* (1960) and David Parry's *The Trouble With Our Ivy* (1960), in which an ivy plant intended to block the sunlight from snobbish neighbours ends up destroying the entire suburb.

Such examples of the domesticisation of continental absurdism serve well enough to illustrate how versions of the well-made play resurfaced as a 'serious' challenge to the standard West End fare of the early 1960s. These plays no doubt found a new kind of audience, one less interested in real social change than in seeing its own more middle-class preoccupations enacted on stage. These new audiences were representative of a widening social base produced by growing affluence, but they were still a part of an established status quo: the centre of power had just moved slightly down the social scale. But the attack of these plays was a cosy one, not threatening the premises of the world they portrayed, simply satirising some of its more extreme manifestations. And such a relentless concentration on the world of the suburbs and provinces was clearly going to tour well both prior and subsequent to London runs, thus helping in the reanimation of provincial theatre.

Changing mainstream fare

In the ten years between 1965 and 1975 British mainstream theatre accommodated a yet more challenging redefinition of mainstream drama. A brief comparison between Peter Nichols's 1967 *A Day in the Death of Joe Egg* and Peter Shaffer's *Equus* of 1973 can serve to show how popular and avant-garde traditions were newly, and variously, combined. Nichol's play was premièred at the subsidised Glasgow Citizens' Theatre, later opening in the same year at the commercial Comedy Theatre in London. This move is significant in view of the play's style and subject matter: it is a dark comedy about a young couple, Sheila and Bri, struggling to bring up a severely brain-damaged child, the 'Joe Egg' of the title. The play opens with Bri, a schoolteacher, addressing the audience as if they were his class at school, in a routine derived from the populist forms of stand-up comedy and the music hall – 'Another word and you'll all be here till five o'clock.'[41] Sheila and Bri also act out a variety of playful scenarios which frequently offer the non-speaking 'Joe Egg' imaginary responses, so that the audience is forced to move between seeing the production as 'slice-of-life' naturalism and consciously constructed theatre in the manner, almost, of Pirandello.

The most extreme use of avant-garde appropriation in *A Day in the Death of Joe Egg* comes at the interval break when, after the cameos from Joe's short life have been re-enacted comically by the parents, Joe Egg herself impossibly skips into a lighting change, and Sheila announces a pause in the narrative: 'Ladies and gentlemen, there will now be an interval. Afterwards the ordinary play, with which we began the performance, will continue.'[42] Here then is a highly successful and absolutely mainstream play that draws heavily from both avant-garde and populist sources.

Peter Shaffer's *Equus* achieves a similar appropriation of popular and avant-garde techniques, but on an edge much closer to tragedy. It concerns the efforts of a psychiatrist, Martin Dysart, to understand why his young patient, Alan Strang, should have blinded six horses with a metal spike. In format it has connections with the popular thriller genre, in which a mystery is to be unravelled by the superior intellect of the detective. However, the play concentrates more on Strang's creation of a 'strange' world of religious ritual centred on the horse-god Equus, from a detritus of familial contradictions involving pubescent sexual repression, Christianity and consumerism. Much of the power of the production derived from the ritual display of the masked actor-horses on stage.

The play opens at the conclusion of the narrative. After Strang is seen tenderly embracing one of the horse-actors, Dysart addresses the audience direct about his loss of faith in his vocation, before offering them the play's events as a series of flash-backs. The actors are always on stage and simply move to and from the various performance spaces; the play is constructed as a collage, with scenes crossing from one to another, sometimes in a stage present and sometimes in a recalled and enacted past. The form recalls Brecht, but the emphasis always falls solidly on the psychology of the individual character. The

41 Peter Nichols, *A Day in the Death of Joe Egg* (London: Faber & Faber, 1967), p. 43.
42 *Ibid.*, p. 45.

Figure 14.1 The mainstream in the regions – trauma as spectacle. Peter Shaffer's *Equus* at the Bristol Old vic, Theatre Royal, Bristol, 1972–3 season.

combination made it a popular choice for mainstream houses across Britain in subsequent years, making just sufficient use of avant-garde techniques to offer an apparently new theatrical path. Like *A Day in the Death of Joe Egg*, *Equus* sought to extend the parameters of the domestic drama in order to raise larger issues. Its uniqueness came from its presentation of the dilemma in a non-comedic mode. In the years that followed, it would become less a model than an indicator that the new mainstream could, like the one it had replaced, treat essentially liberal issues in a serious as well as a comic way. Perhaps most significantly, it became a part of the staple diet of just about every regional repertory theatre in the country.

This indicates a very significant development of the mainstream in this period. At its outset, almost without exception, the plays that defined the new mainstream were comedies, but the comedy becomes more problematic as a result of the plays' continuing emphasis on the domestic. This is because, as the early 1970s unfolded, the domestic focus increasingly meant an inevitable grappling with the problems of the dysfunctional family, gender and sexual issues, and so on – subjects that were part of a much larger public mainstream discourse.

Into the seventies

In the late 1960s and early 1970s momentous events had taken place outside British mainstream theatre and these were to affect not only the dramatic fare it offered but also the way in which new theatres were structured and older theatres reconfigured. The counter-cultural movement that grew in Britain and abroad throughout the 1960s led to the creation of an 'alternative' theatre movement whose success produced many new performance spaces. In the history of the mainstream, it was, most importantly, the regional rather than the London theatres that first reacted to this development. So, when the new Crucible Theatre in Sheffield opened in 1971, for instance, it did so with a smaller studio space to present new and experimental work, alongside the main auditorium in which, it was assumed, more conventional mainstream fare would be produced. Even as the Crucible opened, many older regional theatres had incorporated alternative spaces into their buildings. In 1969 the Royal Court opened the Theatre Upstairs. By 1974 the Royal Shakespeare Company had opened the Other Place in Stratford as an 'alternative' to the Memorial Theatre, followed in 1977 by the Warehouse in London. When, in 1982, the RSC finally opened their London base at the Barbican Theatre, a studio theatre, the Pit, was belatedly added, based in an underground rehearsal space.

Through the 1970s the battle between the mainstream and alternative theatres would be about territorial possession, and it is from this point that we can date the true emergence of a modern mainstream tradition, one clearly defined by the existence of a widespread alternative. It was a battle that would not be confined to the studios. It was a measure of the Nottingham Playhouse's continuing sense of its 'mission' that when Richard Eyre took over as director in 1973, for five years he was able to present a succession of contemporary premières – including Howard Brenton and David Hare's *Brassneck* (1973), Brenton's *The Churchill Play* (1974) and Trevor Griffiths's *Comedians* (1975) – which was unmatched in post-war regional theatre. When the National Theatre finally opened on the South Bank in 1976, its first newly commissioned play was Brenton's *Weapons of Happiness*. It was a commission that, symbolically, had been turned down by the veteran of the first 'new wave' of playwrights, John Osborne.

Through the 1970s it appeared that large-scale committed drama was winning the battle for occupation of the main house stages. A listing of these plays would be impressive and would certainly include – beside those mentioned above, Trevor Griffiths's *The Party* (1974), David Edgar's *Destiny* (1976)

Figure 14.2 The mainstream in the regions – a moment of typical embarrassment. Alan Ayckbourn's *How the Other Half Loves*, Bristol Old Vic, Little Theatre, Bristol, 1974–5 season.

the hint of saucy seaside postcards, and comfortable borrowings from absurdist experimentation. *How the Other Half Loves* illustrates the point well, with a punning title that implies the populist urges of its creator. It is a pun, however, that is central to the play. In perfectly conventional form it uses adultery as a plot-mover, but it does so in ways that offer a sharply realised analysis of the way that the two halves of society do both live and conduct love affairs. Where most other contemporary Anglicisations of the absurd had presented a satire of middle-class life and consumerist dreams with a set of characters who were all from precisely the same social class, Ayckbourn is interested in the minute, but vital, distinctions that operate within the parameters of middle England. The characters at the top of Ayckbourn's social world are the managerial bosses and proprietors of small town businesses, and those at the bottom are upwardly aspiring *petit bourgeoisie*. As Ayckbourn explained in an interview, 'I'm very lucky that my particular level of writing, classwise, is slap bang in the middle of the theatre-going public'.[45] The working classes concerned the new mainstream as little as it had the old.

45 Ian Watson, *Conversations with Alan Ayckbourn* (London: Faber, 1988), p. 109.

As usual in Ayckbourn's theatre, the characters of *How the Other Half Loves* hover between fully fleshed-out people and caricature, an effect created by dialogue that moves with ease between a kind of qualified naturalism and the absurdist speech formulae found in early Ionesco. For example, the office clerk Bill's response on discovering that his wife is not having an affair with middle manager Bob moves beyond naturalism to the grotesque in its mechanical dissection of her shortcomings:

> Do you realise, Mrs Foster, the hours I've put into that woman . . . When I met her, she was nothing . . . With my own hands I have built her up. Encouraging her to join the public library and make use of her non-fiction tickets – I introduced her to the Concert Classics Club – I've coaxed her, encouraged her to think – even perhaps bullied her, some might say.[46]

In this diatribe, Ayckbourn raises problems about the nature of the audience for the new mainstream, attempting to appeal to an already existent and identifiable audience but also to respond to new elements in its changing constituency. It was a part of Ayckbourn's particular and remarkable talent that he continued to allow for what was, in effect, an ambiguity of response to his characters in his work through the 1970s and 1980s. In particular, a sense that most of the female (and usually married) women are victimised by inadequate and/or bullying men came to dominate his dramaturgy – a syndrome most graphically realised in *Women in Mind* (1985), where a vicar's wife descends into madness. Ayckbourn had denied wanting to write 'a play about women's liberation',[47] and certainly none of his female characters ever finds a way out of the impasse, but this is a powerful example of how a partial assimilation of oppositional voices is essential to the growth of a mainstream.

A renewed mainstream

The acceptance of the renewed mainstream drama into the theatrical establishment was made easier as a result of developments that are usually dated from 1979 but which were actually building throughout the 1970s. From the oil crisis of 1973 to the 1978 'winter of discontent', pressure was growing on the government and its funding bodies to reduce the amount of direct public subsidy for all the arts. The concerted move to increasingly replace state funding by private (largely corporate) sponsorship began early in the decade. It

---

46 Alan Ayckbourn, *How the Other Half Loves* (London: Samuel French, 1972), p. 64.
47 Watson, *Conversations*, p. 117.

reached its first peak with the formation of the Association for Business Sponsorship of the Arts (ABSA) in 1976, founded in recognition that sponsorship was already playing a major part in the economics of the theatre. A late 1990s survey of public policy and the arts presents the problem succinctly: 'The private sector does not contribute purely for philanthropic reasons, but for what it can receive . . . Pure and simply, sponsorship is about making money for the sponsor'.[48]

In the 1970s the subsidised theatre increasingly had, perforce, to pay more than lip service to the demands of its new sponsors, and productions that both filled the theatres and found favour with their commercial benefactors became ever more the order of the day. In addition, the necessity to achieve regular transfers into the commercial mainstream theatre further added to the pressures. So after 1979 the new mainstream was not only better able to survive in the new market, it was also culturally more in tune with rapidly changing orthodoxies. And as the 1970s gave way to the 1980s, the new mainstream drama would increasingly come to monopolise the mainstream theatre. In the early 1980s, then, British mainstream theatre was revitalised, confident in its access to an audience for whom the anxieties and aspirations of bourgeois life were no longer the stuff of satire or parody, but ideologically central to a modern world as redefined by the new monetarist economics.

The renewed 'serious' mainstream, therefore, was not a direct product of the politics of the 1980s, though it was certainly moulded and shaped by those politics. By 1979 a clearly definable mainstream already existed, with a history and now quite clearly with a future. That it already existed, and in particular that it had succeeded in finding an identification for the audience in its subject matter, makes it evidence, in itself, of the general cultural and social shift that was facilitating the politics of the new right. With the growing importance of the new impresarios, in particular Cameron Mackintosh and Andrew Lloyd Webber of the Really Useful Theatre Group, mainstream theatre began to leave behind the earlier battles, to develop almost independently of an alternative sector under increasing threat. There were to be troubled years ahead, but the model of mainstream British theatre had been refashioned, perhaps irrevocably. However, in its post-war history it had demonstrated a tenacious malleability when faced with threatening cultural forces and it had refined the art of assimilation to ensure survival. It had successfully adapted to change then, and would surely do so again.

48 Ruth-Blandina Quinn, *Public Policy and the Arts* (Aldershot: Ashgate, 1998), p. 171.

15

Alternative theatres, 1946–2000

BAZ KERSHAW

British alternative theatre in the post-World War Two period was, in part, a reaction to 'mainstream theatre'. Of course the 'mainstream' evolved during those turbulent decades, so that the types of theatre that might be counted as part of it varied, but overall it consisted of West End commercial theatre and commercial venues of the regional touring circuits, subsidised regional repertory theatres and other municipal theatres, and the national theatres (Royal National Theatre, Royal Shakespeare Company).[1] Yet the contrast between 'alternative' and 'mainstream', in practice, has rarely been that straightforward.

For example, when the National Theatre staged Howard Brenton's *Romans in Britain* in 1980 it produced a significant 'alternative' in relation to both mainstream and alternative theatre repertoires of the time. Aesthetically, no *alternative* company could have matched its scenographic scale and complexity; politically, few other *mainstream* theatres would have dared to take the legal risks involved in its explicit portrayal of buggery as a metaphor for the British occupation of Northern Ireland.[2] The example underlines the fact that relativity, in art as much as in physics, gradually became a condition of twentieth-century global culture, so that contesting binary opposites – male–female, centre–margins, mainstream–alternative and more – gave way to a plethora of possible performance practices and analytical perspectives. Accordingly, between World War Two and the turn of the millennium British theatre as a

---

1 See John Elsom, *Post-War British Theatre*, rev. edn (London: Routledge & Kegan Paul, 1979); Ronald Hayman, *British Theatre Since 1955: A Reassessment* (Oxford University Press, 1979); John Pick, *The West End: Mismanagement and Snobbery* (Eastbourne: John Offord, 1983); John Bull, *Stage Right: Crisis and Recovery in British Contemporary Mainstream Theatre* (London: Macmillan, 1994); Dominic Shellard, *British Theatre Since the War* (New Haven: Yale University Press, 1999); Richard Eyre and Nicholas Wright, *Changing Stages: A View of British Theatre in the Twentieth Century* (London: Bloomsbury, 2000).
2 Richard Boon, *Brenton: The Playwright* (London: Methuen, 1991), pp. 173–211; Howard Brenton, *Hot Irons: Diaries, Essays, Journalism* (London: Nick Hern Books, 1995), pp. 28–31.

whole increasingly became pluralistic and fragmented. So as well as considering the complexities of a growing variety of alternative theatres in the second half of the twentieth century, this chapter aims to suggest the historiographic difficulties in such a task.

Some measure of those complexities can be gained from the quartet of contesting terms that cultural commentators applied to the expanding number of small theatre groups in Britain in the 1960s and 1970s. In the late sixties they were collectively christened 'underground theatre' by London's listings magazine *Time Out*, romantically linking them to the resistance movements of World War Two and, more plausibly, the 'revolutionary' politics of the newly politicised student movement. Simultaneously, the same groups were frequently called 'experimental' on account of their customary aesthetic iconoclasm. Then, in the seventies, they were more usually identified as 'fringe theatre' – an analogy with the 'fringe' of the official Edinburgh Festival – or as 'alternative theatre'. Partisan critics and historians preferred 'alternative' as a means to indicate broad opposition to the ideological mainstream in theatre and politics; while their less sympathetic (or more cautious) colleagues opted for 'fringe', risking the implication of marginality in order to encompass the diversity of the new movement.

A longer historical perspective brings three other key terms into play. In the immediate aftermath of World War Two writers keen to promote a new start for British theatre frequently called for a 'popular theatre' that would appeal to all, implying a strong contrast to the class-restricted reach of West End and regional repertory venues. Less commonly, the European notion of a 'people's theatre' was used to suggest either a broad, class-based, politicised theatre or a liberal theatrical embrace of the whole population. Then in the final two decades of the century the entrepreneurial ethos of neo-conservatism prompted the recycling of a term first used towards the end of the Victorian era, as new performance groups working mostly, but not always, beyond the mainstream theatres increasingly were claimed to be 'independent'.

This shifting terminology for the unconventional in British theatre *circa* 1946–2000 only partly indicates the actual messiness of its development. New alternative theatres frequently emerged as much in opposition to as in admiration of their predecessors. The ideological, aesthetic and organisational variety of the new groups was consistent only in its growing complexity. So to reflect the unpredictable genealogies of British alternative theatres, this chapter, section by section, adopts a variety of historiographic strategies in describing them; it also keeps to a conventional chronology as the most useful means of indicating their burgeoning diversity. Hence, in turn, it focusses on efforts to forge the sense of a national theatre movement through notions of 'popular' or 'people's' theatre in the 1940s and 1950s; on the community-oriented projects of individual playwrights and the founding of pioneer oppositional groups in the 1960s; on the extending chronicle of different types of emergent groups and genres in the 1970s; and, finally, on the fragmentation produced by the highly contrasting practices of the 'independent' theatres of the 1980s and 1990s.

These contrasting accounts will serve to suggest how volatile British alternative theatre as a whole became in this period, as a consequence of the remarkable proliferation of new approaches to producing and distributing original forms of performance. These included community theatre, women's theatre, feminist theatre, lesbian theatre, gay theatre, queer theatre, black theatre, ethnic theatre, guerrilla theatre, theatre in education, theatre in prisons, disability theatre, reminiscence theatre, street theatre, site-specific theatre, celebratory theatre, theatre of the oppressed, performance art, physical theatre, visual theatre and more.

But why did Britain and other so-called developed countries enjoy such a flourishing of alternative theatres? And in what ways might they be said variously to have cohered into ideological formations or aesthetic movements or industrial sectors? Answers to the first question may be found in the growing instabilities of British society as it engaged fully in the evolution of the highly mediatised and globalised world disorders produced by late capitalist liberal democracies. Answers to the second, however, are bound to beg more questions, as they imply forms of collective agency that those very same disorders made problematic. Still, an analysis of this conundrum might do worse than by starting with a focus on youth: in this period western youth invented and reinvented itself through the creation of successive subcultures and counter-cultures. Whilst previous periods possibly had their equivalents, British society, from the early 1950s to the millennium, shaped and was shaped by the emergence of these new kinds of cultural formation, as they saturated the dominant culture like waves breaking on a beach. Teddy boys, beatniks, hippies, punks, goths and the rest were ripplets, though, compared to the successive rollers of the counter-cultures, the first one originating in the groundswell of the civil rights and anti-Vietnam war movement and peaking in the student revolts of the late 1960s. More followed: women's and black liberation movements and the gay/lesbian/queer movements of the 1970s and 1980s; new social movements fighting for the environment, for human rights, for peace and against globalisation in the 1980s and 1990s.

At least to begin with, these were primarily youthful formations that challenged the old modernist binaries separating art and politics, creativity and analysis, culture and society on the way to creating the complexities of post-modernity. So the alternative theatres – the popular, people's, underground, fringe, alternative, independent theatres – were, in the main, just a part, but an important part, of a huge spread of dancing resistance to the old ideological monoliths of modernism, dancing in a new decentred celebration of difference, dancing into the new millennium, when it seemed there might be nothing left but alternatives to alternatives.

Touring for a people's theatre?

> The wartime Renaissance in the theatre, not only in London but in all parts of Great Britain, is here to stay. Drama has been brought to the British people, many of whom have seen a play performed for the first time in their lives. And both audiences and standards have demonstrated an appreciable growth, culminating in the successful work of . . . the Arts Council . . . The Old Vic, with headquarters in London, Liverpool, Bristol and elsewhere, represents a most important step in making the theatre a people's art.[3]

Nationalistic optimism was endemic in British society immediately following World War Two, so it is not surprising that Laurence Olivier should want to claim theatre as a significant focus for its fulfilment. The populism of these heated hopes for the drama, coming from such a bastion of the theatre establishment, is very telling of the times. Olivier was appealing to the sense of national unity on the 'home front' generated by the horrors of the Blitz, reinforced by propaganda in all the media, and boosted by the euphoria of victory. So exactly how theatre as 'a people's art' fared in the following two decades may be seen as a barometer for the robustness of the imagined community of 'Great Britain'[4] – did it achieve the vision of cultural inclusion enshrined in the first Charter of the Arts Council, or did it, like the new Labour government's cradle-to-grave plans for the unifying welfare state, fall short of that promise?

Major foundations for a dispersed popular national theatre had been laid during the war by the Play Unit of ABCA (Army Bureau of Current Affairs) and by its civilian equivalent, the Drama Section of CEMA (Council for the Encouragement of Music and the Arts). The Drama Section, starting in 1941 with Martin Browne's Pilgrim Players,[5] promoted tours throughout the country

---

3 Laurence Olivier, 'Foreword', in Peter Noble, *British Theatre* (London: British Yearbooks, 1945), p. 3.
4 Benedict Anderson, *Imagined Communities: Reflections on the Origin and Spread of Nationalism*, rev. edn (London: Verso, 1991).
5 Henzie Browne and E. Martin Browne, *Pilgrim Story: The Pilgrim Players, 1939–1943* (London: Frederick Muller, 1945).

by existing companies, most notably from 1942 to many workers' hostels in munitions works, as well as to smaller venues in regional towns and villages. The repertoire was hardly tainted by populism, consisting primarily of plays by Shaw, Goldsmith, Ibsen, Dekker, O'Neill, Wilde and of course Priestley, but it was greeted by large audiences of 'ordinary people' who were 'wonderfully appreciative and capable of boundless understanding and intelligence'.[6] The Play Unit was founded in 1943, and its companies, staffed entirely by armed forces personnel, toured short and serious shows to many thousands of army units throughout the war. A major influence was the 'living newspaper' style of America's Federal Theatre, which was adapted to create a kind of enlightened propaganda that aimed to provoke considered discussion about war issues. Such respect for the audience was a matter of faith for ABCA's leading social-ist artists, such as Ted Willis, André van Gyseghem and J. B. Priestley, who subsequently worked hard to forge a truly popular post-war people's theatre movement.[7] But their labours were eventually compromised by bricks and mortar.

Back in 1942 CEMA had begun tentatively buying into theatrical real estate, in the form of the Lyric Theatre, Hammersmith, and the Theatre Royal in Bristol. This eventually provided the Old Vic companies with the post-war platform needed for Olivier's enormous success and introduced a structural tension into the general theatre ecology of the 1940s and 1950s. The comple-mentary war-time programming of ABCA and CEMA was abandoned as Arts Council subsidy increasingly fostered an imbalance between building-based (expensive and exclusive) and touring (inexpensive and inclusive) production, and that effectively undermined a string of attempts to make British theatre into a genuine 'people's art'. The casualties, ironically given its success during the war, were virtually all on the side of touring.

By the early 1950s there were over 130 touring repertory companies in oper-ation in Britain, playing in theatres in most major towns, but these were com-mercial organisations with their sights firmly set on the West End.[8] A few small studio theatres in London operating as membership societies – for example, the Arts Theatre, the Hampstead Theatre Club, the amateur Questors Theatre – provided experimental plays, with occasional transfers to the West End. A

6 Noble, British Theatre, p. 108.
7 Ibid., p. 96; Richard Fawkes, Fighting for a Laugh: Entertaining the British and American Armed Forces 1939–1946 (London: Macdonald & Jane's, 1978), pp. 103–10.
8 George Rowell and Anthony Jackson, The Repertory Movement: A History of Regional Theatre in Britain (Cambridge University Press, 1984), pp. 84–6; Andrew Davies, Other Theatres: The Development of Alternative and Experimental Theatre in Britain (London: Macmillan, 1987), pp. 148–9.

number of CEMA groups, such as the Adelphi Players, had continued to tour non-commercial shows outside the capital, under the aegis of the Arts Council, until the late 1940s.[9] But the promise of an alternative people's theatre with a national reach is best represented by three groups which received hardly any support from the state in this period: Unity Theatre's Mobile Group, the Compass Players and Theatre Workshop.

A snapshot of their work in early 1951 – Festival of Britain year – shows a lively variety of purpose. Unity Theatre's London-based non-professional mobile group, working mostly at the weekends, toured working-class venues in the capital's suburbs with a version of the classic Labour novel *The Ragged Trousered Philanthropists* – the lead played by a gas-fitter – and *Exhibition 51*, 'a humorous and critical observation on the Festival of Britain'.[10] Compass Players toured secondary schools and colleges from Darlington to Abergavenny with plays by Molière, Marlowe, Shaw and the company's artistic director, John Crockett.[11] Theatre Workshop undertook two tours of mining villages in south Wales and north-east England, and a two-month tour of Scandinavia, with Ewan MacColl's *Landscape with Chimneys* and *Uranium 235*, both directed by Joan Littlewood.[12] Political plays, classical plays, experimental plays with a socio-critical edge – if this theatrical menu had been more widely available, complementing the efforts of the Old Vic and other building-based companies, then Olivier's vision of a popular British people's theatre might have materialised. But the fate of these three companies provides a sharp object lesson in the toughness of such a trade in an age of austerity.

Unity Theatre had been a successful national organisation of left-wing non-professional theatre with groups in most major cities (most notably London, Bristol, Liverpool and Glasgow), many of which toured shows to working-class venues. The London and Glasgow branches created professional groups in 1946–7, the former staging productions at its base in St Pancras, the latter transferring shows to the West End's Garrick Theatre and the Embassy Theatre between 1946 and 1951. These ventures syphoned off energy and talent from their parent organisations, causing closure for Glasgow in the early 1950s[13] and

9 Cecil Davies, *The Adelphi Players: The Theatre of Persons*, ed. Peter Billingham (London: Routledge Harwood, 2002).
10 Colin Chambers, *The Story of Unity Theatre* (London: Lawrence & Wishart, 1989), p. 295.
11 Pamela Dellar (ed.), *Plays Without Theatres: Recollections of the Compass Players, 1944–1952* (Beverley, Yorks: Highgate Publications, 1989), pp. 161–2.
12 Howard Goorney, *The Theatre Workshop Story* (London: Methuen, 1981), pp. 202–3.
13 John Hill, 'Towards a Scottish people's theatre: the rise and fall of Glasgow Unity', *Theatre Quarterly* 7, 27 (autumn 1977), 69.

a discontinuation of touring by London in 1954.[14] This set the pattern for the other, non-professional Unity groups.

The Compass Players was created using John Crockett's private funds in 1944, and it survived on a mixture of eclectic programming, catholic aesthetics and – as with all the touring companies in this period – commitment well beyond the call of duty. It produced up to four new shows a year, which toured throughout England and to Wales, in a style which later would be called 'multi-media': masks, stylised acting, expressionist lighting, dance inspired by Martha Graham. It collapsed in 1952, mainly because of internal differences and growing debts, but it is significant that an overdraft guarantee of just £300 might have secured its survival.[15]

Theatre Workshop was founded in 1945 by Joan Littlewood, Ewan MacColl and others and until 1953 toured highly innovative productions, which drew on the European traditions of expressionism, constructivism and epic theatre, to extensive circuits of working-class venues, mainly in south Wales and the north of England. But the gruelling schedules eventually caused the company to move to a permanent base at the Theatre Royal in London's Stratford East. Until the mid-1960s the company produced shows for Stratford with minimal public funding, becoming increasingly dependent on transfers to the West End. Among these were Brendan Behan's *The Quare Fellow* (1956), Shelagh Delaney's *A Taste of Honey* (1958) and *Oh What a Lovely War* (1963). These successes undermined the ensemble and led to Littlewood's resignation and ultimately the closure of the company in the mid-1970s.

The total collapse of British theatre touring alternatives in the 1950s contrasts starkly with the Old Vic's success in creating 'headquarters' – in theatre buildings – in major cities. The theatrical establishment and the newly formed Arts Council had particular interests in this plan, but even the staunchest left-leaning supporters of a more democratic distribution of theatre subscribed to the bricks-and-mortar vision. J. B. Priestley, for example, advocated a national system of civic theatre buildings, two for each city and major town, one to receive national tours, the other to have a resident company which would in turn tour to surrounding towns and villages.[16] A national theatre conference in 1948, chaired by Priestley, confirmed the attachment to buildings as the heart

---

14 Chambers, *Unity Theatre*, p. 295.

15 Dellar, *Plays Without Theatres*, p. 151; see also Peter Billingham, *Theatre of Conscience 1939–1953: A Study of Four Touring British Community Theatres* (London: Routledge Harwood, 2002).

16 J. B. Priestley, *Theatre Outlook* (London: Nicholson & Watson, 1947), pp. 59–66; see also Norman Marshall, *The Other Theatre* (London: John Lehmann, 1947), pp. 231–5.

of theatrical life, in turn reinforcing this tendency in Arts Council policy (even though it ran against the spirit of its charter).[17]

It is symptomatic of this new orthodoxy that Charles Landstone – Arts Council Drama Director, 1947–52, and simultaneously manager of the Bristol Theatre Royal – makes no mention of the Compass Players or Theatre Workshop in his personal history of the period, *Off Stage*.[18] Reviewing the history of the Arts Council's Drama Department from the vantage point of 1980, N. V. Linklater (Council Drama Officer, 1952–77) states that its support of touring up until 1960 'was very much a transitional measure'.[19] The management of culture by agencies appointed by government was a small but highly significant factor in the emergent bureaucracies needed to foster the welfare state. In such an environment the waywardly democratic experiments of innovative touring companies were bound to be a precarious and, ultimately, an impossible business.

Experiments in the 1960s

The building of a popular theatre is a question of opening new doors. With new material and actors of wit and invention working on it, it is only a matter of time now before we have an extensive new dramaturgy . . . This future great theatre will, and can, arise everywhere, its achievement requires only work and patience.[20]

Despite the doubled-edged success of Theatre Workshop, there were few indications before the late 1960s that Joan Littlewood's optimism in 1960 was well founded. Local pride, steered by Arts Council policy, did ensure that doors were opened at over a dozen new civic theatres in regional cities between 1958 and 1968,[21] but from the perspective of subsequent alternatives this seemed more like a process of containment than expansion. On the margins of this new repertory system a few determined directors – Littlewood herself, Peter Cheeseman at Stoke-on-Trent, Alan Dosser at the Liverpool Everyman – ruffled

---

17 Davies, *Other Theatres*, pp. 147–8.
18 Charles Landstone, *Off Stage: A Personal Record of the First Twelve Years of State-Sponsored Drama in Great Britain* (London: Paul Elek, 1953); see also, Dellar, *Plays Without Theatres*, p. 45.
19 N. V. Linklater, 'The achievement in drama', in *The State and the Arts*, ed. John Pick (Eastbourne: John Offord, 1980), p. 79.
20 Joan Littlewood, 'Plays for the people', *World Theatre* 7, 4 (1960), 290; quoted in Davies, *Other Theatres*, p. 158.
21 Rowell and Jackson, *Repertory Movement*, pp. 193–4.

its growing middle-class complacency.[22] But the harbingers of the first post-war alternative theatre *movement* were lodged well beyond the soft-carpeted and shiny-chromed foyers.

In the early 1960s the first experiments of the new movement occurred in especially unlikely places, and they were decidedly home-grown in their ambitions and eccentricities. But as the decade lengthened and the West became prosperous, a flourishing international traffic in culture – still largely dominated, though, by the Atlantic axis – stimulated youthful artists in the first counter-culture to pioneer startlingly fresh kinds of performance. For the emergent alternative groups of the second half of the 1960s, aesthetic iconoclasm and unconventional venues were, paradoxically, *de rigueur*. Inspired by the revolutionary fervour of the student, civil rights and anti-war movements, the theatre-makers of the baby boom generation attacked the public sphere of culture as if it were a playground without rules. Here, for the first time since World War Two, was a widespread potential for a robust people's theatre.

Diverse sources can be cited in the first half of the sixties for these new alternative theatres, among them Joan Littlewood's anarchic theatrical enhancement of a CND (Campaign for Nuclear Disarmament) rally in the Royal Albert Hall in 1961; the founding by expatriate American Jim Haynes of the Edinburgh Traverse Theatre in 1963; John Calder's staging of the first British happening at the Edinburgh Festival in the same year; Peter Brook and Charles Marowitz's Artaud-inspired 'Theatre of Cruelty' season with the Royal Shakespeare Company in 1963–4; the visit of America's Living Theatre to London's Mermaid Theatre in 1964, and so on.[23] The new repertory system mustered little to match the excitement of these interventions, despite Peter Cheeseman's growing success, from 1962, in making a truly popular repertoire at Stoke-on-Trent and the founding of the first theatre-in-education team by the Coventry Belgrade Theatre in 1965.

But initiatives by two English playwrights born before World War Two, both with national reputations earned through productions in mainstream theatres, showed how much could be at stake in the making of new models for an alternative people's theatre. In founding the high-profile multi-arts Centre 42 project, Arnold Wesker aimed to gain substantial backing for the

22 Peter Cheeseman, 'A community theatre-in-the-round', *Theatre Quarterly* 1, 1 (Jan.–March 1971), 71–82; John McGrath, *A Good Night Out – Popular Theatre: Audience, Class and Form* (London: Eyre Methuen, 1981), pp. 49–53.
23 Joan Littlewood, *Joan's Book: Joan Littlewood's Peculiar History As She Tells It* (London: Minerva, 1994), pp. 622–3; Sandy Craig (ed.) *Dreams and Deconstructions: Alternative Theatre in Britain* (Oxford: Amber Lane Press, 1980), pp. 18–20.

arts from the trade unions; while John Arden, with his partner Margaretta D'Arcy, unostentatiously crafted highly innovative grass-roots theatre, particularly through two extraordinary experiments in rural villages at opposite ends of England.

Centre 42 was named after a Trades Union Congress resolution of 1960, secured by skilful lobbying by Wesker and backed by future Labour prime minister Harold Wilson.[24] It pledged the unions' support for 'the arts in the life of the community'[25] and represented a major political breakthrough: the last such cultural commitment had been a small-scale sponsorship from the Amalgamated Engineering Union for a disastrous season of leftist plays at the West End's Scala Theatre in 1946.[26] Ambitious to a fault, perhaps, Centre 42 in 1961 and 1962 mounted arts festivals in populist venues in several regional cities, involving art exhibitions, folk music, poetry and jazz, and a singular theatrical breakthrough in Charles Parker's participatory multi-media documentaries about local industries.[27] But most of the festival events emanated from London and the project was dogged by rising accusations of patronising the workers from critics across the political spectrum. Despite an imaginative plan in 1964 to occupy the Camden Town Round House as a permanent base, the organisation dwindled amid all-round acrimony, finally closing in 1970.[28] Besides reinforcing the rift between the arts and the trade unions, this spectacular decline offered a sharp object lesson to the rising generation of theatre workers, already suspicious of organised politics and party lines.

In total contrast, Arden and D'Arcy's modest community drama projects enjoyed a success that was to prove prophetic for later efforts to create a radical people's theatre. In 1960 they lived in the village of Brent Knoll in north Somerset, where a conversation with the vicar led Arden to write and stage *The Business of Good Government*, a gently devastating nativity play performed in the church by villagers as a Christmas festivity.[29] The play is a remarkable retelling of the traditional story as an allegory that shadows the Cold War. It portrays Herod's slaughter of the innocents as good politics in a topsy-turvy world, with a subtlety worthy of Brecht at his best: '[it] shows us why Herod acted as

24 Frank Coppieters, 'Arnold Wesker's Centre Forty-Two: a cultural revolution betrayed', *Theatre Quarterly* 5, 18 (June–Aug. 1975), 37–54.
25 Catherine Itzin, *Stages in the Revolution: Political Theatre in Britain Since 1968* (London: Eyre Methuen, 1980), p. 102.
26 Davies, *Other Theatres*, p. 139.
27 Alan Filewood and David Watt, *Workers' Playtime: Theatre and the Labour Movement Since 1970* (Sydney: Currency Press, 2001), pp. 89–90.
28 Coppieters, 'Centre Forty-Two', p. 51.
29 John Arden and Margaretta D'Arcy, *The Business of Good Government: A Christmas Play* (London: Methuen, 1963).

he did – but leaves us to judge the actions'. [30] Such openness of judgement was paramount in Arden and D'Arcy's next community venture, mounted in 1963 in the small Yorkshire market-town of Kirbymoorside. The event offered an ironical parody of Centre 42, taking the form of a free festival in and around Arden's tiny terraced house: poetry readings, improvised 'living newpapers', dialect storytelling, music from jazz to pop, community films, play readings and performances – a creative free-for-all in which local talent mattered just as much as national or even international reputation. Arden's contribution, *Ars Longa, Vita Brevis*, was performed by the Kirbymoorside Girl Guides only months after – and, according to Arden, much better than – its staging by Peter Brook as part of the RSC's 'Theatre of Cruelty' season.[31] The festival's anarchic sense of fun, informal organisation, aesthetic playfulness – as well as its deliberate blurring of genres, everyday life and art, professional and 'amateur' creativity – prefigured the main features of the alternative theatres of the late 1960s.

But two companies founded in 1965 are conventionally cited as the first fore-runners of the new movement: CAST (Cartoon Archetypal Slogan Theatre) and the People Show. 'Now I don't believe in secret police and I don't believe in torture, but if that bastard doesn't come back I believe we should secretly torture him' ranted CAST's Roland Muldoon in the late 1970s,[32] a parodic attack, addressed straight at the audience, that exactly captures the spirit of revolution gone delightfully mad that infused its productions from the outset. Expelled from Unity Theatre in 1964 for, allegedly, being 'part of an enormous resistance to established politics',[33] Muldoon and Claire Burnley founded the first Marxist-inspired theatre company that did not take sides, at least in the sense that it cheerfully attacked targets from every political camp. In the theatrical equivalent of a surreal comic strip, drawing inspiration as much from the media as from theatre, the company lampooned anything that smacked of po-faced political correctness. They were, in Muldoon's words, the first 'rock and roll theatre group' and purveyed a distinctly sixties style of 'agit-pop'.[34]

The People Show staged its first event – Show No. 1 – in the basement of Better Books in London's Charing Cross Road in 1966.[35] One of the group's founders, Jeff Nuttall, described his colleagues as an 'improbable collection of

30 Albert Hunt, *Arden: A Study of his Plays* (London: Eyre Methuen, 1975), p. 114.
31 Charles Marowitz and Simon Trussler (eds.), *Theatre at Work: Playwrights and Productions in the Modern British Theatre* (London: Methuen, 1967), p. 53.
32 CAST (Cartoon Archetypal Slogan Theatre), *Confessions of a Socialist* (London: Pluto Press, 1979), pp. 16–17.
33 Itzin, *Stages in the Revolution*, p. 12.
34 *Ibid.*, p. 14.
35 Roland Rees, *Fringe First: Pioneers of the Fringe on Record* (London: Oberon Books, 1992), pp. 29–36.

wayward oddballs',[36] a quality that was troublingly apparent in their shows. In 1969, for example, they could be found outside the Royal Court Theatre inviting passers-by into a telephone box to sample dirty postcards; once inside, patrons were offered 'two sugar lumps . . . coloured with red ink or, alternatively, a bra stuffed with baked beans'.[37] Such neo-Dadaist gestures were the founding stuff of British performance art, and would seem to set the People Show in another aesthetic universe from CAST. Indeed, the contrast has drawn several historians of the alternative theatre movement of the 1960s and 1970s to construct genealogies that schizophrenically split it between the political and the performance art groups, between agit-prop and avant-garde.[38] But the symbiotic inversions that link these two founding companies suggest a different alternative story. For whilst the overtly political CAST was expelled from Unity, the overtly a-political People Show moved into the New Left venue of Better Books! More crucially, both groups acknowledged a singular influence in the American comedian Lenny Bruce: Muldoon called him 'the Shakespeare of entertainment', while Nuttall identified with his bitterly comic honing of 'a razor's edge between public ritual and private ceremony'.[39] This is more than significant detail, for Bruce's compulsion to break all rules and boundaries made him a Janus of the permissive sixties: a demonised scourge of 'straight' society and an icon admired to excess by the youthful counter-culture.[40] Viewed from this perspective, these prankster primogenitors of the first alternative theatre movement of the second half of the twentieth century can be seen as united in their differences.

The first alternative theatre movement

In the evening the theatre could go on from 5 or 6 o'clock to 1 or 2 in the morning and at weekends we were open all night long. I would go through the [Arts] Lab warning that in one hour, thirty minutes, or right now, in the theatre so-and-so was going to perform or something and people would just drop in to see what was going on.[41]

36 Jeff Nuttall, *Performance Arts*, vol. *II*, *Memoirs* (London: John Calder, 1979), p. 46.
37 Peter Ansorge, *Disrupting the Spectacle: Five Years of Experimental and Fringe Theatre in Britain* (London: Pitman, 1975), p. 38.
38 See, for example, John Bull, *New British Political Dramatists* (London: Macmillan, 1984), p. 25; David Edgar, *The Second Time as Farce: Reflections on the Drama of Mean Times* (London: Lawrence & Wishart, 1988), pp. 163–4; Shellard, *British Theatre*, pp. 150–3.
39 Ansorge, *Disrupting the Spectacle*, p. 53.
40 Baz Kershaw, *The Politics of Performance: Radical Theatre as Cultural Intervention* (London: Routledge, 1992), pp. 70, 78.
41 Jim Haynes, *Thanks for Coming* (London: Faber & Faber, 1984), p. 153.

The London Drury Lane Arts Lab, founded by Jim Haynes in 1968, was every-thing that conventional theatres aimed *not* to be: scruffy, unpredictable, cheap (and cheerful), noisy, disorganised, disturbing, radical – the late 1960s west-ern counter-culture in a nutshell. Theatre historians have often cited it as *the* seedbed for the alternative theatre of the next two decades, just as 1968 has become *the* turning-point year for the counter-culture's 'expressive rev-olution'.[42] The range and number of influential groups that performed at the Arts Lab would seem to bear this out: Steven Berkoff's London Theatre Group, David Hare and Howard Brenton's Portable Theatre, the Pip Simmons Theatre Company, the Will Spoor Mime Company from Amsterdam, Geoff Moore's Moving Being, the Brighton Combination, the Sensual Laboratory, Yoko Ono, the People Show.[43] The creative iconoclasm these all shared – all out for all-out experiment, all determined on difference – was a key charac-teristic of the emergent movement, as were collaborations between unlikely partners. Thus, in 1968 CAST joined with Arden and D'Arcy, Albert Hunt (founder of the influential Bradford College of Art Group) and John Fox (soon to found Welfare State) to produce *Harrold Muggins is a Martyr* at the Unity Theatre.[44]

Such collaborations ensured a remarkable efflorescence of alternative ways of making performance in the late 1960s, as well as new places for showing it. As the decade ended an informal Arts Lab network numbered at least twenty venues, the college and university union circuit provided more outlets, and shows were staged in places as diverse as the municipal skating rink in Leeds and a crumbling north country monument identified by Britain's leading architectural historian as 'England's grandest folly'.[45] By 1970 the number of new producing groups – permanent and temporary – had reached over forty.[46] The speed of growth continued through almost the whole of the 1970s, as early directories testify. *The Theatre in Education Directory* of 1975 includes community and children's theatre and lists 77 companies; the *Alternative Theatre Handbook 1975–76* has 133 listings, ranging from the Phantom Captain, who described

42 See Bernice Martin, *A Sociology of Contemporary Cultural Change* (Oxford: Blackwell, 1981); Arthur Marwick, *The Sixties* (Oxford University Press, 1998), pp. 584 *passim*.
43 Arts Lab Programmes, 1968.
44 Simon Trussler, 'Political progress of a paralysed liberal: the community dramas of John Arden', *Drama Review* 13, 4 (1969); see also Kershaw, *Politics of Performance*, pp. 95–131.
45 Respectively, Howard Brenton's *Scott of the Antartic*, Portable Theatre, and Boris and Maggie Howarth's Lancaster Street Theatre, a ritual at the Ashton Memorial, Lancaster, both 1970.
46 Jonathon Hammond, 'A potted history of the fringe', *Theatre Quarterly* 3, 12 (Oct.–Dec. 1973), 40.

themselves as 'Vision Mongers and Environ Mentalists', to Rough Theatre, which, typical of many and without a trace of irony, claimed to make 'Theatre for the non-theatregoers'.[47] A slight slow-down occurred towards the end of the decade, yet still the 1980 *British Alternative Theatre Directory* lists 224 groups (plus 181 'small-scale touring' venues) in categories such as community theatre, performance art, dance, mime and youth theatre.[48] The statistics, directory information and professional associations formed by the groups go some way to justify calling this a 'movement'.[49] But it was characterised by a rich, ideologically contradictory, theatrical turbulence that matched the political and social instabilities of the decade: from the miners' strikes of 1972 and 1973, through riots at the Notting Hill Carnival in 1976, to the 'Winter of Discontent' of 1979.

Yet in the first half of the 1970s the main general trend for all types of groups was towards a greater clarity of purpose and refinement of artistic identity. This produced five or six approaches that were distinctive enough to shape *Time Out*'s 'underground' theatre listings even in the early 1970s.[50] The performance art groups, following on from the People Show, developed multi-media dramaturgies of non-narrative imagery, reflecting roots in the visual arts colleges: Welfare State (1968) was one of the earliest, to be joined in extravagant aesthetic anarchy by the likes of Cameron and Miller (1970), the Yorkshire Gnomes (1971), the Birmingham Performance Group (1973), Forkbeard Fantasy (1975) and IOU (1976). The physical theatre groups drew inspiration from UK visits by American and European companies – Living Theatre (1964, 1968, 1971), La Mama (1967, 1969), Jérome Savary's Théâtre Panique (1967 – from 1968 Le Grand Magic Circus), and Grotowski's Theatre Laboratory (1968, 1969) – and they included Freehold (1969), Triple Action (1969), London Mime Theatre (1971) and RAT Theatre (1972). A few groups concentrated mainly on new writing, such as Wakefield Tricycle (1972), Major Road (originally Magic Bus – 1973), Avon Touring (1974) and Paines Plough (1975). Circus, cabaret, melodrama and pantomime were the most common sources for the popular theatre companies, including the Ken Campbell Roadshow (1970), Footsbarn Theatre (1971), Salakta Balloon Band (1973) and Shared Experience (1975).

47 Claire Chapman and Pam Schweitzer (eds.), *Theatre in Education Directory* (London: Theatre Quarterly Publications, 1975); Catherine Itzin (ed.), *Alternative Theatre Handbook* (London: Theatre Quarterly Publications, 1976).
48 Catherine Itzin (ed.), *British Alternative Theatre Directory 1980* (Eastbourne: John Offord, 1980).
49 See Itzin, *Stages in the Revolution*, for TACT (The Association of Community Theatres), ITC (Independent Theatre Council) and TW (Theatre Writer's Union), pp. 176–81, 211–15, 306–15.
50 Time Out, 'Guide to underground theatre', *Theatre Quarterly* 1, 1 (Jan.–March 1971), 61–5.

Virtually all these groups were 'alternative' mainly in a broad cultural sense, but a sharper ideologically oppositional edge could be found in the community, political, women's, gay and black theatre companies. Such groups tended to tailor their shows to suit the audience, leading to a common accusation by mainstream critics that they 'preached to the converted', but why this was a bad thing in community centres, labour clubs and women's refuges when it was perfectly acceptable in churches and West End theatres is never made plain.

In the early 1970s at least thirty-six community theatre groups were set up, most of which, forever fearful of rejection by host constituencies, typically purveyed a disguised or 'soft' radicalism. But blandness of purpose was more apparent than real. City-based groups such as Interplay (Leeds), Attic (Winchester) and the Natural Theatre Company (Bath) – all 1970 – were usually committed to working-class neighbourhoods and estates. Companies touring shows in rural areas – Orchard Theatre (north Devon, 1968), EMMA (west Midlands, 1972), Medium Fair (east Devon, 1972), Pentabus (east Midlands, 1974) – typically saw themselves as serving deprived communities. The extraordinary proliferation led to imaginative specialisation. Interaction toured with its double-decker Fun Art Bus, Bubble Theatre with an inflatable tent and Mikron Theatre plied the canal system on a forty-foot narrow-boat. 'Special needs' communities welcomed projects from Stirabout (1974) in prisons and remand centres, from Matchbox (1974) for people with physical and mental impairments and from Fair Old Times (part of Medium Fair, 1978), which created the new genre of reminiscence theatre. Rarely didactic, these companies frequently adapted theatre-in-education techniques to include creative participation by communities in their projects; but the underlying links with political theatre emerged when, for example, the short-lived Community Theatre (1972) staged *The Motor Show* for striking car workers and Covent Garden Community Theatre (1975) campaigned with local residents against the insensitive redevelopment of the central London market area.[51]

The overtly political theatre groups extended the long tradition of European people's theatre, with clear left-leaning commitments ranging from liberal socialism to hard-line Maoism. Over fifteen were set up by 1975, including, in 1971, Foco Novo, 7:84 Theatre Company (England), General Will; in 1973, Belt and Braces, 7:84 (Scotland), Joint Stock; in 1974, Broadside Mobile Worker's Theatre (formed in a break-away from Red Ladder, 1968) and Centre 42 veteran

---

51 Steve Gooch and Paul Thomson, *The Motor Show* (London: Pluto Press, 1975); Tony Howard, 'Theatre of urban renewal: the uncomfortable case of Covent Garden', *Theatre Quarterly* 10, 38 (summer 1980).

Figure 15.1 Spectacular protest as entertainment: Welfare State International's *Parliament in Flames*, Catford, London, 1981.

ground.[59] Meanwhile, in rural Dorset the playwright-director Ann Jellicoe staged the fourth of a series of 'community plays' involving over 150 local people in a promenade production that in its two-week run sold out to an audience of more than 3,500.[60] Welfare State's spectacular lead was followed by at least a dozen environmental/technological theatre companies in the years that followed. Groups such as Emergency Exit Arts (1981) and Station House Opera (1981) staged shows in venues as varied as swimming pools and multi-storey car parks. And by 1985 Jellicoe had produced a further seven community plays, including Edgar's *Entertaining Strangers*, which, improbably, was restaged by the National Theatre in 1987.[61] As the decade drew to a close her success had spawned the beginnings of a community play movement, with shows in Newcastle, Basildon, Carlisle and elsewhere. The populism, and apparent lack of political edge, of these new alternatives generated accusations of carnival

59 Tony Coult and Baz Kershaw (eds.), *Engineers of the Imagination: The Welfare State Handbook*, rev. edn (London: Methuen, 1990), pp. 88–92; Bim Mason, *Street Theatre and Other Outdoor Performance* (London: Routledge, 1992), pp. 133–5.
60 Ann Jellicoe, *Community Plays: How To Put Them On* (London: Methuen, 1987).
61 Susan Painter, *Edgar: The Playwright* (London: Methuen, 1996), pp. 114–27.

escapism, though spectacle was often a thin disguise for social and political criticism.[62]

Many companies were still aligned with the radical causes of the counter-cultures, but many more of the new ones showed few or no signs of clear oppositional commitment. There was a general weakening of alternative politics as companies competed for diminishing audiences,[63] so that almost all the new trends of the 1980s were clearly marked by the disciplines of the marketplace. Above all, new companies aimed to 'brand' themselves as distinctive or, if possible, unique. Hence, the fragmentation of alternative theatre as a movement and its growing strength as an industrial sector – perhaps now best named 'fringe theatre' – were two sides of the same neo-conservative cultural coin.

At least half of the fringe theatre groups of the 1980s did not overtly proclaim a clear critical political or social position. Instead they defined themselves through a lively variety of theatrical interests, as new writing or repertory-style ventures, as music theatre or 'experimenting with classics' companies, as visual-physical performance or popular theatre groups. The last category was the most popular, with over forty new ones touring a wide spectrum of genres to venues ranging from outdoor festivals to studio theatres. Thus Ra Ra Zoo (1984) pioneered new circus (strictly no animals, other than human) while Mummerandada (1985) combined clowning and *commedia dell'arte*; Trestle Theatre (1981) produced masked comedy, while the Grand Theatre of Lemmings (1981) echoed the anarchic humour of the People Show in promising 'to bring the concept of catharsis to a new meaning, by destroying large numbers of our cast'.[64] A few longer-lived groups achieved mainstream status, most notably Theatre de Complicite (1983), a highly disciplined physical ensemble whose wonderfully fluid *mises-en-scène* were eventually performed at the National Theatre in the 1990s.[65] Unsurprisingly, similar elevation was commoner for young directors who 'radicalised' the classics, such as Deborah Warner and Declan Donnellan – founders of Kick Theatre (1980) and Cheek

62 See Peter Reynolds, 'Community theatre: carnival or camp?', in *The Politics of Theatre and Drama*, ed. Graham Holderness (London: Macmillan, 1992); Graham Woodruff, 'Community, class and control: a view of community plays', *New Theatre Quarterly* 5, 20 (Nov. 1989).

63 Andrew Feist and Robert Hutchison (eds.), *Cultural Trends in the Eighties* (London: Policy Studies Institute, 1990), pp. 29–45.

64 Catherine Itzin, ed., *British Alternative Theatre Directory, 1982* (Eastbourne: John Offord, 1982), p. 28.

65 Theodore Shank (ed.), *Contemporary British Theatre*, updated edn (London: Methuen, 1996), pp. 212–15.

by Jowl (1981), respectively – who were among the exceptions proving the rule that preferment is a prerogative of the privileged few.[66]

These institutional blurrings of cultural hierarchy were reflected in the aesthetics of the visual-physical theatre groups, which could be called 'neo-expressionist', as subjectivity was central to their style. Eschewing the 'subject as tortured individual' of modernist expressionism, they represented the dispersed and fragmented consciousness of post-modernism through a *bricolage* that treated all cultural texts as equivalently quotable. The physically oriented studio-experimentalist groups, such as Theatre Babel (1982), Leda Theatre Collective (1985) and DV8 (1986) drew inspiration anywhere from Grotowski to extreme sports, while the visual companies, such as Intimate Strangers (1983) and Shadow Syndicate (1984), often pursued a slippery romance with the more lurid obsessions of art house films and the popular media.

The most influential of these groups was Impact Theatre Co-operative, founded by Pete Brooks in 1978. By the mid-1980s Impact was producing stunningly dense and dystopic multi-media collages: *The Carrier Frequency* (1985) had performers flailing in the waters of a totally flooded stage as if engulfed in the toxic slime of a post-apocalypse nightmare. The intricate intertextuality – and ideological ambivalence – of Impact's aesthetic was adopted by newer groups, such as Forced Entertainment (1984) and Dogs in Honey (1985), which threw yet wider nets of reference to haul in the semiotic detritus of late eighties consumer culture for more post-modern recycling, laying the shifting foundations for a resurgence of performance art in the 1990s.

The ambivalent subversions of the neo-expressionists were matched by the 'soft ideology' of the growing number of companies touring nationally, such as Tic Toc Theatre (1983) and Meeting Ground (1985), with shows that dealt liberally with 'social questions'. Stronger stuff was offered by a few new Marxist/socialist groups. Tropical Theatre (1980) opened with the appropriately named *Thumbscrews are Getting Tighter*, but by mid-decade – despite some brave projects with the striking miners[67] – only four or so more were proudly waving the red flag. This is hardly surprising, given that leading left-wing companies such as 7:84 (England), Foco Novo and Joint Stock had been forced to close as a result of grant cuts.[68]

The strongest opposition to Thatcherism came in the issue-based shows produced by the growing number of community, women's, feminist, gay/queer,

---

66 *Ibid.*, pp. 206–9, 215–18.
67 Filewood and Watt, *Workers' Playtime*, pp. 109–11.
68 John McGrath, *The Bone Won't Break: On Theatre and Hope in Hard Times* (London: Methuen, 1990), pp. 29–41.

black and special needs groups. The first signs of influence by Augusto Boal's 'theatre of the oppressed' appeared in the mid-1980s with new community groups such as Gusto Theatre (1984), and in the community plays of All Change Arts (1985). In addressing a widening range of constituencies the community-based companies became increasingly specialised, as in, for example, the reminiscence theatre of Bedside Manners (1981) and Age Exchange (1983). In both London and the regional cities black and gay theatre flourished, though often on a semi-professional basis. A notable growth of Asian and African groups, including Theatre of Black Women (1982) and Asian Co-Operative Theatre (1985), was reinforced through the creation of the Tara Arts Centre in 1983. In that year the Greater London Council sponsored a gay arts festival: Hard Corps and Re-Sisters were among the lesbian groups set up in its wake. By the mid-1980s the tragedy of AIDS had met with a tough response from the predominantly male queer groups, whose names signalled a truly impressive resilience: New Heart, Consenting Adults, Hormone Imbalance, Brixton Fairies, Sexual Outlaws.

The stylistic eclecticism of fringe theatre was reflected in the steady rise of women's and feminist companies throughout the 1980s. The Raving Beauties (1981) made cabaret for fringe venues and television; Scarlet Harlets (1981) toured multi-media neo-expressionist shows to community and women's centres, as well as studio theatres; Female Trouble (1981) and No Boundaries (1984) produced plays by women writers; Sensible Footwear (1983) specialised in movement-based satirical storytelling; Beavers and Sphinx Theatre (both 1984) experimented with popular forms for outdoor and community venues. More groups with a highly gendered creative agenda were set up in the 1980s than in the previous two decades. A UK survey covering 1987–90 identified 161 'feminist or pro-feminist companies', of which 33 were mixed gender and 64 were women-only groups.[69] With such a large proportion of the sector – possibly about one-third – crusading for the cause of democratic difference, there were bound to be healthy disputes between radical, bourgeois, liberal and materialist feminisms. But these were subsumed, and sustained, by a widespread hatred of Thatcher as a false icon of femininity, strengthening the resistant resolve of other companies opposed to the 'Iron Lady's' policies.

Hence in the 1980s alternative/fringe theatre partly mirrored the divided culture – between north and south, people in and out of work, rich and poor – fostered by the Conservative government's policies. And, symptomatically, the riven nation enjoyed its most ideologically ambivalent public art in the form

---

69 Goodman, *Contemporary Feminist Theatre*, p. 39.

of 'alternative comedy'. From the founding of the Comedy Store in Soho in 1979, the popularity of a new – and initially mostly politically correct – style of stand-up satire quickly mushroomed into a national orthodoxy. By mid-decade no self-respecting borough was without its upstairs pub room that every Friday and Saturday night was devoted, in some part at least, to the vilification of the great and the good. Early survivors of the Comedy Store's infamously lethal gong quickly became well-loved names through television shows such as *The Young Ones* (1982) and *Girls on Top* (1985): Alexei Sayle, Rik Mayall, Jennifer Saunders, Dawn French and the rest. But it was perhaps Ben Elton's 'radical rhetoric of humour'[70] that best captured the widespread outrage at the outrageous selfishness stimulated by Thatcherism. That this humour hinged on a performative trope that inescapably celebrated radical individualism was one of the more telling paradoxes of that divided decade. But perhaps even this was topped by Thatcher's resignation as Prime Minister in 1990, forced on her by the party she brought to power in the wake of riots against a Poll Tax that she had herself authored.

A plurality of alternatives

> What's interesting about the theatre now is that people still get more offended at watching real people fucking, nudity or violence onstage than people ever will watching a funny little box in the corner of the room or even on celluloid, so it is a more immediate form of expression.[71]

If social division was the British disease of the 1980s, then it was replaced by the delirium of cultural slippage in the 1990s. Theatre director Stephen Daldry's defensive reference to the media, though oddly quaint in mentioning only television and film, is key to this. As everyday life became ever more saturated by personal computers, cell-phones, swipe-card machines and pixelated simulators of anything from skiing to holocausts, so the boundaries between public and private, mediated and live, fantasy and reality, permissible and forbidden increasingly were fabulously blurred. In this newly anarchic environment the aesthetics of British theatre enjoyed a refreshing liberation as the creative iconoclasm of alternative / fringe performance spilled over into mainstream practices. So, for example, Daldry's neo-expressionist production

---

70 Simon Trussler, *The Cambridge Illustrated History of British Theatre* (Cambridge University Press, 1994), p. 372.
71 Stephen Daldry, 'There is a new audience out there', in *Live 1: Food for the Soul – A New Generation of British Theatre Makers*, ed. David Tushingham (London: Methuen, 1994), p. 97.

of J. B. Priestley's *An Inspector Calls* (1993) drew on eighties groups such as Impact to transform the socialist thriller into a sophisticated, reflexive theatrical game: it played at the National Theatre, in the West End and on Broadway – and was still touring as the millennium turned.[72] Through such means, the brave new world of post-modern culture productively undermined the distinctions that had sustained a sense of alternative theatre as a movement or fringe theatre as a sector during the previous three decades.

Traditional political theatre of the left, at least in England, all but disappeared. Community theatre performed by professionals was much reduced. Even the feminist, gay / queer and black groups were diminished by funding cuts and troubled by growing uncertainty about the benefits of a gender, sexual or racial politics which placed solidarity before individual difference. Identity politics bit back, so to speak, at the theatres that had fostered it. By 1995 a leading black artist, Michael McMillan, could write: 'Disillusioned by the straight-jacket of black theatre's conventionality, and desiring to take risks with politicised performance, I was influenced by critical debates in cultural studies, film theory and black visual arts and stumbled upon performance art.'[73] The force of that 'stumbled' – an accidental salvation, perhaps – drives home how far the 'fringe' theatres of the 1990s had fallen from a shared sense of purpose. By mid-decade claims for a cohesive alternative theatre movement in the 1970s were beginning to look like nostalgic myth-making, as experimental practitioners increasingly embraced the pluralism of post-modern theory and culture, often under the banner of 'independent theatre'.

So in the early years of the 1990s there was 'a new spirit of innovation' in British theatre, which reverberated through the rest of the decade.[74] In 1994 a collection of interviews with 'a new generation of British theatre-makers' included director Simon McBurney describing the ascendance of Theatre de Complicite to the National Theatre; performance artist Bobby Baker discussing the presentation of her one-woman food show in her own kitchen; writer-director Neil Bartlett – founder of the queer theatre group Gloria (1988) – explaining his take-over of the Lyric Theatre, Hammersmith; and playwright Jeremy Weller championing the Edinburgh Grassmarket Project, which mounted shows at the Traverse Theatre that were created and performed by the homeless, young offenders and people with mental illnesses.

---

72 Wendy Lesser, *A Director Calls: Stephen Daldry and the Theatre* (London: Faber, 1997), pp. 15–36.
73 Michael Macmillan, quoted in Catherine Ugwu (ed.), *Let's Get It On: The Politics of Black Performance* (London: Institute of Contemporary Art, 1995), p. 202.
74 Tushingham (ed.), *Live 1*, back cover.

By mid-decade, according to prominent arts entrepreneur Neil Wallace, the alternative–mainstream distinction was well and truly crumbling as a result of British-based co-productions, creative exchanges with innovative companies in Europe and visits by high-profile international experimental companies, such as the Wooster Group from New York, Robert Lepage's Ex Machina from Quebec and the Maly Theatre from St Petersburg. As a result, argued Wallace, 'what we're watching is the decline of the *playgoer* . . . the well-crafted play text, brilliantly interpreted . . . that's no longer *enough*'.[75]

The spread of new theatre festivals in the 1990s would seem to bear out at least the second part of this claim. Throughout the 1980s London had enjoyed a bi-annual LIFT (London International Festival of Theatre), which in the following decade continued as a major conduit of influence for experimental groups from around the world. Since the late 1980s the Third Eye Centre in Glasgow had organised an annual National Review of Live Art, a showcase for the more extreme experiments in British performance, often compèred by Neil Bartlett in 'a Coco Chanel "little black frock" and beads'.[76] The high success of these pioneers was infectious: festival fever spread to local authorities increasingly keen to promote their towns to tourists through distinctive events, such as the Stockton International Riverside Festival (street theatre) (1987) and It's Queer Up North in Manchester (1992). Even Barclays Bank joined in, sponsoring the annual New Stages Festival (1990) at the Royal Court Theatre and elsewhere, its participants rebranded as 'independent theatres'. Marketplace mentality met radical imagination to produce a theatre taxonomist's nightmare.

A sense of the mesmerising proliferation of British performance in the 1990s can be gained from the contrasts between two prominent and popular types of practice: live art and community plays. Live art – or time-based art, or performance art – became the new 'political theatre' of the rising generation of artists, celebrated for its lack of rules, disdain of all boundaries, in-yer-face aggression and/or take-it-or-leave-it cool. Paradoxically, creative collaboration and ensemble performance were rediscovered by groups such as Blast Theory (1991), Stan's Cafe (1991) and Third Angel (1995). The deliberate aesthetic over-coding and skilful avoidance of narrative closure of their shows explored the impossibility of theatre as a system for representing anything except its own failure to represent. The theatre of the absurd was reinvented as a species of performance addicted to infinitely recursive irony. At its most disturbing this rising millennial angst produced – depending on the strength of your stomach – a

---

75 *Ibid.*, p. 121, emphasis Tushingham.
76 Alasdair Cameron, 'Experimental theatre in Scotland', in Shank, *British Contemporary Theatre*, p. 135.

messy sublimity or an eerie depravity in the extremes of body-based art. Hence, the facial operations of French flesh-artist Orlan and the skin-hooks of Australian suspension-specialist Stelarc[77] were evoked in 1997 by British body artist Franko B as he stood naked in the Institute of Contemporary Arts, the pure white stage liberally stained by his blood as it dripped from many self-pierced veins, ironic stigmata of a voided identity.[78]

Apparently in another universe, local distinctiveness as a source of collective identity was the motor that drove the community play movement, as it grew steadily throughout the 1990s. In 1992 the inaugural conference of a new national association of community-play-makers took place at the Belgrade Theatre in Coventry, following productions of two large-cast historical-documentary plays – In Search of Cofa's Tree and Diamonds in the Dust – performed by local non-professional participants. These differed from the model refined by Ann Jellicoe in the 1980s in being devised by the performers and staged in a theatre. More innovations testing a form that too often had become a cosy excuse for shallow celebration of a deodorised past seemed designed to capture the distemper of the 1990s. At Bridlington on the north Yorkshire coast in 1995, Remould Theatre produced Come Hell or High Water, the 'first community play with a tragic ending'.[79] And by 1998 a trio of plays showed how elastic this genre had become, though its defining feature continued to be performance by non-professionals: The Visitor at Hereford Shire Hall involved 137 participants in a multi-media mixture of 'science fiction and fictitious history'; Chasing Toplis was toured by thirty performers out of the Derbyshire mining village of Blackwell and focussed on an historic dispute between the BBC and Thatcher's government by framing the story of World War One deserter and local anti-hero Percy Toplis as 'a play about a TV play in a play'; in Travelling Through the Paradise Fields community play finally met live art through an installation in a derelict mill in Batley, Yorkshire, involving ninety local people who played ghosts of communities past for an audience which made 'individual journeys through space . . . each one unique'.[80] A celebration of that quintessential nineties icon, the sovereign consumer? An ironic meditation on the loneliness of life in the millennial global village? The paradoxes

77 Philip Auslander, From Acting to Performance: Essays in Modernism and Postmodernism (London: Routledge, 1997), pp. 126–36; J. D. Paffrath and Stelarc, Obsolete Body/Suspensions (Davis, Calif.: JD Publications, 1984).

78 John Daniel, 'Baying for blood', interview with Franco B, Total Theatre 9, 4 (winter 1997–8), 14–15.

79 David Jones, 'Community plays: two cultures', Mailout: Arts Work with People (Aug.–Sept. 1995), 13.

80 Gee, Emma and Richard Hayhow, 'Community plays', Mailout: Arts Work with People (Feb.–March 1999), 6–11.

Figure 15.2 Live art meets community play: *Travelling Through the Paradise Fields*, Batley, Yorkshire, 1998.

of post-modernity shimmered through every element of British independent theatre as the millennium drew near.

The extreme contrasts between these two tendencies in the new theatre of the 1990s signal the dangers of drawing maps of a territory still under formation. The spirit of innovation, sometimes desperate, sometimes sublime, seemed to delight in producing incommensurate alternatives, especially strange bed-persons. Hence, site-specific performance, in the work of companies such as Brith Gof and Station House Opera,[81] segued into heritage theatre as Shakespeare increasingly was staged in the grounds of stately homes. A

81 Nick Kaye, *Site-Specific Art: Performance, Place and Documentation* (London: Routledge, 2000), pp. 52–7, 163–8.

remarkable range of black performance artists were promoted by the Institute of Contemporary Art in London, but Tara Arts director Jatinder Verma describes the staging of his productions by the Royal National Theatre as a 'pragmatic appropriation' and a 'false dawn'.[82] Stephen Daldry's 'fucking, nudity and violence' had plenty of exposure in the rawness of the more experimental groups, some of which scotched traditional demarcation lines by taking part in events such as the annual Manchester Festival of Community Arts. Aesthetic echoes of the few surviving groups from the alternative theatre movement of the late 1960s – most notably the People Show and Welfare State International – could be detected in the work of many new companies that emerged in the decade, yet the term that they increasingly used to describe themselves – independent theatre – had been recoined by Barclays Bank.

When New Labour under Tony Blair gained government with a landslide victory over the Tories in 1997, a so-called 'third way' of politics, beyond left and right, was proclaimed.[83] This post-modern Parliament immediately created a Secretary of State for Culture, Media and Sport, the first in the nation's history. Almost overnight the arts were recruited to the battle against social exclusion in the name of democratic participation, and a well-knotted nationwide network of theatre of the oppressed agitants, virtually invisible during the eighteen years of Tory rule, emerged to take up the challenge. In 1999, in a cheerful ceremony of 'legislative theatre' conducted by Augusto Boal himself, London's County Hall, closed by Margaret Thatcher with the dissolution of the Greater London Council in 1986, was temporarily reopened for democratic business. Certainly this was not a rehearsal for the all-out revolution envisaged by the 1960s founders of the alternative theatre movement and their immediate precursors; nor was it a foundation stone for a people's theatre as dreamed up by leftist radicals in the 1940s. Rather, the event was a serious sign that its ultimate sponsors – the state – saw huge potential in the links between, in the first Culture Secretary's phrase, 'Culture, Creativity and Social Regeneration'.[84]

The post-war history of British people's-experimental-underground-alternative-fringe-independent theatres placed youthful *fin-de-siècle* practitioners in a strong position to make performances dedicated to justice, freedom and equality. But given the pressures and paradoxes of a highly mediatised and globalised world, such a project was likely to be fraught with ironic opportunities of the kind that even New Labour was having to grasp. Hence in

82 Ugwi, *Let's Get It On*; Shank, *British Contemporary Theatre*, p. xiii.
83 Anthony Giddens, *Beyond Left and Right: The Future of Radical Politics* (London: Polity, 1994).
84 Chris Smith, *Creative Britain* (London: Faber, 1998), p. 129.

September 1999, on the critical issue of the switch-over of the nation to the massive expansion of cultural choice apparently promised by non-terrestrial television, the Culture Secretary pronounced that there would be no switch-off of earth-bound analogue services until '95% of people have *bought into* digital'.[85] It would seem that in the brave new world of the new millennium there would always be a price to pay – in the media, in the theatre, in every cultural form – for genuinely popular 'alternatives'.

85 Chris Smith, interview, BBC Radio 4, *Today Programme*, 17/9/99.

16

Developments in the profession
of theatre, 1946–2000

COLIN CHAMBERS

In February 1948 nearly 500 delegates gathered in London for an unprecedented four-day meeting designed to tackle no less a task than the complete regeneration of British theatre. The British Theatre Conference attracted a broad sweep of interests: London and regional theatres, drama schools and training colleges, plus national institutions, such as the actors' union Equity and the umbrella body for amateur theatre, the British Drama League. Some were present as individuals, among them leading West End theatre managers, who collectively had refused to send a representative when they learned that theatre ownership was on the agenda.[1]

Here was an historic opportunity for the British theatre to redefine itself and its relationship to society. The upsurge of interest in culture during World War Two had survived into peacetime, and Labour's nationalisation programme offered the promise of significant state funding for the arts. The conference, chaired by the writer J. B. Priestley, passed an astonishing array of far-sighted resolutions: on strengthening the Arts Council, establishing a national theatre, reducing and controlling theatre rents and costs through a public authority entertainment tax, renovating theatre buildings, reforming safety and licensing regulations – including a call for Sunday opening and an end to censorship – expanding drama in education, increasing co-operation between amateur and professional theatre, improving professional training and – most contentious of all – regulating entry and re-entry into 'the profession' through training or apprenticeship.

Although this impressive roll-call of concerns prefigured the major debates that defined British theatre during the following half-century, the moment of radical change was lost. National economic stringency and the reassertion of conservatism within the theatre itself pushed the profession of theatre down a

1 Anon., *New Theatre* 4, 9 (March 1948), 6–11.

different path. The standing committee established by the conference quickly went into recess and planning for a follow-up gathering was abandoned. In the subsequent fifty years, however, British theatre – and what was *meant* by British theatre – did change dramatically, albeit more haphazardly than in the 'planned culture' called for by the conference resolutions. The volatile theatrical marketplace was marked by the advance (1940s–50s), ascendancy (1960s–70s) and rolling back (1980s–90s) of state patronage. Government ideology and fierce competition from the other arts – especially film, television and, later, digital entertainment media – plus the burgeoning 'leisure industries' forced theatre from its 'elevated' status in the national culture. Increasing diversification and specialisation, often stimulated by new technologies, reshaped every aspect of theatre work. The idea of theatre as a profession, together with its social and cultural functions, was transformed.

That transformation is the subject of this chapter: the evolution of theatre from a fairly homogenous and autonomous crafts-based industry comprising a small number of closely related systems of artistic production to a highly differentiated and complex industry with a growing number of overlapping sectors all more or less embedded in a technology-driven, mass leisure-culture. In this perspective the environment of the theatre professional changed enormously through various processes of 'professionalisation', in which the theatre profession as a whole increasingly embraced many subsidiary and often independent professions. Growing ambiguities and tensions in job functions, as well as more practical matters such as the frequency of employment opportunities and availability of career structures, made a considerable impact on these historical changes. Relationships between individual and collective creativity and the control of the means of production became critical issues, particularly for those many theatre practitioners, such as actors or playwrights, who had to negotiate a path between being both autonomous artist and hired worker. Ironically, by the end of the century, the theatre professional, long used to surviving on an uneven succession of short-term engagements, had become the paradigm of employment in the new world of economic globalisation.

This chapter focusses on four main areas: first, the general infrastructure and organisation of theatre and theatre companies; second, the new and changing occupational roles within theatre; third, patterns of employment and training; and fourth, professional organisations. Each section has its own chronology, reflecting the different pace of change and weave of influences within each of these areas.

Infrastructure and organisation

An alliance between London theatre managers, dominated by a wartime consortium that became known as the Group, and the newly established Arts
Council (founded 1946) ensured a consolidation of the established order of
theatre in the first decade following World War Two. The methods of control
of commercial theatres after the war were complicated, but their extent can be
gauged by the progress of Prince Littler, who was *the* major figure in the Group.
Littler took over Stoll Theatres Corporation in 1942. He then became head
of Associated Theatre Properties (London) Ltd in 1943, a director of Howard
& Wyndham in 1945 and chair of Moss Empires in 1947. He bought theatres
cheaply in the war and by 1949 he owned 18 of the 42 active West End theatres
and 57 of the 81 main regional touring theatres, including 34 of the 53 theatres
on the No. 1 Circuit, as it was called, of largest venues.[2]

Given such concentrations of power, it is not surprising that the managers
collectively denounced the British Theatre Conference as a 'red front'. At the
same time they successfully opposed parliamentary measures that they feared
would lead to competition from municipal theatres and won the halving of
Entertainment Tax levied on tickets, which was finally abolished in 1957. The
rituals of bourgeois theatre-going (in dress code, timing of shows, marketing
and choice and style of plays) were reinstated and the number of lower-priced
tickets reduced, thus ensuring that the theatre was sealed off from most of the
nation's citizens. In a theatre system that was almost wholly commercial, the
Group's position of strength allowed it, however, to streamline the industry
and to win the support of the unions in order to maintain their 'closed-shop'
agreements, which gave only union members access to work. In ending the
pre-World War Two proliferation of theatre ownership by companies whose
main financial interests lay outside the theatre, the Group was in a position to
turn British theatre into a modern and relatively coherent industry.[3]

The other half of the alliance, the Arts Council of Great Britain, was born
out of wartime initiatives to tour 'theatre-less' areas and support amateur
activity as a basis for a 'people's theatre', yet in peacetime it took an opposite
direction. Instead of encouraging expansion and innovation, it sanctified the
narrow professional order and promoted a paternalistic, patrician view of

2 See John Elsom, *Post-War British Theatre*, rev. edn (London: Routledge & Kegan Paul,
1979); Ronald Hayman, *The Set-Up: An Anatomy of the English Theatre Today* (London: Eyre
Methuen, 1973).
3 Federation of Theatre Unions, 'Theatre ownership in Britain – a report' (London: Federation of Theatre Unions, 1953).

excellence. It opposed state control, believed major public patronage should come from local authorities, and saw its function as correcting temporary imbalances in the marketplace. Its grant to drama was less than that to opera and ballet, and popular forms such as circus (in the land that gave birth in the eighteenth century to its modern incarnation) were excluded altogether.

Whilst London's suburban theatres and large-scale tours to the regions declined after World War Two, repertory theatres (familiarly called 'reps' in the industry) prospered briefly before the rise of television in the mid-1950s lured audiences away. In this period, there were two types of rep: first, theatres with policies like those of the pioneers of the movement in the early decades of the century that challenged the values of the commercial theatre and served their local middle classes; second, the commercially oriented weekly reps that filled the gaps left by the demise of big, and costly, national tours to No. 1 Circuit theatres. Despite their differences, both types reinforced the prevailing hierarchies within the industry in terms of roles in the profession, the status of venues and the habits of theatre-going.

With the break-up of the Group in the mid 1950s due to competition from television, it fell to forces outside the commercial system to revitalise British theatre. The resident company ideal associated with the non-commercial reps retained its inspirational force and was given renewed local and regional civic support and then, from the 1960s, central state support in a process of piecemeal 'nationalisation'. New theatres were built in a spirit of public service in numbers unprecedented since the turn of the century, beginning with the Belgrade Theatre, Coventry, in 1958, which was the first theatre subsidised wholly from the public purse constructed since World War Two. Others were extensively refurbished. By 1970 twenty new theatres had been built and by 1980 the figure had risen to over forty, including conversions such as the Royal Exchange Theatre, Manchester (1976). Of these, thirty-four were located outside London.[4]

Modern democratic ideals were inscribed in the new theatre architecture as well as in changes in working patterns, however limited; artistic standards were raised by longer rehearsal periods and a greater emphasis on the play than on the lead actor. This trend was epitomised by the reinvention, in 1961, of the resident company at Stratford-upon-Avon, in the form of the Royal Shakespeare Company (RSC), a 'national' theatre in all but name, and, two years later, by the creation of the National Theatre (NT) itself. In the 1960s the

---

4 See George Rowell and Anthony Jackson, *The Repertory Movement: A History of Regional Theatre in Britain* (Cambridge University Press, 1984), pp. 99–110.

two national companies brought new prestige to the theatre profession and set new benchmarks: richer repertoire, better working conditions, higher technical quality, new relationships between practitioners and new and expanded roles within the production process. They and the reps, which the Arts Council saw as feeder satellites of the national 'centres of excellence', became the dynamo of quality theatre.

However, in the economic downturn of the 1970s the national/repertory sector failed to produce significant structural or aesthetic developments, and the focus of innovation shifted to the new fringe (or alternative) theatres. The fringe challenged the conservatism of the reps and redrew the map of the profession in a new era of democratisation and diversity. Aided by technological advance, the fringe bypassed the constraints of the reps' building-based economy with readily available transport (the Transit van), flexible new materials (e.g., fabrics and alloys) and lighter, more powerful lighting and sound systems.

The fringe's vitality and broad geographical reach won it public subsidy, but in a period when Britain's economic troubles put future levels for the whole subsidised sector in doubt. Taking its cue from the USA, and presaging a trend that would dominate financial policy for the arts in the following decade, the government helped establish the Association for Business Sponsorship of the Arts (ABSA) in 1976 (renamed as Arts and Business in 1999). With the dominance of monetarism in the 1980s and a lowering of the value of public subsidy, theatres had to negotiate an increasingly intricate network of different funding sources. In this heterogeneous environment, new forms of ownership and management, such as non-profit boards and profit-sharing collectives, flourished and the definition of what constituted theatre simultaneously expanded and blurred, embracing many kinds of performance from dance to live art.

In the 1980s the publicly subsidised sector – the civic reps, the national companies, the fringe – helped to regenerate the commercial theatre by supplying it with productions and personnel, and the remarkable popularity of the exportable modern mega-musical (powered by computer-aided technology) reinforced this resurgence. As sponsorship and marketing became the twin pillars supporting theatrical 'success', the differences between the subsidised and commercial sectors were eroded and all but vanished in the 1990s. Yet the very ease of starting a small theatre group and the relatively small sums of money involved (compared to, say, the recorded arts in this period) made theatre especially adaptable and responsive to the enormous socio-economic changes occurring as the millennium approached.

Figure 16.1 Theatre as heavy industry: Strand Electric lighting controls at Bristol Princes'
Theatre, *circa* 1940. Chief electrician Harry Wood at the helm.

New and changing roles

The job of acting after World War Two was determined by the changing
demands of 'the drama'. The skills an actor was asked to deploy did not
alter a great deal until the mid-1950s when the new drama – Brecht, Beckett,
Littlewood, American and British realism – required new performing and production styles. The actor was given more interesting things to say, in more
voices (including the actor's own accent instead of standard Received Pronun-
ciation) and with more things to do (moving props and scenery, for instance).
The expansion of art theatre in the 1960s brought a new concentration on the
exploitation of the actor's 'self' as the source and instrument of communication. This expansion also broadened the range of the repertoire, which might
run from Euripides, Shakespeare and Wycherley to Coward, Pinter and Bond,
thereby demanding further extension of the actor's technique. The arrival

of the fringe in the 1970s heralded the acquisition of techniques drawn from different disciplines (such as the circus), a wider interest in 'physical' theatre (associated with the work of directors and teachers such as Jerzy Grotowski and Jacques Lecoq) and a temporary preference for the term 'performer' instead of 'actor' to signal an embrace of this new heterodoxy. The diversification continued to the end of the century and brought with it not only input from other art forms, such as dance and fine art, but also borrowings from non-western traditions by inter-cultural theatres.

The actor's work also, for some, became politicised, initially in relatively isolated examples, such as Joan Littlewood's Theatre Workshop in the 1950s, but subsequently through the spread of the fringe on a much broader front, ranging from theatre in education through community theatre to feminist, gay and black theatre. Some actors, especially those inspired by the director Augusto Boal, sustained this commitment through the 1980s and 1990s, but generally this period of 'commodification' undermined the overt political potential of acting. The most significant shift overall for actors, however, was a decline of controlling power over the production, as the last actor-managers of the inter-war period gave way to the theatre-owning entrepreneurs of post-World War Two, who in turn were joined by the producer and the stage director in the 1950s and 1960s. Though there were a few remarkable exceptions to this pattern – say, Donald Wolfit, Laurence Olivier or Kenneth Branagh – they serve, in this context, mainly to prove the general rule.

The rise of the stage director and of 'directors' theatre' had been occurring across mainland Europe throughout the century as art theatre grew in importance and influence.[5] In Britain, with rare exceptions such as Tyrone Guthrie at the Old Vic, this phenomenon was confined to the small or experimental theatres before World War Two. For two centuries or so the term 'producer' had been loosely applied to leading actors, actor-managers, playwrights, stage-managers (and even prompters) who exercised a controlling function, but after the war increasingly it was ousted by the American term 'director'. A new distinction was made between management and financial responsibility for the whole production process and interpretative and co-ordinating responsibility for what appeared on the stage: to produce is to bring forth, to direct is both to guide and control. The career of Peter Brook from the late 1940s to the 1960s was emblematic of this new directorial power, as he blazed his way with dazzling skill through the commercial and the subsidised theatre, often

---

5 See David Bradby and David Williams, *Directors' Theatre* (London: Macmillan, 1988); Edward Braun, *The Director and the Stage* (London: Methuen, 1982).

composing the production's music, designing its sets and editing texts to suit his own views.

The growing power of the *stage* director was reinforced in the 1960s and 1970s by the rise of the *artistic* director, in charge not only of individual productions but also of the entire programme presented by a theatre. There was sufficient stability within the subsidised sector to allow a handful of directors to create a career path in this role, instead of the more usual freelance route. In some theatres the post was also combined with that of chief executive, conferring an even greater degree of control and duty. When the National Theatre opened in 1963, the appointment of Laurence Olivier as its first artistic director was a farewell gesture to the old order. All the subsequent directors at the NT, as well as all those at the RSC – the two most powerful theatrical organisations in Britain – were stage directors. Peter Hall was the great exemplar of this trend. As founder and head of the RSC from 1961 to 1968, then head of the NT from 1973 to 1988, he became, like the earlier actor-managers, a star in his own right, frequently pictured and feted in the news and leisure media (including advertising wallpaper, 'very Peter Hall'), the most influential British theatrical figure of his time.

This shift in the balance of roles between actors and directors was complex and rarely clear-cut. The playwright, for instance, also contested the actor's hegemony. The subsidised sector in the 1950s and 1960s followed the lead given by George Devine at the Royal Court Theatre and promoted a pre-eminent status for the writer (in principle if not always in practice). Subsidised theatres challenged the commercial sector's remuneration of writers through royalties by offering instead a range of financial guarantees through commissions. The Arts Council awarded its first playwright's bursary in 1952, to Leo Lehman (£500 for one year). In the wake of Osborne's *Look Back in Anger* (1956), which encouraged a new and socially broader group of writers to pen plays, playwriting joined directing as both a possible and an attractive full-time career, no longer the part-time escapade of actors, stage-managers, novelists, poets or professors. A panoply of further Arts Council mechanisms was subsequently introduced: guarantees against loss incurred by new work, grants for commissions, and grants for writers in residence at theatres.

The professionalisation of the playwright was reflected in the growth of play publishing. In the late 1940s the few new plays that were published followed in the train of a successful production, most usually in the form of the publisher Samuel French's 'acting edition'. Designed for amateur groups, they provided a text that reconstructed the original production, complete with moves, set design, props list and even laughs. Then in 1959 Penguin launched its New

Figure 16.2 Theatre and new technologies: John Leonard, Head of Sound, at a new lighting board – Bristol Old Vic, *circa* 1976.

English Dramatists series, each volume usually featuring three or four plays by different writers. It had grown to fourteen volumes by 1970, by which time the play publishing market had expanded with the increasing ranks of full-time playwrights, who could now make a living working in film and television as well as theatre.[6]

The professionalisation of directors and playwrights was not an isolated trend. Greater differentiation occurred in the whole range of production skills. The number and function, and sometimes the title, of jobs changed as individual members of the artistic team asserted the value of their contribution and sought more control over, and recognition of, their expertise. The demands of the new drama accelerated the process. For example, the designer became more important as the single set gave way to more complex requirements. Specialist lighting and sound designers replaced electricians and stage-managers as they exploited progress in technology to maximise their particular and increasingly specialised roles. Stage management, a predominantly male domain until shortly after World War Two, ceased to be the preserve of actors who had apprenticed as assistant stage-managers in rep. A team of three became the norm: a stage-manager (also company manager if business duties were involved), a deputy and an assistant, with a clear delineation of duties and career path. Prop-making, until the 1960s part of scenic construction, became a distinct area, and expert technicians in hairdressing, wig-making, prosthetics and cosmetic art took over the actors' traditional responsibility for their own

6 See also Dan Rebellato, *1956 and All That: The Making of Modern British Drama* (London: Routledge, 1999).

make-up. Artistic directors with proliferating responsibilities were able, thanks to subsidy, to increase the numbers of workers in support roles, such as casting directors, literary managers and voice teachers.

The most powerful backstage figure, however, became the specialist administrator. A few were employed in the early post-war period, such as Elizabeth Sweeting (Aldeburgh Festival, Oxford Playhouse) and Hazel Vincent Wallace (Leatherhead), but numbers expanded with the regional theatre-building programme of the late 1950s and 1960s. In large organisations such as the RSC and the NT they became highly influential.

The pressures of specialisation in the increasingly diversified and variegated process of making British theatre increased still further in the 1980s and 1990s. The tightening of state subsidy paradoxically produced a 'bureaucratisation' of theatre. More sophisticated and specialised skills were required to deal with the ever more complex funding arrangements of the bidding culture – dogged by form-filling, especially after the introduction of the National Lottery in 1995, as well as the demands of legislation on pay, contracts, trade unions, employment protection, health, safety and gender, race and disability equality. Ironically, the initial egalitarian 'anti-professionalism' of the fringe, which had tended to collapse roles and encourage multi-skilling, provided excellent training for the fluidity of the new jobs market. Additionally, market deregulation encouraged theatres to hire private service providers, such as consultants, accountants, booking agencies, transport firms and design, marketing and publicity companies. The demands of administration expanded almost exponentially, creating new hierarchies of power. A fresh breed of managerial entrepreneur – the executive producer – rivalled and sometimes supplanted the dominance of the artistic director: a well-suited bulwark of financial and managerial rectitude holding back the fabled profligacy of artistic, especially theatrically artistic, temperament.

Patterns of employment and training

Since the start of the century the oldest of theatrical jobs – acting – had been known in Britain as 'the Profession'. By World War Two, despite residual puritan suspicion, it had become a respectable, middle-class form of employment, a status that was then enhanced during wartime when actors 'did their duty' at home and abroad. Throughout the post-war period the profession attracted legions of new recruits and yet was racked by high levels of unemployment or, rather, underemployment – hence the pragmatic view of mortgage lenders and insurance companies that acting was a high-risk occupation. In the early 1950s, 30–40 per cent of actors were underemployed, working on average thirty-five weeks in the year. By the end of the century, following considerable expansion, 80–90 per cent were underemployed as the average year's work had dropped to twelve and a half weeks. Predictably, there was also a high drop-out rate: about 20 per cent left the profession in the immediate post-war years, although new entrants usually outnumbered the leavers. The figure fell to 10 per cent by the millennium but against a background of higher joblessness.

Earnings generally were consistently below the national average, but there was a high variation in income earned and numbers employed between the top and bottom of the pay scale rarely found in other professions. In the early 1950s the West End minimum wage for a conventional play was £8 a week and in the regions £4.10s. Above that was a scale that grew significantly steeper towards the top: a well-known actor of the second rank, which accounted for no more than 10–15 per cent of the 'talent pool', might earn up to £50 a week in the West End, while a star actor in the highest handful could earn 10 per cent of gross box office income, say about £75–£100 a week. By the 1970s, when the minimum pay was £25, weekly earnings for the élite could be £4,000–£10,000 while the next tier down brought in £1,500–£4,000.[7]

Although television began to attract actors in the mid 1950s, the rise of art theatre in the subsidised sector enhanced the status and relevance of British acting. Reflecting this new confidence, in 1961 the RSC introduced the first long-term contracts for actors (three years), aiming to balance coherence and continuity with flexibility. At the end of the 1960s the RSC contract was reduced to two years while NT contracts differed little from others in the subsidised sector. The national companies offered only a small, albeit significant, number of new jobs overall and at a lower rate of pay than for equivalent work in the commercial sector. The fringe provided more jobs but at even poorer rates.

In the financial recessions of the 1980s many of the larger regional theatres looked for salvation in a new star system based on popularity in television and film, and employed fewer actors in a narrowing range of parts. Market

---

7 Sources for statistics include: British Actors' Equity Association, annual reports; Michael Sanderson, *From Irving to Olivier: A Social History of the Acting Profession in England, 1880–1983* (London: Athlone Press, 1985); Colin Chambers, unpublished interviews with Peter Finch, Assistant General Secretary of Equity (1999). Statistical comparisons between different eras for theatre in this period should be treated circumspectly, as employment patterns in the industry, differences in data collecting and other factors make them unreliable.

forces eventually caused even the more successful fringe groups to employ celebrities, while government 'welfare to work' policies undermined others by making it harder for unemployed actors to undertake unpaid or voluntary work. The availability of work in theatre in general also continued to fall towards the end of the century, a process intensified on the production side by increased mechanical handling and computer-operated control. By the millennium, cross-media work had become the norm: one-quarter of Equity members worked in four or more media and more than a third ranked television as their main area of employment.[8]

Training is central to the definition of a profession: to become a professional requires an appropriate qualification. This relationship, despite a massive expansion of training and educational opportunities, remained contentious in British theatre throughout the second half of the twentieth century thanks to antagonism between the main providers: the drama schools, traditionally considered part of the industry, and the universities, which were not. By the end of the century, however, it was rare for anyone to enter any aspect of the theatrical profession without a certified period of education or training and an acknowledged qualification.

In acting, belief in the supremacy of innate talent ('actors are born, not made') remained strong and the traditional emphasis on informal, job-based training survived even in the era of the drama school. In the immediate post-war period, the reps were the main arena for the experiential, practical learning of theatre crafts, continuing the semi-apprentice arrangements of the old actor-manager system. The resident repertory companies – especially the major ones such as Birmingham, Bristol, Glasgow or Liverpool, which ran repertoires in three or four weekly blocks – offered a relatively stable professional environment. This was the training ground for leading actors such as Albert Finney, Joan Plowright, Ian Richardson and Paul Scofield. Commercial weekly reps in the regions were less well ordered. Absentee managers such as Harry Hanson and Frank Fortescue, who offered poor conditions of work and pay, often ran these from London. Actors could learn a great deal in such reps if they had the stomach for twice-nightly performances, but standards were rudimentary, contracts rare and turnover high due to a proliferation of instant dismissals. Alec McCowen fondly recalls his first job, in this type of set-up in Macclesfield, as a 'splendid introduction to the theatre'. The director

> taught me everything from tying a cleat to mascaring [sic] my eyelashes. I
> collected furniture and props from shops and friends of the theatre . . . There

8 Equity, 'Report on a survey of members' (London: Equity, 1999), p. 5.

were no dressing-rooms – only a curtained partition under the stage to separate the men from the women . . . I changed the scenery, worked the switchboard, pulled the curtain up and down, and in the lunch hour sometimes sold tickets in the box-office. On Sundays, I cleaned up the previous week's play, swept the stage and helped to paint the flats for the coming attraction.[9]

John Osborne, though, remembers this system with scorn as 'the last funk-hole for any actor'.[10]

This approach to 'on the job' training was sustained from the late 1950s to the 1970s by the subsidised reps and national companies, which employed specialists in voice, movement and other aspects of the actor's craft. In the 1970s and 1980s the fringe inherited the system, though the great majority of companies did not enjoy the same close relationship to their host community as the reps, nor offer the same scale of opportunity. Fringe company workers had mostly, though not exclusively, attended university or college, benefiting from the 1944 Education Act, especially through drama training and in the provision of theatre for children and young people. This provision grew in importance following the pioneering projects of Caryl Jenner's Unicorn Theatre for children (founded in 1947), Brian Way and Margaret Faulkes's Theatre Centre (1949), which toured to schools, and Michael Croft's National Youth Theatre (1956). Following the founding of the first theatre-in-education (TIE) company in 1965 at Coventry's Belgrade Theatre, an imaginative TIE movement flourished in the late 1960s and 1970s; an Arts Council report on 'Theatre for Young People' in 1966 led to the allocation of new funds, and there was a thriving national youth theatre sector before the cuts of the 1980s undermined much of its promise.

As for formal training, for nearly two decades after World War Two the drama schools predominated and they mostly produced practitioners in accord with a consensual definition of the profession. There were exceptions, such as the Old Vic School, which was short-lived (1947–51) though highly influential. The older schools – the London Academy of Music and Dramatic Art (1861), the Royal Academy of Dramatic Art (1904) and the Central School of Speech Training and Dramatic Art (1906) – were joined by longer-lasting post-war arrivals such as the Mountview Theatre School (1945), the Bristol Old Vic Theatre School (1946), the Royal Scottish Academy of Music and Drama (1950), Rose Bruford College (1950), the East 15 Acting School (1961), the Drama Centre (1963) and the Guildford School (1964). Local education authorities, which in

9 Alec McCowen, *Young Gemini* (London: Elm Tree Books, 1979), pp. 68–9.
10 John Osborne, *A Better Class of Person: An Autobiography 1929–1956* (London: Faber & Faber, 1982), p. 246.

the 1950s had created a national network of drama advisers that lasted into the early 1980s, raised their discretionary grants in the 1960s to meet a new demand for vocational study at drama schools; the resulting growth led to the founding in 1969 of the Conference of Drama Schools (CDS). Of the forty or so drama schools in the 1970s, fourteen were included in the CDS.

In 1972 concern about links between a lack of coherence in training provision and high underemployment in the profession led the CDS, with support from the industry (including Equity and the Council for Regional Theatres), to ask the Calouste Gulbenkian Foundation to conduct a survey of Britain's drama training. Its report, 'Going on the Stage', resulted in the founding in 1975 of the National Council for Drama Training (NCDT), charged with the accreditation of training courses. The drama schools, however, generally proved unable to update their training to meet developments in the industry. Critics of the NCDT system in the drama schools, and in the universities, viewed its criteria as an obstacle to the modernisation of training. The NCDT framework was also seen as a barrier to widening access to students from diverse backgrounds, a problem exacerbated by the lack of mandatory grants for drama school applicants. Several schools set up to circumvent the high fees charged for full-time courses, such as the Poor School (1986), had to operate outside the NCDT, so that students financing themselves through daytime work could train in the evenings and at weekends. By 2000, the number of CDS drama schools had risen to just twenty-one, out of more than sixty schools.[11]

Although universities had provided a tributary into the professional theatre for talented students throughout the century, it was not until the 1960s that they began to take theatre as a discipline seriously. As higher and further education expanded, especially in the 1960s and 1970s, increasing numbers of university graduates entered the profession, and this provided an important stimulus for both the new drama and the emergence of the fringe. Student theatre was widespread from the 1950s: in the colleges, at the National Student Drama Festival (established in 1955 as an annual event by Clive Wolfe, when the *Sunday Times* sponsored it), at the Edinburgh Fringe and at festivals abroad. Oxbridge continued to provide unsurpassed facilities and opportunities for its theatre-minded undergraduates, but it also refused to recognise theatre as worthy of academic study, regarding drama still as a branch of literature. Bristol University was the first to establish a drama department – in 1947 – and in 1960 it created the first professorship in drama. Other universities

---

11 Figures provided by the Conference of Drama Schools.

followed suit, with drama departments opening at Manchester (1961), Hull (1963), Birmingham (1964), Bangor (1965), Glasgow (1966) and Exeter (1968). These institutions, and subsequently the polytechnics and colleges of higher education, offered courses on many aspects of theatre, from arts administration and stage management to dramaturgy and voice teaching, as well as more adventurous academic scrutiny of performance practices than in most drama schools.

In parallel, some drama schools offered academically validated courses and became part of the higher education network. This began in 1976 when Rose Bruford College recruited students to the first vocational acting degree. By 2001, boosted by government initiatives to promote vocational education and the introduction the year before of student scholarships to replace the discretionary grant system, fifteen of the twenty-one CDS schools were offering acting degrees.

Nevertheless, mutual suspicion between university drama departments and drama schools remained. Criticism of the intellectual content of drama school courses, often seen as narrowly functional and driven by an outdated view of the industry, was matched by criticism of university provision as deficient in technical training. At the turn of the millennium, government demands for greater contact between institutions from different traditions aimed to encourage the two sides to contemplate greater co-operation in the twenty-first century.[12]

Professional organisations

British theatre workers have a long history of creating organisations to protect their interests. Towards the end of the nineteenth century, when British theatre was already a national industry, all the major 'players' – owners, managers, workers – had organised into associations or unions. The basic pattern for the century was set, even though the organisations subsequently followed a path of amalgamation and international alliance, developing interests in discrete areas of professional activity.[13]

Following World War Two the main unions were the Musicians' Union (MU), the National Association of Theatrical and Kine Employees (NATKE)

12 See Ben Francombe, 'Falling off a wall – degrees of change in British actor training', *Studies in Theatre and Performance* 21, 3 (2001).
13 Information in this section is provided by the organisations mentioned; see also Joseph Macleod, *The Actor's Right to Act* (London: Lawrence & Wishart, 1981) and Sanderson, *From Irving to Olivier*.

and British Actors' Equity Association. The MU, founded in 1893, became the principal organisation of musicians in Britain, with a significant representation beyond the theatre. NATKE's roots stretched back to the National Association of Theatre Employees of 1890; since then it has represented mainly craft, technical and general workers. In 1991 it became the Broadcasting Entertainment Cinematograph and Theatre Union (BECTU), reflecting theatre's changing relationship to the electronic media.

Equity was founded in 1930 from two actors' associations; the Variety Artistes' Federation (1906) amalgamated with it in 1967. Equity's membership rose from about 4,000 at the start of World War Two to 20,000 in the early 1970s and to nearly 36,000 by the end of the century. Since the 1930s Equity had established 'closed-shop' agreements with managers' organisations, which enforced standard contracts. In order to protect state welfare benefits for actors, in 1949 the union won the right for them to be taxed as if self-employed while paying National Insurance as if an employee. By the mid-fifties virtually every paid performer was unionised and had a minimum salary as a starting point for their agents to negotiate individual deals. Even after the 'closed shop' arrangements were ended in the 1980s, Equity maintained its position as the industry's organisation for actors, focussing on its core activities of industrial negotiation and services for members. These ranged from distributing royalties earned from foreign broadcasts or reruns to welfare provision, such as caring for the elderly and the sick, and offering pension plans and insurance cover for health and safety at work.[14] Although the union had a wide-ranging membership, including dancers, stage-managers, directors and designers as well as actors, it remained a specialist body, resisting absorption into bigger general unions.

Equity's role as a union, however, was the subject of fierce internal debate. It always had a powerful constituency that saw it as a body of non-political practitioners combining simply to defend their craft and status. Also there had always been proponents of a contrary view, that Equity was a union of workers like any other, trade unionists who necessarily had to be political to win their just demands or to show solidarity. The union went through its own 'red scare' in the Cold War atmosphere of 1949 when three Equity organisers resigned in fear of Communist influence in the union. An *ad hoc* group, including Richard Attenborough, was formed to return Equity to 'non-political' status. The elections to the union's Council that year saw the removal of

14 Interview with Peter Finch.

left-wingers, including Peggy Ashcroft and two former union presidents, Beatrix Lehmann and Sir Lewis Casson.[15] The union stabilised in the following years and even progressed to take 'political' decisions, such as the instruction in 1956 that members should not work where a 'colour bar' – theatrical apartheid – operated. In the 1970s arguments for widening the scope of the union from the politicised fringe generation coalesced with calls for its radical democratisation. A process of reform based on increasing accountability led, in 1978, to the sanctity of the referendum being enshrined in the rule book and, in 1995, to the replacement of the Annual General Meeting by an Annual Representative Conference, to which all participants had to be elected.

On the other side of the employment fence, interest groups created organisations that often had overlapping membership and titles which changed as rapidly as the industry. During World War Two regional organisation was improved under the umbrella of the managers' Conference (later Council) of Repertory (later Regional) Theatres (CORT), which was formed in 1944. The growth of the fringe in the early seventies provided origins for several new organisations. The Association of Lunch Time Theatres, founded in 1972, included some forty groups aiming 'to promote lunchtime theatre, to present principally new and neglected plays and playwrights, to provide alternative venues for actors, directors and designers, and to encourage audiences by making theatre more accessible'.[16] It was also the first organisation to campaign for more subsidies for the fringe as a sector, closely followed, in 1973, by the London Association of Community Theatre Groups, which in 1974 became the Association of Community Theatres (TACT), a campaigning umbrella group that quickly spawned the less openly political and broader-based Independent Theatre Council (ITC), representing mostly small touring groups. TACT campaigned for a minimum wage, for recognition of the fringe by Equity, for the Arts Council to fund community theatre companies sufficiently for them to pay the Equity minimum, and for the Regional Arts Associations to negotiate with the Arts Council on their behalf for revenue grants. TACT achieved its aims by the end of the 1970s, by which time it had affiliated to its progeny, the ITC. Lobbying by the fringe also reshaped the structure of subsidy provision, with greater emphasis being placed on the role of local arts officers. Fringe advocacy also won a twenty-fold increase in Arts Council funding and, in 1979,

---

15 Sanderson, *From Irving to Olivier*, p. 309.
16 Quoted in Catherine Itzin, *Stages in the Revolution: Political Theatre in Britain Since 1968* (London: Eyre Methuen, 1980), p. 136.

a grant towards the ITC's own administration costs. By 2000 the ITC had 450 members.[17]

Equity initially had problems with fringe theatre because of the potential impact on union membership: qualification for membership would be difficult to regulate and verify, and working conditions would be hard to monitor. After extensive internal and external pressure, however, Equity established a Fringe Committee and in 1978 began block unionisation of the fringe. The union provided a 10 per cent per annum quota for new members, changing its qualifying rules to accommodate fringe conditions, and agreed a fringe contract.

The fringe also gave rise to an alternative playwrights' organisation, the approximately thirty-strong Theatre Writers' Group (TWG), formed at the ITC annual conference in 1975. This was the year the Arts Council announced severe cuts, including a freeze on writers' bursaries, on guarantees against royalties for new plays and on production grants for new plays. A failure to challenge these proposed cuts by the literary-based Society of Authors (founded 1884) and the more recently established Writers' Guild of Great Britain (1958 – with interests especially in relation to film and television), stimulated the TWG to grow within a year into the 150-strong Theatre Writers' Union (TWU).[18] The TWU was run by its members in a highly democratic way: general meetings were held every three months and elected a mandated committee, which was responsible to and could be dismissed by the next general meeting. No committee member could serve for more than six months.

The TWU was dedicated to bridging the gap between a system that placed writers' work at the heart of theatre and the realities they faced in terms of power in the workplace, conditions of work (e.g., access to rehearsals) and financial reward. Under the banner of 'A Living Wage for Theatre Writers!' the TWU insisted that writing be acknowledged as work and be properly remunerated. The TWU's central campaign was to establish a minimum standard contract. The union signed interim agreements with a number of fringe groups straight away, which resulted in ratification in 1979 of a basic contract for all companies affiliated to the ITC. The TWU's parallel attempts to negotiate with the major subsidised theatres, led by the National Theatre, hit huge obstacles, however. Neither the NT (bound by the conditions of its membership of the commercially dominated Society of West End Theatre) nor the

---

17 Figures provided by the Independent Theatre Council.
18 See Itzin, *Stages in the Revolution*, pp. 306–15.

Writers' Guild recognised the TWU as a negotiating body. The only way the TWU could get a seat at the table was to use the power it possessed – namely a clutch of playwrights whose work the NT wanted to present. They included Howard Brenton, Edward Bond, Trevor Griffiths, Christopher Hampton and Robert Holman. The TWU voted in 1977 to boycott the NT and was backed by the writers' section of the cine technicians' union ACTT. Four months later, the TWU was accepted in talks alongside the Writers' Guild and the boycott was lifted. Eventually, in 1979, a minimum standard contract was agreed. It included the right to attend rehearsals and to be paid subsistence for so doing, involvement in major artistic decisions concerning casting, choice of director and publicity, and access to higher royalty and subsidiary rights, which could be particularly lucrative. In 1997 the TWU merged with the Writers' Guild, which, largely thanks to TWU activity, had changed its approach to stage writers.

Conclusion

Many positive changes occurred within the professions of theatre in the half-century after World War Two, especially following the campaigns of the fringe in the 1970s and 1980s on an array of issues, from gender and sexuality to ethnicity and disability. By the end of the century, though, much remained to be achieved on all these fronts. Women were breaking the 'glass ceiling' of management in many employment sectors, but none was running a national theatre company and theatres still had not taken on board issues such as child care. With a few notable exceptions, such as Tara Arts co-productions with the National Theatre, multi-cultural society was barely represented in the mostly white as well as male-led theatre.

In common with other branches of culture, the theatre had become more professionalised as it became more specialised, driven by changes in its social and economic status and the possibilities opened up by technological advance. It is an art, but also in the fifty years following World War Two it became a different kind of industry, a vital element of Britain's tourism, export trade and international reputation. The profession, however, had lost a sense of coherence as it fragmented, first with the displacement of the heroic leading actor and subsequently with the spread of a diversified fringe; symptomatically, both national companies became trapped in production-line culture and ceased to be aesthetic pacesetters. The multiplicity of styles, genres and venues embraced by theatre reflected the loss of social homogeneity in a post-imperial, post-industrial Britain. Theatre no longer held the centre of the cultural stage,

sentimental – articulated a century-long experience of coping with capitalism. As with Brechtian and Piscatorian theatre, irony in these genres was a way of hitting back at the dominant class and its ideology. But Theatre Workshop took a robust attitude to bourgeois hypocrisy and working-class sentiment alike; in *Oh What a Lovely War* this enabled a classic critical stance to be taken towards the 'Great War' – World War One.

This war cast a long shadow on the twentieth century. It is often seen as a turning point in western history, its horrors exacerbated and deepened by World War Two's principal traumas – the Holocaust and Hiroshima. Paul Fussell calls the Great War 'a hideous embarrassment to the prevailing Meliorist myth which had dominated the public consciousness for a century. It reversed the Idea of Progress'.[4] Irony became the accepted means of articulating World War One's modernity; Fussell calls it 'a terrible irony',[5] capable simultaneously of acknowledging the horror of mechanised, industrialised war, and of marking art's inadequacy in the face of such horror.

By the end of the twentieth century, *Oh What a Lovely War*'s interpretation of World War One as a catastrophic blunder by the 'old' European ruling classes had become an orthodoxy, but it was new in the 1960s. The show's revaluation allowed the Common Soldier's voice back into history. All this was integral to the historical books of the 1960s that formed the backbone of research for the play. It enacts the 'progress' from optimistic innocence (Act 1) to pessimistic experience (Act 2) that became the accepted interpretation of the war. As they looked back in horror from a Cold War present, many saw the promise of a Doomsday future in the build-up of nuclear weapons on both sides of the Iron Curtain. CND (Campaign for Nuclear Disarmament) was founded in 1958. The original theatre programme for *Oh What a Lovely War* contained anti-nuclear facts and figures as an integral part of its overall anti-war argument. Like CND, Theatre Workshop's production was profoundly oppositional, part of a political voice heard more vehemently as the 1960s progressed. Somewhat unreliable as a source of information about World War One, it is an excellent source for the 'revolutionary sixties'. Like Walter Benjamin's famous 'Angel of History', it was being blown backwards into the future.[6]

---

4 Paul Fussell, *The Great War and Modern Memory* (Oxford University Press, 1975), p. 8. 'Meliorist' indicates a worldview that sees everything consistently getting better over time.
5 *Ibid.*, p. 3.
6 See Derek Paget, 'Remembrance play: *Oh What a Lovely War* and history', in *Acts of War: The Representation of Military Conflict on the British Stage and Television Since 1945*, ed. Tony Howard and John Stokes (Aldershot: Scolar, 1996), pp. 82–97; Walter Benjamin, 'Theses on the philosophy of history', in *Illuminations* (London: Fontana, 1992) p. 249.

Figure 17.1 'We don't want to lose you . . .' Slide 12: *Oh What a Lovely War*, Theatre Workshop, 1963.

A new political theatre

Although *Oh What a Lovely War* was Joan Littlewood's last major contribution to British theatre, it can be seen as a culmination of the Theatre Workshop project. It was a Trojan horse through which anti-naturalistic, political theatre gained a significant foothold in Britain. As radical politics found its voice (in what became known as 'fringe' or 'alternative' theatre), *Oh What a Lovely War* was often cited as an influence. This was true both for campaigning alternative theatre and for the longer tradition of repertory theatre, itself gaining fresh impetus following the opening of the Belgrade Theatre, Coventry, in 1958. Peter Cheeseman – whose local documentaries at the Victoria Theatre, Stoke-on-Trent, strongly influenced repertory practice – acknowledged in 1970 his debt to 'the didactic Left Wing theatre brilliantly extended by Joan Littlewood out of the German and American documentary traditions'.[7] In 1981, 7:84's John McGrath wrote: 'A new generation of young actors played in it, sang the songs, and heard how Joan's actors had worked on it. The fame of Theatre Workshop spread, and with it a whole set of attitudes to making theatre'.[8]

Oh What a Lovely War's major achievement was to question the long-held national myth that World War One had been won. The production asked: by whom was it won, and on whose behalf? Its cutting edge derived from a combination of inventive theatricality and judiciously selected documentary material. Whilst the play has no hero, it presents an *implied* hero who is a constant presence-in-absence. This shadow figure, simultaneously individual and abstract, is the Unknown Soldier whose eternal flame burns in so many European capital cities. To give stage presence to this complex paradox – memory of the unknown – Theatre Workshop synthesised theatrical methodologies and skills virtually absent from contemporary British mainstream theatre. Charles Marowitz summed up its sources in a 1963 review:

> The technique which produced this result grew out of the Living Newspaper productions of the 30s, the English Music Hall in its pre-War heyday, the satirical revues of the early Unity Theatre, the Pierrot Tradition of the English seaside resorts, the socialistic convictions of the Manchester school (the city where Littlewood began), and the tardy influences of Piscator and Brecht. It is more so than anything now at the Old Vic or Stratford, a production which exemplifies an English tradition; the tradition that grew up alongside the more elegant one that today sustains Shaftesbury Avenue and the Shakespeare Establishment.[9]

Whilst this encapsulates much of the play's theatrical provenance, important structuring devices in the show derived from new, technological media.

Founder members Ewan MacColl and Joan Littlewood had experience of documentary 'Features' radio in the 1930s, with MacColl using traditional and

---

7 Peter Cheeseman, 'Introduction', *The Knotty* (London: Methuen, 1970), p. xi.
8 John McGrath, *A Good Night Out – Popular Theatre: Audience, Class and Form* (London: Eyre Methuen, 1981), pp. 48–9.
9 Charles Marowitz, *Confessions of a Counterfeit Critic: A London Theatre Notebook 1958–71* (London: Eyre Methuen, 1973), p. 67.

folk-revival song for narrative and critique. He eschewed the use of popular song, believing its commercial provenance tainted it irrevocably.[10] But he left the company in 1953 when it moved to Stratford East, and Charles Chilton provided a different kind of musical underpinning for *Oh What a Lovely War*. As a BBC radio producer/deviser since 1945, Chilton had gained a reputation for well-researched, popular documentary radio. His ultimate aim was not dissimilar to MacColl's: to give underheard voices a say in history. His 1962 *The Long, Long Trail* used facts and statistics, with songs as ironic critique, to tell the story of the war on the Western Front. This fired the long-held desire of Theatre Workshop's producer, Gerry Raffles, to make a show about World War One. In tone and structure, radio documentary and theatre piece bear a remarkable resemblance.

Theatre Workshop's founding manifesto of 1945 had proclaimed an additional aspiration: their intention 'to create a flexible theatre-art, as swift moving as the cinema'.[11] Littlewood and MacColl admired cinema's ability to 'cut' rapidly, enabling narrative to be released from the stolidity of stage naturalism. In its technical sophistication, *Oh What a Lovely War* was of its time; in the wake of World War Two, society was becoming technologised as never before. Televisions, for example, were transformed from luxury to essential domestic items.[12] Mass populations were becoming accustomed to different experiences of time and space through a technological revolution.

A new multi-media theatre

The first audiences for *Oh What a Lovely War* watched a production cut like a movie and shaped like a light entertainment, which asked them to pay attention to more than its human agents, the performers. If the performers offered 'songs for you, a few battles and some jokes',[13] there were also facts, statistics and documentary photographs presented as part of a multi-media environment. Above the stage, a 'Newspanel' and a translucent projection

10 See Ewan MacColl, *Journeyman* (London: Sidgwick & Jackson, 1990).
11 Goorney, *Theatre Workshop Story*, p. 42.
12 See Tim O'Sullivan, 'Television memories and cultures of viewing, 1950–65', in *Popular TV in Britain: Studies in Cultural History*, ed. John Corner (London: British Film Institute, 1991), pp. 159–81.
13 Theatre Workshop, *Oh What a Lovely War* (London: Methuen, 1967), p. 12 and (London: Methuen, 2000) p. 2. The play was reprinted, unaltered, frequently between 1965 and 2000, when a new edition was published in the Methuen Modern Plays series. The title page announced 'Revised and restored to the original version by Joan Littlewood'. Subsequent references are to both editions; page numbers refer to discrete scenes rather than to specific quotations.

screen reinforced the information dramatised by the performers in a variety of theatrical styles, including dance-drama, agit-prop, slapstick comedy, direct-address monologue, quasi-naturalism and song-and-dance. *Oh What a Lovely War* offered a thesis about World War One while delighting audiences with its theatrical inventiveness.

The Newspanel was a 'ticker-tape' machine, like those used on buildings in big cities such as London and New York to relay news. It displayed moving messages picked out in light bulbs. Words tracked steadily from audience-right to-left, enabling spectators to read statistics, location, time and sometimes even mood from this technological 'actor'. For example, the first message articulated a commonly held view of a pre-war world of happy innocence:

> SUMMER 1914. SCORCHING BANK HOLIDAY FORECAST . . . GUNBOAT SMITH FOULS CARPENTIER IN THE SIXTH ROUND . . . OPERA BLOSSOMS UNDER THOMAS BEECHAM.[14]

Whilst this flashed across the Newspanel, several other effects were produced on the stage below in a theatrical interaction of undoubted complexity and depth.

First, sound: a little band in the pit was playing a medley of fifty-year-old popular tunes (the 'Overture'). Reinforcing the Newspanel's story of a carefree Edwardian world, it also placed the audience in a quasi-variety 'real-time' setting. Second, vision: the stage directions record: '*The stage is set for a pierrot show of fifty years ago with red, white, and blue fairy lights, twin balconies left and right and coloured circus "tubs"*'. A false proscenium, glittering with lights, led the eye around the stage, beyond two little balconies and towards the Newspanel itself. Third, action: the performers entered, cued by the Newspanel leaping into life. They were dressed as pierrots, charming clownlike seaside entertainers of a previous age.[15] Their silky white blouses were picked out with fluffy black pom-pom buttons, and some wore silly conical hats on their heads. On the opening night they launched into a spirited rendition of the 1911 popular song 'Alexander's Ragtime Band' (later changed to the 1912 'Row, Row, Row' – the song printed in the Methuen text). One pierrot, wearing that index of mock-authority, a mortarboard, began to speak. Self-evidently the 'Master of Ceremonies', he welcomed the audience and chivvied late-comers:

---

14 *Oh What a Lovely War*, p. 9/p. 1.
15 See Bill Pertwee, *Beside the Seaside* (London: Collins & Brown, 1999).

Figure 17.2 'And when they ask us, how dangerous it was . . .' Slide 51: *Oh What a Lovely War*, Theatre Workshop, 1963.

Evening ladies and gentlemen, welcome to our little show: 'The Merry Roost-
ers'. [pause for late-comer] Just in time, madam, all you've missed is a dance,
you're lucky. Alright, then. Welcome to our little show, we've got some songs,
a few jokes for you – a couple of dances. Here we go! [to the wings] Are you
ready? [general shout of 'No!']. Time for a couple of jokes, then . . . [a joke
follows, and more ad-libs with cast] . . . Milords, ladies and gentlemen, we
present: The Ever-Popular War Game! [circus-style music].[16]

This opening, which lasted about four minutes in performance, is significant
in that it so totally worked against the naturalistic conventions of early 1960s
mainstream British theatre, and therefore the expectations of its audiences.
The customary opening ritual of the curtain rising to reveal a recognisable
setting appropriate for naturalistic characters was absent. More importantly,
the direct and unambiguous *address* of performer to audience immediately
constituted the audience as *sharer in*, rather than *observer of*, performance. An
open experience was proposed, with the various media exposed to view – not
concealed by a 'fourth wall'.

Oh What a Lovely War was also thoroughly theatrically inter-textual: for
example, the pierrot show and its sister traditions had driven light entertainment in the new medium of radio since the 1920s, with variety in the 1950s
the latest beneficiary. Hence, *not* knowing about this cultural history would
not disable audience members, for the semiotics of lightness and triviality,
humour and vulgarity were plain enough. The show also invited use of the
audiences' existing knowledge of World War One, however limited, through
its title, in posters, flyers and other publicity, and there was extra information
in the programme. Thus the power of this opening lay in 'not naming', in
concealing the seriousness behind the entertainer's bright smile of welcome.
This 'enacted', metonymically, the myopic Edwardian mood and its known
consequences even before any thesis was presented. It also set up an enigma:
why such triviality when *warfare* was the declared subject?

The production circuit

Littlewood, Raffles, Chilton and John Bury were the primary workers who
provided the raw materials for this production; they built the structure,
selected methods and fashioned a playing space. Raffles and Chilton principally

---

16 From a transcription of an audio recording made on Friday 26 April 1963 at a performance
    at Stratford East; the recording provides the source for timings given in this chapter.
    See also Derek Paget, '*Oh What a Lovely War*: the texts and their context', *New Theatre
    Quarterly* 6, 23 (Aug. 1990), 244–60.

provided historical sources; Bury, the designer, created an environment in which the theatrical elements (human and technological) could 'speak' to each other; Littlewood was editor and animator. But the players and technicians were in charge at the moment of performance; their collective imagination, talent and tact completed the production side of the communication circuit. Crucially, the circuit's completion depended upon the active collusion of audiences.

To an extent, both audience and actors were at the mercy of a technology inspired by Piscator as much as by Brecht.[17] Technology provided a vivid counterpoint between documentary and drama, and its rhythms were as important as those of the actors. Take, for example, the 'Plans' scene,[18] which lasted three minutes in performance. It incorporated the first set of over fifty slides, comprising both graphic and actuality material:

(1) a map depicting the German 'Schlieffen Plan' of 1914
(2) a map for the French 'Plan 17' of 1914
(3) an actuality photograph: 'Russian infantry marching with rifles'
(4) another photograph: 'A British battleship berthed at a pier'

Slide 5 was a blank, jokily illustrating the British Army's *lack* of any realistic plan at the outbreak of war. This scene was 'book-ended' by two Newspanel messages. The first recorded British mobilisation in the months before war was declared: 'Churchill', it announced, 'orders the Fleet to Scapa Flow'. The second said simply 'SARAJEVO', resituating the on-stage *action* through its single word and establishing the *mood* through its invocation of the Balkan city where Archduke Franz Ferdinand was assassinated – the incident popularly supposed to have 'begun' World War One in 1914.

The 'Plans' scene thus illustrated and explained in quite a detailed way the strategies and attitudes of military castes in the combatant nations. At the same time, a lively interaction between performer and technology entertained the audience. The technological *coup de théâtre* of the slides should not be underestimated. According to technician Ivor Dykes, the screen 'was set quite close to the actors midstage and masked the running sign [Newspanel] when flown in . . . It was another part of the rhythmic control, we did a hell of a lot of work on flying that screen – it had to be fast or slow, above all silent!'[19] The subsequent cueing of slides to speech / song also had to be as meticulously timed as any dialogue.

17 See Brecht's acknowledgement of Piscator in John Willett, *Brecht on Theatre: The Development of an Aesthetic* (London: Methuen, 1964), pp. 103–35.
18 *Oh What a Lovely War*, pp. 15–17/pp. 3–6.
19 Letter to the author, 25 April 1999.

Rhythm and *flow* were vital elements in the company's stagecraft, achieved through acute sensitivity to pace. In theatrical performance, pace generates energy where speed produces anxiety; Littlewood's production enabled factual material (often supposed to be inherently dull) to be delivered without alienating the audience. The challenge in documentary theatre has always been to convey facts and information accurately, intelligibly and entertainingly; from the outset, the audience was effectively being given an exercise in Brechtian 'complex seeing'.[20] It was already being asked to read *simultaneously* between several theatrical elements.

The rapid transformations of time, place and character possible in Epic theatre are usually dependent upon technology. Newspanel, slides, lighting and recorded sound effects in *Oh What a Lovely War* facilitated rhythmic movement and control between scenes often sharply different in style. Newspanel and slides were 'in dialogue' with human performers. One particularly poignant example occurred at the end of Act 1.[21] The pierrot-soldiers who had just enacted the Christmas truce of 1914 in naturalistic style then turned 'in silence' to face a Newspanel which 'spoke' non-naturalistically, presenting another 1914 reality:

ALL QUIET ON THE WESTERN FRONT . . . ALLIES LOSE 850,000 MEN
IN 1914 . . . HALF BRITISH EXPEDITIONARY FORCE WIPED OUT.

This switch of mood was managed and articulated by the 'technological actor'. Expansion and diminution of stage space and time, relative to the needs of particular scenes, was made possible by rhythmic co-ordination between the human and the technological. Littlewood conceived this, but in the theatre it depended upon actor, musician and technician working in harmony in real time, and on the audience feeding responses into the rhythm of performance. The comparison always made by ex-Workshop performers is with jazz music and its improvisatory flexibility; audiences, offered something so profoundly alive, were invited to become part of this energy.

The scenes immediately following the War Plans illustrate the rapidity of stylistic change: first came 'a dance-cum-Sunday afternoon promenade' (to music by Smetana) dramatising Sarajevo and the moment of assassination (conveyed economically by a single, off-stage gunshot). The wordless, *commedia*-style, music-and-movement scene lasted over a minute, its mood shifting from composure to foreboding. There followed an epic-comic scene,

20 See Willett, *Brecht on Theatre*, p. 44.
21 *Oh What a Lovely War*, pp. 44–53/pp. 30–8.

anchored in terms of setting by a stall on wheels easily brought on and off the stage. Its lightness of mood played against the nature of its subject, the secret services.[22] This kind of multi-level flexibility is impossible to capture on the printed page, which is why readers often find the text of the play baffling.

A new dramaturgy

The original production modulated seemingly effortlessly between the comic and the grimly authentic, the realistic and the fanciful; stylistic shifts were underpinned by a skilled manipulation of source material, which enabled the war's 'terrible irony' to be eloquently articulated. Within a few minutes of the opening of Act 2, a series of Newspanels established the harsh reality of trench warfare following the initial hostilities of 1914.[23] Whilst listening to the ironically jaunty song 'Oh It's a Lovely War', and watching a lively dance routine, the audience's eyes continuously took in sobering facts about 1915 culminating in:

SEPT 25 . . . LOOS . . . BRITISH LOSS 8,236 MEN IN 3 HOURS . . . GERMAN LOSS NIL.

At the conclusion of the song, 'As each of the girls speaks her line to the audience she throws a white feather' – a Home Front symbol of cowardice. Lines were taken verbatim from recruiting posters. For example, 'What did you do in the Great War, Daddy?' referenced the contemporary poster depicting a guilty father unable to look his daughter in the eye as she puts her question – his infant son, ironically, plays with toy soldiers at their feet. Act 2's opening, then, moved rapidly and succinctly through 1915 establishing, firstly, the grim impasse on the Western Front (the hideous repetitiveness of the 'war of attrition'), and secondly, the very different gung-ho mood of the Home Front.

One of the most difficult scenes in the production was the dramatisation of war profiteering.[24] The scene was played in a two-dimensional agit-prop style well known to Theatre Workshop from the 1930s. Source material, too, was drawn from this period (the 1934 book *Merchants of Death*[25] was crucial to

---

22 *Oh What a Lovely War*, pp. 17–20/pp. 6–9. Both the dance-drama scene and this scene were adapted from Theatre Workshop's various productions of their stage adaptation of Jaroslav Hasek's (1920–3) novel *The Good Soldier Schweik*. See Goorney, *Theatre Workshop Story*, pp. 18–19, 103–4, 152–3; Littlewood, *Joan's Book*, pp. 106–9.

23 *Oh What a Lovely War*, pp. 55–7/pp. 39–41.

24 *Oh What a Lovely War*, pp. 57–63/pp. 41–7.

25 H. C. Englebrecht and F. C. Hanighen, *Merchants of Death: A Study of the International Armament Industry* (London: George Routledge, 1934).

the scene). Such an abstract subject is difficult to stage through naturalistic writing and acting, as the inherent 'facelessness' of the abstract constitutes an elusive theatrical challenge. The personifications of medieval morality plays are one antecedent, but the non-naturalistic styles of Russian and German agit-prop troupes of the 1920s and 1930s were the primary influence. Their cartoon style prevented naturalistic depth, but enabled considerable factual detail to be presented.

The scene's grouse-shooting party allowed five key national stereotypes to be humorously portrayed in an instantly recognisable class situation. Moreover, the shooting party's guns could be 'fired' in *comic* contrast to the realistic sound effects used elsewhere; the sound of shooting in this scene was provided by rim-shots on the drum-kit. Sound tapes of warfare were used in the production, but the music-hall-style comic alternative illustrates further flexibility. The scene actually ended with an audio-tape sound of warfare in order, again, to change mood and place.

The 'Profiteers' scene became less factual during the run of the show. For example, the source material offered this kind of detail:

> In the terrific fighting around Verdun, Fort Douaumont was repeatedly a bone of contention. It changed hands several times. In one of the attacks, the Germans ran into some barbed-wire entanglements which only two months previously had been shipped into Switzerland by a German factory, the Magdeburger Draht-und-Kabelwerke.[26]

Performances at Stratford East duly named fort and company, but the printed text has the later West End version:

AMERICA: You're smart, Count – you know he got a consignment of barbed wire from Germany through for Verdun only two months before the battle. Isn't that right, Comte?
BRITAIN: You mean the German chappies were caught on their own barbed wire? I say that's a bit near the knuckle, what? Dashed clever, though.
SWITZERLAND: We must take some credit for that.
BRITAIN: Yes, ten per cent, no doubt.

In general, then, irony was retained but documentary detail diminished in this scene.

The style was disliked by some contemporary critics. In the *Financial Times*, T. C. Worsley damned its 'crass crudity', while Malcolm Rutherford in *Plays*

---

26 *Ibid.*, p. 172.

and Players commented: 'the scenes with the men are realistic, those with the officers satirical, and the division is a disappointing one. Realism and satire in this production are very far apart.'[27] These critics balked at the scene's tendentiousness, far removed from the subtleties of the naturalistic stage that they conventionally valued. In the *Financial Times*, contrasting praise went to the 'brilliance' of the naturalistic trench scenes. There was a perverse willingness to segment the play in a way that denied the depth achieved through the non-naturalistic 'collision' of montaged material.

Poison gas was first used on the Western Front in 1915, and 'Britain' in the play remarks: 'Well the old chlorine's pretty good. Haig's trying it out this moment at Loos. Mind you, we haven't heard from him. Yet.' The song 'Gassed Last Night' followed as the stage darkened. Slides 22–32, which punctuated the song's mordant lyric, constituted the hardest-hitting documentary evidence in the show.[28] Two key images were a gas-blinded column of British wounded (Slide 26) and a dead German soldier (Slide 32); the first coinciding with the song's line about 'warning', the second with its stark contrast between shell holes and graves ('one of us could fill it all alone'). As the lights changed at the end of the song, taped sound returned the audience to the soldiers from whom the profiteers 'had not heard', and a naturalistic scene followed.

Although radical views became fashionable in both theatre and society in the 1960s (and the play benefited from this), West End success muted the play's original radicalism. Criticism and commercial pressures combined to decrease the political commitment of the show as it moved into the mainstream. In this, too, *Oh What a Lovely War* was quintessentially British and of its time. Ronald Bryden's review of the 1969 revival production brought this out well:

> I am tempted to close the book on the sixties and declare Joan Littlewood's First World War documentary the most important theatrical event of the decade . . . The iron impact of the show Joan Littlewood produced lay in its gradual demonstration that the shape the Great War took was the shape of Britain . . . It was an elegy not just for two-and-a-half million dead, but for a revolution which never happened.[29]

By 1969, then, there were already doubts about the political significance of the 1968 'Student Revolution'. Alternative theatre seemed to be flourishing, but within ten years it began to fade. Left-wing theatre struggled for continuity in

---

27 T. C. Worsley, *Financial Times* (20 March 1963); Malcolm Rutherford, *Plays and Players* 10, 8 (1963), 41.

28 *Oh What a Lovely War*, pp. 63–5/pp. 47–8.

29 Ronald Bryden, *Observer* (14 Dec. 1969).

the twentieth century, but the popularity of *Oh What a Lovely War* extended the possibility of relearning techniques perennially under threat from dominant theatrical styles.

Restaging history?

A late twentieth-century production of *Oh What a Lovely War* demonstrated just how difficult such a continuity is to sustain. In 1998 the Royal National Theatre revived the play first for an educational tour and then for a short season at London's Roundhouse. The production team's principal reinterpretative concept was to place the action inside a circus-style 'Big Top'. The folds and swags of their design had a disastrous effect on one of the principal technological actors, fatally damaging the counterpoint of documentary and drama. Slides were projected on the upper part of a cloth that billowed out towards the audience, so that the images were distorted by this 'screen' and by a poor viewing angle. They were also frequently washed out by bright circus-style lighting. A determination to focus on drama's element of entertainment undermined the documentary significance of the slides. As John Tagg remarks, 'Photographs are never "evidence" of history; they are themselves the historical'.[30] The Common Soldiers, so often the subjects of the slides, were important mute 'actors' in the original production. Archive photographs marked the trace of real human beings who lived through (and died in) the war represented on stage. The RNT's obsession with action for action's sake gave priority to performers and sacrificed the authenticity of the slides. This unbalanced the show and drained sequences like 'Gassed Last Night' of their former political power.

As for the Newspanel, it was miniaturised. The RNT's machine (centre stage, just above the performers' heads) was similar to those found in banks, post offices and railway stations. Its little red lights were puny in comparison to the huge white-light machine that dominated the proscenium at Stratford East and Wyndham's Theatre. Where messages once tracked solemnly across the stage in once only authoritative statements, their seriousness often freezing the smile on your face, the words on the tiny RNT machine skittered about neurotically and repetitiously. Inevitably the serious impact of the Newspanel's factual statements was also diminished. Nothing could better illustrate the inherent fragility of oppositional theatre practice than this (doubtless well-intentioned) travesty of the production which gave such a boost to political theatre in 1963.

30 John Tagg, *The Burden of Representation: Essays on Photographies and Histories* (London: Macmillan, 1988), p. 65.

All theatre productions are locked into their own historical moments, and by 1998 both Theatre Workshop and the 'Great War' itself had become 'heritage' experiences. The Imperial War Museum's major 1990s installation entitled 'Trench Experience' aimed for active simulation rather than relying on passive 'glass case' exhibits. Using uniformed dummies, sound/lighting effects and genuine artefacts, the museum seemed no longer to trust its audience to work things out unaided. Similarly, RNT director Fiona Laird seemed to fear that this ageing play might over-tax her audience unless it was tricked out afresh. The RNT's glittering pastiche of circus and music hall would be called post-modern by some, and Theatre Workshop's use of multi-media was certainly 'proto-post-modern'. But the original *Oh What a Lovely War* challenged received theatrical and historical wisdoms with a potent anti-naturalism and a provocative use of subaltern history. At the turn of the millennium, its oppositional values, displaced and relativised, were consequently enfeebled.

18

1979 and after: a view

VERA GOTTLIEB

Lost and yet to come

> The amorous catastrophe may be close to what has been called, in the psychotic domain, an *extreme situation*, 'a situation experienced by the subject as irremediably bound to destroy him' . . . the image is drawn from what occurred at Dachau. Is it not indecent to compare the situation of a love-sick subject to that of an inmate of Dachau? Can one of the most unimaginable insults of History be compared with a trivial, childish, sophisticated, obscure incident occurring to a comfortable subject who is merely the victim of his own Image-repertoire? Yet these two situations have this in common: they are, literally, panic situations: situations without reminder, without return . . . I am lost, forever.[1]

Barthes's comparison of a rejected lover with a prisoner at Dachau hangs frozen on the page. It *is* indecent, but it is also characteristic of much of the philosophy of the last two decades of the twentieth century in its rejection of history, abuse of scale and hence values, and in the removal of context which, if present, would render the point grossly inappropriate. From the perspective of a materialist history, the two situations have nothing in common.

The comparison is intended to demonstrate the dehumanising loss of 'self', yet, while self-confessedly self-centred, Barthes chooses to ignore the differences between a one-to-one relationship and the state-initiated and state-controlled Holocaust, indeed 'one of the most unimaginable insults of History'. But like so much else in our post-modern culture, and in the arts of the *fin du millennium*, there is a dangerous absence of historical readings, of differences of context. This may also distinguish plays by the older generation of post-World War Two British dramatists – Arden, Bond, Pinter, Griffiths, Edgar, Wesker, Churchill, Hare, Brenton, Barker, Wertenbaker, who variously

---

1 Roland Barthes, 'Catastrophe', in *A Lover's Discourse: Fragments*, trans. Richard Howard (London: Jonathan Cape, 1979), pp. 48–9. The quotation is from Bruno Bettleheim, *The Empty Fortress*.

attempted to use or explain history, and to locate the individual within a social, political and thus often historical context – from those of the younger generation, who seem virtually to have abandoned perspectives on the past (Patrick Marber, Jez Butterworth, Anthony Neilson and others). There are, of course, exceptions, such as Mark Ravenhill, with his significant treatment of the dehumanising effects of consumerism, and Sarah Kane.

Kane's actual starting point for her highly controversial *Blasted* (Royal Court Theatre Upstairs, 1995) was Barthes's comparison:

> When I first read that I was appalled he could make the connection . . . gradually I realised that Barthes is right: it is all about loss of self. When you love obsessively, you lose your sense of self. And if you lose the object of your love, you have no resources to fall back on. It can completely destroy you . . . the concentration camps are about dehumanising people before they are killed.[2]

Although Kane's play does make the comparison between 'incarceration' and 'infatuation', *Blasted* throbs with late twentieth-century historical/political images and metaphors – of 'ethnic cleansing' in Bosnia, of Robben Island's ANC prisoners in Apartheid South Africa, of genocide in Rwanda. Although using allegory, the play nonetheless resonates with specific sources of horror. As a political allegory, it is closer to Edward Bond's *Lear* or Harold Pinter's *Ashes to Ashes* or *Mountain Language* than to the works of Kane's contemporaries: the iron grip of history not only provides the context for the lovers in the play, it also seals their fate. Despite the horrors of *Blasted*, love does offer a faint glimmer of hope. In this sense, Kane – like Martin Sherman in his Holocaust play, *Bent* (Royal Court Theatre, 1979) – tries to offer some positive aspects of human relationships within unimaginable circumstances. Dachau provides the actual setting for the second half of *Bent*, one of the few plays to explore the treatment of homosexuality in Nazi Germany, *and* in a concentration camp where dehumanised human beings are driven to the extremes of love and hatred, of ethical depravity despite the main character's sexual innocence.

It is not accidental that late twentieth-century changes in the perception of the world (significantly often labelled 'post' – post-history, post-feminism, post-post-modernism), and, given the 'end of history', the artistic treatment of individuals in an increasingly vague or undefined context, may be strongly linked, with the benefit of hindsight, to a series of significant dates and the events those dates represent. In 1975, for example, Edward Heath's 'old style'

---

2 Quoted in Aleks Sierz, *In-Yer-Face Theatre: British Drama Today* (London: Faber & Faber, 2000), p. 116.

Conservative government was brought down by the miners' industrial action – resulting in a general election that brought in Harold Wilson's Old Labour government (as distinct from Tony Blair's New Labour). This in turn motivated Margaret Thatcher's vengeful destruction of the miners' strike in 1984 – and emasculation of the trade unions generally – and also helped pave the way for the electoral success of Thatcher and the New Right in 1979, with national and global ramifications continuing into the twenty-first century. In 1989 there was the so-called 'death of Communism' and hence the 'end of history'[3] with the collapse of the Soviet Union; the redefinition of eastern Europe with a unified Germany and newly independent states formerly part of the Soviet Bloc; the end of the (post-1945) Cold War – and seemingly a need for 'new' enemies!

An historical date may characterise a 'climate' that originated earlier, but those particular dates are themselves politically significant. Through to the new millennium, the apparent success of the New Right led to the spread of monetarism and globalisation and to the so-called death of ideologies and – with the evaporation of oppositional language – an increasing absence of 'the political' or even public debate in British theatre and, to a lesser extent, in the cinema. Only television drama continued to provide a forum for debate. As the film critic David Thomson put it, there was an urgent need for 'doubts in the dark'.[4] Whilst Thatcher's Britain, and the world, changed radically, the British theatre generally failed to respond to this – to the serious detriment of its role and significance.

Those 'doubts in the dark' were expressed by the older generation of playwrights – several of whom tried to make sense of Thatcherism and the New Right, a lingering inheritance of 1979. In Caryl Churchill's work, for example, both the historical and the political are organic to the content and structure of the plays. In *Vinegar Tom* (1976) Churchill wrote contemporary-style songs to raise major questions about the seventeenth-century persecution of female witches; in *Light Shining in Buckinghamshire* (also 1976), she used verbatim material from the English civil war Putney debates; while in *Cloud Nine* (1979) she began to create a contrapuntal structure of different historical periods – the colonial late Victorian British Empire contrasted with contemporary London.[5] This structural device was used more effectively in *Top Girls* (1981), in which Churchill focusses on 'top women' (whether fictional, or historical) from

---

3 F. Fukuyama, 'The end of history?', *National Interest* (summer 1989), 3–18.
4 David Thomson, 'Why Dirty Harry beats Harry Potter', *Observer* (13 Jan. 2002), Review section, 8.
5 This influenced Ravenhill's structure in *Mother Clap's Molly House* (2001).

Figure 18.1 Contextualising the Thatcherite woman: Caryl Churchill's *Top Girls*, Bristol Old Vic, Theatre Royal, Bristol, 1983–4.

different periods in order to contextualise Marlene, a 'Thatcherite career woman', and to explore the paradoxes of being a top woman in a man's world. In 1987 she wrote *Serious Money*: originally staged at the Royal Court, it transferred to the West End, where it played to packed houses of the very City trader yuppies which it satirises, partly by means of historical parallels with the stock-jobbers of Thomas Shadwell's *The Volunteers* (1692).

However ambivalently achieved, the popular success of *Serious Money* perhaps no more undermined the power of its political and economic parody than the success of Brecht's *Threepenny Opera* (1928) undermined *his* use of history and political parallels to raise serious issues in Berlin. *Serious Money* was written immediately after the so-called 'Big Bang' when the City collapsed and, contrary to monetarist 'free market' thinking, the Bank of England had to shore up the pound to avoid complete economic disaster. Central to the cultural climate were such films as *Wall Street* (1987) – with Michael Douglas as Gekko, the corporate raider with the credo 'Greed is Good' and Charlie Sheen as the hungry yuppie, caught for insider dealing – and *Other People's Money* (1991 – adapted from Jerry Sterner's Off-Broadway play, subtitled *The Ultimate Seduction*), with Gregory Peck and Danny de Vito, Peck representing the old-style paternalistic capitalist and de Vito the greedy corporate asset stripper.

A political sketch

In an article in the *Observer*, under the headline 'Greed is the Creed', Will Hutton wrote:

> American politicians' need for business donations on a gigantic scale to win their election campaigns now pollutes the discourse of the country's public life, with business writing public policy and corrupting everything it touches. And the noxious consequences, in terms of ideas and business practice, spills over into Britain.[6]

Similarly, over the eleven years of Thatcher's premiership, and eighteen years of radical New Right policies, business priorities consistently wrote the public agenda: privatising the nationalised industries of gas and electricity, telecommunications, water, parts of public transport (such as buses), cleaning and catering in the National Health Service, and even the prisons and, to subsequent disastrous effect, the railways – privatisations that were to be maintained by New Labour. After the elections of 1983 (with a bigger majority) and 1987, Thatcher's radical monetarism closed the shipyards and British Steel and decimated the mining industry, manufacturing and much of the country's infrastructure.

In 1983 London Weekend Television transmitted four programmes on 'Breadline Britain', vividly depicting the plight of the poor. Social Services Secretary Norman Fowler's Green Paper, while claiming to be 'the most substantial examination of the social security system' since World War Two, formed part of a fundamental and damaging reassessment of the post-1945 welfare state.[7] On 28 August 1980 the *Guardian* published the following:

> Britain now endures the highest unemployment figures since 1935. The increase of 545,000 a year is the steepest since the great depression. Our jobless are growing over twice as fast as those in any EEC country; and yet we are still only at the start of a long road . . . *Unemployment is being used as a tool of economic management to an extent that no government since the war has dared contemplate* . . . We are increasingly two nations, riven between employed and unemployed, north and south . . . Our steep rise in unemployment is not the inevitable result of world recession . . . our industries are laying off workers because domestic demand for their products has fallen, and their share of that home market has been eroded by imports. That is directly attributable to government policy. (Author's emphasis)

6 Will Hutton, 'Greed is the creed', *Observer* (13 Jan. 2002), 23.
7 Kay Andrews and John Jacobs, *Punishing the Poor: Poverty under Thatcher* (London: Macmillan, 1990), p. 10. See also Ruth Cohen and Maryrose Tarpey, *Single Payments: The Disappearing Safety Net*, Poverty Pamphlet 74 (London: CPAG Ltd, 1988).

Thus, when Margaret Thatcher famously declared that 'there is no such thing as society', it was not only to bring an ideological and material end to the welfare state; not only to create a new Radical Right emphasis on the individual rather than the collective; not only to reinforce her infamous 'return to Victorian values' in shifting responsibility from society to family, but also because the new *radical* ideology had quite different aims and motives from those of any British government since the 1930s. This included, as senior civil servant Sir Frank Cooper put it, 'the orderly management of decline'.[8]

This was the background to such late 1990s films as Mark Herman's *Brassed Off* (1996), Peter Cattaneo's *The Full Monty* (1997) and Stephen Daldry's *Billy Elliot* (2000), in which the miners' strike, economic decline and northern poverty formed not only the backcloth but also the characters' motivations. It is significant that British television drama continued the treatment of serious issues for which a whole string of Plays for Today in the 1950s and 1960s had once been famous. Hence, in the 1980s and 1990s many of the best writers and directors turned to television drama as the platform for debate, partly because of its tradition of serious drama and partly because – as Trevor Griffiths many times remarked – that is where the audiences were. But there were increasing signs that this very popular 'loophole' was under attack, as Thatcher turned her attention to the BBC. For example, a very public row resulted from the BBC's broadcast of Charles Wood's Falklands War play, *Tumbledown* (30 May 1988 and 8 June 1992), causing the director Richard Eyre to defend the playwright, the production and the BBC when questions were asked in Parliament. The resulting controversy partly motivated the government's investigation into the financing of the BBC in the Peacock Report (1986)[9] and – later – the threatened revocation of the BBC's charter. Eyre's subsequent much reported press conference at the National Theatre made the views of the artistic and political opposition clear:

> I would feel the film a failure if it's not deeply political. I am happy to say I don't think the play *is* balanced . . . *Tumbledown* is meant to be viewed as drama . . . Art is trying to give meaning to facts . . . In contemporary British society we

8 From *Thatcher, the Downing Street Years*, Pt. 1 of a four-part BBC documentary (London: BBC 1, Fine Art Productions for BBC News and Current Affairs, 1993) written and produced by Denys Blakeway. The same remark was attributed to Sir William Armstrong in *Thatcher, the Downing Street Years*, pt. 2; see also Ruth Levitas (ed.), *The Ideology of the New Right* (Cambridge: Polity Press, 1986).
9 For details of the controversy over Charles Wood's *Tumbledown* and Ian Curteis's *The Falklands Play*, see George Brandt (ed.), *British Television Drama in the 1980s* (Cambridge University Press, 1993), ch. 8.

have enjoyed a period of liberal expression. The evidence is mounting that it is coming to an end.[10]

This, however, was one of the most exciting periods of British drama – albeit television drama – in which series after series set itself in opposition to the policies of the radical New Right. There was Troy Kennedy Martin's brilliant political thriller *Edge of Darkness* (transmitted by BBC2, November 1985, repeated December 1985, BBC1, and again in May 1992, BBC2). In 1982 there had been Alan Bleasdale's immensely popular and equally controversial *Boys from the Blackstuff*, promoted by the BBC's producer Michael Wearing as 'a series of five new plays'.[11] Their innovatory use of video (for budgetary reasons) had a major artistic influence on future British television drama, creating a visual quality that deepened the reality of the locations of this black comedy about the 'black economy'. Making serious drama accessible to a popular audience, it coincided with the Falklands War, but brought attention back to the all too real domestic problems of Britain. It reflected the fatalistic mood of the times and 'the widespread disillusionment in socialism that accompanied the failure of the Labour government to arrest Britain's economic decline and that in turn enabled the authoritarian populism of Margaret Thatcher to take power in 1979'.[12] Given the audience it reached, the influence of *Boys from the Blackstuff* was greater than that of any contemporary theatre play: the desperate cry of the disintegrating character, Yosser – 'Gizza-job' – entered the popular contemporary vocabulary. To quote John McGrath, it provided 'a public pronouncement of a widespread public grief'.[13]

Television drama in this period also dealt with the highly controversial subject of Northern Ireland. There was Ronan Bennett and John Hales's adaptation of M. S. Powers's *Children of the North*, Charles Wood's *Breed of Heroes*, the Allen/Loach *Hidden Agenda* and works by Graham Reid, Ann Devlin and Mike Leigh.[14] This was also the period of Bleasdale's controversial *The Monocled Mutineer* (BBC, 1986), Alan Dosser's *The Muscle Market* (BBC, 1981) and the stylistically and politically radical plays of Dennis Potter – plays which changed forever the definitions of television drama. Overtly oppositional to

10 *Ibid.*, pp. 145–6.
11 *Ibid.*, ch. 7, p. 124.
12 *Ibid.*, p. 134.
13 *Ibid.*, p. 135.
14 See Edward Braun, '"What truth is there in this story?": the dramatisation of Northern Ireland', in Jonathan Bignell, Stephen Lacey and Madelaine Macmurraugh-Kavanagh (eds.), *British Television Drama – Past, Present and Future* (New York: Palgrave, 2000), pp. 110–21.

the New Right, BBC drama provoked a vendetta from Thatcher.[15] Meanwhile, the commercial channel Granada produced *Brideshead Revisited* (1981) and the brilliant fourteen-episode dramatisation of Paul Scott's *The Jewel in the Crown* (1984), excellent 'period' drama but not confrontational.

Theatre in a cool climate

Opposition to Prime Minister Margaret Thatcher centred on the economic policies of the New Right – in particular, monetarism and globalisation. The management consultant Adrian Ellis defined monetarism simply:

> A managerial philosophy introduced during a period of retrenchment rather than growth, creating an umbilical link in most people's minds between cuts in available funding and the introduction of private sector management tools and language. An approach informed by an emotional conviction supported by a theoretical framework that, all other things being equal, public sector management is less efficient and effective than private sector management, where the Darwinian operation of the market simultaneously encourages efficiency and punishes inefficiency.[16]

This affected the way the British theatre of the period functioned. For the New Right, 'subsidy' was a dirty word – and it is not accidental that the plays that dealt critically with the Thatcher years were all produced within a subsidised context. Steven Berkoff's Falklands play, *Sink the Belgrano!* (1986), was staged at London's Half Moon Theatre; Howard Brenton and David Hare's *Pravda* (1985), exposing the media tycoon Rupert Murdoch, at the National Theatre; and Hare's *The Secret Rapture* (1988, exploring the psychology of women under Thatcher through the person of a *woman* MP), as well as his 'state of Britain' trilogy – *Racing Demons* (1990), *Murmuring Judges* (1991) and *The Absence of War* (1993) – were all produced at the (by then) Royal National Theatre. Trevor Griffiths's *The Gulf Between Us* (1992) and *Thatcher's Children* (1993) were produced at the West Yorkshire Playhouse and by the Bristol Old Vic company, respectively. London's Royal Court staged Churchill's plays, Timberlake Wertenbaker's vital *Our Country's Good* (1988), and plays by Howard Barker, Gregory Motton and Meredith Oakes.

---

15 See Brandt, *British Television Drama*, pp. 9–11, pp. 16–17 and see K. D. Ewing and C. A. Gearty, *Freedom Under Thatcher: Civil Liberties in Modern Britain* (Oxford University Press, 1990).
16 Quoted by Genista McIntosh, Executive Director of the Royal National Theatre, Annual Marjorie Frances Lecture, Goldsmiths College, University of London, 14/11/01.

In some respects it became easier to write about the collapse of Eastern Europe than about domestic politics (although not ultimately separable): in 1990 there were Caryl Churchill's *Mad Forest, a Play from Romania*, David Edgar's *The Shape of the Table*, and Tariq Ali and Howard Brenton's *Moscow Gold*. The Berlin Wall had come down the previous year, it was the end of the Cold War; but while its passing was being ratified in Paris by Thatcher and other heads of state (21 November), 'the traitors'[21] back home were working to get rid of Thatcher as prime minister and leader of the Conservative Party. This was achieved the day after – Thursday 22 November 1990.

The ramifications of Thatcherism and the Radical Right *were* internationally and nationally pervasive. The effect on British theatre was devastating. Subsidy levels were linked to private sponsorship deals – hard to find, and creating their own forms of 'censorship' in which corporate money could not be used for risk-taking and experiment. There seemed no irony in displaying RSC posters in which the sponsor, Allied-Dunbar, appeared in much larger print than Shakespeare. The emphasis on form to the detriment of content, reinforced by the expansion of live or performance arts in the 1980s and 1990s, left theatre far behind television drama and even the much more expensive film industry, partly because, however strapped for cash, film *is* an industry. Theatre in education virtually disappeared from schools; drama was no longer a formal part of the curriculum; and three decades of potential theatre-goers and theatre-makers were lost. Equally, many of the politically driven theatre groups of the 1970s failed to survive, and Thatcher's rate capping of (largely Labour) local government ensured that local authorities cut money to many regional theatres.

Mustering the opposition

The undermining of British theatre did not, however, pass without opposition. In the late 1980s there was a series of theatre conferences and crisis meetings: 'Theatre in Thatcher's Britain: Organising the Opposition', Goldsmiths College, May 1988,[22] followed by a national conference, 'Theatre in Crisis', Goldsmiths College, December 1988[23] and a major conference in Cambridge, 'Theatre Under Threat', October 1990.[24] More recent – in reaction to the new Labour government – was 'Theatre 2001', attended by David Puttnam,

21 From *Thatcher, The Downing Street Years*, Pt. 4.
22 See *New Theatre Quarterly* 5, 18 (May 1989), 113–23.
23 See *New Theatre Quarterly* 5, 19 (Aug. 1989), 210–16.
24 Reported in *New Theatre Quarterly* 7, 26 (May 1991), 187–90.

Richard Eyre (who famously called British theatre overpriced, uncomfortable and sometimes 'bowel-churningly bad'[25]), Andrew Lloyd Webber, Cameron Mackintosh, Thelma Holt, Philip Hedley, Genista McIntosh, Jude Kelly, Bill Kenwright and Adrian Noble, meeting with Labour's Secretary of State for Culture, Chris Smith. The week before, a delegation had gone to Downing Street to lobby Prime Minister Tony Blair. Pragmatic issues were discussed – from seat prices to lavatories – but little altered, except an increase in costs. Whilst Britain and the world have changed radically since 1979, theatre in the main has not – whether in theatre-going conventions, audiences or form.

And yet the hunger was (and still is) there. As Michael Billington put it, 'At a time when theatre is suffocating from a welter of plays about private experience, the Soho experiment reminds us of how dramatists invariably renew their oxygen-supply when they tackle the public world.'[26] The Soho experiment was a direct response to the terrorist attacks of 11 September 2001: Abigail Morris of London's Soho Theatre commissioned a series of ten-minute plays reacting to the news. This was the first opportunity since 1999 – when London's Tricycle Theatre staged its response to the racist Stephen Lawrence murder, *The Colour of Justice* – for theatre to react spontaneously to political events, and it brought in a range of plays, such as Shan Khan's *Taxi to Queens*, which 'suggested that a city's tragedy is a predator's opportunity'.[27]

Throughout history the most powerful theatre has aimed to make sense of the world. The use of history in drama is itself one way of drawing contemporary parallels, and audiences, whether in the theatre or watching drama at home, are quick to draw their own conclusions. Thatcher's 'populism' insulted millions of intelligent citizens, many of whom also felt a sense of betrayal and disillusionment under the new Labour government. If the theatre was slow to express this, BBC1's two-part drama *The Project,* written by Leigh Jackson and broadcast in November 2002, was essentially concerned to explore whether 'ends justify means' in its charting of the period from 1992 through the run-up to New Labour's landslide victory of 1997, and into the second term of Blair's government from 2001.[28]

However tempting, it is not sufficient to trace all subsequent ills back to 1979. New Labour chose, no doubt to the surprise of many who had voted for it, to leave untouched many of the policies of the New Right. In retrospect, Howard

25 *Independent* (3 March 2001), 'Home news', 3.
26 *Guardian Saturday Review* (24 Nov. 2001).
27 *Ibid.*
28 See Vera Gottlieb, 'Theatre today – the "new realities"', *Contemporary Theatre Review* 13, 2 (2003), 5–14.

Brenton's play *The Romans in Britain* (1980), which drew a parallel between the Roman occupation of Britain and the British occupation of Northern Ireland, still looks bold, and that ought to be surprising, since its political perception is not particularly incisive. In this, as in many historical plays, the use of parallels – as distinct from Brecht's or Bond's or Pinter's use of *parable* – exposes the 'what' and the 'why' of political change, but rarely the 'how'. *Process* is seldom demonstrated – a major exception being Trevor Griffiths in his use of history to dissect contemporary politics, whether in *Occupations* (1970), *The Party* (1973), *Oi for England* (1982), *Real Dreams* (1984) or *Hope in the Year Two* (1994).

More than the play itself, the reception of *Romans in Britain* at the National Theatre demonstrated some of the worst characteristics of Thatcherism. Mrs Mary Whitehouse (self-appointed leader of her own Viewers and Listeners Association) accused Brenton and director Michael Bogdanov of 'procuring an act of gross indecency'. (The play includes a scene of the homosexual rape of a Druid by a group of Roman soldiers, a specifically graphic way of reinforcing the political parallel.) Writer and director found themselves facing an Old Bailey trial. Interviewed outside the National Theatre, Whitehouse was asked what she thought of the play as a whole – and quite unashamedly stated that she had neither seen it nor read it. She did not need to – it was 'obscene'. Whitehouse's influence, greatly strengthened by Thatcher, affected much of what could be performed or broadcast without controversy or even censorship.

The threads of history stretching over the previous twenty-five years were reinforced by the death of Whitehouse in 2001. Her importance to television and theatre was evident in a full-page *Guardian* obituary, in which Richard Hoggart suggested: 'She was . . . the authentic voice of middle England, fearful of the costs and challenges of change, oblivious of its opportunities'.[29] Looking at 1979 and what followed, it is impossible to omit the pervasive self-righteousness voiced by Whitehouse – fostered by Margaret Thatcher, Ronald Reagan and the New Right.

The culture of a country is a barometer of its health. The New Right did everything it could to dismantle the welfare state and consensus government in Britain. In the early stages of the new millennium British theatre learned to live with the largely unopposed results of globalisation and monetarism, and without a coherent language of opposition, since the New Right had hijacked the 'radical' agenda. But the New Right, and New Labour after it, bypassed rather than destroyed British socialism. It was socialism, rather than 'old' or

29 *Guardian* (24 Nov. 2001).

'new' Labour, which provided the shared value system of most of the unaligned oppositional theatre practitioners of the Thatcher period and its aftermath. In the twenty-first century, whether 'socialism' may be still conceivable as a source of opposition and alternatives remains an open question. At the end of *The Romans in Britain*, the First Cook says:

> And when he was dead, the King who never was and the
> Government that never was – were mourned.
> And Remembered. Bitterly.
> And thought of as a golden age, lost and yet to come.

19

British theatre and commerce,
1979–2000

STEPHEN LACEY

We no longer talk of subsidy: we speak of investment. We no longer justify the theatre on grounds of spiritual nourishment, intellectual stimulus or communal pleasure: we talk inevitably of 'an important strand in our export drive' and of 'quick and sizeable returns' that will follow an increase in arts funding.[1]

As Michael Billington indicates here, some of the main developments in British theatre since 1979 did not originate with aesthetics but rather with ideology and economics. Theatre has been a business for centuries, of course, even if its institutional and financial basis was often invisible in the discussion of performances, but it is unlikely that Billington could have written this any earlier in the post-World War Two period. He registers a process of commodification, in which the relationships between plays, practitioners, writers and audiences have become defined by the terms of free-market economics. As a result, from about the early 1980s justifications for theatre as a cultural practice became increasingly determined by its value as a commercial activity, with profound consequences for the kinds of theatre that were produced in the final decades of the twentieth century.

The processes considered here are complex, and to discuss them will involve looking first at the political context for the changing relationship of theatre to commerce and the state, in a climate dominated by government intervention to introduce monetarism and major structural changes to the British economy. This included the forging of a new partnership between 'public' and 'private' sources of funding. The kind of theatre that was produced as a result will then be considered, as will some of the most significant political and cultural consequences of commodification. The history, or histories, outlined here have, as yet, no resolution, and the chapter will conclude with a consideration of the theatrical situation at the beginning of the twenty-first century.

---

1 Michael Billington, *Guardian* (28 Dec. 1985), 13.

Theatre and 'high monetarism': Thatcherism and the assault on subsidy

In 1980 Howard Brenton and Tony Howard argued, in *A Short Sharp Shock*, that Britain was in a cultural and political crisis. In this satirical burlesque that echoed the agitational political theatre of the previous decade, they were in no doubt who was to blame for this: the newly elected Conservative government, and in particular Britain's first woman prime minister, Margaret Thatcher. Mrs Thatcher (later, Lady Thatcher) and the Conservatives came to power in May 1979, and their election provides the main reason why this chapter begins with that year. For good or ill (and for most employees in theatre it was undoubtedly the latter), this was a pivotal point in post-war British history, signalling a radical negation of the political, social and cultural assumptions that had dominated the decades since the end of World War Two.

Margaret Thatcher, who remained in office throughout the 1980s, has the distinction of lending her name to an 'ism' – Thatcherism. However, Thatcherism refers to a phenomenon that cannot be reduced to the personality of Margaret Thatcher; as Andrew Gamble has noted, 'Thatcher is . . . important to Thatcherism. But an analysis of Thatcherism that only concentrated on Thatcher would be seriously inadequate'.[2] Of course, 'Thatcherism' did not spring fully formed on her election to the leadership of the Tory Party in 1975, and did not evaporate when she was summarily ejected from power fourteen years later. Mrs Thatcher was in office for less than half the twenty-two years considered here. But for many on the Left in this period Thatcherism was a nightmare, from which, it was hoped, they would all soon awake and return to normal business. However, placed on a larger canvas, it may be that the Thatcherite policy agenda could be more accurately described as 'the first phase of the development of a new political compromise',[3] which will stretch well into the twenty-first century. From the perspective of the economic liberalism that became the new common sense following New Labour's electoral victory in 1997, it was the 1960s and 1970s – the period of expansion, social liberalism and relatively high levels of state support for the arts – that seems the aberration, not Thatcherism.

Thatcherism articulated a version of economic freedom that connected the supremacy of the individual consumer in the marketplace (a key element of monetarism) to notions of 'freedom' and 'choice'. The main consequence of

---

2 Andrew Gamble, *The Free Economy and the Strong State: The Politics of Thatcherism*, 2nd edn (London: Macmillan, 1994), p. 4.
3 *Ibid.*, p. 209.

this was the redefinition of the role of the state in social life. The welfare state, which alongside health and education included funding for the arts, was a prime target. Thatcher distrusted the very concept of public support for the arts, arguing that 'Artistic talent – let alone artistic genius – is unplanned, unpredictable, eccentrically individual . . . I wanted to see the private sector raising more money and bringing business acumen and efficiency to bear on the administration of cultural institutions.'[4] Like the poor, artists in receipt of government support were accused of becoming 'dependent' on 'hand-outs' from the 'nanny state' created by earlier Labour governments, which was deemed both unethical and antithetical to the true independence of the artist. Hence, one of the central themes of Conservative rule from 1979 to 1997 was the reshaping of the relationship between the 'public' and the 'private' domains of the economy. The balance was decisively tilted towards the latter, and the imposition of the model of the free market – of commerce – into all areas of social and cultural life, including theatre, followed on inexorably.

However, subsidised theatre – like education and the National Health Service – was not simply thrown to the mercy of the market. In practice, Thatcherism was always more pragmatic than its rhetoric suggested, accepting (grudgingly) that the state would have a role to play in funding the arts, even if the machinery, purpose and amount of government support would have to alter.[5] Virtually all of the most significant and influential theatre of the post-war period had been produced with the aid of public subsidy, and – with the possible exception of the modern musical – this continued to be the case in the UK and in most other European countries.

The reshaping of the relationship between the arts and government and the shift from public subsidy to private patronage did not happen all at once, nor was its success smooth and assured. The role of the then Arts Council of Great Britain as the main channel of public subsidy to the theatre was crucial in this process. During the period of initial ideological fervour (the early and mid-1980s) the Conservative government's objectives were achieved partly by 'encouraging' companies to seek private sources by attacking levels of subsidy or withdrawing it altogether. In 1980 the government imposed a cut in the Arts Council's budget of £1 million, which led it to withdraw grants from forty-one arts organisations, eighteen of which were theatre companies, amidst a great

---

4 Quoted in Ruth-Blandina M. Quinn, *Public Policy and the Arts: A Comparative Study of Great Britain and Ireland* (Aldershot: Ashgate, 1998), p. 179.
5 Actual levels of public subsidy since 1979 are controversial, partly because of disagreement over how the rate of inflation should be measured. See D. Keith Peacock, *Thatcher's Theatre: British Theatre and Drama in the Eighties* (London: Westport Press, 1999), p. 44.

deal of opprobrium. In 1983 the Council – getting into its ideological stride – published *The Glory of the Garden*, a policy document that signalled a desire to decentralise the arts, but within existing, if not declining, resources. The report also recommended the closure of the Royal Court Theatre in London, since the 1950s the theatre most consistently associated with new writing, and of several other companies. The Royal Court survived, but others were not so lucky, and by the middle of the decade the casualty list – which included 7:84 Theatre Company (England), one of the most influential socialist companies of the 1970s – had begun to lengthen.

By most indicators, the level of subsidy rose (though not substantially) in the early 1990s, as the monetarism of the Thatcher years was modified in the face of recession and the cooling of ideological fervour that accompanied her departure. By the mid-1990s, however, the cumulative effect of stand-still, or reduced, funding was hard to avoid. In 1993, for example, faced with the necessity of making cuts totalling £5 million across the board for the following year, the Arts Council proposed to remove entirely grant aid from ten theatres, mostly in the regions (Bristol Old Vic; Belgrade Theatre, Coventry; Palace Theatre, Watford; Plymouth Theatre Royal were among those targeted). The Council withdrew the plan following considerable public and press criticism, opting instead to impose a 2 per cent cut on all its drama clients – the familiar tactic of 'equal misery' for all.

The situation for particular companies was often complicated by the fact that they also relied on funding from local authorities. In some cases – the Greater London Council (GLC) in the early 1980s is the best example – authorities more than compensated for the decline in central funding. But controls on local spending and the abolition in the mid-1980s of the large (and Labour-dominated) Metropolitan Authorities in Britain's major urban areas curtailed these sources as well. The combination of restrictions on funding from both central and local government was felt most acutely by building-based companies and receiving theatres, particularly outside London. Between 1988 and 1993 an estimated twenty-one theatres, in places as geographically and socially diverse as Lowestoft, Edinburgh, Basildon and Rhyl, had either gone dark or were being used for other purposes.[6]

Theatre and the new economics

The struggle over subsidy did not, of course, occur in a vacuum, and by the mid-1980s the terms of reference of the new economics-led debates about arts

6 *Guardian* (29 Nov. 1993), 8.

funding were altering rapidly. The Thatcher governments pursued economic policies that led to the decimation of traditional manufacturing industry, leaving a chasm to be filled by the new service industries, which included the arts. As John Myerscough, who produced the first rigorous attempt in the UK to measure the economic benefits of the arts to society, argued:

> We live in an era of industrial restructuring characterised by the growing importance of the service industries (especially in the areas of finance, knowledge, travel and entertainment), and of industries based on new technologies exploiting information and the media . . . regional policy must concentrate on attracting service industries as a more urgent aim than winning manufacturing plant. The arts fit naturally into this frame.[7]

Myerscough and his team at the Policy Studies Institute estimated that £10.5 million was spent on the 'cultural leisure market' between 1974 and 1984, about 5.4 per cent of total consumer spending.[8] His arguments provided a strong case for both public and private patronage, using a language that both the government and business could understand. However, his analysis rests on a very broad definition of what constitutes a 'benefit', and – more importantly – what constitutes 'culture'. For the arts as traditionally conceived only account for a relatively small part of the 'cultural leisure market', and Myerscough's model has been attacked for its expansive reach.[9] His analysis also masked an increasing diversification, even fragmentation, within the ecology of theatre, and did not distinguish in any significant sense between the economic structure and cultural objectives of a small touring company and those of, say, a large commercial management controlling several West End theatres.

However, the wider implications of Myerscough's arguments were pervasive, and they resonated with other kinds of political and policy initiatives. In 1988 the Arts Council published *An Urban Renaissance. The Role of the Arts in Urban Regeneration: The Case for Increased Public and Private Sector Co-Operation*, which argued that the arts were vital to the regeneration of Britain's decaying and crisis-ridden inner cities. 'The arts create a climate of optimism', the report insisted, and provide a means of 'helping people believe in themselves and their community again.'[10] The political case for accepting this policy was not lost on a government anxious about both the state of British cities and

---

7 John Myerscough, *The Economic Importance of the Arts in Britain* (London: Policy Studies Institute, 1988), p. 2.
8 *Ibid.*, p. 12.
9 See Robert Hewison, *Culture and Consensus: Arts and Politics Since 1940* (London: Methuen, 1997), pp. 277–8.
10 Quoted in Peacock, *Thatcher's Theatre*, p. 54.

its own popularity, and major cities were quick to capitalise on it. Glasgow, for example, seized the opportunity to rebrand itself during its year as the European City of Culture (1990), instigating a twelve-month programme of arts (and especially theatre) activities as the 'flagship' of its attempts to attract new economic investment. Likewise, the regeneration of Birmingham and Manchester in the 1990s included major arts developments.

A further important factor in the funding equation was the establishment of the National Lottery. Neither wholly 'private' nor 'public' in the traditional sense, the Lottery had a significant impact on the arts, and especially theatre, from its inception in 1994. Camelot, the company formed to set up and manage its operation, was granted a seven-year licence, which was renewed after a bitter and controversial competition with Richard Branson's contending company, People's Lottery, in 2000. As well as generating healthy profits for Camelot, the Lottery was intended as a means of distributing money to 'good causes' – that is to say, those areas of social and cultural life impoverished by fourteen years of diminishing public funding – including the arts. Camelot had estimated that some £9 billion for 'good causes' would be generated between 1994 and 2000; in fact, in excess of £10 billion was raised in this period.[11] Much of the money intended for the arts was distributed through the Arts Council, which saw its role as a conduit of public funds to the professional arts transformed. In 1995–6, for example, the Council distributed some £340 million of Lottery funds; in the same period, its total grant-in-aid from the Exchequer was £191 million. Lottery money was allocated largely for capital projects (new buildings, the renovation of existing ones and major items of equipment), a policy intended to protect the level of Arts Council funding, which mainly provided revenue grants for running costs. One immediate effect of this policy was an epidemic of new building projects, belatedly remedying the chronic decline in the architectural fabric of British theatre, which was one stark legacy of diminishing public subsidy after 1979. But the fact that the Lottery was prevented from paying for people – artists to work in the new buildings – created a new set of problems, to which I shall return.

Sponsorship

Weaning the arts from their dependence on public subsidy was only one thread of the economic story; another was the promotion of private patronage, or

11 See Quinn, *Public Policy and the Arts*, pp. 258–9; Chris Smith, *Creative Britain* (London: Faber & Faber, 1998), pp. 114–22.

was still forced to close, temporarily, its experimental auditorium, the Theatre Upstairs. These were high-profile examples of a general retrenchment that gripped the theatre for the rest of the decade and beyond, with demonstrable effects on the scale, and type, of theatre produced.

Reshaping the repertoire

In an extensive survey of the theatre repertoire across the country in the 1980s and early 1990s, John Bull noted how reliant the main London and regional subsidised companies had become on the same diet of musicals, West End successes (recent and older), school set texts (usually Shakespeare) and the plays of Alan Ayckbourn.[18] David Edgar observed caustically that 'if you went to the theatre in England [in 1988] and didn't see *The Tempest* or *Gaslight* they gave you a small cash prize'.[19] One effect of this narrowing was to drive new plays off the mainstream stages, particularly in the regions. The problem, which had become apparent by the end of the 1980s, was made worse by the recession of the early 1990s. Between 1978 and 1985 new writing constituted about 12 per cent of the repertoire of the main London and regional repertory theatres; between 1985 and 1990 the figure dropped to 7 per cent. In 1994 eighty-seven playwrights wrote to the *Guardian* protesting at the lack of new work on regional stages, citing the new economics as a principal reason.[20]

However, the decline in new writing was subsequently reversed around the end of the recession of the early 1990s. Between 1993 and 1997 new plays represented over 15 per cent of the repertoire of building-based companies, no doubt contributing to an overall increase in box office takings (rising from below 50 per cent of revenue in the late 1980s to 57 per cent in 1996–7).[21] Beyond the main stages, new work was much better represented in the fringe / alternative touring sector – even if new *writing* was not – through an aesthetic of self-generated theatre, often 'devised' rather than 'scripted', which was largely the product of a collaborative ethic and new kinds of training.

With large casts and multi-location sets becoming economically unviable for many theatres, writers began to trim their ambitions to fit. An Arts Council-funded enquiry into professional theatre chaired by Sir Kenneth Cork in 1986

---

18 John Bull, *Stage Right: Crisis and Recovery in Mainstream British Theatre* (London: Macmillan, 1994). See especially chapter 3.
19 David Edgar (ed.), *State of Play* (London: Faber, 1999), p. 19.
20 *Guardian* (21 Nov. 1994).
21 See *Playwrights: A Species Still Endangered?* (London: Theatre Writers' Union, 1987); Edgar, *State of Play*, pp. 19–20.

reported that 'Theatres do not employ as many actors as they did' and argued that this was the principal reason why productions of classical plays (defined as non-Shakespearean plays written before 1945) had declined from 15 per cent of the national subsidised repertoire in 1979–80 to 8 per cent in 1984–5.[22] A snapshot survey of the Theatre Management Association's play lists for 1986–7 indicated that 'although premières in this period were presented in houses seating more than 500 . . . the average cast size of new plays was 6.9 (men's parts averaging 4.3 and women's parts 2.6) and only 36 per cent were written for more than one set'.[23]

The growing insecurity of many theatre companies in the period was evident in the increase in the number of adaptations (principally of novels), rising from 5 per cent of the repertoire in 1979–80 to 20 per cent in the late 1980s, presented on both main stages and studio floors, often with considerable success. Adaptations were seen as a way of using the past to comment on the present, and companies such as Shared Experience (founded 1975) made them a central part of a successful and well-regarded artistic policy. However, the adaptation may also be the perfect vehicle for a theatre nervously in search of a secure audience. Reliant on a well-known, often canonical text, and frequently related to the current school syllabus, the adaptation is a key post-modern cultural product, combining the 'known' with the 'novel' (pun intended), and offering the audience the pleasure of familiarity with a 'new twist' provided by the transfer to another medium. The Royal Shakespeare Company alleviated its financial problems in the mid-1980s with a string of West End transfers of adaptations, such as *Dangerous Liaisons* (1985, from a novel by de Laclos) and *Les Misérables* (1985, from Victor Hugo's novel).

Both tendencies – to make money and rework a classical text in a modern context – were apparent in the RSC's *Nicholas Nickleby*, adapted from Dickens's novel by David Edgar in 1980. For Edgar, the novel had a great deal to say about Britain in the 1980s; 'the book presents, in a wonderfully rich and vivid way, the social conflicts of a time, the 1830s, that are in many ways comparable to our own'.[24] Written in a fluid narrative style, with minimal sets, the production emphasised the novel's social critique of thrusting individualism, a growing trait in 1980s Britain. Despite its length (eight and a half hours, across three performances) *Nicholas Nickleby* was a critical and commercial success.

22 Sir Kenneth Cork, *Theatre IS for All: Report of the Enquiry into Professional Theatre in England, 1986* (London: Arts Council of Great Britain, 1986), p. 88.
23 *Playwrights: A Species Still Endangered?*, p. 44.
24 David Edgar, 'Adapting Nickleby', in *The Second Time as Farce* (London: Lawrence & Wishart, 1988), p. 145.

Figure 19.1 The modern musical triumphant. On the barricades of *Les Misérables*, Barbican Theatre, London, 1985.

It transferred to America in 1981 and was filmed for television by Channel 4 in 1983. The production may have offered a critique of the values of capitalism, but it also demonstrated how a company like the RSC could adapt to those same values.

Subsidised companies became increasingly ingenious in finding ways to survive and prosper in the new theatrical marketplace. For example, a new spirit of collaboration occurred, often between companies from the same sector of the industry, and the motives for this were not necessarily purely economic. Repertory companies combined to produce plays that subsequently toured: in spring–summer 2000, for example, the Palace Theatre, Watford, the Salisbury Playhouse and the Belgrade Theatre, Coventry, together mounted a production of Brian Friel's *Translations*. There were also imaginative collaborations between different kinds of theatre, particularly building-based companies and smaller, touring theatres. Theatre de Complicite, for example, had a close association with the Royal National Theatre through the 1990s, which saw the company develop work for all three of the National's auditoria; and the RNT had close relations with several regional theatres, showcasing productions from the Sheffield theatres (the Crucible, Lyceum and Studio) and the West Yorkshire Playhouse in 2000.

Other strategies involved collaborations between the commercial and sub-sidised theatre sectors, with private and public monies combining in various approaches to co-production. The long traditions of try-outs and transfers to the West End were augmented by national and, occasionally, regional reper-tory theatres – and linked into the new global economy. The crucial example here was *Les Misérables*, which was staged in 1985 by the Royal Shakespeare Company, directed by Trevor Nunn in a co-production with the commercial producer Cameron Mackintosh. Presented initially at the Barbican, the pro-duction was scheduled for a West End transfer from its inception, and as the millennium turned it was still earning an estimated £1 million a year for the RSC. Stephen Daldry's expressionist reworking of J. B. Priestley's *An Inspector Calls* for the Royal National Theatre was first staged in the Lyttelton audito-rium in 1993, transferred to the West End, and then to Broadway. A touring version has since covered the globe and the production was still in the West End in 2001.

A relationship with a commercial producer was important to smaller, and more financially precarious, subsidised companies as well. The resurrected and reformed Theatre Workshop, based at the Theatre Royal, Stratford East, forged a mutually beneficial relationship with Cameron Mackintosh in order to transfer the musical *Five Guys Named Moe* to the West End in the early 1990s. The critical and commercial success of the production helped to alleviate, though not resolve, the financial difficulties faced by the company. In 1993 Philip Hedley, its artistic director, noted that Theatre Workshop suffered from a mismatch between its level of subsidy and artistic policy, which, reflecting a commitment to its local communities, included eight premières a year. The arrangement with Mackintosh, argued Hedley, 'has paid off our deficit . . . and allowed us to increase our salaries a little . . . But when those profits dry up we will be faced with a quarter of a million pounds annual gap in our finances'.[25]

The fringe and alternative theatre sectors suffered some of the most rad-ical effects of the new economic strictures of the 1980s and 1990s. However, though the philosophical and organisational basis of many companies was challenged by the contraction of public subsidy, several thrived. The new commercially oriented structures favoured some small, flexible and economic companies, driven by a single individual (or small group of collaborators) and with a distinctive 'brand image' – companies such as Theatre de Complicite

25 Philip Hedley, 'Invisible dangers', *Guardian* (10 Feb. 1993), Review section, 4.

and Forced Entertainment in England, Brith Gof in Wales and Communicado in Scotland. Complicite, for example, developed from a small-scale touring company to forge a presence on the international theatre circuit – its 1999 production, *Mnemonic*, was commissioned by the Salzburg Festival – apparently without compromising either its working practices or distinctive artistic policies.

Commercial theatre and the musical

One part of British theatre primed for the new language and priorities of monetarism was the commercial theatre, much of which thrived in the period, although in a very particular genre: the modern international musical. This phenomenon, originating in the West End, was the most visible symbol of the commodification of British theatre, and its commercial success was astonishing. British musicals were seen around the world, dominating the major theatre centres of many capital cities, including Broadway. The phenomenon was initially a handful of extraordinarily omnipresent productions, typified by the shows of composer-producer Andrew Lloyd Webber. More than any other development in the theatre since 1979, the success of the musical was an example of the transformation of the means of cultural production in the global marketplace.

Labour-intensive, often subject to high rents and with a product that cannot be 'reproduced' indefinitely to achieve economies of scale, theatre has often required patronage, public and private, because it seemed a poor commercial prospect. Lloyd Webber, Cameron Mackintosh and others – like Wilson Barrett in the 1890s – demonstrated how the theatre could overcome its traditional economic constraints, this time by mounting several productions of the same show, opening simultaneously in global cities, accompanied by the aggressive marketing of both the show and its spin-off merchandising to increase profitability. These musicals stimulated demand to the point where their longevity, based on guaranteed audiences, was unique in the post-war period. The statistics are impressive. Lloyd Webber's *Cats*, for example, was originally produced (1981) with the financial backing of two hundred investors, some putting in as little as £1,000 each to produce the £450,000 cost of staging the show: by 1994, the investors were rewarded with annual profits of 200 per cent of their original investment.[26] By 1992 *Cats* had grossed more than Steven Spielberg's

26 *Guardian* (12 March 1994), 34.

ET, which was at the time the most profitable film ever made.[27] By 1999 Lloyd Webber's *Phantom of the Opera* had grossed twice as much worldwide as James Cameron's film *Titanic* (1998). Newspaper listings on any day in this period indicated just how central musicals had become to the internationally oriented, tourist-driven metropolitan theatre culture. Of the forty-six London productions listed in the *Guardian* in August 2001, twenty-two were musicals, including *The Lion King*, *My Fair Lady* and *The Witches of Eastwick*, occupying some of the West End's largest theatres (the Lyceum, Drury Lane and the Prince of Wales, respectively). And there were many more musicals about to open, making the first year of the new millennium in this respect an unprecedented one.

Politically, the impact of the West End musical was conservative, largely because the form privileged effect above content. As John Bull has noted: 'The prevailing tone. . . . is one of social irrelevance, of an unwillingness to discuss, or an unconcern with, contemporary political issues.'[28] Instead, it provided audiences with high production values and spectacle, a 'conspicuous consumption' that, irrespective of the specific subject or story of particular shows, was the main source of the genre's appeal. Spectacle of this sort has an ideological impact, since it celebrates absorption over reflection, the impact of the signifier over what it might signify.

The ideology of the 'spectacular' was particularly apparent in musicals that had an ostensible 'content'. *Les Misérables* was a case in point. Produced initially at the RSC's London home, the Barbican, in October 1985, the show transferred – by prior arrangement – to the Palace Theatre in December that year. The popular appeal of *Les Misérables* was undeniable, and it was still running in the early years of the twenty-first century. But the critical response was less enthusiastic and raised important issues, not least of which was the appropriateness of a major subsidised theatre using its resources to mount a show that could have been produced entirely commercially. One consistent criticism was, indeed, that spectacle triumphed over content. Hugo's novel is an impassioned critique of poverty, but, as Suzie Mackenzie commented in *Time Out*: 'You are not asked to like *Les Misérables*. You are asked to admire it . . . on the grounds of melodrama, connivance and artifice . . . We are arrested by the spectacle of what we see, not moved by the pain of human suffering.'[29]

---

27 *Ministering to the Arts*, p. 7.

28 Bull, *Stage Right*, p. 17.

29 Suzie Mackenzie, *Time Out* (17 Oct. 1985), in *London Theatre Record* (25 Sept.–8 Oct. 1985), 993.

Or as Michael Billington argued in the *Guardian*, 'what you will remember is the spectacle, not the spiritual conflict . . . The real excitement comes from watching pure command of theatrical effect'.[30]

The modern international musical illustrates the ways in which the component parts of the British theatre industry were operating in different galaxies. The Really Useful Theatre Company (Lloyd Webber's production group) bears as much relationship to, say, a small touring theatre company as does a multinational corporation to a corner-shop. Yet, whilst theatre became an increasingly fragmented industry, theatre practitioners frequently worked across the commercial and subsidised sectors (and across live and electronic media) and often shared a common education and training. Indeed, the actors, directors and designers who were responsible for some of the most spectacular commercial successes did most of their work in subsidised theatres: Trevor Nunn and Stephen Daldry, for example. But damage to one part of the ecology of theatre has an impact on another. Even Cameron Mackintosh – one of the most successful impresarios of the post-World War Two period, grown very rich from collaborations between the commercial and subsidised sectors – found himself writing in 1996:

> The health of our national arts is now at a watershed. Over the last few years, the fabric of British theatre, built up over so many decades, has been eroded to a point where the system is like a worn sock . . . Theatre's grass roots are [suffering]. Roots that people need and support: theatre in education, school's programmes, flourishing regional theatres where Shakespearean productions are properly cast, grants for drama students.[31]

Yet the relationship between different sectors was not one between equals. With an emphasis on profit for its own sake, on spectacle and social irrelevance, the musical became a paradigm of late twentieth-century theatre, and the 'leakiness' between different sectors of the industry ensured that the practices that made the musical so successful seeped into British theatre culture as a whole.

David Edgar has argued that the musical was 'the Trojan horse by which the consumer-oriented principles of the market were infiltrated into the subsidised theatre'.[32] This was particularly true of the major subsidised theatre companies, which operated, at least partially, in the same economic league as

30 Michael Billington, *Guardian* (10 Oct. 1985), in *London Theatre Record* (25 Sept.–8 Oct. 1985), 996.
31 Sir Cameron Mackintosh, 'No public subsidy, no West End', *Arts Council of England: Annual Report 1995–96* (London: Arts Council of England, 1996), p. 12.
32 Edgar, *State of Play*, p. 21.

the larger commercial managements. The RNT's rediscovery of the virtues of the American musical – *Carousel* (1992) and *Sweeney Todd* (1993), for example – was simultaneously an acknowledgement of the artistic vitality of a popular form and a shrewd commercial move in a London theatre market in which American tourists were a significant target. Indeed, the musical became a regular feature in the RNT's repertoire (five were produced between 1999 and 2001). The form also affected the repertoire of theatres outside London, anxious to find a 'success' that would please local audiences and generate a West End/London transfer: for example, the West Yorkshire Playhouse's *Singing in the Rain*, which transferred to the RNT in 2000.

Commerce and cultural politics

The commodification of contemporary theatre had an impact on the ways in which theatre was thought of as a political, social and cultural intervention. Since the eruption of the new wave playwrights in 1956 at the Royal Court and Joan Littlewood's productions with the first Theatre Workshop, one of the main achievements of post-war theatre was its challenge to dominant ideological assumptions about class, gender and politics from a variety of political and cultural perspectives. These were both liberal and reformist (social realism of the 1950s), revolutionary (the Marxist touring companies of the 1970s, such as 7:84) or variously radical (most feminist, gay and black theatre since 1970). In questioning many of the common-sense assumptions of post-war politics and culture, much of British theatre was firmly anti-hegemonic. From 1979 that function was more difficult to maintain. Commodification was not likely to have made theatre *generally* more independent in a free market, but ironically it may have provided conditions for the fulfilment of some of the political objectives of companies that opposed it, by partly redrawing the space in which a politically and culturally oppositional theatre could operate. Commodification has not been a simple or remorseless process, nor has it made such theatre impossible. However, the reshaping of the cultural politics of theatre under the pressure of the new economics was felt across the board.

The demise of large-cast plays in the drive to save money, for example, meant that one kind of political play all but disappeared, with only a very few such productions appearing on the largest subsidised stages. Several of the key left-wing theatre figures of the 1970s had used the resources of the larger provincial theatres and the national companies to mount plays conceived on a large canvas. These 'State of the Nation' plays, such as Howard Brenton and David Hare's *Brassneck* (1973) and David Edgar's *Maydays* (1981), represented the complexities of social and political change in a direct way. However, whilst the 1980s and 1990s saw the continuation and development of other kinds of political writing, the prevailing ideological climate made such drama liable to misinterpretation. A salutary example of how monetarism shaped the reception, as well as the production, of theatre in this period was the fate of Caryl Churchill's *Serious Money* (1987). The play is a satire on Thatcherism set in the heart of the new financial economy of the City of London. Modelled on seventeenth-century city comedies (which dealt with the manifestations of early capitalism), it is a high-energy thriller with songs. Produced initially at the Royal Court, it was a critical and popular success and transferred to the West End. In this new context, the play attracted an audience of the people it attacked, causing several reviewers to comment that its energy and wit – though clearly intended as a critique of Thatcherite values – was enjoyed as a celebration of them. As Steve Grant noted in his review of a Wyndham Theatre performance in *Time Out*, 'The braying, knowing laughter that greeted some of the more telling and cynical one-liners . . . provides the key to its problem'.[33]

The smaller-scale touring sector of theatre suffered particularly from the new demands from the Arts Council and other grant-giving bodies. Often collectively organised, with clear cultural and political objectives, many fringe/alternative companies found that the 'administrative' changes demanded by the Arts Council had political effects. John McGrath describes how the Scottish Arts Council in 1989 threatened the removal of its grant from 7:84 (Scotland) unless the company agreed to replace 'most of the company's board with people with – and I quote – "business skills, public relations expertise, and accountancy and legal skills; people who would be politically objective about the work of the company"'.[34] Repudiating such 'objectivity', McGrath resigned as Artistic Director.

At another level, the cultural politics of theatre was affected by the new Lottery money, which did not change the priorities of the funding system or resolve many of its contradictions. Indeed, one effect of the first wave of Lottery awards was to draw attention to the bias in arts funding towards the established 'high' arts and London. The decision to award the Royal Opera House a total of £78.5 million in 1995 was greeted with hostility and derision (although in that same year the Arts Council awarded £41.1 million to the Lowry Centre in Salford and £20 million towards the creation of a theatre and gallery complex in Milton Keynes).[35] The Council/government had also insisted on a policy

33 Steve Grant, *Time Out* (15 July 1987), in *London Theatre Record* (2–15 July 1987), 824.
34 John McGrath quoted in Lavender, 'Theatre in crisis', p. 211.
35 See *Arts Council of England: Annual Report 1995–96* for further details.

of matched funding, whereby 25 per cent of the costs of a Lottery-approved project had to come from other sources, mirroring a principle adopted in distributing other arts funding. This continued a strategy of favouring those organisations that were successful enough to have access to other sources, and it placed organisations in competition with each other for the same limited resources – thus reproducing many of the same contradictions and tensions caused by the rush for sponsorship a decade earlier. As Ian Rickson, artistic director of the English Stage Company at the Royal Court, noted: 'If all the current Lottery projects were to be realised, private funding would have to increase by 15 times its present amount'.[36]

The example of the Royal Court illustrates other, yet more political, ironies. In 2000 the theatre completed a major refurbishment with the assistance of a Lottery award and a large grant from the Jerwood Foundation, a charitable trust with strong connections to the Court. At one point in the process, however, the Foundation insisted that a £3 million grant would be dependent on the theatre changing its name to the Royal Court Jerwood Theatre – a particularly difficult condition for a theatre with a putative radical identity, and one which exemplified the political dimensions of the funding system in a spectacular way (eventually, the Foundation settled for the naming of one of the two auditoria in the revamped building as the Jerwood).

The impact of commerce on the cultural politics of theatre was also registered in the transformation of theatre's institutional and presentational practices. Again, the modern international musical led the way. Cameron Mackintosh is reputed to have said that the 'real star of *Cats* is the poster',[37] a comment that indicated just how important merchandising had become to fixing the meanings of the theatrical performance. The poster creates a logo, which both signals and 'stands in for' the show, offering a vicarious experience of the original that aspires to continue the purchaser's consumption of the performance. Such logos are the mark of 'brands' in the sense that Naomi Klein uses the word in her discussion of the marketing strategies of modern multi-nationals: 'rather than serving as a guarantee of value on a product, the brand itself has increasingly become the product, a free-standing idea pasted onto innumerable surfaces'.[38]

The 'branding' of theatres was also evident in the transformation of theatre architecture that accompanied the rash of new, largely Lottery-funded,

---

36 Quoted by Michael Billington in 'Thanks but . . .', *Guardian* (25 Nov. 1998), 13.
37 Quoted in BBC Radio 4, *Ministering to the Arts*, p. 7.
38 Naomi Klein, 'The tyranny of the brands', *New Statesman* (24 Jan. 2000), 25; also Naomi Klein, *No Logo* (London: Flamingo / HarperCollins, 2000).

theatre building that took place in the second half of the 1990s. There was a new emphasis on the front stage areas – foyers, bookshops, cafés – as a means of providing a visual identity as well as attracting audiences. This undoubtedly improved the appearance and accessibility of many theatres, although the appeal was often to the young and professional classes. Theatres also began to present other kinds of activities, and foyer cabaret, film screenings and the presentation of concerts became familiar parts of the annual programme of many regional playhouses. In the rush to be venues of general social interaction, theatres perhaps lost something of their specific identities as theatres. One result of this may have been, as Baz Kershaw has argued, the privileging of 'theatre-going' as a self-sufficient social activity over 'any enjoyment of the production and performance itself'.[39]

In a context where the single-purpose theatre building began to give way to multi-purpose venues, companies became very adept at presenting themselves in different ways to diverse constituencies. The self-confident and well-regarded West Yorkshire Playhouse, the last civic theatre built without Lottery money (1990), was clear that its role was not only to provide for the general 'community' of Leeds, but also to target specific groups. It was apparent from the theatre's web site, for example, that it was seeking to address a range of interests, from the business community to local schools and teenagers.[40] To an earlier generation of theatre directors, this would have seemed contradictory, but in the post-Thatcher era it looked like a sensible strategy to increase audiences, make the best use of the building and pursue a socially relevant policy.

A living theatre?

Many theatre companies survived the new economic policies and commercial imperative inaugurated by monetarism, though they may not have thrived. Yet also for many as the millennium approached, the long-term future was in doubt. Accepting that 'the theatre was in crisis partly as a result of years of inadequate funding',[41] the Arts Council began to put a new national policy into place, financed by increased public subsidy. It was encouraged in this

---

39 Baz Kershaw, *The Radical in Performance: Between Brecht and Baudrillard* (London: Routledge, 1999), p. 46.
40 West Yorkshire Playhouse (Nov. 2001): http://www.wyp.co.uk/ (30 Nov. 2001).
41 Arts Council of England, 'The next stage: Arts Council sets out new vision for theatre', press release (28 May 2000).

by the new Labour government, elected in 1997 and re-elected in 2001. The transformation of the existing Department of Heritage into the Ministry of Culture, Arts, Media and Sport was one of the first acts of the incoming government, enshrining an inclusive definition of culture in state structures and policies. Chris Smith, the first secretary of state for the new ministry from 1997 to 2001, was an enthusiastic champion of the 'cultural industries', seeing the inclusiveness of the definition of the term as necessary to the success of its component parts. This thinking provided a new justification for public subsidy, in which the older arguments about excellence and access were inserted into a new, forward-looking post-industrial framework. 'The intrinsic cultural value of creativity sits side by side with, and acts in synergy with, the economic opportunities that are now opening up',[42] and governments, once more, need not be ashamed of subsidising the arts.

Although constrained by a commitment to contain government finances within existing limits for the first two years of its life, Labour announced in 2000 a 'Comprehensive Spending Review', which set out a phased increase in public spending across the board, including for the arts. In its response to the new dispensation, *A Living Theatre – Delivering the National Policy for Theatre in England*, the Arts Council announced that theatre would be a major beneficiary of this state largesse, with a planned increase of £12 million in 2002–3 rising to £25 million in 2003–4 (and after).[43] The policy aimed to benefit over 190 organisations, with the majority of funding going to companies that demonstrated innovation and 'audience development'. This went some way towards rebalancing the theatre ecology, distorted by the emphasis on capital spending within Lottery schemes. Beneficiaries included the Oxford Playhouse (£201,000 for new in-house and touring productions), Theatre de Complicite (£113,529 to develop its international collaborations) and the Afro-Caribbean-led Talawa (£124,128 for its educational programme and producing capability). In arguing and winning the case for increased funding the Council accepted, somewhat belatedly, the consequences of policies that earlier it had been happy to pursue. This was unlikely, however, to alter the power relationship between subsidised theatres and the Council, which seemed determined to centralise and consolidate its power. For example, in 2001 it circulated for consultation plans (since enacted) to disband the Regional Arts Boards, replacing them with slimmed-down regional offices under its control.

---

42 Smith, *Creative Britain*, p. 26.
43 Following statistics from Arts Council of England, *A Living Theatre – Delivering the National Policy for Theatre in England* (London: Arts Council of England, 2001).

Despite these cavils, the 'new money' was undoubtedly welcomed by the theatre industry, but it may have been too late to repair the damage done to its political and cultural role by the processes of commodification. One defence of the new economic régime was that the emphasis on commercial viability made managements and artistic directors more responsive to their audiences, the 'consumers'. This may, in certain instances, have been so, but the price for pursuing audiences in this way was high, for the commodification of theatre did not only involve a reconstruction of the relationship between practitioner and funder, but also between theatres and audiences.

Within the ideology of the market, the theatre audience became a kind of abstraction, in which people are consumers, atomised and individuated, their collectivity written out of the story. This can be seen as a democratic development, an empowerment of the individual spectator, since the market does not (or does not appear to) recognise any other value than the power of individual consumer choice. From one point of view, questions of class, politics, gender and ethnicity are removed from the debate: we need not concern ourselves with them, for if we only follow the logic of the market and pursue the biggest audience compatible with the greatest profit, then everyone will be satisfied. From another viewpoint, such distinctions between consumers are vitally important, for to be successful theatre companies must become ever more sophisticated in their means of targeting the 'right' audience for particular shows. Hence, new technologies, as well as new marketing strategies, allowed the amorphous 'audience' to be conceived as a highly differentiated collection of interest groups, each of which could be individually addressed. However, audiences constituted in this way are not identified with particular social values or a specific cultural identity, but conceived mainly in terms of patterns of consumption.

Paradoxically, despite two decades of market-driven reforms, theatre audiences were getting smaller: it has been estimated that between 1991 and 1998 theatre attendances fell by 30 per cent while ticket prices rose by 50 per cent.[44] There is a deep-rooted historical problem indicated here, for the long-term decline of theatre audiences in an electronic age predates 1979 and is not amenable to easy solutions. The British theatre often found its audience, or rather audiences, in the post-war period, but – with the telling exception of the modern musical – it normally achieved this when it forged a distinctive political (in the broadest sense) and cultural relationship with specific constituencies – women's/feminist theatre, for example, or black or gay

---

44 Quoted in Edgar, *State of Play*, p. 3.

theatre – that is to say, when it recognised that questions about audience are ultimately, and intimately, connected to a cultural politics. The processes of commodification have not secured financial independence for the theatre based on increased audiences within the market. They may, however, prove yet to be a very effective way of containing theatre's radical, noisy, disruptive and anti-hegemonic possibilities.

20

New theatre for new times: decentralisation, innovation and pluralism, 1975–2000

SIMON JONES

1988: the style and substance of 'New Times'

In 1988 three events took place that characterised the *Zeitgeist* of the decade and marked as clear a break with the cultural and theatrical practices of the 1960s and 1970s as the Conservative Party victory in May 1979 had signalled in British politics. Firstly, in October the magazine *Marxism Today* produced an overview of the impact of recent developments in industrial capitalism on global economies and societies: it provocatively entitled its survey 'New Times'. This followed hard upon its response to the successes of the 'new' and 'radical' Right, whose figureheads were President Ronald Reagan and Prime Minister Margaret Thatcher: a revised programme for the British Communist Party, which the *Morning Star* newspaper described as the 'final abandonment of . . . Marxist-Leninist principles'.[1] Secondly, that same month the style magazine *The Face* published its 'Killer 100th Issue!', offering 200 pages of quintessentially post-modern bricolage, in which Becks beer sponsorship was effortlessly sutured to harrowing images of famine victims, and lists of sound-bites haphazardly juxtaposed London's Docklands with Japan and Reagan with Trouble Funk, the 'hippest groove on the globe'.[2] Its art director, Neville Brody, had famously described this wilful deconstruction of journalistic and narrative coherence as 'Every typeface tells its own lie'.[3] Remarkably, the magazine's penchant for abandoning conventional journalistic analysis in favour of lists of 'bullet-points' was echoed in *Marxism Today*'s 'New Times' binary listing:

Fordism	Post-Fordism
Modern	Post-modern
Futurism	Nostalgia

1 Richard Gott, 'A new way forward', *Guardian* (Oct., 1988).
2 *The Face* 100 (Oct. 1988), 18, 88, 110–11.
3 *Ibid.* p. 8–9.

Production	Consumption
Self-control	Remote control
Depth	Surface
Belief	Credit
Elvis	Michael Jackson
Determinism	The arbitrary
Angst	Boredom
Free Love	The free market[4]

And the list went on. In effect, both *The Face* and *Marxism Today* – two very different publications with very different readerships – came to surprisingly similar conclusions, in surprisingly similar forms, about the paradigm shifts underway in late capitalism and its cultures.

The third event had happened in August, unremarked except by a few theatre reviewers. Howard Barker's four-and-a-half-hour epic rewriting of the Helen of Troy myth, *The Bite of the Night*, had its première in the Pit at London's Barbican Theatre in a production by the Royal Shakespeare Company. Variously described by the critics as a 'monumental slab of self-indulgence' or 'a sternly demanding evening of bunker theatre in the aftermath of war, dispiritingly bolted to the Barbican vaults in the wretched Pit',[5] this play, more than any other theatrical opening of the decade, marked a truly radical break with its progenitors and the past. From where had this monster of performance emerged? Why did it provoke such passionate responses? And how did its aesthetics express the broader cultural and economic shifts more completely and disturbingly than the provocations in *Marxism Today* and *The Face*? Can any coherent set of features be said to characterise such cultural decentring, fragmentation, pluralism?

Political antecedents: the Brechtian legacy

In the 1970s Trevor Griffiths's plays, such as *The Party* (1973) and *Comedians* (1975), had been both highly successful on stage and television *and* highly rigorous in their broadly Marxist account of how contemporary social crises could be fully understood only through a class-based analysis of their historical causes.[6] Griffiths perhaps spoke on behalf of other socialist playwrights, and

---

4 Table prepared by Chris Granlund, *Marxism Today* (Oct., 1988).
5 Respectively, Charles Spencer, *Daily Telegraph* (7 Sept. 1988); Michael Coveney, *Financial Times* (16 Aug. 1988).
6 See John Bull, *New British Political Dramatists* (London: Macmillan, 1984), pp. 118–50; Colin Chambers and Mike Prior, *Playwright's Progress: Patterns of Postwar British Drama* (Oxford: Amber Lane, 1987), pp. 53–7; Janelle Reinelt, *After Brecht: British Epic Theatre* (Ann Arbor: University of Michigan Press, 1996), pp. 143–76.

gestured towards a broader consensus amongst radical theatre-makers, when in 1976 he said:

> I think, morally, capitalism was exhausted fifty to one hundred years ago . . . That's why my plays are never about the battle between socialism and capitalism. I take that as being decisively won by socialism. What I'm really seeking is a way forward. How do we transform the husk of capitalist meaning into the reality of socialist enterprise? The socialist future.[7]

David Edgar later described this consensus as 'homogeneous', implying that the majority of radical theatre practitioners believed in the progressive character of socialism and the value of attacking the 'false' ideology of 'bourgeois capitalism'. He admitted that much of this theatre preached largely to the converted, addressing 'middle-class' audiences in 'Arts Council-funded' theatres, many of whom worked in state institutions, such as education, local government or healthcare. It also indulged in biting the hand that fed it, as state-funded theatre-makers attacked the state.[8] Ironically, a direct result of such views was that playwrights like Griffiths began to see theatre as a lost cause, either politically 'safe' in West End musicals and revivals from the classical repertoire, or politically 'neutered' in playing radical new work to already radicalised 'old' audiences. State funding became a sign of political ineffectiveness: it demonstrated capitalism indulging its artists as proof that its values were 'superior' to those of Eastern Bloc Communism. Consequently, for any playwright with radical ambitions, theatre could only be the apprentice's art form, a stepping-stone to the really 'new' audience which was, unknowingly, in need of political education: the television viewers.

This kind of analysis galvanised radical theatre-makers into two types of response. First, there were those who aimed ultimately to reach mass audiences. For instance, many of Griffiths's and Edgar's plays were adapted for television and radio, such as the latter's *Destiny* (1976), an epic analysis of post-colonial Britain and the relationship between bourgeois democracy and the rise of neo-Nazis, premièred by the RSC and produced by the BBC as part of its flagship series *Play for Today*. These writers characterised their deployment of television's dominant mode – a profoundly conservative amalgam of

---

7 Trevor Griffiths, 'Transforming the husk of capitalism', in *New Theatre Voices of the Seventies*, ed. Simon Trussler (London: Methuen, 1981), p. 133.
8 David Edgar, 'Public theatre in a private age', *British Theatre Institute: Special Report 1* (London: British Theatre Institute, 1984); reprinted in an expanded version in David Edgar, *The Second Time as Farce: Reflections on the Drama of Mean Times* (London: Lawrence & Wishart, 1988), pp. 160–74.

theatrical naturalism and Hollywood narrative cinema – as an aesthetics of 'social realism'. Edgar's articulation is a model of clarity:

> Social-realism is obviously a synthesis of the surface perception of naturalism and the social analysis that underlies agit-prop plays. To explain, it is first necessary to be recognisable, and only then, having won the audience's trust, to place those recognisable phenomena within the context of a perceived political truth. It is indeed in this combination of recognition with perception that the political power of theatre lies.[9]

Griffiths was even more explicit:

> When you're trying to speak to large numbers of people who did not study literature at university, because they were getting on with productive work, and you're introducing fairly unfamiliar, dense and complex arguments into the fabric of the play, it's just an overwhelming imposition to present those arguments in unfamiliar forms.[10]

Radical form had to be abandoned in favour of radical content. The former could not be allowed to confuse the latter.

The second distinct kind of response had its most coherent advocate in Edward Bond, whose developing aesthetic shifted the political project in British theatre from hyper-naturalistic plays of contemporary working-class life to a developed form of Brechtian epic parable. *The Pope's Wedding* (1962) and *Saved* (1965), depicting the lives of the young working class, a subject familiar to both Bond and Royal Court audiences, emerged in the wake of the English Stage Company's championing of 'kitchen-sink' naturalism in the late 1950s and early 1960s. However, one notorious scene in *Saved* proved a turning point in the development of Bond's aesthetics. The ferocity of audience and critical reaction to the stoning to death of a baby in a pram by a group of young men surprised Bond, who had assumed spectators would be 'sympathetic to almost everyone in it'.[11] He said later in an interview: 'I know largely I'm writing for people who are not going to understand what I want to say, so this gives me a very difficult problem, because I know that all my plays have to go through the critical filter before they get to the audience.'[12] So, to tame the obfuscating hysteria provoked by these potential 'misreadings', he turned to the model

---

9 Edgar, *Second Time*, p. 171.
10 Quoted in Mike Poole and John Wyver, *Powerplays: Trevor Griffiths in Television* (London: British Film Institute, 1984), p. 3.
11 'A discussion with Edward Bond', *Gambit* 17 (1970), 20–2.
12 'Interview with Edward Bond', *Gambit* 17 (1970), 32.

of 'objective' spectatorship espoused by Brecht and sought progressively to incorporate a critical function into his drama, sometimes literally to bring the critic onto the stage.

This wariness of an audience's capacity for making a variety of interpretations of the same event, a fear of possible 'misunderstandings', was shared by many politically motivated playwrights, such as Edgar, Griffiths and John McGrath of 7:84 Theatre Company. Some, such as Howard Brenton, David Hare and McGrath, responded strategically by casting themselves in the role of director, then critic. And as interpretation became the key *political* dramaturgical problem, as it had been for earlier writers such as Shaw, their plays came to deal more frequently and explicitly with the function of art and the role of the artist. For example, Bond's *The Fool* (1975) was about the poet John Clare, Griffiths's *Comedians* (1975) about stand-up comedians and *Fatherland* (1981) about a singer-songwriter, and Brenton's *Bloody Poetry* (1984) about Byron and the Shelleys. Howard Barker's radio play *Scenes from an Execution* (1984), about a painter upsetting her patron the Doge of Venice, and his television play *Pity in History* (1985), about a stonemason during the English civil war, can be seen, in part, as responses to this sub-genre concerned with the political efficacy of the artist. Tellingly, even Tom Stoppard tackles the phenomenon – from an entirely different political perspective – in *The Real Thing* (1983), which includes a parody of a left-wing playwright whose political agenda is revealed as driven by 'private derangement'.[13]

Edward Bond's account of Shakespeare's final days in *Bingo* (1973) is a prescient and prime example of this sub-genre. The play opens with *the* iconic writer of English literature (read 'culture' and 'humanity') sitting alone in his Warwickshire garden as all around him forced enclosures of common lands produce social upheaval and nascent class struggle. Ironically, in order to present his political interpretation as *the* stable version of those momentous events, Bond has to, as it were, abstract the pivotal action of the play, by leaving the hectic and unmanageable flow of the enclosures largely unseen off stage. Although compromised by his involvement in these events and, in Bond's terms, a failure due to his refusal to express publicly his incisive critique of the enclosures, Shakespeare epitomises the writer's function as socio-political organiser-stabiliser. In this lonely and failed figure, Bond reproduces *the function of the critic* on stage *in* the play, playing back to the audience their allotted role through a technique of reflective doubling: they see the

13 Tom Stoppard, *The Real Thing* (London: Faber & Faber, 1986), p. 33.

actor presenting a labour of critique which challenges them to speak out at the point Shakespeare chose to remain silent.

Hence, in a series of parable plays (with explanatory prefaces) Bond progressively removed the clutter and distraction of naturalistic detail, so that the audience could judge coolly and dispassionately the validity of his assessment of modern capitalist society as profoundly violent. Significantly, he developed a theory for the cause of this violence: the 'gap' or mismatch between human nature and culture. Increasingly, he came to require of human nature a fixity, grounded in simple biological needs, such as food and shelter, and the capacity to socialise. He based his aesthetics for a Rational Theatre on the idea of *justice as a need* currently unsatisfied by society. Capitalist culture becomes the problem: it has to be corrected to fit our needs. But the proposed correction not only removes hunger and violence from society, it also removes desire, since it is desire that exceeds our needs and brings the irrational or unjust into existence.[14] Unfortunately, the very desire that Bond had so accurately identified as the engine of late capitalism was itself altering the political landscape outside the theatre, brushing aside the solidarities of class and economics which he hoped would provide the foundations for a new culture.

Meanwhile, the other end of the stylistic spectrum of the social-realist project reached its apotheosis in such television dramas as Jim Allen and Roland Joffé's *Spongers*, with its unblinking camera, its use of authentic council-estate locations and an improvisational acting style that was intensified by the high degree of correspondence between its actors' actual lives and those of their characters. This harrowing story of a family living on social security handouts, broadcast in 1977 – the year of the Queen's Silver Jubilee – was intended to intervene in a debate on the Left about the Labour government's spending cuts. Eighteen months later, in May 1979, the Tories won their landslide election victory.

Paradigm under pressure: class, desire and the political

In 1982 the Young Writers' Festival at the Royal Court brought Andrea Dunbar's sex play *Rita, Sue and Bob Too* to London. Its style of 'naughty

---

14 See Terry Eagleton, 'Nature and violence: the prefaces of Edward Bond', *Critical Quarterly* 26 (1984), 127–37.

Northern naturalism'[15] was, according to the Court's literary manager, Rob Ritchie, 'as remote as a piece of anthropology' to its southern audiences.[16] The play focussed on the burgeoning underclass created by the Conservative government's liberalisation of markets and employment legislation, and thus anticipated a shift from 'class' represented in terms of industrial or political issues to what Dick Hebdige called 'communities of affect', recreating on stage a voyeuristic (and safely distanced) account of the new poor.[17] This underclass was not brought together by sustained common concerns, created through consciousness-raising and collective action, but gathered fleetingly around disparate responses to specific cultural or social issues. Dunbar's characters' lives have been reduced to getting 'a jump' (a fuck), avoiding pregnancy or being caught out by the law – 'Fuck the world. As long as you're alive, that's all that matters'[18] – and they mark the failure of the social-realist project to raise class-consciousness as a basis upon which art could intervene in political life.

Interestingly, the more the Royal Court stressed Dunbar's biography – Lancashire born, working class, unemployed, a 'raw' talent (albeit carefully supervised by artistic director Max Stafford-Clark) – and sought to locate an authenticity, a veracity, an 'aura' of the real in the person of the author, the more the representation of class seemed problematic. Paradoxically, class on stage became notable for its *lack* of political resonance or social contention. For instance, John Godber's Hull Truck Theatre (founded by Mike Bradwell in 1971) toured extensively throughout the 1980s with a successful series of plays based on specific working-class and lower-middle-class occupations. Deliberately eschewing any form of overt class analysis, a generalised left-of-centre liberalism produced a popular comedy of manners that combined broadbrushstroke characterisation with high-energy sequences of non-verbal, physical movement: *Bouncers* (1983), *Shakers* (1984), *Teechers* (1987). Dramatically, and perhaps politically, Godber owed much more to his northern middle-class counterpart at Scarborough's Stephen Joseph Theatre – Alan Ayckbourn, who had been writing since the early 1960s – than he did to earlier, more class-conscious precursors, such as Arnold Wesker or John Arden. In related vein, Steven Berkoff's twinned plays *East* (1975) and *West* (1983) turned the 'class struggle' into a forum of sexual perversions and linguistic outrages which was removed from any specific historical setting and neutered by knowing

15 Ann McFerran, quoted on back cover of Andrea Dunbar, *Rita, Sue and Bob Too* (London: Methuen, 1988).
16 Rob Ritchie, 'Introduction', in Dunbar, *Rita, Sue and Bob Too*, p. vii.
17 Dick Hebdige, 'After the masses', in *New Times: The Changing Face of Politics in the 1990s*, ed. Stuart Hall and Martin Jacques (London: Lawrence & Wishart, 1989), pp. 76–93.
18 Dunbar, *Rita, Sue and Bob Too*, p. 61.

allusions to Greek and Shakespearean literary canons, seemingly designed to titillate and shock middle-class audiences. In these plays, quoted blank verse and updated mythic narratives served both to distance the audience from the characters' predicament and to render them either absurd or unchangeably universal, as well as giving author-actor-director Berkoff plenty of opportunity for show-stopping set-speeches.

But it was Jim Cartwright's *Road* (1986) that most clearly signalled the profound shift away from earlier representations of class. In some respects, Cartwright's depiction of the new underclass echoes that of Bond in *The Pope's Wedding* (1962) and *Saved* (1965), with feckless, unmotivated, poorly educated, inarticulate and violent characters engaging in wanton acts of self-abasement and self-destruction. It had been the dramaturgical shortcomings of this type of hyper-naturalism that had obliged Bond to return to Brecht's Epic Theatre as a way of dealing with the nihilism produced by such environmental causality: if class-consciousness did not emerge 'naturally' from the character's predicament then the on-stage critic was there to suggest how it might. However, whilst Cartwright's characters possess a chilling awareness of their immediate circumstances, they have no faith in any ideological overview from which to formulate a socially coherent means of changing those conditions for the better. For example, Linda, struggling in desperate poverty to cope with her mother's alcoholism, at one point turns to the audience and bitterly taunts them with 'Poor little me', at once making them grasp both her awareness of her position and the futility of any middle-class sympathy they might feel. Likewise, the promenade staging of the first production at the Royal Court Theatre, with the narrator Scullery ironically leading London audiences around the set – 'Don't feel awkward wi' us, make yoursels at home'[19] – encouraged both an intimacy of engagement with this representation of a northern town's underclass, and a mockery of the theatrical environmentalism that seemed to invite such 'false' empathies. However close the audience got to the actors physically, however seduced by the verisimilitude of their performances, the theatricality of the technique ensured that they remained worlds apart from the actual lives from which such 'representations' were drawn.

At the climax of *Road* four drunken youngsters bellow out a mantra for change over the nostalgic soundtrack of Otis Reading's 'Try a Little Tenderness'. In a way not dissimilar to the novelistic genre of magical realism, the sheer metaphoric force of this hedonistic and hopeless chant marks the aesthetic shift into 'New Times': self-consciousness is not linked by necessity

19 Jim Cartwright, *Road* (London: Methuen, 1990), p. 5.

to any social or political agenda, but rather to desire – personal, idiosyncratic, often non-rational and self-defeating, even super-natural. This produces a poetic space where characters might imagine a transcendence of their cultural, political and social conditions, beyond any conception of class.

If the efficacy of a class-based politics was seriously questioned (or simply ignored) by theatre-makers in the immediate aftermath of Thatcher's election victories, then the social expression and impact of desire increasingly became the focus of attention: the personal became political in new ways. The first significant attempt to accommodate representations of 'class' and 'gender' to the erotic and voyeuristic dimensions of sexuality was Caryl Churchill's *Cloud Nine* (1979). In this play the sexual demon is scandalising because it pervades all the characters and events, but it is finally captured and straitjacketed by ideology, by the overdetermining force of capital: 'You can't separate fucking and economics.'[20] 'Sex' becomes 'sexual practice', subject to observation, objectified in political discourse, and subsequently required to behave itself. Despite jokes that turn sexuality every which way – such as the gay-identified Edward who, falling for a woman, describes himself as 'lesbian' – the argumentative and dialectical strategies adopted from Brecht eventually resolve to *determine* sex all over again. For, as much as it is liberating in revisioning sexual propriety, this process of redefinition is also a reinscription of sex into a set of normative sexualities (albeit decidedly more 'liberal'), which in turn contains and inhibits the possibilities of human behaviour.

The stylistic shift between Acts 1 and 2 in *Cloud Nine* emphasises this process of recuperation, as it moves from the ambiguities of cross-dressing based in pantomime to the more constricted possibilities of psychological realism, full of 'essential' selves, introspection and the finality of 'coming out'. Hence, Churchill's play dramatises the key problem of identity politics: any redefinition both allows a person to come into a novel kind of being, by inventing a category such as the 'homosexual', and simultaneously condemns that person to a label that connotes, if not insists on, certain life-choices, behaviours and etiquettes.[21] Such naming inaugurates both an act of liberation from the past and a definition of conditions that inhibit possible futures.

Churchill returned to the epic-influenced aesthetics of *Cloud Nine* in *Top Girls* (1982), *Fen* (1983) and *Serious Money* (1987), a virulent attack on Thatcherism and yuppiedom written as a pseudo-Restoration farce, with biting political

---

20 Caryl Churchill, *Plays: One* (London: Methuen, 1985), p. 309. See also Howard Brenton, *Sore Throats* (London: Methuen, 1979) and *Romans in Britain* (London: Methuen, 1980).

21 See Michel Foucault, *The History of Sexuality, An Introduction*, trans. Robert Hurley (Harmondsworth: Penguin, 1979).

satire and accurate caricature, reminiscent of Brecht's early expressionistic fables. But rather than confining desire to sexual politics, she also sought in the 1980s a theatre suffused with sexuality's possibilities for confusion: an aesthetics of desire that empowered and encouraged individual expression and social complexity. In collaboration with choreographer David Lan and the dance company Second Stride (founded 1982), she began to write more poetic texts, such as A Mouthful of Birds (1986), Lives of the Great Poisoners (1993) and The Skriker (1994), in which language functioned as one part among many elements of a total-theatre event, including highly choreographed movement and expressionistic design. These were not scripts that were templates for performances. They were allusive in their inclusion of events and identities, of feelings and dreams, of unresolved, extraordinary and often supernatural stories, such as that of Herculine Barbin, an hermaphrodite who lived in France in the nineteenth century. Their dramaturgy rarely resolved into plots, or (sometimes) even characters, let alone arguments putting forward clearly established positions. They reached for what could not be touched by words, what was most pertinent to theatre as a medium, figuring a clear attempt on Churchill's part to create a post-political style of performance, adequate to express the awkward in-betweenness of 'New Times'. They aimed to roll with the seismic shifts in the cultures of advanced capitalism: from collective to personal interests, from needs and rights to desires and wants.

The plurality of the new

Other artists took this deconstruction of the traditional hierarchies of production even further, suffusing theatre with practices and skills from adjacent art forms, including dance and music, and particularly the visual arts. Companies such as Hesitate and Demonstrate (founded 1975) and Intimate Strangers (1983) experimented with highly visual styles, often borrowing wildly from the iconic images of Hollywood cinema for shows like the former's Goodnight Ladies (1982), in which an intricate choreography of mise-en-scène and soundtrack realised a dreamlike series of actions that foregrounded objects, often animated by stage machinery. It relegated the performer to a supporting role, or to a kind of quasi-object status equal to the moving prop-images of the dreamscape. Other companies, such as the People Show (founded 1965), Lumière & Son (1973), Impact Theatre Co-Operative (1978), Rational Theatre (1978) and Station House Opera (1981), emphasised visual images, shifting the theatre goer closer to the spectatorship of cinema and also further problematising the dominance of the verbal text in the performance event.[22]

Choreographic and systematic, often repetitive, movement sequences were generated through improvisation out of the relationship of either performer to performer, or performer to object or space. For instance, Station House Opera's *Cuckoo* (1987) was performed on a platform precariously suspended several metres above the stage floor, a complex set of ropes and counter-weights balancing pieces of furniture and the performer alike in an aerial dance, a kind of meditation on the illusory nature of the solidity we like to believe our living spaces possess.[23] Verbal language was entirely absent from this piece, but emerged variously as heightened prose in the work of David Gale for Lumière & Son, modernised Jacobean tragedy in Hidden Grin's *Suburbs of Hell* (1985, after John Webster) and scientific text in the same company's *Parasite Structures* (1984), post-apocalyptic argot in Impact Theatre's *Carrier Frequency* (1984, based on a text by Russell Hoban), or fragmentary, dreamlike grabs from cinema and popular culture in Forced Entertainment's *200% & Bloody Thirsty* (1987, founded 1984).[24]

Despite the continuing activity of community-based theatre groups, whose vibrant expressions of social agency critiqued the politics of class as a collective force – including the interventionist site-specific and street spectacles of Welfare State International (founded 1968), such as *Raising the Titanic* (1983), and the plays commissioned by Ann Jellicoe, director of the Colway Theatre Trust (founded 1980), such as David Edgar's *Entertaining Strangers* (1985) – it was theatre that focussed on the event-hood and fleshiness of performance, emphasising the visceral presence of the performer before a 'live' audience-spectatorship, making the (often individuated) performer's body both its active subject and its object of study, which came to represent for many people the post-political of 'New Times'. The differing agendas of body-based and issue-based performance work from the 1970s (e.g., companies such as Theatre of Mistakes, Pip Simmons Theatre Group, Gay Sweatshop and Women's Theatre Group) intensified in the 1980s into two predominant sets of related and over-lapping concerns: *physical theatre*, that explored a hybridisation of art forms, such as circus, dance and music theatre (DV8 Physical Theatre, Gloria, Second

---

22 See Theodore Shank, *Contemporary British Theatre*, updated edn (London: Macmillan, 1994), especially Pt. 3.
23 See Nick Kaye (ed.), *Art into Theatre: Performance Interviews and Documents* (Amsterdam: Harwood Academic Press, 1996); Nick Kaye, *Site-Specific Art: Performance, Place and Documentation* (London: Routledge, 2000).
24 See Alison Oddey, *Devising Theatre: A Practical and Theoretical Handbook* (London: Routledge, 1994), pp. 157–9.

Stride and many street performance groups, such as Emergency Exit Arts, Neighbourhood Watch Stilts International, Avanti Display, Scarabeus); and *identity theatre*, that emerged from the 'marginal' communities formed by women with a variety of feminist politics (Bobby Baker, Scarlet Harlots), by 'ethnic' writers and groups who redefined race within the British context (Hanif Kureishi, Winsome Pinnock, Tara Arts, Temba), by gays and lesbians through the reclaiming of the homosexual subject (Neil Bartlett, Split Britches) and by groups formed by people with disabilities to establish themselves as speaking subjects and artists in their own right (Graeae Theatre, Candoco Dance).[25] It was this myriad of small- and medium-sized companies, loosely formed co-operatives and solo artists, performing in a range of small-scale venues (e.g., the Drill Hall and Battersea Arts Centre in London, the Traverse in Edinburgh), festivals (e.g., London International Festival of Theatre, National Review of Live Art) and gallery spaces (e.g., Arnolfini Gallery in Bristol, ICA in London), that surprisingly provided the most radical and robust resistance to the by then glib litany of the post-modern. They variously challenged its fascination with surface (levelling out all descriptions as rhetorical performances of repertoires of sign systems), its belief that there was no depth to this surface because there was no cause to the effect, no referent to the sign, no history to the present and no essence to the body.

These artists and groups flourished in the second half of the 1980s and into the 1990s, despite deepening uncertainty and growing political contention over funding, both nationally and regionally.[26] They were able to reinvent

25 For feminist theatre, see Elaine Aston, *Feminist Theatre Practice* (London: Routledge, 1999); Lizbeth Goodman, *Contemporary Feminist Theatres: To Each Her Own* (London: Routledge, 1993); Lizbeth Goodman and Jane de May, *Feminist Stages* (Amsterdam: Harwood Academic Press, 1996); Geraldine Harris, *Staging Femininities* (Manchester University Press, 1999). For gay and lesbian theatre, see Sue-Ellen Case, *Split Britches: Lesbian Practice/Feminist Performance* (London: Routledge, 1996); Nicholas de Jongh, *Not in Front of the Audience: Homosexuality on Stage* (London: Routledge, 1992); Sandra Freeman, *Putting your Daughters on the Stage: Lesbian Theatre from 1970s to 1990s* (London: Cassell, 1997); Ian Lucas, *Impertinent Decorum: Gay Theatrical Manoeuvres* (London: Cassell, 1994); Philip Osment (ed.), *Gay Sweatshop: Four Plays and a Company* (London: Methuen, 1989); Alan Sinfield, *Out on Stage: Lesbian and Gay Theatre in the Twentieth Century* (New Haven: Yale University Press, 1999). For black and Asian theatre, see Kwesi Owusu, *The Struggle for Black Arts in Britain: What Can We Consider Better Than Freedom?* (London: Comedia, 1986); Catherine Ugwu (ed.), *Let's Get It On: The Politics of Black Performance* (London: Institute of Contemporary Art Publications, 1995). For disability theatre, see Richard Attenborough, *Arts and Disabled People: Report of a Committee of Inquiry under the Chairmanship of Sir Richard Attenborough* (London: Bedford Square Press, 1985); Richard Tomlinson, *Disability, Theatre and Education* (London: Souvenir Press, 1982).

26 See D. Keith Peacock, *Thatcher's Theatre: British Theatre and Drama in the Eighties* (London: Greenwood Press, 1999), pp. 33–64; Baz Kershaw, 'Discouraging democracy: British theatres and economics, 1979–1999', *Theatre Journal* 51, 3 (Oct. 1999), 267–84.

the relationship of theatre to the very idea of the political at a time when many artists and companies from the previous generation found it increasingly difficult to survive, some abandoning theatre, the very art form whose revolutionary function they had championed a decade before. So, from various directions, this intensification effectively downgraded or rejected debate as theatre's strength – its *modus operandi* – and the macro-political as its topic. Instead, resistance formed around and between the twinned poles of an aesthetics and micro-politics of flesh and subjectivity, energy and spectacle in performance: that which precedes argument and remains after it has done its worst – the body and consciousness, specifically that of the performer.

This theatre's resistance to the seemingly overwhelming forces of late capitalism was focussed on the exploration of, and experimentation in, the unique situation that occurs during performance itself. This 'presence' of the performer's body and subjectivity witnessed in the 'here and now' by the audience-spectator became one of the key sites of radicalising activity.[27] Performers sought ever more challenging ways of achieving this effect of presence, seemingly eradicated forever by the absence engendered by contemporary mass media. Almost as if for the first time since the development of cinema and the television / video technologies and industries, here was a resistance to commodification and reproduction, hence industrialisation and trade, that was predicated on the undecidable relationship between the uniqueness of the performance event, its liveness, *and* a contested sense of the self – the subject – as living amongst and between the competing discourses and rhetorics of contemporary culture. This resistance was not a simple rejection of modern living, an attempt to return to an essentialist or biologically grounded prelapsarian utopia, but a profound reworking of the political: not as a collective response, based on a particular class analysis, but as a highly disparate and volatile set of *aesthetic* concerns, of contingent and local 'marginal' communities, of that audience – gathering on that particular occasion in that particular place, however fleetingly, and then dispersing. This was the kind of union of politics and art envisaged by Oscar Wilde or the futurists, by Dada or Artaud, or even by the younger Brecht.

So, the body and the web of discourses that enmeshed the subject became the focus of radical potentiality in a prolific plurality of works, each depending for its full political impact upon the unique combination of its performers,

27 See Philip Auslander, *Liveness* (London: Routledge, 1999); Stanton B. Garner, *Bodied Spaces: Phenomenology and Performance in Contemporary Drama* (Ithaca: Cornell University Press, 1994); Peggy Phelan, *Unmarked: The Politics of Performance* (London: Routledge, 1993).

Figure 20.1 Bobby Baker, performance artist, displaying the Sunday dinner, 1998.

its place and its time. There was the grand scale of the Welsh company Brith Gof (founded 1981), whose *Goddodin* (1988), staged in a disused car factory in Cardiff, was made in collaboration with the music group Test Department (founded 1981), which transformed industrial scrap into percussion instruments and used extreme amplification. There was the 'domestic' placing of Bobby Baker's *The Kitchen Show* (1991) in people's homes in various towns, that fused anecdotes from her own experiences of cooking and mothering with disturbing 'actions' in which familiar domestic objects were made strange and potentially violent. Here the housewife's multi-tasking tricks became a quintessentially performative, 'private' knowledge that marked (as she would say) or defined her body with their routine, aiming to generate wonder in the audience: the everyday transformed into the sublime. Or, at another extreme, consider Franko B's performances (*I Miss You*, 1999) – placed in gallery spaces at the ICA, limited in number due to their impact on his health – which consisted of opening his veins and draining his blood onto the stage, defining his own body by risking its destruction in a way analogous to the high-wire act. Here the everydayness of the body's biological and subconscious functioning – the blood in the veins – was offered up as a quasi-sacrificial gift to the spectator, the performer daring his own demise and disappearance in order to render sublime the everyday fragility of the living organism.

Two companies from the late 1980s particularly expressed the breadth of aesthetics emerging from these radical responses to 'New Times'. Even though both chose to use predominantly conventional performance spaces, their differing approaches to the complex inter-relationship of the post-modern body and discourses of the subject represent two distinct emphases among the theatre groups for whom identity and physicality were critical categories: the limits of the body as a physical entity and as a theoretical proposition.

DV8 Physical Theatre was founded by dancer-choreographer Lloyd Newson with Nigel Charnock and Michelle Richecœur in 1986. In works such as *Dead Dreams of Monochrome Men* (1988), based on the murders of young men by Dennis Nilsen, and *Strange Fish* (1992), where performers danced some of the time underwater in a large glass-fronted tank on stage, DV8 connected the performer's fascination with pushing the physical limits of his/her capabilities – to jump, to run, to carry other performers, to hold their breath – to the outcast's unending paranoia and self-obsession. Newson rendered the everydayness of sexuality as disturbing and unavoidably extreme by implying that these extraordinary individuals – the serial killer and the virtuoso performer – are but extensions of ourselves, his performers acting as post-modern shamans to reveal worlds of terrible possibilities, bodily transformations that defy both the moral force of decency and the physical force of gravity.

Whilst DV8 used physical prowess and brute force as tropes in the exploration of the limits of the performer's body, Gloria produced a dazzling series of works in the late 1980s and early 1990s that, at first glance, might comfortably have appeared on any West End commercial stage. Founded in 1988 by performer-writer-director Neil Bartlett, with composer Nicholas Bloomfield and producer Simon Mellor, Gloria borrowed feverishly from such genres as the cabaret revue (*Sarrasine*, 1990) or the musical (*Night after Night*, 1993). Here the body's limits were realised in the ineluctable gap that opens between the 'magic of theatre' – suddenly to transpose mood and point to the uncanny – and the slipperiness of language. For instance, in *Sarrasine* the performers listed the many synonyms of 'homosexual' then currently in everyday use. The harshness of this mainly abusive catalogue was coupled with the titillating cabaret antics of the performers, who simultaneously displayed rings they had received from hapless lovers. Moreover, this sequence was a knowing reference to the post-structuralist analysis of the Proper Name carried out by Roland Barthes in *S/Z*, which uses for *its* source the Balzac short story that *Sarrasine*, in turn, referenced.[28] In creating this montage of high-brow and low-brow cultural 'grabs', the performers appeared to label or, as it were, to 'clothe' the undecidability of their post-modern bodies / identities by using terms that were themselves highly unstable, as they alluded to the marginalised, usually 'invisible' body of 'the homosexual'. In the fan dance of the cabaret or the torch-song of the diva, they revealed their 'as-if-naked' bodies as potentially coupled to both feminine and masculine subjectivities, therefore doomed to be misrecognised in the gap between theatrical storytelling and representing 'themselves' on stage. So, in the work of both companies, at very different limits of the physical and the philosophical, the body put before the eyes and ears of audience-spectators appeared to dissolve and transform, to become a space of new potentialities that were both deeply and idiosyncratically personal *and* profoundly and radically political.

The Bite of the Night: a 'classic' of New Times

So the global and national, economic and political upheavals of the late 1970s and early 1980s, as well as the cultural shock of punk rock, encouraged a

---

28 Roland Barthes, *S/Z*, trans. Richard Miller (Oxford: Blackwell, 1990).

Figure 21.1 Theatre in Scottish schools. Anthony Strachan as Ivan and Raymond Suart as Jakob in David Grieg's *Petra*, TAG Theatre Company, Glasgow, 1998.

loss and death. Whilst it is certainly witty, fun and engaging, it is also honest, moving and demanding in its interrogation of nationalism.

Petra is the reluctant storyteller confronting the chain of events that led to the death of her young son. Their story is revealed to the audience of young children – classes gathered in-the-round in school gym halls and assembly rooms – through the use of fable and legend: Petra meets three ghosts – Ilka, Jakob and Ivan – who explain that her son must understand why he died in order for his soul to rest.

> ILKA: If you can tell your son the story of how he came to be dead. Then
>   he can drift to sleep, contented and calm.
> PETRA: . . . You died because . . . Because . . . A soldier killed you.
> JAKOB AND IVAN: Why?
> PETRA: There was a war.
> JAKOB AND IVAN: But why?
> PETRA: Because . . . Because . . . Just because.
> JAKOB AND IVAN: But why? But why? But why?[8]

The play inter-weaves storytelling with a challenging interrogation of images of difference and prejudice: the mountain people have their traditional songs, costume and architecture, and have always been at odds with the sea people, with their different accents, music and customs. It is the 'plain people' who are, quite literally, caught in the middle. The negative and destructive elements of racial and cultural difference are explored in the play as Greig depicts a society collapsing into violence and unthinking and uncritical nationalism:

> Law number one: punish the non-singers . . . Law number two: death to
> the non-hat wearers . . . Law number three: send the sea people back to the
> sea . . . Law number five was that anyone who disagreed should be thrown
> into prison. It's just . . . we don't want arguments. Arguments are bad. We
> want everyone to agree.[9]

At the root of the narrative and the political agenda of *Petra* is, paradoxically, Scottish theatre's preoccupation with debates about institutions, organisation and funding. These debates are, finally, about how different groups win a stake in the production and the dissemination of culture, and in the interpretation of representations of the nation.

The scope of David Greig's career demonstrates something of the diversity of theatre in Scotland in the 1990s. He wrote for the Traverse – *Europe* (1994), *The Architect* (1996) and *The Speculator* (for the Edinburgh International

---

8 David Greig, 'Petra', unpublished typescript, p. 11.
9 *Ibid.*, pp. 32–3.

Figure 21.2 An upfront moment in David Grieg's *Caledonia Dreaming*, 7:84 Theatre Company (Scotland), 1997.

Festival in 1999) – and for 7:84 – *Caledonia Dreaming* (1997, 1999). For Suspect Culture, the company he founded with director-actor Graham Eatough, he wrote *Airport* (1996), *Timeless* (1997, 1998) and *Mainstream* (1999). Greig was also commissioned by English theatres, writing *The Cosmonaut's Last Message to the Woman He Once Loved in the Former Soviet Union* (Paines Plough, 1999) and *Victoria* (RSC, 2000).

In common with so much of Scottish theatre in the final decade of the twentieth century, Greig's plays confronted issues of contemporary identity politics and the politics of representation. For a society engaging with and experiencing new structures of government, of course, 'representation' is a weighty and challenging motif. It encompasses issues of political and legislative structures; it impacts on the specifics of the constitutions and policies of cultural institutions; it questions who and what is heard within the key decision-making agencies; and, perhaps most important of all, it is debated in the metaphorical and mythic images and identities of contemporary cultural practice.

Image and genre

There were, of course, significant representations in Scottish culture that challenged the optimism of political change. Novelists such as James Kelman,

Alan Warner, Des Dillon and Irving Welsh; television programmes such as Jed Mercurio's *Cardiac Arrest* (BBC, 1994–6) and Frank Deasy's *Looking after JoJo* (BBC, 1998); films such as *Trainspotting* (Danny Boyle, 1996) and *Small Faces* (Gillies and Billy Mackinnon, 1996) – all gained mainstream success with their tendency towards depicting a self-destructive, urban drug culture and had an impact on Scottish theatre. Bleakly nihilistic versions of the modern metropolis cast Scotland as a society collapsing in on itself because of drugs, unemployment and poverty. The stage version of *Trainspotting* (Traverse, 1994) brought a young and non-traditional audience into theatres across the whole of Scotland, but it has also tended to overshadow the impact of other Scottish playwrights dealing with similar issues of the contemporary urban experience: Iain Heggie's *A Wholly Healthy Glasgow* (Royal Exchange, 1987) and *Clyde Nouveau* (Tron Theatre, 1989), Simon Donald's *The Life of Stuff* (Traverse, 1992), Mike Cullen's *The Cut* (Wiseguise, 1993) and *The Collection* (Traverse, 1995) were all narratively and linguistically distinctive plays and were all, like *Trainspotting*, set in a heightened, but recognisable, contemporary cityscape. This urban milieu was also a potent feature of Chris Hannan's revisionary city comedies *The Evil Doers* (Royal Exchange, 1990) and *Shining Souls* (Traverse, 1996), David Greig's *The Architect*, David Harrower's eclectic and idiosyncratic *Kill the Old Torture their Young* (Traverse, 1998) and Anthony Neilson's violent extra-realistic *Penetrator* (Traverse, 1993) and *The Censor* (The Red Room at the Finborough Theatre, London, 1997), each of which offers varyingly bleak views of the contemporary urban experience.

Harrower's *Kill the Old Torture their Young* is typical in its portrayal of the contemporary cityscape as a topography of psychological unease and moral uncertainty. The play deconstructs the quintessential tropes of Scottish nostalgia by expunging sentimentalism, replacing it with a coolly analytical attitude towards place and ideas, myths and memories of place. This shift is established through four characters – Robert Malloch, Steven, Paul and Darren – and framed by the choric figure of the Rock Star.

Malloch is a successful London-based film-maker, returning to the unnamed city of his birth to make a documentary about the place for television executive Steven. This 'prodigal son' figure is a recognisable one within all marginalised and peripheral cultures, the economic emigrant whose return is celebrated and valorised, mythologised and demonised. Malloch claims:

> I know what I'm doing. You don't. This's the reason I left. These people who say look, look at what's ours. This is what we're known for. Let's keep it that way. The only thing they care about – the only reason they look at anything

is to make sure it hasn't changed since the last time they looked. Because if it changes they're lost.[10]

Malloch is matched by Steven, the 'good brother', who stayed at home and was loyal to his father(land). He repeatedly declares his love of the city and demonstrates his increasing bemusement with Malloch's vision of it: his camera exposes the listings magazines, café society and art exhibits as a fragile veneer which barely conceals the city's violence and isolation. As the truth is revealed, Steven's own sense of self seems to collapse: 'I don't recognise my own city. Where I was born. All dark, sinister. All shadows. Browns and greys. I don't know where I am.'[11]

Paul is the old man who has lived his whole life in the city. His relationship to it is predicated on memory and disillusionment. He remembers a time when eagles flew over the city, he remembers Malloch as a child: metaphor and narrative in close alignment. His disillusionment is symbolised in the dead bird caught in the guttering outside the window of his flat and signalled in the fear with which he initially meets his young neighbour Angela.

Darren has clear, if unlikely, expectations about the city and his place in it. He expects that, through the sheer force of willing it to happen, the city and his life there will be transformed: 'I'm always telling myself I need to get to know more interesting people.'[12] Darren's tragedy is that he cannot see that the 'ordinary' people he meets can validate and affirm his life and his identity more readily than his fantasies.

The Rock Singer is beyond these conflicting and essentially emotional reactions to place. The cultural itinerant, constantly travelling from one city to the next, he attracts none of the detritus of psychological engagement or personal involvement (this is highlighted by the fact that he only refers to himself in the third person): 'The rock singer', he says at the opening of the play, 'is flying out of one country and time zone, across land and sea, to get to . . . some others somewhere.'[13]

Kill the Old deconstructs the allure of belonging while simultaneously interrogating the theme of dislocation and alienation through metaphors of flight and flying: birds, aeroplanes, panoramas, bird's-eye views and other elevated perspectives. The competing claims of the authority of the rhetoric of documentary, the rights of residence and economic or career commitment, the familiarity of longevity, are all shown to fall short of an 'authentic' vision

---

10 David Harrower, *Kill the Old Torture their Young* (London: Methuen, 1998), p. 68.
11 *Ibid.*, p. 60.
12 *Ibid.*, p. 63.
13 *Ibid.*, p. 3.

of the city – each is partial, incomplete and resistant. Comprehension, even interpretation, slips from reach, and Harrower's point is that the city remains intangible and, finally, unknowable.

This Scottish theatre of urban angst was, however, quite different to the contemporary metropolitan plays of Jez Butterworth, Mark Ravenhill, David Eldridge, Nick Grosso, Simon Bent and even Sarah Kane and Tracey Letts. The only Scottish playwrights who fitted neatly into their London cultural milieu are Anthony Neilson and, to a lesser extent, Irvine Welsh. Neilson's plays – which include *Penetrator* (Traverse, 1993), *Year of the Family* (Finborough Theatre, 1994) and *The Censor* (Finborough Theatre, 1997) – are violently and sexually explicit, even misogynistic in their bravura linguistic sophistication. Welsh was a similarly imponderable figure in Scottish theatre in the 1990s. Although *Maribou Stork Nightmares* (Citizens', 1996), *Headstate* (devised with Boilerhouse, 1994) and his first original play, *You'll Have Had Your Hole* (West Yorkshire Playhouse, 1998) increased his engagement with theatre, the misogyny, homophobia and dramaturgical naïvety that critics perceived in the latter piece showed that the bid to shock can too easily remove storytelling, communication and humanity from the stage. Nevertheless, it remains the case that his name attracted audiences to theatres – in September 1999 the Glasgow Citizens' adaptation of his novel *Filth* was a popular success in its smallest studio space.

In contrast to these urban dramas there remained, infusing all of Scottish culture, a parallel and potent tendency to acknowledge the history of Scotland as an immediate and meaningful presence, and especially to present the rural experience as impacting on the imaginary and moral well-being of *all* of the nation. Underlying both these trends is a tendency to depict Scotland as magically transformative and psychologically healing – quintessentially described in films like *Brigadoon* (Vincente Minnelli, 1954), *The Maggie* (Alexander MacKendrick, 1954) and *Local Hero* (Bill Forsyth, 1983) – wherein the physical experience of being in Scotland, and, of course, being connected with a woman who functions as the personification of Scotland, returns urban man to his contented, complete and natural self. This familiar trope was not much advanced in Stephen Greenhorn's nonetheless delightful 'road movie for the stage', *Passing Places* (1997).

The play recounts a mythic journey from Motherwell to Thurso, from the decaying central belt into a diverse and vibrant rural and Highland Scotland, undertaken by two young men. Alex and Brian are unlikely explorers, and their journey is uncanny. Historically, this is a journey between the two key mythologised spaces of imagined Scotland: from the twentieth-century cityscape of industrial Clydeside and into the nineteenth-century savage and romantic Scotland imagined by Sir Walter Scott and debased as 'heritage' Scotland through discourses of Balmorality and tartanry.[14] It is a journey of unexpected incongruities.

> BRIAN (*in guidebook mode*): Inverary. A picturesque township on the shores of Loch Fyne. Notable for its carefully planned layout, its church tower and its historic court-house, now an award-winning museum.
> ALEX: White-washed tourist hell-hole.
> BRIAN: Excellent sea-fishing opportunities. In season.
> ALEX: We're not stopping . . . We're not tourists, Brian.
> BRIAN: I've not been here before.
> ALEX: We live here.
> BRIAN: Not here.
> ALEX: We're only a hundred miles from Glasgow.
> BRIAN: Yeah? Look though. See anything familiar?
> ALEX: Only you talking shite.[15]

Travelling *up* the west coast (as opposed to the classic road movie motif of travelling *to* the west coast) Alex and Brian are challenged to reconsider what it means, not just to be 'Scottish', but to belong anywhere at all. As they navigate their way north the quixotic pair meet with an eclectic group of new Scots, all of whom seem much more knowledgeable about and comfortable in this modern version of Scotland than the two urban-native Scots. Guided by slacker drop-out Mirren, they encounter an ex-army new-ager in Loch Creran, a Canadian geologist on Skye, a French sculptor-cum-handyman and Ukrainian workers from a factory ship in Ullapool, and in Thurso they meet a Cornish surfer-chick working as a hotel receptionist; all the while being trailed by Binks, the quintessential late twentieth-century Scottish theatrical stereotype, the psychopathic Glasgow hardman. These encounters lead Greenhorn's characters to reinterpret and renegotiate the contrasts and dissonances of contemporary Scotland in the extended metaphor of 'Zen and the art of single-track roads', wherein one travels 'Optimising the way you

---

14 See Tom Nairn, *The Break-Up of Britain: Crisis and Neo-Nationalism* (London: Verso, 1981); Colin McArthur (ed.), *Scotch Reels: Scotland in Cinema and Television* (London: British Film Institute, 1982); Ian Donnachie and Christopher Whatley (eds.), *The Manufacture of Scottish History* (Edinburgh: Polygon, 1992); David McCrone, *Understanding Scotland: The Sociology of a Stateless Nation* (London: Routledge, 1992), especially ch. 7, 'Scottish culture: images and icons', pp. 174–96.
15 Stephen Greenhorn, *Passing Places*, in *Scotland Plays*, ed. Philip Howard (London: Nick Hern Books, 1998), pp. 155–6.

meet other traffic. Minimising the disturbance to either side', aspiring towards 'Oneness'.[16]

New beginnings

All these determinedly male-centred narratives found a qualifying and alternative response in plays about the lives of women. *The Trick is to Keep Breathing* (adapted from Janice Galloway's novel by Michael Boyd for the Tron in 1995) presented one woman's mental and emotional breakdown in an imploding Scottish society, and provided Siobhan Redmond with a role of extraordinary power and purpose. Nicola McCartney's *Easy* (1995, initially presented as an amateur production but subsequently restaged for Lookout Theatre, the small-scale touring company McCartney founded in 1997) and *The Hanging Tree* (Lookout, 1997) matched this production's urban voice with female characters of youthful verve and distinction. Her Traverse Theatre commission *Heritage* (1999) tells of Ulster immigrants in Saskatchewan in the period 1914–20 and debates how long-held beliefs, politics and prejudices shape and skew even the strongest of relationships, while *Home* (Lookout, 2000) was an ambitious and coruscating investigation of family, memory and regret, again set in contemporary Scotland.

During this same period a number of more established women writers in Scotland experimented with different media. From her early feminist pieces, *Chiaroscuro* (Theatre of Black Women, 1985) and *Twice Over* (Gay Sweatshop, 1987), to her gay romance *Twilight Shift* (7:84, 1993), the dramas of poet and novelist Jackie Kay have been constantly unexpected and challenging of her audience's prejudices and expectations. Rona Munro wrote for film and television, including *Biting the Hands* (BBC, 1989), *Men of the Month* (BBC, 1994), *Ladybird, Ladybird* (Ken Loach, 1994) and *Bumping the Odds* (BBC, 1997). The novelist Kate Atkinson wrote *Abandonment* (2000) for the Traverse. Meanwhile, after a gap of eight years, Liz Lochhead re-emerged as a crowd-pleasing populist with *Perfect Days* (1998). In a slick and large-scale production by the Traverse, this play was a huge hit in the Edinburgh Fringe Festival, before touring across Scotland and transferring to the West End. It also signalled a significant shift in Lochhead's dramaturgy: her contemporary and charismatic characters are trapped in an extended sitcom that demonstrates none of the formal experimentation of, say, *Blood and Ice* (Traverse, 1982) or *Mary Queen of Scots got her Head Chopped Off* (Communicado, 1987).

16 *Ibid.*, p. 170.

This range of productions, writers and companies ably demonstrates the trend that the critic Peter Zenzinger celebrated:

> ... while the new works are informed by an artistic vision that is distinctively Scottish, they have largely moved beyond the self-conscious Scottishness of the earlier dramatic tradition, which often hampered its artistic realisation and limited its appeal outside Scotland.[17]

This shift – in particular, the look beyond Scotland – was encapsulated in the cycle of political productions by 7:84 in the period leading up to the referendum and the election. Under the artistic directorship of Iain Reekie the company staged a multi-part investigation into political and cultural nationalism, power, responsibility and the nation-state. Beginning with Greig's *Caledonia Dreaming* and Greenhorn's *Dissent* (1998), followed by two devised projects, *Election 99* and *Outside Broadcast* (both 1999), which reimagined the living newspaper for a new political and artistic environment, the project culminated in 2000 with Peter Arnott's lyrical and dryly ironic *A Little Rain*. Alongside TAG's *Making the Nation*, the 7:84 cycle underlined Scotland's growing cultural confidence and willingness to question, challenge and test its new models of political and social organisation.

In a period of transition, creation and recreation within Scottish society, the demands on Scotland's artists were never more pressing. Scottish theatre took on new responsibilities by being *both* international and outward looking *and* essentially and immediately committed to work within and about Scottish society. Political devolution and the new Scottish Parliament were significant factors in setting the scene for the successful coming together of these two dynamics. The ambitions of the producing companies and the diversity of new writing challenge assumptions about Scottish theatre, about social expectations and about political orthodoxies. Perhaps through the promise of the new democracy Scotland, like its theatre-makers, might emerge as more critically aware and culturally questioning.

17 Peter Zenzinger, 'The new wave', in Randall Stevenson and Gavin Wallace (eds.), *Scottish Theatre Since the Seventies* (Edinburgh University Press, 1996), p. 125.

22

Theatre in Wales in the 1990s and beyond

ROGER OWEN

There is a chilling phrase in Gwyn A. Williams's seminal historical study of Welsh culture and identity, *When Was Wales?* (1985), that suggests something of the character of Welsh theatre in the late twentieth century. Baffled and disheartened by the results of the 1979 general election, which saw significant advances by the Conservative Party throughout the principality, Williams foresaw 'the elimination of Welsh peculiarities' and a *'powerful simplification'* of political consciousness in Wales – a disastrous state of affairs which 'strongly suggested an integration into Britain more total than anything yet experienced'.[1]

By the turn of the millennium it was clear, though, that this vision of a 'powerful simplification' had not emerged and that rumours of the imminent death of Wales had been greatly exaggerated. Wales was not assimilated by Britain, not in the political sense at least. Rather, it clawed its way back into existence, so that the sumptuous eleven-seat Tory rump of Welsh MPs returned in 1979 had withered away to nought by 1997, and a new National Assembly for Wales – rejected by the electorate in the referendum of 1979 – convened for its inaugural session in May 1999. Williams's fear that the Welsh political map would lose its diversity and local complexity, leading to 'standard British two-party contests'[2] in most Welsh constituencies, was also misplaced. In the National Assembly elections of 1999 such constituencies were largely confined to the extreme south-east and north-east of the country. More significant still, Plaid Cymru/The Party of Wales made astonishing gains in some of the former industrial heartlands of south Wales and became the main opposition party to Labour in the Assembly, guaranteeing that the internal politics of Wales had a radically different character to those of Britain as a whole. Williams's worries had come to nothing: quite simply, he got it wrong.

---

1 Gwyn A. Williams, *When Was Wales?* (London: Black Raven Press, 1985), pp. 296–7.
2 *Ibid.*, p. 296.

Except, of course, he did not entirely. In some crucial aspects of Welsh life the 'powerful simplification', I will argue, has in fact occurred. Whilst it did not result in the assimilation of Wales as a political entity, it nonetheless impacted on the cultures and, in particular, the theatres of Wales. It led to a *faux*-populist institutionalisation of Welsh theatre, the impoverishment of its local diversity and the marginalisation of intellectually challenging and stimulating work.

Restructuring the theatre

The ingredients for such a powerful simplification had been in place for a long time. In the second half of the twentieth century the theatre had changed at a startling pace, leading to an obviation of its traditional social role and an obscuring of its own history. The collapse of the amateur theatre movement after World War Two and the subsequent creation of a number of modern medium-scale theatre buildings during the 1960s and 1970s, coupled with the growth of electronic media – which diverted funds, audiences and creative talent into broadcasting – disrupted any binding sense of aesthetic or social continuity in Welsh theatre. No wonder, then, that it became common for theatre practitioners and critics to assert, quite wrongly, that 'Wales has almost no theatre history to speak of'.[3] Without a clear social role, and without a binding historicity, the medium was ripe for simplification. Indeed, the only real impediments to such a development was the complexity of Welsh cultural politics after 1979 – when, according to Gwyn A. Williams, a 'crisis of representation' arose from the 'paralysis of parliamentary democracy'[4] – plus the lack of a suitably simplified approach to policy on the part of the theatre's major sources of public funding, respectively, the Welsh Committee of the Arts Council of Great Britain (1946–67), the Welsh Arts Council (1967–94) and the Arts Council of Wales (ACW).

Significantly, both these impediments were removed in the late 1990s. In politics, the creation of the Assembly conclusively reactivated the Welsh scene, and in the field of public arts funding, the ACW instigated major changes. In 1999 it conducted a radical administrative reorganisation and review of policy, which excited a great deal of debate and argument amongst theatre companies and commentators. Those changes were outlined in its report, *The Drama Strategy for Wales*, which recommended the removal of regular

---

3 Carl Tighe, 'Theatre (or not) in Wales', in T. Curtis (ed.), *Wales: The Imagined Nation* (Bridgend: Poetry Wales Press, 1986), p. 242.
4 Williams, *When Was Wales?*, p. 297.

revenue funding from around half of the ACW's longest-standing clients. The Council characterised this as an attempt to ensure 'that fewer organisations may be funded better' in order to improve quality and accessibility.[5] The chief beneficiaries of this new system were the two companies designated as WNPACs, or 'Welsh National Performing Arts Companies', designed to represent the theatre of Wales alongside several other major national arts organisations, such as the National Orchestra of Wales, Welsh National Opera and the Diversions Dance Company.

The designation of an English-language theatre WNPAC in 1999 proved relatively unproblematic (indeed, there was suspicion that the whole reorganisation of the ACW's funding policy had been conceived in order to facilitate that end). Clwyd Theatr Cymru in Mold, Flintshire – which, as the Clwyd Theatre Company, had gained a reputation for popular and innovative main-stage productions during the 1990s, with a number of its shows transferring to the West End – received an allocation of £2 million under the new arrangement and duly began touting its high-gloss, high-profile wares around Wales. However, the creation of an equivalent (though significantly smaller) WNPAC for Welsh-language theatre proved considerably more problematic, because no obvious recipient of ACW's beneficence could be agreed upon. In 1997 the most likely candidate, Cwmni Theatr Gwynedd in Bangor, following a gradual downturn in its audience numbers, had been downgraded by the ACW through an imposition of its policy of creating 'stronger strategic partnerships . . . between producers and presenters' (i.e., between theatre companies and theatre buildings) and a reduction in touring. Eventually, following further negotiations and the intervention of the National Assembly for Wales, a flagship Welsh-language theatre company was established, Theatr Genedlaethol Cymru ('The Welsh National Theatre'), to be based at an entirely new 'culture village' near Carmarthen.

One can hardly blame the ACW, in reformulating its drama strategy, for attempting to extricate itself from a funding dilemma which, according to the strategy document, had produced 'a general picture of a large portfolio of clients characterised by erosion in artistic standards and flexibility due to underfunding with few opportunities for new ideas and talent to emerge'.[6] However, the new Drama Strategy had far wider consequences for the general ecology of theatre in Wales than the ones expressed in the document itself.

5 Arts Council of Wales, *The Drama Strategy for Wales* (Cardiff: Arts Council of Wales, 1999), p. 1.
6 *Ibid.*, p. 2.

Those consequences may well have contributed significantly to the powerful simplification of theatre in Wales as a whole.

The Council had noted that '[one] of the main strengths of drama in Wales has been its diversity', and declared its intention to find 'a better balance between diversity, quality and sustainability'.[7] Anna Holmes, Chief Officer for Drama and Dance at the time, argued that the new policy would protect theatrical diversity because, while the number of companies in receipt of revenue funding might decrease, the range of styles and practices would be maintained.[8] However, the circumstances in which the policy review had been conceived unquestionably committed the Council to a quite contrary course; namely, a process of corporate branding. At the heart of the policy was an attempt to ensure the revival of the theatre's appeal to an audience that had been gradually declining for years. The Council calculated that the public would respond positively to 'cultural product' with which it could readily identify.[9] Thus, the ACW's support for WNPACs and partnerships may be seen as an attempt to create distinctive product in several quasi-industrial theatre plants around Wales in order to increase the profile of theatre as a *nationally branded* art form. The simplification inherent in this definition of the audience as consumer, and of art works as consumables, was strongly in keeping with the temper of the times, not only in Wales but in Britain as a whole. The New Labour government of Tony Blair was particularly adept at such branding; for example, through its enthusiasm for the media slogan 'Cool Britannia' as a general tag for the most marketable and exportable products of Britain's creative industries, such as rock music, film, fashion design and leisure-orientated computer software. The Welsh variant, 'Cool Cymru', was also surprisingly effective, as it celebrated some highly conspicuous successes in rock music and film.

The ideological origins of this late twentieth-century consumer culturalism can be found, ironically, in Thatcherism, which sought the depoliticisation of the public and a subversion of their sense of history. Hence, the renewed sense of national confidence that flowed from the marketability and export potential of new Welsh culture in the 1990s was inextricably tied to a disavowal of the beleaguered social and historical mythology of previous decades. Many in

7 *Ibid.*
8 Interview with author, Cardiff, 7/7/99; see also, Heike Roms, 'Tried and tested', *Planet* (April–May 1999), 121.
9 Cf. Terry Hands, 'Who has the vision to revive our future?', *Western Mail* (14 Nov. 1998): 'The public and the young people are more likely to respond to a home team than to increasingly desperate administrators and increasingly disparate programming.' Hands was Artistic Director of Clwyd Theatr Cymru.

Wales seemed to feel that they could represent themselves more confidently and more assertively, if not to others, then at least to themselves, and this was, of course, welcome: but such a sense of freedom always carries a cost. Perhaps this could be glimpsed in the ACW's attempts to promote theatrical diversity by creating an undifferentiated, monolithic organisational structure.

Unity through diversity in Welsh theatre

The question of diversity was vitally important for the theatre of Wales, as it was through diversification that the theatre had renewed itself and made a fresh appeal to audiences in the early 1980s. Significantly, this politically difficult period saw the creation of a number of innovative and highly committed theatre companies, working in both Welsh and English. These included Welsh-language groups such as Theatr Bara Caws (1977), Theatr Crwban (1978), Cwmni Cyfri Tri (1980), Hwyl a Fflag/Sgwar Un (1981) Whare Teg (1983) and Theatrig (1984); bilingual groups such as Brith Gof and Theatre West Glamorgan/Theatr Gorllewin Morgannwg (both 1981); and English-language groups such as Hijinx Theatre and Made in Wales (both 1981) and Volcano Theatre (1983). Collectively, much of their project was characterised by a determination to create a theatre relevant to the needs and aspirations of specific 'communities', whether defined by geography or by beliefs. There was little consensus among these companies concerning the specifics of theatre style and technique: the values that their work espoused were to do with relevance and social effectiveness rather than, say, the aesthetic traditions of mainstage theatre practice. As Theatr Bara Caws argued in 1980: 'Nid ffyr minks a bocsys siocled ddylai'r theatr fod' ('Theatre should not be all mink furs and chocolate boxes').[10]

During this same period several eminent Welsh historians and cultural commentators argued that diversity was an inherent characteristic of the Welsh. Major studies – such as Kenneth O. Morgan's *Rebirth of a Nation: Wales 1880–1980*,[11] Gwyn A. Williams's *When Was Wales?*, John Davies's *A History of Wales*[12] and Emyr Humphreys's *The Taliesin Tradition*[13] – described the Welsh experience as comprising fundamental divisions, and Welshness as a contradictory experience, always open to contestation and reappraisal. This approach posited the people of Wales as having the capacity to remake their history, to start anew

---

10 *Y Cymro* (22 Jan. 1980), 13.
11 Kenneth O. Morgan, *Rebirth of a Nation: Wales 1880–1980* (Oxford University Press, 1981).
12 John Davies, *A History of Wales* (Harmondsworth: Penguin, 1994).
13 Emyr Humphreys, *The Taliesin Tradition* (London: Black Raven Press, 1983).

and to interpret any signs of breakdown as portents of reincarnation. It also placed an important emphasis on *performance*. Williams and Humphreys were particularly influential in this respect, as their accounts of Welsh history carried within them an implicit sense of theatre. 'Wales', according to Williams 'has always been now'; it is 'an artefact which the Welsh produce'.[14] Welshness was defined as essentially performative, a set of dramaturgical manoeuvres. Thus Humphreys detected a recurring narrative in Welsh history, presented by a succession of charismatic 'actors', drawn from a cast as diverse as the Renaissance magus John Dee, the great Methodist revivalists of the eighteenth century, and British Prime Minister Lloyd George.[15]

From this perspective it was just a small imaginative step to arrive at an interpretation of Wales and Welsh identity *as theatre*, comprising a narrative which was at once a living reality and a metaphor for dogged, disrupted continuity, whose presentation was paradoxically dynamised by a *lack* of cultural and political self-determination. Hence the work of Welsh theatre companies in effect took place on the broadest, most diverse national stage possible: Wales itself. And if the nation could be interpreted thus, the theatre did not need to be constituted as a unified institution in order to have national significance. Dafydd (later Lord) Elis Thomas, when asked 'whether there should be some form of national theatre' after the bankruptcy in 1984 of the national Welsh-language theatre company, Cwmni Theatr Cymru, encapsulated the new thinking by asserting that 'it existed already in the form of a diversity of companies'.[16] According to this logic, local innovation could be claimed *as* national in a way that was becoming increasingly difficult in the regions of England as a result of the centralising influence of the Thatcher government. Hence, theatre could offer a way out of the contemporary 'crisis of representation' and an alternative to the powerfully simplified vision of an undifferentiated British state.

A number of companies formed at this time, and whose work continued to be influential throughout the 1990s, profited greatly from these ideas of contested national identity and of malleable, theatrical self-definition. For example, Brith Gof explored the particular significance that performance had exerted on all aspects of Welsh life. The company's early work often appropriated the forms of traditional social practices and customs; or as company founder/director Mike Pearson put it, the 'particular patterns of cultural

14 Williams, *When Was Wales?*, p. 304.
15 Humphreys, *Taliesin Tradition*, pp. 42–3, 91–100, 198–207.
16 Dafydd Elis Thomas, quoted by Emyr Edwards, 'Tristwch ein theatr', *Y Faner* (5 Sep. 1986), 4.

behaviour specific to Welsh gatherings'.[17] Strongly opposing any essentialist or 'folkloric' tendencies, Brith Gof actively sought to trouble traditional material through deploying obviously alien or unfamiliar acting and staging techniques. Cliff McLucas, artistic director of the company in the late 1990s, described this as an attempt at hybridisation:

> Brith Gof deals with subject matter from Welsh literary, historical, social, political, mythical sources. But what they've done is to weld on to those sources a form of theatre entirely alien, and made a hybrid. The idea of hybridisation is very important and is entirely opposite to ideas of purity and authenticity.[18]

Hybridisation was at the heart of Brith Gof's work during the 1990s. Through the making of theatre for specific sites, the use of multiple stages, the juxtaposition of texts, the integration of able-bodied and disabled or amateur and professional performers, the company presented a series of radically disrupted spectacles. Their work was both communally orientated and challengingly individualistic. For example, *Haearn* (1992), in a semi-derelict industrial plant in Tredegar, Gwent, or *Lla'th (Gwynfyd)* (1998), at an abandoned upland farm near Bwlch-llan, Ceredigion, attracted a number of local spectators, possibly curious about this new use of old places, but the structural complexity of these shows resisted any possibility of a common response or even a common interpretation. The form and context of this theatre presented an implicit argument for the preservation of distinct local identities, and simultaneously challenged and affirmed the view that a distinctive localism allows the spectator a window on the wider world.

A similar case can be made for the plays of Ed Thomas, another important practitioner of the 1980s and 1990s, who became one of the major representative voices of contemporary theatre in Wales. Like Brith Gof, Thomas emphasised the hybridity and eclecticism of Welsh identity, and exhorted the Welsh to celebrate the irregularity and incongruity of their cultures. His notion of Welshness is one of distinctive fragmentation: 'people can wear flowers, a red beach jumper, have spiky hair, listen to . . . hymns and drop acid all at the same time without any contradictions. Wales is all inside-out, back-to-front and postmodern without even knowing it'.[19] Thomas used theatre as a means

---

17 Mike Pearson, 'Special worlds, secret maps: a poetics of performance', in *Staging Wales: Welsh Theatre, 1979–1997*, ed. Anne-Marie Taylor (Cardiff: University of Wales Press, 1997), p. 98.

18 Quoted in Charmian C. Savill, 'Dismantling the wall', *Planet* (Feb.–March 1990), 28.

19 Ed Thomas, 'Not much of a dream then, is it?', in Hazel Walford Davies (ed.), *State of Play* (Llandysul: Gomer, 1998), p. 117.

Figure 22.1 The cast of *Gas Station Angel*, written and directed by Ed Thomas in a Fiction Factory/Royal Court Theatre co-production, London, 1998.

of exciting new myths for Wales, by releasing any previously held view of Welsh identity from its historical shackles, and by injecting an anarchically playful, consciously self-inventive element into his dramatic dialogue and its performance. Following the enthusiastic response to *House of America* (1988), Thomas and his company – then known as Y Cwmni (The Company), later renamed Fiction Factory (1994) – adopted a far more improvisatory style, with a distinctively rough and disorientating dynamic of its own. This theatre largely sacrificed regularity or symmetry of form in favour of spontaneity and surprise, portraying characters who were often displaced or dissatisfied and who attempted to reintegrate themselves into a collective through force of argument or just chaotic, poetic exuberance. It was the dramatic style of plays such as *East from the Gantry* (1992) and *Song from a Forgotten City* (1995) that produced the strongest criticism of Thomas's work. He was derided as verbose and lacking any sense of theatrical economy, while some metropolitan critics particularly relished the prospect of demolishing his supposedly lofty national reputation. The presentation of *Gas Station Angel* (1998) at London's Royal Court Theatre Downstairs provided such an occasion, with criticism of Thomas's trenchantly uneconomic style closely associated with his nationality: 'Celtic windbaggery' was the *Daily Telegraph*'s verdict, while Michael Billington

Figure 22.2 Adam and Eve are reborn into the midnight hour of the twentieth century. *After the Orgy*, Volcano Theatre, 1994/8.

in the *Guardian* derided this 'Welsh rabbit rabbit rabbit'.[20] However, the ease with which Thomas's reputation was built and sustained within Wales suggests that the self-confident embrace of occasionally reviled national icons promoted by his plays may well be a fruitful theatrical tactic.

An 'Anglo-Welsh' Welsh company

The ascription of theatrical characteristics to the very nature of Welsh identity seemed to figure, astonishingly, in the appropriation of performances created in Wales which claimed no special affinity with the nation at all. Swansea-based Volcano Theatre, for example, did not promote itself as distinctively Welsh in any way, actively disavowing any discussion of the 'problem of Welsh-ness'[21] and touring extensively in Britain, Europe and beyond (most of its performances have been staged outside Wales). Yet the company made a significant impact in Wales in the 1980s and 1990s, and was often discussed as an

20 Charles Spencer, 'Celtic windbaggery that's worthy of the Welsh bard himself', *Daily Telegraph* (11 June 1998), 27; Michael Billington, 'Welsh rabbit rabbit rabbit', *Guardian* (13 June 1998), 5; see also 'London critics shoot *Gas Station Angels* down in flames', *Western Mail* (15 June 1998), 10.
21 Paul Davies, 'Physical theatre and its discontents', in Taylor, *Staging Wales*, p. 163.

integral part of the Welsh theatre scene. Its relationship with Wales was therefore complex. Based in the principality since its formation in 1983, and referring to itself as an 'Anglo-Welsh' theatre company, it pursued a programme of politically motivated theatre which placed it at odds with many notions of national culture and identity.

Volcano could be described as representative of a Marxist and 'old' Labour tradition, important in South Wales for much of the twentieth century, that sought commonality in like-minded (socialist or working-class) communities regardless of their regional or national identity. The company opposed the increasing tendency to deny or gloss over questions of class identity and social justice when describing the condition of contemporary society. One of Volcano's directors, Paul Davies, argued in 1997 that the company had been motivated by

> a feeling that theatre had, unfortunately, turned its back on what was an increasingly complex political situation [in Britain] . . . the success of New Right ideology [during the 1980s] and the collapse of the Communist utopia signalled the end of one way of looking at, and living in, the world. Radical rethinking of a Marxist and non-Marxist hue declared we were living in 'new times'.[22]

These 'new times' were characterised by the rise of post-modernism and a deadeningly vague approach to matters of cultural and artistic policy. Volcano, he says, had determined to pitch its work in order to disturb the notion of a classical tradition, and in order to reveal 'the market system of production, exchange and ideology' which underlies that tradition, as 'differentiated but universal'. As such, 'the Anglo-Welsh experience can be seen within the logic of late twentieth-century capitalism.'[23] Hence, while not subscribing to any specifically Welsh cultural agenda, Volcano had many of the attributes of those that did: a commitment to their chosen community, an unorthodox affinity with a historical and political tradition which has played a vital role in the creation of modern Wales, and an antipathy towards some of the institutions of contemporary theatre. It was not difficult, therefore, to place them amongst the companies from Wales that had been responsible for advocating a vision of a theatre and a nation sustained by diversity.

These theatre companies, significantly more so than their main-stage counterparts, sought to address complex issues of identity, history and social responsibility through performance, and many of them were conspicuously

---

22 *Ibid.*, pp. 163–4.
23 *Ibid.*, p. 165.

successful, both aesthetically and in terms of popular appeal. Their work was especially notable for its willingness to engage with the vicissitudes of a culture in crisis. However, another ominous phrase from Gwyn A. Williams suggests that many such efforts may have been undermined by the events that spawned the 'crisis of representation' in the first place. The sea change of 1979, he claims, 'cut off of an intelligentsia from its people':

> While the ideologies of technical, managerial and administrative groups remained opaque but clearly without any Welsh specificity, the most visible and creative formers of educated opinion among the Welsh were rejected by their people, tossed into a ditch of irrelevance.[24]

In other words, there was a rejection both of cultural tradition and of the specific dilemmas faced by a marginal national community in defence of its own sense of history. And, whilst the political paralysis caused by long-term Tory rule continued (sometimes referred to as 'the democratic deficit'), this complex theatre of diversity did not – could not, perhaps – create for itself a coherent or singular identity that would secure a wide audience. This was, perhaps from the outset, a theatre for converts.

Conclusion

At the start of the twenty-first century the effects of the 'crisis of representation' described above led to a resurgent but intellectually impoverished notion of nationhood that may have gained the upper hand in the theatre of Wales. I think that three main consequences could ensue. First, it is possible that a powerfully simplified national theatre culture, which capitalises on a growing feeling of national self-confidence, could be successfully created. However, given that theatre is a form that must be appropriated by its audience, and given the fact that a number of managed strategies such as that proposed by the ACW have failed in the past, this is not the likeliest outcome for the medium. Second, the link between theatre and nationhood could be severed completely, with the extant model of national self-assertion and self-interrogation being passed over in its entirety to the media. In some ways this had already largely happened during the second half of the twentieth century, with the sudden growth in the media sector in Wales, representing both the Welsh- and English-speaking communities. Regardless of the bitter debates sometimes caused by the relative level of public funding given to each, it is safe to say that the mass

24 Williams, *When Was Wales?*, p. 297.

495

media were vital to the generation of a modern 'national consciousness' in Wales. As Kevin Williams argued in 1997:

> The mass media play a central role in the construction of Welsh identity, what it means to be Welsh in today's rapidly changing world . . . the media are the main means by which Wales represents itself to the outside world as well as defining what it is to be Welsh to the people who live in Wales.[25]

In similar vein, the television producer and executive Euryn Ogwen Williams argued in his 1998 National Eisteddfod lecture that the Welsh (along with everyone else) were 'living in the midst of a revolution',[26] in which the capacity to predict the future – even the very near future – was severely constrained by remarkably rapid advances in telecommunications and computer technology. The marginal status of Welsh culture, he claimed, would not present a problem if the society as a whole accepted the fact of change and made use of the tools that were facilitating it. The essence of the information revolution is 'the destruction of any power that does not arise out of the willingness of individuals to sign up to a community'.[27] If those who subscribed to a Welsh identity were to make common cause, believing that the social, national and historical value of Welsh culture could embrace such change, then there may be a bright future ahead: 'Our strength in the digital age is that we are small. A revolution which, in essence, gives control to the individual and depends on creating networks of individuals to create a community favours the small rather than the large.'[28]

The third possibility might be that a genuinely popular theatre could emerge in a completely different context – one that is willed into existence by an audience. It might even have been the case that at the end of the twentieth century such a theatre already existed in embryo, in examples of the most simple and aesthetically unpremeditated acts of 'theatre'. Some of these events were extremely unsophisticated in their dramaturgy, and yet, in their wider significance as theatre, were also extraordinarily rich and complex. Whilst they would not be classed as drama, the pre-match entertainments at international rugby fixtures during 1998 and 1999 – particularly at Wembley Stadium in London – were striking examples of a kind of spontaneous, ecstatic theatre, which, for all their poverty of narrative ideas, encompassed many different views and versions of Welsh identity.

25 Kevin Williams, *Shadows and Substance* (Llandysul: Gomer, 1997), p. 5.
26 Euryn Ogwen Williams, *Byw yng Nghanol Chwyldro/Living in the Midst of a Revolution* (Eisteddfod Genedlaethol, 1998).
27 *Ibid.*, p. 18.
28 *Ibid.*

Two examples are worth noting in conclusion. The Wales versus England international at Wembley in April 1999 featured the back-to-back appearance of comedian Max Boyce and singer Tom Jones, from whom the crowd gleefully appropriated national cliché upon cliché in what appeared to be an extravagant attempt to inaugurate the shrine of English sport as the location for a Welsh home game. Two months later, Wales and South Africa played the first rugby match at the new Millennium Stadium in Cardiff. Just before kick-off time, a previously little-known Pontypridd supporter, Andrew Harry, invaded the pitch in the guise of the 'Ginger Monster', and became the first person to score a converted try at the new stadium. Grotesquely bedecked in ginger wig, false ears and kilt, and carrying a stuffed sheep under his arm in place of a ball, this was both a celebratory caricature of current rugby hero Neil Jenkins *and* an assertively comic reappropriation of derogatory national stereotypes. The crudeness of the Monster's act – weaving his way to the try line, and then kicking the sheep over the crossbar – paradoxically was crucial to the complexity and effectiveness of the action, instantly appreciated by the mass audience. This was light years away from the careful deliberations of a committee about the application of public funds, but perhaps it is at least as likely that such wild and anarchically unforeseeable actions will lead to the creation of a new kind of theatre for Wales, a theatre which can only be developed and refined according to its own creative premises.

23

English theatre in the 1990s and beyond

LIZ TOMLIN

In the twenty-first century the concept of national identity is likely to be increasingly overshadowed by the global and post-industrial, or post-modern, cultural landscape. By the end of the twentieth century the omnipresence of worldwide mass media and multi-national conglomerates was already ensuring that potentially fashionable and profitable influences spread far beyond the national boundaries of their origin, blurring hitherto culturally distinct borders. Moreover, in this age of mass communication, 'reality' itself may be increasingly experienced through the mediations of communication and information technologies. Scott Lash and John Urry, drawing on the theories of Jean Baudrillard, argue that the post-modern anxiety surrounding the nature of representation is the consequence of living in a society

> in which the boundary between the cultural and life, between the image and the real, is more than ever transgressed. Or because of a semiotics in which already cultural images, that is, what are already representations in television, advertisements, billboards, pop music, video, home computers and so on, themselves constitute a significant and increasingly growing portion of the 'natural' social reality that surrounds people.[1]

Where the distinction between the 'real' and the representation of that 'real' begins to disappear, the possibility of an identity that might exist outside of Baudrillard's simulacrum – the world as no more than appearance – becomes severely threatened.[2] Consequently, the search for 'communal' identities that dominated new theatre in England in the 1970s and much of the 1980s has been replaced by a preoccupation with individual identities. When 'The Personal is Political' became a slogan in the 1970s it indicated an argument which claimed that the everyday lives of those communities largely 'occluded' from

---

1 Scott Lash and John Urry, *The End of Organised Capitalism* (Cambridge: Polity, 1987), p. 287.
2 Jean Baudrillard, *Simulacra and Simulation*, trans. Sheila Faria Glaser (Ann Arbor: University of Michigan Press, 1994).

the cultural mainstream – women, gays, ethnic minorities and so on – were valid as public cultural statements. The 'personal' proposed in the 1990s, however, was more often a confession of self-fascination or private obsession than a statement of interests made on behalf of, or coming from, an oppressed or marginalised community.

Such individualistic tendencies were well in line with the prevailing political climate. The unified 'opposition' of socialism, so paramount to the theatre movements of earlier decades, gave way to an overriding acceptance of capitalist neo-liberalism. As Leo Panitch and Colin Leys, discussing the New Labour Party's rhetoric in the late 1990s, observe:

> The result is a distinctive kind of idealism, co-existing with the insistence on 'realism' about the new globalised economy. The realism consists essentially of the assertion that global capitalism is a permanent and irremovable fact of life, not an inhuman and ultimately self-destructive system: correspondingly, politics is the art of living with it, not a vocation to overcome it.[3]

In this chapter I will argue that the generally coherent political protest of much of English theatre in the 1970s and 1980s was replaced in the 1990s by a diversity of political positions that replicated, rejected or challenged *fin-de-siècle* post-modernism. The chapter therefore makes no claims to be definitive, nor does it promise a generally 'true' picture of theatrical activity in that decade and beyond; rather, it discusses practices already selected as significant by the cultural, economic and political powers that promoted theatre and supported its continuation. However, I hope to demonstrate that there was a surprisingly common preoccupation, across diverse types of theatre, with problems surrounding the post-modern crisis of identity and a consequent anxiety about the inefficacy of theatre in an age shaped by mass-mediated cultural forms.

The touch of technology

Live performance is rarely, if ever, untouched by technology, and one of the largest growth areas in new performance in the 1990s was in the field defined by funding bodies, such as the Arts Council of England, as 'multi-media' or 'combined arts'. At its best, the combination of video and live performance

---

3 Leo Panitch and Colin Leys, *The End of Parliamentary Socialism: From New Left to New Labour* (London: Verso, 1997), p. 248; see also Mark Hayes, *The New Right in Britain* (London: Pluto Press, 1994); Tudur Jones, *Remaking the Labour Party: From Gaitskell to Blair* (London: Routledge, 1996).

indicated the increasing difficulty of distinguishing between the simulated and the real. The 'new' identity politics was no longer concerned with the disjunction between society's simulated representations – or media distortions – and the reality of those identities (mis)represented; rather, such politics became obsessed with the failure of 'reality' to provide any stable counterpoint to the 'simulated' where the self's identity might be found.

Many English experimental theatre companies of the 1990s wrestled with this dilemma. In Blast Theory's (founded 1991) *Something American* (1996) the performers adopted seemingly random roles from Hollywood films, such as Rocky or the clichéd American cop; Gobsquad's (1994) *Safe* (1999) featured 'rock stars' and 'airpilots'; Third Angel's (1995) *The Killing Show* (1996) focussed on an 'ordinary' woman who finds media fame through being brutally murdered, while performers in that company's *Experiment Zero* (1997–8) struggled to attain 'B-movie-star status'. In all of these productions the attempts to realise representations of celebrity status were designed to fail. The 'American cop' constantly had to battle with reminders to the audience that he wasn't a real policeman; the cartoonish 'Rocky' wasn't a very good boxer; the bad B-movie dialogues, out of tune rock songs and embarrassed 'rock stars' all served as ironic examples of the failed attempt to represent, or to embody the 'other'.

If the 'famous' persona is acknowledged to be no more than a construct, something entirely 'other' to the celebrity's 'real' self, then these works dealt with the failure to achieve a simulation of representation, ignoring even the possibility of any underlying reality. Such productions largely turned away from 'public' themes, engaging instead with the private domains of fantasy and narcissism, looking for the individual's significance and 'identity' through role-playing the desired 'other'. The pessimism in this trope – glimpsed in the usually grim humour of these shows – derives from the post-modern assumption that role-play is always inadequate, 'identity' is 'always already' lost in the performers' failing attempts to find it.

The failure of theatrical performance to successfully replicate the mass media's simulations was further accentuated by the technological aspects of such productions, which paradoxically and intentionally appeared much more 'authentic' than their 'live' counterparts. Philip Auslander explains how the 'simulations' of mass media may come to be the models for a reality which reality itself inevitably fails to live up to: 'whereas mediatized performance derives its authority from its reference to the live or the real, the live now derives its authority from its reference to the mediatized, which derives its authority from its reference to the live'.[4] The film footage used in *Experiment Zero* showed one performer as a B-Movie actress, a role and status she finds impossible to attain in her 'live' performance; the film, slickly shot and edited, stood in stark and deliberate contrast to the 'inadequate' attempts at 'live' representation. Similarly, in *The Killing Show* the 'home video' footage leading up to the woman's murder gestured to a landscape more familiar and convincing than the actor's on-stage monologue. The atmospheric soundtrack, the slow-motion footage, the victim's clichéd responses to the camera were common conventions that aimed to draw the spectator into the 'world' of the film, while the 'voice-over' narration of the on-screen events by the on-stage actor was an ironic alienation device, questioning its own authority through its deadpan delivery. It is significant that in both these productions performers were placed in positions of extreme discomfort in an effort to pull focus from the lure of the filmed events to the 'actually happening' on-stage action: in *The Killing Show* the performer choked on blood-red treacle poured down her throat, while in *Experiment Zero* handfuls of pill-shaped sweets were used to the same effect.

This theatrical trend underlined Auslander's claim that unmediated 'reality' was becoming less familiar than the mediated version. At the beginning of Gobsquad's *Safe*, images on a screen seemed to be provided by a performer videoing bodies lying on the stage, yet deliberately altered details of the pictured 'corpses' demonstrated that the footage was pre-shot. This ironically gave far more 'authenticity' to the screened images, as the 'corpses' were made up more realistically in the film than they were on the stage, a point emphasised by close-ups. The set suggested a fading and out-of-date theatricality, the fairy lights which surrounded the stage giving the effect of a tacky cabaret or cheap cruise-ship entertainment. At one point a 'comic turn' was presented with the female performer's voice amplified and distorted to an accompaniment of canned laughter: an implicit 'confession', perhaps, of the failure of theatre's ability to entertain, never mind convince, its audience.

The work of these companies forcefully suggested that the rejection or suspicion of the possibility of 'reality' in a post-modern era had undermined theatre's general social or political relevance, and implied that the characters and plots of conventional plays in mainstream theatres were just remnants of the modernist nightmare. When the 'liveness' of the live event is questionable,

---

4 Philip Auslander, 'Liveness: performance and the anxiety of simulation', in *Performance and Cultural Politics*, ed. Elin Diamond (London: Routledge, 1996), pp. 202–3.

if the best it can do is simulate technology's representations of a reality which itself is becoming a simulation of its own technological image, where can theatre's artistic or political significance be found? That question was like a ghost which haunted the performances of leading experimental company Forced Entertainment in the late 1990s. Always an underlying concern of the company's work, it became the central fear around which *Showtime* (1996–7), *Pleasure* (1997–8) and *Dirty Work* (1998–9) revolved.

Showtime opened with one of the performers talking to the audience about what a 'good show' should be. His performance was deliberately inadequate, and humorous in its failure to deliver the conventions he proposed as essential to the theatre. The show continued with pantomime trees which squabble and fall over, upsetting the 'badly' constructed set, and a performer who opened a tin of spaghetti, which he pours onto his bare stomach so that he can clutch at his spilled-out 'guts' and slowly 'die' throughout the performance. Meanwhile another performer wearing a pantomime dog's head answered questions about the way she would commit suicide. In *Dirty Work* the concerns are the same, but even darker. Three performers sit on a small, 'burnt-out' scaffold stage, its false proscenium arch framed by ripped and stained velvet drapes. One of the performers sits alone upstage with an old gramophone player, punctuating the dialogue, every now and then, with the same mournful tune. She never speaks, nor in any way relates to the other performers, who are sitting downstage on chairs facing the audience. They talk to the audience, not to each other, and describe the events of a five-act play, introducing each act and including the interval, which of course is not a feature of *Dirty Work* itself. The play they describe is full of personal anecdote and epic events from sleazy sex shows to atomic explosions, and quite obviously unstageable. In contrast to the company's earlier work, the performers make little attempt to charm the audience, the understated acting is no longer playful, but downbeat and distant. There is humour in many of writer-director Tim Etchell's textual juxtapositions and ironic counterpoints, but it is always tinged with the intermittent and melancholy echoes of the gramophone music. The piece had an apocalyptic feel, as if it might be the last show on earth; the death of theatre seemed absolute, as if there was nothing left but its burnt-out shell filled only with impossible fantasy and nostalgia.

In much of this 1990s experimental theatre the post-modern temptation to accept everything as simulation, to believe that nothing exists beyond mediated representations that cannot hold any claim to 'truth', led to a political stalemate. At its best, there was charm in the performers' heroic efforts to find meaning and significance in a postmodern void, which the audience might recognise as its own. At its worst, this theatre reached the depths of pessimism as, obsessed with its own inadequacy, it spiralled deeper and deeper into meta-theatrical angst, unable to gesture towards anything beyond its own ever-decreasing field of self-reference.

In the mainstream

Despite the very different theatrical conventions in the mainstream traditions of theatres such as London's Royal Court, the thematic concerns of high-profile new playwrights in the 1990s, such as Mark Ravenhill and Sarah Kane, bore some significant resemblances to the work discussed above. In *Faust: Faust is Dead* (Actors' Touring Company, 1997) Ravenhill's protagonist philosopher, Alain, argues that 'at some point, at a moment at the end of the twentieth century, reality ended . . . and simulation began'.[5] Yet the play, in apparent opposition to the post-modernist truisms of the time, aims to emphasise a dark 'reality' when a young boy stabs himself to death in the motel chalet occupied by Alain and his young protégé, Pete. Donny's suicide is an attempt to prove to Pete that his earlier self-wounding, broadcast on the Internet, was 'real' and not a simulation. Ironically, Pete can only cope with such reality by viewing it through the lens of his video camera, and the audience see the 'reality' of Donny's death mediated on a video screen.

Where Ravenhill differed from many of the experimental artists of the period was in his conviction that post-modernism is not so much a philosophical condition as a political one. If simulation is replacing reality, then Ravenhill aimed to make it clear where the ownership of simulation, and consequently the control over perceived realities, lies. Hence, as Brian points out in Ravenhill's *Shopping and Fucking* (1996), the first words in the bible of contemporary society are 'Get. The Money. First.'; he continues, 'It's not perfect. I don't deny it. We haven't reached perfection. But it's the closest we've come to meaning.'[6] The fear that global capitalism's commodification of human life and emotion is endangering the human potential of love is evident in much of Ravenhill's work. His plays are peopled with the unloved and forgotten children of society: 14-year-olds who practice 'Lick and Go'[7] sex for money, or sometimes use sex *as* money, looking to purchase the parental care they never had. Rent boys, like *Shopping and Fucking*'s Gary, are condemned to crave violent abuse because

---

5 Mark Ravenhill, *Faust: Faust is Dead* (London: Methuen, 1997), p. 30.
6 Mark Ravenhill, *Shopping and Fucking* (London: Methuen, 1996), pp. 86, 87.
7 *Ibid.*, p. 17.

it stands as the closest thing to 'love' they know. Human feelings and emotions are reduced to chemical effects – 'the coffee, the fags, the . . . ozone, the smack, the Nutra-sweet' – and even Robbie's dramatic gesture of pitting love of mankind against the power of money – 'the suffering . . . the wars . . . and the grab, grab, grab' – is induced by the drug ecstasy.[8] Whilst Pete can only deal with the reality around him by looking at life through a camcorder, Gary describes the horror of what he craves through narrating an imaginary filmscape in which he is the central protagonist. Similarly, in *Handbag* (1998) Phil attempts to deal with his past abuse of his young daughter by resorting to a fairy-tale ending:

> And finally the dealer comes for the kid and the dad says: 'I'm free of you. I've got no habit and I'm free of you and I never want to see you again.' And the dealer starts to shake, and then he turns red like a furnace and then smoke comes out of his ears and he burns up until there's just a pair of shoes lying there and they're full of ash and that's the end.[9]

The stark reality of these characters' lives, Ravenhill implies, is only bearable when mediated as fiction, yet he never denies that such a reality exists.

In 'Cool Britannia? "In-Yer-Face" Writing in the British Theatre Today' Aleks Sierz suggests that the 'critiques of modern society' in Ravenhill's plays are 'muffled by their subjectivity – and by their attraction to a distinctly postmodern sensibility'.[10] I would argue, on the contrary, that Ravenhill far from accepts the desirability of the soul-less post-modern landscape that his work explores. The isolated individualism of his characters and their enslavement to a simulated life-once-removed is not presented as an inevitability, but as the consequence of a society that has rejected humanist values in favour of the 'religion' of money, and the power over other people's lives that money brings. So, at the close of *Shopping and Fucking* the image of the three friends feeding each other from individually portioned take-away food cartons perhaps is meant to conjure up the biblical parable of hell and heaven, in which everyone has six-foot-long spoons for eating their food – in hell they starve, in heaven they provide each other's succour. This faint gesture towards the possibilities of human contact and community – reminiscent, perhaps, of the yet bleaker image of Len mending a chair at the end of Edward Bond's *Saved* (1965) – stands as the only way out of the nightmare picture Ravenhill paints of

---

8 *Ibid.*, pp. 32, 38.
9 Mark Ravenhill, *Handbag* (London: Methuen, 1998), p. 72.
10 Aleks Sierz, 'Cool Britannia? "In-yer-face" writing in the British theatre today', *New Theatre Quarterly* 14, 56 (Nov. 1998), 332.

contemporary society. And if we adopt playwright David Greig's definition of political theatre as one which 'posits the possibility of change',[11] then Ravenhill's condemnation of much of the cultural landscape of the 1990s, and his identification of its causes, is no less a political protest of its time than the work of Bond in the days when socialism was still perceived as a real possibility.

The plays of Sarah Kane, and in particular *Blasted* (1995), also referenced and critiqued the cult of the individual. In *Blasted* the journalist Ian points out that the true horror of war, unlike the 'stories' of heroic individuals so loved by the tabloid press, 'isn't a story anyone wants to hear . . . it has to be . . . personal'.[12] And as the play's two main characters, Ian and Cate, are forced to experience such horrors at first hand, there is an implication that humanity has to pay for its crimes. Ian's abuse of Cate, a young woman with the vulnerability of a child, is turned back on him when he is raped by the soldier who invades his bombed-out hotel room. The soldier also sucks out Ian's eyes, suggesting the justice of the Old Testament, and then Ian descends into the depths of human depravity, finally eating Cate's dead baby to stay alive. Soon after this Cate returns with food, but it is too late, the worst has already happened. The play ends with Cate sucking her thumb and drinking gin, sitting apart from Ian, both alone in a nightmare world that will not let them die. The highly graphic nature of Kane's use of violence may be interpreted as an attempt to 'force' her audience to confront the 'real' horrors it more commonly experiences as 'simulated'. It aims, perhaps, through the illusion and the 'liveness' of theatre, to bring home the atrocities that the media broadcast on a daily basis – atrocities that were suffered by somebody somewhere, unmediated and terrifyingly real.

However much *Blasted* might suggest that there are human causes to brutality, Kane offers little hope that change will occur, and in her final two plays the picture becomes even bleaker. *Cleansed* (1998) is set in an institution run by Tinker, a sadist reminiscent of Howard Barker's protagonists, whose torturing of his inmates seems designed to test the limits of love by pushing their lives to the extremes of human endurance. Carl's betrayal of Rod is extracted by a beating, and his tongue is then cut out so that he can no longer make vows of love which he is unable to keep. As he persists in expressing this love through other parts of his body they – like Helen's in Barker's *The Bite of the Night* – are severed too, until he is no more than a trunk, even his genitals removed, yet he is forced to stay alive even beyond the end of the play.

11 David Greig, quoted in Aleks Sierz, 'About now', *New Theatre Quarterly* 13, 51 (Aug. 1997), 290.
12 Sarah Kane, *Blasted* with *Phaedra's Love* (London: Methuen, 1996), pp. 45–6.

Kane's nihilistic and Beckett-like image of life as torture continued in *Crave* (1998), which explores the terrain of desire and despair through the stories of four personae – C, M, B, A – who sit in a line behind a table, as if at a public debate or trial. Sometimes addressing the audience, sometimes each other, their speech evokes an interminable craving for the things that will destroy them. Thus Kane defines the search for human love in a barren landscape that renders love impossible. The one-line, sometimes monosyllabic, dialogue between the four figures is broken only by A's intense, unpunctuated two-page monologue as he attempts to communicate his 'overwhelming undying overpowering unconditional all-encompassing heart-enriching mind-expanding on-going never-ending love'; yet C's chorus of 'this has to stop this has to stop this has to stop' is omnipresent throughout.[13]

In Sarah Kane's universe, it seems that love is the torture endured by the living, both craved and impossible, and death is the only way out. Hence *Cleansed* closes with a parody of hope: the two dismembered bodies of the characters denied even death watch the rain stop and the sun gets 'brighter and brighter, the squeaking of rats louder and louder, until the light is blinding and the sound deafening'.[14] This touches a nihilism that goes beyond Kane's earlier work. The characters in *Cleansed* can bear no responsibility for their tortured lives as they are victims of a cruel and inescapable establishment. Rob's claim that 'death isn't the worst thing they can do to you'[15] resonates beyond the asylum, turning it into a metaphor for a human existence that promises, at best, death as a release, at worst, unspeakable and never-ending torture. There is a movement here away from *Blasted*'s portrayal of atrocities committed in human *extremis*, towards an inner, more personal territory of existential despair. Kane's own suicide in February 1999 seemed the tragic and inevitable consequence of her work's philosophical conclusions.

On the edge of the real

Ironically, the simulated acts of graphic sex and violent atrocity that littered productions of Ravenhill's and Kane's plays demonstrated a continuing faith in the efficacy of theatre's ability to 'shock' its audience through a skilful representation of the 'real'. Conversely, tactics such as the choking incidents in Third Angel's work suggest a suspicion of representation's ability to 'move' an audience and resort, instead, to presenting actual bodily discomfort to elicit

---

13 Sarah Kane, *Crave* (London: Methuen, 1998), p. 18.
14 Sarah Kane, *Cleansed* (London: Methuen, 1998), p. 44.
15 *Ibid.*, p. 30.

Figure 23.1 Recycling in the avant-garde. Stan's Cafe's revival of Impact Co-operative Theatre's *The Carrier Frequency*, 1999 – original production 1985.

a reaction. The early productions of Forced Entertainment placed a similar emphasis on the 'real': the smell of beer pervaded *200% and Bloody Thirsty* (1987–8); in *Club of No Regrets* (1993) performers were tied to chairs with strong sticky-tape and water was hurled at them by 'stage-hands'. Impact Theatre Co-Operative's celebrated *The Carrier Frequency* (1985, restaged in 1999 by Stan's Cafe) took place in knee-deep water and heralded the excess of undeniably 'real' substances in subsequent works by experimental companies throughout the nineties, placing an emphasis on the 'physical' reality and 'presence' of the theatre event as something which mediatised performance could not offer. This emphasis was most effective when exploited by shows which also celebrated a high level of technical control, such as in the throwing of eggs in Vincent Dance Theatre's (founded 1994) *Falling from the High Rise of Love* (1999), or the water and mud splattered onto the audience during Northern Stage Ensemble's (founded 1987) *Animal Farm* (1993, see Fig. 23.2).

Admittedly, at the turn of the millennium this tradition was tenuous and still emergent. The continental anarchy of La Fura del Baus (Spain) or Archaos (France) was still largely unmatched in England; Theatre de Complicite (founded 1983), the most successful British physical theatre company in tune with European developments, seemed primarily at the pinnacle of

Figure 23.2 A moment of filthy triumph. Northern Stage Ensemble's *Animal Farm*, 1993.

performance influenced by the charismatic French trainer Jacques Lecoq, rather than heralding a new kind of 'indigenous' movement. Of more interest in the emerging highly physicalised theatre in England at this time was its fascination in juxtaposing high levels of technical virtuosity with physical and performative failure. Whereas the absence of physical training/technique in companies such as Forced Entertainment was presumed to validate the endurance of the performers and provide the audience with a 'real' experience of human struggle, companies like DV8 (founded 1986), Frantic Assembly (1994), Vincent Dance Theatre (1994) and Point Blank (2000) used high levels of bodily accomplishment to explore a similar post-modern terrain. In Frantic Assembly's *Generation Trilogy* (1995–98), highly skilful, high-energy movement sequences were set against the performers' banal confessions of personal weakness; in Vincent Dance's *Drop Dead Gorgeous* (2001) actual physical danger was used to expose the fragility of the body through highly technical dance sequences performed on a bed of broken slate by performers in high heels; and in Point Blank's *Dead Causes* (2000), performers who tried to 'speak the truth' to the audience were brutally silenced by the others in a frantic movement sequence which released clouds of ash into the auditorium.

Another development in this exploration of the 'real' was provided by companies that explored the potential of theatricality in the unique context of the live event, especially through the dangers of the unexpected and the possibility of including the audience in the action. Stan's Cafe's *It's Your Film* (1999) could be seen by only one spectator at a time, who was installed in a photo booth, eye-level positioned facing the centre of a small screen. To a ten-minute soundtrack, performers on the other side of the screen acted out a *film noir* sequence, the lighting design creating cinematic effects such as close-ups and long shots, enabling seeming 'cuts' and 'fades' between scenes. This was a self-aware experiment in simulation, live actors replicating 'filmed' sequences of 'live' action that had never taken place. Yet when the piece ended with a 'close-up' of an actor's sinister stare straight into the eyes of the spectator, the knowledge of his proximity on the other side of the screen, the feeling that this 'fourth wall' could so easily be broken, induced the pleasure of danger, the possibility that – unlike in watching a film – transgression could – at this very moment and no other – occur.

Reflex Theatre (founded 1995) performed a trilogy of pieces set in and around their audiences in pub, café and cabaret spaces (1996–8). In these the fictional and actual locations were identical, allowing the performers to mix freely with the audience/other patrons in and around the tables and along the bar. This created a unique viewpoint on the performers for each spectator – an intimate moment for one, for another was a 'long shot', framed by other performers and the environment itself. In addition to the pleasure of 'uniqueness' – the sense of individual attention so lacking in the mass media – the staging in a common social setting gave access to a community of involvement; the proximity of other spectators encouraged shared responses and post-show debate in ways rarely available in conventional theatres.

For example, towards the end of Lock In (1997) a 'spectator' suddenly challenged the action, then was joined by others, as local workshop participants got up to perform alongside the company. Each contribution had been devised by the performer, and they gained in significance partly because it was clear that the 'additional' actors were from constituencies virtually unrepresented in English theatre, whether mainstream or alternative. Whilst it could be said that Reflex Theatre's 'mediation' of such identities diminished the 'authenticity' of these participants, participatory strategies in performance were becoming a crucial means of challenging a post-modernism which, in celebrating a 'neo-liberal interest group pluralism', had few means for effectively addressing major structural inequalities in society.[16] Precisely because post-modernism undermines the authority of the subject-of-community, such inequalities are, as Dean MacCannell observes, 're-inscribe(d) as mere difference, drained of all specificity'.[17] From this perspective, it is significant that much of the performance work of the 1990s and early 2000s that struggled to realise meaningful collective identities was practised by artists from constituencies still largely marginalised in English theatre – artists of the new economic underclass, or with disabilities, or from black, Asian and other ethnic cultures. Active participation became a vital means to enable these voices to be heard speaking about their specific – and often communal – 'subjective' realities in order to counterbalance the dominant 'subjective' – and primarily individualist – realities of the white, middle-class, able-bodied artist.

Access and ownership for the future

Northern Stage Ensemble's adaptation of Anthony Burgess's A Clockwork Orange (1998–9) was informed by a parallel project in which members of the company worked with young offenders to make a film reflecting their experiences. In the touring production Burgess's anti-hero Alex and his friends,

16 Seyla Benhabib, 'Epistemologies of postmodernism: a rejoinder to Jean-François Lyotard', New German Critique 33 (1984), 124.
17 Dean MacCannell, Empty Meeting Grounds: The Tourist Papers (London: Routledge, 1992), p. 196.

played by professional actors, courted and charmed the audience with direct address and skilfully choreographed fighting. Their victims were presented as grotesque, luridly costumed cartoon characters, undermining – though not entirely – audience sympathy and shifting the focus firmly onto the authorities' subsequent treatment of Alex. This included his torture – tied into a wired-up chair – and subsequent humiliation on a chat show, one semi-human surrounded by grotesquely performed public figures. Without a doubt this interpretation derived directly from the real young offenders' slant on the issues involved. Hence, *A Clockwork Orange* was an expression of their vision, transparently mediated by a professional director and an ensemble company of quality actors. Similarly, *A Factory Romeo and Juliet* (1999) began as a joint project with Shadowdance, a special-needs dance group based in Newcastle-upon-Tyne, in which the impaired dancers led workshops for the Northern Stage performers, exploring their contrasting interpretations of Shakespeare's text. In the ensuing production the principal characters were shaped by the discoveries in the workshops. This created a moving attempt to express how love and passion are experienced by many people who, for whatever reason, have difficulty in communicating love, or even feeling – as a result of widespread prejudice – that they have no right to experience it at all.

The questions raised by this type of mediation, and the problems of determining ownership in such practices, entail sophisticated means of analysis. However, the fact remains that, in a culture so heavily weighted towards the already privileged, those artists who enjoy a relatively high profile are increasingly faced with a choice: do they simply ignore the occlusion of so many marginalised or dissident 'voices', or attempt, through empathic mediation, to reveal how they might 'speak'. The nature of each individual's active engagement with the processes of such performance itself constitutes the politics of these artistic practices. This engagement in performance explicitly challenges the scepticism and apathy fostered by the post-modern. For, whilst a spectator can disengage and remain unmoved by this (or any other) type of performance, a responsible 'actor' has to be committed to his or her action as well as a belief in its consequences and validity.

In the early years of the twenty-first century the post-modern conventions established by Forced Entertainment and others in the 1980s and 1990s became widespread and commonplace in English experimental theatre, and in parts of the mainstream, in the process losing their artistic and political edge. Consequently, companies such as Frantic Assembly, Third Angel, Point Blank and Unlimited Theatre (founded 1997) revisited narrative and character through a 'post' post-modern perspective. This tactic allowed a much broader spectrum of voices to be heard in the mediation of character, so that concerns beyond the purely formalist and philosophical could be addressed. By combining these 'traditional' conventions with an increased awareness of form, performativity and meta-narrative the new theatre of the new millennium found, perhaps, one route out of the nihilistic stalemate of much of the earlier post-modern performance.

Equally encouraging were the new priorities of arts funding agencies, which increasingly favoured theatre made by artists from marginalised communities or made specifically for those communities. Two of the revised five main aims of the Arts Council of England focussed on cultural diversity and social change, partly resulting from a major review of theatre provision in the late 1990s.[18] Unfortunately, media profiling and academic analysis of theatre addressing these and related areas of concern did not keep pace with the opportunities opened up by New Labour's cultural policies, and English theatre committed to the democratisation of performance was still having to rely on labels such as 'black', 'Asian', 'community' or 'disability' to justify its existence alongside the less contentiously labelled work – experimental, multi-media, independent – of the white, middle-class and able-bodied artist.

Nevertheless much was achieved in the 1990s and beyond to establish some equality of status for previously under-represented communities. Increasingly, women and gay men in particular occupied positions of influence in the systems of cultural production, and in the various sectors of English theatre, on stage and off. Still, the same rights and responsibilities needed to be won for and by those groups held at the margins. To deny such rights would have manifold social effects, not least of which would be the continuation of a blinkered view of what 'English' theatre, in its totality, might constitute in the new millennium.

18 Arts Council of England, *The Boyden Report* (London: Arts Council of England, 1999).

Bibliography

Adams, David, *Stage Welsh. Nation, Nationalism and Theatre: The Search for Cultural Identity*, Llandysul: Gomer, 1996.

Agate, James, *A Short View of the English Stage, 1900–1926*, London: Herbert Jenkins, 1926.

Aitcheson, J. W. and H. Carter, *A Geography of the Welsh Language 1961–1991*, Cardiff: University of Wales Press, 1994.

Aitcheson, J. W. and H. Carter, *The Welsh Language 1961–1981: An Interpretive Atlas*, Cardiff: University of Wales Press, 1985.

Anderson, Benedict, *Imagined Communities: Reflections on the Origin and Spread of Nationalism*, London: Verso, 1983; rev. edn 1991.

Anderson, Lindsay, 'Vital theatre', *Encore* 4, 2 (Nov.–Dec. 1957).

Anderson, William C., '"Diana of Dobson's": the shopgirl's characteristics and conditions', in Mary R. Macarthur (ed.), *The Woman Worker* 2 (12 June 1908).

Andrews, Kay and John Jacobs, *Punishing the Poor, Poverty under Thatcher*, London: Macmillan, 1990.

Anon , *The Mabinogion*, trans. Gwyn Jones and Thomas Jones, London: Everyman, 1992.

Ansorge, Peter, *Disrupting the Spectacle: Five Years of Experimental and Fringe Theatre in Britain*, London: Pitman, 1975.

Ansorge, Peter, *From Liverpool to Los Angeles: On Writing for Theatre, Film and Television*, London: Faber & Faber, 1997.

Archer, William, *The Old Drama and the New*, London: William Heinemann, 1923.

Archer, William, *The Theatrical World of 1893–1897*, 5 vols., London: Walter Scott, 1894–8.

Archer, William and Harley Granville Barker, *A National Theatre: Scheme and Estimates*, London: Duckworth, 1907.

Arden, John and Margaretta D'Arcy, *The Business of Good Government: A Christmas Play*, London: Methuen, 1963.

Arts Council of England, *The Boyden Report*, London: Arts Council of England, 1999.

Arts Council of England, *A Living Theatre – Delivering the National Policy for Theatre in England*, London: Arts Council of England, 2001.

Arts Council of England, 'The next stage: Arts Council sets out new vision for theatre', London: Arts Council of England (press release, 28 May 2000).

Arts Council of England, *51st Annual Report and Accounts 1996–97*, London: Arts Council of England, 1997.

Arts Council of England, '£100 million more for the arts', *Arts Council News* (August 2000).

Arts Council of Great Britain, *Ends and Means: 18th Annual Report*, London: Arts Council of Great Britain, 1963.

Arts Council of Great Britain, *The Glory of the Garden: The Development of the Arts in England*, London: Arts Council of Great Britain, 1984.

Arts Council of Great Britain, *Housing the Arts in Great Britain: Parts I and II*, London: Arts Council of Great Britain, 1959/1961.

Arts Council of Great Britain, *Key Year: 21st Annual Report*, London: Arts Council of Great Britain, 1965–6.

Arts Council of Great Britain, *State of Play: 19th Annual Report*, London: Arts Council of Great Britain, 1963–4.

Arts Council of Great Britain, *A Year of Achievement: 33rd Annual Report and Accounts 1977/78*, London: Arts Council of Great Britain, 1978.

Arts Council of Great Britain, *43rd Annual Report and Accounts*, London: Arts Council of Great Britain, 1988.

Arts Council of Wales, *The Arts in Wales: Priorities into Practice 7*, 2 (July 1984).

Arts Council of Wales, *The Drama Strategy for Wales*, Cardiff: Arts Council of Wales, 1999.

Asche, Oscar, *Oscar Asche, his Life, by Himself*, London: Hurst & Blockett, 1929.

Ashley, David, *History without a Subject: The Postmodern Condition*, Oxford: Westview Press, 1997.

Ashwell, Lena, *Myself a Player*, London: Michael Joseph, 1936.

Ashwell, Lena, 'Scrapbooks: 1907–April 1909, and 1908', unpublished material, Theatre Museum, London.

Aston, Elaine, *Feminist Theatre Practice*, London: Routledge, 1999.

Attenborough, Richard, *Arts and Disabled People: Report of a Committee of Inquiry under the Chairmanship of Sir Richard Attenborough*, London: Bedford Square Press, 1985.

Auden, W. H. and Christopher Isherwood, *The Dog Beneath the Skin: Or, Where is Francis?*, London: Faber & Faber, 1935.

Auslander, Philip, *From Acting to Performance: Essays in Modernism and Postmodernism*, London: Routledge, 1997.

Auslander, Philip, *Liveness: Performance in a Mediatised Culture*, London: Routledge, 1999.

Ayckbourn, Alan, *How the Other Half Loves*, London: Samuel French, 1972.

Ayckbourn, Alan, *Relatively Speaking*, London: Evans, 1968.

Bablet, Denis, *The Theatre of Edward Gordon Craig*, trans. Daphne Woodward, London: William Heinemann, 1966.

Bailey, Peter, *Popular Culture and Performance in the Victorian City*, Cambridge University Press, 1998.

Bailey, Peter (ed.), *Music Hall: The Business of Pleasure*, Milton Keynes: Open University Press, 1986.

Balfour, Michael (ed.), *Theatre and War 1933–1945: Performance in Extremis*, Oxford: Berghahn, 2001.

Banham, Martin (ed.), *The Cambridge Guide to Theatre*, updated edn, Cambridge University Press, 1995.

Bannister, Winifred, *James Bridie and his Theatre*, London: Rockcliff, 1955.

Barbor, H. R., *The Theatre: An Art and an Industry*, London: Labour Publishing, 1924.

Barker, Clive, 'From fringe to alternative theatre', *Zeitschrift für Anglistick und Amerikanistick* 26, 1 (1978).

Barker, Clive and Maggie B. Gale (eds.), *British Theatre Between the Wars, 1918–1939*, Cambridge University Press, 2000.

Barker, Howard, *Arguments for a Theatre*, 2nd edn, Manchester University Press, 1993.

Barker, Howard, *The Bite of the Night*, London: John Calder, 1988.

Barnes, Philip, *A Companion to Post-War British Theatre*, London: Croom Helm, 1986.

Barthes, Roland, *A Lover's Discourse: fragments*, trans. Richard Howard, London: Jonathan Cape, 1979.

Barthes, Roland, *S/Z*, trans. Richard Miller, Oxford: Blackwell, 1990.

Bason, Fred, *Gallery Unreserved*, London: John Heritage, 1931.

Bate, Jonathan and Russell Jackson (eds.), *Shakespeare: An Illustrated Stage History*, Oxford University Press, 1996.

Baudrillard, Jean, *Simulacra and Simulation*, trans. Sheila Faria Glaser, Ann Arbor: University of Michigan Press, 1994.

Beauman, Sally, *The Royal Shakespeare Company*, Oxford University Press, 1982.

Beerbohm, Max, *Around Theatres, 1924*, London: Rupert Hart-Davis, 1953; reprinted, New York: Simon & Schuster, 1954.

Beerbohm, Max, *Last Theatres, 1904–1910*, New York: Taplinger, 1970.

Bell, Sam Hanna, *The Theatre in Ulster*, Totowa, N.J.: Rowan & Littlefield, 1972.

Benhabib, Seyla, 'Epistemologies of postmodernism: a rejoinder to Jean-François Lyotard', *New German Critique* 33 (1984).

Benjamin, Walter, *Illuminations*, trans. Harry Zohn, London: Fontana, 1992.

Bennett, Arnold, *Cupid and Commonsense*, London: Frank Palmer, 1909.

Bignell, Jonathan, Stephen Lacy and Madelaine Macmurraugh-Kavanagh (eds.), *British Television Drama – Past, Present and Future*, New York: Palgrave, 2000.

Billingham, Peter, *Theatres of Conscience 1939–1953: A Study of Four Touring British Community Theatres*, London: Routledge Harwood, 2002.

Bond, Edward, 'A discussion with Edward Bond', *Gambit* 17 (1970).

Bond, Edward, 'Interview with Edward Bond', *Gambit* 17 (1970).

Boon, Richard, *Brenton: The Playwright*, London: Methuen, 1991.

Booth, Michael R. and Joel H. Kaplan (eds.), *The Edwardian Theatre: Essays on Performance and the Stage*, Cambridge University Press, 1996.

Bourchier, Arthur, *Art and Culture in Relation to Socialism*, London: ILP, 1926.

Bourdieu, Pierre, *Distinction: A Social Critique of the Judgement of Taste*, trans. Richard Nice, London: Routledge & Kegan Paul, 1984.

Bradby, David and David Williams, *Directors' Theatre*, London: Macmillan, 1988.

Brandane, John, *The Glen is Mine*, London: Constable, 1939.

Brandt, George (ed.), *British Television Drama in the 1980s*, Cambridge University Press, 1993.

Branson, Noreen, *Britain in the Nineteen Twenties*, London: Weidenfeld & Nicolson, 1975.

Branson, Noreen and Margot Heinemann, *Britain in the Nineteen Thirties*, London: Weidenfeld & Nicolson, 1971.

Bratton, J. S. (ed.), *Music Hall: Performance and Style*, Milton Keynes: Open University Press, 1986.

Bratton, J. S., Richard Allen Cave, Breandan Gregory, Heidi J. Holder and Michael Pickering, *Acts of Supremacy: The British Empire and the Stage, 1790–1930*, Manchester University Press, 1991.

Braun, Edward, *The Director and the Stage*, London: Methuen, 1982.

Brenton, Howard, *Hot Irons: Diaries, Essays, Journalism*, London: Nick Hern Books, 1995.

Brenton, Howard, *The Romans in Britain*, London: Methuen, 1980.

Brenton, Howard, *Sore Throats*, London: Methuen, 1979.

Bridges-Adams, William, *Looking at a Play*, London: Phoenix House, 1947.

Brith Gof, *Brith Gof – A Welsh Theatre Company: 1981–85*, Cardiff: Brith Gof, 1985.

Brith Gof, *Brith Gof – A Welsh Theatre Company: 1985–88*, Cardiff: Brith Gof, 1988.

Brith Gof, *Brith Gof – y llyfr glas: 1988–95*, Cardiff: Brith Gof, 1995.

Brookfield, Charles H. E., 'On Plays and Play-Writing', *National Review*, 345 (November 1911).

Brown, Muriel and Nicola Madge, *Despite the Welfare State*, London: William Heinemann, 1982.

Browne, Henzie and E. Martin Browne, *Pilgrim Story: The Pilgrim Players, 1939–1943*, London: Frederick Muller, 1945.

Bull, John, *New British Political Dramatists*, London: Macmillan, 1984.

Bull, John, *Stage Right: Crisis and Recovery in Mainstream British Theatre*, London: Macmillan, 1994.

Burns, Tom and Elizabeth Burns (eds.), *The Sociology of Literature and Drama*, Harmondsworth: Penguin, 1973.

Butler, Nicholas, *John Martin-Harvey: The Biography of an Actor Manager*, Wivenhoe: Nicholas Butler, 1997.

Cameron, Alasdair, *Twentieth-Century Scottish Theatre: A Study Guide*, Department of Scottish Literature, University of Glasgow, 1988.

Carey, John, *The Intellectuals and the Masses*, London: Faber & Faber, 1992.

Carson, L. (ed.), *The Stage Yearbook 1928*, London: The Stage, 1928.

Cartwright, Jim, *Road*, London: Methuen, 1990.

Case, Sue-Ellen, *Split Britches: Lesbian Practice/Feminist Performance*, London: Routledge, 1996.

CAST (Cartoon Archetypal Slogan Theatre), *Confessions of a Socialist*, London: Pluto Press, 1979.

Chambers, Colin, *Other Spaces: New Theatre and the RSC*, London: Eyre Methuen, 1980.

Chambers, Colin, *The Story of Unity Theatre*, London: Lawrence & Wishart, 1989.

Chambers, Colin and Mike Prior, *Playwrights' Progress: Patterns in Post-War British Drama*, Oxford: Amber Lane, 1987.

Chapman, Claire and Pam Schweitzer (eds.), *Theatre in Education Directory*, London: Theatre Quarterly Publications, 1975.

Chapman, Mave and Ben Chapman, *The Pierrots of the Yorkshire Coast*, Beverley: Hutton Press, 1988.

Cheeseman, Peter, 'A community theatre-in-the-round', *Theatre Quarterly* 1, 1 (Jan.–March 1971).

Cheeseman, Peter, 'Introduction', in *The Knotty*, London: Methuen, 1970.

Child, Harold, *A Poor Player: The Story of a Failure*, Cambridge University Press, 1939.

Chisholm, Cecil, *Repertory: An Outline of the Modern Theatre Movement*, London: Peter Davies, 1934.

Chothia, Jean, *English Drama of the Early Modern Period 1890–1940*, Harlow: Longman, 1996.

Churchill, Caryl, *Plays: One*, London: Methuen, 1985.

Cima, Gay Gibson, *Performing Women: Female Characters, Male Playwrights and the Modern Stage*, Ithaca: Cornell University Press, 1993.

Citizens' Theatre Company: A Conspectus to Mark the Citizens' 21st Anniversary, Glasgow: Citizens' Theatre Ltd, 1964.

Clarke, Jon and Margot Heinemann, *Culture and Crisis in Britain in the 1930s*, London: Lawrence & Wishart, 1970.

Cochrane, Claire, *Shakespeare at the Birmingham Repertory Theatre 1913–1929*, London: Society for Theatre Research, 1993.

Cockrell, Dale, *Demons of Disorder: Early Blackface Minstrels and their World*, Cambridge University Press, 1997.

Cohen, Ruth and Maryrose Tarpey, *Single Payments, the Disappearing Safety Net* (Poverty Pamphlet 74), London: CPAG Ltd, 1988.

Collins, L. J., *Theatre at War 1914–18*, London: Macmillan, 1998.

Coppetiers, Frank, 'Arnold Wesker's Centre Forty-Two: a cultural revolution betrayed', *Theatre Quarterly*, 5, 18 (June–Aug. 1975).

Cork, Sir Kenneth, *Theatre IS for All: Report of the Enquiry into Professional Theatre in England, 1986*, London: Arts Council of Great Britain, 1986.

Corner, John (ed.), *Popular TV in Britain: Studies in Cultural History*, London: British Film Institute, 1991.

Corrie, Joe, *In Time o' Strife*, Edinburgh: 7:84 Theatre Company, 1982.

Cotes, P. *George Robey*, London: Cassell, 1972.

Coult, Tony and Baz Kershaw (eds.), *Engineers of the Imagination: The Welfare State Handbook*, rev. edn, London: Methuen, 1990.

Coveney, Michael, *The Citz: 21 Years of the Glasgow Citizens' Theatre*, London: Nick Hern Books, 1990.

Coveney, Michael, 'Pushing on to a national theatre', *Plays and Players*, 21, 7 (April 1974).

Cox, R. Douglas, C. Douglas Stuart and William Martin, *Theatrical, Variety & Fit-Up Directory*, London: Whitton & Smith, 1904, 1905, etc.

Craig, Cairns, *Out of History*, Edinburgh: Polygon, 1996.

Craig, Edward Gordon, *On the Art of the Theatre*, London: William Heinemann, 1911.

Craig, Sandy (ed.), *Dreams and Deconstructions: Alternative Theatre in Britain*, Ambergate, Derbys.: Amber Lane, 1980.

Curtis, T. (ed.), *Wales: The Imagined Nation*, Bridgend: Poetry Wales Press, 1986.

Daldry, Stephen, 'There is a new audience out there', in *Live 1: Food for the Soul – A New Generation of British Theatre Makers*, ed. David Tushingham, London: Methuen, 1994.

Dale, Antony, *The Theatre Royal Brighton*, Stocksfield: Oriel Press, 1980.

Daniel, John, 'Baying for Blood' (interview with Franco B.), *Total Theatre*, 9, 4 (winter 1997–8).

Davies, Andrew, *Other Theatres: The Development of Alternative and Experimental Theatre in Britain*, London: Macmillan, 1987.

Davies, Cecil, *The Adelphi Players: The Theatre of Persons*, ed. Peter Billingham, London: Routledge Harwood, 2002.

Davies, D. Jacob, 'Llwyfannu Meini Gwagedd', *Y Gehinen* (Haf 1954).

Davies, George, 'Drama yr Ymylon', *Drama* (Gwanwyn 1960).

Davies, Walford, *Saunders Lewis a Theatr Garthewin*, Llandysul: Gomer, 1995.

Davies, Hazel Walford (ed.), *State of Play*, Llandysul: Gomer, 1998.

Davies, Janet, *The Welsh Language*, Cardiff: University of Wales Press, 1993.

Davies, John, *A History of Wales*, Harmondsworth: Penguin, 1994.

Davis, Tracy C., *The Economics of the British Stage, 1800–1914*, Cambridge University Press, 2000.

Dean, Anthony (ed.), *Street Arts: A User's Guide*, Winchester: King Alfred's College Press/International Street Arts Network, 2003.

Dean, Basil, *The Theatre at War*, London: George Harrap, 1956.

De Jongh, Nicholas, *Not in Front of the Audience: Homosexuality on Stage*, London: Routledge, 1992.

De Jongh, Nicholas, *Politics, Prudery and Perversions: The Censoring of the English Stage 1901–1968*, London: Methuen, 2001.

Dellar, Pamela (ed.), *Plays without Theatres: Recollections of the Compass Players, 1944–1952*, Beverley, Yorks: Highgate Publications, 1989.

Devine, T. M. and R. J. Finlay (eds.), *Scotland in the 20th Century*, Edinburgh University Press, 1996.

Diamond, Elin (ed.), *Performance and Cultural Politics*, London: Routledge, 1996.

Dick, Eddie (ed.), *From Limelight to Satellite*, London: British Film Institute and Scottish Film Council, 1990.

Dickinson, Thomas H., *The Changing Theatre in Europe*, London: Putnam, n.d., *c.*, 1937.

Donnachie, Ian and Christopher Whatley (eds.), *The Manufacture of Scottish History*, Edinburgh: Polygon, 1992.

Donohue, Joseph, 'What is the Edwardian theatre?', in Michael R. Booth and Joel H. Kaplan, eds., *The Edwardian Theatre: Essays on Performance and the Stage*, Cambridge University Press, 1996.

Downing, Dick, *In our Neighbourhood: A Regional Theatre and its Local Community*, York: Joseph Rowntree Foundation, 2001.

Dukes, Ashley, *Drama*, London: Williams & Northgate, 1926.

Dukes, Ashley, *The World to Play With*, Oxford University Press, 1928.

Du Maurier, Daphne, *Gerald, A Portrait*, London: Victor Gollancz, 1934.

Dunbar, Andrea, *Rita, Sue and Bob Too*, London: Methuen, 1988.

Duncan, Robert and Arthur McIvor (eds.), *Labour and Class Conflict on the Clyde 1900–1950*, Edinburgh: John Donald, 1992.

Duvignaud, Jean, *Le Sociologie du théâtre*, Paris: Presses Universitaires de France, 1965.

Dyhouse, Carol, *Feminism and the Family in England 1880–1939*, Oxford: Blackwell, 1989.

Eagleton, Terry, 'Nature and violence: the Prefaces of Edward Bond', *Critical Quarterly* 26 (1994).

Edgar, David, 'Public theatre in a private age', *British Theatre Institute: Special Report 1* (1984).

Edgar, David, *The Second Time as Farce: Reflections on the Drama of Mean Times*, London: Lawrence & Wishart, 1988.

Edgar, David (ed.), *State of Play*, London: Faber & Faber, 1999.

Edwards, Emyr, 'Tristwch ein theatr', *Y Faner* (Sept. 1986).

Edwards, Hywel Teifi, *Codi'r Llen*, Llandysul: Gomer, 1998.

Edwards, Hywel Teifi (ed.), *A Guide to Welsh Literature c. 1800–1900*, 5 vols., Cardiff: University of Wales Press, 2000.

Elder, Eleanor, *Travelling Players: The Story of the Arts League of Service*, London: Frederick Muller, 1939.

Elsom, John, *Post-War British Theatre*, rev. edn, London: Routledge & Kegan Paul, 1979.

Englebrecht, H. C. and F. C. Hanighen, *Merchants of Death: A Study of the International Armament Industry*, London: George Routledge, 1934.

Equity, 'Report on a survey of members', London: Equity, 1999.

Ervine, St John, 'British Drama League lecture', *Times* (1 Jan. 1926).

Evans, Eric J. and Jeffrey Richards, *A Social History of Britain in Postcards 1870–1930*, Harlow: Longman, 1980.

Ewing, K. D. and C. A. Gearty, *Freedom under Thatcher: Civil Liberties in Modern Britain*, Oxford University Press, 1990.

Eyre, Richard and Nicholas Wright, *Changing Stages: A View of British Theatre in the Twentieth Century*, London: Bloomsbury, 2000.

Fawkes, Richard, *Fighting for a Laugh: Entertaining the British and American Armed Forces 1939–1946*, London: Macdonald & Jane's, 1978.

Federation of Scottish Theatre, *Proposal for a National Theatre for Scotland*, Edinburgh: Federation of Scottish Theatre Limited, 2000.

Federation of Theatre Unions, 'Theatre ownership in Britain – a report', London: Federation of Theatre Unions, 1953.

Feist, Andrew and Robert Hutchison (eds), *Cultural Trends in the Eighties,* London: Policy Studies Institute, 1990.

Feist, Andrew and Robert Hutchison (eds.), *Cultural Trends 1990*, London: Policy Studies Institute, 1990.

Ferguson, J. A., *Campbell of Kilmohr*, London: Gowans & Gray, 1915.

Filewood, Alan and David Watt, *Worker's Playtime: Theatre and the Labour Movement Since 1970*, Sydney: Currency Press, 2001.

Findlater, Richard, *Banned! A Review of Theatrical Censorship in Britain*, London: MacGibbon & Kee, 1967.

Findlater, Richard, *The Unholy Trade*, London: Victor Gollancz, 1952.

Findlay, Bill (ed.), *A History of Scottish Theatre*, Edinburgh: Polygon, 1998.

Forbes-Winslow, D., *Daly's, The Biography of a Theatre*, London: W. H. Allen, 1944.

Foucault, Michel, *The Archaeology of Knowledge*, trans. A. M. Sheridan Smith, London: Tavistock, 1972.

Foucault, Michel, *The History of Sexuality, An Introduction*, trans. Robert Hurley, Harmondsworth: Penguin, 1979.

Foulkes, Richard (ed.), *British Theatre in the 1890s: Essays on Drama and the Stage*, Cambridge University Press, 1992.

Francis, J. O., 'The deacon and the dramatist', *Welsh Outlook* (June 1919).

Francombe, Ben, 'Falling off a wall – degrees of change in British actor training', *Studies in Theatre and Performance* 21, 3 (2001).

Freeman, Sandra, *Putting your Daughters on the Stage: Lesbian Theatre from 1970s to 1990s*, London: Cassell, 1997.

Fukuyama, Francis, 'The end of History?' *National Interest* (Summer 1989).

Fukuyama, Francis, *The End of History and the Last Man*, Harmondsworth: Penguin, 1992.

Fussell, Paul, *The Great War and Modern Memory*, Oxford University Press, 1975.

Gale, Maggie B., *West End Women: Women on the London Stage 1918–1962*, London: Routledge, 1996.

Gale, Maggie B. and Viv Gardner (eds.), *Women, Theatre and Performance: New Histories, New Historiographies*, Manchester University Press, 2000.

Gamble, Andrew, *The Free Economy and the Strong State: the Politics of Thatcherism*, 2nd edn, London: Macmillan, 1994.

Gardner, Lyn, 'Just sit down and shut up', *Guardian Saturday Review* (14 Oct. 2000).

Gardner, Viv, 'No flirting with philistinism: Shakespeare production at Miss Horniman's Gaiety Theatre', *New Theatre Quarterly* 14, 55 (Aug. 1998).

Gardner, Viv (ed.), *Sketches from the Actresses' Franchise League*, Nottingham: Nottingham Drama Texts, 1985.

Garner, Stanton B., *Bodied Spaces: Phenomenology and Performance in Contemporary Drama*, Ithaca: Cornell University Press, 1994.

Gee, Emma and Richard Hayhow, 'Community plays', *Mailout: Arts Work with People* (Feb./March 1999).

Giddens, Anthony, *Beyond Left and Right: The Future of Radical Politics*, London: Polity, 1994.

Giesekam, Greg, 'Review of *The Politics of Alternative Theatre in Britain 1968–1990*, by Maria DiCenzo', *Comparative Drama* 33, 3 (fall 1999).

Gifford, Douglas and Dorothy McMillan (eds.), *A History of Scottish Women's Writing*, Edinburgh University Press, 1997.

Gill, Maud, *See the Players*, London: Hutchinson, 1938.

Godfrey, Philip, *Back Stage*, London: George Harrap, 1933.

Goldie, Grace Wyndham, *The Liverpool Repertory Theatre 1911–1935*, London: Hodder & Stoughton, 1935.

Gooch, Steve and Paul Thomson, *The Motor Show*, London: Pluto Press, 1975.

Goodman, Lizbeth, *Contemporary Feminist Theatres: To Each Her Own*, London: Routledge, 1993.

Goodman, Lizbeth and Jane de May, *Feminist Stages*, Amsterdam: Harwood Academic Press, 1996.

Goodwin, Tim, *Britain's Royal National Theatre: The First Twenty-Five Years*, London: National Theatre with Nick Hern Books, 1988.

Goorney, Howard, *The Theatre Workshop Story*, London: Eyre Methuen, 1981.

Goorney, Howard and Ewan MacColl (eds.), *Agit-Prop to Theatre Workshop: Political Playscripts 1930–50*, Manchester University Press, 1986.

Gottlieb, Vera, 'Thatcher's theatre – or, after *Equus*', *New Theatre Quarterly* 4, 14 (May 1988).

Gottlieb, Vera, 'Theatre Today – the "new realism"', *Contemporary Theatre Review* 13, 1 (Feb. 2003).

Gottlieb, Vera and Colin Chambers (eds.), *Theatre in a Cool Climate*, Oxford: Amber Lane, 1999.

Granville Barker, Harley, 'Preface', in *Laurence Housman's Little Plays of St Francis*, 2nd series, London: Sidgwick & Jackson, 1931.

Granville Barker, Harley, 'Repertory theatres', *New Quarterly* 2 (1909).

Gray, Terence, *Dance-Drama: Experiments in the Art of the Theatre*, Cambridge: Heffer & Sons, 1926.

Great Britain Board of Education, Adult Education Committee, *The Drama in Adult Education*, London: HMSO, 1926.

Greig, David, 'Petra', unpublished typescript.

Greig, David, 'Petra's Explanation', unpublished typescript.

Griffiths, Trevor, 'Author's preface', in *Through the Night*, London: Faber & Faber, 1977.

Gruffydd, W. J., 'Drama i Gymru', *Y Beirniad* 1 (1911).

Guthrie, Tyrone, *A Life in the Theatre*, London: Hamish Hamilton, 1960.

Guttmann, Alan, *Sports Spectators*, New York: Columbia University Press, 1986.

Hall, Stuart and Martin Jacques (eds.), *New Times: The Changing Face of Politics in the 1990s*, London: Lawrence & Wishart, 1989.

Hamilton, Cicely, *Diana of Dobson's: A Romantic Comedy in Four Acts*, New York: Samuel French, 1925.

Hamilton, Cicely, *Life Errant*, London: J. M. Dent, 1935.

Hamilton, Cicely, *Marriage as a Trade*, London: Chapman & Hall, 1909; rpt. London: Women's Press, 1981.

Hamilton, Cicely and Lilian Baylis, *The Old Vic*, London: Jonathan Cape, 1926.

Hammond, Jonathan, 'A potted history of the fringe', *Theatre Quarterly* 3, 12 (Oct.–Dec. 1973).

Hands, Terry, 'Who has the vision to revive our future?', *Western Mail* (14 Nov. 1998).

Hannan, Chris, *Shining Souls*, London: Nick Hern Books, 1996.

Harris, Geraldine, *Staging Femininities*, Manchester University Press, 1999.

Harrower, David, *Kill the Old Torture their Young*, London: Methuen, 1998.

Harrower, David, *Knives in Hens*, London: Methuen, 1995.

Harrower, David and David Greig, 'Why a new Scotland must have a properly-funded theatre', *Scotsman* (25 Nov. 1997).

Hartnoll, Phyllis (ed.), *The Oxford Companion to the Theatre*, 4th edn, Oxford University Press, 1983.

Harvie, Christopher, *No Gods and Precious Few Heroes: Scotland 1914–1980*, London: Edward Arnold, 1981.

Harvie, Christopher, *Scotland and Nationalism*, 3rd edn, London: Routledge, 1998.

Hawkes, Terence, *Meaning by Shakespeare*, London: Routledge, 1992.

Hay, Malcolm and Philip Roberts, 'Interview with Howard Brenton', *Performing Arts Journal*, 3, 3 (1979).

Hayes, Mark, *The New Right in Britain*, London: Pluto Press, 1994.

Hayman, Ronald, *British Theatre Since 1955: A Reassessment*, Oxford University Press, 1979.

Hayman, Ronald, *The Set-Up: An Anatomy of the English Theatre Today*, London: Eyre Methuen, 1973.

Haynes, Jim, *Thanks for Coming*, London: Faber & Faber, 1984.

Hewison, Robert, *Culture and Consensus: England, Art and Politics Since 1940*, London: Methuen, 1997.

Hewison, Robert, *Under Siege: Literary Life in London 1939–45*, rev. edn, London: Methuen, 1988.

Hill, John, 'Glasgow Unity Theatre: the search for a "Scottish People's Theatre"', *New Edinburgh Review* 40 (Feb. 1978).

Hill, John, 'Towards a Scottish people's theatre: the rise and fall of Glasgow Unity', *Theatre Quarterly* 7, 27 (autumn 1977).

Hobsbawm, Eric, *The Age of Empire, 1876–1914*, London: Weidenfeld & Nicolson, 1987.

Hodgson, Terry (ed.), *The Batsford Dictionary of Drama*, London: Batsford, 1988.

Holderness, Graham (ed.), *The Politics of Theatre and Drama*, London: Macmillan, 1992.

Hollege, Julie, *Innocent Flowers: Women in the Edwardian Theatre*, London: Virago, 1981.

Holroyd, Michael, *Bernard Shaw*, 4 vols., New York: Random House, 1988–92.

Homden, Carol, *The Plays of David Hare*, London: Routledge, 1996.

Honri, Peter, *Working the Halls*, London: Futura, 1976.

Hooper, Ewan, 'A new Scottish theatre', unpublished typescript, Scottish Theatre Archive, Special Collections Department, Glasgow University Library, 1981.

Howard, Diana, *London Theatres and Music Halls, 1850–1950*, London: Library Association, 1970.

Howard, Philip (ed.), *Scotland Plays*, London: Nick Hern Books, 1998.

Howard, Tony, 'Theatre of urban renewal: the uncomfortable case of Covent Garden', *Theatre Quarterly* 10, 38 (summer 1980).

Howard, Tony and John Stokes (eds.), *Acts of War: The Representation of Military Conflict on the British Stage and Television Since 1945*, Aldershot: Scolar, 1996.

Howe, P. P., *Dramatic Portraits*, London: Martin Secker, 1913.

Howe, P. P., *The Repertory Theatre: A Record and A Criticism*, London: Martin Secker, 1910.

Hudson, Lynton, *The Twentieth-Century Drama*, London: George Harrap, 1946.

Huggett, Richard, *Binkie Beaumont: Eminence Grise of the West End Theatre 1933–1973*, London: Hodder & Stoughton, 1989.

Humphreys, Emyr, *The Taliesin Tradition*, London: Black Raven Press, 1983.

Hunt, Albert, *Arden: a Study of his Plays*, London: Eyre Methuen, 1975.

Hunt, Hugh, Kenneth Richards and John Russell Taylor, *The Revels History of Drama in English*, vol. VII, *1880 to the Present Day*, London: Methuen, 1978.

Hutchison, Robert, *The Politics of the Arts Council*, London: Sinclair Browne, 1982.

Hynes, Samuel, *The Edwardian Turn of Mind*, Princeton University Press, 1968.

Innes, Christopher, *Edward Gordon Craig*, Cambridge University Press, 1983; 2nd edn, Amsterdam: Harwood Academic Press, 1998.

Irving, G. *Great Scot!*, London: Leslie Frewin, 1968.

Itzin, Catherine (ed.), *Alternative Theatre Handbook*, London: Theatre Quarterly Publications, 1976.

Itzin, Catherine (ed.), *British Alternative Theatre Directory, 1980*, Eastbourne: John Offord, 1980.

Itzin, Catherine (ed.), *British Alternative Theatre Directory, 1982*, Eastbourne: John Offord, 1982.

Itzin, Catherine, *Stages in the Revolution: Political Theatre in Britain Since 1968*, London: Eyre Methuen, 1980.

Jellicoe, Ann, *Community Plays: How To Put Them On*, London: Methuen, 1987.

Jones, Alun R. and Gwyn Thomas (eds.), *Presenting Saunders Lewis*, Cardiff: University of Wales Press, 1973.

Jones, David, 'Community plays: two cultures', *Mailout: Arts Work with People* (Aug./Sept. 1995).

Jones, D. Llwyd, 'Drama Arwyddocaol', *Y Faner* 23, 5 (1945).

Jones, Nerys Ann, 'Golwg Newydd ar Flodeuwedd', *Taliesin* 65 (1988).

Jones, Tudur, *Remaking the Labour Party: From Gaitskell to Blair*, London: Routledge, 1996.

Jones, R. Tudur, *John Elias: Prince Amongst Preachers*, Bridgend: Welsh Evangelical Society, 1975.

Kane, Sarah, *Blasted* with *Phaedra's Love*, London: Methuen, 1996.

Kane, Sarah, *Cleansed*, London: Methuen, 1998.

Kane, Sarah, *Crave*, London: Methuen, 1998.

Kane, Whitford, *Are We All Met?*, London: Elkin Mathews & Marrot, 1931.

Kaplan, Joel H. and Sheila Stowell, *Theatre and Fashion: Oscar Wilde to the Suffragettes*, Cambridge University Press, 1994.

Kaye, Nick (ed.), *Art into Theatre: Performance Interviews and Documents*, Amsterdam: Harwood Academic Press, 1996.

Kaye, Nick (ed.), 'British Live Art: Essays and Documentation', *Contemporary Theatre Review* 2, 2 (1994).

Kaye, Nick, *Postmodernism and Performance*, London: Macmillan, 1994.

Kaye, Nick, *Site-Specific Art: Performance, Place and Documentation*, London: Routledge, 2000.

Keat, Russell, Nigel Whiteley and Nicholas Abercrombie (eds.), *The Authority of the Consumer*, London: Routledge, 1994.

Kelsall, Moultrie, *The Twelve Seasons of the Edinburgh Gateway Company, 1953–1965*, Edinburgh: St Giles Press, 1965.

Kennedy, Dennis, *Granville Barker and the Dream of Theatre*, Cambridge University Press, 1985.

Kennedy, Dennis, *Looking at Shakespeare: A Visual History of Twentieth-Century Performance*, 2nd edn, Cambridge University Press, 2001.

Kennedy, Dennis (ed.), *The Oxford Encyclopedia of Theatre and Performance*, Oxford University Press, 2003.

Kennedy, Dennis, 'Sports and shows: spectators in contemporary culture', *Theatre Research International* 26, 3 (2001).

Kershaw, Baz, 'Building an unstable pyramid: the fragmentation of British alternative theatre', *New Theatre Quarterly* 9, 36 (Nov. 1993).

Kershaw, Baz, 'Discouraging democracy: British theatres and economics, 1979–1999', *Theatre Journal* 51, 3 (Oct. 1999).

Kershaw, Baz, 'Dramas of the performative society: theatre at the end of its tether', *New Theatre Quarterly* 17, 67 (Aug. 2001).

Kershaw, Baz, *The Politics of Performance: Radical Theatre as Cultural Intervention*, London: Routledge, 1992.

Kershaw, Baz, *The Radical in Performance: Between Brecht and Baudrillard*, London: Routledge, 1999.

Kilroy, Thomas, 'Groundwork for an Irish theatre', *Studies: An Irish Quarterly Review of Letters, Philosophy and Science* 48 (summer 1958).

King, Elspeth, *The Hidden History of Glasgow Women: The New Factor*, Edinburgh: Mainstream, 1993.

King, Robert, *North Shields Theatres*, Gateshead: Northumberland Press, 1948.

King, W. Davies, *Henry Irving's Waterloo: Theatrical Engagements with Arthur Conan Doyle, George Bernard Shaw, Ellen Terry, Edward Gordon Craig, Late-Victorian Culture, Assorted Ghosts, Old Men, War, and HISTORY*, Berkeley: University of California Press, 1993.

Kirwan, Bernadette, 'Aspects of Left Theatre in England in the 1930s', unpublished Ph.D. thesis, Loughborough University, 1989.

Klein, Naomi, *No Logo*, London: Flamingo / HarperCollins, 2000.

Klein, Naomi, 'The tyranny of the brands', *New Statesman* (24 Jan. 2000).

Knoblock, Edward, *Round the Room: An Autobiography*, London: Chapman & Hall, 1939.

Kracauer, S., *The Mass Ornament*, trans. Thomas Y. Levin, Cambridge, Mass.: Harvard University Press, 1995.

Kustow, Michael, *Theatre@Risk*, London: Methuen, 2000.

Lamb, Charles, *Howard Barker's Theatre of Seduction*, Amsterdam: Harwood Academic Press, 1996.

Landstone, Charles, *Off Stage: A Personal Record of the First Twelve Years of State-Sponsored Drama in Great Britain*, London: Paul Elek, 1953.

Lash, Scott and John Urry, *The End of Organised Capitalism*, Cambridge: Polity, 1987.

Lavender, Andy, 'Theatre in crisis: conference report, December 1988', *New Theatre Quarterly* 5, 19 (Aug. 1989).

Lesser, Wendy, *A Director Calls: Stephen Daldry and the Theatre*, London: Faber & Faber, 1997.

Levitas, Ruth (ed.), *The Ideology of the New Right*, Cambridge: Polity Press, 1986.

Lewis, Saunders, 'By way of apology', *Dock Leaves* 6 (1955).

Lewis, Saunders, *Gymerwch Chi Sigaret?*, Llandybie: Llyfrau'r Dryw, 1956.

Lewis, Saunders, 'The present state of Welsh drama', *Welsh Outlook* 6 (1919).

Lewis, Saunders, 'Rhai Amhenon', *Y Llwyfan* 4, Media Gorfferat (June/July 1928).

Lewis, Mair Saunders, *et al.* (eds.), *Letters to Margaret Gilcriest*, Cardiff: University of Wales Press, 1933.

Linklater, N. V., 'The achievement in drama', in *The State and the Arts*, ed. John Pick, Eastbourne: John Offord, 1980.

Littlewood, Joan, *Joan's Book: Joan Littlewood's Peculiar History As She Tells It*, London: Methuen, 1994; London: Minerva, 1995.

Littlewood, Joan, 'Plays for the people', *World Theatre* 8, 4 (1960).

Lloyd, D. Tecwyn, 'Daniel Owen ar y Llwyfan', *Llên Cymru* 10 (1968–9).

Lloyd, Tecwyn D., 'Gwir gychwyn busnes drama 'ma', *Llyfan* 8 (spring/summer 1973).

Lochhead, Liz, *Mary Queen of Scots got her Head Chopped Off*, Harmondsworth: Penguin, 1989.

Lott, Eric, *Love and Theft: Blackface Minstrelsy and the American Working Class*, Oxford University Press, 1993.

Loveman, Jack, Letter to the editor, *Young Worker* (9 Oct. 1926).

Lucas, Ian, *Impertinent Decorum: Gay Theatrical Manoeuvres*, London: Cassell, 1993.

Lucas, John (ed.), *The 1930s. A Challenge to Orthodoxy*, Brighton: Harvester Press, 1978.

MacCannell, Dean, *Empty Meeting Grounds: The Tourist Papers*, London: Routledge, 1992.

MacColl, Ewan, *Journeyman*, London: Sidgwick & Jackson, 1990.

MacDonald, Robert David, *ChinCilla*, in *A Decade's Drama*, Todmorden, Lancs: Woodhouse Books, 1980.

MacLennan, Elizabeth, *The Moon Belongs to Everyone: Making Theatre with 7:84*, London: Methuen, 1990.

Macleod, Joseph, *The Actor's Right to Act*, London: Lawrence & Wishart, 1981.

Macqueen-Pope, Walter James, *The Footlights Flickered*, London: Jenkins, 1959.

Macqueen-Pope, Walter James, *Gaiety: Theatre of Enchantment*, London: W. H. Allen, 1949.

Macqueen-Pope, Walter James, *Shirt Fronts and Sables: A Story of the Days when Money could be Spent*, London: Hale, 1953.

Mackintosh, Cameron, 'No public subsidy, no West End', in *Arts Council of England: Annual Report 1995–96*, London: Arts Council of England, 1996.

Maguire, Tom, 'Under new management: the changing direction of 7:84 (Scotland)', *Theatre Research International* 17, 2 (summer 1992).

Mais, S. P. B., 'A short view of the modern English stage', *Theatre World* (Dec. 1926).

Maitland, S., *Vesta Tilley*, London: Virago, 1986.

Malleson, Miles, *The Fanatics*, London: Ernest Benn, 1924.

Malleson, Miles, *The ILP Arts Guild: The ILP and its Dramatic Societies: What They Are and Might Become*, London: ILP Publications, 1925.

Maltby, H. F., *What Might Happen: A Piece of Extravagance in Three Acts*, London: Stage Play Publishing Bureau, 1927.

Mander, Raymond and Joe Mitchenson, *The Lost Theatres of London*, London: Rupert Hart-Davis, 1968; rev. edn, London: New English Library, 1976.

Mander, Raymond and Joe Mitchenson, *Musical Comedy: A Story in Pictures*, London: Peter Davies, 1969.

Mander, Raymond and Joe Mitchenson, *The Theatres of London*, 1st edn, London: Rupert Hart-Davis, 1961; 3rd edn, London: New English Library, 1975.

Marowitz, Charles, *Confessions of a Counterfeit Critic: A London Theatre Notebook 1958–71*, London: Eyre Methuen, 1973.

Marowitz, Charles and Simon Trussler (eds.), *Theatre at Work: Playwrights and Productions in the Modern British Theatre*, London: Methuen, 1967.

Marshall, Norman, *The Other Theatre*, London: John Lehmann, 1947.

Marshalsay, Karen, '"The quest for a truly representative Scottish national drama": the Scottish National Players', *Theatre Research International* 17, 2 (summer 1992).

Martin, Bernice, *A Sociology of Contemporary Cultural Change*, Oxford: Blackwell, 1981.

Marwick, Arthur, *British Society Since 1945*, Harmondsworth: Penguin, 1982.

Marwick, Arthur, *The Sixties: Cultural Revolution in Britain, France, Italy and the Uniterd States, c. 1958–c. 1974*, Oxford University Press, 1998.

Mason, Bim, *Street Theatre and Other Outdoor Performance*, London: Routledge, 1992.

Mayer, David (ed.), *Playing out the Empire: Ben Hur and other Toga Plays and Films, 1883–1908; A Critical Anthology*, Oxford University Press, 1994.

Mazer, Cary M., *Shakespeare Refashioned: Elizabethan Plays on Edwardian Stages*, Ann Arbor: UMI Research Press, 1981.

McArthur, Colin (ed.), *Scotch Reels: Scotland in Cinema and Television*, London: British Film Institute, 1982.

McCann, Paul, 'The trouble starts with a million pound windfall', *Independent on Sunday: Focus* (24 Aug. 1997).

McCarthy, Desmond, *The Court Theatre, 1904–1907*, London: A. H. Bullen, 1907; rpt. Stanley Weintraub and Coral Gables (eds.), Florida: University of Miami Press, 1966.

McCoola, Ros, *Theatre in the Hills*, Chapel-en-le-Frith: Caron Publications, 1984.

McCowen, Alec, *Young Gemini*, London: Elm Tree Books, 1979.

McCrone, David, *Understanding Scotland: The Sociology of a Stateless Nation*, London: Routledge, 1992.

McDonald, Jan, 'The Citizens' Theatre Glasgow, 1969–1979 – a house of illusion', *Maske und Kothurn* 29 (1983).

McGrath, John, *The Bone Won't Breath: on Theatre and Hope in Hard Times*, London: Methuen, 1990.

McGrath, John, *A Good Night Out – Popular Theatre: Audience, Class and Form*, London: Eyre Methuen, 1981.

McLeish, Robert, *The Gorbals Story*, Edinburgh: 7:84 Publications, 1985.

McMillan, Joyce, *The Traverse Theatre Story 1963–1988*, London: Methuen, 1988.

Meisel, Martin, *Shaw and the Nineteenth-Century Theater*, Princeton University Press, 1963.

Mellor, Geoff J., *They Made Us Laugh*, Littleborough, Lancs: George Kelsall, 1982.

Mellor, Geoff J., *Pom-Poms and Ruffles: the Story of Northern Seaside Entertainment*, Clapham, Yorks: Dalesman, 1966.

Merkin, Ros (ed.), *Popular Theatres?*, Liverpool: John Moores University Press, 1996.

Moore, Geoff, *Moving Being: Two Decades of Theatre Ideas*, Cardiff: Moving Being Ltd., n.d.

Morgan, Edward, *John Elias: Life, Letters and Essays*, Edinburgh: Banner of Truth Trust, 1973.

Morgan, Kenneth O., *The People's Peace: British History 1945–1990*, Oxford University Press, 1992.

Morgan, Kenneth O., *Rebirth of a Nation: Wales 1880–1980*, Oxford University Press, 1981.

Morley, Malcolm, *Margate and its Theatres*, London: Museums Press, 1966.

Moussinac, Leon, *The New Movement in the Theatre. A Survey of Recent Trends in Europe and America*, London: Batsford, 1931.

Mowat, Charles L., *Britain Between the Wars, 1918–1940*, London: Methuen, 1955.

Murdoch, Helen, *Travelling Hopefully. The Story of Molly Urquart*, Edinburgh: Paul Harris, 1981.

Myerscough, John, *The Economic Importance of the Arts in Britain*, London: Policy Studies Institute, 1988.

Myerscough, John, *The Economic Importance of the Arts in Glasgow*, London: Policy Studies Institute, 1988.

Myerscough, John, *Monitoring Glasgow 1990*, Glasgow: Glasgow City Council, 1991.

Nairn, Tom, *The Break-Up of Britain: Crisis and Neo-Nationalism*, London: Verso, 1981.

Newton, H. Chance, *Idols of the Halls*, London: Heath Cranton, 1928; facsimile reprint 1975.

Nichols, Peter, *A Piece of my Mind*, London: Methuen, 1987.

Nichols, Peter, *A Day in the Death of Joe Egg*, London: Faber & Faber, 1967.

Nicholson, Steve, *British Theatre and the Red Peril: The Portrayal of Communism 1917–1945*, Exeter University Press, 1999.

Nicholson, Steve, 'Montagu Slater and the theatre of the thirties', in *Recharting the Thirties*, ed. Patrick J. Quinn, London: Associated Universities Press, 1996.

Nicholson, Steve, 'Unneccessary plays: European drama and the British censor in the 1920s', *Theatre Research International* 20, 1 (1995).

Nicoll, Allardyce, *English Drama 1900–1930: The Beginning of the Modern Period*, Cambridge University Press, 1973.

Noble, Peter, *British Theatre*, London: British Yearbooks, 1946.

Nowell-Smith, Simon (ed.), *Edwardian England, 1901–1914*, Oxford University Press, 1964.

Nuttall, Jeff, *Performance Art, vol. II, Memoirs*, London: John Calder, 1979.

Oddey, Alison, *Devising Theatre: A Practical and Theoretical Handbook*, London: Routledge, 1994.

Oliver, Paul (ed.), *Black Music in Britain*, Milton Keynes: Open University Press, 1990.

Orme, Michael [Alix A. Grein], *J. T. Grein: The Story of a Pioneer, 1862–1935*, London: J. Murray, 1936.

Osborne, John, *A Better Class of Person: An Autobiography 1929–1956*, London: Faber & Faber, 1982.

Osment, Philip (ed.), *Gay Sweatshop: Four Plays and a Company*, London: Methuen, 1989.

Overton, Grace, *Drama in Education: Theory and Technique*, New York and London: Century Co., 1926.

Owain, O. Llew., *Hanes y Ddrama yng Nghymru 1850–1943*, Lerpwl: cyhoeddwyd ar ran Cyngor yr Eisteddfod Genedlathol, 1948.

Owen, Roger, 'Y ddefod golledig?: Theatr, cymdeithas a chymreictod yn y Gymru Gymraeg 1945–1990', unpublished Ph.D. Thesis, University of Wales, Aberystwyth, 1999.

Owusu, Kwesi, *The Struggle for Black Arts in Britain: What Can We Consider Better Than Freedom?*, London: Comedia, 1986.

Packman, R. H., 'Introduction' in Leon Moussinac, *The New Movement in the Theatre. A Survey of Recent Trends in Europe and America*, London: Batsford, 1931.

Paffrath, J. D. and Stelarc, *Obsolete Body/Suspensions*, Davis, Calif.: JD Publications, 1984.

Paget, Derek, '*Oh What a Lovely War*: the texts and their context', *New Theatre Quarterly* 6, 23 (Aug. 1990).

Paget, Derek, 'Theatre Workshop, Moussinac, and the European connection', *New Theatre Quarterly* 11, 43 (Aug. 1995).

Painter, Susan, *Edgar: The Playwright*, London: Methuen, 1996.

Palmer, John, *The Future of the Theatre*, London: G. Bell, 1913.

Panitch, Leo and Colin Leys, *The End of Parliamentary Socialism: From New Left to New Labour*, London: Verso, 1997.

Parker, Derek and Julia Parker, *The Natural History of the Chorus Girl*, London: Trinity Press, 1975.

Parker, Derek and Julia Parker, *The Story and the Song: A Survey of English Musical Plays, 1916–78*, London: Chappell, 1979.

Peacock, D. Keith, *Thatcher's Theatre: British Theatre and Drama in the Eighties*, London: Westport Press, 1999.

Pearson, Hesketh, *The Last Actor-Managers*, London: Methuen, 1950.

Pearson, Lynn, *The People's Palaces: Britain's Seaside Pleasure Buildings 1876–1914*, Buckingham: Barracuda, 1991.

Pearson, Meic, 'Welsh heterotopias', *New Welsh Review* 21 (1993).

Pellizzi, Camillo, *The English Drama: The Last Great Phase*, London: Macmillan, 1935.

Pertwee, Bill, *Beside the Seaside*, London: Collins & Brown, 1999.

Pertwee, Bill, *Pertwee's Promenades and Pierrots: One Hundred Years of Seaside Entertainment*, Newton Abbot, Devon: Westbridge, 1979.

Peters, John, 'Meet the wild bunch', *Sunday Times* (11 July 1976).

Phelan, Peggy, *Unmarked: The Politics of Performance*, London: Routledge, 1993.

Phillpotts, Eden and Adelaide Phillpotts, *Yellow Sands*, London: Duckworth, 1926.

Pick, John (ed.), *The State and the Arts*, Eastbourne: John Offord, 1980.

Pick, John, *West End: Mismanagement and Snobbery*, Eastbourne: John Offord, 1983.

Pickering, Michael, '"A jet ornament to society": black music in nineteenth-century Britain', in *Black Music in Britain*, ed. Paul Oliver, Milton Keynes: Open University Press, 1990.

Pickering, Michael, 'White skin, black masks: "nigger" minstrelsy in Victorian England', in *Music Hall: Performance and Style*, ed., J. S. Bratton, Milton Keynes: Open University Press, 1986.

Poggi, Valentina and Margaret Rose (eds.), *A Theatre that Matters: Twentieth-Century Scottish Drama and Theatre*, Milan: Unicopli, 2001.

Pogson, Reg, *Miss Horniman and the Gaiety Theatre*, Manchester: Rockcliff Press, 1952.

Poole, Mike and John Wyver, *Powerplays: Trevor Griffiths in Television*, London: British Film Institute, 1984.

Price, Cecil, *The English Theatre in Wales in the Eighteenth and Early Nineteenth Centuries*, Cardiff: University of Wales Press, 1948.

Price, Cecil, 'Portable theatres in Wales', *National Library of Wales Journal* 9 (summer 1955).

Price, Cecil, *The Professional Theatre in Wales*, University College of Swansea Press, 1984.

Price, Cecil, 'Some Welsh theatres 1844–1870', *National Library of Wales Journal* 12 (winter 1961).

Priestley, J. B., *The Plays of J. B. Priestley*, vol. III, London: William Heinemann, 1950.

Priestley, J. B., *Theatre Outlook*, London, Nicholson & Watson, 1947.

Quinn, Patrick (ed.), *Recharting the Thirties*, London: Associated Universities Press, 1996.

Quinn, Ruth-Blandina M., *Public Policy and the Arts: A Comparative Study of Great Britain and Ireland*, Aldershot: Ashgate, 1998.

Rabey, David, *Howard Barker, a Study*, London: Macmillan, 1989.

Ravenhill, Mark, *Faust: Faust is Dead*, London: Methuen, 1997.

Ravenhill, Mark, *Handbag*, London: Methuen, 1998.

Ravenhill, Mark, *Shopping and Fucking*, London: Methuen, 1996.

Read, Donald, *England 1868–1914*, London: Longman, 1979.

Read, Jack, *Empires, Hippodromes and Palaces*, London: Alderman Press, 1985.

Rebellato, Dan, *1956 and All That: The Making of Modern British Drama*, London: Routledge, 1999.

Rees, Roland, *Fringe First: Pioneers of the Fringe on Record*, London: Oberon Books, 1992.

Rees W., (Gwilym Hiraethog), 'Helyntion hen deiliwr', *Y Tyst a'r Dydd* (29 Dec. 1871–2 Feb. 1877).

Reinelt, Janelle, *After Brecht: British Epic Theatre*, Ann Arbor: University of Michigan Press, 1996.

'Report from the Joint Select Committee of the House of Lords and the House of Commons on the Stage Plays (Censorship)', in *Reports from Committees*, 1909 Parliamentary Papers, vol. 3, 214, London: HMSO, 1909.

Reynolds, Ernest, *Modern English Drama: A Survey of the Theatre Since 1900*, London: George Harrap, 1950.

Reynolds, Harry, *Minstrel Memories: The Story of Burnt Cork Minstrelsy in Great Britain from 1836 to 1927*, London: Alston Rivers, 1928.

Rice, Margery Spring, *Working-Class Wives: Their Health and Conditions*, 2nd edn, London: Virago, 1981.

Ritchie, Rob (ed.), *The Joint Stock Book: The Making of a Theatre Collective*, London: Methuen, 1987.

Roberts, Philip, *The Royal Court Theatre and the Modern Stage*, Cambridge University Press, 1999.

Roms, Heike, 'Tried and tested', *Planet* (April–May 1999).

Rowell, George, *Theatre in the Age of Irving*, Oxford: Blackwell, 1981.

Rowell, George and Anthony Jackson, *The Repertory Movement: A History of Regional Theatre in Britain*, Cambridge University Press, 1984.

Salmon, Eric (ed.), *Granville Barker and his Correspondents*, Detroit: Wayne State University Press, 1986.

Samuel, Raphael, Ewan MacColl and Stuart Cosgrove, *Theatres of the Left, 1880–1935: Workers' Theatre Movements in Britain and America*, London: Routledge & Kegan Paul, 1985.

Sanderson, Michael, *From Irving to Olivier: A Social History of the Acting Profession in England, 1880–1983*, London: Athlone Press, 1985.

Sandison, G, *Theatre Ownership in Britain*, London: Federation of Theatre Unions, 1953.

Savill, Charmian C., 'Dismantling the Wall', *Planet* (Feb.–March 1990).

Saville, Ian, 'Ideas, forms and developments in the British workers' theatre, 1929–1935', unpublished Ph.D. thesis, City University, 1990.

Schechner, Richard. 'A new paradigm for theatre in the academy', *Drama Review* 36, 4 (1992).

Schneer, Jonathan, *London 1900, The Imperial Metropolis*, New Haven: Yale University Press, 1999.

Scottish Arts Council / Ruth Wishart, *Scottish Arts in the 21st Century: A Report on the Consultation Process*, Edinburgh: Scottish Arts Council, 1999.

Scottish Executive, *Scottish National Theatre: Report of the Independent Working Group* (May 2001).

Scullion, Adrienne, 'Self and nation: issues of identity in modern Scottish drama by women', *New Theatre Quarterly* 17, 68 (Nov. 2001).

Shank, Theodore (ed.), *Contemporary British Theatre*, updated edn, London: Macmillan, 1996.

Shaw, Bernard, *Bernard Shaw: The Drama Observed*, 4 vols., ed. Bernard F. Dukore, University Park: Pennsylvania State University Press, 1993.

Shaw, Bernard, *Collected Plays with their Prefaces*, 7 vols., ed. Dan H. Laurence, London: Max Reinhardt, Bodley Head, 1971–4.

Shaw, Bernard, *Letters to Granville Barker*, ed. C. B. Purdom, London: Phoenix House, 1956.

Shaw, Bernard, *Our Theatres in the Nineties*, vol. ii, London: Constable, 1931.

Shaw, Roy, *The Arts and the People*, London: Jonathan Cape, 1987.

Shiubhalaigh, Maire Nic, *The Splendid Years*, Dublin: James Duffy, 1955.

Shellard, Dominic, *British Theatre Since the War*, New Haven: Yale University Press, 1999.

Shellard, Dominic (ed.), *Theatre in the 1950s*, Sheffield: Sheffield Academic Press, 2000.

Shepherd, Simon and Peter Womack, *English Drama: A Cultural History*, Oxford: Blackwell, 1996.

Shiach, Morag, *Discourse on Popular Culture: Class, Gender and History in Cultural Analysis, 1730 to the Present*, London: Polity, 1989.

Short, Ernest, *Sixty Years of Theatre*, London: Eyre & Spottiswoode, 1951.

Sidnell, Michael J., *Dances of Death: The Group Theatre of London in the Thirties*, London: Faber & Faber, 1984.

Sierz, Aleks, '"About Now" in Birmingham', *New Theatre Quarterly* 13, 51 (Aug. 1997).

Sierz, Aleks, 'Cool Britannia? "In-yer-face" writing in the British theatre today', *New Theatre Quarterly* 14, 56 (Nov. 1998).

Sierz, Aleks, *In-Yer-Face Theatre: British Drama Today*, London: Faber & Faber, 2000.

Sinfield, Alan, *Out on Stage: Lesbian and Gay Theatre in the Twentieth Century*, New Haven: Yale University Press, 1999.

Slater, Montagu, 'Stay down miner', in *The 1930s. A Challenge to Orthodoxy*, ed. John Lucas, Brighton: Harvester Press, 1978.

Smith, Anthony, *Software for the Self: Culture and Technology*, London: Faber & Faber, 1996.

Smith, Chris, *Creative Britain*, London: Faber & Faber, 1998.

Socrates [pseud., anon.], *An Oration Over the Dead Body of a Miner: With Apologies to the Shade of Shakespeare*, London: Workers' Publications, 1926.

Speaight, Robert, *William Poel and the Elizabethan Revival*, London: Society for Theatre Research, 1954.

Stephens, Meic (ed.), *The Arts in Wales*, Cardiff: Welsh Arts Council, 1979.

Stephens, Meic (ed.), *The Welsh Language Today*, Cardiff: University of Wales Press, 1973.

Sterne, Ashley and Archibald de Bear, *The Comic History of the Co-Optimists*, London: Herbert Jenkins, 1926.

Stevenson, John and Chris Cook, *Britain in the Depression: Society and Politics 1929–39*, 2nd edn, London: Longman, 1994.

Stevenson, Randall and Gavin Wallace (eds.), *Scottish Theatre Since the Seventies*, Edinburgh University Press, 1996.

Stewart, Ena Lamont, *Men Should Weep*, London: Samuel French, 1983.

Stokes, John, *Resistible Theatres: Enterprise and Experiment in the Late Nineteenth Century*, London: Paul Elek, 1972.

Stokes, John, Michael Booth and Susan Bassnett, *Bernhardt, Terry, Duse: The Actress in her Time*, Cambridge University Press, 1988.

Stoppard, Tom, *The Real Thing*, London: Faber & Faber, 1986.

Stourac, Richard and Kathleen McCreery, *Theatre as a Weapon: Workers' Theatre in the Soviet Union, Germany and Britain, 1917–1934*, London: Routledge & Kegan Paul, 1986.

Stowell, Sheila, *A Stage of their Own: Feminist Playwrights of the Suffrage Era*, Manchester University Press, 1992.

Stuart, Aimée and Philip Stuart, *Nine Till Six*, London: Samuel French, 1930.

TAG (Theatre About Glasgow), 'Making the Nation' (press release) (17 March 1999).

Tagg, John, *The Burden of Representation: Essays on Photographies and Histories*, London: Macmillan, 1988.

Taylor, Anne-Marie (ed.), *Staging Wales: Welsh Theatre 1979–1997*, Cardiff: University of Wales Press, 1997.

Taylor, John Russell, *The Rise and Fall of the Well Made Play*, London: Methuen, 1967.

Theatre Workshop, *Oh What a Lovely War*, London: Methuen, 1967; rev. edn, London: Methuen, 2000.

Theatre Writers' Union, *Playwrights: A Species Still Endangered?*, London: Theatre Writers' Union, 1987.

Thomas, Dylan, *Under Milk Wood*, ed. Hazel Walford Davies and Ralph Maud, London: J. M. Dent, 1995.

Thomas, James, *The Art of the Actor-Manager: Wilson Barrett and the Victorian Theatre*, Ann Arbor: UMI Research Press, 1984.

Thompson, Paul, *The Edwardians: The Remaking of British Society*, 2nd edn, London: Routledge, 1992.

Tich, M. and R. Findlater, *Little Tich: Giant of the Music Hall*, London: Elm Tree Press, 1979.

Time Out, 'Guide to underground theatre', *Theatre Quarterly* 1, 1 (Jan.–March 1971).

Tomlinson, Richard, *Disability, Theatre and Education*, London: Souvenir Press, 1982.

Trewin, J. C., *Drama 1946–50*, London: Longmans, Green, 1951.

Trewin, J. C., *The Theatre Since 1900*, London: Andrew Dakers, 1951.

Trussler, Simon, *The Cambridge Illustrated History of British Theatre*, Cambridge University Press, 1994.

Trussler, Simon, 'Political progress of a paralysed liberal: the community dramas of John Arden', *Drama Review* 13, 4 (T44) (1969).

Trussler, Simon (ed.), *New Theatre Voices of the Seventies*, London: Methuen, 1981.

Turner, Victor, *Dramas, Fields and Metaphors*, Ithaca: Cornell University Press, 1974.

Tushingham, David (ed.), *Live 1: Food for the Soul – A New Generation of British Theatre Makers*, London: Methuen, 1994.

Tushingham, David (ed.), *Live 4: Freedom Machine*, London: Nick Hern Books, 1996.

Tynan, Kenneth, *Curtains*, London: Longmans, Green, 1961.

Tynan, Kenneth, 'The royal smut hound', in Micheline Wandor, *Look Back in Gender: Sexuality and the Family in Post-War British Drama*, London: Methuen, 1987.

Tynan, Kenneth, *Tynan Right and Left*, London: Longman, 1967.

Tynan, Kenneth, *A View of the English Stage*, London: Davis-Poynter, 1975.

Ugwu, Catherine (ed.), *Let's Get It On: The Politics of Black Performance*, London: Institute of Contemporary Art Publications, 1995.

Van Druten, John, 'The sex play', *Theatre Arts Monthly* (11 Jan. 1927).

Veitch, Norman *The People's: Being a History of the People's Theatre, Newcastle upon Tyne 1911–1939*, Gateshead on Tyne: Northumberland Press, 1950.

Vernon, Frank, *The Twentieth-Century Theatre*, London: George Harrap, 1924.

Walker, Brian (ed.), *Frank Matcham: Theatre Architect*, Belfast: Blackstaff Press, 1980.

Walton, John and James Walvin (eds.), *Leisure in Britain 1780–1939*, Manchester University Press, 1983.

Wandor, Michelene, *Carry on Understudies: Theatre and Sexual Politics*, 2nd edn, London: Routledge & Kegan Paul, 1986.

Wardle, Irving, *The Theatres of George Devine*, London: Eyre Methuen, 1978.

Wareing, Alfred, 'The little theatre movement. Its genesis and its goal', in *The Stage Yearbook 1928*, ed. L. Carson, London: The Stage, 1928.

Watson, Ian, *Conversations with Alan Ayckbourn*, London: Faber & Faber, 1988.

Wearing, J. P., *The London Stage 1900–1909*, 2 vols., Metuchen, N.J. and London: Scarecrow Press, 1981.

Wearing, J. P., *The London Stage 1920–1929: A Calendar of Plays and Players*, Metuchen, N.J. and London: Scarecrow Press, 1984.

Webster, Margaret, *The Same Only Different: Five Generations of a Theatre Family*, London: Victor Gollancz, 1969.

Whitaker, Wilfrid B., *Victorian and Edwardian Shopworkers: The Struggle to Obtain Better Conditions and a Half-Holiday*, Newton Abbot: David & Charles, 1973.

Whittaker, Thomas, *Tom Stoppard*, London: Macmillan, 1983.

Whyte, Christopher (ed.), *Gendering the Nation*, Edinburgh University Press, 1995.

Willett, John (ed.), *Brecht on Theatre: The Development of an Aesthetic*, London: Methuen, 1964.

Willett, John, *The Theatre of Erwin Piscator: Half a Century of Politics in the Theatre*, London: Methuen, 1986.

Williams, Euryn Ogwen, *Byw yng Nghanol Chwyldro/Living in the Midst of a Revolution*, Eisteddfod Genedlaethol, 1998.

Williams, Gwyn A., *When Was Wales?*, London: Black Raven Press, 1985.

Williams, Ioan, *Capel a Chomin*, Caerdydd: Gwasg Prifysgol Pantycelyn, 1991.

Williams, Ioan, *Capel a Chomin Astudiaeth o ffugchwwedlau pedwar llenor'*, Cardiff: University of Wales Press, 1989.

Williams, Ioan, *A Straitened Stage: A Study of the Theatre of J. Saunders Lewis*, Bridgend: Seren Books, Poetry of Wales Press, 1991.

Williams, J. Ellis., *Inc yn fy Ngwaed*, Llandybie: Llyfrau'r Dryw, Christopher Davies, 1963.

Williams, Kevin, *Shadows and Substance*, Llandysul: Gomer, 1997.

Williams, Raymond, *Culture*, London: Fontana, 1981.

Williams, Raymond, *Culture and Society 1780–1950*, Harmondsworth: Penguin, 1958.

Williams, Raymond, 'Social environment and theatrical environment: the case of English naturalism', in *Problems in Materialism and Culture*, London: Verso, 1980.

Williams, Raymond, *Writing in Society*, London: Verso, 1991.

Wilmut, Roger, *Kindly Leave the Stage: The Story of Variety 1919–1960*, London: Methuen, 1985.

Wilson, A. E., *Edwardian Theatre*, London: Arthur Barker, 1951.

Wilson, A. E., *Playgoer's Pilgrimage*, London: Stanley, Paul & Co., 1938.

Woodfield, James, *English Theatre in Transition, 1881–1914*, London: Croom Helm, 1984.

Woodruff, Graham, 'Community, class and control: a view of community plays', *New Theatre Quarterly* 5, 20 (Nov. 1989).

Woolf, Virginia, *The Captain's Death Bed and other Essays*, London: Hogarth Press, 1950.

Wright, D. G., *Popular Radicalism: The Working-Class Experience 1780–1880*, London: Longman, 1988.

Index

Note: Italicised page numbers refer to illustrations.